The Book of Jewish Knowledge

The Book of Jewish Knowledge

a multifaceted exploration
of the teachings, observances,
and history of Judaism

THE ROHR JEWISH LEARNING INSTITUTE

THE ROHR JEWISH LEARNING INSTITUTE
Chairman: **Rabbi Moshe Kotlarsky**
Principal Benefactor: **Mr. George Rohr**
Executive Director: **Rabbi Efraim Mintz**

THE BOOK OF JEWISH KNOWLEDGE
Editor / Compiler: **Rabbi Yanki Tauber**
Creative Director / Designer: **Baruch Gorkin**
Project Chairman: **Rabbi Shmuel Kaplan**

© Published and Copyrighted 2022 by The Rohr Jewish Learning Institute
832 Eastern Parkway, Brooklyn, NY 11213

Library of Congress Control Number: 2020924045

ISBN 978-1-63668-012-5 — Slipcase deluxe edition
ISBN 978-1-63668-011-8 — Flexcover edition

(888) YOUR-JLI / 718–221–6900
myJLI.com

For any questions, comments, and feedback,
or to order a replacement bookmark,
please email us at: thebook@myJLI.com

COLOPHON
Typeface: Tenso, by Jos Buivenga, The Netherlands
Cover: cold-foil stamping, embossing
Paper: 100 gsm Gardapat 13 Kiara, Italy

Printed and bound in China

COVER IMAGES
Clockwise from top right: Bar Kokhba coin (see pp. 1-2); Mishnah manuscript (see p. 185);
Jewish wedding ceremony (see p. 409); Esther and Ahasuerus (see p. 361);
Tefillin infographic (see p. 322); Festival icons (see p. 329)

BACK COVER IMAGE
Shabbat table (see p. 298)

TITLE PAGE IMAGE
Torah case (see p. 156)

PRINCIPAL SPONSORS

*In loving memory of our dear parents,
Eugene, Doris, Joseph, and Vivian, who were our
family's esteemed and beloved "learning institutes,"
and in honor of our dear children, Nick, Sam, Libby,
and Laura, who continue to grow in the light of that
transgenerational insight.*

– Lee and Patti Schear

FUNDING PARTNERS

*In loving memory of our dear parents,
Howard Joseph (Chaim Yosef) and Bernice (Perel) Cohen,
and Edwin (Eliyahu Chaim) and Shirley (Sarah) Schoen.
May the knowledge gained, pride rekindled, and heritage practiced
through this splendid publication amplify their merit.*

– Isadore and Roberta Schoen

PREFACE

What is Judaism? What does it mean to be a Jew? What is the secret of our survival, for thirty-eight centuries, through attempts to destroy us too numerous and varied to recount? What is Judaism's message to the world?

The Book of Jewish Knowledge *does not attempt to answer these questions with a single answer or set of answers. Rather, this volume offers 1,200 answers in 1,200 voices, presenting the story of Judaism via the variety of media that capture the Jewish experience: a Biblical account, a traditional Jewish practice, a painting by a Jewish artist, a Midrashic parable, a Talmudic discourse, a historical document, a poignant photograph, a gefilte fish recipe, a prayer from Psalms, a Scriptural aphorism, a Halachic responsum, a Kabbalistic diagram, a philosophical essay, a 12th-century travelogue. Collectively, these present the reader with an encyclopedic overview of Jewish history, an in-depth examination of four millennia of Jewish wisdom, and an intimate tour of Jewish traditions and observances.*

Our aim in compiling this volume was to create a single book that surveys the full scope of Jewish teaching and Jewish life, yet also does justice to the depth and beauty of Judaism. Our hope is that whether this is your first book on Judaism, or if you are approaching it with a lifetime of learning and engagement, you will gain a new appreciation of the range and grandeur of Jewish knowledge and experience.

ON THE STRUCTURE AND USAGE OF THIS BOOK

The Book of Jewish Knowledge consists of five sections: Jewish History, Jewish Teaching, Jewish Practice, The Jewish Year, and Lifecycle Milestones. These are further divided into 160 subsections and topics (e.g., "The First Jews," "The Exodus," "The Weekly Parashah," "Business Ethics," "The Synagogue," "Shabbat," "The Passover Seder," "Education," "Marriage," etc.).

There is, however, considerable overlap between the categories. In "Jewish History," for example, our interest is not only to chronicle the events, but also to explore their significance through the lens of more than one hundred generations of Jewish learning, and how these events impacted the Jewish psyche and the Jewish experience. In "The Jewish Year," we also explore the history of the festivals and special days that mark our annual cycle, and the observances by which we relive and internalize these events. Indeed, all five sections contain elements of Jewish teaching, Jewish observance, and Jewish history, much as Jewish life incorporates learning, practice, and experience as an integral whole.

Our approach is unabashedly traditional. We are more interested in what Judaism has to say about itself than what others have said about it. While the latter are also featured in this book for context and perspective, our primary frame of reference are the traditional source texts of Judaism: the Torah (Bible), the Talmud, and the teachings and writings of the sages of Israel. Yet, as the sages repeatedly emphasize, "there are seventy faces to the Torah." Judaism speaks in a medley of voices, each complementing and fulfilling the others. In these pages, the reader will find a broad range of perspectives and viewpoints on virtually any topic in Judaism.

Each section and subsection opens with a short introductory overview of the topic. Beyond that, we have preferred to allow the quotes, citations, artworks, and infographics to tell their story without undue editorialization and commentary, encouraging the reader to create their own narrative with these original texts and visuals. Every item on the page was carefully selected as a potential contributor to this narrative. This includes the numerous paintings, artifacts, and photographs that populate these pages, which rather than merely illustrating the text introduce additional information and insight to the topic being addressed.

Each of the citations in this book is marked with an icon indicating its source and type, identifying it as a Scriptural passage, a historical document, etc. A description of the eight icons and the categories they represent follows this preface on page xiii.

A short biographical description of each of the 225 personalities and works cited in this book is presented on pages 435–443.

As a rule, the Hebrew and Yiddish words and other specialized terms used in this book are explained where they are introduced. For those cases in which such terms appear outside of their primary context, consult the *Glossary* on p. 444 for a brief explanation and/or reference to the pages in this book where the term is discussed.

A NOTE ON THE DATES AND OTHER DATA IN THIS BOOK

In keeping with our traditionalist approach, the historical dates in this book follow the records and calculations presented in the traditional Jewish source texts (the Talmud, *Seder Olam, Seder ha-Dorot,* etc.). In some cases, these dates will differ somewhat from the accepted standard in modern academic sources. Specifically, there is a 164-year discrepancy between the traditional and the modern-academic calculations for the First Temple era and the earlier part of the Second Temple era. For example, the date given by contemporary historians for the destruction of the First Temple is 587 BCE, while the date according to the Talmud and *Seder Olam* is 423 BCE. The dates for the reigns of kings David and Solomon will show a similar discrepancy. The reader is reminded to take this discrepancy into account when encountering historical dates that differ from some common conventions.

Also within the context of Jewish tradition, many of the data presented in this book are the subject of differing opinions among scholars, differences in custom among communities, and multiple perspectives by sages and thinkers. As the Talmud famously avers, "These and these are both the words of the living G-d," as all derive from the same source and strive toward the same goal. In the texts presented in this book, we aimed for a cross-section of source texts and perspectives that would represent the rich variety of Jewish teaching. On the other hand, in the graphs, tables, and maps created for this volume—many of which present complex and multifaceted information—this could not be achieved without significantly compromising clarity and usability. We therefore chose, in most cases, to represent only one of several alternative views, not as an endorsement over the others, but simply as a matter of practicality. In such cases, additional information and references are provided in the *Additional Notes* on pages 448–451.

An important disclaimer must also be made in regard to any texts, lists, and infographics in this book that pertain to the practice of Halachah (Torah law). The detailed laws of Shabbat, kosher, prayer, mikveh, etc., and the variations in practice by different communities, are beyond the scope of this volume. The reader is therefore advised to see all Halachic information in this book as intended solely for the purpose of general edification, and to refer to authoritative Halachic sources for more detailed guidance.

SPELLING OF THE DIVINE NAME

In this book, "G-d" is written with a hyphen instead of an 'o.' According to Torah law, the divine name is sacred, and great care must be taken to accord it proper care and reverence. For this reason, it is best to avoid writing or printing the word "G-d" in its full spelling in all but the most recognizably sacred books (e.g., a Bible or prayer book), lest it be unwittingly defaced or treated irreverently.

This practice also serves to remind us that even as we discuss G-d and His influence in our lives, He is above and beyond our words; that even as we are enjoined, by the Almighty Himself, to seek Him with our thought, speech, and deeds, He transcends all human effort to name and describe His reality.

IN CONCLUSION

Any attempt to encapsulate the whole of Judaism in a single volume is a most ambitious endeavor; at most, we can build a portal. If this is your first encounter with Judaism, our hope is it will be the first of many; that this sampling of the range, depth, and beauty of the ideas and ideals taught and lived by the Jewish people for 3,800 years will encourage you to further your knowledge of and engagement with Judaism.

The Rohr Jewish Learning Institute (JLI)

ABOUT JLI

The Rohr Jewish Learning Institute (JLI) has been at the forefront of Jewish education since 1999, and serves as the adult education arm of the worldwide Chabad-Lubavitch movement. The scholars, educators, writers, editors, designers, and videographers of JLI have created hundreds of courses on Jewish history, Talmudic law, Biblical commentary, Jewish philosophy, Jewish mysticism, medical ethics, business ethics, mental health, and many other topics. The courses are translated into nine languages, offer continuing educational credits for multiple professions, and are taught in more than 2,000 communities worldwide by JLI-trained and certified instructors. It was by drawing on the prodigious content in these courses that *The Book of Jewish Knowledge* could be produced.

ACKNOWLEDGEMENTS

This volume includes texts and citations from 225 different authors, and works by more than 100 artists and photographers. As a rule, these are credited on the page where their contribution appears. The *Appendices* section of this book contains additional sourcing information and credits.

The Book of Jewish Knowledge was a multi-year effort involving many dedicated individuals, all of whose contributions are considerable and greatly appreciated. In the following lines, we note the key figures that played significant roles in bringing this work to fruition.

This book was conceived by **Rabbi Shmuel Kaplan,** regional director of Chabad Lubavitch in Maryland, whose unflagging efforts drove the project to its conclusion.

Rabbi Yanki Tauber developed the structure and content of the book, selected and translated the source texts, and wrote the introductory paragraphs to each section. **Baruch Gorkin** designed the interior and the cover of the book, curated the art and photography, and created the diagrams, maps, and other graphic elements.

Rabbi Nissen Mangel served as the rabbinic advisor for the project, reviewing the material and offering his invaluable guidance. Associate editor **Dr. Shmuel Klatzkin** made significant contributions to the research and drafting of portions of the book, particularly its "Diaspora" section. **Rivki Mockin** served as the book's project manager, and **Adina Posner** helped coordinate the production process. **Mrs. Shaina B. Mintz,** JLI's director of operations, oversaw the logistics of the book's development.

Rabbis Zalman Abraham, Mordechai Dinerman, Yosef Gansburg, Naftali Silberberg, and **Avraham Sternberg** reviewed and critiqued the work and were instrumental in directing its editorial vision. **Professor Lawrence Schiffman** provided valuable editorial input. **Carolyn Hessel,** director emerita of the Jewish Book Council, guided and advised the project. **Rabbis Gershon Grossbaum, Gad Sebag,** and **Mrs. Rivkah Slonim** also advised on portions of the book, and **Rabbi Chaim Nochum Cunin** generously shared his knowledge and expertise.

A significant portion of the material in this volume was drawn from the JLI courses that are taught by more than 2,000 JLI instructors around the world. The steady stream of feedback provided by these instructors and their students has greatly enhanced the quality of JLI's courses—and by extension, of this book as well.

The research compiled by JLI's **Machon Shmuel: The Sami Rohr Research Institute** was a most valuable resource. Significant research and editorial contributions were provided by **Rabbi Yakov Gershon,** Machon Shmuel's lead researcher. **Aliza Mayteles** also assisted with various research tasks.

Chana Tauber assisted in creating the bibliography, as well as in obtaining images and artwork and securing permissions from the relevant archives, museums, libraries, etc.; **Mussi Abelsky, Mushka Grossbaum,** and **Shulamis Nadler** also devoted time and effort to permissions and image acquisition. **Racheli Tauber** helped compile the index, **Shimon Gorkin** assisted with the book layout, and **Rabbis Mendel Rosenfeld** and **Mendel Sirota** helped with the marketing and publishing logistics. The text was proofread by **Lynne Clamage**, **Rachel Musicante**, **Mimi Palace**, and **Ya'akovah Weber**.

We are eminently grateful to the principal sponsors of this project, **Lee and Patti Schear**, who are dedicating the *Book of Jewish Knowledge* to the loving memory of their parents, and in honor of their beloved children. Lee and Patti have translated their commitment to passing the torch of Jewish learning across the generations into a vehicle to bring that wisdom and passion to the whole of the Jewish people and beyond.

Isadore and Roberta Schoen invested most generously in this project. We are grateful to them for their support, which enabled years of research, editing, and design.

Gary and Carol Berman provided the seed funding that enabled the launch of this project. Generous contributions by **Cheston and Lara Mizel, Abraham Podolak, Moshe and Rebecca Bolinsky,** and **David Shinefeld** helped bring the project to fruition.

Rabbi Moshe Kotlarsky, JLI's visionary chairman, was a pillar of support for this project, as for all of JLI's programs. The generous support of JLI's principal benefactor, **Mr. George Rohr,** enables all of JLI's work, growth, and expansion, and is largely responsible for the Jewish renaissance that is being spearheaded by JLI and its affiliates across the globe.

JLI's executive board—**Rabbis Chaim Block, Hesh Epstein, Ronnie Fine, Yosef Gansburg, Shmuel Kaplan, Yisroel Rice,** and **Avraham Sternberg**—devote countless hours to the development of JLI and drive the vision, growth, and success of the organization. We also are grateful to **Rabbi Yaakov Fellig** for his guidance and support.

JLI is indebted to its philanthropic pillars. We'd like to particularly note the generosity of **Jake Aronov, Gordon and Leslie Diamond, Francine Gani, Zalman and Mimi Fellig, Yitzchok and Julie Gniwisch, Edwin and Arlene Goldstein, Yosef and Chana Malka Gorowitz, Carolyn Hessel, Barbara Hines, Joe and Shira Lipsey, David and Debra Magerman, David and Harriet Maldau, David Mintz, Eyal and Aviva Postelnik, Eliezer and Denise Robbins, Clive and Zoe Rock, Michael and Fiona Scharf, Judy Schulich,** and **David and Helen Zalik.** We also thank **Rabbis Sholom Deitch** and **Nochum Mangel** for their continuous support and partnership.

Rabbi Efraim Mintz
Executive Director
The Rohr Jewish Learning Institute

CITATION TYPES

 SCRIPTURE

The icon for Scripture is based on the images of a scroll and a spiral. The scroll is a literal reference; the spiral symbolizes Scripture's role as the singular source from which all subsequent Torah knowledge emanates.

 TALMUD & MIDRASH

The Talmud and Midrash expound the many layers of meaning and the plurality of viewpoints implicit in the the Torah. The icon for these works evokes the classical "daf" format for presenting multiple commentaries on a central text.

 SAGES

Many generations of Jewish sages devoted their lives to elucidating and expounding the texts of the Torah. The quill symbolizes the product of their toil.

 MYSTICS

The mystics explore the inner, esoteric aspect of Torah. The icon for mystical texts is based on the "*sefirot* tree" commonly present in Kabbalistic charts.

 LAWS & CUSTOMS

Ultimately, the teachings emerging from Scripture, Talmud, and the writings of the later sages find expression in Torah law—known as *halachah*, "the way"—and the customs adopted by Jewish communities through the generations.

 PERSPECTIVES

Personal perspectives expressed in essays, diaries, and other works, both from within the Jewish world and by those who observed it from without, serve to illuminate the total Jewish experience.

 HISTORICAL DOCUMENTS

Historical edicts, proclamations, and other archival texts are indicated with the "document" icon.

 STORIES & PARABLES

Often, the best way to convey an idea is to tell a story or weave a parable. Indeed, stories and parables, with their emphasis on the telling and listening experience, occupy an important place in Jewish teaching.

Contents

diagrams, tables, and maps

Jewish History

1

It has been posited that "history"—in the sense that the events, lifetimes, and epochs that transpire in the world form a cohesive narrative—is a distinctly Jewish idea. The Jewish people were the first to profess, and to tell the world, that the universe has a purposeful Creator, that our lives have meaning, and that the human story has a goal toward which it progresses.

Our section on Jewish History *presents some of the signature events in the four-thousand-year trajectory of the Jewish story, and their significance in the words of their actors and observers.*

 GENESIS 12:1–3

And G-d said to Abram: "Go you from your land, and from your birthplace, and from your father's house, to the land that I will show you.

"I will make you a great nation … and all the families of the earth will be blessed through you."

 ISAIAH 42:6

I have given you as a people's covenant, as a light unto the nations.

 MIDRASH TANCHUMA, *TOLEDOT 5*

Hadrian said to R. Joshua: "How great is the lamb that survives amongst seventy wolves."

Said he to him: "How great is the shepherd who saves her and guards her."

 MARK TWAIN, *HARPER'S MAGAZINE, MARCH, 1898*

If the statistics are right, the Jews constitute but one per cent. of the human race. It suggests a nebulous dim puff of star-dust lost in the blaze of the Milky Way. Properly the Jew ought hardly to be heard of; but he is heard of, has always been heard of. He is as prominent on the planet as any other people, and his commercial importance is extravagantly out of proportion to the smallness of his bulk. His contributions to the world's list of great names in literature, science, art, music, finance, medicine, and abstruse learning are also away out of proportion to the weakness of his numbers.

He has made a marvelous fight in this world, in all the ages; and has done it with his hands tied behind him. He could be vain of himself, and be excused for it. The Egyptian, the Babylonian, and the Persian rose, filled the planet with sound and splendor, then faded to dream-stuff and passed away; the Greek and the Roman followed, and made a vast noise, and they are

The Sassoon Haggadah, Spain or Southern France, circa 1320

gone; other peoples have sprung up and held their torch high for a time, but it burned out, and they sit in twilight now, or have vanished.

The Jew saw them all, beat them all, and is now what he always was, exhibiting no decadence, no infirmities of age, no weakening of his parts, no slowing of his energies, no dulling of his alert and aggressive mind. All things are mortal but the Jew; all other forces pass, but he remains. What is the secret of his immortality?

 FRANZ ROSENZWEIG
LETTER TO MARTIN BUBER, 1923

The fact of our everlastingness renders all the phases of our history simultaneous. In the history of other peoples, reaching back for what has been left behind is only necessary from time to time; for us, it is a constant, vital necessity … for we must be able to live within our everlastingness.

 MAIMONIDES, *END OF MISHNEH TORAH*

In those times [of the future Messianic era], there will be no hunger or war, no jealousy or rivalry. For the good will be plentiful, and all delicacies available as dust. The sole occupation of the world will be only to know G-d.… As it is written (Isaiah 11:9): "For the world will be filled with the knowledge of G-d, as waters cover the sea."

timeline of Jewish history

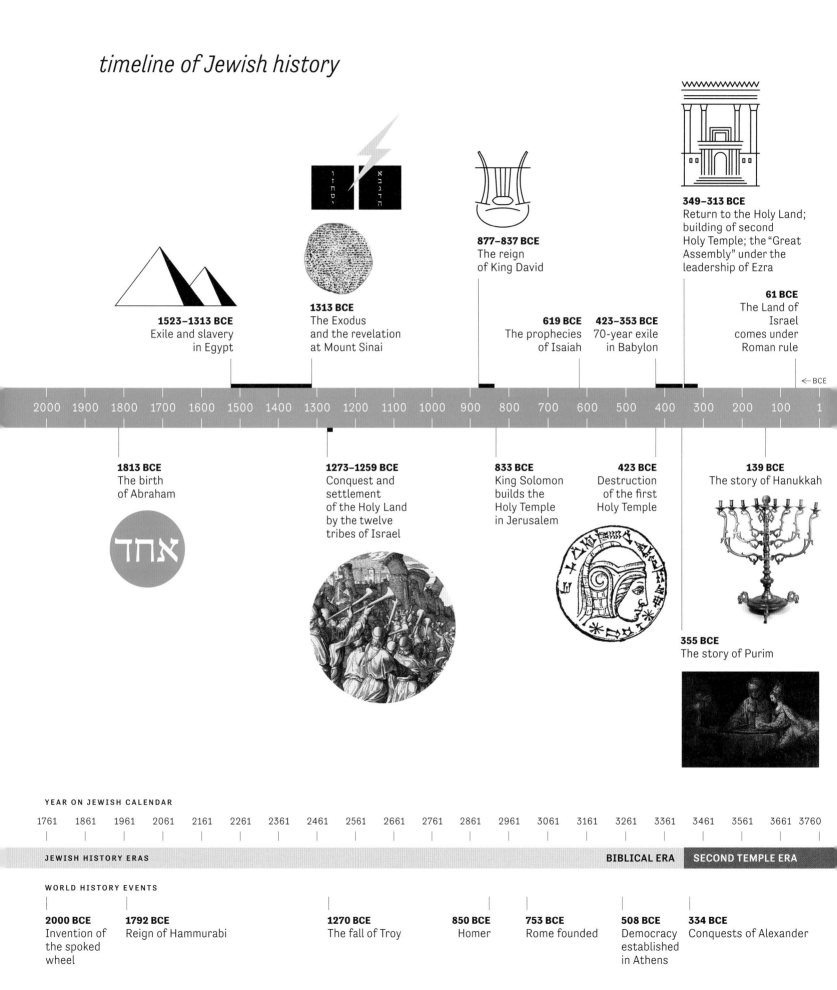

1523–1313 BCE
Exile and slavery
in Egypt

1313 BCE
The Exodus
and the revelation
at Mount Sinai

877–837 BCE
The reign
of King David

349–313 BCE
Return to the Holy Land;
building of second
Holy Temple; the "Great
Assembly" under the
leadership of Ezra

61 BCE
The Land of
Israel
comes under
Roman rule

619 BCE
The prophecies
of Isaiah

423–353 BCE
70-year exile
in Babylon

← BCE

2000 1900 1800 1700 1600 1500 1400 1300 1200 1100 1000 900 800 700 600 500 400 300 200 100 1

1813 BCE
The birth
of Abraham

1273–1259 BCE
Conquest and
settlement
of the Holy Land
by the twelve
tribes of Israel

833 BCE
King Solomon
builds the
Holy Temple
in Jerusalem

423 BCE
Destruction
of the first
Holy Temple

139 BCE
The story of Hanukkah

355 BCE
The story of Purim

YEAR ON JEWISH CALENDAR

1761 1861 1961 2061 2161 2261 2361 2461 2561 2661 2761 2861 2961 3061 3161 3261 3361 3461 3561 3661 3760

JEWISH HISTORY ERAS   BIBLICAL ERA   SECOND TEMPLE ERA

WORLD HISTORY EVENTS

2000 BCE
Invention of
the spoked
wheel

1792 BCE
Reign of Hammurabi

1270 BCE
The fall of Troy

850 BCE
Homer

753 BCE
Rome founded

508 BCE
Democracy
established
in Athens

334 BCE
Conquests of Alexander

1734
R. Israel Baal Shem Tov
founds the Hasidic movement

882–942
R. Saadia Gaon

1648
Chmielnicki massacres

1967
Six Day War;
liberation
of Jerusalem

69
Destruction of the Second Temple

רש"י

1563
R. Joseph Caro
completes the
Shulchan Aruch

1040–1105
Rashi

1948
Establishment
of the modern
state of Israel

189
Completion of the Mishnah
by R. Judah ha-Nasi

637
Muslim
conquest of
the Holy Land

1135–1204
Maimonides

1492
The Spanish
Expulsion

1897
Zionist
movement
launched

CE →

1 100 200 300 400 500 600 700 800 900 1000 1100 1200 1300 1400 1500 1600 1700 1800 1900 2000

219–475
Compilation of the Babylonian Talmud

912–1172
The golden age
of Jewish life
and scholarship
in Spain

1242
Burning of
the Talmud
in Paris

1570
Ari and
the Safed
Kabbalists

1933–1945
Holocaust

133
The Bar Kochba revolt;
R. Akiva killed by the Romans

c.1960
"Return
to roots"
teshuvah
movement

1654
First Jews settle in
New Amsterdam (New York)

1770
The Enlightenment
movement

1989–2000
Mass
exodus of
Soviet Jewry

3761 3860 3960 4060 4160 4260 4360 4460 4560 4660 4760 4860 4960 5060 5160 5260 5360 5460 5560 5660 5760

TALMUDIC ERA   **SAVORAIC & GEONIC ERA**   **RISHONIM (EARLY SAGES)**   **ACHARONIM (LATER SAGES)**

33
Founding
of Christianity

476
Dissolution of
the Roman
Empire

610
Founding
of Islam

1066
Norman conquest
of England

1096–1291
The Crusades

1450
Invention
of printing

1492
The voyage
of Columbus

1776
American
Revolution

The first Jews

The fathers and mothers of the Jewish people—Abraham and Sarah, Isaac and Rebecca, and Jacob, Rachel, and Leah—are more than individuals who lived some 3,800 years ago. They are icons of Jewish identity, and their beliefs, character traits, and achievements form the spiritual DNA of the Jewish soul.

 NACHMANIDES, *COMMENTARY TO GENESIS 12:6*

Our sages have said: "All that happened to the Patriarchs is a signpost for the children" (*Midrash Tanchuma, Lech Lecha* 9). This is why the Torah elaborates in its account of their journeys, their well-digging, and other events of their lives…. For when something occurs to one of the [Patriarchs], one understands from it what is decreed to occur to their descendants.

 ZOHAR, *VOL. 3, 302a*

Each of the Patriarchs knew G-d from within their own essential character. Abraham personified Love; Isaac personified Awe; and Jacob personified Truth.

 R. MENACHEM M. SCHNEERSON
BASED ON *LIKUTEI SICHOT, VOL. 30, PP. 239–240*

The lives of the Patriarchs, as related by the Torah, are primarily an account of their achievements. The lives of the Matriarchs, on the other hand, are the story of the sacrifices they made for the sake of their children. Indeed, this is the essence of motherhood: the giving of one's very being and self to create and nurture another life.

This is why, according to Jewish tradition, the various *qualities* of a person's Jewishness—their tribal identity, or whether they are a Kohen, Levite, or Israelite—follows that of the father. But the essence of one's Jewishness—the question of whether a person is Jewish or not—is determined by the mother's identity.

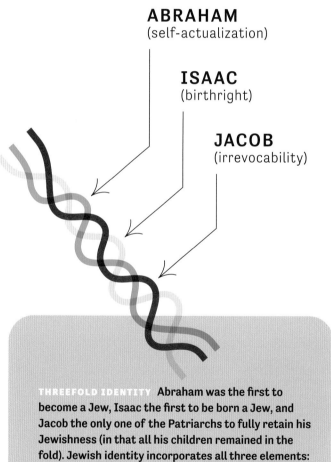

ABRAHAM
(self-actualization)

ISAAC
(birthright)

JACOB
(irrevocability)

THREEFOLD IDENTITY Abraham was the first to become a Jew, Isaac the first to be born a Jew, and Jacob the only one of the Patriarchs to fully retain his Jewishness (in that all his children remained in the fold). Jewish identity incorporates all three elements: self-generated values; recognizing and cultivating one's spiritual birthright; and the assurance that no Jew is ever irrevocably lost to their people. (*R. Yitzchak Hutner, 1906–1980*)

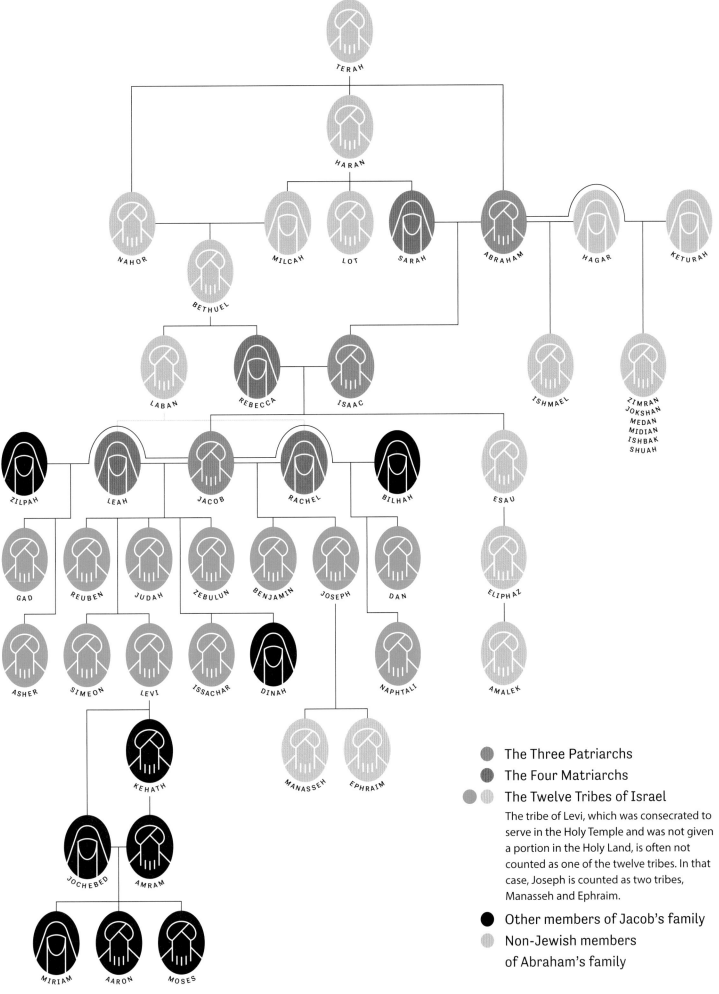

The Three Patriarchs

The Four Matriarchs

The Twelve Tribes of Israel

The tribe of Levi, which was consecrated to serve in the Holy Temple and was not given a portion in the Holy Land, is often not counted as one of the twelve tribes. In that case, Joseph is counted as two tribes, Manasseh and Ephraim.

Other members of Jacob's family

Non-Jewish members of Abraham's family

ABRAHAM AND SARAH

 MIDRASH RABBAH, *BEREISHITH 39:1*

There was once a man who was traveling from place to place, and he saw a mansion alight. Said he, "Can it be that this mansion has no master?" So the owner of the mansion looked out to him and said, "I am the master of the mansion."

In the same way, Abraham would go around saying, "Can it be that the world has no master?" So the Almighty looked out and said: "I am the master of the world."

 MAIMONIDES
MISHNEH TORAH, LAWS OF IDOLATRY, 1:3

No sooner was [Abraham] weaned, and he was but a child, that his mind began to seek and wonder: How do the heavenly bodies circle without a moving force? Who moves them? They cannot move themselves! Immersed amongst the foolish idol-worshippers of Ur Casdim, he had no one to teach him anything; his father, his mother, and his countrymen, and he amongst them, all worshipped idols. But his heart sought, until he comprehended the truth and he understood the way of righteousness by means of his sound wisdom. He came to know that there is one G-d who created all, and that in all existence there is no other. He came to know that the entire world erred.

At the age of forty Abraham recognized his Creator. He began to debate with the people of Ur Casdim, saying to them: This is not the way of truth that you are following. He smashed the idols, and began to teach the people that it is fitting to serve only the one G-d. When he began to defeat them with his arguments, the king wished to kill him; he was miraculously saved. He departed to Charan and continued to call in a great voice to the world, teaching them that there is one G-d.

 MIDRASH RABBAH, *SHIR HASHIRIM, 1:22*

Regarding Abraham and Sarah it is written, "the souls that they made in Charan" (Genesis 12:5). Yet if the entire world would convene they could not create a single flea! Rather, these are the converts whom Abraham and Sarah converted. Said R. Chunya: Abraham would convert the men, and Sarah would convert the women.

Abraham would invite them into his home, give them to eat and to drink, show them love and fellowship, and bring them under the wings of the Divine Presence. This teaches us that whoever brings a person close to the Almighty, it is considered as if they have created them.

 MIDRASH RABBAH, *SHEMOT 1:1*

The Almighty said to Abraham, "All that Sarah says to you, hearken to her voice" (Genesis 21:12). This teaches us that Sarah was superior to Abraham in prophecy.

 ETHICS OF THE FATHERS, *CH. 5, MISHNAH 3*

With ten trials our father Abraham was tried, and he withstood them all, in order to make known how great was the love of our father Abraham.

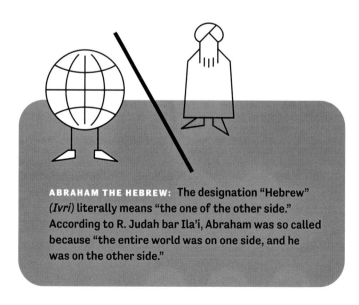

ABRAHAM THE HEBREW: The designation "Hebrew" (*Ivri*) literally means "the one of the other side." According to R. Judah bar Ila'i, Abraham was so called because "the entire world was on one side, and he was on the other side."

the ten trials of Abraham

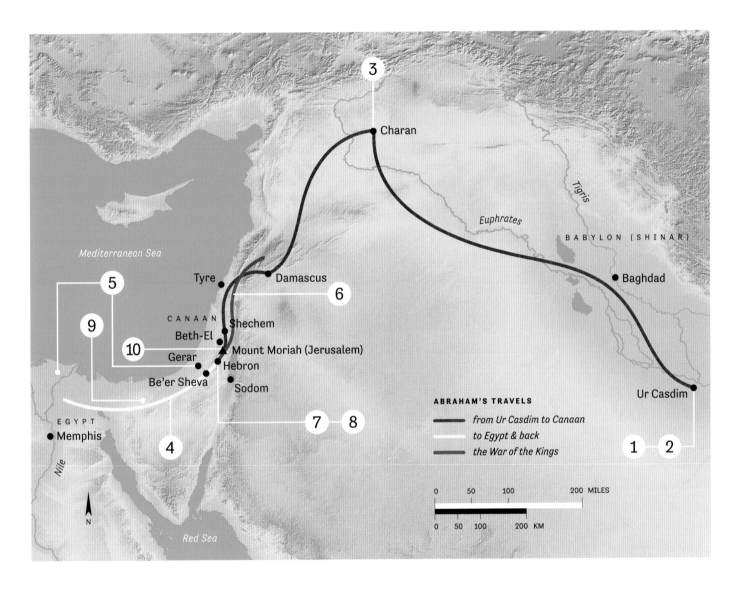

① **Abraham narrowly escapes being killed at birth by the Babylonian king Nimrod, and is subsequently hidden underground for many years.** (*Pirkei d'Rabbi Eliezer, 26*)

② **Abraham is imprisoned by Nimrod for smashing the idols of Ur Casdim and professing belief in the Creator. Nimrod has him thrown into a burning furnace, but he is miraculously saved.** (*Midrash Rabbah, Bereishith 38:13*)

③ **G-d commands Abraham to leave everything behind and set out to an unknown "land that I will show you."** (*Genesis 12:1*)

④ **A famine forces Abraham and Sarah to leave the Holy Land soon after their arrival there.** (*Genesis 12:10*)

⑤ **The abductions of Sarah by Pharaoh and by Abimelech.** (*Genesis 12:11–20 and 20:1–18*)

⑥ **Abraham goes to war against four mighty kings to rescue his nephew Lot.** (*Genesis 14:13–24*)

⑦ **The "Covenant Between the Parts," at which Abraham is informed of the exile and hardship destined for his descendants.** (*Genesis 15:7–21*)

⑧ **Abraham is commanded to circumcise himself at the advanced age of ninety-nine.** (*Genesis 17:9–27*)

⑨ **The banishment of Hagar and Ishmael.** (*Genesis 21:9–14*)

⑩ **The Binding of Isaac.** (*Genesis 22*)

THE BIRTH OF ISAAC

Abraham and the Three Angels (detail),
Marc Chagall, France, 1966

 GENESIS 17:17–19, 18:9–14, 21:1–6

Abraham fell upon his face, and he laughed. And he said in his heart: "Shall a child be born to a one-hundred-year-old man? And if Sarah, shall a ninety-year-old woman give birth?"...

G-d said: "But your wife Sarah will give birth to a son unto you, and you shall call his name Isaac ('will laugh'). And I will establish my covenant with him, as an everlasting covenant for his descendants after him."

They said to him, "Where is your wife Sarah?"; and he said, "Here in the tent." And he said: "Return I will return to you at this time next year, and behold, your wife Sarah will have a son." And Sarah was listening at the doorway of the tent.... Sarah laughed within herself, saying: "After I have withered would there be rejuvenation for me...?"

G-d said to Abraham: "Why is this that Sarah laughed, saying, 'Would I then truly give birth, and I have grown old?' Is anything beyond G-d? At the appointed time I will return to you, at this time next year, and Sarah will have a son."

G-d remembered Sarah as He had said; and G-d did unto Sarah as He had spoken. Sarah conceived and gave birth to a son ... at the appointed time, which G-d had spoken. Abraham called the name of the son that was born to him ... Isaac. Abraham circumcised his son Isaac at the age of eight days, as G-d had commanded him....

And Sarah said: "G-d has made laughter for me; everyone who hears will laugh for me."

⊘ R. SAMSON RAPHAEL HIRSCH
COMMENTARY TO GENESIS 17:17 AND 18:1

There seems to be no getting away from laughter when it comes to Isaac's birth: Abraham laughed, Sarah laughed, the whole world laughed.... For the very existence of this child and the people he would engender is, in its essence, a divine absurdity. The notion that a 100-year-old man and his 90-year-old wife, who have never had a child in the course of their long married life, should bear a son, and to place the hopes of the whole future of mankind on this child!

According to all natural conditions of cause and effect, the entire existence of the Jewish people, its history, its hopes, its expectations, must appear as the most laughable pretension. It only makes sense when it reckons on the deeply infringing, completely free almighty will of the Almighty G-d.

That was why G-d waited for the first seed of this nation to be laid until the "absurd" old age of its ancestors; that was why He waited to fulfill His promise until all human hopes for its realization had ended. For it was a question of creating a nation which, from the very beginning of its existence, was to be in opposition to all the ordinary laws of world history—an intimation of the divine in the midst of mankind.

THE BINDING OF ISAAC

The "Binding of Isaac" is one of the most dramatic narratives in the Torah. It is also one of the most disturbing. It is true, as many of the commentaries point out, that its final message is that the Almighty does *not* desire that Isaac be killed. The closing verses of the Torah's account, however, make it clear that the "Binding" is more than a statement against human sacrifice. In these verses G-d vows that Abraham's deed will serve as the foundation of His relationship with Abraham and Isaac's descendants. In the words of Don Isaac Abarbanel, "This chapter constitutes the entire capital of Israel's merit before their Father in heaven."

Abraham's supreme test offers the following challenge to his heirs: To live a G-dly life with the same passion with which the martyr embraces death. To cultivate a commitment so absolute that one is literally prepared to lay down one's life for it, and then apply the full brunt of that commitment not toward the annihilation of life, but to its development and perfection.

GENESIS 22:1–18

It was after these things that G-d tested Abraham. And He said to him, "Abraham!" And he said, "Here I am."

And He said: "Please take your son, your only one, whom you love, Isaac, and go you to the land of Moriah; and bring him up there as an ascent-offering upon one of the mountains, which I will say to you."

Abraham arose early in the morning, and he saddled his donkey, and he took his two lads with him, and his son Isaac; he split wood for the ascent-offering, and he arose and he went to the place which G-d said to him.

On the third day, Abraham lifted his eyes and he saw the place from afar. And Abraham said to his lads: "Sit you here with the donkey, and I and the lad will go until like so; and we will worship, and we will return to you."

Abraham took the wood for the ascent-offering and he placed it on his son Isaac, and he took in his hand the fire and the slaughtering-knife; and the both of them went together.

Isaac spoke to his father Abraham, and he said, "My father." And he said, "Here I am, my son." And he said, "Here are the fire and the wood, but where is the lamb for the ascent-offering?"

And Abraham said: "G-d will see to Himself the lamb for the ascent-offering my son"; and the both of them went together.

They came to the place which G-d said to him. Abraham built there the altar, and he arranged the wood; and he bound his son Isaac, and he placed him upon the altar, above the wood.

Abraham sent forth his hand, and he took the slaughtering-knife, to slaughter his son.

And an angel of G-d called to him from the heavens, and he said, "Abraham! Abraham!"; and he said, "Here I am." And he said, "Do not send forth your hand to the lad, and do not do anything to him; for now I know that you fear G-d, and you did not withhold your son, your only one, from Me."

After that, Abraham lifted his eyes and he saw, behold, a ram is caught in the thicket by its horns; Abraham went and took the ram, and he brought it up as an ascent-offering in place of his son.

Abraham called the name of that place *Ado-nai Yir'eh* ("G-d will see"); as it is said today, "In the mountain of G-d it shall be seen."

An angel of G-d called to Abraham a second time from the heavens. And he said: "By Myself I have sworn, says G-d, that because you have done this thing, and did not withhold your son, your only one. That bless will I bless you, and multiply will I multiply your descendants as the stars of the heavens, and as the sand that is on the shore of the sea; and your descendants shall inherit the gate of their enemies. And in your descendants will be blessed all nations of the world, because you have listened to My voice."

The Binding of Isaac, mosaic pavement by Marianos and Hanina, Beth Alpha Synagogue, Land of Israel, 6th century CE

What was the purpose of Abraham's "test"?

■ Up to this point, Abraham served the Almighty exclusively with the attribute of *chesed* (love and benevolence). There was no *gevurah* (rigor and awe) in him. In order to achieve wholeness, both in himself and in his source above, Abraham had to bind his *chesed* to the *gevurah* of Isaac. (*Zohar, 2nd century CE*)

■ Abraham's test demonstrated two fundamental truths to all mankind: (a) The extent to which a person's love and awe of G-d can reach. (b) The veracity of prophecy; for had there been the slightest doubt in Abraham's mind that the Almighty had spoken this command to him, he would not have rushed to commit an act so extremely opposed to his every natural instinct. (*Maimonides, 1135–1204*)

■ G-d obviously does not need to test a person in order to know the extent of their faith; rather, the purpose of a "test" is to bring a person's potential goodness into actuality, as the value of a good deed is greater than a good intention. (*Nachmanides, 1194–1270*)

■ In the same way that exercising one's physical strength makes one stronger and exercising one's wisdom makes one wiser, so is the quality of a person's divine service developed by the difficulties it encounters. A test not only actualizes a person's faith but also increases it. (*R. Nissim Gerondi, 1320–1376*)

■ In offering up Isaac as a sacrifice to the Almighty, Abraham elevated all of Isaac's descendants to the height of closeness to the Divine. With this act, the people of Israel were liberated from the hegemony of all natural influences and placed under G-d's particular providence. (*R. Hasdai Crescas, c. 1349–1410*)

■ The instinct that sets devotion to G-d above every other love and desire is an inherently positive one. In Abraham's time, however, this instinct was expressed in reprehensible ways by those who offered human sacrifices to pagan gods. The Binding of Isaac established that G-d does not desire to be served in such a manner—that in its true, uncorrupted guise, the passion to serve G-d is in harmony with the natural morality of man, driving not the destruction of life but its elevation and enhancement. (*R. Abraham Isaac Kook, 1865–1935*)

■ The Binding of Isaac introduced true self-sacrifice into the human experience. As long as a person's sacrifice is for the sake of a certain goal or cause, it is still, if only in the most subtle way, a "selfish" act, as the person is personally invested in this cause. Only when a person can see no positive result from their action—as was the case when Abraham was called upon to sacrifice his son—and does it solely to carry out the divine will, has a truly selfless act taken place. Abraham's act empowered us, who follow in the path that he blazed, to attain true selflessness in our service of the Creator. (*R. Menachem M. Schneerson, 1902–1994*)

REBECCA

The twenty-fourth chapter of Genesis presents a detailed account of how Rebecca became the second of the four founding mothers of the Jewish people. It describes how Abraham sent his trusted servant, Eliezer, back to the land of his birth to find a wife for Isaac. The method employed by Abraham's servant has served as guidance for subsequent generations of Jewish spouse-seekers: beyond beauty and wisdom, look for a person with a kind heart and a generous spirit.

🎧 GENESIS 24:10–26

The servant took ten camels from his master's camels … and all the bounty of his master in his hand; and he arose and went to Aram Naharaim….

He kneeled the camels outside the city, at the water well, at evening time, the time when the water-drawers go out.

And he said: "Lord, the G-d of my master Abraham, please make happen before me today; and do a kindness with my master Abraham.

"Here I am standing upon the wellspring of water; and the daughters of the people of the city are going out to draw water.

"Let it be that the girl to whom I will say, 'Please tip your jug that I may drink,' and she will say, 'Drink, and also your camels I will give drink'; it is she whom you have proven for your servant, for Isaac…."

He had yet to finish speaking, and behold, Rebecca was going out … and her jug was on her shoulder. The girl was very beautiful, a virgin, and no man had known her. She went down to the wellspring, filled her jug, and came up.

The servant ran toward her, and he said: "Please sip me a bit of water from your jug."

And she said, "Drink, my master." She hurried and took down her jug upon her hand, and she gave him drink.

When she finished to give him drink, she said: "Also for your camels I will draw, until they have finished drinking."

She hurried and poured her jug into the trough, and ran again to the well to draw; and she drew for all his camels.

The man, wondering at her, held his peace, waiting to discern whether G-d has made his way successful or not…. And he said, "Whose daughter are you? Please tell me…." And she said to him, "I am the daughter of Bethuel the son of Milcah, to whom she gave birth unto Nahor [the brother of Abraham]."

🎧 GENESIS 24:67

Isaac brought her in to the tent [of] his mother Sarah. He married Rebecca, and she became his wife, and he loved her; and Isaac was consoled after his mother.

⬛ MIDRASH RABBAH, *BEREISHITH 60:16*

As long as Sarah was alive, there was a cloud hovering over the doorway of her tent. When Sarah died, that cloud departed. When Rebecca came, that cloud returned.

As long as Sarah was alive, her doors were open wide. When she died, that openness ended. When Rebecca came, that openness resumed.

As long as Sarah was alive, there was a blessing in the dough. When she died, that blessing departed. When Rebecca came, that blessing returned.

As long as Sarah was alive, there was a lamp burning from one Shabbat eve to the following Shabbat eve. When she died, that lamp ceased. When Rebecca came, it resumed.

Clay bottle, Eastern Mediterranean, 4th–3rd century BCE

JACOB

In the life of Abraham, we recognize a paradigm of Jewish generosity and social commitment. In the personality of Isaac, we discern the Jew's fear of Heaven and silent sacrifice. In Jacob, who closes the triad of the "Patriarchs," we see a prototype of his descendants' devotion to learning. Jacob spends the first half of his life as "a dweller in the tents of learning," and his first act upon his arrival in Egypt—where he would live his final 17 years—was to establish a house of study. Jacob is also an archetype for the Jew's epochal perseverance under conditions of exile and adversity: in foreign Charan, in the employ of the deceitful Laban, he built his family and fortune; in alien Egypt, he imparted a lasting legacy to the fledgling nation of Israel.

If Abraham exemplified love and Isaac personified awe, Jacob epitomized truth: the incessant quest for truth, and the consistency and persistency of truth.

Contemporary view of Harran, Turkey (the Biblical "Charan"), birthplace of Leah and Rachel

CORNFIELD

events and periods in Jacob's life

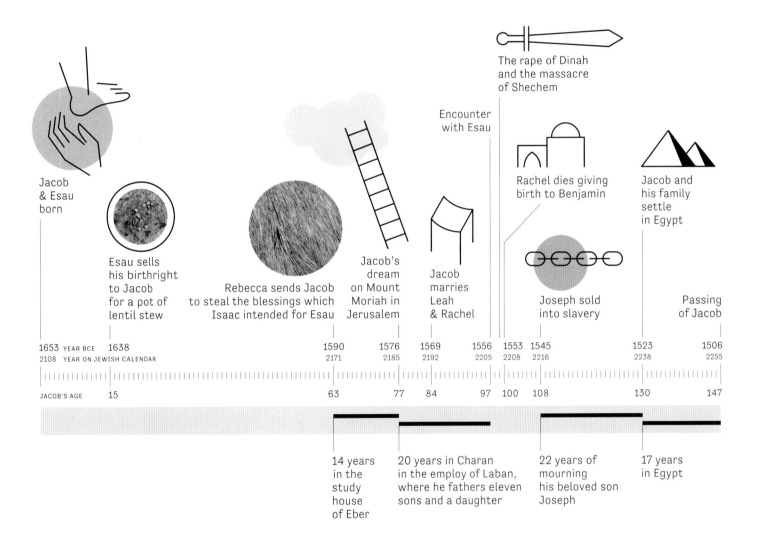

Jacob & Esau born

Esau sells his birthright to Jacob for a pot of lentil stew

Rebecca sends Jacob to steal the blessings which Isaac intended for Esau

Jacob's dream on Mount Moriah in Jerusalem

Jacob marries Leah & Rachel

Encounter with Esau

The rape of Dinah and the massacre of Shechem

Rachel dies giving birth to Benjamin

Joseph sold into slavery

Jacob and his family settle in Egypt

Passing of Jacob

1653	1638		1590	1576	1569	1556	1553	1545		1523	1506

YEAR BCE

YEAR ON JEWISH CALENDAR

| 2108 | | | 2171 | 2185 | 2192 | 2205 | 2208 | 2216 | | 2238 | 2255 |

JACOB'S AGE

| 15 | | 63 | 77 | 84 | 97 | 100 | 108 | | 130 | 147 |

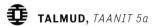

14 years in the study house of Eber

20 years in Charan in the employ of Laban, where he fathers eleven sons and a daughter

22 years of mourning his beloved son Joseph

17 years in Egypt

GENESIS 25:27

Jacob was a wholesome man, a dweller of tents.

MIDRASH RABBAH, *BEREISHITH 63:10*

"A dweller of tents"—of the houses of learning of Shem and Eber.

PIRKEI D'RABBI ELIEZER, *CHAPTERS 37–38*

"Like a man who flees from a lion and a bear encounters him; he enters his house and leans his hand against the wall, and a snake bites him...." (Amos 5:19). This is Jacob. He flees from Laban, and Esau ambushes him on the road like an aggrieved bear. He enters his home, the land of Canaan, and the snake Shechem bites him...

GENESIS 32:29

No longer shall your name be called "Jacob," but rather "Israel." For you have wrestled with the divine and with men, and you have prevailed.

TALMUD, *TAANIT 5a*

Our father Jacob did not die. As his seed is alive, he too is alive.

THE WRESTLING TWINS

The Jacob-Esau contest is a recurring theme in the words of the prophets and sages of Israel. On the historical level, it represents the conflict of Judea and Rome—the clash of word and sword that has defined the Jewish people's encounter with the gentile world for millennia. On a more universal plane, Esau embodies the materialism and violence of the present world, and Jacob the spirituality and perfection of the World to Come. And in the internal world of the human psyche, Esau and Jacob represent the dichotomy between our "animal soul" and "divine soul"—between our drive for self-gratification and our striving for union with our source in our Creator.

A divide so primal and prevalent could not be resolved in the lifetimes of the original Jacob and Esau. Rather, it awaits its final resolution when "the saviors shall ascend Mount Zion to judge the Mountain of Esau" (Obadiah 1:21) in the Messianic age.

 GENESIS 25:21–28

Isaac supplicated to G-d facing his wife, as she was barren; G-d acquiesced to him, and his wife Rebecca conceived.

The children struggled inside her, and she said: "If so, why am I thus?" And she went to inquire of G-d. G-d said to her:

Two nations are in your belly
and two kingdoms from your innards will diverge;
kingdom will overpower kingdom
and the greater will serve the younger.

Her days to give birth were fulfilled, and behold, twins were in her belly.

The first one came out ruddy, his entirety as a hairy mantle; and they called his name Esau.

After that his brother came out, his hand holding-fast to the heel of Esau, and he called his name Jacob; Isaac was sixty years old when she gave birth to them.

The lads grew. Esau was a man who knows game, a man of the field; and Jacob was a wholesome man, a dweller of tents.

Isaac loved Esau for the game in his mouth; and Rebecca loved Jacob.

 GENESIS 27:22

The voice is the voice of Jacob, and the hands are the hands of Esau.

 TALMUD, *GITTIN 57b*

"The voice is the voice of Jacob": this teaches us that no prayer is effective unless the descendants of Jacob have a part in it. "And the hands are the hands of Esau": this teaches us that no war is successful unless the descendants of Esau have a share in it.

 MAIMONIDES, *INTRODUCTION TO AVOT, SECTION 6*

The philosophers say that a perfectly pious person who desires only good is greater than a person who is drawn to immoral deeds yet conquers their desires. But when we examine the words of the sages of the Talmud on this matter, we find that one who craves sinful things, yet resists them, is more worthy and more fulfilled than one who does not desire them. They went so far as to say (Talmud, *Sukkah* 52a): "The greater a person is, the greater is their evil inclination."

R. MENACHEM M. SCHNEERSON
BASED ON *IGROT KODESH, VOL. 22, PP. 360–361*

Jacob is born grasping Esau's heel because this is the purpose for which "Jacob" comes down to the world. The divine soul is perfect, and perfect in its relationship with its Creator; for itself, it lacks for nothing. The purpose of its terrific descent into physical life is to rectify and elevate "Esau"—the animal soul, the physical body, and the material world.

JACOB'S DREAM

 GENESIS 28:10–14

Jacob went out from Be'er Sheba; and he went to Charan.

He encountered the place, and he lodged the night there for the sun had come down; and he took of the stones of the place, and he placed at his head. And he lay in that place.

He dreamed: Behold, a ladder was stood to the earth and its head reached the heavens. And behold, angels of G-d were ascending and descending on it.

And behold, G-d was standing over him, and He said: "I am G-d, the G-d of your father Abraham and the G-d of Isaac; the land upon which you lie, to you I will give it, and to your descendants.

"Your descendants shall be as the dust of the earth. You will break out to the west and to the east, to the north and to the south; and all the families of the earth will be blessed through you and your descendants."

What do the ladder in Jacob's dream and its ascending and descending angels represent?

■ The rise of and fall of empires and world powers. *(Pesikta d'Rav Kahana, 5th century)*

■ The altar in the Holy Temple, upon whose ramp the priests ascended and descended to bring offerings to the Almighty. *(Bar Kapara, 3rd century)*

■ Mount Sinai, where Moses ascended to heaven and the Torah was brought down to earth. *(Bereishith Rabbah, 3rd century)*

■ Prayer. *(Zohar, 2nd century)*

■ Prophecy. *(Maimonides, 1135–1204)*

■ Material wealth, by means of which a person can ascend to the greatest heights or descend to the lowest depths. *(R. Jacob ben Asher, c. 1270–1345)*

Jacob's Ladder, Shalom Moskovitz, Israel, before 1980

■ The ladder is the soul of man, by means of which good deeds are raised up to the heavens and divine blessings are brought down to earth. *(R. Chaim ibn Attar, 1696–1743)*

■ The cycle of "rushing and returning" that drives the whole of Creation. Every created thing is constantly striving to be subsumed within its source in G-d, only to be driven back to its place and task in the world. *(R. Moses Chaim Luzzatto, 1707–1746)*

■ The ladder is man's service of the Creator, whose ups and downs are both integral to a person's journey. *(R. Shalom Noach Beresovsky of Slonim, 1911–2000)*

RACHEL AND LEAH

Jacob's partners in generating the Jewish people are two matriarchs: Rachel and Leah. The beautiful and charismatic Rachel represents the pursuit of spirituality and self-perfection, while the underappreciated yet fruitful Leah is the commitment to good deeds and to the rectification of the physical world.

The nation of Israel is not a homogeneous whole. It incorporates twelve tribes, each with its distinct character and calling, which are more generally grouped as "the children of Leah" and "the children of Rachel." Indeed, the rivalry between these two factions runs a seam through the whole of Jewish history. For both endeavors, and even the conflict between them, are indispensable to the mission of Israel.

GENESIS 29:16–30

Laban had two daughters; the name of the elder was Leah, and the name of the younger was Rachel. The eyes of Leah were tender, and Rachel was beautiful of form and beautiful of appearance.

Jacob loved Rachel. And he said, "I will serve you seven years for Rachel your younger daughter." And Laban said, "Better I give her to you than I give her to another man; stay with me."

Jacob worked for Rachel seven years. They were in his eyes as a few days, in his love of her.

And Jacob said to Laban, "Bring-here my wife, as my days are fulfilled, and I will come to her." Laban gathered all the people of the place, and he made a feast. And it was in the evening, and he took his daughter Leah and he brought her in to him; and he came to her.

It was in the morning, and behold, she was Leah! And he said to Laban: "What is this you have done to me? Have I not served with you for Rachel? Why have you deceived me?"

And Laban said: "It is not so done in our place, to give the younger before the firstborn. Fulfill this one's week, and we will give you also this one, for the service which you will serve with me for an additional seven years."

Jacob did so … and he gave him his daughter Rachel as a wife for him…. He came also to Rachel, and he loved also Rachel more than Leah; and he served with him an additional seven years.

 MIDRASH RABBAH, *EICHAH, PREFACE 24*

On the day that the Holy Temple was destroyed and the people of Israel were driven into exile, the Almighty was weeping: "Woe is to Me for my home! My children, where are you? My priests, where are you? My beloved ones, where are you? What can I do for you? I warned you, and you did not repent…!"

Immediately, Abraham spoke up and said: "Master of the world! You gave me a son when I was one hundred years old. When he matured and was a young man of thirty-seven, You said to me, 'Bring him up as an offering to Me.' I made myself cruel, showing him no mercy. I myself bound him. Will You not remember this for me, and have mercy on my children?"

Isaac spoke up and said: "Master of the world! When father said to me, 'G-d will see to Himself the lamb for the ascent-offering my son,' I did not hesitate over Your words. I was bound with a willing heart upon Your altar, and stretched out my neck under the knife. Will You not remember this for me, and have mercy on my children?"

Jacob spoke up and said: "Master of the world…! Did I not stay in Laban's house for twenty years? And when I left, and the wicked Esau approached me and wished to kill my children, I was prepared to die for them…. For the majority of my days, I suffered greatly on their behalf. Will You not remember this for me, and have mercy on my children?"

Moses spoke up and said: "Master of the world! Was I not a faithful shepherd of Israel for forty years, running before them like a horse in the wilderness? When the time came for them to enter the Land, You decreed

Tomb of Rachel, Bethlehem, Land of Israel, 1890s

that my bones shall remain fallen in the wilderness. And now that they have been exiled, You send for me to weep over them...?"

But a heavenly voice came forth and said: "This is My decree...!"

At that moment, our mother Rachel leaped forward and said: "Master of the world! It is known to You that your servant Jacob loved me with a great love, and he labored seven years for my sake. When the time of my marriage to my husband arrived, my father plotted to exchange me for my sister. This was a most difficult thing for me, as the plot became known to me; I informed my husband, and I gave him a signal so that he could distinguish between me and my sister.... But

then I reconsidered my action, and I suppressed my desire, because I had compassion for my sister that she should not be disgraced. In the evening ... I gave my sister all the signals I had given to my husband, so that he should think that she was Rachel....

"Now if I, who am but flesh and blood and dust and ashes, was not jealous of my rival and did not allow her to be shamed and disgraced, You, who are a living, everlasting, and compassionate king, why are You jealous of the worship of idols that are of no substance, that You exiled my children and had them killed by the sword, and allowed their enemies to do with them as they wished...?"

Immediately the Almighty's compassion was aroused and He said: "For your sake, Rachel, I will restore Israel to their place."

JOSEPH AND HIS BROTHERS

Joseph is one of the most fascinating characters in Jewish history. He suffers the indignities of slavery and unjust imprisonment, yet he finds a way to harness those very conditions to achieve his successes, rising to become the de facto ruler of a mighty empire and the one who saves the entire region from famine. We observe his spiritual growth from a favorite son engaging in "youthful frivolities," whose behavior so enraged his brothers that they sold him into slavery, to the magnanimous leader who comforts his shame-stricken brothers when he reveals his identity to them. It is not forgiveness that Joseph offers his brothers, but something far deeper: the assurance that in his eyes, everything that happened to him was ordained by G-d for the sake of a greater good, so that he bears them no ill will in the first place.

 GENESIS 45:1–8

Joseph was not able to constrain himself … and he called: "Remove every man from my presence!" And no man stood with him when Joseph made himself known to his brothers.

He put his voice to weeping; and Egypt heard, and the house of Pharaoh heard.

Joseph said to his brothers: "I am Joseph, is my father still alive?"; and his brothers could not answer him, as they were bewildered before him.

And Joseph said to his brothers, "Please approach me," and they approached. And he said, "I am Joseph your brother, whom you sold to Egypt.

"And now, do not be distressed, and it should not be irate in your eyes, that you sold me here; for as a source of livelihood, G-d has sent me before you. It is now two years of famine within the land; and another five years,

in which there is no plowing and harvest….

"It is not you who sent me here, but G-d; He set me as a patron to Pharaoh, and as master of his entire house, and a ruler in all the land of Egypt."

 MIDRASH TANCHUMA, *VAYEISHEV 4*

To what is this comparable? To a cow who needed to be yoked to the plow, but was withholding her neck from the yoke. So they took her calf from behind her and drew it to the place where they wanted her to plow. When the cow heard her calf bleating, she went, despite herself, because of her child.

So too, the Almighty sought to fulfill the decree of the exile in Egypt prophesied to Abraham. So He contrived all the events [of the selling of Joseph], in order to cause Jacob to go down to Egypt.

the saga of Joseph and his brothers

1562 BCE

Joseph is born. He is the youngest of the children Jacob fathers in Charan, but the first to be born to Jacob's most beloved wife, Rachel.

1553 BCE

Rachel dies while giving birth to her second son, Benjamin, shortly after Jacob returns with his family to the Holy Land.

1545 BCE

The brothers become jealous of Jacob's preferential treatment of Joseph, and Joseph fuels their jealousy by relating his dreams, which foretell that he will rule over them. Prompted by Judah, the brothers sell Joseph into slavery, and make Jacob believe that Joseph was killed by a wild animal.

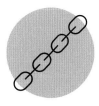

1544 BCE

Joseph is purchased by Potiphar, a minister in the Egyptian royal court, and rises to become the administrator of all of Potiphar's affairs. But when Joseph rejects the advances of Potiphar's wife, she libels him and has him thrown into the royal dungeon.

1534 BCE

Joseph earns the trust of the royal prison warden, who puts him in charge of all the prisoners' affairs. Imprisoned with Joseph are two of Pharaoh's ministers, the chief butler and the chief baker. Joseph interprets their dreams, and asks the chief butler to intervene on his behalf.

1532 BCE

Joseph is taken from prison to interpret Pharaoh's dreams. He predicts the coming of seven years of plenty followed by seven years of famine, and proposes a plan for surviving the famine by storing grain during the years of plenty. Pharaoh appoints Joseph viceroy of Egypt.

1525–1523 BCE

Joseph's brothers come to Egypt to purchase grain during the famine, but fail to recognize the Egyptian ruler as the lad they sold into slavery. Joseph first compels them to bring Benjamin to Egypt, and then accuses Benjamin of stealing his silver goblet and threatens to make Benjamin his slave. This time, the brothers do not abandon Rachel's child. Judah pleads for Benjamin, and offers himself as a slave in his place.

1523 BCE

Joseph reveals his identity to his brothers. Jacob and his seventy descendants settle in the Egyptian province of Goshen.

1506 BCE

Jacob dies in Egypt. The brothers fear that Joseph will now take revenge on them, but Joseph again reassures them, saying: "You plotted evil upon me, but G-d plotted it for the good."

1452 BCE

Joseph dies at the age of 110, after serving as viceroy of Egypt for 80 years.

Exodus and Sinai

In this section, we look at the events and processes by which the seventy souls of Jacob's family developed into the nation of Israel: the "smelting pit" of the Egyptian bondage that forged them into a people; the Exodus from Egypt, which the prophet Ezekiel describes as the "birth" of Israel; the revelation at Mount Sinai, where the people of Israel received the Torah and entered into a covenant with G-d; and the events of Israel's forty-year journey through the wilderness, in the course of which a new generation, born in freedom and reared on miracles, prepared to enter the land promised to their ancestors.

DEUTERONOMY 4:32–35

Ask now after the early days that came before you, from the day that G-d created man upon the earth, and from one end of the heavens to the other: Has there ever been the likes of this great thing, or has anything like it been heard?

Have a people heard the voice of G-d speaking from within the fire, as you have heard, and lived?

Or has G-d endeavored to take for Himself a nation from the bowels of a nation, with trials, with signs and with miracles, with battles, with a mighty hand and with an outstretched arm, and with great awesome deeds, as all that the Lord your G-d has done for you in Egypt before your eyes?

You were shown to know that G-d is the G-d, there is none else besides Him.

Exodus, Isac Friedlander, United States, 1931

THE QUEST FOR FREEDOM The Biblical account of the Exodus has served as a source of inspiration for numerous liberation movements, from the abolitionist movement in 18th- and 19th-century America to human rights struggles around the world (see p. 145).

Recreation of ancient Egyptian brick mold

ENSLAVEMENT IN EGYPT

EXODUS 1:1–22

These are the names of the children of Israel, those coming into Egypt; with Jacob, each with their household they came.

Reuben, Simeon, Levi, and Judah. Issachar, Zebulun, and Benjamin. Dan and Naphtali, Gad and Asher. All souls that were the issue of the loins of Jacob were seventy souls; and Joseph was in Egypt.

Joseph died, and all his brothers, and all that generation.

And the children of Israel were fruitful, and swarmed, and multiplied, and grew strong, exceedingly-exceedingly; and the land was filled with them.

A new king arose over Egypt who did not know Joseph. And he said to his people: "Behold, the people of the children of Israel are more numerous and mighty than us. Let us wisen ourselves to them, lest they multiply, and it will be that when there happens a war, they will also be added on to our enemies, and they will wage war with us, and they will go up from the land."

They placed taskmasters upon them, in order to afflict them with their burdens; and they built storage cities for Pharaoh—Pithom and Raamses.

But as much as they afflicted them, so did they multiply and so did they expand; and they were frustrated before the children of Israel.

The Egyptians enslaved the children of Israel with crushing labor. They made bitter their lives with hard labor, with mortar and with bricks, and with every labor in the field....

And Pharaoh commanded all his people, to say: "Every son that is born, throw him into the river; and every daughter you shall make live."

Door jamb relief,
Memphis, Egypt, 1213–1204 BCE

MIDRASH RABBAH, MIDRASH TANCHUMA, AND RASHI, *EXEGESES TO EXODUS 1 AND 38*

R. Akiva taught: In the merit of the righteous women of that generation the Israelites were delivered from Egypt.

At first, Pharaoh only insisted that they make the prescribed number of bricks each day. Then he commanded that they should not be allowed to sleep in their homes, so that they should not be able to procreate. The taskmasters said to them: "If you go home to sleep, you will lose a few hours each morning from your work when we send for you, and you will not complete the allotted number." So they made them sleep on the ground out in the field.

What did the daughters of Israel do? They would go down to draw water from the river, and the Almighty would send small fish into their pitchers, which they drew up half water and half fish. They then set two pots on the fire, one for hot water and the other for the fish. They sold the fish and bought wine, which they carried to their husbands in the field. They washed and anointed them, and fed them and gave them to drink. They would then take out their mirrors and look into them with their husbands, teasing them, "Look, I'm more beautiful than you…" thus arousing their desire and cohabitating with them. The Almighty caused them to conceive immediately, and they gave birth to multiple children in each pregnancy.

When Moses was commanded to build the Tabernacle in the wilderness, all the Israelites contributed. Some brought silver, others brought gold…. Said the women: What do we have to contribute to the making of the Tabernacle? They went and brought their mirrors to Moses. When Moses saw those mirrors, he rejected them, as they are instruments of licentiousness. Said G-d to Moses: "Accept them, as these mirrors are more precious to Me than everything else. With these mirrors, the women raised up hosts of children in Egypt."

MAIMONIDES
MISHNEH TORAH, LAWS OF IDOLATRY, 1:3

As the Israelites' years in Egypt grew long, they regressed to learn from [the Egyptians'] ways and to worship idols like them…. A little bit longer, and the sapling that Abraham planted would have been uprooted, and the children of Jacob would have reverted to the error and confusion of the world. It was out of the Almighty's love for us, and His keeping of the oath He made to our father Abraham, that He made Moses the master of all prophets and sent him.

R. MENACHEM M. SCHNEERSON
BASED ON *LIKUTEI SICHOT, VOL. 1, PP. 111–113*

In Egypt, where very little rain falls, agriculture is completely dependent on the Nile, whose overflow fills a network of irrigation canals. The ancient Egyptians therefore deified the Nile, worshipping it as the ultimate endower of life.

Thus, Pharaoh's decree to drown the Hebrew children in the Nile had both a physical and a spiritual significance. In addition to the threat of physical annihilation, our ancestors in Egypt faced the threat of having their children drowned in the Nile in the spiritual sense—of becoming completely submerged in the Nile-cult that regards the natural means of sustenance as gods.

Today's "Pharaoh"s are the more benign forces that claim to rule our life—the conventions of modern society. These, too, threaten to drown our children in their Nile—in the educational priorities and career choices that society venerates as the providers of sustenance and life. These are only tools of sustenance, as the Nile is an instrument of the Creator's sustenance of those who dwell along its banks. But when a person invests their choicest energies in the instrument rather than in their relationship with their Creator and Source, they are succumbing to the Pharaonic decree to be "drowned in the Nile."

MOSES

 EXODUS 2:1–10

There went a man from the house of Levi, and he married the daughter of Levi.

The woman conceived and gave birth to a son. She saw him that he was good, and she hid him for three months.

When she was no longer able to hide him, she took for him a papyrus box, and plastered it with plaster and pitch. She placed the child in it, and she placed it in the reeds on the edge of the river.

His sister stood herself from afar, to know what would be done to him.

The daughter of Pharaoh went down to bathe on the river, and her girls were going alongside the river. She saw the box in the midst of the reeds, and she sent forth her handmaiden, and she took it.

She opened and she saw him, the child, and behold, a weeping lad; and she had mercy on him, and she said: "This is of the children of the Hebrews...."

The child grew up ... and he became a son to her; she called his name Moshe ("drawn"), as she said: For I have drawn him from the water.

 TALMUD, *SOTAH 12a–13a*

Amram was the leader of the generation. When he saw that the wicked Pharaoh had decreed, "Every son that is born you shall throw into the river," he said: In vain do we labor. He went and divorced his wife. Whereupon all the Israelites went and divorced their wives.

His daughter [Miriam] said to him: "Father, your decree is worse than Pharaoh's decree. Pharaoh decreed against the males; you have decreed against the males and the females. Pharaoh decreed regarding this world; you have decreed regarding this world and the World to Come. In the case of the wicked Pharaoh, there is a doubt as to whether his decree will be fulfilled or not; you are a righteous person, and your decree will certainly be fulfilled...."

So Amram went with the counsel of his daughter and remarried his wife; and they all went and took back their wives.... Aaron and Miriam danced before her, and the ministering angels proclaimed (Psalms 113:9), "The mother of children rejoices...."

It is written (Exodus 15:20), "Miriam the prophetess, the sister of Aaron...." This tells us that Miriam was already a prophetess when she was Aaron's sister only [i.e., before Moses was born]. She prophesied: "My mother is destined to give birth to a son who will save the people of Israel." When Moses was born, the entire house was filled with light. Her father stood and kissed her on the head, saying, "My daughter, your prophecy has been fulfilled!" Then, when Moses was placed in the Nile, her father stood and berated her over the head, saying, "My daughter, where is your prophecy?" Thus it is written, "His sister stood herself from afar, to know what would be done to him"—to know what would become of her prophecy....

Why did the hand of divine providence contrive that Moses should be raised in Pharaoh's palace?

■ So that the oppressors of Israel should be defeated from within, and that Pharaoh should be dethroned by the child he raised in his own home. (*Midrash Tanchuma, 3rd century*)

■ So that Moses should possess the mentality of a prince and ruler, rather than the docile nature of one who is raised in slavery. (*R. Abraham ibn Ezra, c. 1089–1164*)

■ The development of anything that is true and deep emerges from the shell that is extraneous to it, like a fruit that matures within its husk. (*R. Judah Loew of Prague, 1520–1609*)

EXODUS 2:11–21

Moses grew up, and he went out to his brethren; and he saw their sufferings. He saw an Egyptian man beating a Hebrew man of his brethren. He turned this way and that way, and saw that there was not a man; and he smote the Egyptian and buried him in the sand.

He went out on the second day, and behold, two Hebrew men were fighting; and he said to the wicked one, "Why would you smite your fellow?" And he said, "Who placed you as a man who is ruler and judge over us? Do you say to kill me, as you killed the Egyptian?" Moses was afraid and he said, "Indeed, the matter has become known!"

Pharaoh heard of this matter, and he sought to kill Moses; Moses fled from before Pharaoh, and he settled in the land of Midian, and he sat at the well.

The priest of Midian had seven daughters; they came and they drew up water and filled the gutters, to give drink to the flock of their father. The shepherds came and drove them away; Moses arose and rescued them, and he gave drink to their flock.

They came to Reuel their father, and he said, "Why have you hastened to come today?" And they said, "An Egyptian man saved us from the hand of the shepherds; and also draw did he draw up for us, and he gave drink to the sheep."

And he said to his daughters, "And where is he? Why is this that you have forsaken the man? Call him and he shall eat bread." Moses was willing to settle with the man; and he gave his daughter Zipporah in marriage to Moses.

R. SIMCHA ZISEL ZIV OF KELM
CHOCHMAH UMUSAR, CHAPTER 3

Before relating Moses' encounter at the burning bush, the Torah devotes an entire section to four events in Moses' early years.

First we are told that "Moses grew up," which Rashi explains as meaning that he came into greatness, as Pharaoh had appointed him to run his household. It would have been natural for Moses to be loyal to Pharaoh. Yet "he went out to his brethren and he saw their sufferings," which Rashi explains to mean that "he set his eyes and heart on them to feel their pain."

The Torah then tells us that not only did Moses identify with the sufferings of the community, but also with those of an individual. "He saw an Egyptian man beating a Hebrew man of his brethren" and acted to save the oppressed from the oppressor.

After this, the Torah tells us that not only did Moses do so in the case of an Egyptian beating a Hebrew, but also when "two Hebrew men were fighting." Also when the oppressor was a fellow Hebrew, he took up the burden of the oppressed and endeavored to rescue him.

Finally, the Torah tells us that not only in the land of his birth, where he enjoyed peace and tranquility, did Moses act this way, but also in another land, in Midian, as a foreigner, a fugitive from Pharaoh and from a death sentence, a wanderer burdened with his own troubles. Yet when he saw what the shepherds were doing to the Midianite women, unjustly driving them from the well, he rose up and came to their rescue, and also helped them give water to their flock.

Scripture elaborates in describing Moses' early life to inform us that it was for good reason that Moses was chosen to take the people of Israel out of Egypt and for the Torah to be given through him. In a profound way, Moses "assumed the burden of his fellow" (*Ethics of the Fathers*, 6:6)—which our sages list as one of the necessary qualities one must possess in order to acquire Torah.

R. JONATHAN SACKS, *CHABAD.ORG, PARASHAH COLUMNISTS, SHEMOT*

It was Freud's greatest Freudian slip, and for some reason his commentators, at least those that I've read, haven't noticed it.

In his last book, *Moses and Monotheism*, Freud notes that several scholars have identified a common theme in stories about the childhood of heroes. The hero's birth is fraught with danger. As a baby, he is exposed to the elements in a way that would normally lead to death—sometimes by being placed in a box and thrown into the water. The child is rescued and brought up by adoptive parents. Eventually, he discovers his true identity. It is a story told about Sargon, Gilgamesh, Oedipus, Romulus, and many others. It is also the story of Moses.

At this point, however, Freud notes that in one respect, the story of Moses isn't like the others at all. In fact, it's the opposite. In the conventional story, the hero's adoptive parents are humble, ordinary people. Eventually he discovers that he is actually of royal blood, a prince. In the Moses story, the reverse is the case. It is his adoptive family that is royal. He is brought up by the daughter of Pharaoh. His true identity, he discovers, is that he belongs, by birth, to a nation of slaves.

Freud saw this and then failed to see what it meant. Instead he changed tack and concluded that the story is a fabrication designed to conceal the fact that Moses was the son of Pharaoh's daughter; he really was a prince of Egypt. What Freud failed to realize is that the story of Moses is not a myth but an anti-myth.

Its message is simple and revolutionary. True royalty is the opposite of our conventional wisdom. It isn't privilege and wealth, splendor and palaces. It's moral courage. Moses, in discovering that he is the child of slaves, finds greatness.

Freud failed to see that he had come face to face with one of the most powerful moral truths the Bible ever taught. A child of slaves can be greater than a prince. G-d's standards are not power and privilege. They are about recognizing the divine image in the weak, the powerless, the afflicted, the suffering, and fighting for their cause.

 MIDRASH RABBAH, *SHEMOT 2:2*

It is written (Psalms 11:5), "G-d examines the righteous." And how does the Almighty examine them? With the shepherding of flocks.

Our sages taught: When Moses was tending the flock of Jethro in the wilderness, a young kid escaped. Moses ran after the kid until it reached a shady place with a pool of water and stopped to drink. When Moses approached it, he said, "I did not know that you ran away because of thirst! You must be weary." He placed the kid on his shoulder and walked back.

Said the Almighty: You are merciful in leading the flock of a mortal—you shall tend My flock, the people of Israel.

WHAT'S IN A NAME We know our greatest leader not by the name given to him by his biological parents, but by the name he was called by the Egyptian princess who saved his life and raised him as her own son, naming him "Moses" because "I drew him from the water" (Exodus 2:10). Indeed, the sages cite the case of Pharaoh's daughter as one of the examples that teach us that, "One who raises a child in their home, it is considered as if they have given birth to that child." *(Talmud, Sanhedrin 19b)*

THE BURNING BUSH

 EXODUS 3:1–17

Moses was shepherding the flock of his father-in-law…. He led the flock after the wilderness, and he came to the mountain of G-d, to Horeb.

An angel of G-d appeared to him in a heart of fire from within the thornbush; and he saw that, behold, the thornbush was burning with fire, and the thornbush was not consumed….

G-d called to him from within the thornbush, and He said: "Moses! Moses!" And he said, "Here I am."

And He said: "Do not come near to here; shed your shoes from your feet, as the place upon which you are standing is holy ground."

And He said: "I am the G-d of your father, the G-d of Abraham, the G-d of Isaac, and the G-d of Jacob"; and Moses hid his face, as he was afraid to look toward G-d.

And G-d said: "I have seen the affliction of My people who are in Egypt; I have heard their cries before their taskmasters; I know their hurt…. Now go, and I will send you to Pharaoh, and you shall take out My people, the children of Israel, from Egypt."

And Moses said to G-d: "Who am I that I should go to Pharaoh, and that I should take out the children of Israel from Egypt?"

And He said: "For I will be with you. And this is your sign that I Myself have sent you: When you take the people out of Egypt, you will serve G-d on this mountain….

"Go and gather the elders of Israel, and say to them: G-d, the G-d of your fathers appeared to me, the G-d of Abraham, Isaac, and Jacob, saying: Remember I have remembered you, and what is being done to you in Egypt…. I shall bring you up from the afflictions of Egypt, to the land of the Canaanite … to a land that flows with milk and honey."

Burning Bush, Robert Shore, New York, 2012

Why did G-d appear to Moses in a burning thornbush?

■ To teach us that no place, no matter how lowly, is devoid of the divine presence. (*R. Joshua ben Korchah, 2nd century*)

■ In order to convey that "I am with them in their distress." (*Psalms 91:15; Midrash Tanchuma, 3rd century*)

■ As the thornbush burned but was not consumed, so will the people Israel never be destroyed, despite all the persecutions to which they are subjected. (*Shemot Rabbah*)

■ The "heart of fire" in the thornbush represents the simple Jew's insatiable yearning for G-d. (*R. Israel Baal Shem Tov, 1698–1760*)

THE TEN PLAGUES

The plague		Purpose and message
1	The Nile turned into **BLOOD**.	The Nile was worshipped by the Egyptians, as it was the sole source of water in their rain-starved land. The plague of blood served to discredit the god of Egypt in the eyes of both the Egyptians and the Israelites.
2	Swarms of **FROGS** covered the whole of Egypt, invading the Egyptians' homes, beds, cooking ovens, and utensils.	Even a creature as innocuous as the frog, which presents no visible benefit or threat to man, was enlisted to carry out the divine will.
3	**LICE** infested the Egyptians.	Pharaoh's magicians were able to replicate the first two plagues, but their sorcery was unable to manipulate a creature as small as a louse, forcing them to concede that "this is the finger of G-d" (Exodus 8:15). The plague of lice demonstrated that the divine province extends even to the most miniscule entity.
4	**HORDES OF WILD ANIMALS** invaded the cities and homes of the Egyptians.	This plague demonstrated the Almighty's special providence over the people of Israel, when the hordes of wild beasts, whose nature is to roam indiscriminately, did not venture into the province of Goshen, where the Israelites lived.
5	**PESTILENCE** decimated all the livestock that were outside in the Egyptians' pastures and fields.	Those Egyptians who heeded Moses' warning, and did not leave their animals out in the field, had their herds spared, demonstrating that the divine justice rewards even as it punishes.

The ten plagues that Moses and Aaron wrought upon Egypt served not only to punish the Egyptians for the sufferings they inflicted on the Israelites and to force Pharaoh to allow the Israelites to go, but also to demonstrate to the Egyptians—and, even more importantly, to their Hebrew slaves—the hollowness of Egypt's power, the fallacy of its nature-worship, and that the Creator's authority and power is exclusive and all-embracing.

 EXODUS 5:1–2, 7:1–3

And after that, Moses and Aaron came and said to Pharaoh: "So said G-d, the G-d of Israel: 'Let My people go, to worship Me in the wilderness.'"

And Pharaoh said: "Who is G-d, that I should heed His voice…? I do not know G-d, and neither will I let Israel go…."

G-d said to Moses: "See, I have made you a judge over Pharaoh, and Aaron your brother will be your spokesman. You will speak all that I will command you, and

The plague		Purpose and message
6	The Egyptians were covered with **BOILS**.	Plagues 4, 5, and 6 represent a progression in the plagues' reach, from the abstract, to the tangible, to the personal. First the Egyptians were terrorized by the hordes, then their property was damaged by the pestilence, and finally their own bodies were covered with painful and humiliating boils.
7	An unearthly **HAIL**, consisting of ice and fire, rained down on Egypt.	Fire and ice collaborated in this plague, demonstrating that not only are the forces of nature subservient to the Creator, they will also transcend their most fundamental characteristics to serve the divine will.
8	A cloud of **LOCUSTS** descended upon Egypt and consumed all of the land's vegetation.	This was the point at which the Egyptians' resistance began to falter. For the first time, Pharaoh's servants urged him to let the Israelites go, and Pharaoh began to negotiate with Moses on who should be allowed to leave.
9	Utter **DARKNESS** prevailed throughout Egypt for seven days, while the Israelites moved freely in the light, even inside the Egyptians' homes.	On the very first day of Creation, G-d created light, separated between light and darkness, and set the cycle of day and night (Genesis 1:3–5). In the plague of darkness the most primal cycle of existence was turned on end, demonstrating that the Creator of nature wields it and contravenes it at will.
10	All **FIRSTBORN** Egyptians died at the stroke of midnight of Nisan 15.	In Egypt, the firstborn held the key positions in the government and the priesthood. Their sudden death struck a crippling blow to the very infrastructure of Egyptian society, and forced Pharaoh to literally drive the Israelites out of Egypt.

Aaron your brother will speak to Pharaoh…. And I will harden Pharaoh's heart, so as to multiply My signs and My wonders in the land of Egypt."

 EXODUS 12:29–39

It was midnight, and G-d struck every firstborn in the land of Egypt. From the firstborn of Pharaoh who sits on his throne, to the firstborn of the captive that is in the dungeon; and every firstborn of the cattle.

Pharaoh got up in the night, he and his servants and all of Egypt, and there was a great cry in Egypt; for there was no house without one dead. And he called to Moses and to Aaron in the night, and he said: "Get up, go out from the midst of my people, also you, also the children of Israel, and go serve G-d, as you spoke…."

The Egyptians pressed strongly on the people, to hurry and send them off from the land; for they said: We shall all die!… So they baked the dough which they brought out from Egypt as matzah cakes, as it did not leaven; for they were chased out from Egypt and could not tarry.

THE EXODUS

The Exodus is more than the birth of the Jewish people. It is a perpetual event, referred to in many Jewish rituals, recalled in almost every Jewish prayer. For the journey from slavery to freedom is the story of our national history, of each individual's life-trajectory, and the stated purpose of each day of our lives. The process by which the original Exodus unfolded—from Moses' encounter at the burning bush, to the plagues that loosened the shackles of Egypt, to the splitting of the sea that removed the final obstacle on the road to Sinai—informs each of our personal pathways to redemption.

 DEUTERONOMY 16:3

Remember the day that you went out of Egypt, all the days of your life.

 PASSOVER HAGGADAH

We were slaves to Pharaoh in Egypt, and the Almighty took us out from there with a mighty hand and with an outstretched arm. If G-d had not taken our ancestors out of Egypt, we, our children, and our children's children would still be enslaved to Pharaoh in Egypt....

In every generation, a person must see themselves as if they, personally, went out of Egypt.

 R. ABRAHAM SABA
TZROR HAMOR, EXODUS 12:40

When the time came for the people of Israel to leave Egypt, their exodus occurred in great haste, without even allowing time for the dough they were preparing to bake for their journey to rise. For if the redemption had not come at that very instant, the Israelites would have become so deeply enmeshed in the depravity of Egypt as to be irredeemable. This is why we say that

"if G-d had not taken our ancestors out of Egypt, we ... would still be enslaved to Pharaoh in Egypt."

 R. JUDAH LOEW OF PRAGUE
GEVUROT HASHEM, CH. 61

There are those who ask: What use is the Exodus to us, if today we are subjugated by other nations? But when the people of Israel were taken out of Egypt, freedom was made an inherent quality of their nature. After the Exodus, no circumstantial subjugation has the power to alter the essential state of the Jew, which is that of freedom and sovereignty. We might be physically enslaved, but our spirit remains free.

 R. SCHNEUR ZALMAN OF LIADI
SEFER HAMAAMARIM, HANACHOT HARAP, P. 9

The Hebrew word for Egypt, *Mitzrayim*, means "boundaries" and "narrow straits." We each need to achieve a personal "exodus from Egypt" every day of our lives—to free ourselves from that which limits and constrains us in our service of our Creator.

Escape from Egypt, The Golden Haggadah, Catalonia, 1320—1330

THE SPLITTING OF THE SEA

 EXODUS 12:37, 13:18–21, 14:5–31

The children of Israel journeyed from Rameses to Succoth, about six hundred thousand on foot, the men, besides the young children....

G-d led the people around by way of the desert to the Sea of Reeds.... G-d went before them by day in a pillar of cloud to lead them on the way, and at night in a pillar of fire to give them light; to travel day and night....

And Pharaoh and his servants had a change of heart toward the people, and they said: "What is this that we have done, that we have released Israel from serving us?" [Pharaoh] harnessed his chariot, and took his people with him. He took six hundred select chariots, and all the chariots of Egypt, with officers over them all.... And the Egyptians chased after them, and overtook them encamped by the sea....

Pharaoh drew near. The children of Israel lifted up their eyes, and, behold, the Egyptians were advancing after them. They were very frightened, and the children of Israel cried out to G-d.

And they said to Moses, "Are there no graves in Egypt, that you have taken us to die in the wilderness? What is this that you have done to us, to take us out of Egypt? Is this not the thing that we spoke to you in Egypt, saying, 'Leave us alone, and we will serve the Egyptians, as we would rather serve the Egyptians than die in the wilderness'?"

Moses said to the people, "Do not be afraid. Stand firm and see the salvation of G-d, which He will do for you today. For as you have seen the Egyptians today, you shall not see them again anymore, forever. G-d will fight for you, and you shall be silent."

And G-d said to Moses, "Why do you cry out to Me? Speak to the children of Israel, and they should move forward!

"And you, raise your staff and stretch out your hand over the sea, and split it; and the children of Israel will come within the sea on dry land...."

Moses stretched out his hand over the sea. And G-d led the sea with the strong east wind all night, and He made the sea into dry land; and the waters split.

The children of Israel entered within the sea on dry land; and the waters were for them as a wall, to their right and to their left.

The Egyptians pursued and came after them; all Pharaoh's horses, his chariots, and his horsemen, into the midst of the sea.... And G-d said to Moses, "Stretch out your hand over the sea...." And the waters returned and covered the chariots and the horsemen, the entire force of Pharaoh ... not even one of them survived....

On that day, G-d saved Israel from the hand of the Egyptians; and Israel saw the Egyptians dead on the shore of the sea. Israel saw the great hand that G-d had wrought upon the Egyptians; and the people feared G-d, and they believed in G-d and in Moses, His servant.

 MECHILTA, *BESHALACH, SECTION VAYEHI, 2*

As they stood at the shore of the sea, the people of Israel split into four factions. One faction said, "Let us throw ourselves into the sea." A second faction said, "Let us return to Egypt." A third said, "Let us wage war against the Egyptians." A fourth said, "Let us cry out to G-d."

To those who said, "Let us throw ourselves into the sea," Moses responded: "Do not be afraid. Stand firm and see the salvation of G-d." To those who said, "Let us return to Egypt," he said: "As you have seen Egypt this day, you shall not see them again anymore, forever." To those who said, "Let us wage war against the Egyptians," he said: "G-d will fight for you." And to those who said, "Let us cry out to G-d," he said: "And you shall be silent."

 R. MENACHEM M. SCHNEERSON
BASED ON *LIKUTEI SICHOT, VOL. 3, PP. 876–887*

The people of Israel had departed Egypt and were moving toward Mount Sinai, when they reached an impasse: the sea was in front of them, and the Egyptians were

Rolling Surf, Milton Avery, United States, 1958

closing in from behind. The "four factions" that formed among them represent four possible responses that a person or community might have when they find their path to carrying out the divine will obstructed by the prevailing reality.

One possible reaction is, "Let us throw ourselves into the sea." Let us submerge ourselves within the sea of Torah, the sea of religious life. Let us create our own closed communities, insulating ourselves and our families from the profane world out there.

At the other extreme is the reaction, "Let us return to Egypt." Let us accept the reality that it is the Pharaohs who wield the power in this world. We will do whatever we can, under the circumstances, to do what is right; but it is futile to imagine that we can change the way things are.

A third reaction is to "wage war against them"—to assume a confrontational stance against the hostile reality, battling it despite all odds.

A fourth reaction is to say, "Let us cry out to G-d." It is wrong to abandon the world, or to succumb to it, or to fight it; instead, we should deal with it on the spiritual plane. A single prayer can achieve more than the most secure fortress, the most servile appeasement, or the most aggressive army.

Moses rejected all four approaches. While each has its time and place, none of them represents the vision that should define our relationship with the world we inhabit. Rather, when we find our progress toward Sinai impeded by a hostile or indifferent world, we should heed the divine directive, "Speak to the children of Israel, and they should move forward!" Do one more mitzvah. Take one more step toward your goal.

And when we move forward, we will see that insurmountable barrier yield and that ominous threat fade away. We will see that the prevalent reality is not so real after all, and that it is in our power to reach our goal. Even if we have to split seas to get there.

GIVING OF THE TORAH

 EXODUS 19:1–9

In the third month from the exodus of the children of Israel from the land of Egypt; on this day, they arrived in the desert of Sinai…. Israel encamped there, opposite the mountain.

Moses ascended to G-d. And G-d called to him from the mountain, saying, "So shall you say to the house of Jacob, and tell the children of Israel:

"You have seen what I did to Egypt, and I have carried you on eagles' wings, and I have brought you to Me.

"And now, if you will listen to My voice and keep My covenant, you shall be to Me a special treasure out of all peoples, for Mine is the entire earth. You shall be to Me a kingdom of priests and a holy nation…."

And G-d said to Moses: "Behold, I am coming to you in the thickness of the cloud, in order that the people should hear when I speak to you, and they will also believe in you forever."

 EXODUS 24:4–7

Moses wrote all the words of G-d…. He took the book of the covenant and read it in the ears of the people; and they said: "All that G-d has spoken, we will do and we will hear."

 EXODUS 19:16–20:15

It was on the third day, when it was morning; there was thunder and lightning, and a thick cloud was upon the mountain, and the sound of the shofar, exceedingly powerful…. Moses brought the people out toward G-d from the camp; and they stood beneath the mountain….

G-d spoke all these words, saying:

I am the Lord your G-d, who took you out from the land of Egypt, from the house of slavery….

And all the people saw the voices, and the flames, the sound of the shofar, and the mountain smoking; and the people saw and trembled, and they stood from afar.

 EXODUS 24:12–18, 31:18

G-d said to Moses: "Come up to Me to the mountain … and I will give you the stone tablets, and the *torah* [teaching], and the *mitzvah* [commandment]…." And Moses was on the mountain for forty days and forty nights….

And He gave to Moses, when He had finished speaking with him on Mount Sinai, the two tablets of the testimony; tablets of stone, inscribed by the finger of G-d.

 TALMUD, *SHABBAT 88a*

When the people of Israel said, "We will do and we will hear"—placing "we will do" before "we will hear"—a heavenly voice proclaimed: "Who revealed to My children this secret, which the ministering angels employ?"

It is written (Song of Songs 2:3), "As an apple tree among the trees of the wood, so is my beloved among the lads." Why are the people of Israel compared to an apple tree? As the apple tree gives forth its fruit before its leaves, so did Israel set "we will do" before "we will hear."

REVERSE PERCEPTION Citing the verse (Exodus 20:15), "the people saw the voices …" the Midrash comments: "They saw what is ordinarily heard, and they heard what is ordinarily seen" (R. Akiva in *Mechilta*). The Lubavitcher Rebbe explains the mystical significance of this phenomenon. To those who stood at Sinai, divinity and spirituality, which are ordinarily only "heard" as abstract ideas, were as tangible and real as what a person sees with their own eyes. Conversely, the material world, which is ordinarily "seen" as a concrete reality, was no more than a concept that a person hears about and understands.

Jabal Musa ("Mount Moses") in the Sinai Peninsula, believed by many to be the Biblical Mount Sinai where Moses received the Torah

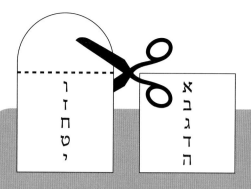

SHAPE OF A TABLET According to the Talmud (*Bava Batra*, 14a) the tablets did not have rounded tops, as commonly depicted. Each was a even-sided square, measuring six handbreadths in height and six handbreadths in width, and three handbreadths thick. (A "handbreadth" is the width of a closed fist, or between 8 and 9 centimeters.)

 MAIMONIDES, *MISHNEH TORAH, LAWS OF THE FUNDAMENTALS OF THE TORAH, 8:1–3*

The people of Israel did not believe in Moses our teacher because of the miracles he performed. Indeed, the person whose belief is based on miraculous signs will always have some skepticism in their heart, as the sign might have been done through trickery or sorcery.... What, then, was the source of our belief? The revelation at Mount Sinai ... Moses entered the thick cloud, and the voice of the Almighty spoke to him—and we heard it—saying: "Moses, go and say to them so and so." ... The whole of Israel are firsthand witnesses to the revelation at Sinai, so that no further proof is required....

Therefore, if a prophet comes and performs miraculous signs, and attempts to abrogate the prophecy of Moses, we do not listen to him, and we know with certainty that he performed those signs through trickery or sorcery ... [as he is attempting to dispute] what we saw with our own eyes and heard with our own ears.

 MECHILTA D'RASHBI, *EXODUS 19:2*

The Torah was given to the people of Israel in the ownerless desert. For if it were given in the Land of Israel, the residents of the Land of Israel would say, "It is ours"; and if it were given in some other place, the residents of that place would say, "It is ours." Therefore it was given in the wilderness, so that anyone who wishes to acquire it may acquire it.

 ZOHAR, *VOL. 2, 93b*

These Ten Commandments encompass the whole of the Torah. They include all that is above and below. They incorporate the ten utterances with which the Almighty created the world.... All the secrets they contain were revealed to all who looked upon them, who saw in them the 613 commandments of the Torah that they include.

Why does G-d proclaim at Sinai, "I am the Lord your G-d, who took you out from the land of Egypt" rather than "... who created the heavens and the earth"?

■ G-d as creator is equally the G-d of all peoples of the world. That the Almighty took the people of Israel out of Egypt speaks to His unique relationship with the Jewish people. (*R. Judah Halevi, 1075–1141*)

■ G-d as creator is better appreciated by the intellectually advanced, less so by the common folk. G-d as redeemer is equally appreciated by everyone. (*R. Abraham ibn Ezra, 1089–1164*)

■ There are those who acknowledge that the natural reality was created by the Almighty, yet erroneously regard it as autonomous and immutable. The miracles of the Exodus demonstrate that G-d is both the originator and the master of nature, who contravenes it at will. (*Nachmanides, 1195–1270*)

■ The G-d of Creation is beyond our understanding—as the creation of "something from nothing" is utterly beyond our ken—and thus impersonal. In the Exodus, we experienced G-d as one who descends into our most constrained and spiritually compromised circumstances, concerns Himself with our troubles and needs, liberates us, and establishes a personal bond with us. (*R. Schneur Zalman of Liadi, 1745–1812*)

{FOR MORE ON THE SIGNIFICANCE OF THE REVELATION AT MOUNT SINAI, SEE CITATIONS ON P. 314}

the ten commandments

1

I am the Lord your G-d

who took you out from the land of Egypt,
from the house of slavery.

2

Do not have any other gods before Me

Do not make for yourself a carved figure or any
image that is in the heavens above, on the earth
below, or in the water beneath the earth. Do not
bow to them and do not serve them; for I, G-d your
G-d, am a zealous G-d, calling to account the
iniquity of the parents upon the children, upon the
third and the fourth generations, for those who
hate Me; and acting with lovingkindness for
thousands of generations, for those who love
Me and keep My commandments.

3

Do not take the name of G-d your G-d in vain

for G-d will not absolve the one
who takes His name in vain.

4

Remember the Sabbath day

to sanctify it. Six days you shall labor and do all
your work. The seventh day is a Sabbath to the
Lord your G-d; do not do any work—you, your son,
your daughter, your manservant, your
maidservant, your beast, or your sojourner who is
within your gates. For six days G-d made the
heaven, the earth, the sea, and all that is in them;
and He rested on the seventh day. Therefore, G-d
blessed the Sabbath day and sanctified it.

5

Honor your father and your mother

in order that your days be lengthened on the land
that the Lord your G-d is giving to you.

6

Do not murder

7

Do not commit adultery

8

Do not steal

9

Do not bear false witness against your fellow

10

Do not covet

your fellow's house; do not covet your fellow's
wife, his manservant, his maidservant, his ox, his
donkey, or anything that is your fellow's.

Exodus 20:1–14

THE GOLDEN CALF AND THE BREAKING OF THE TABLETS

Jews Praying in the Synagogue on Yom Kippur,
Maurycy Gottlieb, Austria, 1878

THE FIRST YOM KIPPUR The day on which the Almighty
forgave the sin of the Golden Calf and granted us the Second
Tablets—the 10th day of Tishrei on the Jewish calendar—
is observed each year as Yom Kippur, our annual "day of
atonement" and return to G-d (see p. 338). Yom Kippur is "the
singularity of the year" (as per Leviticus 16:34)—the day on
which we connect with the singular essence of our soul and its
intrinsic oneness with G-d, drawing its inviolable integrity
to repent the transgressions and redeem the failings that mar
the more extrinsic areas of our lives.

The Torah's account of the formative generation of
Israel is not one of unadulterated heroism and success.
It chronicles their sins as well as their virtues, their
debacles alongside their triumphs, the quarrels and the
kvetching that intersect their progress to freedom and
enlightenment.

A case in point is the incident of the Golden Calf.
Just forty days after experiencing the divine revelation at Mount Sinai, the people of Israel reverted to
the idolatry of Egypt and worshipped an idol of molten
gold. Yet the story of the Golden Calf is also the story
of our repentance and rehabilitation, and of "broken
tablets" that attest to the immutability of our bond
with our Creator no less than the "second tablets" of
our renewed covenant.

EXODUS 32:1–6

The people saw that Moses was delaying in coming
down from the mountain; and they congregated upon
Aaron, and they said to him: "Come, make for us a god
that will go before us; because this man Moses who
brought us up from the land of Egypt, we do not know
what has become of him...."

All the people stripped themselves of the golden
earrings that were in their ears ... and he made it into
a molten calf. And they said: "This is your god, O Israel,
who brought you up from the land of Egypt." ... They
arose early on the morrow, and they brought up offerings.... And the people sat down to eat and to drink,
and they got up to make merry.

NECHAMA LEIBOWITZ
BASED ON *NEW STUDIES IN EXODUS, KI TISA 2*

How is it possible that a generation who saw the
plagues wrought upon Egypt and the splitting of the
sea, who stood at Mount Sinai and heard the voice of
G-d proclaim "I am the Lord your G-d ... Do not have any
other gods before Me ..." should go and worship an idol?
Perhaps this is what the Torah wishes to teach us, as a

40+40+40

FORTY TIMES THREE Moses spent a total of 120 days on Mount Sinai: forty days (Sivan 7 to Tamuz 17), during which he received the Torah from the Almighty; forty days (Tamuz 19 to Av 29) to plead for forgiveness for the Children of Israel for the sin of the Golden Calf; and a third forty days (Elul 1 to Tishrei 10) to receive the second tablets.

lesson for future generations: that indeed, such a thing is possible. Miracles, no matter how magnificent, do not change a person's nature and habits. As Maimonides writes, "A person who was raised as an unskilled laborer cannot suddenly jump up, rinse the dirt off his hands, and march into battle with seasoned warriors…. This is why the Almighty in His wisdom circled them about in the wilderness [for forty years], so that they may learn greatness … and so that a new generation should be born that was not acclimated in slavery and humiliation."

No one-time event, not even hearing the voice of the Almighty Himself, will instantly change a person from a worshipper of idols to a servant of G-d. Only a sustained habituation in a life of Torah and mitzvot, which embraces the totality of a person—ordinary days and festivals, home life and work life, day after day and hour after hour—will engender true change and prevent regression to a decadent past.

 EXODUS 32:15–19, 32:31–32

Moses turned and went down the mountain, and the two tablets of the testimony were in his hand…. And it was when he drew closer to the camp, and he saw the calf and the dances … he flung the tablets from his hands, and he shattered them at the foot of the mountain….

Moses returned to G-d, and he said: "I implore! This nation has committed a grave sin…. And now, if You will forgive their sin— But if not, please erase me from Your book that You have written."

 MIDRASH RABBAH, *SHEMOT 43:1*

There was once a prince who sent a messenger to betroth a wife for him. The messenger went, and discovered that the woman had been unfaithful. What did he do? He took the marriage contract that the prince had entrusted to him and tore it up, saying, "Better that she be judged as an unattached woman than as a married wife."

This is what Moses did. When Israel committed that deed, he took the tablets and broke them.

 EXODUS 34:1–3

G-d said to Moses: "Carve yourself two stone tablets like the first ones; and I will inscribe upon the tablets the words that were on the first tablets, which you broke … and ascend Mount Sinai in the morning….

"No man shall go up with you, neither shall anyone be seen anywhere on the mountain; neither shall the sheep and the cattle graze facing that mountain…."

 RASHI, *COMMENTARY TO EXODUS 34:3*

[This is in contrast to] the first tablets, which were accompanied by commotion, noise, and crowds; hence the evil eye affected them [and they were destroyed]. For there is no greater virtue than modesty.

 MIDRASH RABBAH, *SHEMOT 46:1*

The Almighty said to Moses: Do not be distressed over the first tablets, which contained only the Ten Commandments. In the second tablets I am giving you also Halachah, Midrash, and Agadah.

 TALMUD, *MENACHOT 99a*

Both the [Second] Tablets and the Broken Tablets were kept in the Ark.

FORTY YEARS IN THE WILDERNESS

Year	Date	Observed as	Event	Location
2448 (1313 BCE)	Nisan 15	Passover	The Exodus	Ⓐ
	Nisan 21	7th day of Passover	Splitting of the sea	Ⓑ
	Iyar 16		Manna begins to fall	Ⓒ
	Sivan 6	Shavuot	Giving of the Torah	Ⓓ
	Tamuz 17	Fast day of Tamuz 17	Worship of the Golden Calf; Moses breaks the Tablets	
2449 (1313–1312 BCE)	Tishrei 10	Yom Kippur	G-d forgives the people of Israel; grants Moses the Second Tablets	
	Kislev 25	Hanukkah	Making of the Tabernacle completed	
	Nisan 1		Tabernacle erected	
	Iyar 14	Pesach Sheini	"Second Passover" instituted	
	Sivan 29– Av 9	Tish'ah B'Av	Mission of the Spies	Ⓔ
2487 (1274 BCE)	Nisan 10		Passing of Miriam	Ⓕ
	Av 1		Passing of Aaron	Ⓖ
	Av 15	Tu B'Av	End of decree that the generation of the Exodus would die in the desert	Ⓗ
2488 (1273 BCE)	Adar 7		Passing of Moses	Ⓘ
	Nisan 10		Children of Israel enter the Holy Land	Ⓙ
		Sukkot	The festival of Sukkot, celebrated on Tishrei 15–21, commemorates the "clouds of glory" that protected the people of Israel throughout their journey	

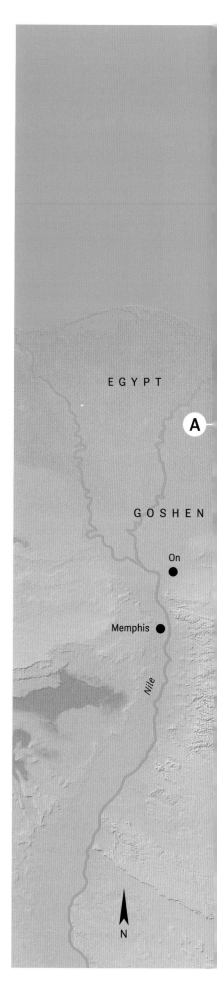

EGYPT

Ⓐ

GOSHEN

On

Memphis

Nile

N

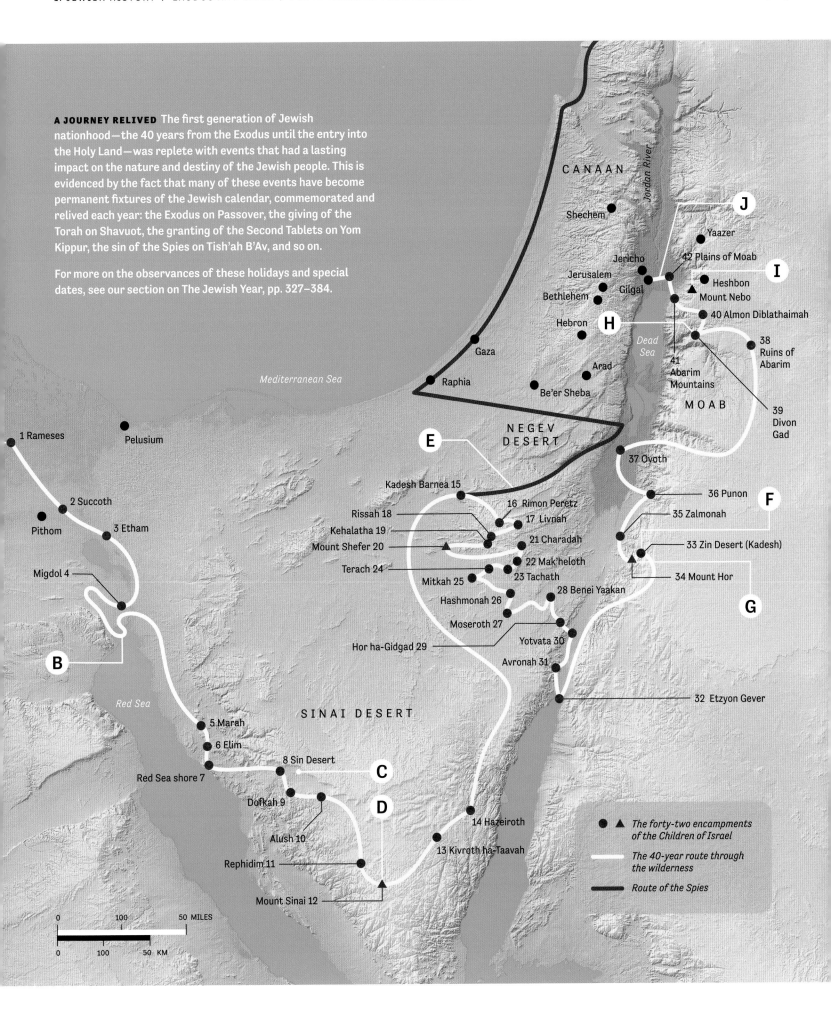

A JOURNEY RELIVED The first generation of Jewish nationhood—the 40 years from the Exodus until the entry into the Holy Land—was replete with events that had a lasting impact on the nature and destiny of the Jewish people. This is evidenced by the fact that many of these events have become permanent fixtures of the Jewish calendar, commemorated and relived each year: the Exodus on Passover, the giving of the Torah on Shavuot, the granting of the Second Tablets on Yom Kippur, the sin of the Spies on Tish'ah B'Av, and so on.

For more on the observances of these holidays and special dates, see our section on The Jewish Year, pp. 327–384.

CANAAN

Jordan River

Shechem

Yaazer

J

Jericho

42 Plains of Moab

I

Jerusalem

Gilgal

Heshbon

Bethlehem

Mount Nebo

Hebron

H

40 Almon Diblathaimah

Dead Sea

Gaza

41 Abarim Mountains

38 Ruins of Abarim

Raphia

Arad

Be'er Sheba

MOAB

39 Divon Gad

Mediterranean Sea

NEGEV DESERT

37 Ovoth

1 Rameses

Pelusium

E

36 Punon

F

Kadesh Barnea 15

35 Zalmonah

2 Succoth

16 Rimon Peretz

Pithom

17 Livnah

33 Zin Desert (Kadesh)

3 Etham

Rissah 18

Kehalatha 19

21 Charadah

34 Mount Hor

Mount Shefer 20

Terach 24

22 Mak'heloth

G

Migdol 4

Mitkah 25

23 Tachath

Hashmonah 26

28 Benei Yaakan

Moseroth 27

Yotvata 30

Hor ha-Gidgad 29

Avronah 31

Red Sea

SINAI DESERT

32 Etzyon Gever

5 Marah

6 Elim

8 Sin Desert

C

Red Sea shore 7

Dofkah 9

D

Alush 10

14 Hazeiroth

Rephidim 11

13 Kivroth ha-Taavah

Mount Sinai 12

The forty-two encampments of the Children of Israel

The 40-year route through the wilderness

Route of the Spies

0   100   50 MILES

0   100   50 KM

THE MANNA

 EXODUS 16:4–35

G-d said to Moses, "Behold, I will rain down for you bread from heaven. The people will go out and gather each day's portion on its day...."

In the morning, there was a layer of dew around the camp. The layer of dew ascended, and behold, on the surface of the desert was a fine substance, fine as frost upon the ground.

The children of Israel saw it and they said to one another, "It is *manna* (food)," as they did not know what it was. And Moses said to them: "It is the bread that G-d has given you to eat.

"This is the thing that G-d has commanded: Gather of it, each one according to their eating-need, an *omer* for each head; according to the number of souls that each has in their tent, you should take."

The children of Israel did so; they gathered, both the one who gathered much and the one who gathered little. They measured it by the *omer*, and the one who gathered much did not have more, and the one who gathered little did not have less; each one according to their eating-need, they gathered.

And Moses said to them: "No person shall leave over any of it until morning." But they did not listen to Moses; people left over from it until the morning, and it bred worms and became putrid; and Moses was angry with them....

It was on the sixth day, that they gathered a double portion of bread, two *omers* for each one. And all the leaders of the community came and told Moses.

And he said to them: "That is what G-d has spoken. Tomorrow is a rest day, a holy Sabbath to G-d. Bake that which you would bake, and cook that which you would cook, and all the remainder leave over to keep until morning." They left it over until morning, as Moses

had instructed; and it did not become putrid, and no worm was in it.

And Moses said: "Eat it today, for today is a Sabbath to G-d. Today you will not find it in the field...." And the people rested on the seventh day....

Moses said to Aaron: "Take one jar, and put there the fill of an *omer* of manna; and deposit it before G-d, to be preserved for your generations...."

The children of Israel ate the manna for forty years, until they came to an inhabited land ... until they came to the border of the land of Canaan.

 DON ISAAC ABARBANEL
COMMENTARY TO EXODUS 16:16

The manna was a lesson in the true nature of sustenance and wealth. No matter how much effort and toil a person expends, everything that they earn in this world is ordained from Above. So when the time comes for a person to depart from this world, we discover that "the one who gathered much" has not gained anything, as their wealth does not follow with them to the grave. We also discover that "the one who gathered little did not have less," as the Almighty provides to every individual everything that is required for their sojourn on earth.

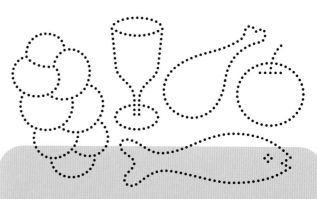

ETHEREAL FOOD   In many ways, the manna was the ultimate food. The Talmud (*Yoma* 75a–b) relates that the manna contained no waste and was fully absorbed by the body, and that a person was able to taste in it any food they desired.

THE SPIES

At the people's behest, Moses sent twelve spies to scout the land of Canaan, the land promised to the Patriarchs. Upon their return, ten of their number dissuaded the people from trusting the divine promise. As a result, it was decreed that the generation who left Egypt would die out in the wilderness. It would be left to their children—a generation formed by freedom and miracles—to realize the goal of nationhood in the Jewish homeland.

 NUMBERS 13:25–14:34

They returned from scouting the land at the end of forty days.... And they said, "We came to the land to which you sent us, and indeed it flows with milk and honey; and this is its fruit.

"However, the people who dwell in the land are powerful, and the cities are fortified and exceedingly great.... We are not able to go up against these people, as they are stronger than us."

They put out an evil report of the land that they had scouted to the children of Israel, saying, "... It is a land that consumes its inhabitants.... We saw there the giants ... and we were in our own sight as grasshoppers, and so we were in their sight."

The entire community raised their voices and cried, and the people wept on that night. And all the children of Israel complained against Moses and Aaron, "... If only we had died in the land of Egypt, or if only we had died in this wilderness! Why is G-d bringing us to this land to fall by the sword, and that our wives and infants will be [our enemy's] spoils? Is it not better for us that we return to Egypt...?"

Joshua the son of Nun and Caleb the son of Jephunneh, who were among those who had scouted the land, tore their clothes. They spoke to the entire congregation of the children of Israel, saying: "The land that we passed through to scout it—the land is exceeding, exceedingly good! If G-d desires us, He will bring us to this land and give it to us, a land flowing with milk and honey. Only do not rebel against G-d. Do not fear the people of that land ... G-d is with us; do not fear them!"

The entire congregation threatened to pelt them with stones; and the glory of G-d appeared in the Tent of Meeting to all the children of Israel.

G-d spoke to Moses and Aaron.... "Say to them: If not as you have spoken in My ears, so will I do to you.

"In this wilderness your corpses shall fall, your entire number who were counted, all those from the age of twenty and up ... except for Caleb the son of Jephunneh and Joshua the son of Nun.

"As for your infants, of whom you said that they will be as spoils, I will bring them, and they will know the land that you despised....

"Your children will wander in the wilderness for forty years ... according to the number of days that you scouted the land ... a day for a year, a day for a year..."

R. SCHNEUR ZALMAN OF LIADI
BASED ON *LIKUTEI TORAH, SHELACH, 36c–38b*

The Torah tells us that the Spies were holy and righteous men, the "heads of the children of Israel" (Numbers 13:2). Why did they not wish to enter the Holy Land?

The source of their error was that they wished to relate to the Almighty solely via the more spiritual realm of thought—through study and meditation. They did not want to lower themselves to the realm of action, as a life on the land would require. They wanted to remain in the wilderness, secluded from the world and sustained by the miraculous "bread from heaven," rather than occupy themselves with plowing and sowing and the other demands of earthly life.

Their mistake was that the divine desire is that we serve the Creator in the land, through our physical actions. For the loftiest truths can be actualized only in the lowest realm of creation, the realm of action.

BALAAM'S BLESSINGS

One of the most beautiful odes to the people of Israel was uttered by their enemy, the Aramean prophet Balaam, who was summoned by Balak the king of Moab to curse the Israelites in the final year of their journey through the wilderness. Three times Balaam attempted to curse the Israelite camp, and each time blessings emerged from his mouth instead.

 NUMBERS 23:9, 23:21, 24:5-9

From the mountain peaks I see him
from the hills I behold him;
lo, it is a people who dwells alone
and is not reckoned amongst the nations....

He sees no iniquity in Jacob
and He perceives no perversity in Israel
the Lord his G-d is with him
and the King's friendship is his....

How goodly are thy tents, O Jacob
your dwelling places, O Israel!
As streams they extend
as gardens by the riverside
as aloes that G-d planted
as cedars upon the waters....

He crouched, he lay down like a lion, like a great lion
who shall dare to rouse him?
Those who bless you are blessed
and those who curse you are cursed.

 MIDRASH RABBAH, *DEVARIM 1:4*

It would have been fitting for the reproofs [of the book of Deuteronomy] to have come from the mouth of Balaam, and for Balaam's blessings to have come from the mouth of Moses.... But the Almighty said: Let Moses, who loves them, rebuke them; and let Balaam, who hates them, bless them.

A TALKING DONKEY The Biblical account (Numbers 22) of Balaam's trip to the Israelite camp includes the curious incident of the talking ass. Three times an angel blocks Balaam's path, causing the donkey he is riding to turn off the road, then press against a wall, and finally stop in its tracks; on each occasion Balaam beats his beast. The donkey then berates Balaam for his behavior, and Balaam is forced to concede that he failed to see the divine messenger that his animal had perceived.

Not lost on Balaam was the message that the prophet is but a tool of the divine will; that when the Almighty wills it, an ass will see angels, and rebuke its rider for his failings. *(Nachmanides, 1194–1270)*

Meanings of the statement, "How goodly are thy tents O Jacob":

■ Balaam saw that the doorways of the tents in the Israelite camp were not aligned one opposite the other, attesting to the integrity of their home life and their respect for each other's privacy. *(R. Jochanan, c. 180–279)*

■ These are the synagogues and study halls of the Jewish people, which will always remain with them through all the devastations of the exile. *(R. Aba bar Kahana, 3rd century)*

THE PASSING OF MOSES

 DEUTERONOMY 34:1–12

Moses went up from the plains of Moab to Mount Nebo, to the top of the summit, facing Jericho. And G-d showed him the entire land … until the western sea....

G-d said to him: "This is the land I swore to Abraham, to Isaac, and to Jacob, saying: I will give it to your offspring. I have made you see it with your eyes, but you shall not cross over there."

And Moses, the servant of G-d, died there, in the land of Moab, by the mouth of G-d … and no person knows the place of his burial, to this day.

Moses was one hundred and twenty years old when he died. His eye had not dimmed, nor had his freshness departed....

There arose not a prophet in Israel like Moses, whom G-d knew face to face; for all the signs and wonders which G-d had sent him to perform in the land of Egypt … and all the strong hand, and all the great awe, which Moses did before the eyes of all Israel.

 MIDRASH TANCHUMA, *CHUKAT 10*

A shepherd was given the king's flock to feed and care for, but the flock was lost. When the shepherd sought to enter the royal palace, the king refused him entry....

So, too, the Almighty said to Moses: You took the six hundred thousand out of Egypt, and you buried them in the wilderness; now you want to bring a different generation into the Land? If you do so, it will be said that the generation of the wilderness has no share in the World to Come. Rather, remain by their side and bring them with you.

Panoramic view of the Promised Land from Mount Nebo

EMANUELE MAZZONI

In the Jewish Homeland

The Land of Israel is integral to Jewish identity, ideology, and observance. G-d's covenant with the Patriarchs, and Moses' mission to redeem the Children of Israel from Egypt, are both framed in the context of the divine promise of the Land. The Torah itself is formulated as a program for living in the Land: the fulfillment of many mitzvot, and the ideal fulfillment of all mitzvot, are possible only in the Land of Israel and with the presence of the Holy Temple in Jerusalem. And while Judaism has adapted itself and its people to diaspora life, it is an overtly temporary adaptation, referring at every turn to the restoration of national life in "the land that G-d seeks."

 GENESIS 15:18

On that day, G-d made a covenant with Abram, to say: To your seed I have given this land.

 EXODUS 6:6–8

Therefore, say to the children of Israel: I am G-d. I will take you out from under the suffering of Egypt … I will take you to Me as a people, and I will be a G-d to you…. And I will bring you to the land that I raised My hand in oath to give it, to Abraham, to Isaac, and to Jacob, and I will give it to you as a heritage; I am G-d.

 DEUTERONOMY 11:10–12

The land into which you are coming to inherit it, it is not like the land of Egypt out of which you came, where you sow your seed and water it by foot like a vegetable garden…. It is a land of mountains and valleys, that drinks water from the rains of the heavens.

   A land that G-d seeks; the eyes of G-d are always upon it, from the beginning of the year to the end of the year.

 TALMUD, *SOTAH 14a*

Why did Moses our teacher yearn to enter the Land of Israel? Did he want to partake of its fruits or to be satiated by its bounty? Rather, Moses said: Many of the mitzvot commanded to the people of Israel can only be fulfilled in the Land of Israel. I wish to enter the Land so that they may all be fulfilled by me.

 TALMUD, *BAVA BATRA 158b*

The very air of the land of Israel makes a person wise.

 R. JUDAH HALEVI, *KUZARI, 2:14–16*

When a farmer finds a choice root buried in barren soil, he will transfer it to a fertile field, where it will develop into a great fruit-bearing tree—which in turn spawns many other trees like itself…. In the same way, Abraham became attached to divinity, and became worthy of the divine covenant, only after G-d brought him to the Land…. Hence this land, which is particularly suited to providing spiritual guidance to the world, was reserved for the people of Israel.

Summer Landscape (detail), Anna Ticho, Israel, 1978

 RASHI, *COMMENTARY TO GENESIS 1:1*

Said R. Yitzchak: The Torah ought to have begun [with the verse] "This month shall be to you...." (Exodus 12:2), which is the first mitzvah commanded to the people of Israel. Why, then, does it begin with "In the beginning [G-d created the heavens and the earth]"? ... So that if the nations of the world would say to Israel, "You are thieves, for having conquered the lands of the seven nations," they would reply to them: The entire world is G-d's; He created it, and He grants it to whomever He desires. It was His will to give it to them, and it was His will to take it from them and give it to us.

 R. MENACHEM M. SCHNEERSON
BASED ON *LIKUTEI SICHOT, VOL. 30, P. 250*

Virtually every nation in the world occupies land that it conquered from those who lived there before them. Why is it only against the Jewish nation that the accu-sation is leveled, "You are thieves, for having conquered the lands of the seven nations"?

But the Jew is different. We are a spiritual people, whose primary concern is with matters of the soul rather than the body. The nations of the world sense this, and this is the subtext of their complaints against us: The Jewish people belong in the heavens; what business have they laying claim to a parcel of physical earth?

The answer, as Rashi says in his commentary to the first verse of Genesis, is that the Torah begins with the statement, "In the beginning G-d created the heavens and the earth." The Almighty created the world because He desired that the divine reality should permeate not just the spiritual heavens, but also, and especially, the material earth. The Torah was therefore given not to the supernal angels, but to the people of Israel—human beings charged to live a G-dly life within a physical existence.

the Land of Israel through the ages

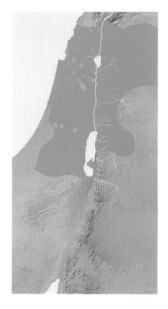

1738–1523 BCE
The Patriarchs in
the Holy Land

1258 BCE
Settlement of the
Land under Joshua

877–797 BCE
The Kingdom of David and Solomon

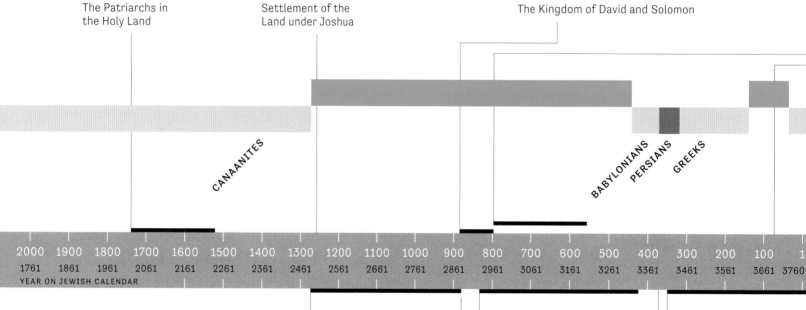

CANAANITES

BABYLONIANS

PERSIANS

GREEKS

2000	1900	1800	1700	1600	1500	1400	1300	1200	1100	1000	900	800	700	600	500	400	300	200	100	1
1761	1861	1961	2061	2161	2261	2361	2461	2561	2661	2761	2861	2961	3061	3161	3261	3361	3461	3561	3661	3760

YEAR ON JEWISH CALENDAR

1273–879 BCE
Era of the Judges

833–423 BCE
First Temple era

349 BCE–69 CE
Second Temple era

879 BCE
Coronation of Saul,
the first Jewish
king of Israel

372 BCE
Cyrus calls on Jews
to return to
their homeland

Areas and periods of Jewish rule

0   50 MILES

0   50 KM

N

797–556 BCE
The Divided Kingdom

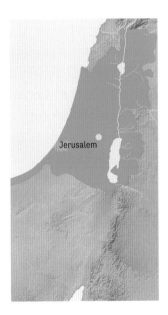

73 BCE
The Hasmonean Kingdom
at its greatest extent

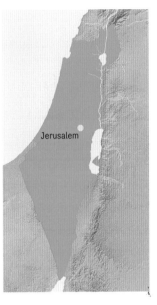

The State of Israel today

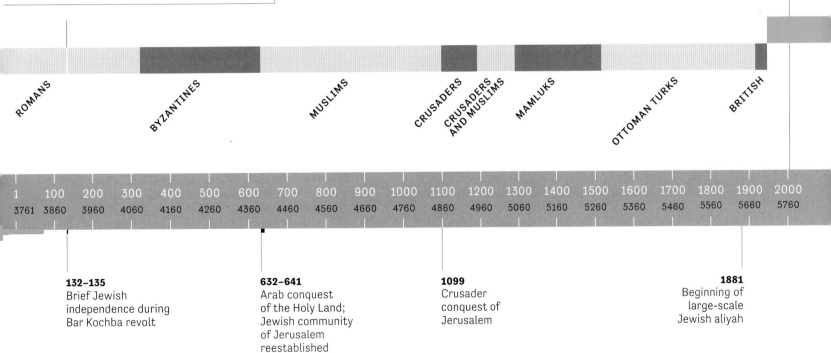

ROMANS   BYZANTINES   MUSLIMS   CRUSADERS   CRUSADERS AND MUSLIMS   MAMLUKS   OTTOMAN TURKS   BRITISH

1	100	200	300	400	500	600	700	800	900	1000	1100	1200	1300	1400	1500	1600	1700	1800	1900	2000
3761	3860	3960	4060	4160	4260	4360	4460	4560	4660	4760	4860	4960	5060	5160	5260	5360	5460	5560	5660	5760

132–135
Brief Jewish
independence during
Bar Kochba revolt

632–641
Arab conquest
of the Holy Land;
Jewish community
of Jerusalem
reestablished

1099
Crusader
conquest of
Jerusalem

1881
Beginning of
large-scale
Jewish aliyah

CONQUEST AND SETTLEMENT

One month after the passing of Moses, the people of Israel crossed the Jordan River under the leadership of Moses' disciple, Joshua. The Biblical book of Joshua describes the battles, marked by divine miracles on the one hand and brilliant military stratagems on the other, in which the Israelites conquered 31 city-states within the land of Canaan.

 JOSHUA 10:5–14

The day the sun stood still

Five Amorite kings—the king of Jerusalem, the king of Hebron, the king of Jarmuth, the king of Lachish, the king of Eglon—gathered together ... and they encamped upon Gibeon and made war against it....

Joshua went up from Gilgal, he, and all the men of war with him.... And G-d said to Joshua: "Do not fear

them, for I have delivered them into your hand; not a man of them shall stand before you."

Joshua came to them suddenly; he had gone up from Gilgal all night. G-d confused them before Israel, and they smote them with a great smiting at Gibeon. They chased them by the way that goes up to Beth-Horon, and smote them to Azekah, and to Makkedah....

Then Joshua did speak to G-d, on the day when G-d delivered up the Amorites before the children of Israel; and he said in the sight of Israel: "Sun, stand still upon Gibeon; and moon, in the valley of Ayalon."

The sun stood still, and the moon halted, until the nation avenged themselves on their enemies.... There was not a day like that, before it or after, that G-d hearkened to the voice of a man, as G-d did battle for Israel.

 JOSHUA 24:1–22

Joshua gathered all the tribes of Israel to Shechem ... and he said to all the people: "So said the Lord, G-d of Israel: Your forefathers dwelt on the other side of the river from the earliest time—Terah, the father of Abraham and the father of Nahor—and they served other gods.

"I took your father Abraham from the other side of the river, and I led him throughout all the land of Canaan, and I multiplied his descendants.... I took your fathers out of Egypt ... and I have given you a land for which you did not labor, cities which you did not build ... vineyards and olive groves which you did not plant....

"And now ... if it displeases you to serve G-d, choose this day whom you will serve, whether the gods that your ancestors who were on the other side of the river served, or the gods of the Amorites in whose land you dwell...."

The people responded ... "We shall serve G-d, for He is our G-d!"

And Joshua said to the people, "You are witnesses unto yourselves that you have chosen G-d for yourselves, to serve Him." And they said, "We are witnesses."

Battle of Jericho, Julius Schnorr von Carolsfeld, Germany, 1860

THE CONQUEST OF JERICHO The first Canaanite city to be conquered by Joshua was the heavily fortified city of Jericho. For seven days, a procession led by priests sounding *shofarot* (ram's horns) and carrying the Ark of the Covenant marched around the walls of Jericho. The entire people then "shouted with a great shout; and the wall fell down in its place ... and they took the city" (Joshua 6:20).

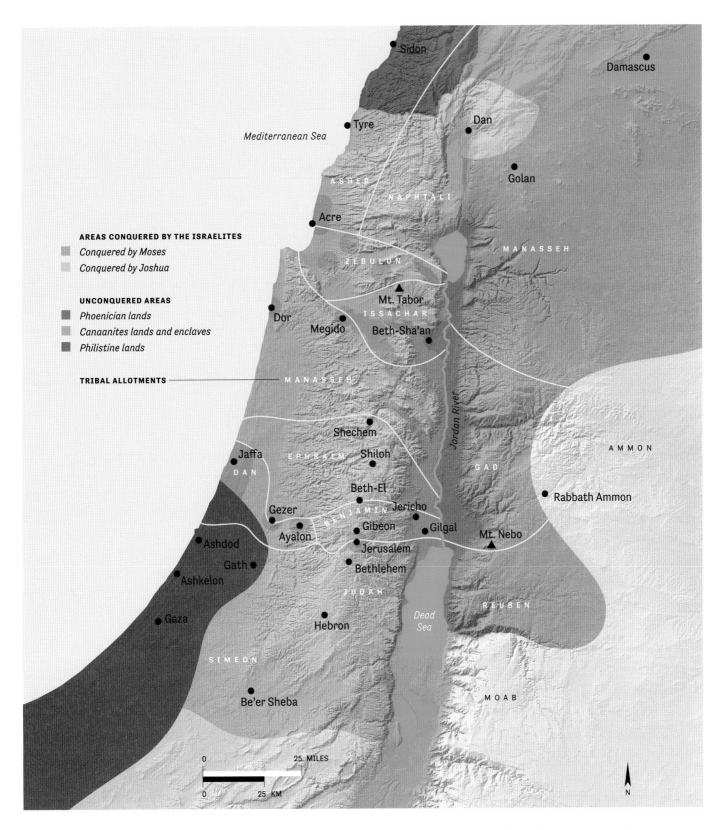

Sidon

Damascus

Tyre

Mediterranean Sea

Dan

Golan

ASHER

NAPHTALI

Acre

AREAS CONQUERED BY THE ISRAELITES
- Conquered by Moses
- Conquered by Joshua

MANASSEH

ZEBULUN

UNCONQUERED AREAS
- Phoenician lands
- Canaanites lands and enclaves
- Philistine lands

Mt. Tabor ▲
ISSACHAR

Dor

Megido

Beth-Sha'an

TRIBAL ALLOTMENTS ———————

MANASSEH

Shechem

AMMON

Jaffa

EPHRAIM

Shiloh

DAN

GAD

Beth-El

Gezer

Jericho

Rabbath Ammon

BENJAMIN

Ayalon

Gibeon

Gilgal

Mt. Nebo ▲

Jerusalem

Ashdod

Bethlehem

Gath

Ashkelon

JUDAH

REUBEN

Gaza

Hebron

Dead Sea

SIMEON

MOAB

Be'er Sheba

Jordan River

0   25 MILES

0   25 KM

N

THE TWELVE TRIBAL TERRITORIES IN THE LAND OF ISRAEL Under the leadership of Joshua, the boundaries of the tribal territories were demarcated, assigning to each of the twelve tribes their portion in the Holy Land and allotting a homestead to each of the 600,000 households of Israel. However, Joshua did not complete the conquest of the Land; at the time of his passing, there remained extensive areas in the southwest and in the north that were not conquered, as well as Canaanite enclaves within the area of Jewish settlement. Throughout the era of the Judges, the Jewish people would suffer military oppression by their Canaanite neighbors, as well as from the Canaanites' pagan influence. It was only under the kingship of David that the entire Land was brought under Jewish sovereignty (see map on p. 61).

ERA OF THE JUDGES

 JUDGES 21:25

In those days there was no king in Israel; each man did what was right in his eyes.

 SHMUEL KLATZKIN

The turbulence of freedom

The Biblical book of Judges chronicles a turbulent and highly significant stage in Jewish history. The era of the Judges—roughly, the four centuries between the passing of Joshua and the crowning of King Saul as the first monarch of the nation of Israel—stands in contrast to both the era that preceded it and the era that followed.

In earlier Biblical books, we learn of the Patriarchs and Matriarchs, in whose lives the Almighty was a living presence who instructed them and blessed them. We then read how Moses was sent to lead their descendants, the Children of Israel, out from Egypt to Sinai, where the people entered into a covenant to become G-d's subjects. The Torah was the new nation's constitution and law code, and Moses its chief magistrate. By the end of his forty years as prophet and leader, Moses had so thoroughly internalized the divine meaning and message that almost the entire Book of Deuteronomy is said in his voice; Moses speaks, and as the sages put it, "the Divine Presence speaks from his mouth" (*Zohar*, 3:232a).

As Moses had taken up leadership by divine command, so was Joshua installed as his successor. G-d instructed Moses to place his hands on Joshua's head in the presence of all the people (Numbers 27:18–23), and the Book of Joshua (1:16–18) tells us how his leadership was accepted by the people just as Moses' had been.

The Book of Judges begins with the death of Joshua. That passing marked a profound change, for unlike Moses, Joshua had not been told of a successor. With Joshua's death, there was no transference of leader-

DEBORAH & YAEL While the Biblical narrative includes many strong and influential women, the case of Deborah—prophetess, judge, and military leader—stands out as one of the few instances in which a woman served as the leader of the entire nation of Israel.

The extent of Deborah's influence can be discerned in the following exchange recorded in the Book of Judges. When Deborah charged the Israelite warrior Barak ben Abinoam to raise an army to battle the Canaanites, Barak insisted: "If you will go with me I will go; but if you will not go with me I will not go." Deborah's response was: "I shall go with you. However, your glory will not be on the road you are taking, as G-d will surrender Sisera into the hands of a woman" (Judges 4:8–9). The prophetess was referring not to herself, but to the second female hero of the battle, Yael, who killed the feared Canaanite general Sisera by hammering a spike through his temple as he lay sleeping in her tent.

The song sung by Deborah in celebration of Israel's salvation (recorded in Chapter 5 of the Book of Judges) is one of the "Ten Songs" marking ten celebratory milestones in the story of the Jewish people.

ship onto a single person. Significantly, in response to the people's request for someone to lead them in battle against the Canaanites that Joshua had not subdued, the Almighty responded by designating leadership to an entire tribe: "Judah should go up" (Judges 1:2).

It seems a reasonable development. Our history is meant to be the story of our internalization of G-d's message and our identification with the divine plan. It seems perfectly apt that after some training under our great teacher, Moses, and his successor, it would be time to assume an egalitarian responsibility as a people who accept the Almighty as their king and need no other authority. Thus, as we enter the period of the Judges, there is no king-figure. The people were being given the chance to show how well they had internalized their relationship with G-d.

Egalitarian responsibility is a thrilling thought. It inspired the founders of modern democracy to say that we are given the right to govern ourselves by the Deity—in Jefferson's words, we are endowed with unalienable political rights by "Nature and Nature's G-d." But great ideas rarely translate smoothly from the realm of thought to the realm of practical human affairs. Jefferson himself balanced his home budget by breeding and selling slaves; eventually a bloody civil war would be fought before non-whites had their inalienable rights recognized in the United States.

How did Israel's first attempt at a monarch-less society unfold? At the beginning, it goes well; but not for long. With an unblinking eye, the Book of Judges chronicles it all: the successes and the failures, the hope, its betrayal, and its rebirth—time and time again.

The many and varied tribulations of this period are summarized in the followings verses from the book's second chapter (Judges 2:12–20):

The children of Israel would forsake the G-d of their ancestors, who had taken them out of the land of Egypt, and follow the gods of others…. Then the wrath of G-d would flare against Israel and He would deliver them into the hands of their plunderers….

G-d raised up judges, and they saved them from the hands of those who had spoiled them…. For G-d retracted [from His anger], because of [their] cries….

And it was when the judge died, that they would return and deal more corruptly than their forefathers, going after the gods of others to serve them….

Among the "judges" (as the leaders of this period are referred to in the text), are some well-known names. The Song of Deborah is read in the synagogue as a *haftarah* every year, as is the story of the brave but headstrong Jephthah; the exploits of Gideon and his fearless leadership are striking. And who has not heard of the mighty Samson? A fierce warrior for G-d who was defeated by his own craving after Delilah, he redeemed himself by a supreme act of self-sacrifice, taking out his Philistine captors at the cost of his own life. The stories of other judges are less well-known—Othniel, the first judge, who successfully fights the Canaanites; Ehud, who saves Israel from the tyranny of Moab; and the judges Shamgar, Tola, Jair, Ibzan, Elon, Abdon, and Samuel.

Each judge's period of leadership follows the pattern the Book of Judges lays out at its start. The people would begin to worship alien gods, and an enemy would get the upper hand; sometimes it was a Canaanite nation, sometimes it was Moab, sometimes it was Midian or Ammon. In their trouble, the people would turn to the Almighty, and G-d would save them through a leader who would emerge from one of the twelve tribes of Israel. The "judge" would rally the nation to a renewed commitment to their covenant with the Almighty, and to a unified defense against their enemies—only to have the same cycle of events repeat itself after the judge's passing.

The Book of Judges ends with two stories illustrating the chaotic nature of the times. The story of Micah and his idol being adopted by the tribe of Dan, which presages all the troubles of the Northern Kingdom in later days; and the disturbing story of the concubine at Gibeah. Both show, in different ways, how far the people were yet from self-governance. In the latter incident, the tribe of Benjamin was nearly lost to Israel in a bloody civil war. At last, a solution was reached that left the people whole, but shaken.

Thus the stage was set for the emergence of the kings of Israel, who would bring order to the national life, unprecedented glory, and an undying hope that would shine brightly even in the darkness of the bitter and prolonged exiles that would follow.

THE KINGDOM OF ISRAEL

The first Israelite king, Saul, was not crowned until nearly four hundred years after the people had settled the Land of Israel. Saul's kingship was short-lived: scarcely had he taken the throne when the prophet Samuel informed him that, due to his failure to fully abide by G-d's instructions regarding the war against Amalek, the sovereignty would be transferred to another. Samuel then secretly anointed David as the future king, and the kingship passed to the House of David.

This account emphasizes two central themes in the Torah's conception of the Jewish kingship. First, that it is to arise only out of the people's desire and need:

it was not until the nation requested that a king be appointed over them that the Almighty instructed Samuel to do as they asked. Second, that the king's authority, and his very seat upon the throne, are wholly dependent on his fidelity to Torah law and his adherence to the divine instructions conveyed by the prophets.

DEUTERONOMY 17:14–20

When you come to the land that the Lord your G-d is giving you, and you take possession of it and dwell in it, and you will say: "I will set a king over myself, like all the nations around me."

Then you shall set a king over you, one whom the Lord your G-d chooses. From among your brethren, you shall set a king over yourself; you cannot place a foreigner over yourself, one who is not your brother.

Only he should not acquire many horses for himself, so that he will not bring the people back to Egypt in order to acquire many horses; for G-d has said to you, "You shall not return that way anymore."

He should not take many wives for himself, so that his heart should not turn astray; and he should not acquire much silver and gold for himself.

And it shall be, when he sits upon his throne of his kingship, that he should write for himself two copies of this Torah on a scroll.... It should be with him, and he should read from it all the days of his life, in order that he may learn to fear the Lord his G-d, to keep all the words of this Torah and these statutes, to do them.

And so that his heart should not be haughty over his brethren, and so that he should not turn away from the commandments, either to the right or to the left; in order that his days in his kingship may be prolonged, for him and for his descendants, among Israel.

King David playing a harp,
Ethiopia, 15th century

Seal of King Hezekiah,
Land of Israel, 6th century BCE

Epitaph of King Uzziah of Judah, who reigned in Jerusalem in the 7th century BCE. The text, inscribed when the king's remains were moved in the first century CE, reads (in Hebrew and Aramaic): "Here were brought the bones of Uzziah king of Judah. Not to be opened."

 TALMUD AND RASHI, *BERACHOT 34a–b*

When should a person bow during prayer? At the beginning and the end of the "forefathers" blessing, and at the beginning and the end of the "gratitude" blessing.... The high priest, however, bows at the beginning and the end of each blessing. And a king, once he bows, does not stand up until he concludes his prayers; as it is written (I Kings 8:54), "When Solomon finished praying ... he stood up from kneeling before the altar of G-d...." For the higher one's station, the more one needs to subjugate oneself to the Almighty.

 R. ELIJAH OF VILNA
COMMENTARY TO PROVERBS 27:27

The Hebrew term *melech*, "king," applies only to one who is appointed by a people who willingly submit to his sovereignty. One who conquers a land or a nation and imposes his will upon them by superior force is not a *melech*, but a *moshel* ("ruler").

We say in our prayers, "The kingship is G-d's; He rules the nations" (Psalms 22:29); and then we say, "G-d will be king over the entire world" (Zechariah 14:9). Is G-d not already king? Indeed we, the people of Israel, have submitted to the Almighty's kingship; not so the idol-worshipping nations, though G-d rules over them by force. Thus we say, "The kingship is G-d's," in reference to our relationship with G-d; but "He rules the nations"—as regards the nations who have not willingly accepted Him, G-d is only their "ruler." In the future, however, all will unite to serve G-d and crown Him as their king; then, "G-d will be king over the entire world."

 TZEMACH TZEDEK, *DERECH MITZVOTECHA 108a*

The purpose of appointing a king is so that through the king, the nation is subservient to the Almighty. For the nation is subservient to the king and must obey all his decrees ... and the king himself is subservient to G-d.... Thus, by extension, the people are subservient to G-d.

kings and prophets of Israel

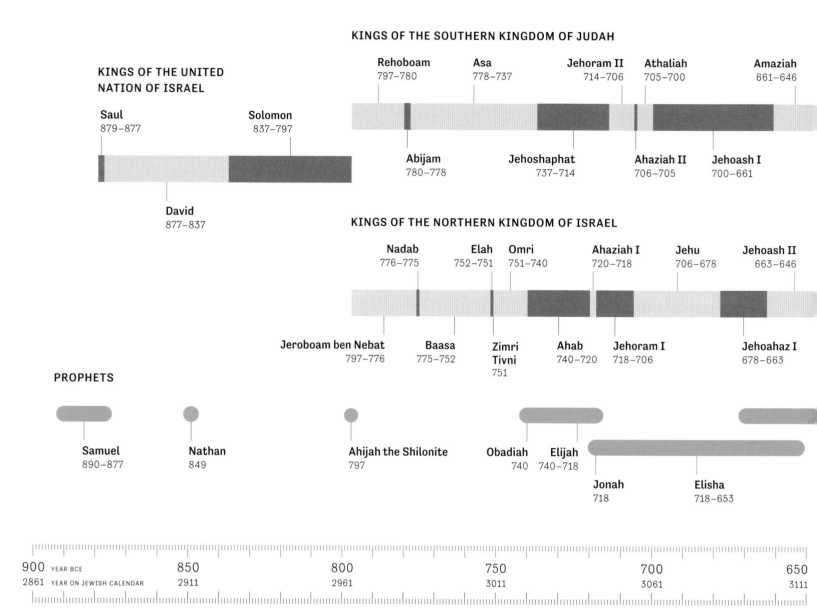

 R. ADIN EVEN-ISRAEL (STEINSALTZ)
EXCERPTED FROM *BIBLICAL IMAGES, PP. 177–180*

Jezebel, the wife of the Israelite king Ahab, can be understood only in light of the fact that she was a stranger coming from a world with an outlook radically different from that of the kings of Israel, the good and the bad alike. Jezebel was quite unable to understand the uniqueness of Israel where the king was a kind of constitutional monarch, his power limited by judicial authority. Jezebel epitomizes a worldview which sees the king as more than an absolute ruler, as being, more or less, a god; where the king's will was not only law, but also the determining morality.

Ahab was perhaps not a good Jew, he sinned and caused others to sin, but he was still Jewish in terms of his sensitivity to the rule of law, and to the idea that he was not merely the overlord of the people but also their servant. Hence, his behavior over Naboth's vineyard (I Kings, chapter 21). This is a case where the law of property rights prevails—the right of a man to retain

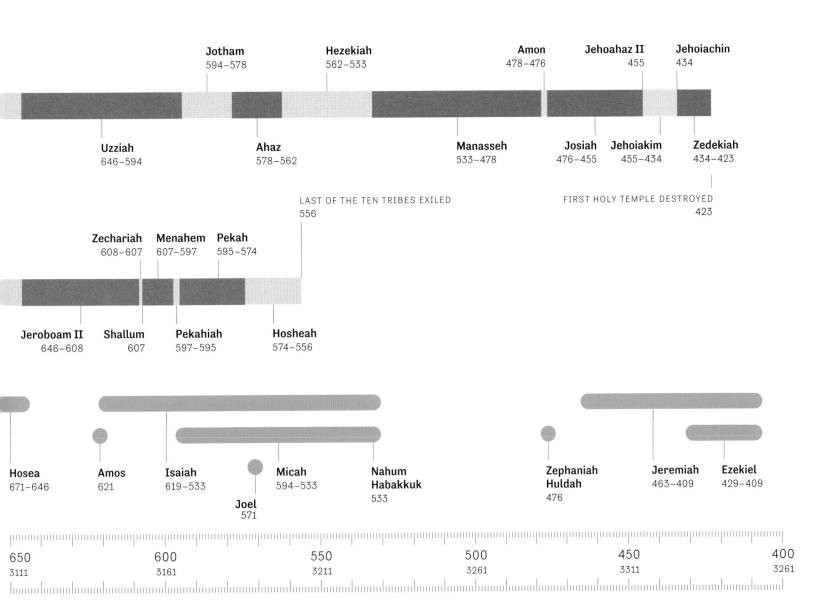

the estate of his fathers. Ahab could commit the sin of covetousness, could coax, threaten, and do his utmost to try to circumvent this law, but it never occurred to him that it could be altogether ignored. And it certainly did not occur to him that the king could unhesitatingly use any means at his disposal to gain his ends.

In contrast, Jezebel was amoral. She was not simply an evil woman, but a woman with no notion of morality. In a certain sense, she was a remarkably good wife; and when she saw her husband downcast because he could not satisfy his caprice, she carried out the most complex maneuvers to satisfy his whim. In all that she did—in bribing the judges, in conspiring with false witnesses, and in killing Naboth—Jezebel apparently had no stirrings of conscience, while Ahab could not withstand the prophet's rebuke. In this passage, the difference between the husband and the wife is very sharp: Jezebel remains true to a consistent, pagan idea, whereas Ahab, also when he sins, sins in the context of a man with a moral sense.

DAVID AND SOLOMON

It was under David's kingship that the whole of the Land of Israel came under Jewish sovereignty; that Jerusalem was conquered and made the national capital; and that the site of the Holy Temple was acquired and readied for the construction of the glorious edifice that would serve for centuries as the epicenter of the relationship between G-d and Israel. The dynasty founded by David and Solomon produced the kings, sages, and communal leaders that have led the people of Israel in sovereignty and in exile to this very day, and is destined to produce the Messiah, the final redeemer of Israel.

But it is more than these achievements that have secured King David such a central place in the Jewish consciousness. The many facets of David's personality—beautiful youth, fearless warrior, musician and poet, jurist and scholar, remorseful penitent, fervent petitioner and passionate lover of G-d—have made the very name "David" the embodiment of the yearnings and hopes of the Jewish people, and of the divine promise of Israel's eternity.

 GENESIS 49:10

The scepter shall not depart from Judah, nor the lawgiver from between his feet, until the Messiah comes, and to him will be a congregation of peoples.

 I SAMUEL 17:4–51

David and Goliath

There emerged a champion from the Philistines' camp, named Goliath, from Gath; his height was six cubits and a span. A helmet of bronze was on his head, and he was wearing a coat of mail; the weight of the coat was five thousand shekels of copper. Greaves of bronze were on his legs, and a bronze javelin was between his shoulders. The shaft of his spear was like a weaver's beam, and the spear's head was six hundred shekels of iron, and the shield-bearer went before him.

He stood and called to the armies of Israel, and he said to them: "Why should you come out to wage war? Am I not the Philistine, and you the servants of Saul? Choose for yourselves a man, and let him come down to me. If he be able to fight with me and kill me, we shall be slaves to you; and if I overcome him and kill him, you shall be slaves to us and serve us." And the Philistine said: "I taunt the ranks of Israel this day; give me a man, and let us fight together."

Saul and all Israel heard these words of the Philistine, and they were panic-stricken and very much afraid.

David was the son of an Ephrathite man from Bethlehem of Judah, whose name was Jesse. [Jesse] had eight sons ... the three eldest had followed Saul to the battle ... and David was the youngest....

Jesse said to David his son, "Take now to your brothers an *ephah* of this parched corn and ten loaves of this bread, and rush them to the camp ... and bring these ten cheeses to the captain of the thousand. And see how your brothers are faring...." David arose early in the morning, and left the sheep with a keeper.... He came to the barricade ... and he greeted his brothers.

While he was speaking with them, behold, the champion, named Goliath ... was coming up from the ranks of the Philistines, and he spoke the same words; and David heard.... And David said to the men who were standing before him.... "Who is this uncircumcised Philistine, that he should taunt the ranks of the living G-d....?" The words which David had spoken were heard; and they related them before Saul, and he summoned him.

David said to Saul, "Let no man's heart fail because of him. Your servant will go and battle with the Philistine."

Saul said to David, "You are unable to go to this Philistine to battle with him, for you are a lad, and he is a warrior since his youth."

Said David to Saul, "Your servant was a shepherd of sheep for his father, and there came a lion and also a bear, and carried off a lamb from the flock. I went out after him and I smote him, and saved [the lamb] from

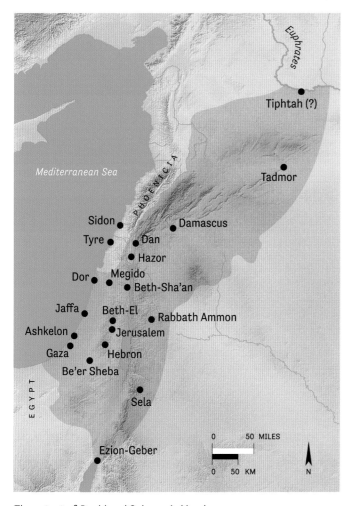

The extent of David and Solomon's kingdom

his mouth…. G-d, who saved me from the paw of the lion and from the paw of the bear, He will save me from the hand of this Philistine." And Saul said to David, "Go, and may G-d be with you."

Saul dressed David with his armor, and he placed a bronze helmet on his head, and he dressed him with a coat of mail, and David girded his sword upon his armor … and David said to Saul, "I cannot go with these, for I am not accustomed." And David took them off.

He took his staff in his hand, and he chose for himself five smooth stones from the brook, and he placed them in the shepherd's bag that he had … and his sling was in his hand; and he approached the Philistine….

The Philistine looked and saw David, and he despised him, for he was a youth, ruddy and beautiful. And the Philistine said to David, "Am I a dog, that you come to me with sticks? … Come to me, and I shall give your flesh to the fowl of the air and to the beasts of the field."

And David said to the Philistine, "You come to me with sword, spear, and javelin; and I come to you with the name of the Lord of Hosts, the G-d of the armies of Israel that you have taunted. This day, G-d will deliver you into my hand, and I shall slay you and take off your head … and all the world will know that there is a G-d in Israel…. For the battle is the Lord's, and He will deliver you into our hand…."

David stretched his hand into the bag and took a stone from it, and he slung it; he hit the Philistine in his forehead, and the stone sank into his forehead, and he fell on his face to the ground. David overpowered the Philistine with a sling and with the stone, and he smote the Philistine and slew him; and no sword was in the hand of David.

David ran and stood over the Philistine. He took the Philistine's sword and drew it from its sheath, and cut off his head with it. And the Philistines saw that their hero was dead, and they fled.

 MIDRASH RABBAH, *SHEMOT 2:2*

It is written, "[He chose His servant David] and took him from the sheepcotes" (Psalms 78:70)…. David would first let out the lambs, so that they could graze on the softest grasses. He then let out the old sheep to graze on the intermediate grasses. Then he let out the young sheep to graze on the tough grasses. Said the Almighty: The one who knows to nurture sheep, each according to its ability—he shall be the shepherd of My people.

 TALMUD, *BERACHOT 3b*

A harp would hang above David's bed, opposite his window. As soon as midnight would arrive, a north wind would come and blow on it, and it would play on its own. Immediately [David] would arise and occupy himself in Torah until dawn.

{ALSO SEE "PSALMS" ON P. 176}

I KINGS 3:5–14

And G-d appeared to Solomon in a dream of the night; and G-d said, "Ask what I shall give you."

Solomon said, "You have done Your servant David my father a great kindness, as he walked before You in truth … You have given him a son to sit on his throne….

"And now, O Lord my G-d … I am but a young lad; I do not know how to go out or come in…. Grant Your servant an understanding heart to judge Your people, that I may discern between good and bad; for who is able to judge this formidable people of Yours?"

It was pleasing in the eyes of G-d that Solomon had asked this thing. And G-d said to him: "Because you have asked this thing, and have not asked for yourself long life; neither have you asked riches for yourself, nor have you asked for the life of your enemies; but have asked for yourself understanding to discern judgment.

"Behold, I have done according to your word: I have given you a wise and understanding heart, so that there was none like you before you, nor after you shall any arise like you.

"I have also given you that which you have not asked, also riches, also honor…. And if you walk in My ways, to keep My statutes and My commandments, as your father David did walk, then I will lengthen your days."

{SEE "THE WISDOM OF SOLOMON," PP. 180–183}

I KINGS 5:5–14

Judah and Israel dwelled secure, each man under his vine and under his fig tree, from Dan to Be'er Sheba, all the days of Solomon…. And they came from all the nations to hear the wisdom of Solomon.

MIDRASH RABBAH, *SHEMOT 15:26*

The moon begins to shine on the first [of the month], its light growing for fifteen days, until its sphere is full. Then, from the fifteenth to the thirtieth, its light is diminished, and on the thirtieth it isn't seen.

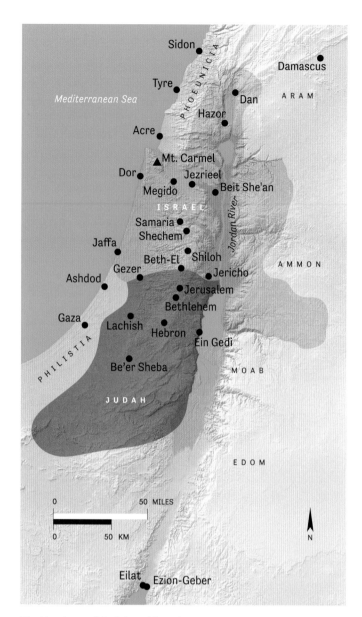

The kingdoms of Judah and Israel

So too with the people of Israel. There were fifteen generations from Abraham to Solomon. Abraham began to shine…. Then came Isaac, who also illuminated…. Jacob came and increased the light…. After that were Judah, Perez, Hezron, Ram, Aminadab, Nahshon, Salmon, Boaz, Obed, Jesse, and David. When Solomon came, the orb of the moon was full….

From that point on, the kings [of Israel] declined: Solomon's son Rehoboam, Rehoboam's son Abijah, his son Asa, Jehoshaphat, Jehoram, Ahaziah, Jehoash, Amaziah, Uzziah, Jotham, Ahaz, Hezekiah, Manasseh, Amon, Josiah, Jehoiakim … until Zedekiah, whose eyes were blinded and in whose days the Temple was destroyed.

A NATION DIVIDED

After the passing of King Solomon, the people of Israel split into two kingdoms. The southern kingdom of Judah, consisting primarily of the tribes of Judah and Benjamin, remained loyal to the House of David. The other ten tribes, led by Jeroboam ben Nebat of the tribe of Ephraim, formed the kingdom of Israel in the north.

Jeroboam did more than divide the nation of Israel. In order to prevent his subjects from making the thrice-yearly pilgrimages to the Holy Temple in Jerusalem, where the superior status of the royal House of David would be emphasized, he imposed the worship of pagan idols on his people, a practice that was reinforced by most of his successors.

The Kingdom of Israel lasted about 250 years, until its destruction by King Shalmaneser of Assyria, who exiled the ten tribes to a place or places unknown. The Kingdom of Judah survived a century longer, until its conquest by the Babylonian emperor Nebuchadnezzar, who destroyed the Holy Temple and exiled the people of Judea to Babylon.

LOST TRIBES One of the enduring mysteries of Jewish history is the fate of the "ten lost tribes" exiled during the Assyrian conquest of the Northern Kingdom. A number of isolated communities—the Beta Israel of Ethiopia, the Bnei Menashe and Bene Israel of India, and the Igbo Jews of Nigeria—hold traditions that trace their descent to one or more of the lost tribes. Eldad the Danite, who lived in the 9th century and corresponded with the sages of his day, described the locations and lifestyles of a number of the lost tribes, including those who live behind the legendary Sambatyon River that rages all week and rests only on the Shabbat. Speculations have also been raised regarding various peoples and tribes whose customs resemble traditional Jewish practices. Ultimately, the resolution of the mystery of the lost tribes of Israel awaits their restoration to the Jewish people in the Messianic era, as prophesied by Ezekiel (see citation on this page).

 TALMUD, *SANHEDRIN 102a*

The Almighty Himself grabbed Jeroboam by the robe and said to him: "Repent, and I, you, and [David] the son of Jesse will stroll together in the Garden of Eden."

Asked Jeroboam: "Who will walk first?"

Said G-d to him: "The Son of Jesse."

Said Jeroboam: "If so, I am not interested."

 EZEKIEL 37:15–27

The word of G-d came to me, saying:

Son of man! Take one stick and write upon it, "For Judah and for the children of Israel, his fellows." And take another stick and write upon it, "For Joseph, the stick of Ephraim, and all the house of Israel, his fellows." Join them one to the other to make one stick, and they shall become one in your hand.

When your people will say to you, "Will you not tell what these are to you?" say to them: "So said G-d: Be-hold, I will take the children of Israel from among the nations into which they have gone, and I will gather them from all around, and I will bring them to their land. I will make them into one nation.... No longer will they be two nations; no longer will they be divided into two kingdoms....

"They will dwell on the land ... wherein your ancestors lived ... they and their children and their children's children, forever; and My servant David will be their prince forever.

"I will form a covenant of peace for them ... and I will place My sanctuary in their midst forever. My dwelling shall be over them; I will be their G-d, and they will be My people."

THE HOLY TEMPLE

*"They shall make for Me a sanctuary, and I will dwell within them"
(Exodus 25:8). With these words, G-d commissioned Moses to build
the first physical "dwelling place" (mishkan, or "tabernacle") for the
divine presence.*

*The original Tabernacle—also called the "Tent of Meeting"—
accompanied the Children of Israel in their travels through the
wilderness. It was subsequently erected in a variety of places in the
Holy Land, until King Solomon built the permanent Holy Temple in its
designated place on Mount Moriah in Jerusalem.*

*A basic tenet of Judaism is that G-d is everywhere, both transcending
and pervading all of existence. But the everyday physical reality
obscures this fundamental truth. The Holy Temple was a breach in
this concealment, a place where the divine presence could be tangibly
experienced.*

*The Holy Temple is the prototype for a more universal goal: that
every individual life should likewise become a "dwelling place" for the
goodness and truth of the divine. As the mystics point out, the divine
promise, "I will dwell within them," can also be understood in its most
literal sense—that G-d will dwell "within each and every one of them."*

*Parapet fragment from the
Temple Mount, Jerusalem,
Land of Israel, 1st century BCE.
The Hebrew inscription reads,
"To the place of trumpeting …"*

Model of the Second Temple, Israel Museum, Jerusalem, Israel

 **MAIMONIDES,** *MISHNEH TORAH, LAWS OF THE HOLY TEMPLE, 2:1*

The location of the altar [in the Holy Temple] is very exact, and should never be changed.... It was [on the future site of] the Holy Temple that our father Isaac was bound. As it is written (Genesis 22:2), "Go you to the land of Moriah"; and in the book of Chronicles it says, "Solomon began to build the house of G-d in Jerusalem on Mount Moriah ..." (II Chronicles 3:1).

GENESIS 28:16–17

Jacob awoke from his sleep, and he said: "Indeed there is G-d in this place, and I myself did not know.... How awesome is this place; this is naught but the house of G-d, and this is the gate of the heavens."

I KINGS 8:13–29

I have built a home for You, a base for Your dwelling forever.... Behold, the heavens and the heaven of heavens cannot contain You; how more so this house that I have built! ... May Your eyes be open toward this house night and day, toward the place of which You said, "My name will be there," to listen to the prayer that Your servant will pray toward this place.

From King Solomon's prayer at the dedication of the Holy Temple in Jerusalem

 SHULCHAN ARUCH, *ORACH CHAYIM, 94:1*

When praying, a person who is outside of the Land of Israel should face toward the Land.... One who is in the Land should face Jerusalem.... One who is in Jerusalem should face the Holy Temple. One who is in the Holy Temple should face the Holy of Holies.

the temple and the mount

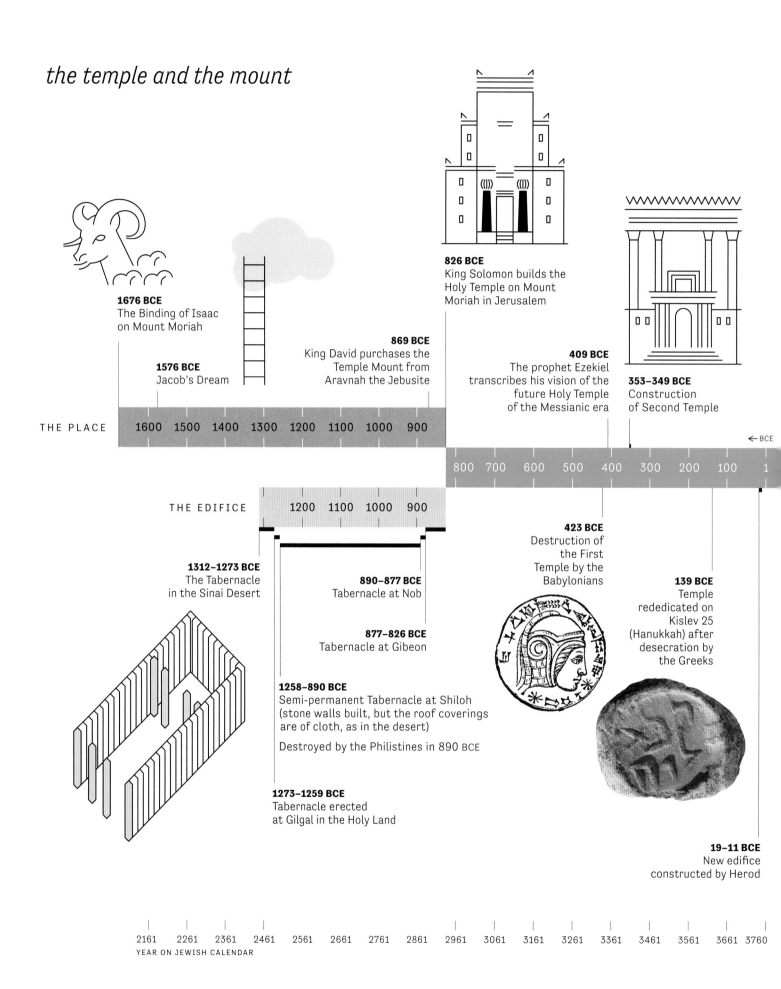

1676 BCE
The Binding of Isaac
on Mount Moriah

1576 BCE
Jacob's Dream

869 BCE
King David purchases the
Temple Mount from
Aravnah the Jebusite

826 BCE
King Solomon builds the
Holy Temple on Mount
Moriah in Jerusalem

409 BCE
The prophet Ezekiel
transcribes his vision of the
future Holy Temple
of the Messianic era

353–349 BCE
Construction
of Second Temple

THE PLACE | 1600 1500 1400 1300 1200 1100 1000   900 |

← BCE

| 800 700 600 500 400 300 200 100   1 |

THE EDIFICE | 1200 1100 1000   900 |

1312–1273 BCE
The Tabernacle
in the Sinai Desert

890–877 BCE
Tabernacle at Nob

877–826 BCE
Tabernacle at Gibeon

1258–890 BCE
Semi-permanent Tabernacle at Shiloh
(stone walls built, but the roof coverings
are of cloth, as in the desert)

Destroyed by the Philistines in 890 BCE

1273–1259 BCE
Tabernacle erected
at Gilgal in the Holy Land

423 BCE
Destruction of
the First
Temple by the
Babylonians

139 BCE
Temple
rededicated on
Kislev 25
(Hanukkah) after
desecration by
the Greeks

19–11 BCE
New edifice
constructed by Herod

2161 2261 2361 2461 2561 2661 2761 2861 2961 3061 3161 3261 3361 3461 3561 3661 3760
YEAR ON JEWISH CALENDAR

69
Second Temple destroyed
by the Romans

361 and 610
Failed attempts to rebuild the Temple during the reign of the
Roman emperor Julian and during the Sassanian conquest

1967
Israeli Defense Forces
recapture the Old City and
the Temple Mount during
the Six Day War

CE →

| 1 | 100 | 200 | 300 | 400 | 500 | 600 | 700 | 800 | 900 | 1000 | 1100 | 1200 | 1300 | 1400 | 1500 | 1600 | 1700 | 1800 | 1900 | 2000 |

637–691
Muslims build a mosque on the
Temple Mount, as well as the "Dome of
the Rock," believed to be situated above
the site of the Temple

1948
Jordanian conquest of the
Old City of Jerusalem

Jews denied access to the
Western Wall, the sole
surviving remnant of the
Temple, for nineteen years

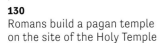

130
Romans build a pagan temple
on the site of the Holy Temple

| 3761 | 3860 | 3960 | 4060 | 4160 | 4260 | 4360 | 4460 | 4560 | 4660 | 4760 | 4860 | 4960 | 5060 | 5160 | 5260 | 5360 | 5460 | 5560 | 5660 | 5760 |

components of the temple

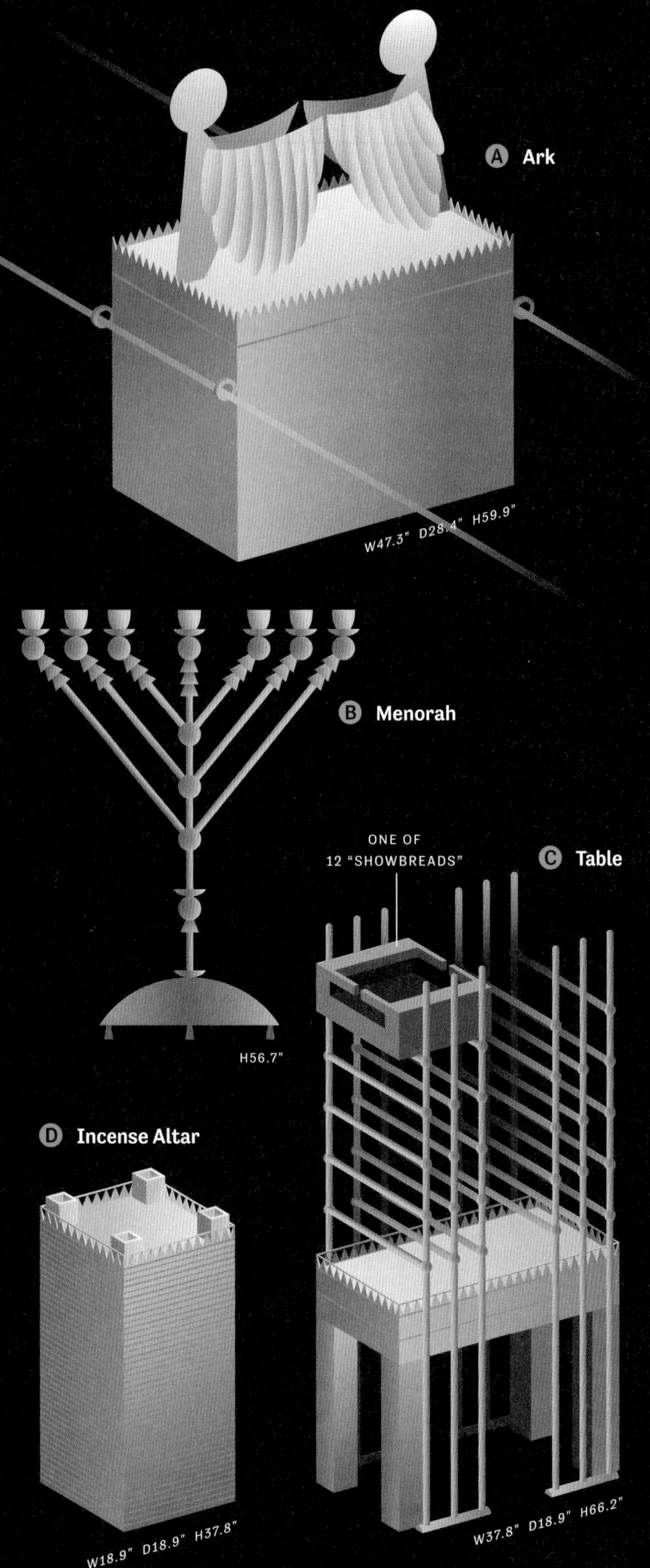

A Ark

W47.3" D28.4" H59.9"

B Menorah

H56.7"

D Incense Altar

W18.9" D18.9" H37.8"

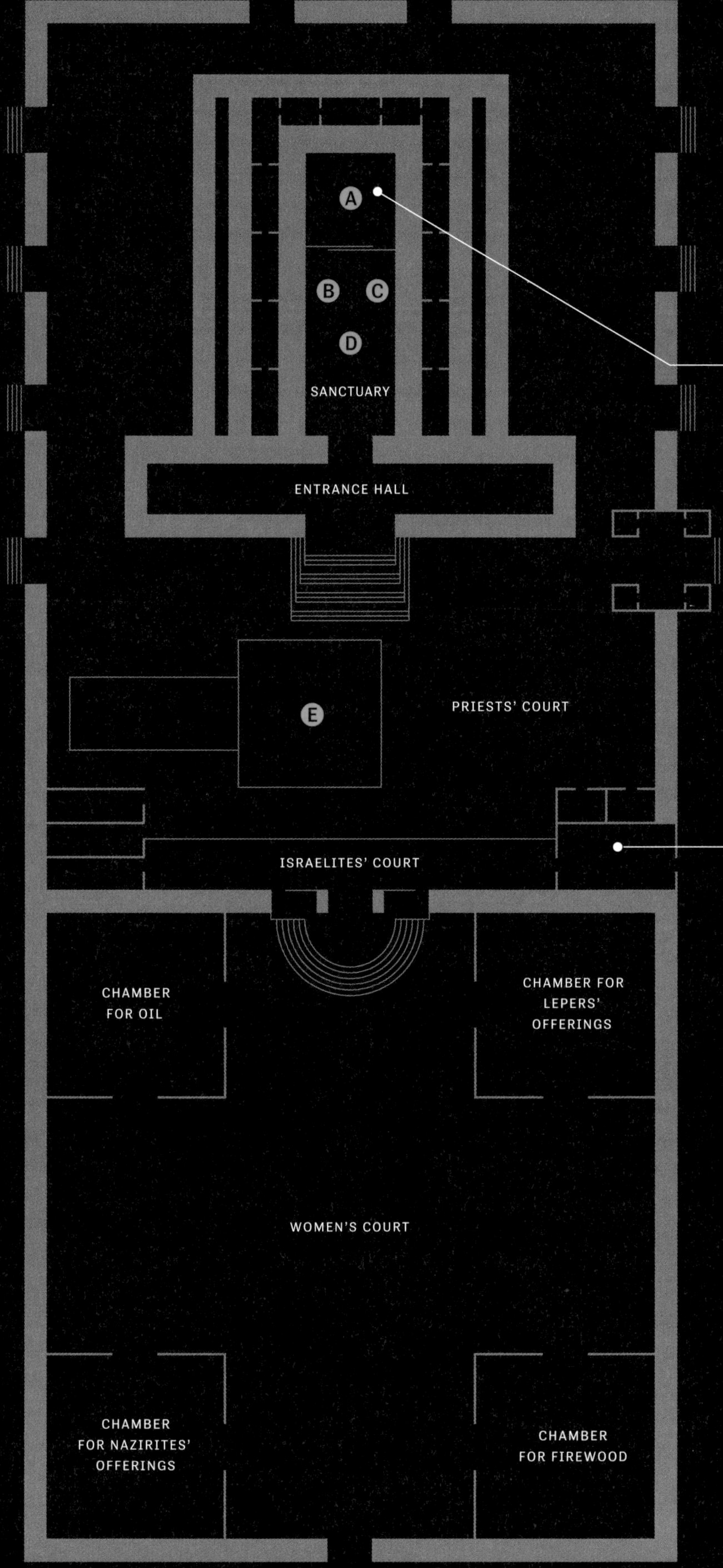

ONE OF
12 "SHOWBREADS"

C Table

W37.8" D18.9" H66.2"

SANCTUARY

A
B   C
D

ENTRANCE HALL

PRIESTS' COURT

E

ISRAELITES' COURT

CHAMBER
FOR OIL

CHAMBER FOR
LEPERS'
OFFERINGS

WOMEN'S COURT

CHAMBER
FOR NAZIRITES'
OFFERINGS

CHAMBER
FOR FIREWOOD

THE SANCTUARY AND THE COURTYARDS
W228.4' X D530.8'

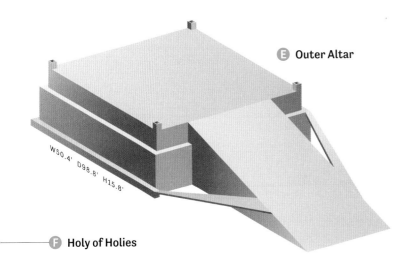

 Outer Altar

W50.4' D98.8' H15.8'

 Holy of Holies

SEVENTY-ONE JUDGES

THREE ROWS OF
DISCIPLES

 Chamber of the Sanhedrin

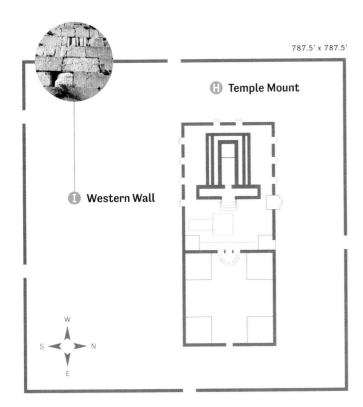

787.5' x 787.5'

 Temple Mount

Western Wall

W
S — N
E

NOTE: Measurements shown on these pages are based on a calculation of the Biblical "cubit" at 18.9 inches.

A Ark

The most sacred object in the Temple, the "Ark of the Covenant," contained the two stone tablets, inscribed with the Ten Commandments, that Moses brought down from Mount Sinai. It also held the Torah scroll written by Moses on the last day of his life. The Ark thus served as a receptacle for the Torah, embodying the very soul of the bond between the Almighty and the Jewish people. Topping the cover of the Ark were two winged figures (*keruvim*, or "cherubs"), one male and the other female, symbolizing the marriage of G-d and Israel.

NUMBERS 7:89

When Moses would enter the Tent of Meeting to speak with [G-d], he heard the voice speaking to him from above the cover that is on the Ark of Testimony, from between the two *keruvim*; and He spoke to him.

TALMUD, *BAVA BATRA 99a*

In one place it says that the *keruvim* "faced each other" (Exodus 25:20); in another place it says that "they faced the room" (II Chronicles 3:13). For when the people of Israel did the will of the Almighty, the *keruvim* faced each other; and when the people of Israel did not do the will of G-d, they faced away from each other.

B Menorah

The Menorah was a seven-branched candelabra, made of pure gold and standing eighteen handbreadths high. Its lamps were filled with the purest olive oil and lit each afternoon to burn through the night.

The Menorah represents the people of Israel, who serve as a "lamp of G-d" (Proverbs 20:27) and "a light unto the nations" (Isaiah 42:6). Its seven branches,

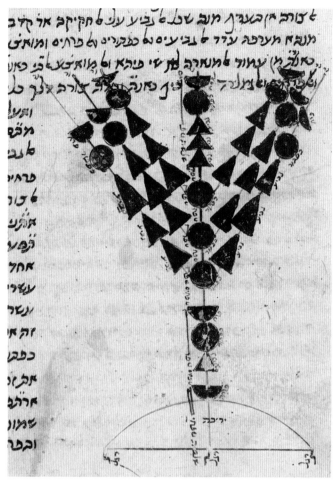

Maimonides' drawing of the Menorah, from a manuscript of his commentary on the Mishnah, circa 1168

corresponding to the seven fundamental character traits (love, awe, compassion, etc.—see pp. 372–373), allude to the variety of souls that comprise the Jewish people. The Torah (Exodus 25:31–40 and Numbers 8:1–42) instructs that the entire Menorah should be hammered out of a single block of gold, and that all its lamps should face the center stem of the Menorah—attesting both to the underlying unity of Israel and to how its diversity of individuals and life-callings are all oriented to a shared mission.

 MIDRASH RABBAH, *BAMIDBAR 15:2*

When a person builds a house, they make the windows narrow on the outside and wider on the inside so that the light should enter from the outside and illuminate the interior. But when King Solomon built the Temple, he made its windows narrow on the inside and wider on the outside, so that its light should illuminate the world.

 Table

The Table stood at the northern wall of the Sanctuary, opposite the Menorah. Each Shabbat, twelve specially baked loaves of unleavened "showbread" were arranged on the Table's golden posts and shelves, where they remained until the following Shabbat, when they were distributed to the priests serving in the Temple that week. Miraculously, the bread remained fresh despite its seven-day display, and it fully satiated those who ate of it, despite the fact that it was apportioned among thousands of priests.

⚡ **BECHAYEI,** *COMMENTARY TO EXODUS 25:23*

The Table served as the source of divine sustenance. G-d dispatched His blessing to the bread placed on the Table, and from there the divine blessing extended to all foods, bringing sustenance to the world.

 Incense Altar

This was a small (1 x 1 x 2 cubits) gold-plated altar, used solely for the burning of the *ketoret*, an "incense" made from a mixture of eleven spices and herbs. The twice-daily burning of *ketoret* was one of the most sacred and mysterious services performed in the Temple; the Talmud relates that it was considered a special privilege if a Kohen (priest) performed this service once in his lifetime.

In his *Guide for the Perplexed* (3:45), Maimonides describes the function of the *ketoret* as follows: "Since many animals were slaughtered in the sacred place each day, their flesh butchered and burnt and their intestines cleaned, its smell would doubtless have been like the smell of a slaughterhouse.... Therefore, the Almighty commanded that the *ketoret* be burned twice a day, each morning and afternoon, to lend a pleasing fragrance to [the Holy Temple] and to the garments of those who served in it."

Bechayei vehemently objects: "Heaven forbid that the great principle and mystery of the *ketoret* should be reduced to this mundane purpose.... [Rather,] *ketoret* means 'to bind' ... the one who offers *ketoret* binds the divine attribute of judgment to its Source above, bringing down a bestowal of blessing" (commentary to Exodus 30:1 and to Leviticus 10:1).

The mystics, however, see these two explanations as complementary: the burning of the *ketoret* represents the power of the soul to bind itself with its source in its Creator, thereby sublimating the "stench" of one's evil inclination (the "animal soul" within a person) and transforming the negative in one's life into a force for good (*Zohar Chadash, Shir ha-Shirim,* 83a).

 ## Outer Altar

The altar on which the *korbanot* (animal and meal offerings) were brought stood outside of the Sanctuary, in the Temple courtyard. It was built of whole stones, and a long ramp served the priests to access the fire that was kept constantly burning on its top.

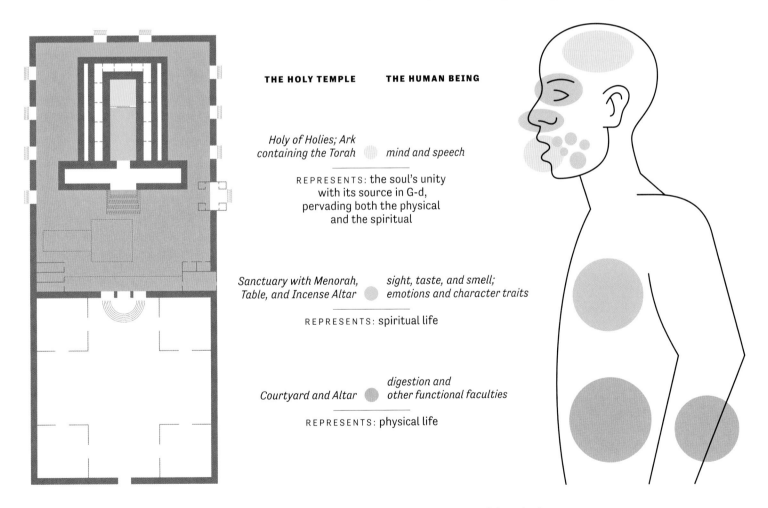

THE HOLY TEMPLE	THE HUMAN BEING
Holy of Holies; Ark containing the Torah	mind and speech
REPRESENTS: the soul's unity with its source in G-d, pervading both the physical and the spiritual	
Sanctuary with Menorah, Table, and Incense Altar	sight, taste, and smell; emotions and character traits
REPRESENTS: spiritual life	
Courtyard and Altar	digestion and other functional faculties
REPRESENTS: physical life	

THE ANATOMY OF THE TEMPLE In the writings of Bechayei, R. Moses Isserlis, Tzemach Tzedek, and others, the Holy Temple is seen as mirroring the human form, with the Temple's various components corresponding to the different areas of human life. Presented here is a generalized summary of the "anatomy" of the Temple.

NACHMANIDES, *COMMENTARY TO LEVITICUS 1:9*

The purpose of the *korbanot* ... is that the person [bringing the offering] should contemplate that they have sinned to their Creator with their body and their soul, and that they are in truth deserving that their own blood should be spilled and their own body burned, were it not for the benevolence of the Creator who accepted this offering from them in their stead.

 R. SCHNEUR ZALMAN OF LIADI
LIKUTEI TORAH, VAYIKRA 2b–c

It is known that every person has two souls: a divine soul, and an animal soul.... The purpose of the soul's descent into this world is to refine the animal soul, to conquer it and transform it.... Thus it says, "A person who will offer from you a *korban* to G-d, from the animal..." (Leviticus 1:2). The offering to the Almighty is literally "from you"—from the animal in yourself.

Maimonides' sketch of the sanctuary floor plan, from a manuscript of his commentary on the Mishnah, circa 1168

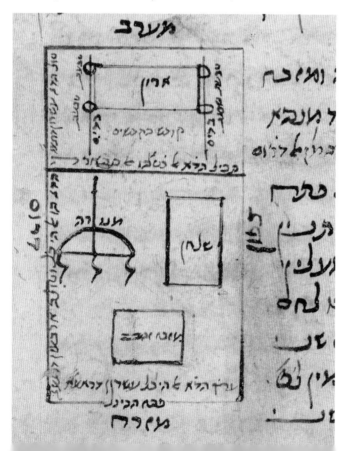

 ## Holy of Holies

The Holy of Holies was the innermost chamber of the Temple and its most sacred space. Only one person, the *kohen gadol* (high priest), entered this chamber, and only on Yom Kippur, the holiest day of the year.

The Book of Kings (II Kings 11:2) refers to the Holy of Holies as "the bedroom," alluding that this was the most intimate space in the marital home of the Divine Groom and the Bride Israel. This was also the place of the most profound expression of the divine presence. The Talmud (*Bava Batra* 99a) relates that the "space of the Ark did not take up any space": although the Ark possessed spatial dimensions of its own, it did not take up any of the space in the room. This expressed the truth that G-d does not only transcend the finite but the infinite as well. In the Holy of Holies, finitude and infinitude, nature and the supranatural, space and spacelessness, coexisted as one.

 TOSEFTA, *YOMA 2:12*

There was a stone in the Holy of Holies called *shethiah* ("foundation") which protruded from the ground the height of three finger-widths. Originally the Ark was placed on top of it. After the Ark was hidden away, the high priest would offer the incense [of the Yom Kippur service] on this stone.

R. Yosei said: From this stone the world was founded.

 **MAIMONIDES,** *MISHNEH TORAH, LAWS OF THE HOLY TEMPLE, 4:1*

When King Solomon built the Holy Temple, he knew that it was destined to be destroyed. So he built a place beneath it to hide the Ark [at the end of] hidden, deep, winding passageways. King Josiah instructed that it be hidden there.... Also hidden were: Aaron's staff, the jar [of manna], and the anointing oil. None of these were brought back when the Second Temple was built.

The Temple Mount today, view from the south. Western Wall plaza is at left edge of photo, toward the bottom.

 ## Chamber of the Sanhedrin

In addition to its role as the focal point of the people's service of G-d, the Holy Temple was also a center of learning and jurisprudence.

In the desert, the Tabernacle served as the "Tent of Meeting," where G-d communicated the Torah's laws to Moses. In Jerusalem, it was the seat of the Sanhedrin, a tribunal of seventy-one sages which served as the highest court of Torah law. All matters of national importance (appointing a king, the decision to go to war, etc.) were decided by the Sanhedrin. To the Sanhedrin's chamber on the north wall of the Temple courtyard were also brought all issues that the lower courts were unable to decide (see citation from Deuteronomy on p. 186).

 ## Temple Mount

The Temple Mount was—and remains—sacred ground, and according to Torah law, only those who are in a state of ritual purity are permitted to enter it. Archaeological digs have unearthed numerous mikvehs (ritual immersion pools—see p. 410) just outside the Temple Mount walls that appear to have served the many thousands who came to the Holy Temple on the three annual pilgrimage festivals of Passover, Shavuot, and Sukkot.

 ## Western Wall

In 69 CE, the Romans torched the second Holy Temple and then razed its charred ruins to the ground. In the 2,000 years since, Jews have cherished the western wall of the Temple Mount as the sole surviving remnant of the Temple, and have come there to pour out their hearts in prayer (see p. 85 and p. 383).

THE SECOND COMMONWEALTH

historical milestones of the Second Temple era

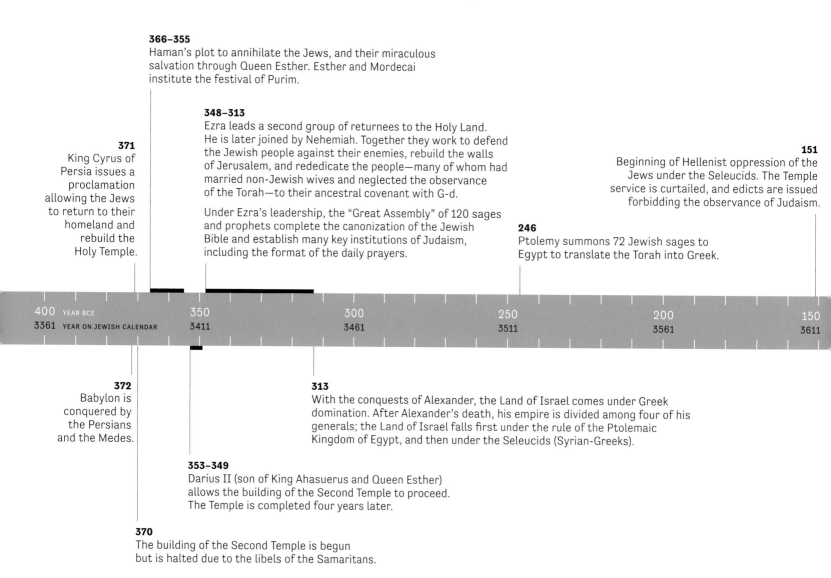

366–355
Haman's plot to annihilate the Jews, and their miraculous salvation through Queen Esther. Esther and Mordecai institute the festival of Purim.

348–313
Ezra leads a second group of returnees to the Holy Land. He is later joined by Nehemiah. Together they work to defend the Jewish people against their enemies, rebuild the walls of Jerusalem, and rededicate the people—many of whom had married non-Jewish wives and neglected the observance of the Torah—to their ancestral covenant with G-d.

Under Ezra's leadership, the "Great Assembly" of 120 sages and prophets complete the canonization of the Jewish Bible and establish many key institutions of Judaism, including the format of the daily prayers.

371
King Cyrus of Persia issues a proclamation allowing the Jews to return to their homeland and rebuild the Holy Temple.

151
Beginning of Hellenist oppression of the Jews under the Seleucids. The Temple service is curtailed, and edicts are issued forbidding the observance of Judaism.

246
Ptolemy summons 72 Jewish sages to Egypt to translate the Torah into Greek.

400 YEAR BCE	350	300	250	200	150
3361 YEAR ON JEWISH CALENDAR	3411	3461	3511	3561	3611

372
Babylon is conquered by the Persians and the Medes.

313
With the conquests of Alexander, the Land of Israel comes under Greek domination. After Alexander's death, his empire is divided among four of his generals; the Land of Israel falls first under the rule of the Ptolemaic Kingdom of Egypt, and then under the Seleucids (Syrian-Greeks).

353–349
Darius II (son of King Ahasuerus and Queen Esther) allows the building of the Second Temple to proceed. The Temple is completed four years later.

370
The building of the Second Temple is begun but is halted due to the libels of the Samaritans.

Seventy years after the conquest of Judah and the exile of its people to Babylon, a small segment of the Jewish exiles, led by the Judean prince Zerubbabel, returned under a mandate by the Persian emperor Cyrus to re-settle the Land and rebuild the Holy Temple. It was a difficult beginning, plagued by poverty, persecution, and a host of social and spiritual ills; but under the leadership of Ezra and the other members of the "Great Assembly," the community grew and eventually flour-ished. The Holy Land once again became the center of Jewish life, until its catastrophic destruction by the Romans in the first century of the Common Era.

In many ways, the Second Temple era fell short of the glory years of the First Temple. The era of prophecy had come to an end. A sizable portion of the Jewish people remained in the diaspora communities in Babylonia, Egypt, and elsewhere. Other than for a brief period of independence under the Hasmonean dynasty, the Jew-ish homeland was subject to the empires of the time.

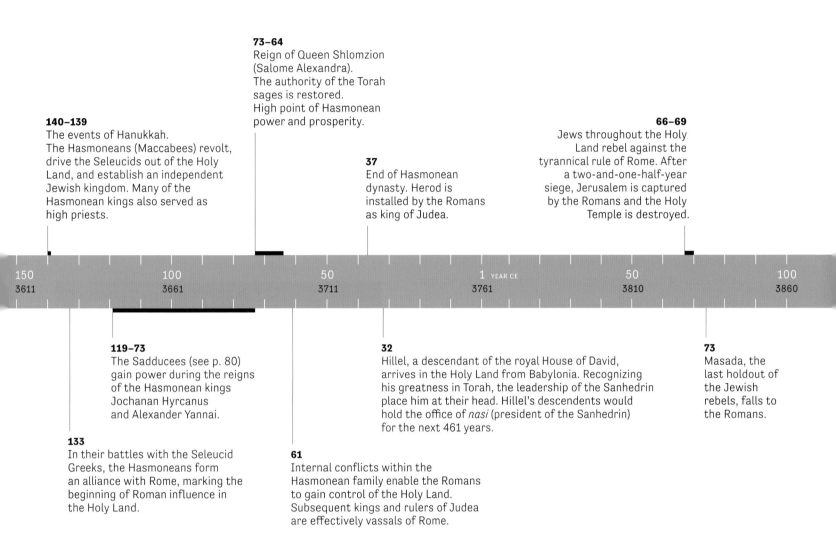

73–64
Reign of Queen Shlomzion (Salome Alexandra).
The authority of the Torah sages is restored.
High point of Hasmonean power and prosperity.

140–139
The events of Hanukkah.
The Hasmoneans (Maccabees) revolt, drive the Seleucids out of the Holy Land, and establish an independent Jewish kingdom. Many of the Hasmonean kings also served as high priests.

37
End of Hasmonean dynasty. Herod is installed by the Romans as king of Judea.

66–69
Jews throughout the Holy Land rebel against the tyrannical rule of Rome. After a two-and-one-half-year siege, Jerusalem is captured by the Romans and the Holy Temple is destroyed.

150	100	50	1 YEAR CE	50	100
3611	3661	3711	3761	3810	3860

119–73
The Sadducees (see p. 80) gain power during the reigns of the Hasmonean kings Jochanan Hyrcanus and Alexander Yannai.

32
Hillel, a descendant of the royal House of David, arrives in the Holy Land from Babylonia. Recognizing his greatness in Torah, the leadership of the Sanhedrin place him at their head. Hillel's descendents would hold the office of *nasi* (president of the Sanhedrin) for the next 461 years.

73
Masada, the last holdout of the Jewish rebels, falls to the Romans.

133
In their battles with the Seleucid Greeks, the Hasmoneans form an alliance with Rome, marking the beginning of Roman influence in the Holy Land.

61
Internal conflicts within the Hasmonean family enable the Romans to gain control of the Holy Land. Subsequent kings and rulers of Judea are effectively vassals of Rome.

Internal conflicts—between traditionalists and Hellenists, between the "Pharisees" who remained faithful to the Sinaic tradition and the anti-rabbinical Sadducees, and, in the era's closing years, between those advocating peace with Rome and the Zealots pursuing rebellion—tore at the people from within.

In other ways, the Second Temple era rivaled, and even surpassed, its predecessor. Jewish learning and influence flourished. It was during this period that the canonization of the twenty-four books of the Jewish Bible was completed, and study halls rang with the discussions that would later form the core of the Mishnah and Talmud. Jewish settlement and commerce carried the ideas and ethos of Judaism to the farthest reaches of the Persian, Greek, and Roman empires, leaving its imprint on numerous cultures and belief systems.

RETURN FROM BABYLON

 EZRA 1:1–3:12

And G-d aroused the spirit of Cyrus the king of Persia, and he issued a proclamation throughout his kingdom, and also in writing, saying:

"So said Cyrus.... All the kingdoms of the earth, the Lord G-d of the heavens has delivered to me, and He commanded me to build Him a house in Jerusalem which is in Judea. Whoever is among you of all His people, may his G-d be with him, and let him ascend to Jerusalem which is in Judea, and let him build the house of the Lord, G-d of Israel...."

These are the people of the province who went up from the captivity of the exile, whom Nebuchadnezzar, the king of Babylon, had exiled to Babylon; and they returned to Jerusalem and Judea, each one to his city. Those who came with Zerubbabel ... the entire congregation together was forty-two thousand, three hundred and sixty....

In the second year of their coming ... the builders laid the foundation of the Temple of G-d.... And many of the priests and the Levites and the patriarchs, old men who had seen the first Temple upon its foundation, [when they saw] this Temple with their eyes, were weeping with a loud voice, and many with a shout of joy to raise their voice....

 NEHEMIAH 3:33–4:16

It came to pass when Sanballat heard that we were building the wall [of Jerusalem], he became wroth and was very angry, and he ridiculed the Jews. And he spoke before his brethren and the army of Samaria, and he said, "What are the feeble Jews doing? Will they let them? Will they sacrifice? Will they finish in one day? Will they revive the stones from the heaps of dust, as they are burnt?" ... But we built the wall, and the entire wall was built to its half, and the people had a desire to build....

They all banded together to come and wage war against Jerusalem and to wreak destruction therein. We prayed to our G-d, and we stationed a watch over them....

And it was from that day on, half of my youths did work, and half of them held spears, shields, bows, and coats of mail.... The builders of the wall and the carriers of the loads were loading, with one hand doing the work and one holding the sword.... The night will be for our watch, and the day for work.

Belshazzar's Feast (detail), Rembrandt van Rijn, Amsterdam, circa 1636

THE WRITING ON THE WALL When an invading Median and Persian force was initially repelled, the Babylonian ruler Belshazzar threw a banquet and brought out the vessels of the Holy Temple, captured by his grandfather Nebuchadnezzar, so that "the king, his dignitaries, his queen, and his concubines should drink from them" (Daniel 5:2). A hand appeared and wrote a cryptic message on the wall, which the Judean prince Daniel deciphered as *mene, mene, tekel, ufarsin* (counted, counted, weighed, and divided), to say: "G-d has counted the days of your kingdom, and ended it; your deeds have been weighed on the scales of justice, and were found wanting; and your kingdom will be divided between Media and Persia." That very night the invaders returned, and Belshazzar was assassinated by his own men. One year later, the Persian emperor Cyrus issued the historical proclamation calling on the exiled Jewish people to return to their homeland and rebuild the Holy Temple.

THE GREEKS AND THE HASMONEANS

 JOSEPHUS, *ANTIQUITIES OF THE JEWS, 11:8*

Alexander came into Syria and took Damascus; and when he had obtained Sidon, he besieged Tyre, and he sent an epistle to the Jewish high priest, to send him some auxiliaries, and to supply his army with provisions…. But the high priest answered the messengers that he had given his oath to Darius not to bear arms against him; and he said that he would not transgress this while Darius was in the land of the living. Upon hearing this answer, Alexander was very angry … and threatened that he would make an expedition against the Jewish high priest, and through him teach all men to whom they must keep their oath. So when he had, with a good deal of pains during the siege, taken Tyre and had settled its affairs, he came to the city of Gaza…. When he had taken Gaza, he made haste to go up to Jerusalem….

When [the high priest] heard of this he was in an agony, and under terror, not knowing how he should meet the Macedonians, since the king was displeased at his foregoing disobedience. He therefore ordained that the people should make supplications and should join with him in offering sacrifice to G-d, whom he besought to protect that nation and to deliver them from the perils that were coming upon them. Whereupon G-d warned him in a dream … that he should take courage, and adorn the city, and open the gates; that the rest should appear in white garments, but that he and the priests should meet the king in the habits proper to their order, without the dread of any ill consequences, which the providence of G-d would prevent. Upon which, when he rose from his sleep, he greatly rejoiced, and declared to all the warning he had received. According to which dream he acted entirely, and so waited for the coming of the king.

When he understood that [Alexander] was not far from the city, he went out in procession, with the priests and the multitude of the citizens. The procession was venerable, and the manner of it different from that of

Gold stater of Alexander the Great, Memphis, Egypt, circa 323 BCE

other nations. It reached to a place [from which you have] a prospect both of Jerusalem and of the Temple. And where the Phoenicians and the Chaldeans that followed [Alexander] thought they should have liberty to plunder the city, and torment the high priest to death, which the king's displeasure fairly promised them, the very reverse of it happened. For Alexander, when he saw the multitude at a distance, in white garments, while the priests stood clothed with fine linen, and the high priest in purple and scarlet clothing, with his mitre on his head, having the golden plate whereon the divine name was engraved, he approached by himself, and adored that name, and first saluted the high priest. The Jews also did all together, with one voice, salute Alexander, and encompass him about; whereupon the kings of Syria and the rest were surprised at what Alexander had done, and supposed him disordered in his mind. However, Parmenio alone went up to him, and asked him how it came to pass that, when all others adored him, he should adore the high priest of the Jews? To whom he replied, "I did not adore him, but that G-d who has honored him with his high priesthood; for I saw this very person in a dream, in this very habit, when I was at Dios in Macedonia, who, when I was considering with myself how I might obtain the dominion of Asia, exhorted me to make no delay, but boldly to pass over the sea thither, for that he would conduct my army, and would give me the dominion over the Persians...."

When he had said this to Parmenio, and had given the high priest his right hand, the priests ran along by him, and he came into the city. And when he went up into the Temple, he offered sacrifice to G-d, according to the high priest's direction, and magnificently treated both the high priest and the priests. The Book of Daniel was shown to him, wherein Daniel declared that one of the Greeks should destroy the empire of the Persians, he supposed that himself was the person intended....

 TALMUD, *MEGILAH 9a*

King Ptolemy gathered together seventy-two sages and placed them in seventy-two rooms, without telling them why he had assembled them. He went in to each one of them and said to him: "Translate for me the Torah of Moses your master." The Almighty put counsel into the heart of each one of them, and they all agreed to the same mind.

 MAX I. DIMONT, *JEWS, G-D AND HISTORY, P. 109*

The Greeks believed in the holiness of beauty; the Jews believed in the beauty of holiness.

 SIDDUR, *AL HANISIM PRAYER*

In the days of Mattityahu the son of Jochanan the High Priest, the Hasmonean, and his sons ... the wicked Hellenic government rose up against Your people Israel to make them forget Your Torah and to violate the decrees of Your will. But You, in Your abounding mercies, stood

by them in the time of their distress. You waged their battles, defended their rights, and avenged the wrong done to them. You delivered the mighty into the hands of the weak, the many into the hands of the few, the impure into the hands of the pure, the wicked into the hands of the righteous, and wanton sinners into the hands of those who occupy themselves with Your Torah. You made a great and holy name for Yourself in Your world, and effected a great deliverance and redemption for Your people Israel to this very day. Then Your children entered the shrine of Your House, cleansed Your Temple, purified Your Sanctuary, and kindled lights in Your holy courtyards; and they instituted these eight days of Hanukkah to give thanks and praise to Your great name.

{FOR MORE ON THE HASMONEAN REVOLT
AND THE FESTIVAL OF HANUKKAH, SEE PP. 350–357}

 NACHMANIDES, *COMMENTARY TO GENESIS 49:10*

The Hasmoneans who assumed the kingship during the Second Temple era were pious and holy men, and were it not for their valor, the Torah and its mitzvot would have been forgotten from Israel. Nevertheless, they were punished for taking the throne, as they were not descendants of David and Judah. Furthermore, the Hasmoneans were priests, who are enjoined to devote themselves solely to serving the Almighty in the Holy Temple, and should have eschewed the monarchy. The four Hasmonean brothers who reigned over Israel, notwithstanding their might and military successes, were all felled by the sword of their enemies. In the end, the Hasmonean dynasty was wiped out by their own slaves who usurped their throne, as they had usurped the throne of Judah.

the Hasmonean dynasty

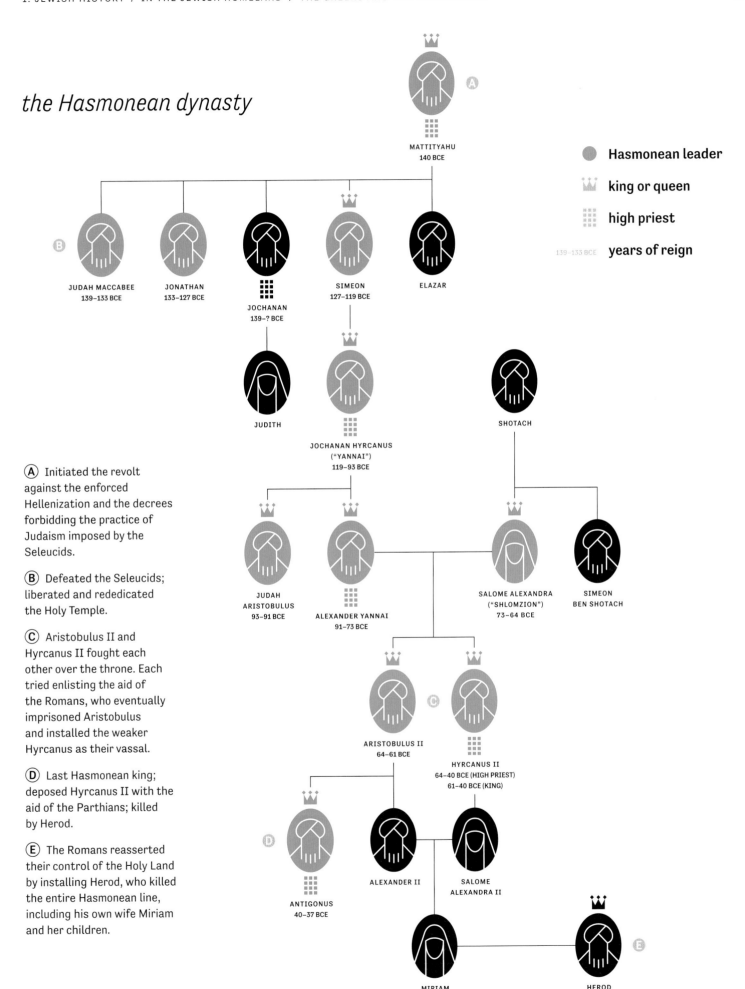

Hasmonean leader

king or queen

high priest

139–133 BCE **years of reign**

MATTITYAHU
140 BCE

Ⓐ

Ⓑ

JUDAH MACCABEE
139–133 BCE

JONATHAN
133–127 BCE

JOCHANAN
139–? BCE

SIMEON
127–119 BCE

ELAZAR

JUDITH

JOCHANAN HYRCANUS
("YANNAI")
119–93 BCE

SHOTACH

JUDAH
ARISTOBULUS
93–91 BCE

ALEXANDER YANNAI
91–73 BCE

SALOME ALEXANDRA
("SHLOMZION")
73–64 BCE

SIMEON
BEN SHOTACH

ARISTOBULUS II
64–61 BCE

Ⓒ

HYRCANUS II
64–40 BCE (HIGH PRIEST)
61–40 BCE (KING)

Ⓓ

ANTIGONUS
40–37 BCE

ALEXANDER II

SALOME
ALEXANDRA II

MIRIAM

HEROD
37 BCE–1 CE

Ⓔ

Ⓐ Initiated the revolt against the enforced Hellenization and the decrees forbidding the practice of Judaism imposed by the Seleucids.

Ⓑ Defeated the Seleucids; liberated and rededicated the Holy Temple.

Ⓒ Aristobulus II and Hyrcanus II fought each other over the throne. Each tried enlisting the aid of the Romans, who eventually imprisoned Aristobulus and installed the weaker Hyrcanus as their vassal.

Ⓓ Last Hasmonean king; deposed Hyrcanus II with the aid of the Parthians; killed by Herod.

Ⓔ The Romans reasserted their control of the Holy Land by installing Herod, who killed the entire Hasmonean line, including his own wife Miriam and her children.

PHARISEES AND SADDUCEES

The split between the Pharisees, who accepted the "Oral Torah" (see pp. 186–190) and the authority of the Torah sages, and the Sadducees, who rejected the rabbinic tradition and interpreted the Torah after their own understanding, plagued the people of Israel during the latter part of the Second Temple era. There were periods when the high priesthood, and even the Sanhedrin, were in the hands of the Sadducees, and times when the Pharisees regained control of the leadership. On the whole, the population at large was loyal to the rabbinic tradition, while portions of the upper classes associated with the Sadducees.

 AVOT D'RABBI NATHAN, *CHAPTER 5*

Antigonus of Socho received the tradition from Simeon the Just. He would teach: "Do not be like servants who serve their master in order to receive a reward; rather, be like servants who serve their master not for the sake of receiving a reward; and the fear of Heaven should be upon you...."

Antigonus had two disciples, [Zadok and Boethus,] who repeated this teaching to their disciples, and their disciples to their disciples. They rose up and examined the matter, saying: Why did our predecessors say this? Is it right for a laborer to toil all day and not receive their reward in the evening? Had our predecessors known that there was another world and that there would be a resurrection of the dead, they surely would not have said this! So they arose and turned away from the Torah. Two sects sprang from them: the Sadducees and the Boethusians, the Sadducees named after Zadok and the Boethusians after Boethus. All their lives they used vessels of silver and gold, because they were arrogant in mind. The Sadducees said that it was a tradition of the Pharisees to subject themselves to austerity in this world, and in the world to come they possess nothing at all.

 JOSEPHUS
ANTIQUITIES, 13:10 AND 18:1; WARS, 2:8

The Pharisees have delivered to the people a great many observances by succession from their predecessors which are not written in the laws of Moses; and for that reason it is that the Sadducees reject them, saying that we are to esteem those observances that are in the written word to be obligatory, but are not to observe those that derive from the tradition of our forefathers....

The doctrine of the Sadducees is this: that souls die with the bodies; nor do they regard the observation of anything besides what the law enjoins them....

The Pharisees are friendly to one another, and are for the exercise of concord and regard for the public. But the behavior of the Sadducees one toward another... and their conversation with those that are of their own party, is as barbarous as if they were strangers to them.

While the Sadducees are able to persuade none but the rich, and have not the populace obsequious to them, the Pharisees have the multitude on their side.

 TALMUD, *KIDUSHIN 66a*

King Yannai went to Kohalith in the wilderness and conquered sixty towns there. On his return he was in high spirits and summoned all the sages of Israel. Said he to them: "Our forefathers [in their poverty] ate mallows when they were engaged in the building of the [second] Holy Temple; let us too eat mallows in remembrance of our forefathers." So mallows were served on tables of gold, and they ate.

Now, there was a frivolous, evilhearted, worthless man there named Elazar ben Po'irah, who said to King Yannai: "King Yannai, the hearts of the Pharisees are against you." "Then what shall I do?" "Raise them up with the [high priest's] golden plate between your eyes."

[Yannai appeared before them with the high priests'] golden plate between his eyes, causing them to rise [to

SADDUCEE CALENDAR? A fragment of a 2,100-year-old calendrical text discovered near Qumran in the Judean Desert on the shore of the Dead Sea, home to a Jewish sect that seems to have followed Sadducee applications of Torah law. The text in the fragment sets the date of the annual barley offering, as well as the festival of Shavuot, on the first day of the week, although Passover falls on the third day of the week. This is consistent with the Sadducee interpretation of Leviticus 23:15–16, in contrast to the rabbinic interpretation, which sets these events on the first and 50th days following the first day of Passover, regardless of the day of the week.

their feet]. There was an elder named Judah ben Gedidiah who was present there. Said Judah ben Gedidiah to King Yannai: "King Yannai! Let the crown of kingship suffice you, and leave the crown of priesthood to the seed of Aaron." For it was rumored that [Yannai's] mother had been taken captive in Modi'in. The matter was investigated, but it was not found to be so. And the sages of Israel departed under [the king's] anger.

Said Elazar ben Po'irah to King Yannai: "King Yannai! Would the most humble man in Israel be treated thus? And you, a king and a high priest, shall be treated thus?" "Then what shall I do?" "If you would take my advice, trample them." "But what shall happen with the Torah?" "It is here, rolled up and lying in the corner; whoever wishes to study it can come and study it!"

(Said R. Nachman bar Isaac: At that point, a spirit of heresy was instilled into [Yannai]. For he should have responded: "That is well for the Written Torah; but what of the Oral Torah?")

Straightway, the evil was ignited by Elazar ben Po'irah. All the sages of Israel were massacred, and the world was desolate until Simeon ben Shotach came and restored the Torah to its former glory.

 MIDRASH RABBAH, *VAYIKRA 35:10*

It happened in the days of Simeon ben Shotach and Queen Shlomzion that the rains would fall on Shabbat nights, until the wheat grew large as kidneys, the barley as olive-pits, and the lentils as gold dinars. The sages stocked [these grains] for future generations, to show the divine blessings that are lost due to sinfulness.

The nine-year reign of Queen Shlomzion (Salome Alexandra) was an island of tranquility in the tumultuous century of Hasmonean rule. She ended persecution of the rabbis that had been conducted during the reigns of her father-in-law and husband, and the Sanhedrin was reconstituted under the righteous leadership of her brother, Simeon ben Shotach.

THE DESTRUCTION

 TALMUD, *YOMA 9b*

Why was the first Holy Temple destroyed? Because of three things that prevailed there: idolatry, immorality, and bloodshed…. But the Second Temple, when they were occupied with Torah, mitzvot, and the practice of charity, why was it destroyed? Because there was baseless hatred amongst them.

 TALMUD AND RASHI, *SOTAH 49b*

When the Hasmonean brothers Hyrcanus and Aristobulus were battling each other over the throne, Hyrcanus brought Roman legions with him and was besieging Jerusalem from the outside, and Aristobulus was inside the city. Each day, they would lower a basket with money from the Temple treasury, and in return, they would send up two lambs for the daily offerings.

There was an old man inside the city who was versed in Greek wisdom. Speaking in Greek, he said to those outside the city: "As long as they are conducting the service in the Temple, you will not defeat them." So the next day, when the money was sent down in a basket, they sent up a pig. When it was halfway up, the pig stuck its hooves into the city wall. At that moment, the Land of Israel shook for a distance of four hundred parasangs.

At that time they declared: "Cursed be the person who raises pigs, and cursed be the person who teaches their son Greek wisdom."

 TALMUD, *GITTIN 56a–b*

"Give me Yavneh and its sages"

Vespasian came and besieged Jerusalem for three years…. The Zealots were then in the city. The rabbis said to them: "Let us go out and make peace with [the Romans]." They would not let them, but on the contrary said, "Let us go out and fight them." The rabbis said: "You will not succeed." The [Zealots] then rose up and burned the stores of wheat and barley (in order to force the people to fight), and a famine ensued….

Abba Sikra, the head of the Zealots in Jerusalem, was the son of the sister of Rabban Jochanan ben Zakai. [R. Jochanan] sent to him, saying, "Come to visit me privately." When he came he said to him, "How long are you going to carry on in this way, and kill all the people with starvation?" He replied: "What can I do? If I say a word to them, they will kill me." He said: "Devise some plan for me to escape. Perhaps I will be able to save something." He said to him: "Pretend to be ill, and let everyone come to inquire about you. Bring something evil-smelling and put it by you so that they will say you are dead…."

When they reached the city gate, [the Zealots] wanted to put a lance through the bier. [Abba Sikra] said to them: "Shall [the Romans] say, 'They have pierced their Master'?" They wanted to give it a shove. He said to them: "Shall they say that they shoved their Master?" They opened a gate for them and they got out.

When [R. Jochanan] reached [the Roman camp], he said [to Vespasian]: "Peace to you, O king!" He said: "Your life is forfeit on two counts. First, because I am not a king and you call me king. And again, if I am a king, why did you not come to me before now?"

He replied: "As for your saying that you are not a king, in truth you are a king, because if you were not a king, Jerusalem would not be delivered into your hand. As it is written (Isaiah 10:34), 'The Lebanon (i.e., the Holy Temple, as in Deuteronomy 3:25) shall fall by a mighty one.' As for your question, 'If I am a king, why did you not come to me till now?,' the answer is that the Zealots among us did not let me."

Said he to him: "If there is a jar of honey around which a serpent is wound, should one not break the jar to get rid of the serpent?" [R. Jochanan] was silent.

(R. Yosef—some say R. Akiva—applied to R. Jochanan the verse (Isaiah 44:25), "[G-d] turns wise men backward and makes their knowledge foolish." For he ought

ANDREW SHIVA

An aerial view of the Masada fortress, Judean Desert, Israel

to have said to him: "One takes a pair of tongs and removes the snake and kills it, and leaves the jar intact…")

At this point, a messenger came from Rome saying: "Arise, for the Emperor is dead, and the notables of Rome have decided to place you at the head…."

[Vespasian] said: "I am now going, and will send someone to take my place. But make a request of me, and I will grant it."

He said to him: "Give me Yavneh and its sages, and the dynasty of Rabban Gamliel, and physicians to heal Rabbi Zadok."

R. Yosef—some say R. Akiva—applied to him the verse, "[G-d] turns wise men backward and makes their knowledge foolish." He ought to have asked him to spare Jerusalem! R. Jochanan, however, thought that so much he would not grant, and so even a little would not be saved.

THE LAST HOLDOUT The Masada fortress, overlooking the Dead Sea in the Judean desert, was the last holdout of the Jewish rebellion against the Romans. Following the conquest of Jerusalem and the destruction of the Holy Temple in 69 CE, the fortress was seized by a determined rebel leader named Elazar. Occupying a high plateau surrounded by sheer cliffs from all sides, equipped with an underground network of water cisterns and well-stocked with food and arms, the 967 men, women, and children on Masada held out against the Roman legions for many months. When the Romans finally succeeded in breaching the fortress, they met only with a deathly silence; the entire community on Masada had chosen to die by their own hands rather than to be massacred or enslaved by their enemies. The sole survivors were two women and five children who had hidden in an underground cavern.

THE BAR KOCHBA REVOLT

MIDRASH RABBAH, *EICHAH 2:4*

When R. Akiva saw the successes of Bar Koziba [Bar Kochba], he would say, "This is the Messiah." Said R. Jochanan Torta to him, "Akiva! Grass will grow on your cheeks, but the Messiah will not yet have come." ...

Bar Koziba had 200,000 warriors with severed fingers. The sages sent a message to him: "How much longer will you maim the people of Israel?" Said he to them, "So how should their bravery be tested?" Said they to him, "Anyone who cannot uproot a Cedar of Lebanon, do not sign him up in your army." So he had 200,000 of the former and 200,000 of the latter. When they went out to battle, they would say, "G-d, don't help us, just don't hinder us." ...

For three and one half years, Hadrian besieged Betar. R. Elazar of Modi'in was there, engaged in fasting and sackcloth; each day he would pray: "Master of the World! Do not sit in judgment today." In the end, [Hadrian] was thinking of going back [to Rome]. A Cuthian came to him and said, "As long as this hen wallows in the ashes, you will not be able to conquer the city. Wait here for me, and I will arrange for you to conquer it this day."

[The Cuthian] entered the city through a sewer trench, and found R. Elazar standing and praying. He then acted as if he was whispering something in R. Elazar's ear. People went and said to Bar Koziba, "Your friend Rabbi Elazar is conspiring to hand over the city to the Romans." So he had the Cuthian brought to him, and said, "What did you say to him?" Said he to him, "If I tell you, the emperor will kill me; and if I don't tell you, you will kill me. Better that I kill myself, and not divulge the king's secrets." Bar Koziba thought that [R. Elazar] wanted to deliver the city.

When R. Elazar finished praying, Bar Koziba summoned him before him. Said he to him: "What did that Cuthian say to you?" Said he to him: "I do not know what he whispered in my ear; I did not hear anything,

Rebel tunnel, part of a network of underground cisterns and connecting tunnels used during the Bar Kochba revolt, 132–135 CE

as I was praying." Bar Koziba was filled with rage; he gave R. Elazar one kick with his foot, killing him.... Immediately the sins caused Betar to be conquered, and Bar Koziba was killed.

They brought his head to Hadrian. Said he: "Who killed him?" A legionnaire said, "I killed him." Said he to him, "Bring me his neck." They brought it, and they found a serpent wound around it. Said [Hadrian]: "Had his G-d not killed him, who could have defeated him?"

The Romans were slaughtering the Jews until the horses sank to their noses in blood.... Hadrian did not allow the Jews to bury their dead, until another king decreed [fifteen years later] that they could be buried. Said R. Huna: On the day that the dead of Betar were allowed to be buried, the sages instituted the blessing, "He who is good, and who does good."

THE MEDIEVAL ERA

 GEDALIAH ALON, *THE JEWS IN THEIR LAND IN THE TALMUDIC AGE, P. 37*

It would be inaccurate to see [the post-Talmudic period in the Holy Land, 420 to 640 CE] as an age that was more concerned with preserving the work of previous generations than with creating anything of its own. Indeed, there is an area of original spiritual creativity which is the special mark of these declining years. For this was the time when *piyyut*—the unique liturgical poetry of the synagogue—made its first appearance. In the *piyyutim* of Yannai, from all indications composed in the Land of Israel at the end of the Byzantine period, we discover this wonderful new literary genre already in full flower, combining halakhah, aggadah, prayer and art. It was to flourish for generations to come in many and varied forms, becoming a significant element in the blood-stream of Jewish life.

 ZEV VILNAY, *LEGENDS OF PALESTINE, PP. 63–64*

One day when Sultan Selim was in Jerusalem, he saw an old Christian woman who brought a mass of garbage and cast it upon a spot near his palace. Angrily, he sent one of his men to bring the woman before him. The woman explained that she lived two days' journey from Jerusalem, and had come in obedience to a long-standing custom instituted by the bishops: that a mass of ordure be brought once in thirty days and cast on the spot where the house of the G-d of Israel had formerly stood. If they could not destroy it in its entirety, they wished it to be swamped and forgotten.

The Sultan on inquiry found that she spoke the truth. So he took many coins of gold and silver and, with basket and shovel in hand, issued the following proclamation to his people: "Whosoever loves the king and desires to give him pleasure, let him see his actions and do likewise." Going to the dunghill, the sultan threw into different parts of it many purses of coins, so that the poor might dig away the rubbish in order to find the treasure. The Sultan himself stood by them, urging them on. Finally more than 10,000 men worked for thirty days until the dunghill was completely removed, and the *Kotel ha-Ma'aravi*, the Wailing Wall, stood revealed as it is seen today.

 BENJAMIN OF TUDELA *TRAVEL JOURNAL, CIRCA 1173*

From Tyre it is one day's travel to Acre, the Acco of Scripture, on the boundary of the tribe of Asher. It is the frontier of the Land of Israel. Because of its situation on the shore of the Mediterranean and its large port, it is the principal place of disembarkation of all pilgrims who come to Jerusalem by sea.... There are about two hundred Jewish inhabitants here, whose leaders are R. Zadok, R. Jepheth, and R. Jonah.

Three parasangs farther is Haifa.... One side of this city is situated on the coast, on the other it is overlooked by Mount Carmel. Under the mountain are many Jewish gravesites, and near the summit is the cavern of Elijah the Prophet. The Christians have built a place of worship near this site, which they call St. Elias. On the summit of the hill you may still trace the site of the altar that was built by Elijah in the time of King Ahab, and the circumference of which is about four yards. The Kishon River runs down the mountain and along its base.

It is four parasangs hence to Kfar Nachum, identical with Meon, the place of abode of Nabal the Carmelite. Six parasangs brings us to Caesarea ... inhabited by about ten Jews and two hundred Samaritans.... To Kakun, the Keilah of Scripture, is half-a-day's journey; in this place are no Jews. To St. George, the ancient Luz, half-a-day's journey; one Jew only, a dyer, lives here. To Sebaste, one-day's journey. This is the ancient Samaria, where you may still trace the site of the palace of the Israelite king Ahab. It was formerly a very strong city, and is situated on a mount, in a fine country, richly watered, and surrounded with gardens, orchards, vineyards, and olive groves. No Jews live here.

historical milestones, 1st to 18th centuries

69–74
R. Jochanan ben Zakai establishes a center for Torah learning at Yavneh, and guides the adjustment of Jewish religious life in the absence of the Holy Temple.

219–279
Deliberations in the academy of R. Jochanan bar Naphcha in Tiberias form the basis for the "Jerusalem Talmud."

359–363
The *nasi* Hillel II establishes the continuous Jewish calendar (see p. 330–331).

Brief respite from persecution during the rule of the anti-Christian emperor Julian—who at one point authorized the rebuilding of the Holy Temple—ends when he dies in battle in 363.

4th—7th Centuries
The classical Holy Land *payyetanim* compose the liturgical poems incorporated in Jewish prayers.

634–638
Muslim conquest ends six centuries of Roman and Byzantine rule over the Holy Land. Jewish community reestablished in Jerusalem.

1	YEAR CE	100	200	300	400	500	600	700	800	900
3761	YEAR ON JEWISH CALENDAR	3960	4060	4160	4260	4360	4460	4560	4660	

132–135
Bar Kochba rebellion: Initial success in liberating Jerusalem and other parts of Judea is followed by crushing defeat at the hands of the Romans. The Romans intensify their decrees against the study of Torah and the practice of Judaism, and many sages and leaders are executed. Jews are banned from living in Jerusalem, and Judea is renamed "Syria Palaestina."

148–200
Romans relax some of the anti-Jewish decrees. The Sanhedrin and the office of the *nasi* are reestablished in the Galilee. Compilation of the Mishnah by R. Judah ha-Nasi (see pp. 186—187).

429
Roman Emperor Theodosius II forbids the appointment of a successor to R. Gamliel VI, ending the office of *nasi* in the Holy Land.

7th—10th Centuries
Work of the "Masoretes," centered in Tiberias and Jerusalem (see note B on p. 154).

324–358
Christianity becomes the dominant religion of the Roman Empire. Increased persecution causes many Jews to emigrate and settle in Babylonia, which has been gradually replacing the Holy Land as the center of Torah learning and Jewish life. The activity of the Sanhedrin is curtailed by the Romans, and then banned altogether.

Detail from a map of the Holy Land published in the beginning of the 19th century, after a drawing by R. Elijah of Vilna, Lithuania, circa 1790

985

Arab geographer Al-Muqaddasi reports that in the coastal plains of the Holy Land, "for the most part the assayers of corn, dyers, bankers, and tanners are Jews."

1266

The Mamluk Sultan Baybars converts the Cave of the Patriarchs in Hebron into an Islamic sanctuary and bans Jews from entering. The ban remains in place until Israel gains control of the site in 1967.

1755–1800

Throughout the centuries, rabbinical emissaries, called *shadarim*, traveled to the Diaspora to raise funds for the support of the Jewish communities in the Holy Land. Beginning in the 18th century, various diaspora communities established *colelim* ("collectives") for this purpose.

A notable *shadar* was R. Chaim Yosef David Azulai ("Chida"), who traveled throughout Europe and North Africa in the years 1755–1806.

901	1000	1100	1200	1300	1400	1500	1600	1700	1800
4661	4760	4860	4960	5060	5160	5260	5360	5460	5560

1517

Following the Ottoman conquest of the Holy Land, Jews from across the Ottoman Empire immigrate to the Land. These include many refugees from the Spanish and Portuguese expulsions of 1492 and 1497.

c. 1540–1620

The city of Safed flourishes as a center of Jewish learning, with 32 registered synagogues, a Hebrew printing press (established in 1577), and the seat of the Kabbalistic schools of Cordovero and Ari (see pp. 230–231). R. Joseph Caro completes his *Shulchan Aruch* (codification of Jewish law) in 1563.

1099–1291

Two centuries of Christian crusades to the Holy Land. The entire Jewish population of Jerusalem is slaughtered upon the city's conquest in 1099. Battles rage throughout the Land as various regions pass back and forth between the warring Christian and Muslim armies. Nevertheless, many Jews continue to make aliyah from the Diaspora (see pp. 92–95).

Josaphat Valley near Jerusalem, Land of Israel, circa 1870

It is two parasangs farther to Shechem (Nablus), situated in the valley between Mount Gerizim and Mount Ebal. It is the abode of about one thousand Cuthians, who observe the Mosaic law only, and are called Samaritans…. On Passover and holidays they offer burnt-offerings on the altar which they have erected on Mount Gerizim … which they claim is the Holy Temple….

Jerusalem is a small city strongly fortified with three walls. It contains a numerous population, composed of Arabs, Jacobites, Arameans, Greeks, Georgians, Franks, and indeed of people of all tongues. The dyeing-house is rented by the year, and the exclusive privilege of dyeing is purchased from the king by the Jews of Jerusalem, two hundred of whom dwell in one corner of the city, under the tower of David…. The city contains no edifice stronger than the tower of David. There are two buildings there. One is a hospital that affords shelter to the sick; these are provided with everything they may want, both during life and in death. The second they call "Temple," being the palace originally built by King Solomon, which harbors and furnishes four hundred knights, who are ever ready to wage war…. In Jerusalem is the large place of worship, called Sepulchre, containing the sepulcher of "that man," visited by all [Christian] pilgrims.

Jerusalem has four gates, called the gates of Abraham, David, Zion, and Josaphat. The latter stands opposite the site of the Holy Temple…. Omar Ben Al-Khataab erected a large and handsome cupola over it; the gentiles do not put any idols or images in this place, but only come there to pray. In front of it you see the Western Wall, one of the walls of the Holy Temple…. It is called the Gate of Mercy, and all Jews come there to pray…. Very little water is found at Jerusalem; the inhabitants generally drink rainwater, which they collect in their houses.

From the Valley of Josaphat the traveler immediately ascends the Mount of Olives…. From hence the Dead Sea is distinctly visible. Two parasangs from the sea stands the salt pillar into which Lot's wife was metamorphosed; and although the goats continually lick it, the pillar grows again and retains its original state. You also have a prospect over the whole valley of the Dead Sea, and of the brook of Shittim, even as far as Mount Nebo….

Two parasangs from Jerusalem is Bethlehem of Judea; and within half a mile of it, at a crossroads, stands the monument of the grave of Rachel. This monument is constructed of eleven stones, equal to the number of the children of Jacob. It is covered by a cupola, which rests upon four pillars; and every Jew who passes there inscribes his name on the stones of the monument. Twelve Jews, dyers by profession, live at Bethlehem. The country abounds with rivulets, wells, and springs of water.

Six parasangs farther is Hebron. The ancient city of that name was situated on the hill, and lies in ruins at present; in the valley is the Machpelah field and cave, and there the city is situated today. Here is the large place of worship called St. Abram de Bron, which during the time of the Muhammedans was a synagogue. The gentiles have erected six sepulchers in this place, which they pretend to be those of Abraham and Sarah, of Isaac and Rebecca, and of Jacob and Leah; the pilgrims are told that they are the sepulchers of the Patriarchs, and money is extorted from them. But if any Jew comes, who gives an additional fee to the keeper of the cave, an iron door is opened, which dates from the times of our forefathers who rest in peace, and with a burning candle in their hand the visitor descends into a cave, which is empty, traverses a second cave in the same state, and at last reaches a third, which contains six

graves, those of Abraham, Isaac, and Jacob, and of Sarah, Rebecca, and Leah…. A lamp burns in the cave and upon the graves continually, both night and day; and you there see tubs filled with the bones of Israelites, for it was their custom to bring there the bones of their ancestors and to leave them there….

In Ramleh you still find walls erected by our ancestors, as is evident from the inscriptions on the stones. The city contains about three hundred Jews. It was formerly very considerable, for a Jewish cemetery in its vicinity is two miles in extent.

Five parasangs hence to Jaffa, the Yaffo of Scripture, on the coast; one Jew only, a dyer by profession, lives here. Three parasangs to Ibelin, the ancient Yavneh, where the site of the school may still be traced; it contains no Jews….

Ascalon, which is in fact the New Ascalon, built on the coast by Ezra the Priest … is very large and handsome; and merchants from all parts resort to it, on account of its convenient situation on the border of Egypt. There are here about two hundred Jews, of whom the principals are R. Tzemach, R. Aaron, and R. Solomon, besides about forty Karaites, and about three hundred Samaritans. In the city is a fountain called Bir Ibrabim-al-Khahil, and it is said that this is the well dug by Abraham in the time of the Philistines.

In Sepphoris, the Tzipori of antiquity, are the gravesites of R. Judah ha-Nasi; Rabban Gamliel; R. Chiya, who came back from Babylon; and of Jonah the son of Amittai the prophet…. From Sepphoris it is five parasangs to Tiberias, a city situated between two mountains on the shore of the Sea of Kinereth, which is a river large and wide as a lake; the Jordan flows into it, and then emerges from it and flows through plains to a place called Ashdoth-Pisgah, and then empties itself into the Dead Sea. Tiberias contains about fifty Jews, the leaders of whom are R. Abraham the astronomer, R. Muchthar, and R. Isaac. The hot waters, which spout forth from underground, are called the hot springs of Tiberias….

ZECHARIAH AL-DHAHIRI
SEFER HAMUSAR, CHAPTER 6

Safed, circa 1567

I journeyed from the province of Syria, through Upper Galilee, to the city of Safed…. I came into the city, and behold, within it dwelt the divine presence. For there is a large community, crookedness being far removed from them, about fourteen thousand in number. In eighteen academies they pursue the study of the Talmud. There I saw the light of Torah, and the luminance that was to the Jews. They surpassed all other communities, as they are the most praiseworthy of the praiseworthy. They break breaches in the boundaries of wisdom, and nary an ignoramus is to be found amongst them. I contemplated their learning in the inner and the outer, and behold, my own knowledge was less than a shepherd's….

I had come to hear the expositors who expound a subject in multiple ways, as they know every secret thing, from its ceiling to its foundation. Especially the great luminary, the sage Rabbi Joseph Caro, from whose seat of learning the wise men of Safed do not quit themselves. For in his heart the Talmud is stored, having sat learning for seven years in seclusion; in addition to the many wisdoms, hidden and revealed, that are sealed within his heart.

I went one Sabbath to his yeshivah, to see the preciousness and glory of his greatness…. The sage sat upon a chair, and with his mouth he did amplify his subject. With an utterance he would draw a man away from the yoke of time, bringing him near to the faithful G-d; he would clothe him in garments of freedom, as in the verse (Psalms 19:7), "G-d's Torah is whole, restoring the soul." The dear and exalted sage deliberated on a matter in both its plain and esoteric sense. Before him were about two hundred precious and distinguished pupils, sitting on benches.

When he had finished his words of wisdom, he gestured to a disciple before him to speak of the soul and its faculties, its character and purpose. [The student] stood before him with the sweetness of his learning, and said: "You have already taught us, our master—this is not from our own wisdom—that the soul has ten faculties, five inner and five outer. The inner are movement and sense, which permeate the body… and three that reside in the mind: imagination, thought, and memory…. The faculty of thought has four tributaries: reception, retention, knowledge, and discrimination…. And the five external faculties are: sight, hearing, smell, taste, and touch…. From these branch out four faculties by which the body endures: procreation, growth, nourishment, and enjoyment. All these derive from desire, from which extend the roots and branches of the soul. There is also another faculty, that of anger and wrath, which endangers the soul, and by which all treasure is lost; regarding it the prophet declared (Psalms 81:10), 'There shall be no alien god within you.' Its utility is for every animal and beast to gain its prey; and for the destroyers among men to be removed through it.

"Now these three, namely thought, desire, and wrath, might be deficient, or excessive, or median. Their deficiency or excess is ruinous; in their median, they are balanced and constructive…. These are the soul's faculties and their measure. But she, the soul, remains preserved for eternal life, when she fulfills the commandments of her Creator. So have you taught us, our master, meriting us the World to Come; thus you have supported us and empowered us."

I waited for a while, until the sage indicated to his disciples to rise and assigned them each a *mishnah* to study…. [The student] took me to his place; I went with him to a meager house, where he spread a worn cloth. And he said to me: "This is the manner of the Torah and those who study her, those who suckle at her breasts. As the merciful sage declared (*Ethics of the Fathers*, 6:4): 'Bread with salt you shall eat, and sleep on the ground, as in the Torah you toil.'"

Interior of the Ari Synagogue, Marc Chagall, Safed, Land of Israel, 1931

CHAGALL IN SAFED Although he considered his work "not the dream of one people but of all humanity," Marc Chagall (1887–1985) is widely regarded as the quintessential Jewish artist of the 20th century. Chagall visited Israel numerous times, often in connection with monumental projects such as his stained-glass windows for the synagogue of the Hadassah Hospital (1960–62) and his large tapestries and mosaics for the Knesset building (1965–69). According to the artist, however, it was his three-month stay in 1931 that left the most vivid impression. Chagall worked incessantly, recording his impressions of Tel Aviv, Jerusalem, and Safed. In Safed, he painted several views of synagogue interiors.

ALIYAH

Aliyah—*Hebrew for "ascent"—is the term used throughout Jewish history to describe the immigrations of the Jewish people to the Land of Israel.*

From the time that the people of Israel settled their ancestral homeland in the 13th century BCE, *there has been a continued Jewish presence in the Land. Also when we were exiled by foreign conquerors—by the Babylonians in the fifth century* BCE *and again by the Romans in the first century* CE—*there remained Jewish communities that braved hardship and poverty to live in the Holy Land. And throughout the Jewish diaspora, the Land was ever foremost in the minds and hearts of its people. Three times a day, Jews faced in the direction of Jerusalem and prayed: "Sound the great shofar for our freedom, raise a banner to gather our exiles, and gather us from the four corners of the earth to our land."*

In every generation there were those who translated yearning into action and ascended to the Land of Israel. Presented in these pages is a sampling of some of the notable aliyahs of Jewish history.

WHICH WAY IS "UP"? The term "aliyah" is Biblical in origin. The sages note that throughout the Bible, journeys to the Holy Land are referred to as "going up," and departures from the Land are described as "going down," implying that "the Land of Israel is higher than all other lands." Maharal (R. Judah Loew of Prague, 1520–1609) remarks that because the earth is a sphere, every point on its surface can be seen as the top of the sphere; accordingly, the designation of a particular place as the "top" of the world is a purely spiritual concept. Because the sacred is higher than the mundane, the Holy Land is regarded as the highest of all lands, to which one ascends from every other part of the world.

Mizrach sign, Poland, circa 1890. Many Jewish homes have a decorative sign with the Hebrew word mizrach *("east") to indicate the direction for prayer.*

The Jewish National Fund was established in 1901 to purchase land in the Holy Land for Jewish settlement. Many Jewish homes throughout the world kept a JNF charity box, into which even the most impoverished families would put a few coins each week.

 **MAIMONIDES,** *MISHNEH TORAH, LAWS OF KINGS, 5:10–11*

The great sages would kiss the boundaries of the Land of Israel [upon their arrival], kiss its stones, and roll in its dust. Indeed it is written (Psalms 102:15), "Your servants cherish her stones and favor her dust." ...

Although one cannot compare being received by the Holy Land during one's lifetime to being received by it after death, nevertheless, the greatest sages would bring their dead to be buried in the Holy Land, as can be also learned from the example of our father Jacob and the righteous Joseph.

Maimonides resided briefly in the Holy Land in 1165, before circumstances compelled him to move to Egypt. Upon his passing in 1204, his body was brought to the Land and buried in Tiberias.

 **R. JUDAH HALEVI**
MY HEART IS IN THE EAST

לִבִּי בְמִזְרָח וְאָנֹכִי בְּסוֹף מַעֲרָב
אֵיךְ אֶטְעֲמָה אֵת אֲשֶׁר אֹכַל וְאֵיךְ יֶעֱרָב
אֵיכָה אֲשַׁלֵּם נְדָרַי וֶאֱסָרַי, בְּעוֹד
צִיּוֹן בְּחֶבֶל אֱדוֹם וַאֲנִי בְּכֶבֶל עֲרָב
יֵקַל בְּעֵינַי עֲזֹב כָּל טוּב סְפָרַד, כְּמוֹ
יֵקַר בְּעֵינַי רְאוֹת עַפְרוֹת דְּבִיר נֶחֱרָב.

My heart is in the East
　　and I am at the ends of West
How can I taste what I eat
　　and how could it be savored?
How shall I render my vows and my bonds
　　while yet
Zion is in the fetters of Rome
　　and I am in the shackles of Arabia?
It shall be as easy for me to forsake
　　all the bounty of Spain, as
It shall be precious for me to behold
　　the dust of the desolate Abode.

notable aliyahs of Jewish history

Abraham is commanded by G-d to leave his birthplace of Ur Casdim and journey to "the land that I will show you," where he will become a great nation. "Abram went…. and [he] traversed the land until the place of Shechem…. And G-d appeared to Abram, and He said: 'To your seed I will give this land'" (Genesis 12:1–7).

After 70 years of exile in Babylonia, about 50,000 Jews return to the Holy Land in a series of aliyahs under the leaderships of Zerubbabel, Ezra, and Nehemiah, and rebuild the Holy Temple in Jerusalem.

In the years 1209–1211, some 300 leading Talmudic scholars, known as "Tosafists," come to the Land of Israel from Western Europe. Many settle in Jerusalem, which was under Muslim rule at the time; others settle in Acre, capital of the Crusader Kingdom, to which the *tosafist* R. Yechiel of Paris also moved with his yeshivah in 1258.

In 1267, Nachmanides made aliyah from his native Spain and resurrected the Jewish community in Jerusalem, which had been ravaged during the Mongol raids 23 years earlier. The synagogue he established in Jerusalem is still in use today.

ABRAHAM'S JOURNEY
18TH CENTURY BCE

RETURN FROM BABYLON
4TH CENTURY BCE

ALIYAH OF THE TOSAFISTS
13TH CENTURY

13TH CENTURY BCE
ISRAELITES SETTLE THE LAND

Forty years after their exodus from Egypt, the people of Israel conquer and settle the Promised Land under the leadership of Joshua.

2ND CENTURY CE
ALIYAHS OF TALMUDIC SAGES

During the Talmudic era, many disapora scholars come to the Holy Land to study at the feet of the great Torah sages of Israel. In the latter part of the second century, R. Chiya "the Great" arrives from Babylonia with his nephews Rabah bar Chana and Aba Arichta ("Rav"). Based in Tiberias, R. Chiya travels throughout the Land to set up a public education system, and is thus credited by the Talmud as the one who "prevented the Torah from being forgotten by Israel."

Other notable aliyahs of the Talmudic era include Hillel's arrival in the Holy Land in 32 BCE, and that of R. Ze'ira in the third century CE.

1740–1816
HASIDIC AND LITHUANIAN ALIYAHS

R. Israel Baal Shem Tov (1698–1760), founder of the Hasidic movement, encouraged many of his followers to settle in the Holy Land. In 1777, an organized aliyah of several hundred Hasidic families travel from Eastern Europe, eventually settling in Safed, Tiberias, and Hebron.

Beginning in 1808, a series of organized groups led by disciples of R. Elijah, the Gaon of Vilna (1720–1797), representing the "Lithuanian" or non-Hasidic communities of Eastern European Jewry, arrive in the Land, settling mostly in Safed and Jerusalem.

With the rise of the modern Zionist movement in the latter part of the 19th century, the migration of diaspora Jews to Israel increases exponentially. Between 1882 and 1939, close to half a million Jews emigrate from Eastern Europe to the Land of Israel. It is during this time that the *moshavot* (agricultural settlements) and kibbutzim are established, the city of Tel Aviv is founded, and the Jewish neighborhoods outside the walls of Jerusalem's Old City are settled.

Beginning in 1934, the British strictly limit the number of Jews allowed to immigrate to the Land of Israel, which was then under their rule. This state of affairs persists throughout the Holocaust, sealing the fate of many Jews seeking to escape Nazi-occupied Europe. Following the war, it shuts the gates of the Land to the many Holocaust survivors seeking to rebuild their lives in the Jewish homeland. More than 100,000 Jews attempt to enter the Land clandestinely during this period; most are intercepted by the British and sent back to Europe, or interned in British detention camps.

Israel's stunning victory in the Six Day War sparks a renaissance of Jewish identity among the Jews of the Soviet Union, as well as a movement to immigrate to Israel. Most of those who apply for exit visas are persecuted by the Soviet regime. Mass demonstrations are held worldwide under the banner, "Let My People Go!" After sustained behind-the-scenes diplomacy by world leaders, the Soviets finally relent, and starting in the early 1970s, tens of thousands are allowed to leave for Israel.

Following the collapse of the Soviet Union in 1991, close to 1,000,000 make aliyah to Israel.

ZIONIST ALIYAHS
1881–1939

THE "ILLEGAL" ALIYAH
1934–1948

THE EXODUS OF RUSSIAN JEWRY
1973–1991

1881–1950
YEMENITE ALIYAH

1948–1971
ALIYAH FROM ARAB COUNTRIES

1984–1991
ETHIOPIAN ALIYAH

For many centuries, Jews traveled to Israel from Yemen, whose ancient Jewish community dates back to the First Temple era. In 1881, when conditions in the Ottoman Empire make travel to Israel less prohibitive, the trickle becomes a flood, with some walking many miles through the desert to realize their lifelong dream of living in the Holy Land. Thousands make aliyah in the ensuing decades. After the establishment of the Jewish state, close to 50,000 Yemenite Jews are airlifted to Israel in "Operation Magic Carpet" (June 1949 to September 1950).

The establishment of the State of Israel in May of 1948 spurs a major wave of Jewish immigration to the Jewish homeland. By 1951, the Jewish population of Israel, which numbered 650,000 at the state's founding, more than doubles. By the early 1970s, around 900,000 Jews leave, flee, or are expelled from Arab and Muslim countries and make aliyah, including 255,000 Jews from Morocco, 128,000 from Iraq, 57,000 from Iran, 83,000 from Libya and Tunisia, and 4,000 from Afghanistan.

In the late 1970s, a clandestine operation by the Mossad (the Israeli intelligence agency) is implemented to rescue the Beta Israel community of Ethiopia, which was threatened by famine and persecution. About 17,000 members of the community are airlifted to Israel in the 1980s, and 45,000 more in the next decade, including 14,325 who are flown on 34 aircraft in a single day, May 24, 1991, in "Operation Solomon."

THE MODERN STATE OF ISRAEL

historical milestones, 1839–1949

1870
Living off the land: A Jewish agricultural school is established on a tract of land southeast of Jaffa. Petah Tikvah, the first Jewish agricultural settlement in the Holy Land of the modern era, is founded in 1878, followed by 27 additional settlements over the next 25 years.

1839–1842
Beginnings of the modern Zionist movement:
In 1839, Balkan rabbi Judah Alkalai publishes a book calling for an activist approach to the restoration of the Jewish people to the Land of Israel. Similar works are subsequently published by a number of Jewish religious and secular figures, such as Moses Hess, R. Zvi Hirsch Kalischer, and Theodor Herzl.
In 1841, Sir Moses Montefiore begins a correspondence with the British consul in Damascus on plans for establishing a Jewish homeland in the Holy Land.

1896–1904
Theodor Herzl meets with world leaders in an effort to obtain support for the establishment of a Jewish homeland in the Land of Israel. In 1897, the first World Zionist Congress convenes in Basel, Switzerland.

1840 YEAR CE	1850	1860	1870	1880	1890	1900
5600 YEAR ON JEWISH CALENDAR 5610	5620	5630	5640	5650	5660

1854
Expansion of Jerusalem: Mishkanot Shaananim, the first Jewish residential settlement outside the old walled city of Jerusalem, is built. More settlements follow, including Nahalat Shiva in 1869, and Me'ah Shearim in 1874.

1882
Increased antisemitism in Europe fuels waves of Jewish immigration to the Land of Israel. About 35,000 immigrants arrive in the Land over the next two decades, more than doubling its Jewish population.

Jewish farmers in the agricultural settlement of Hadera, 1891–1901

*Jewish kindergarten,
Rishon LeZion, circa 1898*

1901
Establishment of the Jewish National Fund to purchase land for Jewish settlement.

1915–1917
The Jewish espionage network NILI assists the British in their conquest of the Land of Israel from the Ottoman Turks during the First World War.

1909
Founding of the first kibbutz, Degania, and the first modern Hebrew city, Tel Aviv.

1919–1928
Third and Fourth Aliyahs: More than 120,000 Jews arrive in the Land of Israel during this decade. Many of the newcomers are young *halutzim* (pioneers), who build roads and towns, and drain the marshes in the Jezreel Valley and the Hefer Plain.

1921
R. Abraham Isaac Kook, a scholar, philosopher, mystic, and poet who was a central figure in the Religious Zionism movement and its leading thinker, is appointed chief rabbi of the Land of Israel.

1947
The United Nations votes to partition the Land of Israel into an Arab and a Jewish state. The compromise is accepted by the Jewish Zionist leadership, but rejected by the Arab leaders, who initiate armed attacks against the Jews.

1929–1939
Some 250,000 Jews, including 55,000 fleeing Nazi persecution, arrive in the fifth wave of Jewish emigration from Europe to the Land of Israel.

1948
On Friday afternoon, May 14, in anticipation of the expiration of the British Mandate at midnight that evening, the Declaration of the Establishment of the State of Israel, signed by 37 representatives of the various Jewish communities in the Land, is proclaimed by David Ben-Gurion in a ceremony in Tel Aviv.

The very next day, the armies of six Arab countries invade in an attempt to strangle the newly born state in its cradle. Miraculously, the Jewish state survives, though it fails to hold on to the Old City of Jerusalem and the Jewish settlements in Gush Etzion and the Gaza Strip (see map on p. 102).

1901	1910	1920	1930	1940	1950
5661	5670	5680	5690	5700	5710

1917–1922
The "Balfour Declaration," expressing support for the establishment of a national home for the Jewish people in the Land of Israel, is subsequently incorporated in the Treaty of San Remo and in the British Mandate for Palestine issued by the League of Nations.

1920
A Jewish defense force, the Haganah, is organized in response to Arab violence against the Jewish settlements.

1931–1947
In response to Arab pressure and violence, the British intensify their restrictions on Jewish immigration and settlement. A number of Jewish groups, including the Irgun (founded 1931) and Lehi (1940), engage in an armed struggle to achieve Jewish independence. After WWII, the Haganah also fights to drive the British from the Land.

1929
Arabs riot against the Jews, massacring and maiming hundreds. The ancient Jewish community of Hebron is completely destroyed, as are 17 other Jewish communities across the Land.

1904–1914
The "Second Aliyah" brings about 40,000 Jews to the Land of Israel.

Tel Aviv's "White City" Bauhaus architecture, The Engel House, architect: Zeev Rechter, 1933

Fighters in the nascent IDF (Israeli Defense Forces) in Israel's war of independence, October 1948

THE OLD YISHUV This term, which means "old settlement," was the name given to the Jewish communities established in the Holy Land prior to 1882, in contrast to the new wave of immigrants who arrived in the Zionist-inspired aliyahs. A number of differences marked these two communities. The former were mainly religious Jews desiring only to live in the holy environment of the Land of Israel; the latter included more secular Jews, and many who were motivated by the dream of creating an independent Jewish state. The Old Yishuv was concentrated primarily in the "four holy cities" of Jerusalem, Hebron, Safed, and Tiberias, and was supported by funds provided by the Jewish diaspora; whereas the "New Yishuv" was engaged in establishing new settlements and towns on land purchased from the local Arab landowners, and living off the land. In truth, however, these distinctions were not absolute. The new immigrants included many religious Jews; the New Yishuv was also supported by philanthrophy, and the Old Yishuv was not wholly reliant on it. In fact, the first Jewish agricultural settlement of the modern era, Petah Tikvah, was a project of the Old Yishuv, as was Nahalat Shiva, the first self-sufficient settlement outside Jerusalem's Old City walls.

 LORD ALEXANDER LINDSAY, *TRAVELOGUE, 1837*

Richly as the valleys wave with corn, and beautiful as is the general aspect of modern Palestine, vestiges of the ancient cultivation are every where visible ... proofs far more than sufficient that the land still enjoys her Sabbaths, and only waits the return of her banished children, and the application of industry commensurate with her agricultural capabilities, to burst once more into universal luxuriance—all that she ever was in the days of Solomon.

 THEODOR HERZL, *THE JEWISH STATE*

The idea that I have developed in this pamphlet is an ancient one; it is the restoration of the Jewish State....

We are a people—one people. We have sincerely tried everywhere to merge with the national communities in which we live, seeking only to preserve the faith of our fathers. It is not permitted us. In vain are we loyal patriots, sometimes superloyal; in vain do we make the same sacrifices of life and property as our fellow citizens; in vain do we strive to enhance the fame of our native lands in the arts and sciences, or her wealth by trade and commerce. In our native lands where we have lived for centuries we are still decried as aliens, often by men whose ancestors had not yet come at a time when Jewish sighs had long been heard in the country....

Oppression and persecution cannot exterminate us. No nation on earth has endured such struggles and sufferings as we have.... Wherever we remain politically secure for any length of time, we assimilate. I think this is not praiseworthy....

Israel is our unforgettable historic homeland.... The Jews who will it, shall achieve their State. We shall live at last as free men on our own soil, and die peacefully in our own homes. The world will be liberated by our freedom, enriched by our wealth, magnified by our greatness. And whatever we attempt there for our own benefit will redound mightily and beneficially to the good of all mankind.

JEWISH ANTI-ZIONISTS? Zionism is as old as Judaism. The belief that the Land of Israel is the birthright of the Jewish people has been integral to the Jewish faith throughout Jewish history. In this sense, "Jewish anti-Zionism" is an oxymoron.

In the more narrow sense of "Zionism" as the political movement that formed in the latter part of the 19th century and was the driving force behind the creation of the modern State of Israel, the picture is more complex. While the movement gained wide support throughout the Jewish world, certain Jewish groups opposed it for a variety of reasons. Many religious Jews were apprehensive of the secular and even anti-religious stance of modern Zionism, fearing that Jewish nationalism was being used to replace, rather than augment, the ethos and observances that have defined the Jewish people for millennia. Some believed that since the exile that placed the Jewish people under the dominion of other nations was a divine decree, it was forbidden to counteract that state before the arrival of the divinely-ordained Messiah. Until 1937, the official position of American Reform Judaism was anti-Zionist, out of fear that it raised the specter of "dual loyalty" on the part of American Jews.

Once the State of Israel became a fait accompli in 1948, the overwhelming majority of the Jewish world has supported its continued existence and success. The internal Jewish debate over Zionism has shifted to the question of the values—secular and religious— the Jewish state should live by and espouse.

 MOSHE ZVI SEGAL
GENERATION TO GENERATION, PP. 75–77

In those years, the area in front of the Kotel (Western Wall) did not look as it does today. Only a narrow alley separated the Kotel and the Arab houses on its other side. The British Government forbade us to place an ark, tables, or benches in the alley; even a small stool could not be brought to the Kotel. The British also instituted the following ordinances, designed to humble the Jews at the holiest place of their faith: it is forbidden to pray out loud, lest one upset the Arab residents; it is forbidden to read from the Torah (those praying at the Kotel had to go to one of the synagogues in the Jewish quarter to conduct the Torah reading); it is forbidden to sound the shofar on Rosh Hashanah and Yom Kippur. The British placed policemen at the Kotel to enforce these rules.

On Yom Kippur of that year [1930] I was praying at the Kotel. During the brief intermission between the *musaf* and *minchah* prayers, I overheard people whispering to each other, "Where will we go to hear the shofar? There are as many policemen as people praying…." The Police Commander himself was there, to make sure that the Jews would not, Heaven forbid, sound the single blast that closes the fast.

I listened to these whisperings, and thought to myself: Can we possibly forgo the sounding of the shofar that accompanies our proclamation of the divine sovereignty? Can we possibly forgo the sounding of the shofar, which symbolizes the redemption of Israel? True, the sounding of the shofar at the close of Yom Kippur is only a custom, but "a Jewish custom is Torah"! I approached R. Yitzchak Horenstein, who served as the rabbi of our "congregation," and said to him, "Give me a shofar."

"What for?"

"I will blow."

"What are you talking about? Don't you see the police?"

"I will blow."

The rabbi abruptly turned away from me, but not before he cast a glance at the prayer stand at the left end of the alley. I understood: the shofar was in the stand. When the hour of the blowing approached, I walked over to the stand and leaned against it. I opened the drawer and slipped the shofar into my shirt.

I had the shofar, but what if they saw me before I had a chance to blow it? I was still unmarried at the time, and following the Ashkenazic custom, did not wear a tallit. I turned to the person praying at my side, and asked him for his tallit. My request must have seemed strange to him, but the Jews are a benevolent people, especially at the holiest moments of the holiest day, and he handed me his tallit without a word.

I wrapped myself in the tallit. At that moment, I felt that I had created my own private domain. All around me, a foreign government prevails, ruling over the people of Israel even on their holiest day and at their holiest place, and we are not free to serve our G-d; but under this tallit is another domain. Here I am under no dominion save that of my Father in Heaven; here I shall do as He commands me, and no force on earth will stop me.

When the closing verses of the *ne'ilah* prayer—"Hear O Israel," "Blessed be the name" and "The Lord is G-d" —were proclaimed, I took the shofar and blew a long, resounding blast. Everything happened very quickly. Many hands grabbed me. I removed the tallit from over my head, and before me stood the Police Commander, who ordered my arrest.

I was taken to the *kishla*, the prison in the Old City, and an Arab policeman was appointed to watch over me. Many hours passed; I was not given any food or water to break my fast. At midnight, the policeman received an order to release me, and he let me out without a word.

I then learned that when the chief rabbi of the Holy Land, R. Abraham Isaac Kook, heard of my arrest, he immediately contacted the secretary of the High Commissioner of Palestine, and asked that I be released. When

NO VOTE ON G-D The thirty-seven signatories of Israel's Declaration of Independence included representatives of a wide array of Jewish parties and groups: secular Zionists, religious Zionists, socialists, the right-wing "revisionists," the orthodox Agudath Israel party, and the atheist Communist party. Arriving at an agreed-upon text necessitated many compromises, which were then put to a vote. A particularly contentious issue was including a mention of G-d in the text: the religious and traditional representatives insisted on a statement that expressed the people's faith and trust in the Almighty and their gratitude for the miracles they were experiencing, while the secularists and atheists were adamantly opposed. In the end, the phrase "Rock of Israel," traditionally a reference to G-d, was proposed. "Each of us believe in the Rock of Israel," said Ben-Gurion, "as he conceives it." Ben-Gurion had one request, however: "Don't allow me to put this phrase to a vote." The phrase was accepted without a vote.

his request was refused, he stated that he would not break his fast until I was freed. The High Commissioner resisted for many hours, but finally, out of respect for the rabbi, he had no choice but to set me free.

For the next eighteen years, until the Arab conquest of the Old City in 1948, the shofar was sounded at the Kotel every Yom Kippur. The British well understood the significance of this blast; they knew that it would ultimately demolish their reign over our land as the walls of Jericho crumbled before the shofar of Joshua, and they did everything in their power to prevent it. But every Yom Kippur, the shofar was sounded by men who knew they would be arrested for their part in staking our claim on the holiest of our possessions.

🄷 DECLARATION OF THE ESTABLISHMENT OF THE STATE OF ISRAEL

The Land of Israel was the birthplace of the Jewish people. Here their spiritual, religious, and political identity was shaped. Here they first attained statehood, created cultural values of national and universal significance, and gave to the world the eternal Book of Books.

After being forcibly exiled from their land, the people kept faith with it throughout their dispersion and never ceased to pray and hope for their return to it and for the restoration in it of their political freedom.

Impelled by this historic and traditional attachment, Jews strove in every successive generation to re-establish themselves in their ancient homeland. In recent decades they returned in their masses…. [They] made deserts bloom, revived the Hebrew language, built villages and towns, and created a thriving community controlling its own economy and culture, loving peace but knowing how to defend itself, bringing the blessings of progress to all the country's inhabitants, and aspiring towards independent nationhood….

The catastrophe which recently befell the Jewish people—the massacre of millions of Jews in Europe —was another clear demonstration of the urgency of solving the problem of its homelessness by re-establishing in the Jewish State in the Land of Israel, which would open the gates of the homeland wide to every Jew and confer upon the Jewish people the status of a fully privileged member of the comity of nations….

On the 29th November, 1947, the United Nations General Assembly passed a resolution calling for the establishment of a Jewish State in the Land of Israel…. This right is the natural right of the Jewish people to be masters of their own fate, like all other nations, in their own sovereign State.

Accordingly we, members of the people's council, representatives of the Jewish community of the Land of Israel and of the Zionist movement … hereby declare the establishment of a Jewish State in the Land of Israel, to be known as the State of Israel….

THE STATE OF ISRAEL will be open for Jewish immigration and for the ingathering of the exiles; it will foster the development of the country for the benefit of all its inhabitants; it will be based on freedom, justice, and peace as envisaged by the prophets of Israel; it will ensure complete equality of social and political rights to all its inhabitants irrespective of religion, race, or sex; it will guarantee freedom of religion, conscience, language, education, and culture; it will safeguard the holy places of all religions; and it will be faithful to the principles of the Charter of the United Nations….

WE APPEAL—in the very midst of the onslaught launched against us now for months—to the Arab inhabitants of the State of Israel to preserve peace and participate in the building of the State on the basis of full and equal citizenship and due representation in all its provisional and permanent institutions.

WE EXTEND our hand to all neighboring states and their peoples in an offer of peace and good neighborliness, and appeal to them to establish bonds of cooperation and mutual help with the sovereign Jewish people settled in its own land….

WE APPEAL to the Jewish people throughout the Diaspora to rally round the Jews of the Land of Israel in the tasks of immigration and building, and to stand by them in the great struggle for the realization of the age-old dream—the redemption of Israel.

Placing our trust in the Rock of Israel, we affix our signatures to this proclamation at this session of the provisional council of state, on the soil of the homeland, in the city of Tel Aviv, on this Friday, the 5th day of Iyar, 5708 (May 14, 1948).

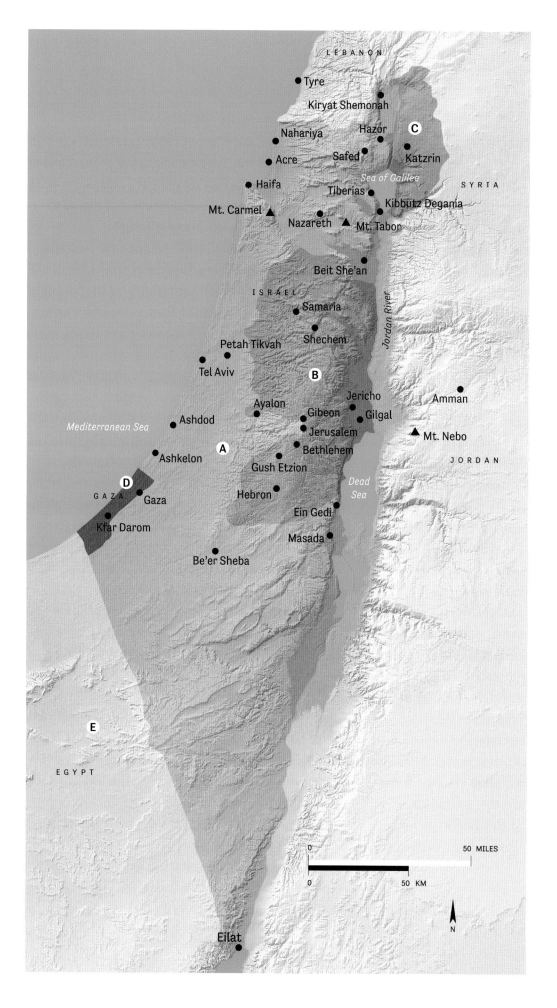

MAP OF ISRAEL TODAY

Ⓐ Territory retained by
Israel in the 1949 armistice
agreements.

Ⓑ Judea and Samaria,
also called "The West
Bank." Occupied by Jordan,
1948–1967; recovered
by Israel in the 1967
Six Day War.

Ⓒ The Golan Heights,
captured from Syria in the
Six Day War. Formally
annexed by Israel in 1981.

Ⓓ The Gaza Strip, occupied
by Egypt 1948–1967, and
recovered by Israel in the
Six Day War. In 2005, Israel
unilaterally "disengaged"
from the Gaza Strip, removing
some 8,000 Jewish residents
and 21 Jewish settlements.
Shortly afterward, the area
fell under the control of
the Islamic terrorist group
Hamas, which uses it to
launch terror and rocket
attacks on Israel.

Ⓔ The Sinai Peninsula,
captured by Israel in 1967.
Returned to Egypt as part
of the 1979 Camp David
peace accords.

THE SIX DAY WAR

Israeli soldiers at the newly liberated Western Wall, June 1967, Jerusalem, Israel

Despite their defeat in the 1947–1949 war, the Arab countries surrounding Israel refused to accept the existence of the Jewish state and continued to plot its annihilation. In the months leading up to June of 1967, they stepped up their guerilla and artillery attacks against Israel, mobilized hundreds of thousands of troops on its borders, and openly boasted of their intention to "drive the Jews into the sea."

On the morning of June 5, 1967, Israel struck preemptively, destroying the Egyptian and Syrian air forces while their planes were still on the ground. When Jordanians joined the fighting, the IDF responded by driving them out of the Old City of Jerusalem and the territory west of the Jordan River, which the Jordanians had been occupying since 1949. In only six days, Israel defeated its enemies, liberated the heartland of the Jewish homeland, and stunned the world with its miraculous victory.

 MICHAEL OREN
SIX DAYS OF WAR, PP. 135–136

Throughout the country, thousands were hurrying to dig trenches, build shelters, and fill sandbags. Schools were refitted as bomb shelters, and air raid drills were practiced daily. Most buses and virtually all taxis were mobilized, and an emergency blood drive launched. Upward of 14,000 hospital beds were readied and antidotes stockpiled for poison gas victims, expected to arrive in waves of 200. Some 10,000 graves were dug.

The sole bright spot in these otherwise morbid preparations was the unprecedented outpouring of sympathy from around the Jewish world. Yet these gestures did little to relieve the sense of approaching catastrophe, of the Jews' abandonment to yet another Holocaust.

 YULI EDELSTEIN
INTERVIEW, TAZPIT NEWS AGENCY, MAY 20, 2012

I was very young when the Six Day War happened and I remember everyone around me being terribly scared. According to reports on Soviet radio, Israel was disappearing....

The reunification of Jerusalem, the Temple Mount in Israel's hands, and the outcome of the Six Day War changed the standing of Israel in the eyes of Jews across the world, but especially for the Jews in the former Soviet Union. For at least two million Soviet Jews, a reunited Jerusalem brought a feeling that there is a homeland and that they must start fighting for it.... There was a whole change of attitude—one from relief to pride.

Diaspora

It is the paradox of the Jewish story that while our identity is inexorably bound to the Land of Israel, for the majority of our history we have lived scattered among the nations and cultures of the world. Indeed, at the very covenant that the Land was promised to us, Abraham was also told that his descendants would experience galut, *the state of physical exile and spiritual displacement that has defined the Jewish experience for millennia.*

The Talmud (Pesachim 87b) states that "G-d dispersed the people of Israel among the nations only so that converts should be added to them." According to the Hasidic masters, this refers not only to those who converted to Judaism or were influenced by its ethos and mores, but also to the sparks of divine potential buried in every part of the world, which are redeemed and elevated when the resources in which they are embodied are utilized to a holy end.

Symbol of the Jewish quarter in the medieval city of Segovia. The emblem is composed of the Hebrew letters that spell Sepharad *("Spain") configured in the shape of the Iberian Peninsula.*

 GENESIS 15:12–14

The sun was coming down, and a slumber fell upon Abram; and behold, a terror, a great darkness, was falling upon him. And [G-d] said to Abram: "Know shall you know that your seed will be sojourners in a land that is not theirs; and they will enslave them and afflict them … and after that they will go out with great wealth."

 DEUTERONOMY 4:27–31

And G-d will scatter you among the peoples, and you will remain few in number among the nations where G-d will lead you. There you will worship gods that are the handiwork of man; wood and stone, which neither see nor hear nor eat nor smell.

And from there, you will seek the Lord your G-d, and you will find Him; as you will seek Him with all your heart and with all your soul…. In the end of days, you will return to G-d and listen to His voice. For the Lord your G-d is a merciful G-d; He will not let you loose and He will not destroy you. He will not forget the covenant of your ancestors, which He swore to them.

 PASSOVER HAGGADAH

This [divine promise] has stood by our ancestors and us. For not one alone rose up against us to annihilate us; rather, in every generation they rise up against us to annihilate us, and the Almighty saves us from their hand.

 MIDRASH RABBAH, *SHEMOT 36:1*

"A leafy olive tree, fair with goodly fruit, has G-d called your name" (Jeremiah 11:16). Why are the people of Israel compared to an olive? Like an olive that is picked

Community event in synagogue, Moscow, 1990

from its tree, and then pounded, then put through the grinder, then bound in ropes and pressed by stones, and only after all this does it yield its oil; so is it with the people of Israel....

Also: All other liquids blend with each other, except for oil, which remains apart. So, too, the people of Israel do not assimilate into the nations.

 R. SHALOM DOVBER OF LUBAVITCH
CITED IN *HAYOM YOM, CHESHVAN 1*

From the time that the Almighty said to our father Abraham, "Go you from your land" (Genesis 12:1), and "Abraham went on, journeying southward" (ibid., verse 9), began the "work of refinement" [i.e., the process of extracting and elevating the sparks of holiness that are scattered throughout the material world]. By the decree of divine providence, a person travels to those places where the sparks that are destined to be refined by them await redemption.... The Causer of all causes contrives the many events and circumstances that will

bring a person to those places where their individual mission in life is to be acted out.

 R. MENACHEM M. SCHNEERSON
BASED ON *LIKUTEI SICHOT, VOL. 15, P. 433*

Joseph, the first Jew to be forcibly exiled from the Jewish homeland, had two sons born to him in his foreign domicile. The first he named Manasseh, meaning "cast off" and "makes forget," as a reminder to persevere in an environment that endeavors to obliterate a person's identity. The second he named Ephraim, "fruitfulness," in recognition that "G-d has made me fruitful in the land of my affliction" (Genesis 41:50–52). In the course of our history, these were to become the dual dividends of *galut*: (a) the reserves of faith and commitment we exact from our souls to survive the horrors of persecution and the enticements of assimilation; and (b) a profound and fruitful influence on the places and peoples with which we come in contact in our exiles.

the spread of the Jewish diaspora

900 BCE—400 BCE

Expansion into Syria under King David. Settlements in Yemen and India under King Solomon. Dispersions in the Assyrian, Egyptian, Babylonian, and Persian empires prior to and following the destruction of the first Holy Temple.

400 BCE—200 CE

Diaspora communities form throughout the Greek and Roman empires—a process accelerated by the destruction of the Second Temple in the first century CE. Jews also migrate to Arabia and Ethiopia.

200—1300

Jewish life flourishes in Babylonia and Persia for 800 years. Spain emerges as a major center of Jewish life, while Ashkenazic Jewry develops in Western Europe. Communities form in North Africa and throughout the Muslim world.

1300—1700

Expulsions and persecution drive many Ashkenazic Jews to more hospitable environs in Eastern Europe. In the wake of the Spanish Expulsion, Sephardic Jews settle in North Africa, Italy, the Netherlands, and throughout the Ottoman Empire. Many *anusim* (Jews forcibly converted to Christianity) seek refuge in the new American colonies; when the Inquisition follows them there, some escape to the Dutch and English colonies in the north. Jews also find new homes in India and the Far East.

1700—1880

As the Jewish population swells from under 2 million to almost 8 million in less than two centuries, new diaspora communities form in the Americas, the Far East, South Africa, and Australia, though the bulk of the Jewish population is concentrated in Eastern Europe. By 1880, some five million Jews reside in the Russian Empire, most of them confined by law to a narrow "pale of settlement."

1880—2020

The upheavals of the last century and a half have resulted in Jews establishing communities in virtually every part of the world. Beginning in the 1880s, millions escaping poverty and persecution in Eastern Europe immigrated to America, Western Europe, and other diaspora locales, while others made aliyah to the Land of Israel. When the Nazi Holocaust all but annihilated the 1,000-year-old European Jewish community, most of its surviving remnants sought new homes outside the blood-soaked continent. Between 1948 and 1960, close to one million North African and Middle Eastern Jews escaped or were driven out of the communities they inhabited for 2,500 years. As these two erstwhile diasporas declined, new centers of Jewish life emerged in Israel and the United States.

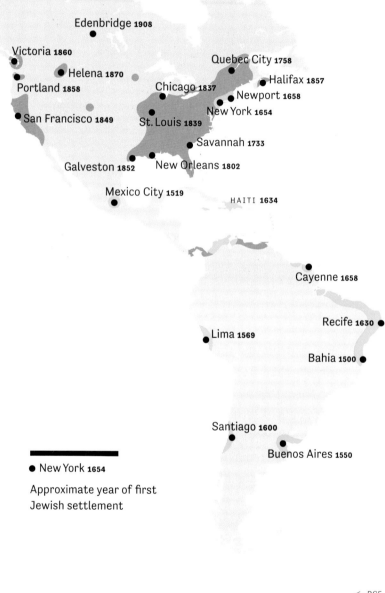

● New York **1654**

Approximate year of first Jewish settlement

Map labels:

Dawson City **1897**
Anchorage **1850**
Edenbridge **1908**
Victoria **1860**
Helena **1870**
Portland **1858**
Quebec City **1758**
Halifax **1857**
Chicago **1837**
Newport **1658**
San Francisco **1849**
New York **1654**
St. Louis **1839**
Galveston **1852**
New Orleans **1802**
Savannah **1733**
Mexico City **1519**
HAITI **1634**
Cayenne **1658**
Recife **1630**
Lima **1569**
Bahia **1500**
Santiago **1600**
Buenos Aires **1550**

900	800	700	600	500	400	300	200	100	← BCE
2861	2961	3061	3161	3261	3361	3461	3561	3661	3760

YEAR ON JEWISH CALENDAR

ICELAND **1624**

Arkhangelsk **1828**

Stockholm **1681**

Edinburgh **1691**   Fredericia **1682** Vilna **1593**   Moscow **1650**

Dublin **1232**   Irkutsk **1818**

Prague **950**   Kiev **1050**   Birobidzhan **1928**

London **100**
Mainz **100**   Przemysl **1085**   Tanais **100**   Harbin **1905**
                                  —— KHAZARIA **700**
Lyon **39**   —— CRIMEA **100 BCE**   Beijing **1605**
Rome **161 BCE**   Zanavi **400 BCE**   Bukhara **712**
Cordoba **200 BCE**   Salonica **50**   Kobe **1905**
                    Sardis **350 BCE**   Kaifeng **750**   Nagasaki **1572**
SICILY **50** →
            CYPRUS **200 BCE** →   Aleppo **850 BCE**   Shanghai **1850**
Tangiers **100**   Djerba **400 BCE**   Babylon **434 BCE**   Multan **712**
            Alexandria **330 BCE**   Jerusalem   Macau **1557**
                                              Kathmandu **2000**
Elephantine **650 BCE**   Hejaz **100**
                                  Mumbai **175 BCE**   Bangkok **1601**
Timbuktu **1500**   Meroe **50**   Sanaa **800 BCE**   PHILIPPINES **1590**
                                        Madras **1640**   Saigon **1870**
Gondar **100**
                    Cochin **800 BCE**
                          SRI LANKA **900**
Nairobi **1899**   Singapore **1800**

Lubumbashi **1907**   Surbaya **1800**

Bulawayo **1890**

                                              Perth **1829**   Sydney **1788**

Cape Town **1820**   Kororareka **1831**

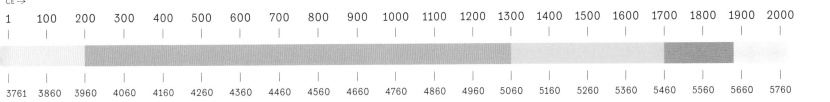

CE →

| 1 | 100 | 200 | 300 | 400 | 500 | 600 | 700 | 800 | 900 | 1000 | 1100 | 1200 | 1300 | 1400 | 1500 | 1600 | 1700 | 1800 | 1900 | 2000 |

| 3761 | 3860 | 3960 | 4060 | 4160 | 4260 | 4360 | 4460 | 4560 | 4660 | 4760 | 4860 | 4960 | 5060 | 5160 | 5260 | 5360 | 5460 | 5560 | 5660 | 5760 |

BABYLONIA

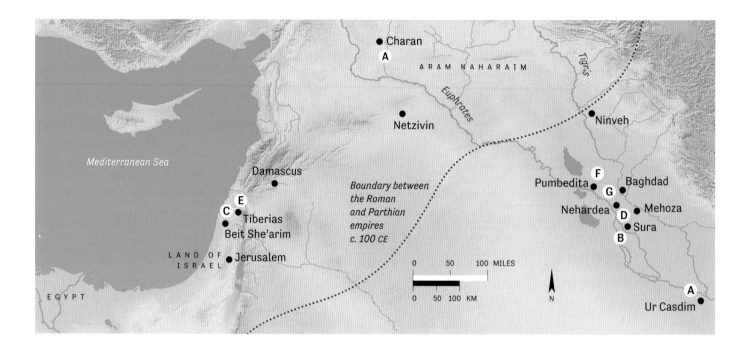

PSALMS 137:1–6

By the rivers of Babylon, there we sat, we also wept, when we remembered Zion.

On the willows in its midst we hung our harps. For there our captors asked us for words of song; our tormentors, for gladness: "Sing for us of the songs of Zion."

How shall we sing the song of G-d on foreign soil? If I forget you, O Jerusalem, may my right hand forget its skill. May my tongue cleave to my palate, if I do not remember you, if I do not raise Jerusalem above my greatest joy.

JEREMIAH 29:4–7

So said the Lord of Hosts, the G-d of Israel, to all the exile community that I have exiled from Jerusalem to Babylon: Build houses and dwell in them, plant gardens and eat their fruit. Take wives and father sons and daughters … multiply there and be not diminished.

Seek the welfare of the city where I have exiled you, and pray for it to G-d; for in its peace you will have peace.

ISAIAH GAFNI, *A HISTORICAL ATLAS OF THE JEWISH PEOPLE, PP. 64–65*

The Babylonian diaspora did not resemble any other. Its antiquity, and the fact that it remained the only large Jewish community outside the Roman Empire, made it a world apart. Since Mesopotamian Jewry was never embraced by the seductive and highly assimilative influence of the Greco-Roman civilization, it could develop its own original forms of social life and autonomous institutions.…

As it grew and prospered, the community tended to emphasize its antiquity. By the time it had produced its own version of the Talmud, it manifested a kind of "local patriotism." Was not Abraham, the father of the nation, born "beyond the river" (Euphrates)? Were not the Euphrates and the Tigris the two rivers which flowed out of Eden? The Jews of Babylon, therefore, considered themselves the aristocracy of the Jewish people. Even the land of Mesopotamia acquired an aura of sanctity in their eyes, second to the Land of Israel, of course, but holier than all other countries.

THE LAND OF THE TALMUD

The map on the left marks some of the foundational events of Jewish history occurring in Babylonia and the Holy Land.

(A) 1813 – 1556 BCE
FIRST JEWS

The Jewish presence in Mesopotamia (roughly, present-day Iraq) reaches back to the very origins of the Jewish people. The first Jew, Abraham, was born in Ur Casdim, and then relocated to Charan, before journeying to the Land of Israel by divine command. Mesopotamia is also the birthplace of the four matriarchs of the Jewish people, Sarah, Rebecca, Rachel, and Leah; and of eleven of the twelve sons of Jacob, born during Jacob's sojourn in Charan.

(B) 434 BCE
THE BABYLONIAN EXILE

Nebuchadnezzar, the Babylonian emperor who conquered Jerusalem and destroyed the first Holy Temple, exiled the bulk of the Jewish people to Babylonia. Seventy years after the Temple's destruction, a relatively small group returned to rebuild the Holy Temple in Jerusalem. Over time, the Holy Land replaced Babylonia as the center of Jewish life, though a sizable part of the Jewish people continued to live in the Babylonian diaspora throughout the Second Temple era.

(C) 189 CE
THE MISHNAH

After the destruction of the Second Temple in 69 CE, the Land of Israel continued to serve as the seat of the Sanhedrin and the center of Jewish learning. Toward the end of the second century, R. Judah ha-Nasi completed his redaction of the Mishnah, which encapsulates 35 generations of legal Torah rulings from Moses to his time (see citation from Maimonides on p. 186 and table on p. 204). But the Roman persecution of the Jewish people and their suppression of the Jewish faith were taking their toll, and in the years following R. Judah's passing, the flourishing Babylonian Jewish community replaced the Holy Land as the center of Torah learning and Jewish life.

(D) 219 – 475
THE BABYLONIAN TALMUD

Two of R. Judah ha-Nasi's disciples, Rav (Abba Aricha) and Shmuel, established Torah academies in Babylonia—the former in Sura and the latter in Nehardea. The academy in Sura would serve as a major center of Torah learning for nearly 1,000 years. Other Babylonian academies included those in the town of Pumbedita (near modern-day Fallujah), headed in the 3rd and 4th centuries by Rav Judah, Rabah bar Nachmani, and Abayei; and in Mehoza, the seat of Abayei's colleague, Rava.

It was in Sura that R. Ashi and Ravina embarked, in the beginning of the fifth century, on the monumental task of compiling the Babylonian Talmud, a task that was completed by their disciples a generation later. The Talmud records three centuries of teachings by the greatest Torah sages of Babylon and the Holy Land, formulated as deliberations on the Mishnah. This vast compendium of legal and moral teachings is second in importance only to the Bible as a foundational text of Judaism (see overview on pp. 184–199).

(E) 200 – 350
THE JERUSALEM TALMUD

During the Talmudic period, Torah learning continued in the Land of Israel, with scholars and students traveling to and from Babylon, although the difficult conditions in the Holy Land prevented its centers from achieving the prominence of the Babylonian academies. The Holy Land produced a sister Talmud of its own—the "Jerusalem Talmud"—whose foundations were laid by the sages R. Jochanan (bar Naphcha), Reish Lakish, and R. Elazar at the Tiberias academy in the third and fourth centuries.

(F) 589 – 1038
THE GEONIC ERA

Babylonian Jewry continued to flourish after the Talmudic era. The Jews of Babylon were granted broad autonomy by the Persian and, subsequently, the Muslim rulers of the region. The *resh galuta* ("head of the diaspora" or "exilarch"), who traced his lineage to the royal House of David, held court as the governor of the Jewish community. The Geonim, who headed the prestigious academies at Sura and Pumbedita, were recognized as the Torah authorities and spiritual leaders for the entire Jewish people, and sent their responsa (written answers for legal and religious questions) to Jewish communities worldwide. A seminal figure of this period was R. Saadia Gaon (882–942), who translated the Torah into Arabic and authored *The Book of Beliefs and Opinions*, a foundational work of Jewish philosophy. Following the passing of R. Hai Gaon of Pumbedita in 1038, the centers of Jewish learning shifted to Spain, North Africa, and Western Europe, even as Babylonia and Persia continued to boast flourishing Jewish communities.

(G) 1941 – 1952
EXODUS OF IRAQ'S JEWS

On Shavuot of 1941, a pogrom against the Jewish community of Baghdad left 180 dead, 1,000 injured, and 900 Jewish homes destroyed. Over the next decade, a series of antisemitic attacks and libels made the position of the Jewish community of Iraq increasingly perilous. In 1951–52, more than 120,000 Iraqi Jews—about 95% of the country's Jewish population—were airlifted to Israel. By the end of the 1960s all but a handful of Jews had left the country, ending 2,500 years of Jewish communal life in Babylonia.

THE GRECO-ROMAN ERA

Upon the destruction of the First Temple in the fifth century BCE, most Jews were exiled eastward to Babylonia; but a sizable portion went south and west to Egypt. That settlement would burgeon and expand, in particular after Egypt was conquered by Alexander the Great in 332 BCE. The new city of Alexandria became a center of Jewish life in exile.

The Jewish diaspora expanded with the development of the Greek and Roman empires, as Jews followed the trade routes and commercial opportunities that were opened. The destruction of the Second Temple and the failed revolts against Rome further accelerated the process. Jews migrated westward throughout the Mediterranean basin, southward into Arabia and Yemen, and northward to Asia Minor and the Caucasus. Wherever they settled, they brought their faith, teachings, and distinct way of life with them, and there are

Portrait of Philo of Alexandria, André Thevet, Paris, 1584

PHILO OF ALEXANDRIA (c. 20 BCE–50 CE) was a leading figure of the thriving Jewish community of Alexandria. Philo's writings, which seek to synthesize Jewish and Hellenist thought, strongly influenced both secular and religious philosophy of subsequent generations. Philo was a staunch advocate of the ideals and morals of Judaism in face of the pagan cultures of his time. In 40 CE, he headed a delegation to Rome petitioning the emperor Caligula to exempt the Jews from an edict mandating that the emperor be worshiped as a deity.

many recorded instances of individuals, and even entire peoples, converting to Judaism during the Greco-Roman period. It is estimated that by the first century CE, some 2 million Jews—out of an estimated world Jewish population of 4.5 million—lived in the Diaspora. Some historians place that estimate even higher, suggesting that Jews constituted ten percent of the 70 million inhabitants of the Roman Empire.

 TALMUD, *MENACHOT 110a*

From Tyre to Carthage, people know of Israel and of their Father in Heaven.

 TALMUD, *SUKKAH 51b*

One who has not seen the great synagogue of Alexandria of Egypt has never seen the glory of Israel. It is said that it was like a large basilica, with a colonnade within a colonnade. At times, it held twice the number of those who left Egypt. It had 71 golden chairs, corresponding to the the 71 members of the Sanhedrin, each of which contained no less than 21 talents of gold. There was a large wooden platform at the center, and the sexton would stand on it with scarves in his hand. When they reached the point for the congregation to respond "Amen," he waved a scarf and all the people would answer "Amen!"

They did not sit intermingled; the goldsmiths sat separately, silversmiths separately, blacksmiths separately, metalworkers separately, and weavers separately. When a poor stranger entered the place, he recognized the members of his craft and turned to them, thereby obtaining a livelihood for his household.

 MAX I. DIMONT, *JEWS, G-D AND HISTORY, PP. 75 AND 115–116*

Though the bulk of the population was still agricultural, many [Jews in the Second Temple era] turned to commerce and industry, which took those so engaged to every outpost of the former Alexandrian empire. The Jews

JEWISH STATES IN THE DIASPORA As a rule, exile from the Land of Israel also meant the loss of Jewish sovereignty. However, history includes a small number of instances of independent Jewish states outside of the Holy Land.

In the first century CE, the kingdom of Adiabene (in today's Kurdistan) was ruled by the Jewish sovereigns Queen Hilni (Helena) and her son Munbaz, who also aided the Jews in the Holy Land in their revolt against Rome. In 495, the Jewish exilarch Mar Zutra led a revolt against the Persian rulers of Babylonia and established an independent Jewish state at Mahoza which lasted for seven years. In the beginning of the 8th century, the king and the ruling classes of the Khazar kingdom (in today's southern Russia) converted to Judaism, and over the next three centuries, Jews from Greece, Asia Minor, Persia, and Mesopotamia found refuge there from persecution.

Roman world, from India to the Atlantic Ocean, over three continents, two empires, and dozens of nations. They had already defied two thousand years of history. Logically and historically the Jews were overdue to lose their ethnic unity and disappear. But they did not disappear. They responded to this new challenge with another formula for survival—"Diaspora Judaism."

We have already defined the word Diaspora as coming from the Greek, meaning "a scattering" or "to scatter about," and today the word has come to signify that body of Jews not living in Israel itself but scattered outside the boundaries of that country. Actually, Diaspora means far more than this. Diaspora is both a way of life and an intellectual concept, a state of being and a state of mind....

A people in exile, banished from its homeland, produces no culture, but gradually either dies out through assimilation, or stagnates by reverting to a nomadic existence. This has been the history of all other exiled peoples. The Jews were the only exception. The Diaspora produced new Jewish cultures. Though the inner core of each Diaspora culture always remained distinctly Jewish, each took on the dominant traits of the host civilization. It was always [G-d] and monotheism, no matter how each such Diaspora culture was packaged—in Greek tunic, in Arab mufti, or in American ivy-league. When a civilization was philosophic, like that of the Greeks, the Jews became philosophers. When it was composed predominantly of poets and mathematicians, like that of the Arabs, the Jews became poets and mathematicians. When it was scientific and abstract, like that of the modern Europeans, the Jews became scientists and theoreticians. When it was pragmatic and suburban, like the American, the Jews became pragmatists and suburbanites. Only when a culture or civilization contradicted the basic ethical monotheism of the Jews were they unable to adapt or be adapted to it. The Jews were part of, yet distinct from, the civilization in which they lived.

prospered and multiplied. "They have penetrated into every state so that it is difficult to find a single place in the world in which this tribe has not been received and become dominant," wrote the Greek geographer and philosopher Strabo in the first century BCE. Every Greek city in Asia Minor had a considerable Jewish population. But underneath the façade of tranquility ... an internal struggle [was taking place] among the Jews themselves against Hellenization....

The [failed revolts] against Rome had brought Jewish political fortunes to the brink of economic and social disaster. In the second century, the majority of Jews were stateless and dispersed into every corner of the

SEPHARDIC JEWRY

The Jewish connection with *Sepharad*—Hebrew for "Spain"—goes back to Biblical times. Some identify Tarshish, the port to which the prophet Jonah attempted to flee, with Tartessus in the south of Spain, and the prophet Obadiah makes mention of the exiles to *Sepharad*. When the Carthaginians and, subsequently, the Romans colonized the Iberian coast, Jewish merchants and settlers came too. The Jewish historian R. Abraham ibn Daud writes that his own ancestors were among a group of noble Jewish families exiled to Spain in the first century CE, and Abarbanel cites traditions dating the Jewish settlement of Spain from the destruction of the First Temple. By the fifth century, Jews constituted a significant portion of the Iberian population.

Following the Visigoth rulers' adoption of Christianity in the sixth century, the Jews of Spain suffered persecution, expulsion, and forced conversions. That changed with the Muslim conquest of Spain, which began in 711 and heralded a "golden age" for Spanish Jewry. Jews were welcomed to participate in the common culture, and served as merchants, physicians, linguists and poets, and even viziers and military commanders. Spain became home to some of the greatest Torah scholars in Jewish history, whose influence spread throughout North Africa, southern Europe, and the Middle East. Ultimately, the distinctive culture and traditions of "Sephardic Jewry" would come to embrace the plurality of Jewish communities in the lands under Muslim rule.

While Sephardic Jews enjoyed relative freedom and prosperity in comparison to other Jewish diasporas, their fortunes nevertheless fluctuated through the generations. The anti-Jewish riots in Granada in 1066 are regarded by many historians as the beginning of the end of the golden age for Spanish Jewry. The Almovarids, who governed Muslim Spain in the 12th century, imposed many restrictions on its Jewish population; matters worsened under the even more fanatical Almohads, who expelled and forcefully converted Jews in many Sephardic communities. Even under the more liberal Muslim rulers, Jews were subject to restrictions and discriminatory laws designed to emphasize their inferior status to the Muslim population.

As the Christians from the north advanced in their reconquest of Spain, many Sephardic Jews came to live under Christian rule. In some cases, they fared as well, or even better, than in the Muslim-ruled areas, while in others they suffered persecution and forced conversion. In 1492, the whole of Spain was in Christian hands, and the infamous *Edict of Expulsion* was issued, decreeing that all Jews must convert to Christianity or leave Spain. Five years later, the forced conversion of all the Jews in Portugal (including many Spanish refugees) spelled the end of centuries of flourishing Jewish life in Iberia.

Hundreds of thousands of Spanish Jews chose the wanderer's staff and migrated to any place that would allow them to live as Jews—to the Muslim-controlled lands in North Africa and the Near East, and the more tolerant Christian lands in parts of Italy and, later, the Netherlands. They fared best in the Ottoman Empire, which was eager to employ their financial, diplomatic, and scientific expertise to the benefit of its developing realm. When the Holy Land came under Ottoman rule in 1517, Sephardic Jews established communities there. But many remained in Spain and Portugal, ostensibly accepting conversion yet continuing to practice Judaism in secret, at times for generations, while awaiting an opportunity to escape the clutches of the Inquisition and openly return to the Jewish faith. Some migrated to the Spanish and Portuguese colonies in South and Central America, in the hope that they could better evade the Inquisition in the New World.

Wherever they went, the Sephardic Jews took their distinct traditions and way of life with them, often establishing Sephardic communities alongside Jewish communities of the Ashkenazic (European) tradition. Today, the two communities exist side by side in almost every place where Jews live.

*Scenes of Jewish life
in the 2,400-year-old
Sephardic community of
Djerba, Tunisia, 2017*

MEIR ALFASI

MEIR ALFASI

key figures of Sephardic Jewry

HISDAI IBN SHAPRUT c. 915–970; Cordoba, Spain. Served as court physician and foreign minister to Caliph Abd-al-Rahman III. Sponsored yeshivahs and intervened on behalf of Jewish communities worldwide. Translated scientific works from Greek into Arabic. Corresponded with the Jewish king of the Khazar kingdom.

MENACHEM IBN SARUK c. 920–970; Tortosa, Spain. Poet and polyglot. Produced the first known dictionary of the Hebrew language (known as *Machberet*) and pioneered the field of Hebrew philology.

R. HANANEL d. c. 1055; Kairouan, Tunisia. The son of one of the legendary "four captives" (see p. 116), R. Hananel was a key link in the transmission of Torah scholarship from the Geonim of Babylon to the "early sages" (*rishonim*) of North Africa and Europe. Authored the first running commentary on the Talmud. His disciples included R. Isaac Alfasi, R. Gershom of Mainz, and R. Nathan ben Yechiel of Rome.

R. SHMUEL HANAGID c. 993–1056; Granada, Spain. Scholar, poet, linguist, governor, and general. Served as the grand vizier for the city-state of Granada and commander-in-chief of its army. Was a disciple (through correspondence) of R. Hai Gaon, serving as an important conduit for the transmission of the teachings of the Babylonian Geonim to Spanish Jewry.

R. ISAAC ALFASI 1013–1103; Morocco and Spain. Known by the acronym RIF. Author of an important work of Halachah (Torah law), written as a digest of the Talmud. R. Isaac studied in Kairouan under R. Nissim Gaon and R. Hananel, and later headed a yeshivah in Fez, Morocco (whence his surname). In 1088 he was forced to flee to Spain, where he founded a yeshivah in Lucena that became one of that country's flagship Jewish institutions.

R. SOLOMON IBN GABIROL c. 1021–1058; Spain. Poet, philosopher, ethicist, and mystic. Known in the Muslim world as "Avicebron." His work, *Font of Life*, is a classic in both Jewish and Muslim ethical philosophy. His mystical-devotional poem, *Royal Crown*, and other lyrical works of his authorship have been incorporated into Jewish liturgy.

R. JUDAH HALEVI c. 1075–1141; Toledo or Tudela, Spain. One of the greatest Jewish poets of all time, R. Judah Halevi also authored one of Judaism's most important theological works, *The Kuzari*, in which he presents the beliefs and ideology of Judaism in the form of a dialogue between a Jewish scholar and the Khazar king who converted to Judaism. R. Judah died shortly after fulfilling his lifelong dream of making aliyah to the Holy Land (see his iconic poem, *My Heart Is in the East,* on p. 93).

MAIMONIDES R. Moses ben Maimon ("Rambam"), 1135–1204; Spain, Morocco, and Egypt. Physician, philosopher, scholar, and communal leader. Forced to flee his native Spain by the Almohads' policy of forcefully converting Jews to Islam, Maimonides lived in Fez, Morocco, before further Almohad persecution forced the family to flee once more, and eventually settle in Fostat (old Cairo), Egypt, where Maimonides served as court physician to Sultan Saladin. Maimonides authored numerous groundbreaking works of Torah scholarship, including a commentary on the Mishnah; a foundational work of Jewish philosophy, *Guide for the Perplexed*; and his *magnum opus*, a comprehensive, 14-volume codification of Torah law which he named *Mishneh Torah*. The epitaph inscribed on his tombstone, "From Moses to Moses none arose like Moses," attests to the peerless place he holds in the history of Jewish learning.

NACHMANIDES R. Moses ben Nachman, c. 1195–1270; Girona, Catalonia and Jerusalem, Israel. One of the preeminent sages of Spanish Jewry, Nachmanides authored prominent works in all areas of Torah scholarship: Biblical commentary, Talmudic analysis, Torah law, Jewish philosophy, ethics, and Kabbalah. Nachmanides was the chief rabbi of Christian-ruled Catalonia, and in 1263, he was forced to defend the Jewish faith in a public disputation before King James I of Aragon. Nachmanides won the debate, but under pressure from the Church, he was banished from the country. After several years of wandering, the 70-year-old sage made aliyah to the Holy Land and took a leading role in resurrecting the Jewish community in Jerusalem.

DON ISAAC ABARBANEL (or Abravanel), 1437–1508; Portugal, Spain, and Italy. Scholar, philosopher, statesman, and financier. Served as treasurer to several monarchs, including Alfonso V of Portugal. Abarbanel had extensive dealings with Ferdinand and Isabella of Spain, whom he attempted to dissuade from their infamous Edict of Expulsion in 1492. He took up the wanderer's staff with his exiled brethren and settled in Italy (see his account on p. 126). Abarbanel authored a series of commentaries on the Bible, and other important Torah works.

R. JOSEPH CARO 1488–1575; Turkey, Bulgaria, and Israel. Born in Spain, R. Joseph was four years old when his family was among those driven from the country in 1492. After living in Turkey and in Bulgaria, he settled in Safed, Israel, where he attained the status of senior sage at a time when the city was home to many great scholars and Kabbalists. His most famous work is the *Shulchan Aruch*, the "Code of Jewish Law" that became the most fundamental guide for Jewish observance and the basis for all subsequent Halachic works.

DOÑA GRACIA MENDES-NASI 1510–1569; Lisbon, Antwerp, Venice, and Istanbul. International businesswoman, philanthropist, diplomat, and Jewish activist. Born to a family of Spanish-Portuguese Jews who were forcefully converted to Christianity but continued to practice Judaism in secret. At age 28, Doña Gracia inherited the fortune of her husband, a trader in black pepper and silver, and became one of the wealthiest women in Europe. She eventually succeeded in leaving Portugal, living for a time in Belgium and Italy before settling in Constantinople (today's Istanbul), the capital of the Ottoman Empire. She became an influential figure in the Ottoman court and a leader of the Sephardic diaspora, and used her wealth and influence to exert financial pressure on the Christian regimes that persecuted Jews. She built synagogues and yeshivahs, sponsored the publication of Jewish books, and developed an escape network that saved hundreds of *conversos* from the Inquisition. She also pioneered the resettlement of Jews in the Holy Land under Ottoman rule, after centuries of desolation following the Crusader conquests.

R. MENASSEH BEN ISRAEL 1604–1657; Amsterdam, Holland. Born on the Portuguese Island of Madeira to secretly Jewish parents fleeing the Inquisition. The family eventually found refuge in Amsterdam, where R. Manasseh gained eminence as a rabbi and author, corresponding with intellectuals and statesmen both within and without the Jewish world. He headed a yeshivah, and established the first Hebrew printing press in Holland. He spent the last two years of his life in England working toward the readmission of the Jews into that country, from which they had been officially banned since 1290.

SIR MOSES MONTEFIORE 1784–1885; London, England. Banker, industrialist, philanthropist, and statesman. Born to an Italian Sephardic-Jewish family, Montefiore retired from his business activities at the age of 36 and devoted the next 65 years of his long life to communal, diplomatic, and philanthropic work on behalf of the Jewish people. He was elected sheriff of London in 1836, and was knighted by Queen Victoria in 1837. He founded and funded numerous settlements in the Land of Israel, and his diplomatic activities laid the foundations for the modern Zionist movement to establish a Jewish homeland in the Holy Land.

R. ISRAEL ABUHATZEIRA 1889–1984; Tafilal, Morocco and Netivot, Israel. A scion of the illustrious Abuhatzeira family of sages, mystics, and miracle-workers who served as leaders of Moroccan Jewish communities for generations. R. Israel, affectionately known as "Baba Sali," settled in Israel in 1964 and was a mentor to the 250,000 Moroccan Jews who were struggling to rebuild their lives in the Jewish homeland.

R. OVADIA YOSEF 1920–2013; Israel. Born in Baghdad, R. Ovadia was raised in Jerusalem and studied in its Sephardic yeshivahs, achieving renown as a Torah scholar and Halachist at a young age, and served briefly as a rabbi and teacher in Cairo, Egypt. In 1973, he was elected as Sephardic chief rabbi of Israel, a position he held for ten years. In 1984, he founded the Israeli political party "Shas," and spearheaded a Sephardic renaissance movement that energized all segments of the Sephardic community. His prolific responsa stress the Sephardic Halachic tradition and often address the juncture of Torah law and modern life. R. Ovadia's funeral in Jerusalem was the largest in Israel's history, with an estimated attendance of 850,000.

R. ABRAHAM IBN DAUD
SEFER HAKABBALAH, PP. 13–14

The four captives

Some time before [the decline of the Babylonian Gaonate], it was ordained by the divine providence that [centers of Torah learning should be established in the west]. This is how it came about.

The commander of a pirate fleet, whose name was Ibn Rumahis, sailed from Cordoba. The fleet sailed as far as the coast of the Land of Israel and swung about to the Greek sea, where it encountered a ship carrying four great scholars, who were traveling from Bari to a city called Sefastin on a fundraising mission.

Ibn Rumahis captured the ship and took the sages prisoner. One of them was R. Hushiel, the father of R. Hananel. Another was R. Moshe, who was taken prisoner with his wife and his young son, R. Hanoch. The third sage was R. Shemariah the son of R. Elchanan. As for the fourth, I do not know his name.

The commander wanted to forcibly violate R. Moshe's wife, as she was exceedingly beautiful. She cried out in Hebrew to her husband, R. Moshe, asking him if those who drown in the sea will be brought back to life at the time of the resurrection of the dead. He replied to her by citing the verse (Psalms 68:23), "Says the Lord: I will bring them back from Bashan; I will bring them back from the depths of the sea." Upon hearing his words, she threw herself into the sea and drowned.

These sages did not tell a soul about themselves or their wisdom. The commander sold R. Shemariah for ransom [to the Jewish community] in Alexandria of Egypt, from which R. Shemariah proceeded to the Egyptian capital where he became head [of the academy]. R. Hushiel was ransomed on the African coast, from which he proceeded to the city of Kairouan, which at that time was the greatest of all Muslim cities in the land of the Maghreb. There R. Hushiel became the head of the academy, and there his son R. Hananel was born.

The commander then arrived at Cordoba, where the local Jews ransomed R. Moshe and his son R. Hanoch. They were under the impression that he was an ignoramus. Now, in Cordoba there was a Torah Academy that was presided over by a magistrate by the name of R. Nathan, who was a very pious person. The Jews of Spain were not thoroughly versed in the words of the sages; nevertheless, with the little knowledge they did possess, they held study sessions and deliberated their meanings.

[One day,] R. Nathan was explaining the law in the Talmudic tractate Yoma that "each sprinkling requires immersion," but he was unable to explain it correctly. Thereupon, R. Moshe, who was seated in the corner like an attendant, arose before R. Nathan and said to him, "Rabbi, this would result in an excess of immersions!" When R. Nathan and the students heard his words, they marveled to each other and asked him to explain the law to them. This he did quite properly. Then each of them asked him all the difficulties which they had, and he replied to them out of the abundance of his wisdom.

When R. Nathan walked out of the study hall and the waiting litigants approached him, he said to them: "I shall no longer be your magistrate. This stranger who is garbed in rags is my master, and I will be his disciple. You ought to appoint him magistrate of the community of Cordoba."

This they did. The community assigned R. Moshe a large stipend and honored him with costly garments and a carriage. As a result, the pirate commander wished to retract his sale. However, the king would not permit him to do so, for he was delighted by the fact that the Jews of his domain no longer had need of the people of Babylonia.

Word spread through all of Spain and the Maghreb, and students came to study under him. Moreover, all questions that had formerly been addressed to the Babylonian academies were now directed to him. This affair occurred in the days of R. Sherira Gaon, in about the year 4750 [990 CE].

ASHKENAZIC JEWRY

Beginning around the year 1000 CE, we find the term *Ashkenaz* being used to refer to Jewish communities living in Europe north of the Pyrenees and the Alps. These communities had developed a set of customs and traditions distinct from the Jews of southern Europe, North Africa, and the Middle East. Another differentiating feature of these communities was that they lived under Christian rule, whereas the great majority of Jews at that time lived in Muslim-ruled lands.

Ashkenazic life was originally centered along the Rhine Valley, in present-day Germany and France. Here Jews prospered commercially and spiritually. The region's thriving viticulture drove commerce, and the financial success supported scholarship. Preeminent yeshivahs and rabbinic courts—spearheaded by the likes of R. Gershom of Mainz (960–1040), Rashi (1040–1105), and R. Tam (1100–1171)—pioneered scholarly methodologies and legal precedents that still guide the observance of Jewish law today.

The First Crusade, declared in 1095, brought violent upheaval to the original communities of Ashkenaz. Mobs massacred Jewish communities along the Rhine Valley, and the situation of Jews in these lands never recovered. Successive waves of violent persecution and expulsions—Jews were expelled from England in 1290, from France in 1306, and from much of Germany by 1573—characterized most of the rest of the Middle Ages.

All this caused a gradual shift of Ashkanazic Jewry toward more hospitable lands in Eastern Europe. The Kingdom of Poland—whose vast territory extended through modern-day Poland, Lithuania, Belarus, and Ukraine—issued statutes guaranteeing rights to Jews and other groups. Given broad autonomy, Jews established self-governing institutions—most famously, the "Council of the Four Lands." They brought their "Germanic" culture, including their vernacular, Yiddish, with them, and became a prosperous middle class that supported Torah scholarship and produced many of the

Green Violinist, Marc Chagall, France, 1923–24

great scholars of Jewish history. Eventually, Eastern Europe would be home to close to eighty percent of the world's Jewish population.

The golden age of Ashkenazic Jewry was disrupted in 1648, when a bloody Cossack revolt brought death, destruction, and dislocation to the Jews of Poland. Some twenty percent of the Jewish population of Poland was massacred, sold into slavery, or fled. Poland itself was to become increasingly less tolerant as the years went on, before it was finally partitioned and absorbed by Russia, Austria, and Prussia in the 18th century. The Russian Empire suddenly found itself home to hundreds of thousands of Jews, upon whom it imposed oppressive economic restrictions, and confined to the infamous "Pale of Settlement."

Around that time, intellectual and political ferment in western and central Europe weakened the religious ideology that had fueled persecution of the Jews for centuries. The Enlightenment brought the opening of economic and social opportunities for Jews, and in a reversal of the trend in earlier centuries, many Jews migrated westwards to take advantage of these developments. Jews in Germany and Britain found their way into the highest ranks in the universities, the sciences, business, the arts, the professions, and even politics.

The majority of Ashkenazic Jews, however, remained in Eastern Europe, where the influence of the Enlightenment was countered by an intense religious revival. The Hasidic movement, which emerged in the mid-1700s in Ukraine and spread rapidly among the Jews of Eastern Europe, revitalized traditional Jewish life with the robust spiritual and devotional mindset it fostered. Other traditionalist movements would follow, lessening the appeal to migrate westward to more secular societies and the assimilation they bred.

Napoleon's conquests led to the demolition of political restrictions of Jews through much of Europe. But Napoleon's final defeat in 1815 led to a resurgence of both nationalism and antisemitism; over the next

century and a half, these forces would surge together, reaching their horrific climax in the Nazi Holocaust. When liberal revolts were crushed throughout central Europe in 1848, Jews suffered from the resultant backlash. Many left for the New World, transforming America's originally Sephardic-dominated Jewish community into a mainly Ashkenazic one, which it has remained to this day. When in the 1880s Tsar Alexander III of Russia instituted a policy designed to make life so difficult for the five million Jews in the Russian Empire that "one-third would convert, one-third would emigrate, and one-third would starve," an even greater wave of emigrants left for the United States. Other Eastern European Jews set their sights on a return to the Holy Land and formed the nucleus of the resurgent Jewish community there.

The cataclysm of World War I destabilized the continent. Armies marched back and forth across the lands of densest Jewish population. Revolution and civil war in Russia brought first slaughter at the hands of the "White" nationalist forces, and then the systematic dismemberment of Jewish life by the new Communist masters of the land. A bitter, defeated Germany turned to Nazism, and the monstrous regime it installed made it its goal to annihilate all of Europe's Jews. More than 90% of the Jews of the great heartland of Eastern Europe were murdered, and Europe ceased to be the center of world Jewry.

Some one million Jews survived World War II in the Soviet Union, only to be persecuted by Stalin and his heirs. Yet despite Soviet repression, Judaism did not die in Russia. Eventually, the fall of Communism and the disintegration of the Soviet Union brought hundreds of thousands of Jews to America, Israel, and other locales, while those who remained have been rebuilding the infrastructure of Jewish life.

A mere shadow of its former glorious self in its native Europe, Ashkenazic Jewry has flourished in America and

*Entrance to Kazimierz,
the Jewish district of Krakow,
Poland, 1935–1938*

ROMAN VISHNIAC

Israel. In the first waves of American immigration of the 19th and early 20th centuries, the development of Torah scholarship and observance lagged far behind the surge of population and the gains in social and economic advancement. But the post-World War II period brought an influx of leadership and religious commitment from Europe, and a binding together of Ashkenazic streams from around the world. Under the conditions of political and religious freedom, American Jewry has found creative new ways to make Jewish teachings and practice widely available and deeply meaningful to a broad swath of its close to six million members.

In the Holy Land, Ashkenazic Jews led the socialist Zionist movements that took the leading roles in the establishment of the state. Other Ashkenazim played major roles in political and religious countercurrents. More recently, however, other streams of Jewry have increasingly stepped to the fore, and a trend of blending together the various communities of world Jewry both within Israel and beyond its borders may lead to a future of increased integration between the Ashkenazic, Sephardic, and other Jewish "subcultures" created by the Jewish diaspora.

notable Ashkenazic communities

MAINZ

The cradle of Ashkenazic Jewry. Historians believe that Jews followed the Roman legions to Mainz, and records show them well established there by the 10th century. In 1013, the first of the Ashkenazic *rishonim* ("early" sages of the post-Geonic period), R. Gershom, founded a yeshivah in Mainz that forged the distinctively Ashkenazic approach to Jewish law and scholarship, earning him the appellation "Light of the Diaspora." Another seminal figure who lived in Mainz was R. Jacob Levi Moelin ("Maharil," c. 1365–1427), known for his authoritative codification of the *minhagim* ("customs") of Ashkenazic Jewry. The Mainz community was massacred during the First Crusade, and when Jewish life returned, it was never with the same confidence. Political emancipation and assimilation came with Napoleon, and a modern Jewish community prospered in Mainz until the rise of Nazism. A small new community was founded after World War II.

PRAGUE

Records attest to the presence of Jewish merchants in Prague as early as 970, though tradition traces its Jewish settlement to centuries earlier. Jews enjoyed great freedom there until the outbreak of the Crusades, after which periodic violence affected the community. Royal protection in the 13th century helped grow the community, and a new Jewish area was built, including the Altneuschul (c. 1270), the oldest still-functioning synagogue in Europe. Prague was a center of Hebrew publication in the early days of the printing press, and was known for a number of great Torah scholars, most famous among them R. Judah Loew, the "Maharal of Prague" (1520–1609). In the 17th century, Prague was home to the largest Ashkenazic-Jewish community in Europe. With the 19th century came political emancipation and assimilation, and Prague's Jews became prominent in business, literature, and the arts. Most of the 52,000 Jews living in Prague in 1939 perished in the Holocaust. The fall of Communism in 1989 brought a revival in Jewish life, and Prague now is home to a small but growing Jewish community.

KRAKOW

This one thousand-year-old Polish city saw Jews arrive in the early 13th century, mostly from German lands, where Jewish life had become precarious. In 1334, King Casimir the Great granted Krakow's Jews broad political rights, sparking growth in both the population and the fortunes of the community. The city became a center of Jewish scholarship; the first yeshivah in Poland was founded here shortly before 1500, and Krakow was home to the most important Ashkenazic Halachist, R. Moses Isserlis (1530–1572, known as "Rema"), and other giants of Torah scholarship. Increasing persecution and economic depression came in the 1600s. In 1846, Krakow came under Austrian rule, which brought political rights and greater assimilation. By the beginning of the 20th century, Jews constituted 25% of Krakow's population. The Holocaust destroyed the community, though Oskar Schindler's activity saved about 1,000 Jews. A postwar pogrom scared away Jews wishing to return. Today, a small community has been reestablished.

VILNA

Jews were granted the right to live in Vilna (Vilnius) in 1593. Fifty years later, the 3,000 Jews living there comprised about a quarter of the city's population. Its well-organized community provided generous support for Torah study, bestowing upon the city the title, "The Jerusalem of Lithuania." Most influential among its rabbinic figures was R. Elijah, the Gaon of Vilna ("Gra," 1720–1797), renowned for his distinctive Halachic approach, his groundbreaking critical Talmudic text analysis, and his intense engagement with Kabbalah. In the controversy over the emergence of Hasidism in the middle of the 18th century, Vilna was famous as the center of opposition to the new movement. In the mid-19th century, Vilna became a center of the Musar movement, which emphasized moral introspection and character refinement as an accompaniment to intellectual Talmudic learning. Nazis and local antisemites devastated the community during World War II, and the absorption of Vilna into Stalin's Soviet empire left the city under a rule hostile to Judaism. Today a small community has returned and is growing.

MEZHIBUZH

The Jewish population of this small Ukrainian town never exceeded a few thousand souls, but it gave birth to one of the most transformative movements in Jewish history. At the time of the Cossack revolt of 1648, Mezhibuzh was home to about 2,500 Jews, nearly all of whom were murdered or taken as slaves by the Chmielnitzki mob. Stability finally returned decades later, and Jews once again settled and flourished there. A little after 1740, the founder of Hasidism (see p. 232), R. Israel Baal Shem Tov, came to Mezhibuzh, which remained the center of the movement until his passing in 1760. Today, many visitors come to pray at the Baal Shem Tov's gravesite in the restored Jewish cemetery, and to visit other historic Jewish sites in the region.

WARSAW

This city was originally inhospitable to Jews, who found a warmer welcome elsewhere in Poland, and it was not until 1862 that Jews were granted the right to settle everywhere in Warsaw. Nonetheless, in the 18th century Warsaw's Jewish population already numbered over 100,000. During the interwar period, Jews constituted as much as 37% of the city's population, reaching a peak of 375,000 in 1939. The Jews of Warsaw were overwhelmingly Hasidic, and traditional Jewish life flourished in hundreds of synagogues and *shtiebles*; but by 1900, Warsaw had become home to many secularist Jews as well, and a center of Yiddishist culture and Zionist activism. After World War I, Warsaw's Jews participated in the politics of the reestablished Poland, with a number of Jewish parties electing representatives to the Polish parliament; but native antisemitism made life precarious by the end of the 1930s. The Nazi conquest of Poland led to the horrific ghettoization and murder of Warsaw's Jews. A small Jewish community of about 3,000 lives in the city today.

ODESSA

Odessa had been a sleepy Black Sea fort under Ottoman rule until it was conquered and settled by Russia in the 1790s. Given status as a free port, it attracted foreign capital as well as Jews, who formed a part of the newly growing city's business and political life in a way not possible in the rest of Russia. By 1912, there were 200,000 Jews living in Odessa, comprising more than 30% of the city's population. As a rule, Jewish life in Odessa was less traditional than in the older areas of Russia. Jews were represented in all economic fields and professions, including the performing arts, music, literature, and journalism; the city was also home to some of the prominent leaders of political Zionism. The advent of Communist rule in 1917 forced the disbanding of traditional institutions and the cessation of most Jewish practice; secularist Jews also suffered, with many Jewish intellectuals executed by Stalin. The heavy hand of Nazi occupation took a deadly toll, but many survived. The opening of the gates for emigration led to a major exodus of Jews after 1990, with thousands going to the United States or Israel. About 35,000 Jews remain in Odessa today.

NEW YORK

Although originally settled by Sephardic Jews in 1654, Ashkenazim were a majority in the New York Jewish community long before the American Revolution. Succeeding waves of Ashkenazic Jewish immigration in the 19th and early 20th centuries made New York the largest Jewish city in the world; well over two million Jews lived in the city, comprising one quarter of its population, and the city became the headquarters of many Jewish organizations and institutions. Rapid assimilation of immigrants and their children led to an explosion of economic and cultural creativity, influence, and achievement. In the wake of World War II, New York became a center of an intense revival of traditional Jewish life in strikingly new environs, as dozens of major yeshivahs and Hasidic communities settled and flourished there.

PERSECUTION AND GENOCIDE

anti-Jewish decrees and violence through the ages

NOTE: The historic instances of persecutions directed against
the Jewish people are far too numerous to list.
Presented here are some of the more blatant and illustrative cases.

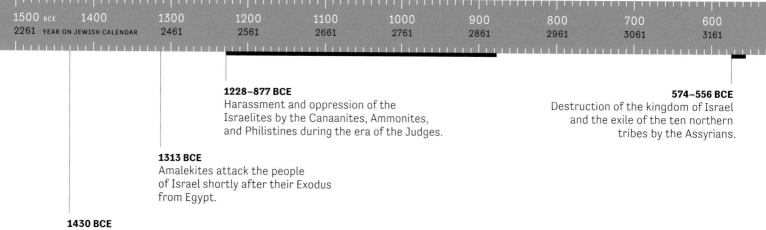

| 1500 BCE | 1400 | 1300 | 1200 | 1100 | 1000 | 900 | 800 | 700 | 600 |
| 2261 YEAR ON JEWISH CALENDAR | 2461 | | 2561 | 2661 | 2761 | 2861 | 2961 | 3061 | 3161 |

1228–877 BCE
Harassment and oppression of the
Israelites by the Canaanites, Ammonites,
and Philistines during the era of the Judges.

574–556 BCE
Destruction of the kingdom of Israel
and the exile of the ten northern
tribes by the Assyrians.

1313 BCE
Amalekites attack the people
of Israel shortly after their Exodus
from Egypt.

1430 BCE
The Egyptians enslave the
people of Israel.

 SIDDUR

Look down from heaven and see
How we have become a mockery among the nations
Regarded as sheep being led to slaughter
To be killed, destroyed, beaten, and humiliated
Yet despite all this, we have not forgotten Your name
Please, do not forget us!

 ESTHER 3:8–9

Haman said to King Ahasuerus: "There is one people,
scattered and divided among the peoples in all the provinces of your kingdom. Their laws differ from those of
every people, and they do not keep the king's laws; it is

therefore of no value for the king to allow them to exist.
"If it pleases the king, may it be decreed to destroy
them; and I will weigh ten thousand talents of silver …
to be brought to the treasuries of the king."

 MACCABEES, *BOOK 1, CH. 1, VERSES 42–59*

King Antiochus … sent letters by the hands of messengers to all the cities of Judah; that they should follow
the law of the gentile nations…. And should profane
the Sabbath and the festival days. And pollute the
Sanctuary and the priests. He commanded altars to
be built, and temples, and idols, and swine's flesh to
be offered…. And that they should leave their children
uncircumcised, and make their souls abominable with

380–480
Christianity, which began as a Jewish sect in the 1st century CE and broke away to form its own religion, becomes the state religion of the Roman Empire. Because the authors of the New Testament placed the responsibility for the killing of Jesus on the Jews, Christians for centuries viewed Jews as "Christ killers," and as "a people condemned forever to suffer exile and degradation," fueling hatred and persecution of Jews. The Christian rulers of the Roman Empire issued numerous anti-Jewish edicts, forbade the construction of synagogues, and disbanded Jewish religious institutions.

117–119
Hundreds of thousands of Jews die in the failed "Revolt of the Diaspora," decimating the populous Jewish communities of Cyprus, Cyrene (Libya), and Alexandria.

68–73
Romans capture Jerusalem and destroy the Second Temple. 1,100,000 Jews are killed, and hundreds of thousands are exiled or sold into slavery.

442–434 BCE
Babylonians conquer the kingdom of Judah, destroy the first Holy Temple, and exile the Jewish people to Babylon.

35
Pogrom against the Jewish population of Alexandria, Egypt.

500	400	300	200	100 BCE	1 CE	100	200	300	400
3261	3361	3461	3561	3661	3761	3860	3960	4060	4160

151–140 BCE
Antiochus IV attempts to forcibly Hellenize the Jewish people, and forbids the observances of circumcision, Shabbat, and the Jewish festivals on pain of death.

357 BCE
Haman plots to kill all the Jews throughout the Persian Empire in a single day.

45
First known case of the infamous blood libels leveled against the Jews, which would claim many Jewish lives through the centuries. Hellenist anti-Semite Apion claims that "each year the Jews kidnap a Greek, fatten him up for a year, and then convey him to the forest where they offer up his body as a sacrifice and eat his internal organs, while swearing an oath of eternal hatred toward all Greeks."

120–135
The Roman emperor Hadrian outlaws the practice of Judaism and builds a pagan temple on the site of the destroyed Jewish Temple.

In the wake of the failed Bar Kochba rebellion—in which 580,000 Jews are killed and 1,000 Jewish towns razed to the ground—the decrees against Judaism are intensified, and prominent Jewish sages and leaders ("the ten martyrs") are cruelly executed.

455–486
Sasanian rulers of Persia and Babylonia forbid the observance of Shabbat and other Jewish precepts as part of a policy of imposing the state religion of Zoroastrianism. The Jewish community in Isfahan is massacred and their children are forcibly converted. Many flee to the Malabar Coast of India.

all manners of uncleanness and profanation. To the end that they should forget the Torah, and should change all the ordinances of G-d.... They drove the Israelites into secret places, even wheresoever they could flee for succor.... They cut to pieces and burned with fire the books of the law of G-d. All who were discovered possessing a copy of the covenant or practicing the Torah, the king's decree sentenced them to death.... Women who had had their children circumcised were put to death according to the edict, their babies hung round their necks, and the members of their household and those who had performed the circumcision were executed with them....

 TALMUD, *BERACHOT 61b*

When [the Romans] took out Rabbi Akiva to be killed, it was the time for the reading of the Shema. They were combing his flesh with iron combs, and he was accepting the yoke of the divine sovereignty with the Shema ("Hear O Israel, the Lord is our G-d, G-d is one").

His disciples said to him: "O master, to such an extent?" Said he to them: "All my life I was pained on account of the verse (Deuteronomy 6:5), 'You shall love G-d ... with all your soul'—meaning, even if you must give up your life. I would say: When will I have the opportunity to fulfill it? Now that I have the opportunity, should I not fulfill it?"

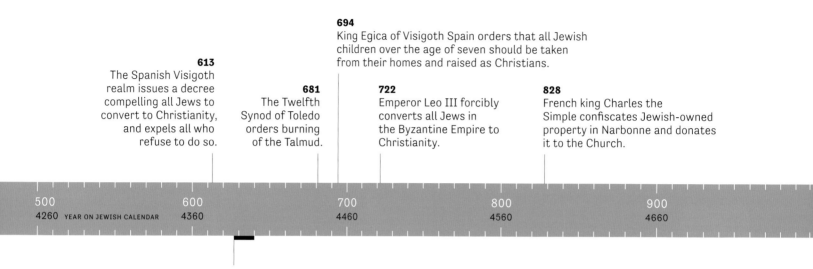

613
The Spanish Visigoth realm issues a decree compelling all Jews to convert to Christianity, and expels all who refuse to do so.

681
The Twelfth Synod of Toledo orders burning of the Talmud.

694
King Egica of Visigoth Spain orders that all Jewish children over the age of seven should be taken from their homes and raised as Christians.

722
Emperor Leo III forcibly converts all Jews in the Byzantine Empire to Christianity.

828
French king Charles the Simple confiscates Jewish-owned property in Narbonne and donates it to the Church.

500	600	700	800	900
4260 YEAR ON JEWISH CALENDAR 4360		4460	4560	4660

627–640
Muhammad, the founder of Islam, initially allied himself with the Jews of Arabia, believing they would accept him as a prophet and convert to the religion he founded. When this hope did not materialize, he turned on the Jews, expelling or killing the Jews in the territories where he gained power. By 640 (three years after Muhammad's death), Jews had been expelled from the entire Arabian Peninsula, where numerous Jewish tribes had flourished for centuries.

Muhammad's successors continued his policy of imposing the new religion by the force of the sword, conquering vast territories and forcefully converting millions of people. Although Muslim rule included periods of tolerance—most notably, the golden age in Spain (912-1172) and the Ottoman Empire in the 16th and 17th centuries—Muhammad's inflammatory statements about the Jews, recorded in the Koran, have stoked Islamic hatred and persecution of Jews for centuries. Jews in Muslim-ruled lands were made to pay special taxes, stripped of many citizens' rights, and subjected to humiliating laws and regulations designed to emphasize their degraded status. At times they were compelled to wear distinctively marked clothing, such as a yellow belt.

 ABBA KOVNER
SCROLLS OF FIRE, SECTION 13

The last stronghold in the wars of Muhammad against the Jewish tribes was Kuraita, a settlement of Jewish date-growers and warriors near Medina. The people of Kuraita did not have the time to strengthen their fortifications before the Muslim forces stormed them. For fourteen days the Jews resisted, and when they were defeated, Muhammad gave the order to massacre the defenders. Six hundred elders of the community were beheaded in the marketplace of Medina in a single day, as Muhammad stood in the square and watched. After them, the rest of the community died a martyr's death; only one man saved his life by converting to Islam.

 R. SOLOMON BAR SIMEON, *EXCERPTS FROM SURVIVORS' ACCOUNTS RECORDED IN 1140 CE*

It was in the 1,028th year of our exile [1096 CE], a year replete with hope for our redemption that turned to agony and grief and howling and weeping, as all the Biblical curses, written and unwritten, were heaped upon our souls.

In France and Germany there arose a throng of harsh, restless, and bitter people who set their hearts to march to Jerusalem to liberate the tomb of their idol and conquer the land from the Ishmaelites. As they passed through the towns where Jews lived, they said to one another: Here we are journeying to a distant land to avenge ourselves on the Muslims, when the Jews,

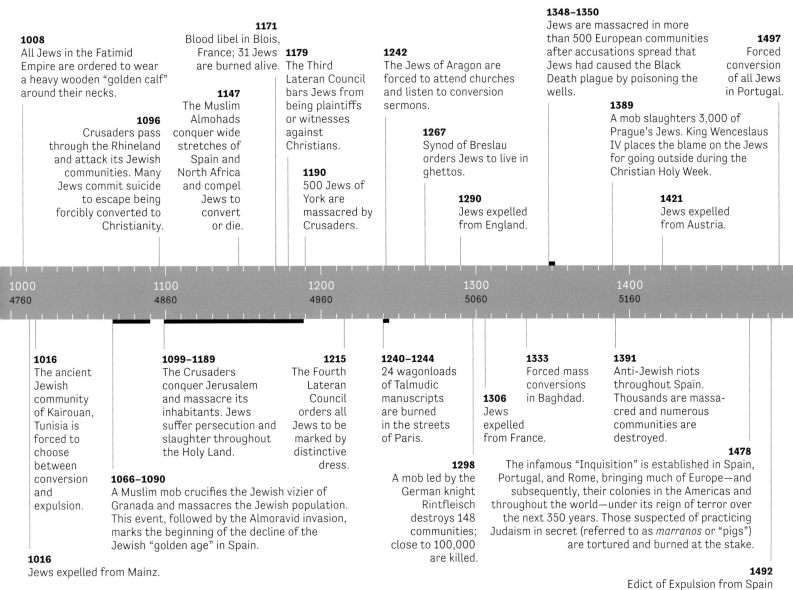

1008
All Jews in the Fatimid Empire are ordered to wear a heavy wooden "golden calf" around their necks.

1171
Blood libel in Blois, France; 31 Jews are burned alive.

1179
The Third Lateran Council bars Jews from being plaintiffs or witnesses against Christians.

1242
The Jews of Aragon are forced to attend churches and listen to conversion sermons.

1348–1350
Jews are massacred in more than 500 European communities after accusations spread that Jews had caused the Black Death plague by poisoning the wells.

1497
Forced conversion of all Jews in Portugal.

1147
The Muslim Almohads conquer wide stretches of Spain and North Africa and compel Jews to convert or die.

1096
Crusaders pass through the Rhineland and attack its Jewish communities. Many Jews commit suicide to escape being forcibly converted to Christianity.

1190
500 Jews of York are massacred by Crusaders.

1267
Synod of Breslau orders Jews to live in ghettos.

1290
Jews expelled from England.

1389
A mob slaughters 3,000 of Prague's Jews. King Wenceslaus IV places the blame on the Jews for going outside during the Christian Holy Week.

1421
Jews expelled from Austria.

| 1000 | 1100 | 1200 | 1300 | 1400 |
| 4760 | 4860 | 4960 | 5060 | 5160 |

1016
The ancient Jewish community of Kairouan, Tunisia is forced to choose between conversion and expulsion.

1099–1189
The Crusaders conquer Jerusalem and massacre its inhabitants. Jews suffer persecution and slaughter throughout the Holy Land.

1215
The Fourth Lateran Council orders all Jews to be marked by distinctive dress.

1240–1244
24 wagonloads of Talmudic manuscripts are burned in the streets of Paris.

1333
Forced mass conversions in Baghdad.

1391
Anti-Jewish riots throughout Spain. Thousands are massacred and numerous communities are destroyed.

1306
Jews expelled from France.

1066–1090
A Muslim mob crucifies the Jewish vizier of Granada and massacres the Jewish population. This event, followed by the Almoravid invasion, marks the beginning of the decline of the Jewish "golden age" in Spain.

1298
A mob led by the German knight Rintfleisch destroys 148 communities; close to 100,000 are killed.

1478
The infamous "Inquisition" is established in Spain, Portugal, and Rome, bringing much of Europe—and subsequently, their colonies in the Americas and throughout the world—under its reign of terror over the next 350 years. Those suspected of practicing Judaism in secret (referred to as *marranos* or "pigs") are tortured and burned at the stake.

1016
Jews expelled from Mainz.

1492
Edict of Expulsion from Spain (see account by Don Isaac Abarbanel on p. 126).

---

whose forefathers killed and crucified our lord, dwell here amongst us. Let us first take revenge on them; let us destroy them as a people so that the name Israel may no longer be remembered, sparing only those who will become like us and profess our belief.

When word reached the Jewish communities of the Rhineland, they turned to the vocation of their ancestors—repentance, prayer, and charity. But their Father in Heaven did not heed their prayers, as this generation had been chosen by Him as one with the strength and fortitude to stand in His royal palace, to do His bidding and sanctify His name in His world....

On Shabbat, the 8th of Iyar of that year, the enemy attacked the community of Speyer. Eleven holy souls were slaughtered when they refused to be baptized.... On the 23rd of Iyar they attacked the community of Worms. Half of the people barricaded themselves in their houses, while the other half sought refuge in the bishop's castle. The beasts overran the town, trampling men, women, and children, looting and destroying the homes. They trampled the Torah scroll in the mud, tore it to pieces, and burned it.

Seven days later, on the 1st of Sivan—the day on which the people of Israel arrived at Mount Sinai to receive the Torah—the mob infiltrated the bishop's courtyard and put us to the sword. Many Jews took their own lives, lest they be contaminated by the enemy's putrid waters.... In Mainz, the most prestigious of the

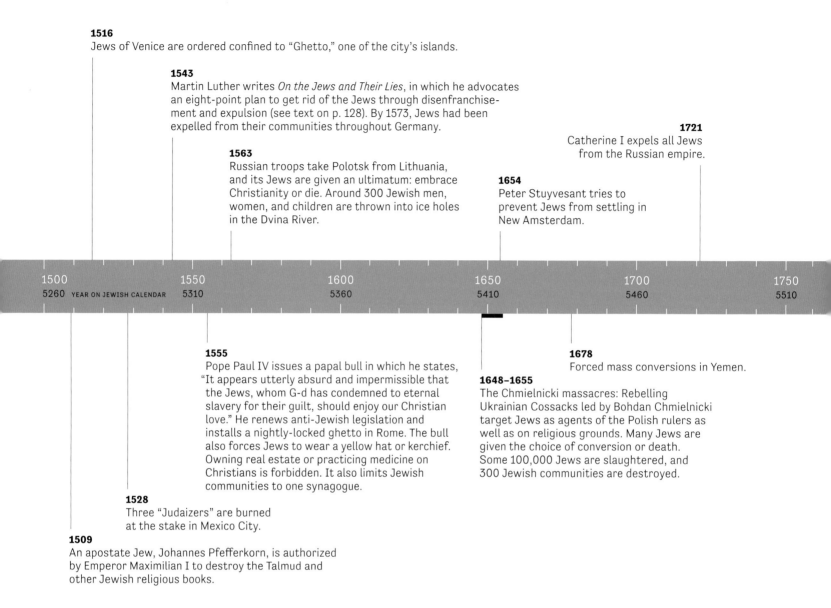

1516
Jews of Venice are ordered confined to "Ghetto," one of the city's islands.

1543
Martin Luther writes *On the Jews and Their Lies*, in which he advocates an eight-point plan to get rid of the Jews through disenfranchisement and expulsion (see text on p. 128). By 1573, Jews had been expelled from their communities throughout Germany.

1563
Russian troops take Polotsk from Lithuania, and its Jews are given an ultimatum: embrace Christianity or die. Around 300 Jewish men, women, and children are thrown into ice holes in the Dvina River.

1721
Catherine I expels all Jews from the Russian empire.

1654
Peter Stuyvesant tries to prevent Jews from settling in New Amsterdam.

1500	1550	1600	1650	1700	1750
5260 YEAR ON JEWISH CALENDAR	5310	5360	5410	5460	5510

1555
Pope Paul IV issues a papal bull in which he states, "It appears utterly absurd and impermissible that the Jews, whom G-d has condemned to eternal slavery for their guilt, should enjoy our Christian love." He renews anti-Jewish legislation and installs a nightly-locked ghetto in Rome. The bull also forces Jews to wear a yellow hat or kerchief. Owning real estate or practicing medicine on Christians is forbidden. It also limits Jewish communities to one synagogue.

1678
Forced mass conversions in Yemen.

1648–1655
The Chmielnicki massacres: Rebelling Ukrainian Cossacks led by Bohdan Chmielnicki target Jews as agents of the Polish rulers as well as on religious grounds. Many Jews are given the choice of conversion or death. Some 100,000 Jews are slaughtered, and 300 Jewish communities are destroyed.

1528
Three "Judaizers" are burned at the stake in Mexico City.

1509
An apostate Jew, Johannes Pfefferkorn, is authorized by Emperor Maximilian I to destroy the Talmud and other Jewish religious books.

Jewish communities, the Jews took up their weapons under their leader R. Kalonymus and battled the mob at the city gates until midnight…. One thousand and one hundred holy souls were martyred on Tuesday, the 3rd of Sivan—1,100 bindings as the binding of Isaac the son of Abraham in a single day.

 DON ISAAC ABARBANEL, *INTRODUCTION TO COMMENTARY ON THE BOOK OF KINGS*

In the 244th year of the sixth millennium from Creation [1484], I was called to serve in the court of the king of Spain, the most powerful of the kings of the land, who ruled over the kingdoms of Castile, Aragon, Catalonia, Sicily, and other islands. The Almighty granted me favor in the eyes of the king and the consort and all the leading ministers. I was occupied in their affairs for eight years. I acquired both wealth and glory….

In the ninth year [of my service], the year [5]252 [1492], the king of Spain conquered the kingdom of Granada…. In his power and pride, his attitude changed…. Esau said in his heart: How shall I appease my deity, who placed this city under my rule? Surely, by gathering under his wing the scattered sheep of Israel and bringing them into his religion and his faith. Thus, the word of the king and his decree went forth, as the decree of Persia and Media of yore, and the pronouncement was tremblingly read: "To you, all the families of the children of Israel, I say: If you will pass under the

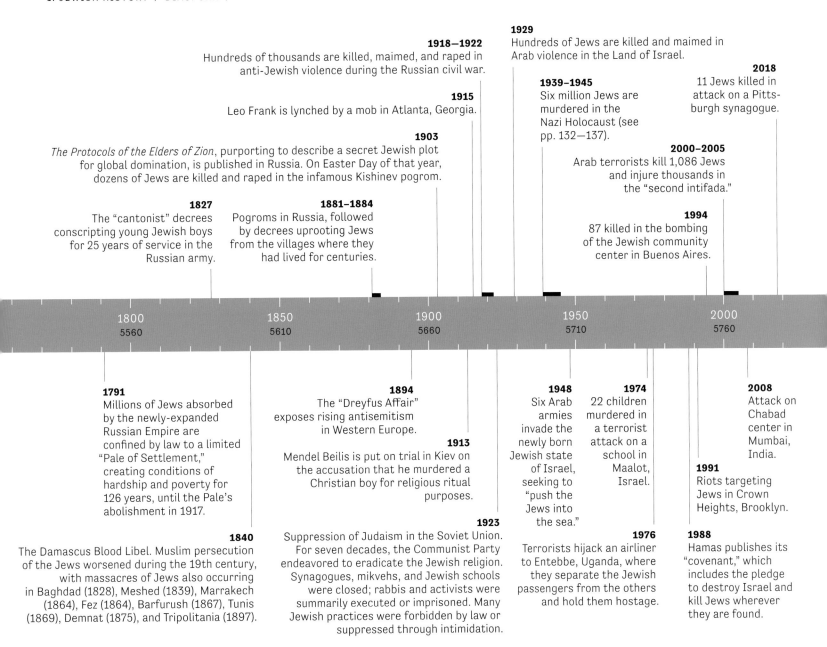

1929
Hundreds of Jews are killed and maimed in Arab violence in the Land of Israel.

1918—1922
Hundreds of thousands are killed, maimed, and raped in anti-Jewish violence during the Russian civil war.

2018
11 Jews killed in attack on a Pittsburgh synagogue.

1939—1945
Six million Jews are murdered in the Nazi Holocaust (see pp. 132—137).

1915
Leo Frank is lynched by a mob in Atlanta, Georgia.

1903
The Protocols of the Elders of Zion, purporting to describe a secret Jewish plot for global domination, is published in Russia. On Easter Day of that year, dozens of Jews are killed and raped in the infamous Kishinev pogrom.

2000–2005
Arab terrorists kill 1,086 Jews and injure thousands in the "second intifada."

1827
The "cantonist" decrees conscripting young Jewish boys for 25 years of service in the Russian army.

1881–1884
Pogroms in Russia, followed by decrees uprooting Jews from the villages where they had lived for centuries.

1994
87 killed in the bombing of the Jewish community center in Buenos Aires.

1800
5560

1850
5610

1900
5660

1950
5710

2000
5760

1791
Millions of Jews absorbed by the newly-expanded Russian Empire are confined by law to a limited "Pale of Settlement," creating conditions of hardship and poverty for 126 years, until the Pale's abolishment in 1917.

1894
The "Dreyfus Affair" exposes rising antisemitism in Western Europe.

1913
Mendel Beilis is put on trial in Kiev on the accusation that he murdered a Christian boy for religious ritual purposes.

1948
Six Arab armies invade the newly born Jewish state of Israel, seeking to "push the Jews into the sea."

1974
22 children murdered in a terrorist attack on a school in Maalot, Israel.

2008
Attack on Chabad center in Mumbai, India.

1991
Riots targeting Jews in Crown Heights, Brooklyn.

1840
The Damascus Blood Libel. Muslim persecution of the Jews worsened during the 19th century, with massacres of Jews also occurring in Baghdad (1828), Meshed (1839), Marrakech (1864), Fez (1864), Barfurush (1867), Tunis (1869), Demnat (1875), and Tripolitania (1897).

1923
Suppression of Judaism in the Soviet Union. For seven decades, the Communist Party endeavored to eradicate the Jewish religion. Synagogues, mikvehs, and Jewish schools were closed; rabbis and activists were summarily executed or imprisoned. Many Jewish practices were forbidden by law or suppressed through intimidation.

1976
Terrorists hijack an airliner to Entebbe, Uganda, where they separate the Jewish passengers from the others and hold them hostage.

1988
Hamas publishes its "covenant," which includes the pledge to destroy Israel and kill Jews wherever they are found.

---

repulsive waters and bow to the gods of the gentiles, you shall eat of the good of the land, like us today, settle the land and do commerce therein. But should you refuse to avow the name of my god and worship him, then you must depart from amongst my people, from the lands of Spain, Sicily, Murcia, and Sardinia, which are under my rule, and within three months, not a single footstep of anyone called by the name Israel may remain in any of the countries of my kingdom."

As I was a member of the royal court at the time, I cried out until my throat was hoarse, speaking to the king twice and thrice, saying, "Why do you do such to your servants? Multiply financial penalties upon us as you wish; every Israelite man would give everything he has for his country!" I called upon my friends who had the king's ear to plead for my people. But he sealed his ears and refused to reconsider. The queen stood by his side to incite him to act with finality. We strove, but no respite was granted us. I did not rest, I did not desist, but I was unable to avert the doom....

We said to each other: "Let us be strong on behalf of our faith, and on behalf of the Torah of our G-d, in the face of the blasphemers and the haters. If they let us live we shall live, and if they slay us we shall die; but we shall not desecrate our covenant, and our heart will not retreat. We shall carry on in the name of G-d our Lord."

They went forth without strength, three hundred thousand of them, on foot—the young and the aged,

infants and women, from all the provinces of the king. Wherever the wind drove them, they went. Their Sovereign went before them, their G-d at their head. They called out, "I am to G-d!" and, "My hand is to G-d!"

Some went to Portugal and to Navarre, which were close by. But many troubles and evils befell them—pillage, destruction, famine, and plague. Some sought a a path through the sea's stormy waters; but the hand of G-d struck at them. Many were captured and sold as slaves throughout the gentile territories. Many drowned in the ocean, and many were consumed by fire and water when the ships caught fire.... I, too, chose the path of the sea. Joining the exiles, I came with my household here, to this lauded city of Naples, whose kings are benevolent rulers.

 R. JOSEPH YAABETZ, *OHR HACHAYIM, CHAPTER 2*

Listen, my brothers! I am one of the exiles of Spain, and I saw how the majority of the cultured, who so glory in their knowledge, became apostates and desecrated their honor in the day of their great misfortune, whereas ordinary women and unlettered men sacrificed their lives and their fortunes for the sanctification of the divine name.

 MARTIN LUTHER, *ON THE JEWS AND THEIR LIES*

What shall we Christians do with this rejected and condemned people, the Jews? Since they live among us, we dare not tolerate their conduct ... [lest] we come to share in their lies, curses, and blasphemy.... I shall give you my sincere advice:

First, to set fire to their synagogues or schools and to bury and cover with dirt whatever will not burn, so that no man will ever again see a stone or cinder of them.... Second, I advise that their houses also be razed and destroyed. For they pursue in them the same aims as in their synagogues. Instead they might be lodged under a roof or in a barn, like the gypsies. This will bring home to them the fact that they are not masters in our country, as they boast, but that they are living in exile and in captivity, as they incessantly wail and lament about us before G-d. Third, I advise that all their prayer books and Talmudic writings, in which such idolatry, lies, cursing, and blasphemy are taught, be taken from them. Fourth, I advise that their rabbis be forbidden to teach henceforth on pain of loss of life and limb.... Fifth, I advise that safe conduct on the highways be abolished completely for the Jews.... Sixth, I advise that usury be prohibited to them, and that all cash and treasure of silver and gold be taken from them.... Such money should now be used in no other way than the following: Whenever a Jew is sincerely converted, he should be handed one hundred, two hundred, or three hundred florins, as personal circumstances may suggest. Seventh, I recommend putting a flail, an ax, a hoe, a spade, a distaff, or a spindle into the hands of young, strong Jews and Jewesses and letting them earn their bread in the sweat of their brow, as was imposed on the children of Adam. For it is not fitting that they should let us accursed Goyim toil in the sweat of our faces while they, the holy people, idle away their time behind the stove, feasting and farting.... [Finally,] let us emulate the common sense of other nations such as France, Spain, Bohemia ... [and] eject them forever from the country.

 BENNY MORRIS, *TRAVELER'S REPORT CITED IN RIGHTEOUS VICTIMS, PP. 11–12*

I have seen a little fellow of six years old, with a troop of fat toddlers of only three and four, teaching [them] to throw stones at a Jew, and one little urchin would, with the greatest coolness, waddle up to the man and literally spit upon his Jewish gaberdine. To all this the Jew is obliged to submit; it would be more than his life was worth to offer to strike a Mahommedan.

 CHAIM NACHMAN BIALIK

Cursed be the one who says, "Avenge!"
Such revenge, revenge for the blood of a little child
Satan himself has yet to devise....
Let the blood pierce the abyss
Let the blood pierce the black depths
Burrowing in the darkness, eating through
The rotting foundations of the earth.

From *On the Slaughter,* written in the wake of the Kishinev Pogrom, April 1903.

 NATAN SHARANSKY
DEFENDING IDENTITY, PP. 17–24

When I was arrested, taken to Lefortovo prison, and accused of high treason, I was told I would never get out alive. The choice the KGB put to me was simple. If I cooperated by condemning Israel, Zionism, and the Jewish emigration movement, I would be permitted to join my wife in Israel relatively quickly. If I refused to cooperate, I would be executed as a spy and traitor....

The Soviet regime was predicated on controlling, largely through fear, the minds and the thoughts of hundreds of millions of people. The existence of even a single person who does not succumb to fear, who publicly defies it, endangers the entire system. The regime had to crush all signs of dissent, however small and seemingly insignificant.

"You should not be so stubborn and inflexible," my interrogators told me. "Cooperate and you will go free. Let's avoid all the unpleasantness. Declare that we are right and you are wrong and then you can go on with your life." In interrogation after interrogation, they repeated the same sugar-coated threat: "Help us so that we can help you. We are not bloodthirsty," they purred, "we do not want you to die. We only want you to cooperate."

This was the typical KGB approach, to make the moment of your destruction the basis of your release. For after you have compromised with them, you are no longer a threat. You are no longer an obstacle in their battle to stamp out any spark of freedom because you have already sacrificed the most powerful freedom of all: inner freedom. The KGB does not need your life, only your soul....

At the time of my interrogations, I did not have the right words to describe this feeling of commitment that provided me with such a powerful sense of inner freedom. But some years later, I found a way to express it. A few days before my arrest, an American tourist gave me a small book of Psalms from my wife.... Back then, my Hebrew was in no way adequate to read that book. After I was arrested, the book, along with all my other belongings, was confiscated.… The book soon took on an almost mystical meaning for me. I started to fight to have it returned, a battle that continued for three years.

I finally recovered the little book of Psalms with the news that my father had passed away. I tried to read it, but I still understood little.… The first lines I understood were those of Psalm 23: "Although I walk through the valley [of the shadow] of death, I fear no evil, for You are with me."

I noticed that in the Psalms, the word *fear* kept appearing. On the one hand, fear was something to be overcome, such as not fearing evil. But as *yirat hashem*, or the fear of G-d, it had a positive connotation. It took me time to understand what this fear of G-d meant. My understanding was at first very vague and uncertain. But at some moment it occurred to me, seeing it many times, that this fear was connected not simply to G-d the Creator but to the image of G-d in which man was created. Mankind was created to be worthy of that image and to be true to it. This required me to go forward in an honest and direct way, without compromising principles. This fear, the fear of not being worthy of the divine image, not the fear of death, was what I was most afraid of in my interrogations with the KGB. I was afraid to lose the world of inner freedom I had found, to fail to stay true to my inner self.

 R. YOSEF YITZCHAK SCHNEERSOHN
LIKUTEI DIBURIM, VOL. 4, PP. 692–693

It was not by our choosing that we left the Land of Israel, nor it is by our own power that we shall return there. G-d has driven us into *galut*, and it is He who will redeem us through Mashiach, the righteous redeemer, speedily in our day, amen.

This, however, all the nations on the face of the earth must know: Only our bodies have been exiled and sub-jugated to the sovereignty of governments. Our souls were not driven into exile, nor were they placed under the dominion of any ruler. We must proclaim openly and publicly that in all that pertains to our religion—the Torah, the mitzvot, and Jewish customs—no one has the authority to dictate to us, and no force may be exerted upon us. We must proclaim [this] with the strongest Jewish stubbornness, with the millennia-old Jewish self-sacrifice.

R. Yosef Yitzchak spoke the above words on the 3rd of Tamuz, 5687 (July 3, 1927) at the Leningrad Railway Station, in open defiance of the Soviet agents present in the crowd. The Rebbe was on his way to Kostrama in Soviet Central Asia, where he had been exiled by the Stalinist regime because of his work to preserve Judaism throughout the Soviet Union. Several days earlier, a death sentence placed upon him had been commuted.

 MAX I. DIMONT
JEWS, G-D AND HISTORY, PP. 215–216

With but one word, with but one gesture—conversion—the Jew could have become the most honored of citizens in Europe.… Though some Jews did take this "passport to European civilization," as Heinrich Heine termed baptism, most Jews did not. They transcended whatever ignominy was heaped upon them with the firm conviction that their values were superior to the values of their detractors.

 SIMON SCHAMA, *THE STORY OF THE JEWS, OXFORD FILM AND TELEVISION PRODUCTION, 2013*

Given the hammer blows of the Roman legions, and coming as they did after century upon century of blows from Egyptians, Syrians, and Babylonians, there would have been scant reason to suppose that the Jews would survive as a people—and yet, two thousand years later the Jews are still here. How?

Well, one answer could be found back at the Arch of Titus—not something that's here, but something that's not. When Josephus describes the procession of loot and prisoners paraded through the streets of Rome,

CAPTIVE AUDIENCE A satirical lithograph depicting Catholic attempts to convert the Jews by forcing them to listen to church sermons. One anonymous pamphleteer cited the account of a traveler through Italy: "They are forced every Friday to listen to the sermons of a Dominican monk concerning their unbelief. The *sbirri* (Roman police) go among them with big sticks to wake those who fall asleep; two clerics take the names of the absentees in order to punish them. They check their ears to see that they haven't stopped them with wool."

The Conversion of the Jews in Rome (detail), Hieronymus Hess, Basel, Switzerland, circa 1821

he says, "And last of all of the spoils was carried the Laws of the Jews." But, where are the laws [on the Arch of Titus]? Where are the Torah scrolls? Conspicuously, tellingly, they are absent.

What were scrolls of law anyway? Just many words on parchment, not really worth the time of a sculptor or the cost of the marble.

But words copied, memorized, internalized, made unforgettable, will beat swords anytime. You can't hold words captive.

The Roman Empire has come and gone, but go into a synagogue any Saturday and you'll still hear those words.

𐤎 MIDRASH RABBAH, *VAYIKRA 27:11*

Said R. Levi: Woe to the wicked! They occupy themselves with plotting against Israel, each of them saying: My plan is better than yours....

Esau said: Cain was a fool. He killed his brother (wanting the world for himself) while his father was still alive. Did he not realize that his father could have

more children? I will not do that. Rather, "The days of my father's mourning will approach, [and I will kill my brother Jacob]" (Genesis 27:41).

Pharaoh said: Esau was a fool. He said, "The days of my father's mourning will approach." Did he not realize that his brother will have broods of children during his father's lifetime? I will not do that. Rather, I will strangle them at birth.... Thus it is written ... "[Pharaoh command to all his people:] Every son that is born, throw him in the river ..." (Exodus 1:22).

Haman said: Pharaoh was a fool. He said, "Every son that is born...." Did he not realize that the females will marry and bear children? I will not do that. Rather, I will decree "to destroy, kill, and annihilate [all the Jews, from young to old, infants and women, in a single day]" (Esther 3:13)....

And in the future, Gog and Magog will say: All of them were fools, plotting against the Jews. Did they not realize that they have a patron in heaven? We will not do that. Rather, first we will destroy their G-d, and then we will deal with them. Thus it is written, "The kings of the earth rise up, and princes take counsel together, against G-d and against His anointed" (Psalms 2:2).

THE HOLOCAUST

The Holocaust was the systematic, state-sponsored murder of six million Jews, including 1.5 million Jewish children, by Adolf Hitler's Nazi regime and its collaborators during the years 1939–1945.

Hitler's war on the Jews was driven by a virulent hate of Judaism, which he saw as standing in direct opposition to his ideology of the supremacy of the Aryan race and its unbeholdenness to morals or conscience. He was convinced that all Jews, regardless of their beliefs or religiosity, carry the ethos of Judaism in their blood, and that unless the Jewish race was annihilated, it would continue to contaminate humanity with "the dirty and degrading self-mortification of a false vision called conscience and morality."

Yellow star-shaped cloth badge that Jews were forced to wear, Germany, circa 1941

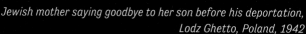
Jewish mother saying goodbye to her son before his deportation, Lodz Ghetto, Poland, 1942

the decimation of European Jewry

Two-thirds of Europe's nine million Jews—or more than one in three of the world's 17 million Jews—were shot, gassed, and starved to death in the ghettos, death camps, and killing sites of the Holocaust.

Every arm of Nazi Germany's sophisticated bureaucracy was involved in the killing process. Parish churches and the Interior Ministry supplied birth records showing who was Jewish; the Finance Ministry confiscated Jewish property; transport offices arranged the trains for deportation to the death camps; German companies disenfranchised Jewish stockholders, availed themselves of Jewish slave labor, tested drugs on camp prisoners, and produced meticulous records of the killings using the nascent computer technology.

While an estimated 200,000 individuals were engaged in the actual killing, it was aided and abetted by the silent compliance of the great majority of Europe's 500 million people. Virtually no social group, religious community, academic institution, or professional association declared its solidarity with the Jews. There were, however, courageous individuals who risked their lives to save Jews. The State of Israel has recognized approximately 25,000 non-Jews as "righteous among the nations," based on the documented testimony of Holocaust survivors.

1939
European Jewish population
9,365,000

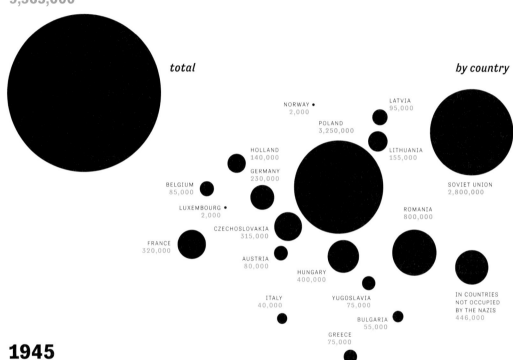

total

by country

NORWAY • 2,000
LATVIA 95,000
POLAND 3,250,000
HOLLAND 140,000
LITHUANIA 155,000
GERMANY 230,000
BELGIUM 85,000
SOVIET UNION 2,800,000
LUXEMBOURG • 2,000
ROMANIA 800,000
CZECHOSLOVAKIA 315,000
FRANCE 320,000
AUSTRIA 80,000
HUNGARY 400,000
ITALY 40,000
YUGOSLAVIA 75,000
IN COUNTRIES NOT OCCUPIED BY THE NAZIS 446,000
BULGARIA 55,000
GREECE 75,000

1945
European Jewish survivors
3,416,000

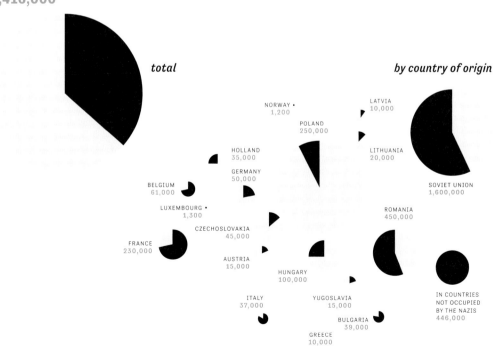

total

by country of origin

NORWAY • 1,200
LATVIA 10,000
POLAND 250,000
HOLLAND 35,000
LITHUANIA 20,000
GERMANY 50,000
BELGIUM 61,000
SOVIET UNION 1,600,000
LUXEMBOURG • 1,300
ROMANIA 450,000
CZECHOSLOVAKIA 45,000
FRANCE 230,000
AUSTRIA 15,000
HUNGARY 100,000
ITALY 37,000
YUGOSLAVIA 15,000
IN COUNTRIES NOT OCCUPIED BY THE NAZIS 446,000
BULGARIA 39,000
GREECE 10,000

VOICES OF THE HOLOCAUST

👁 **ANNE FRANK,** *THE DIARY OF A YOUNG GIRL,*
APRIL 11, 1944

Who has inflicted this upon us? Who has made us Jews
different from all other people? Who has allowed us to
suffer so terribly up till now? It is G-d who has made us
as we are, but it will be G-d, too, who will raise us up
again. If we bear all this suffering and if there are still
Jews left when it is over, then Jews, instead of being
doomed, will be held up as an example. Who knows, it
might even be our religion from which the world and
all peoples learn good, and for that reason and that
reason alone do we have to suffer now. We can never
become just Dutch, or just English, or representatives
of any country for that matter; we will always remain
Jews, but we want to, too.

When the diary of Anne Frank (1929–1945) was published in 1947,
the 15-year-old Jewish schoolgirl became, for many, the face of the
6,000,000 Jews murdered by the Nazis and their collaborators
during the Holocaust. For two years, Anne, her sister Margot, her
parents Otto and Edith Frank, and four other Jews lived in hiding in
the rooms above Otto Frank's offices in Amsterdam, aided by four
of Otto's non-Jewish employees. In August 1944, their hiding place
was discovered, and they were deported to Auschwitz. Anne was
later transported to the Bergen-Belsen concentration camp, where
she and her sister died just weeks before that camp was liberated
in April of 1945. The diary chronicles Anne's daily life from June 12,
1942, a few weeks before the family went into hiding, until August
1, 1944, three days before they were arrested.

👁 **VIKTOR E. FRANKL,** *MAN'S SEARCH FOR MEANING,*
PP. 65–66

We who lived in concentration camps can remember the
men who walked through the huts comforting others,
giving away their last piece of bread. They may have
been few in number, but they offer sufficient proof that
everything can be taken from a person but one thing:
the last of the human freedoms—to choose one's attitude in any given set of circumstances, to choose one's
own way.

Viktor E. Frankl (1905–1997) was an Austrian neurologist and psy-
chiatrist. In 1942, Frankl, his wife, and his parents were deported
to the Theresienstadt concentration camp, and in 1944 they were
transported to Auschwitz; of the four, only Viktor survived. In 1946,
he published *Nevertheless, Say Yes to Life: A Psychologist Experiences
the Concentration Camp*, in which he describes how his travails led
him to understand that a person can find meaning in all situations,
even the most brutal, and thus, a reason to continue living. The book,
subsequently published under the title *Man's Search for Meaning*,
has sold more than 10 million copies worldwide. Frankl became one
of the key figures in existential therapy and a prominent source of
inspiration for humanistic psychologists.

House at Terezin, Hana Kohnová,
Theresienstadt Concentration camp, circa 1942.
Hana was born in 1931 and deported to Auschwitz

 R. KALONYMUS SHAPIRA, *AISH KODESH, P. 191*

How can we encourage ourselves, at least a little bit, while the divine salvation has yet to come?... With the knowledge that we are not alone in our suffering, but that the Almighty Himself, so to speak, suffers with us, as is stated (Psalms 91:15) "I am with them in their distress."

There are times when we suffer for our own sake, because of our sins, or out of G-d's love for us to cleanse us and purify us, and it is only that the Almighty suffers along with us. But there are times when it is we who suffer along with Him, when our suffering is solely for the sanctification of His great name.... How do we know which it is? We know it thus: Is the enemy's hatred only toward us, or is their hatred primarily toward the Torah, and that is why they persecute us? This tells us that they are the enemies of the Jewish people only because they are the enemies of G-d, and that our suffering is wholly for the sanctification of the divine name.

R. Kalonymus Shapira (1889–1943) was a Hasidic rebbe and a pioneer in improving Jewish educational methods. During the Holocaust, he ran a secret synagogue in the Warsaw Ghetto. His only son was killed in the Nazi bombing of Warsaw in 1939, and his only daughter was deported to the death camps in 1942; yet he remained a source of fortitude to his disciples and congregants. In his weekly sermons, he grappled with questions of divine justice and shared words of encouragement and faith. After the ghetto's liquidation, he was sent to the Trawniki concentration camp near Lublin, where he was shot to death together with all remaining Jewish inmates in the summer of 1943. In 1960, a canister in which he had hidden a manuscript of his sermons was discovered in the ruins of the Warsaw Ghetto by a construction worker, and was subsequently published as *Aish Kodesh* ("Sacred Fire").

 HANNAH SENESH, *BLESSED IS THE MATCH*

Blessed is the match that was consumed
    and ignited flames
Blessed is the flame that burned
    in the secret fastness of the heart
Blessed are the hearts who knew
    to cease with honor
Blessed is the match that was consumed
    and ignited flames

Hungarian-born Hannah Senesh (1921–1944) made aliyah to the Holy Land in 1939, and was among the founding members of the kibbutz Sedot Yam. She joined the British army to fight the Nazis, and in March 1944, was part of a group of Jews parachuted into Yugoslavia to assist in an attempt to rescue Hungarian Jews about to be deported to Auschwitz. Senesh was captured and tortured, but refused to supply the information that would compromise other members of the mission. She was executed in the prison courtyard in Budapest. The poem *Blessed Is the Match* was composed in a partisan camp in Yugoslavia several days before Senesh's capture.

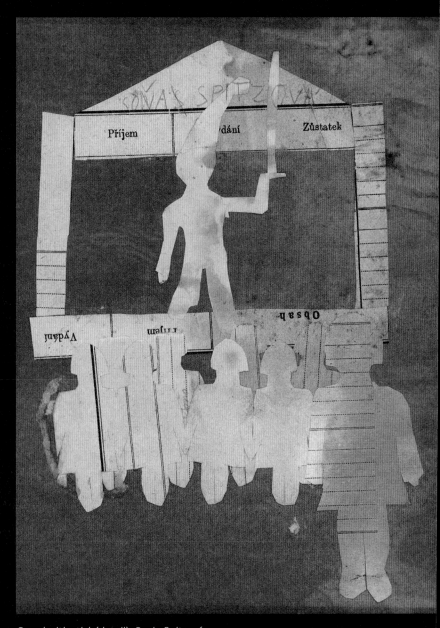

⊙ **ELIE WIESEL**, *INTERVIEW WITH HARRY J. CARGAS*

The only justice would be if I could bring back, if not six million, at least one person to life. But I cannot. The only other justice I would accept would be—and I mean it very profoundly, very sincerely—the coming of the Messiah…. I don't feel any theology of the Holocaust is possible except this one: if the Messiah were to come…. This is the only response possible because otherwise, nothing is a response.

Elie Wiesel (1928–2016) was awarded the Nobel Peace Prize in 1986 for his life's work as a "messenger to mankind" that the lessons of the Holocaust and the voices of its victims should never be forgotten. Wiesel authored more than 50 books, including *Night*, a work based on his experiences as a prisoner in the Auschwitz (to which he was deported at age 15), Buna, and Buchenwald concentration camps; and *The Trial of G-d*, which he based on a scene he witnessed in Auschwitz where three Jews convened a *bet-din* (court of Torah law) and put G-d on trial for the sufferings inflicted on the

Guard with stick (detail), Sonja Spitzová,
Theresienstadt concentration camp, circa 1942.
Sonja was born in 1931 and was deported to Auschwitz
in October of 1944, where she perished.

THE JEW IN THE FREE WORLD

The modern era brought emancipation for the Jew, and an entirely new set of challenges. With the advent of the Enlightenment movement in 18th-century Europe, and the American and French revolutions it spawned, the world was set on a course that would eventually bring civil rights and equal opportunity to the plurality of the Jewish people. But will the Jew who is treated like everyone else become like everyone else? In the "old country," Jewish learning and the traditional Jewish way of life flourished despite—some would say because of—the strictures of discrimination and persecution. Could they flourish in the unfettered freedom of this new world?

 GEORGE WASHINGTON, *LETTER TO THE HEBREW CONGREGATION OF NEWPORT, AUGUST 18, 1790*

The citizens of the United States of America have a right to applaud themselves for having given to mankind examples of an enlarged and liberal policy—a policy worthy of imitation. All possess alike liberty of conscience and immunities of citizenship.

It is now no more that toleration is spoken of as if it were the indulgence of one class of people that another enjoyed the exercise of their inherent natural rights, for, happily, the Government of the United States, which gives to bigotry no sanction, to persecution no assistance, requires only that they who live under its protection should demean themselves as good citizens in giving it on all occasions their effectual support....

May the children of the stock of Abraham who dwell in this land continue to merit and enjoy the good will of the other inhabitants—while every one shall sit in safety under his own vine and fig tree, and there shall be none to make him afraid.

May the father of all mercies scatter light, and not darkness, upon our paths, and make us all in our several vocations useful here, and in His own due time and way everlastingly happy.

 JONATHAN D. SARNA *AMERICAN JUDAISM, PP. 162–163*

Many Jews ... felt that they had no choice when it came to Saturday work.... With the six-day work week commonplace and Sunday closing laws strictly enforced, unsympathetic employers decreed that "if you don't come in on Saturday, don't bother coming in on Monday...." Some pious Jews, of course, continued to preserve their Sabbath at all costs. The courageous tales they told about themselves years later, however, strongly suggest that in an earlier day they stood forlornly in the minority.

The wealthy Orthodox builder and communal leader Harry Fischel (1865–1948), for example, looked back on his "early struggles" over Sabbath observance as the defining "spiritual conflict" of his life.... After weeks of searching for work as a new immigrant, Fischel recalled,

The Butcher Shop,
George Segal,
United States, 1965

he found the job of his dreams in an architecture firm. He worked happily for five days and then requested to take Saturday off at no pay so he could observe the Sabbath. His request was firmly denied, and he was ordered to come into work or lose his job…. After a sleepless night, he resolved to compromise: "He would not give up his position, but before going to work he would attend services in the synagogue." The very existence of early-morning Sabbath services for those who needed to work is, of course, deeply revealing. His worship complete, Fischel prepared to go to his office, but the sight of other Jews observing the Sabbath and the shock that he knew his parents would experience "could they but know the step he contemplated" gave him pause: "Suddenly, although the day was in mid-August and the heat was stifling … [a] chill went through every fibre of his being…." In the clarity of the moment, "he knew that neither then nor later would it ever be

possible for him to desecrate the Sabbath." Fischel lost his job but subsequently prospered—good fortune that he credited to his lifelong "principle" of Sabbath-observance.

 ALAN DERSHOWITZ
THE VANISHING AMERICAN JEW, PP. 1–2

American Jewish life is in danger of disappearing, just as most American Jews have achieved everything we ever wanted: acceptance, influence, affluence, equality. As the result of skyrocketing rates of intermarriage and assimilation, as well as "the lowest birth rate of any religious or ethnic community in the United States," the era of enormous Jewish influence on American life may soon be coming to an end…. One Harvard study predicts that if current demographic trends continue, the American Jewish community is likely to number less than one million and conceivably as few as 10,000 by the time the United States celebrates its tricentennial in 2076….

THE CHABAD PHENOMENON

When the sixth rebbe (Hasidic leader) of Chabad-Lubavitch, R. Yosef Yitzchak Schneersohn (1880–1950), having escaped from both Stalinist persecution in Soviet Russia and the horrors of Nazi-occupied Poland, arrived in New York in the winter of 1940, he was advised by his American supporters that "America is different." Any attempt at resurrecting the traditional Jewish life that flourished in the old country, the Rebbe was told, was doomed to failure. R. Yosef Yitzchak refused to accept this "truism." While other Jewish religious leaders concentrated on nurturing the remnants of their devastated communities, he set his sights outward, dispatching his followers to revive dying communities and seed new ones across the United States and throughout the world. These worldwide outreach and community-building activities increased exponentially under his son-in-law and successor, R. Menachem Mendel Schneerson (1902–1994). Today, the Chabad-Lubavitch movement is recognized as the primary force behind the post-Holocaust renaissance of Jewish life, and has established vibrant Jewish communities in more than 4,000 locales in every part of the globe.

LEVI FREIDIN / JEM

A "mitzvah tank" in the streets of Manhattan, New York, 1975

Emblem of Tzivos Hashem, a New York-based Jewish children's club founded in 1980. Children rise in rank by doing mitzvot and good deeds.

Jews have faced dangers in the past, but this time we may be unprepared to confront the newest threat to our survival as a people, because its principal cause is our own success as individuals. Our long history of victimization has prepared us to defend against those who would destroy us out of hatred…. But today's most serious threats come not from those who would persecute us, but from those who would, without any malice, kill us with kindness—by assimilating us, marrying us, and merging with us out of respect, admiration, and even love.

ARON MOSS

Why be Jewish?

QUESTION: I am teaching a high school class about threats to Judaism in the modern world. What do you see as the biggest threat to Jewish survival—assimilation or antisemitism?

ANSWER: The biggest threat to Jewish survival is confused Jewish identity. Sadly, today in many Jewish schools and families, Jewish identity is built through teaching Holocaust awareness and a fear of marrying out. The Jewish community's preoccupation with assimilation and antisemitism is not the solution, it is the problem.

A pessimistic and negative presentation of being Jewish turns off young Jews more than anything else. When we obsess about antisemitism we paint ourselves as perpetual victims. When we overemphasize the threat of assimilation, it makes us feel like an endangered species. The Jews are alongside the humpback whale and the giant panda in the list of helpless and pitiful communities disappearing from the planet. Is it so surprising that young Jews are opting out of Judaism? Who wants to be a victim?

We have to stop defining ourselves by the way others perceive us. Assimilation is when non-Jews love us so much they want to marry us. Antisemitism is when non-Jews hate us so much they want to kill us. They both just happen to us; but what do we think of ourselves? What reason do *we* have to stay Jewish?

Judaism is the most powerful idea that the world has ever seen. The Jewish people should survive because we have a message that the world needs to hear.

The Jewish way of life is a revolutionary force that can transform ordinary lives into lives of meaning. A family that keeps Shabbat is always reminded of what is really important—that there is more to life than accumulating wealth. The kosher laws teach us that we are not mere animals that must feed our every urge and desire, and that eating itself can be holy. A mezuzah on the door tells the world that this home is built for a higher purpose.

Judaism teaches lessons that the world urgently needs to learn—that every individual person is created in the divine image, and is therefore unique and valuable; that morality is not relative but absolute; that humans are partners with G-d in creation, with a mission to create heaven on earth.

These bold Jewish ideas are more relevant now than ever. But bold Jewish ideas need bold Jewish people to perpetuate them. We can only make the world into a divine home if we start with our own home.

The Jewish feeling we need to develop in ourselves and in our children is not fear of antisemitism, or guilt about assimilation. It is a humble pride in the greatness of the Jewish mission and a confident resolve to fulfill it.

timeline of Jewish population

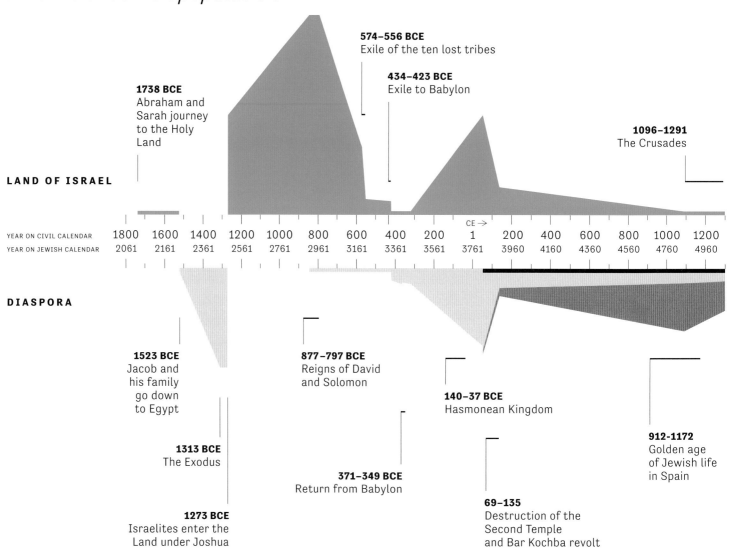

1738 BCE
Abraham and
Sarah journey
to the Holy
Land

574–556 BCE
Exile of the ten lost tribes

434–423 BCE
Exile to Babylon

1096–1291
The Crusades

LAND OF ISRAEL

YEAR ON CIVIL CALENDAR	1800	1600	1400	1200	1000	800	600	400	200	CE → 1	200	400	600	800	1000	1200
YEAR ON JEWISH CALENDAR	2061	2161	2361	2561	2761	2961	3161	3361	3561	3761	3960	4160	4360	4560	4760	4960

DIASPORA

1523 BCE
Jacob and
his family
go down
to Egypt

877–797 BCE
Reigns of David
and Solomon

140–37 BCE
Hasmonean Kingdom

1313 BCE
The Exodus

371–349 BCE
Return from Babylon

912-1172
Golden age
of Jewish life
in Spain

69–135
Destruction of the
Second Temple
and Bar Kochba revolt

1273 BCE
Israelites enter the
Land under Joshua

Jewish population tallies

LAND OF ISRAEL

DIASPORA

TOTAL

	1738 BCE	1273 BCE	800 BCE	423 BCE	50 CE	135	1090
LAND OF ISRAEL			5,000,000	10,000	2,500,000	700,000	35,000
DIASPORA			10,000	310,000	2,000,000	600,000	1,475,000
TOTAL	**2**	**2,500,000**	**5,010,000**	**320,000**	**4,500,000**	**1,300,000**	**1,510,000**

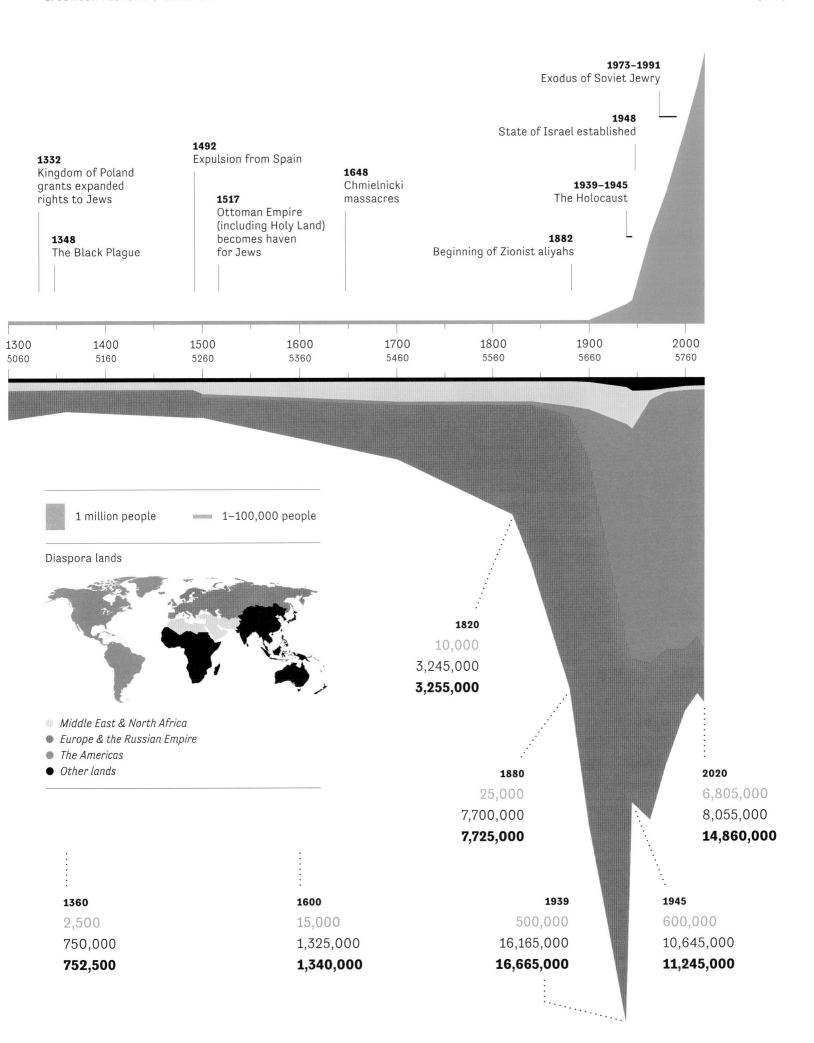

1332
Kingdom of Poland
grants expanded
rights to Jews

1348
The Black Plague

1492
Expulsion from Spain

1517
Ottoman Empire
(including Holy Land)
becomes haven
for Jews

1648
Chmielnicki
massacres

1882
Beginning of Zionist aliyahs

1939–1945
The Holocaust

1948
State of Israel established

1973–1991
Exodus of Soviet Jewry

1300
5060

1400
5160

1500
5260

1600
5360

1700
5460

1800
5560

1900
5660

2000
5760

1 million people

1–100,000 people

Diaspora lands

Middle East & North Africa
Europe & the Russian Empire
The Americas
Other lands

1820
10,000
3,245,000
3,255,000

1880
25,000
7,700,000
7,725,000

2020
6,805,000
8,055,000
14,860,000

1360
2,500
750,000
752,500

1600
15,000
1,325,000
1,340,000

1939
500,000
16,165,000
16,665,000

1945
600,000
10,645,000
11,245,000

THE JEWISH CONTRIBUTION

"I will make you into a great nation," were G-d's words to Abraham as the latter set out on his epochal journey. "And all families of the earth will be blessed through you" (Genesis 12:2–3).

First and foremost, of course, are the spiritual and moral blessings that the Jewish people have imparted to all families of the earth: the truths and ethos of monotheism, upon which the belief systems of half the world's population are founded; and the principles—the sanctity of human life, equality before the law, charity, and the pursuit of peace—that form the bedrock of human civilization.

But the Jewish contribution to the world also includes blessings of a more material nature. Jewish achievements in science, philosophy, medicine, economics, technology, mathematics, literature, art, entertainment, and virtually every other field of human endeavor have enriched the peoples of the world in every era of Jewish history.

 **MAIMONIDES,** *MISHNEH TORAH,*
LAWS OF KINGS, 8:10–11

Moses bequeathed the Torah and the mitzvot only to the people of Israel, as it says (Deuteronomy 33:4), "[The Torah that Moses commanded us] is the inheritance of the congregation of Jacob"; and to all those who desire to convert from among the other nations, as it says (Numbers 15:15), "the convert shall be the same as you." But a non-Jew who does not desire to accept Torah and mitzvot should not be compelled to do so.

Moses also instructed, at G-d's behest, to compel all inhabitants of the world to observe the mitzvot commanded to the children of Noah.... Anyone who accepts these seven mitzvot and is careful to fulfill them is regarded as one of the righteous amongst the nations of the world, and has a share in the World to Come. But they must accept them and fulfill them not merely because their mind agrees with them, but because G-d commanded them in the Torah.

 **JOHN ADAMS,** *LETTER TO FRANÇOIS ADRIAAN*
VAN DER KEMP, 16 FEBRUARY 1809

I will insist that the Hebrews have done more to civilize men than any other nation. If I were an atheist and believed in blind eternal fate, I should still believe that fate had ordained the Jews to be the most essential instrument for civilizing the nations. If I were an atheist of the other sect, who believe or pretend to believe that all is ordered by chance, I should believe that chance had ordered the Jews to preserve and propagate to all mankind the doctrine of a supreme, intelligent, wise, almighty Sovereign of the universe, which I believe to be the great essential principle of all morality, and consequently of all civilization.

 **THOMAS CAHILL,** *THE GIFTS OF THE JEWS,*
PP. 156–157, 239–241, 248–250

The Jews were the first people to develop an integrated view of life and its obligations. Rather than imagining the demands of law and the demands of wisdom as discrete realms (as did the Sumerians, the Egyptians, and the Greeks), they imagined that all of life, having come from the Author of life, was to be governed by a single outlook. The material and the spiritual, the intellectual and the moral were one....

The great formula is not that there is one G-d but that "G-d is One." From this insight will flow not only the integrating and universalist propensities of Western philosophy but even the possibility of modern science. For life is not a series of discrete experiences, influenced by diverse forces. We do not live in a fragmented universe, controlled by fickle and warring gods.... Because G-d is One, life is a moral continuum—and reality makes sense....

The Jews gave us a whole new vocabulary, a whole new Temple of the Spirit, an inner landscape of ideas and feelings that had never been known before.... We dream Jewish dreams and hope Jewish hopes. Most of our best words, in fact—*new, adventure, surprise;*

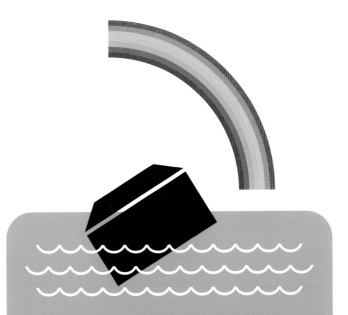

THE NOAHIDE LAWS Judaism famously does not proselytize. This attitude derives from the belief that every human being is created in the divine image, and can fulfill their purpose in life without becoming a Jew or assuming the obligation to fulfill the 613 mitzvot of the Torah.

Yet Judaism does have a universal message. It believes that there is a set of mitzvot—divine commandments—which the Creator gave to the entire human race: a universal moral code, predicated on the acceptance of a Higher Authority to whom every person is accountable for their actions, that is the foundation of a just and civilized society.

There are seven fundamental "Noahide laws," so called in reference to Noah, to whom G-d gave these mitzvot as the basis for a renewed covenant between the Creator and His creation following the turmoil of the Flood. These include prohibitions against idolatry, blasphemy, murder, adultery and incest, and theft; the duty to establish courts of justice; and the prohibition to eat flesh torn from a living animal. The Noahide Code also includes the imperative to procreate and settle and civilize the world; to know and serve G-d; and to practice social justice and charity.

unique, individual, person, vocation, time, history, future; freedom, progress, spirit, faith, hope, justice—are the gifts of the Jews....

Nor can we imagine the great liberation movements of modern history without reference to the Bible. Without the Bible we would never have known the abolitionist movements, the prison-reform movement, the antiwar movement, the labor movement, the civil rights move-

ment, the movements of indigenous and dispossessed peoples for their human rights, the antiapartheid movement in South Africa, the Solidarity movement in Poland, the free-speech and pro-democracy movements in such Far Eastern countries as South Korea, the Philippines, and even China. These movements of modern times have all employed the language of the Bible; and it is even impossible to understand their great heroes and heroines—people like Harriet Tubman, Sojourner Truth, Mother Jones, Mahatma Gandhi, Martin Luther King, Cesar Chavez, Helder Camara, Oscar Romero, Rigoberta Menchu, Corazon Aquino, Nelson Mandela, Desmond Tutu, Charity Kaluki Ngilu, Harry Wu—without recourse to the Bible.

Beyond these movements, which have commonly taken the Book of Exodus as their blueprint, are other forces that have shaped our world, such as capitalism, communism, and democracy. Capitalism and communism are both bastard children of the Bible, for both are processive faiths, modeled on biblical faith and demanding of their adherents that they always hold in their hearts a belief in the future and keep before their eyes the vision of a better tomorrow, whether that tomorrow contains a larger gross domestic product or a workers' paradise. Neither ideology could have risen in the cyclical East, in Hinduism, Buddhism, Taoism, or Shinto. But because capitalism and communism are processive faiths without G-d, each is a form of madness—a fantasy without a guarantee. Democracy, in contrast, grows directly out of the Israelite vision of individuals, subjects of value because they are images of G-d, each with a unique and personal destiny. There is no way that it could ever have been "self-evident that all men are created equal" without the intervention of the Jews.... We are the undeserving recipients of this history of the Jews, this long, excessive, miraculous development of ethical monotheism without which our ideas of equality and personalism are unlikely ever to have matured in the way that they have.

famous Jews

Abraham Zacuto (1452–1515) Astronomer and mathematician.

Baruch Spinoza (1632–1677) Leading figure of modern Western philosophy.

Haym Salomon (1740–1785) Financier of the American Revolution.

Mayer Anschel Rothschild (1744–1812) Founding father of international finance.

David Ricardo (1772–1823) Economist.

Heinrich Heine (1797–1856) Poet and essayist.

Benjamin Disraeli (1804–1881) British prime minister.

Karl Marx (1818–1903) Economic and political theorist; revolutionary socialist.

Jacques Offenbach (1819-1880) Composer.

Levi Strauss (1829–1902) Entrepreneur; inventor of blue jeans.

Camille Pissarro (1830–1903) Impressionist painter.

Sarah Bernhardt (1844–1923) Actress.

Emma Lazarus (1849–1887) Poet; author of *The New Colossus*, inscribed on the base of the Statue of Liberty.

Paul Ehrlich (1854–1915) Nobel laureate; developed cure for syphilis.

Sigmund Freud (1856–1939) Pioneered the field of modern psychiatry.

Louis Brandeis (1856–1941) United States Supreme Court justice.

Emil Durkheim (1858–1917) Founder of sociology.

Henri Bergson (1859–1941) Philosopher; Nobel laureate.

Isaac Levitan (1860–1900) Painter.

Gustav Mahler (1860–1911) Composer and conductor.

Albert Kahn (1869–1942) Architect.

Rose and **Morris Michtom** (1870–1938) Creators of the teddy bear.

Rosa Luxemburg (1871–1919) Socialist revolutionary.

Marcel Proust (1871–1922) Novelist.

Leon Blum (1872–1950) Prime minister of France.

Gertrude Stein (1874–1946) Leading figure of the modernist movement.

Martin Buber (1878–1965) Philosopher and author; popularizer of Hasidism.

Lise Meitner (1878–1968) Physicist; co-discoverer of nuclear fission.

Leon Trotsky (1879–1940) Communist theorist and revolutionary.

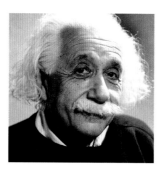

Albert Einstein (1879–1955) Pioneering theorist of modern physics.

Samuel Goldwyn (1879–1974) Pioneering American movie producer.

Fiorello LaGuardia (1882–1947) Reformist mayor of New York City.

Franz Kafka (1883–1924) Writer.

Amadeo Modigliani (1884–1920) Painter and sculptor.

Niels Bohr (1885–1962) Physicist; pioneer of quantum mechanics.

Al Jolson (1886–1950) Entertainer.

Groucho, Harpo, Chico, and **Zeppo Marx** (1887–1979) Comic actors.

Marc Chagall (1887–1985) Painter.

S. Y. Agnon (1888–1970) Hebrew writer; Nobel laureate.

Irving Berlin (1888–1989) Lyricist and composer.

Boris Pasternak (1890–1960) Writer; Nobel laureate.

Henry Morgenthau, Jr. (1891–1967) Secretary of the U.S. Treasury.

Nelly Sachs (1891–1970) Poet; Nobel laureate.

David Sarnoff (1891–1971) Head of RCA; radio and television industry leader.

Jacques Lifschitz (1891–1973) Sculptor.

Walter Benjamin (1892–1940) Philosopher and literary critic.

Isaac Babel (1894-1940) Writer.

Jack Benny (1894–1974) Comedian.

George Gershwin (1898–1937) Composer and songwriter.

Molly Picon (1898–1992) Actress.

Leo Strauss (1899–1973) Philosopher.

Laszlo Biro (1899–1985) Inventor of the ballpoint pen.

Hyman Rickover (1900–1986) Developer of America's nuclear-powered navy.

Moe Berg (1902–1972) Pro baseball player; U.S. intelligence agent.

Isaac Bashevis Singer (1902–1991) Yiddish novelist; Nobel laureate.

Karl Popper (1902–1994) Philosopher of science and social theory.

John von Neumann (1903–1957) Pioneer of computer science.

Vladimir Horowitz (1903–1989) Pianist.

Robert Oppenheimer (1904–1967) Physicist; headed the Manhattan Project.

Jacob Javitz (1904–1986) U.S. Senator.

Ayn Rand (1905–1982) Writer and philosopher.

Moe Asch (1905–1986) Recorder and archiver of folk and ethnic music.

Hannah Arendt (1906–1975) Author and theorist.

Emmanuel Levinas (1906–1995) Philosopher.

Estee Lauder (1906–2004) Businesswoman.

Abraham Joshua Heschel (1907–1972) Author and civil rights activist.

Abraham Maslow (1908–1970) Psychologist; formulated the "hierarchy of needs" pyramid.

Arthur Goldberg (1908–1990) United States Supreme Court justice, cabinet member, and U.N. ambassador.

Claude Levi-Strauss (1908–2009) Anthropologist.

Simone Weil (1909–1943) Philosopher and activist.

Saul Alinsky (1909–1972) Radical labor and community organizer.

Benny Goodman (1909–1986) Musician.

Sir Isaac Berlin (1909–1997) Social philosopher.

Paul Zoll (1911–1999) Pioneering cardiologist; co-developer of the pacemaker and defibrillator.

Milton Friedman (1912–2006) Economist; Nobel laureate.

Richard Tucker (1913–1975) Tenor.

Jonas Salk (1914–1995) Developer of the polio vaccine.

Arthur Miller (1915–2005) Playwright.

Herman Wouk (1915–2019) Author.

Sid Luckman (1916–1998) Pro football quarterback.

Kirk Douglas (1916-2020) Actor, writer, and philanthropist.

Red Auerbach (1917–2006) Record-holding coach of Boston Celtics.

Richard Feynman (1918–1988) Physicist.

Leonard Bernstein (1918–1990) Pianist, composer, and conductor.

Isaac Asimov (1920–1992) Author of science fiction and popular science.

Shelley Winters (1920–2006) Actress.

Thomas Kuhn (1922–1996) Physicist, historian, and philosopher of science.

Joseph Heller (1923–1999) Novelist.

Norman Mailer (1923–2007) Writer.

Henry Kissinger (1923–) U.S. Secretary of State; Cold War strategist.

Ed Koch (1924–2013) Mayor of New York.

Sammy Davis Jr. (1925–1990) Entertainer.

Maya Plisetskaya (1925–2015) Ballet dancer.

Allen Ginsberg (1926–1997) Beat generation poet and mystic.

Mel Brooks (1926–) Actor.

Maurice Sendak (1928–2012) Children's author.

Dolph Schayes (1928–2015) Pro basketball hall-of-famer.

Cynthia Ozick (1928–) Writer.

Jacques Derrida (1930–2004) Founder of Deconstructionism.

Robert Aumann (1930–) Developer of game theory; Nobel laureate.

Leonard Nimoy (1931–2015) Actor, film director, musician, and photographer.

Paul Krassner (1932–2019) Author and radical satirist.

Joan Rivers (1933–2014) Comedian.

Philip Roth (1933–2018) Novelist.

Ruth Bader Ginsburg (1933–2020) United States Supreme Court justice.

Arno Alan Penzias (1933–) Physicist.

Leonard Cohen (1934–2016) Author and musician.

Sandy Koufax (1935–) Major league pitcher.

Woody Allen (1935–) Filmmaker.

Bob Dylan (1941–) Singer and songwriter; Nobel laureate.

Neil Diamond (1941–) Singer-songwriter.

Bernie Sanders (1941–) U.S. Senator.

Paul Simon and **Art Garfunkel** (1941–) Singers and songwriters.

Elizabeth Holtzman (1941–) U.S. Congresswoman.

Barbra Streisand (1941–) Singer and actress.

Carole King (1942–) Songwriter and performer.

Joseph Lieberman (1942–) U.S. Senator; vice-presidential candidate.

Calvin Klein (1942–) Fashion designer.

James Levine (1943–) Conductor.

Itzhak Perlman (1945–) Violinist.

Steven Spielberg (1946–) Filmmaker.

Daniel Libeskind (1946–) Architect.

Billy Joel (1949–) Singer and songwriter.

Mark Spitz (1950–) Olympic swimmer.

Charles Schumer (1950–) U.S. Senate Majority Leader.

Jerry Seinfeld (1954–) Comedian.

Steve Ballmer (1956–) CEO of Microsoft.

Rahm Emanuel (1959–) White House chief of staff; mayor of Chicago.

Larry Page and **Sergey Brin** (1973–) Co-founders of Google.

Volodymyr Zelensky (1978–) President of Ukraine

Ivanka Trump (1981–) Businesswoman and political activist.

Scarlett Johansson (1984–) Actress.

Mark Zuckerberg (1984–) Creator of Facebook.

THE STRIVING FOR REDEMPTION

If the 3,800-year saga of Jewish history has one pervasive theme, it is the unwavering faith in the future of a redeemed and perfected world. First proclaimed by Moses and the prophets of ancient Israel, the hope and striving for the Messianic redemption is immortalized in the words of the *Ani Maamin* ("I believe") declaration included in the Jewish prayer book:

אֲנִי מַאֲמִין בֶּאֱמוּנָה שְׁלֵמָה
בְּבִיאַת הַמָּשִׁיחַ
וְאַף עַל פִּי שֶׁיִּתְמַהְמֵהַּ
עִם כָּל זֶה אֲחַכֶּה לוֹ בְּכָל יוֹם שֶׁיָּבוֹא

I believe with complete faith
  in the coming of Mashiach
Although he may tarry
  nevertheless, I await his coming every day

"The melody is the pen of the soul," say the Hasidic masters, and many songs expressing the all-pervading striving for redemption were composed over the centuries. A particularly poignant example is the tune composed for the words of *Ani Maamin* by Azriel David Fastag in a cattle car on the way to the Nazi death camp Treblinka. Today, Fastag's *Ani Maamin* is sung in Jewish communities throughout the world, and stands as a testament to the inextinguishable faith of the Jewish people.

For more on Mashiach and the future redemption, see pages 225–227 in the "Philosophy and Beliefs" section of this book.

Ani Maamin *composed by Azriel David Fastag*
on the train to Treblinka

MUSIC NOTATION: AVREMI G

Jewish Teaching

286

מאמתי קורין את שמע בערבים
משעה שהכהנים נכנסים לאכל
בתרומתן עד סוף האשמורת
הראשונ֗ דברי אליעזר וחכ אומ
עד חצות רבן גמליאל אומ עד
שיעלה עמוד השחר
מעשה שבאו בניו מבית המשתה
אמרו לו לא קרינו את שמע אמר
להם אם לא עלה עמוד השחר אמ֗

"Torah" means "teaching" and "instruction." In its narrower sense, the term refers to the Five Books of Moses, the core text of Judaism. In its broader sense, the Torah is the entire body of Jewish teaching deriving from the divine communication received by Moses at Mount Sinai and handed down and expounded through the generations.

What is the Torah? Is it the constitution of the Jewish people and their private marriage contract with G-d, or is it the Jew's message to the world?

Is it a chronicle of historical events and practical directives, or a profound parable conveying the meaning of life and a roadmap for its winding pathways?

Is it the revealed word of G-d zealously preserved through the millennia, or the most ambitious human attempt to make sense of ourselves, our Creator, and the world in which we live?

The answer to each of the above questions is: it is both. It is fully the one and it is fully the other. And it is fully the one because it is fully the other.

No single book, much less a section in a book, could possibly survey the whole of Torah, which spans many thousands of works composed in 3,300-plus years since Sinai. Rather, in these pages we offer a representative sampling from some of the many streams that flow from the font of Torah.

Torah pointer, Europe or United States, 19th–mid 20th century

Mishnah, the Kaufmann manuscript, Land of Israel or Italy, 10th or 11th century

Bukharan cheder, Samarkand, Russian Turkestan, 1905–1915

SERGEY PROKUDIN-GORSKY

 TALMUD, *SUKKAH 42a*

From when a child knows how to speak, his father teaches him the verse (Deuteronomy 33:4), "The Torah that Moses commanded us is the inheritance of the congregation of Jacob."

 DEUTERONOMY 4:5–6

See, I have taught you statutes and laws, as the Lord my G-d has commanded me…. Keep them and do them, for this is your wisdom and your understanding in the eyes of the nations, who will hear all these statutes and say: "Only this great nation is a wise and understanding people."

 MIDRASH RABBAH, *BEREISHITH 1:1*

An architect who builds a palace does not do so on his own; he has scrolls and notebooks which he consults on how to place the rooms, where to set the doors. So, too, G-d looked into the Torah and created the world.

 ZOHAR, *VOL. 2, 161b*

G-d looked into the Torah and created the world. Man looks into the Torah and sustains the world.

 R. SCHNEUR ZALMAN OF LIADI
EXCERPTED FROM *TANYA, CHAPTER 5*

When the human mind grasps a certain idea, the idea is held within the mind and enveloped by it, while simultaneously the mind is immersed within the idea and enveloped by it…. Now, a law in the Torah is the wisdom and will of G-d, who desired that if, for example, Reuben will claim such-and-such and Simeon will argue such-and-such, then the ruling should be such-and-such. Consequently, a person who studies this Torah law apprehends, grasps, and envelops within their mind the very wisdom and will of G-d, while at the same time, the person's mind is enveloped by them. This makes for a wonderful union, which has no parallel anywhere in the physical world, whereby two entities attain absolute oneness and unity from every side and angle.

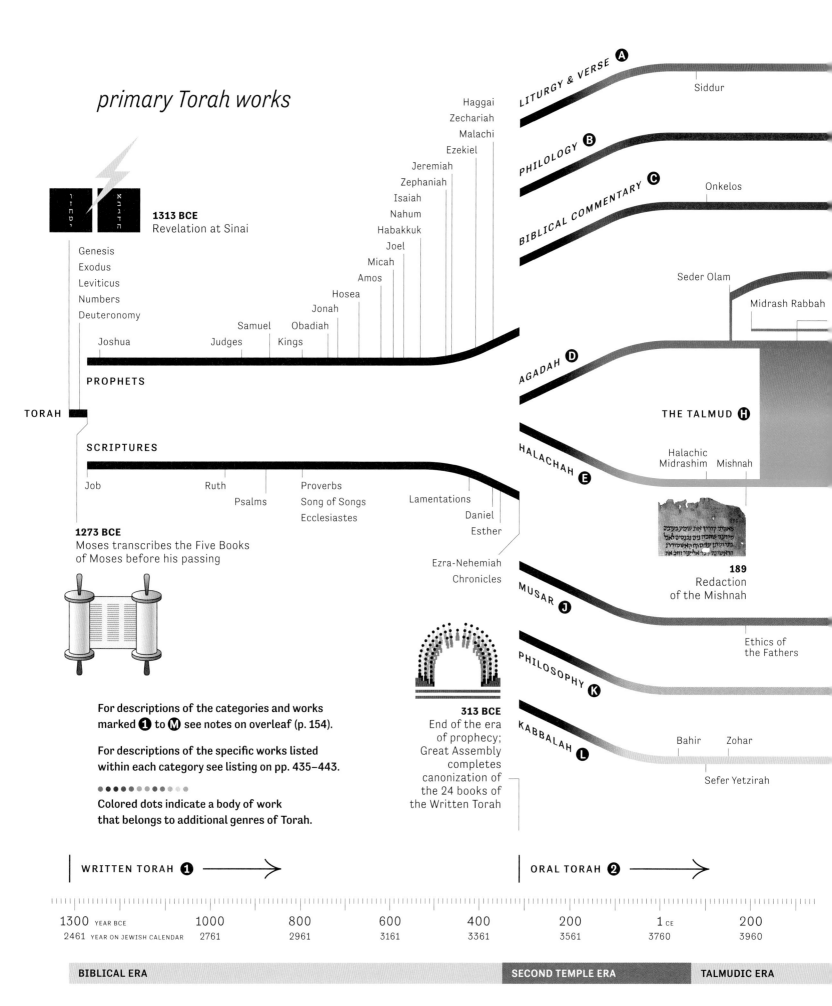

primary Torah works

LITURGY & VERSE Ⓐ
    Siddur

PHILOLOGY Ⓑ

BIBLICAL COMMENTARY Ⓒ
    Onkelos

Haggai
Zechariah
Malachi
Ezekiel
Jeremiah
Zephaniah
Isaiah
Nahum
Habakkuk
Joel
Micah
Amos
Hosea
Jonah
Obadiah

1313 BCE
Revelation at Sinai

Genesis
Exodus
Leviticus
Numbers
Deuteronomy

Joshua   Judges   Kings   Samuel

PROPHETS

Seder Olam

Midrash Rabbah

AGADAH Ⓓ

THE TALMUD Ⓗ

TORAH

SCRIPTURES

HALACHAH Ⓔ

Halachic
Midrashim   Mishnah

Job   Ruth   Proverbs
   Psalms   Song of Songs
        Ecclesiastes

Lamentations
   Daniel
   Esther

1273 BCE
Moses transcribes the Five Books
of Moses before his passing

189
Redaction
of the Mishnah

Ezra-Nehemiah
Chronicles

MUSAR Ⓙ

Ethics of
the Fathers

For descriptions of the categories and works
marked ❶ to Ⓜ see notes on overleaf (p. 154).

For descriptions of the specific works listed
within each category see listing on pp. 435–443.

●●●●●●●●●●● ● ●
Colored dots indicate a body of work
that belongs to additional genres of Torah.

PHILOSOPHY Ⓚ

313 BCE
End of the era
of prophecy;
Great Assembly
completes
canonization of
the 24 books of
the Written Torah

KABBALAH Ⓛ

Bahir   Zohar

Sefer Yetzirah

| WRITTEN TORAH ❶ ⟶ | | ORAL TORAH ❷ ⟶ |

1300 YEAR BCE	1000	800	600	400	200	1 CE	200
2461 YEAR ON JEWISH CALENDAR	2761	2961	3161	3361	3561	3760	3960

| BIBLICAL ERA | SECOND TEMPLE ERA | TALMUDIC ERA |

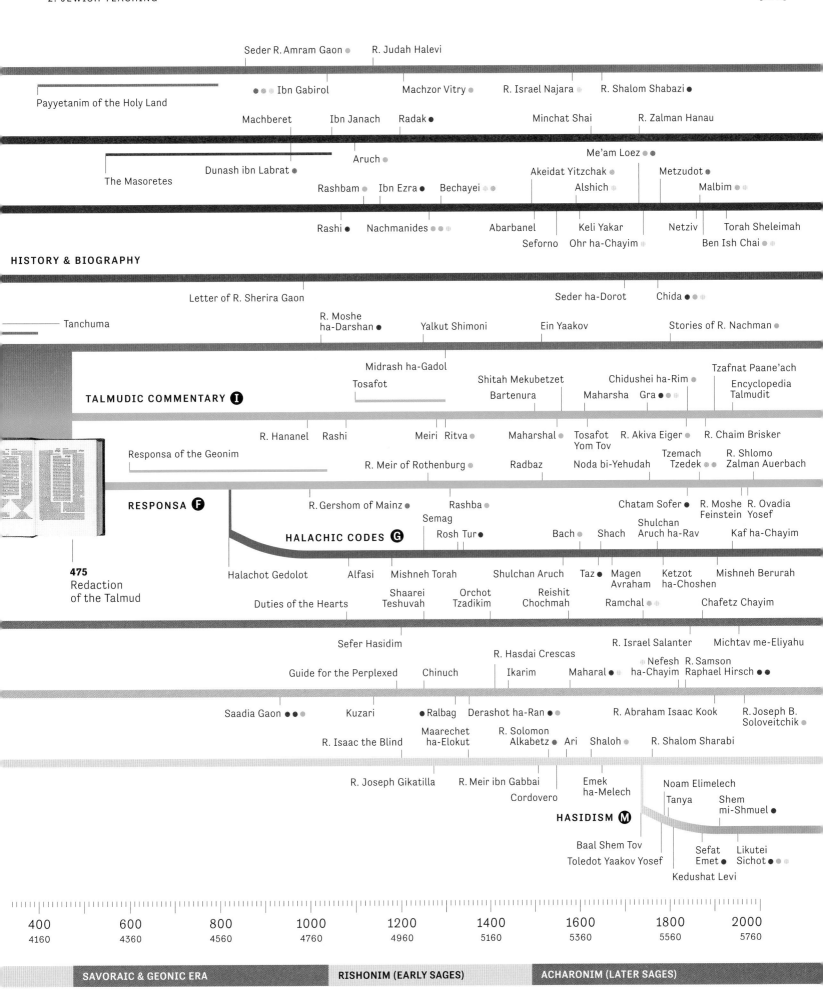

Seder R. Amram Gaon   R. Judah Halevi

Payyetanim of the Holy Land   Ibn Gabirol   Machzor Vitry   R. Israel Najara   R. Shalom Shabazi

Machberet   Ibn Janach   Radak   Minchat Shai   R. Zalman Hanau

The Masoretes   Dunash ibn Labrat   Aruch   Me'am Loez   Metzudot

Rashbam   Ibn Ezra   Bechayei   Akeidat Yitzchak   Malbim
Alshich

Rashi   Nachmanides   Abarbanel   Keli Yakar   Netziv   Torah Sheleimah
Seforno   Ohr ha-Chayim   Ben Ish Chai

HISTORY & BIOGRAPHY

Letter of R. Sherira Gaon   Seder ha-Dorot   Chida

Tanchuma   R. Moshe ha-Darshan   Yalkut Shimoni   Ein Yaakov   Stories of R. Nachman

Midrash ha-Gadol   Tzafnat Paane'ach

Tosafot   Shitah Mekubetzet   Chidushei ha-Rim   Encyclopedia Talmudit
Bartenura   Maharsha   Gra

TALMUDIC COMMENTARY ⓘ

R. Hananel   Rashi   Meiri   Ritva   Maharshal   Tosafot Yom Tov   R. Akiva Eiger   R. Chaim Brisker

Responsa of the Geonim   R. Meir of Rothenburg   Radbaz   Noda bi-Yehudah   Tzemach Tzedek   R. Shlomo Zalman Auerbach

RESPONSA Ⓕ   R. Gershom of Mainz   Rashba   Chatam Sofer   R. Moshe Feinstein   R. Ovadia Yosef
Semag
Rosh Tur   Bach   Shach   Shulchan Aruch ha-Rav   Kaf ha-Chayim
HALACHIC CODES Ⓖ

475
Redaction of the Talmud

Halachot Gedolot   Alfasi   Mishneh Torah   Shulchan Aruch   Taz   Magen Avraham   Ketzot ha-Choshen   Mishneh Berurah

Duties of the Hearts   Shaarei Teshuvah   Orchot Tzadikim   Reishit Chochmah   Ramchal   Chafetz Chayim

Sefer Hasidim   R. Israel Salanter   Michtav me-Eliyahu

Guide for the Perplexed   Chinuch   R. Hasdai Crescas   Nefesh ha-Chayim   R. Samson Raphael Hirsch
Ikarim   Maharal

Saadia Gaon   Kuzari   Ralbag   Derashot ha-Ran   R. Abraham Isaac Kook   R. Joseph B. Soloveitchik

R. Isaac the Blind   Maarechet ha-Elokut   R. Solomon Alkabetz   Ari   Shaloh   R. Shalom Sharabi

R. Joseph Gikatilla   R. Meir ibn Gabbai   Emek ha-Melech   Noam Elimelech
Cordovero   Tanya   Shem mi-Shmuel

HASIDISM Ⓜ

Baal Shem Tov   Sefat Emet   Likutei Sichot
Toledot Yaakov Yosef
Kedushat Levi

400	600	800	1000	1200	1400	1600	1800	2000
4160	4360	4560	4760	4960	5160	5360	5560	5760

SAVORAIC & GEONIC ERA   **RISHONIM (EARLY SAGES)**   **ACHARONIM (LATER SAGES)**

Notes for *Primary Torah Works* chart on the previous pages:

❶ WRITTEN TORAH The twenty-four books of the Jewish Bible. Also called *Tanach*, which is an acronym for its three components: *Torah* (the Five Books of Moses, also known as the *Chumash* and as the Pentateuch), *Nevi'im* ("prophets"), and *Ketuvim* ("writings" or "scriptures"). For specific descriptions of the 24 books, see table on pages 158–159, and the overview on pages 156–183.

❷ ORAL TORAH Collective name for the entire body of interpretation, exposition, and commentary that is part of the Torah's chain of transmission from Moses onward—in contrast to the "Written Torah" that was put into writing by Moses and the Biblical prophets. For more of the nature, role, history, and composition of the Oral Torah, see overview on pages 186–190.

Ⓐ LITURGY & VERSE The core texts of the **SIDDUR** (Jewish prayer book) were created by the sages of the Great Assembly in the 4th century BCE. Following the destruction of the Second Temple, R. Gamliel of Yavneh gave the Siddur its present structure and form (circa 76 CE). Later generations of Torah scholars composed prayers and *piyyutim* (liturgical poems) that were incorporated into the Siddur. Others composed devotional poetry as literary and inspirational works unto themselves.

Ⓑ PHILOLOGY The Masoretes were scholars and scribes, active in Tiberias, Jerusalem, and Babylonia between the 6th and 10th centuries, who preserved and recorded the tradition (*mesorah*) for the precise wording, spelling, pronunciation, and punctuation of the Written Torah, and produced manuscripts renowned for their accuracy. Most famous of these is the Aleppo Codex edited by Aaron ben Asher of Tiberias, c. 920 (see image and description on p. 157). Later philologists produced works systemizing Hebrew grammar and the philology of the Bible, which the Biblical commentaries would draw on in their explanation and analysis of the text.

Ⓒ THE BIBLICAL COMMENTARIES The words of the Written Torah are sometimes ambiguous, often concise, and always encapsulate many layers of meaning. Throughout the generations, numerous Torah scholars wrote commentaries on the Written Torah, as well as commentaries on their predecessors' commentaries.

Ⓓ AGADAH & MIDRASH The term *agadah* ("telling") denotes the non-legal teachings of the sages. These include ethical aphorisms, homilies, parables, and historical and biographical narratives. *Midrash* ("exposition") is a general name for expositions of Biblical verses cited by the sages of the Mishnah and the Talmud (c. 100 BCE to 400 CE). There are Halachic (legal) Midrashim as well as Agadic Midrashim. The **TALMUD** (see Ⓗ below) is a mix of both genres of Midrash, but the term is usually applied to anthologies not included in the Talmud itself.

Ⓔ HALACHAH ("the way"). The field of Torah law. Includes rulings pertaining to the details of the Biblical commandments (mitzvot) and the rabbinical ordinances, and the deliberations leading to these rulings (see overview on pages 202–213). The **MISHNAH**, compiled by R. Judah ha-Nasi in c. 189 CE, was the first official transcription of the Oral Torah (see table on p. 204, and description by Maimonides on p. 186).

Ⓕ HALACHIC RESPONSA A vast body of rabbinic literature documenting queries in Torah law sent to Halachic authorities, and their detailed reasoned responses. See pp. 206–207 for a sampling of the types of questions that these responsa addressed.

Ⓖ HALACHIC CODES Works that organize the legal rulings and practical instructions derived from Talmudic and Halachic literature, and the commentaries on these codes that discuss and debate the rulings they contain. See overview on pp. 204–205.

Ⓗ TALMUD ("learning"). The most important work of Judaism after the Bible. The Talmud is a multivolume compilation that incorporates the Mishnah (see entry for **HALACHAH** above) and appends to it teachings and deliberations (called *gemara*) by hundreds of sages over a period of close to 300 years, from the 3rd through 5th centuries. There are two versions of the Talmud—a "Jerusalem Talmud" compiled in the Holy Land in the 4th century, and the more comprehensive "Babylonian Talmud," completed toward the end of the 5th century. See pages 108–109 and pages 184–199.

Ⓘ TALMUDIC COMMENTARY The many thousands of works devoted to analyzing the laws, reasonings, and debates in the Talmud are among the most innovative and mind-sharpening areas of Torah learning (see infographic on pp. 192–193).

Ⓙ MUSAR ("exhortation" or "discipline"). Moral and ethical teachings addressing a person's inner life and the quest for piety and character refinement. See pages 244–256.

Ⓚ PHILOSOPHY Works exploring the beliefs, axioms, and philosophical reasonings implicit in the Torah. See overview on pp. 214–227.

Ⓛ KABBALAH ("received"). The mystical dimension of the Torah transmitted by tradition from master to disciple. See pages 228–243.

Ⓜ HASIDISM ("piety" and "benevolence"). Incorporating elements of the Torah's mystical, philosophical, and psychological teachings, Hasidism endeavors to reveal the "soul of Torah," thereby illuminating and integrating all genres of the Torah. See pages 232–236 and 242–243.

TALMUD, *BERACHOT 61b*

Once, the wicked government [of Rome] decreed that the Jewish people were forbidden to study the Torah. Papus ben Judah saw R. Akiva convening gatherings in public and studying Torah with them. Said he to him: "Akiva, are you not afraid of the government?"

Said R. Akiva to him: "I will answer you with a parable.

"A fox was walking along a river and saw fish rushing to-and-fro. Said he to them, 'What are you fleeing?'

"Said they to him, 'The nets that the humans spread for us.'

"Said he to them, 'Why don't you come out onto the dry land? We will live together, as my ancestors lived with your ancestors.'

"Said they to him, 'Is it you whom they call the wisest of animals? You're not wise, but foolish! If in our environment of life we have cause for fear, how much more so in the environment of our death!'

"The same applies to us. If now, when we sit and study the Torah, of which it is said (Deuteronomy 30:20), 'It is your life and the lengthening of your days,' such is our situation, how much more so if we neglect it."

MIDRASH RABBAH, *SHIR HASHIRIM 1:19*

The words of the Torah are compared to water, as it is written (Isaiah 55:1), "Ho! All who thirst, come to the waters."

As water extends from one end of the world to the other, so does the Torah extend from one end of the world to the other.

As water is life for the world, so is Torah life for the world.

As water is free for all, so is Torah free for all.

As water comes from heaven, so does Torah come from heaven.

As water comes with thunderous noise, so did Torah come with thunderous noise.

As water refreshes a person's soul, so does Torah refresh a person's soul.

As water purifies a person from uncleanliness, so does Torah purify a person from uncleanliness.

As water descends drop by drop and then becomes streams upon streams, so it is with Torah: a person learns two laws today and two laws tomorrow, until it becomes a flowing torrent.

As water leaves a high place and flows to a low place, so does Torah leave a haughty-minded person and cling to a humble person.

As water is best not stored in silver or gold but in the lowliest of vessels, so is Torah only preserved in a person who is unpretentious as a clay jug.

And just as with water, a great person is not ashamed to ask a lowly person for a drink of water, so too a great person is not ashamed to ask a lowly person, "Teach me a chapter, an idea, a word, or even a letter of Torah."

 R. ELIEZER PAPO
PELEH YO'ETZ, S.V. SEFER

Essential to Torah learning is the acquisition of *sefarim* (Torah books), both for the scholar—as the sages have declared, "As there cannot be a craftsman without tools, so there cannot be a scholar without books"—and for the layman, who also requires many books: the Biblical commentaries, works of moral teaching, handbooks of Torah law (in Hebrew for those who are proficient in the holy tongue, and in the vernacular for those who read the vernacular), as well as volumes of Tanach, Mishnah, the holy *Zohar*, and the like…. Spare no expense, "for love is fierce as death" (Song of Songs 8:6), and the love of G-d can only be achieved through the love of Torah.

The Bible

The Torah was communicated in two forms: written and spoken. Moses came down from Mount Sinai with two stone tablets, upon which the Ten Commandments were engraved by the divine hand—ten precepts that encapsulate the whole of Torah (see pp. 36–39 above). Over the course of the next 40 years, G-d communicated to Moses, and Moses transcribed, a more detailed articulation of the divine law, in the form of five books containing 613 commandments. These, and the writings of the prophets who followed Moses, constitute the "Written Torah," known to the world as "the Jewish Bible."

Moses also taught and explained the meaning of the text as he received it from G-d, along with the principles and methodology by which future generations should interpret and apply it. This is the "Oral Torah," which imparts authoritative meaning and perpetual relevance to the written text.

NOTE: THROUGHOUT THIS BOOK, THE SYMBOL 🕉 INDICATES A CITATION FROM THE WRITTEN TORAH

Torah case and finials, India, 1876

THE TORAH SCROLL The holiest object in Judaism is the *Sefer Torah*, a parchment scroll containing the Five Books of Moses. Each of the 304,805 letters of the text is meticulously written by hand by a trained religious scribe, called a *sofer*; if even a single missing, extra, or incorrectly formed letter is discovered in a Torah scroll, it is set aside and disqualified from use until the error is corrected. The result of this vigilance is a phenomenon unparalleled in the history of the written word: the Torah is a document that predates the printing press by more than 2,500 years, yet thousands of Jewish communities dispersed across the globe, many of which had little or no contact with each other for centuries, all possess the same text.

VOWEL AND CANTILLATION MARKS

The 22 letters of the Hebrew *aleph-bet* are all consonants, and in its basic written form (such as in a Torah scroll), the Written Torah is transcribed without vowels or punctuation marks. Supplementing the text are vowel points (*nekudot*) and cantillation marks (*taamim*) indicating the proper pronunciation and syntax, which are part of the Sinaic tradition. But the fact that these are not incorporated into the foundational text allows for alternative readings that provide additional layers of meaning beyond the plain sense of the text.

The Aleppo Codex (c. 920) is the oldest surviving manuscript containing the text of the Torah with the traditional vowel and cantillation markings.

OUT OF RESPECT FOR ITS SANCTITY, THE DIVINE NAME IS NOT FULLY REPRODUCED IN THESE IMAGES

THE 24 BOOKS OF THE WRITTEN TORAH

name of book		primary topics and themes	transcribed/authored
TORAH			
Genesis		Creation of the world; early human history; lives of the patriarchs and matriarchs of the people of Israel	transcribed by Moses
Exodus		The Exodus from Egypt; the giving of the Torah at Mount Sinai; the construction of the Tabernacle	
Leviticus		The Temple service; festivals of the Jewish year; legislation of ritualistic, social, and civil laws	
Numbers		Events of the Israelites' 40-year journey through the wilderness	
Deuteronomy		Moses' final address to the people of Israel before his passing; a review of many of the events and laws of the previous three books	
PROPHETS			
Joshua		Conquest of the Holy Land and its apportionment among the 12 tribes of Israel	Joshua
Judges		Events of the era of the Judges (see pp. 54–55)	Samuel
Samuel (I & II)		Lives and deeds of the prophet Samuel, King Saul, and King David	Samuel, Gad, and Nathan
Kings (I & II)		The reign of King Solomon and the building of the Holy Temple in Jerusalem; history of the kingdoms of Judah and Israel	Jeremiah
Isaiah		Prophecies of consolation over the Destruction and Exile; the reconciliation between G-d and Israel; the coming of Mashiach and the future Messianic age of peace, perfection, and divine revelation	authored by Isaiah; transcribed by Hezekiah and his court
Jeremiah		Warnings of the destruction of Jerusalem because of the people's sins and injustices; promise of the return of the Babylonian exiles after 70 years	Jeremiah
Ezekiel		Vision of the "divine chariot" that is the source for many of the mystical teachings of Kabbalah; prophecies of the future redemption, including a description of the third Holy Temple	authored by Ezekiel; transcribed by the Great Assembly
The Twelve	Hosea	The prophet Hosea is told to marry an unfaithful woman in order to experience firsthand G-d's interminable love for His people despite their unfaithfulness	transcribed by the Great Assembly
	Joel	The future day of judgment of the nations who persecuted the people of Israel; the divine enlightenment of the Messianic era	
	Amos	Denunciation of the exploitation of the weak and poor by the rich and powerful; the hypocrisy in serving G-d while failing to practice justice and charity	
	Obadiah	Establishment of the divine sovereignty in the Messianic era	

name of book	primary topics and themes	transcribed/authored
Jonah	The story of Jonah (see p. 333)	
Micah	Denunciation of moral and social corruption; a call to practice justice, kindness, and humility; the Messianic redemption	
Nahum	Prophecies delivered to the people of Israel, as well as to the Assyrian empire	
Habakkuk	The rise and fall of the Babylonian empire; the Messianic redemption	
Zephaniah	The future day of judgment; the time when all nations will unite to serve G-d	
Haggai	The return to Zion and the building of the second Holy Temple	
Zechariah	Mystical visions of angels and celestial worlds; the peace, prosperity, and spiritual renaissance of the future redemption	
Malachi	G-d's love for the people of Israel; rebuke of corrupt priests; Elijah's heralding of the future redemption and the reconciliation of parents and children	

SCRIPTURES

name of book	primary topics and themes	transcribed/authored
Psalms	Lyrical prayers and praises of G-d (see pp. 176–179)	composed by King David; includes psalms by Abraham, Moses, and other poets
Proverbs	Aphorisms on the virtues of wisdom, hard work, and a moral life	King Solomon
Job	Job and his three friends debate the question, "Why do the righteous suffer?"	Moses
Song of Songs	A love song that metaphorically describes the relationship of G-d and Israel	King Solomon
Ruth	The story of the Moabite princess who converted to Judaism and became the ancestor of King David	Samuel
Lamentations	Elegies mourning the destruction of the Holy Temple and the exile of Israel	Jeremiah
Ecclesiastes	Insights into the transience of life and the futility of worldly pursuits	King Solomon
Esther	The story of Purim (see pp. 360–365)	Esther and Mordecai
Daniel	Life and visions of Daniel, a Judean prince who served in the courts of Babylonian and Persian emperors; prophecies on the historical rise and fall of nations and on the timing of the Messianic redemption	authored by Daniel; transcribed by the Great Assembly
Ezra-Nehemiah	Describes the Jewish people's return from Babylon, the reestablishment of their commitment to the Torah, and the building of the second Holy Temple	Ezra and Nehemiah
Chronicles (I & II)	Summary of the whole of Biblical history	Ezra

THE WEEKLY PARASHAH

 MAIMONIDES, *MISHNEH TORAH,*
LAWS OF PRAYER, 12:1

Moses instituted for the people of Israel that they should read from the Torah in public each Shabbat, as well as on Monday and Thursday mornings, so that they should never go for three days without hearing the Torah. Ezra instituted they should also read from it on Shabbat afternoon.

 SHULCHAN ARUCH, *ORACH CHAYIM, 285:1–3*

In addition to listening to the public Torah readings in the synagogue, a person should also review the weekly reading on their own, in a manner of "twice scripture and once *targum*" (i.e., to read the Hebrew text of each verse twice, and its Aramaic translation by Onkelos one time).

Studying the weekly portion with Rashi's commentary is also considered as having reviewed it with the *targum*. A G-d-fearing person should read both the *targum* and Rashi.

 HAYOM YOM, *CHESHVAN 2*

In the early years of his leadership, R. Schneur Zalman of Liadi said to his disciples, "A person should live with the times." He later explained: One should live with the Torah portion (*parashah*) of the week, and with the section of the *parashah* that relates to each particular day; not just to study the daily section, but to also live with it.

THE ANNUAL TORAH READING CYCLE In order to complete the reading of the Torah in the course of the year, the Five Books of Moses are divided into 54 weekly readings called *parashiyot*. Each *parashah* is further divided into seven parts, for the seven people who are called up to read from the Torah during the Shabbat morning reading. This division also serves to allocate a specific portion of the *parashah* to each day of the week.

Because the number of weeks in the Jewish year varies (see "The Jewish Calendar" on p. 331), there can be anywhere between 48 and 54 weekly Torah readings in a given year. Therefore, certain *parashiyot* are sometimes paired with other *parashiyot* to form a joint two-*parashah* reading.

2,100-YEAR-OLD BIBLE "In the beginning G-d created the heavens and the earth..." A fragment of a parchment scroll from the late Hasmonean period (approx. 100–63 BCE) containing the opening verses of the Book of Genesis. Discovered in the Qumran Caves in the Judean desert in 1952.

the 54 parashiyot of the Torah

parashah name	verses	topics & themes
BOOK OF GENESIS		
Bereishith *"In the beginning"*	1:1 to 6:8	G-d creates the world; Adam and Eve in the Garden of Eden; Cain murders Abel; the ten generations from Adam to Noah.
Noach *"Noah"*	6:9 to 11:32	The great Flood; the tower of Babel; the 70 nations; the ten generations from Noah to Abraham.
Lech Lecha *"Go you"*	12:1 to 17:27	Abraham and Sarah journey to the Holy Land; G-d's covenant with Abraham and his descendants; Hagar and Ishmael; Abraham's circumcision.
Vayeira *"And he revealed himself"*	18:1 to 22:24	Visit of the three angels; destruction of Sodom; birth of Isaac; the binding of Isaac; the birth of Rebecca.
Chayei Sarah *"The life of Sarah"*	23:1 to 25:18	The passing and burial of Sarah; the marriage of Isaac and Rebecca.
Toledot *"Progeny"*	25:19 to 28:9	Jacob and Esau; Isaac in the land of the Philistines; Jacob steals the blessings.
Vayeitzei *"And he went out"*	28:10 to 32:3	Jacob's dream; Jacob's 20 years in Charan; his marriages to Leah and Rachel; the birth of eleven of the twelve tribes of Israel.
Vayishlach *"And he sent"*	32:4 to 36:43	Jacob's encounter with Esau; the rape of Dinah and the massacre of Shechem; Jacob is given the name "Israel"; the progeny of Esau.
Vayeishev *"And he settled"*	37:1 to 40:23	Joseph is sold into slavery by his brothers; the incident of Judah and Tamar; Joseph is libeled and imprisoned after rejecting the advances of Potiphar's wife.
Mikeitz *"At the end"*	41:1 to 44:17	Pharaoh's dreams; Joseph is appointed viceroy of Egypt; Joseph's brothers come to Egypt to purchase grain during the seven years of famine; Joseph tests his brothers by threatening to keep Benjamin as a slave.
Vayigash *"And he approached"*	44:18 to 47:27	Joseph reveals his identity to his brothers; Jacob and his family come down to Egypt.
Vayechi *"And he lived"*	47:28 to 50:26	Passing of Jacob and his blessings to his children; passing of Joseph; the promise of redemption.

parashah name	verses	topics & themes
BOOK OF EXODUS		
Shemot *"Names"*	1:1 to 6:1	Enslavement in Egypt; birth and early years of Moses; Moses at the burning bush; Moses and Aaron confront Pharaoh.
Va'eira *"And I revealed myself"*	6:2 to 9:35	The first seven plagues brought upon Egypt.
Bo *"Come in"*	10:1 to 13:16	The last three plagues; the Exodus from Egypt; the observances of Passover, consecration of the firstborn, and the mitzvah of *tefillin*.
Beshalach *"When he sent out"*	13:17 to 17:16	Splitting of the sea; the manna; the war with Amalek.
Yitro *"Jethro"*	18:1 to 20:23	Jethro visits the Israelite camp; the giving of the Torah at Mount Sinai; the Ten Commandments.
Mishpatim *"Judgments"*	21:1 to 24:18	Civil laws and torts given at Mount Sinai.
Terumah *"Uplifting"*	25:1 to 27:19	G-d instructs Moses on the building of the Tabernacle.
Tetzaveh *"You shall command"*	27:20 to 30:10	The instructions to Moses on the making of the priestly garments and on the inauguration of the Tabernacle.
Ki Tisa *"When you raise"*	30:11 to 34:35	Worship of the Golden Calf; Moses breaks the Tablets of the Covenant; the Second Tablets.
Vayak'hel *"And he assembled"*	35:1 to 38:20	Making of the Tabernacle.
Pekudei *"Accountings"*	38:21 to 40:38	Making of the priestly garments; Tabernacle assembled.

parashah name	verses	topics & themes

BOOK OF LEVITICUS

parashah name	verses	topics & themes
Vayikra *"And he called"*	1:1 to 5:26	Laws of the *korbanot* (animal and meal offerings brought in the Tabernacle and in the Holy Temple).
Tzav *"Command"*	6:1 to 8:36	More laws of *korbanot*; preparations for the Tabernacle's inauguration.
Shemini *"Eighth"*	9:1 to 11:47	Inauguration of the Tabernacle; death of Nadab and Abihu; the kosher dietary laws.
Tazria *"She shall seed"*	12:1 to 13:59	Laws pertaining to childbirth; laws of *tzaraat* ("leprosy") .
Metzora *"Leper"*	14:1 to 15:33	Purification process of the leper; laws of *nidah* (menstruant).
Acharei Mot *"After the death of"*	16:1 to 18:30	Yom Kippur service in the Holy Temple; prohibitions against incest and other forbidden relations.
Kedoshim *"Holy ones"*	19:1 to 20:27	Numerous mitzvot, including laws pertaining to honesty in business, agricultural gifts to the poor, the prohibition of gossip and slander, and the rule "Love your fellow as yourself."
Emor *"Say"*	21:1 to 24:23	Laws pertaining to the *kohanim* (priests); the festivals of the Jewish year.
Behar *"On the mountain"*	25:1 to 26:2	Laws pertaining to the observance of the sabbatical and jubilee years, the sale of land, and prohibitions against fraud and usury.
Bechukotai *"In my statutes"*	26:3 to 27:34	The rewards for keeping the Torah's commandments, and the catastrophes destined to befall the people should they abandon their covenant with G-d; laws of pledges to the Temple and animal tithes.

BOOK OF NUMBERS

parashah name	verses	topics & themes
Bamidbar *"In the wilderness"*	1:1 to 4:20	The census taken of the people of Israel in the Sinai Desert.
Naso *"Lift up"*	4:21 to 7:89	Populations of the Levite families; laws of the nazirite and of the *sotah* (wayward wife); the priestly blessing; gifts brought by the tribal leaders for the dedication of the Tabernacle.
Behaalotecha *"When you elevate"*	8:1 to 12:16	Kindling of the menorah; inauguration of the Levites' service in the Tabernacle; the Second Passover; description of the Israelites' encampment and journeys in the wilderness; the people criticize the manna and demand meat; Miriam is punished for speaking negatively of Moses.
Shelach *"Send"*	13:1 to 15:41	Spies sent to explore the Promised Land dissuade the people from entering the Land, and it is decreed that the generation of the Exodus will die out in the wilderness; the libations brought with the Temple offerings; the mitzvah of tzitzit.
Korach *"Korah"*	16:1 to 18:32	Korah's rebellion against Moses; the gifts and tithes given to the Kohen and Levite.
Chukat *"The statute of"*	19:1 to 22:1	Law of the Red Heifer; the passing of Miriam; Moses strikes the rock; the passing of Aaron; conquest of the Emorite lands east of the Jordan.
Balak *"Balak (Moabite king)"*	22:2 to 25:9	Balaam's curses are transformed into blessings; the Israelites sin with the daughters of Moab and worship the idol Pe'or; Phinehas stops the plague by killing Zimri and the Midianite woman.
Pinchas *"Phinehas"*	25:10 to 30:1	Phinehas is rewarded for his act of zealotry; allotment of the Land of Israel among the tribes and families; the second census; the petition of daughters of Zelophehad and the laws of inheritance; the daily and seasonal offerings brought in the Temple.
Matot *"Tribes"*	30:2 to 32:42	Laws of the annulment of vows; the war on Midian; the tribes of Reuben and Gad ask to be granted the eastern territories.
Massei *"Journeys"*	33:1 to 36:13	List of the 42 encampments of the Israelites in the 40-year journey from Egypt to the Promised Land; the boundaries of the Land; the "Cities of Refuge" set aside for one who kills by accident.

parashah name	verses	topics & themes

BOOK OF DEUTERONOMY

parashah name	verses	topics & themes
Devarim *"Words"*	1:1 to 3:22	Moses begins his "repetition of the Torah" five weeks before his passing; he recounts the incident of the spies, and the conquests of the lands of Sichon and Og.
Va'etchanan *"And I implored"*	3:23 to 7:11	Moses implores G-d to allow him to enter the Land; the unity and exclusivity of G-d; description of the revelation at Mount Sinai and repetition of the Ten Commandments; the Shema.
Eikev *"In consequence of"*	7:12 to 11:25	The blessings of the Land of Israel; Moses recounts the people's 40-year journey through the wilderness; the second portion of the Shema.
Re'ei *"See"*	11:26 to 16:17	The blessings and curses to be given on Mt. Gerizim and Mt. Ebal; worship in a Holy Temple in "the place that G-d will choose to make dwell His name"; the eradication of idolatry; the laws of prophecy; repeat of the kosher dietary laws; the mitzvah of charity; the three pilgrimage festivals.
Shoftim *"Judges"*	16:18 to 21:9	Establishment of a justice system; the principle of equality before the law; laws governing the conduct of a king; laws of warfare.
Ki Teitzei *"When you go out"*	21:10 to 25:19	Contains 74 mitzvot including the laws of marriage and divorce, employee rights, return of a lost object, burial and dignity of the dead, and forbidden plant and animal hybrids (*kilayim*).
Ki Tavo *"When you come in"*	26:1 to 29:8	The gift of "first fruits" brought to the Temple; warning of the calamities to befall the people of Israel if they fail to keep the Torah.
Nitzavim *"Standing erect"*	29:9 to 30:20	The unity of Israel; the future redemption; the principle of free choice.
Vayeilech *"And he went"*	31:1 to 31:30	On the last day of his life, Moses transfers the leadership to Joshua, and transcribes the Torah and presents it to the people.
Haazinu *"Listen"*	32:1 to 32:52	The song delivered by Moses recounting the history of the people of Israel and their future travails.
Vezot Haberachah *"And this is the blessing"*	33:1 to 34:12	Moses' blessings to the twelve tribes of Israel; the passing of Moses.

Mikraot Gedolot (Rabbinic Bible), published by Daniel Bomberg, Venice, 1524

BIBLE WITH COMMENTARIES "There are seventy faces to the Torah," declared the great sage R. Akiva, and Torah scholars of every generation labored to explicate the meanings, insights, and lessons implicit within the text. The very earliest printed versions of the Jewish Bible were set in the now ubiquitous format that facilitates multifaceted learning, by placing the Biblical text in the center of the page and surrounding it with commentaries from different eras and genres.

THE 613 MITZVOT

The Hebrew word *torah* means "instruction," and the Torah's most overt purpose is to define "the path in which they should go, and the deeds which they should do" (Exodus 18:20). The gist of the Torah, therefore, is the mitzvot, the 613 divine commandments contained in the Five Books of Moses. Everything else—the historical accounts, the prophetic exhortations, the philosophical and mystical expositions—is to establish, enable, and drive the fulfillment of the mitzvot.

 TALMUD, *MAKOT 23b–24a*

R. Simlai expounded: Six hundred and thirteen commandments were communicated to Moses: 365 prohibitions, corresponding to the number of days in the solar year; and 248 positive commandments, corresponding to the number of organs and limbs in the human body.

Said R. Hamnuna: This is alluded to in the verse (Deuteronomy 33:4), "Moses commanded us Torah." The word *torah* (תורה) has the numerical value of six hundred and eleven. For two commandments—"I am the Lord your G‑d" and "You shall have no other gods before Me"—we heard directly from the Almighty [at Mount Sinai].

 R. ISAIAH HOROWITZ
SHENEI LUCHOT HABERIT, 1:51b

The word *mitzvah* is related to *tzavta*, meaning "union" and "attachment," as the act of doing a mitzvah creates a union with the Creator.

 ZOHAR, *VOL. 1, 27a*

"And G‑d Almighty took man, and He put him in the Garden of Eden to work it and to keep it" (Genesis 2:15). "To work it"—these are the positive commandments of the Torah; "to keep it"—these are the prohibitions.

 R. SCHNEUR ZALMAN OF LIADI
BASED ON *LIKUTEI TORAH, PEKUDEI 3c–4a*

The mitzvot come in two forms: actions and prohibitions. For each accomplishes something the other does not.

The advantage of an action is that the person doing the mitzvah actualizes the divine will in their behavior, character, and environment. The divine desire has not only been obeyed, it has also been made real in the world.

But an action is, by definition, limited. It occurs in a particular place and time, involves particular materials, generates particular feelings, creates a particular consciousness. It actualizes the divine desire in a specific, finite part of created reality.

On the other hand, *not* doing something carries no such limitation. When we fulfill the divine will by refraining from doing, it is an unbounded event, relating to the full infinity of the mitzvah and its Commander.

 R. MENACHEM M. SCHNEERSON
LIKUTEI SICHOT, VOL. 4, P. 1193

There are two aspects to every mitzvah. One is the fact that by doing a mitzvah, we fulfill the divine desire. In this, all mitzvot are equal. The qualities of the particular mitzvah are irrelevant; what is significant is that the divine will was done. It is regarding this aspect of the mitzvah that it is said that "if we were commanded to chop wood," we would do it with the same enthusiasm and obedience to the divine will as the most spiritually fulfilling mitzvah.

The second aspect of a mitzvah is the way that it affects the person who does it. It is regarding this aspect of the mitzvah that our sages have said: "Does the Almighty care if you slaughter an animal from the throat or from the back of the neck? But the mitzvot were given to refine the person" (*Midrash Rabbah, Bereishith* 44:1). In this regard, each mitzvah serves as a different "garment" (i.e., enhancement) for the soul.

{ALSO SEE CITATIONS ON PP. 258–259 AND 314}

the 613 commandments of the Torah

COUNTING THE COMMANDMENTS   An entire body of Torah scholarship is devoted to identifying the 613 mitzvot spoken of in the Talmud, and the specific Torah verses from which they are derived. The list below presents, in a generalized form, the 248 positive commandments and the 365 prohibitions as identified, numbered, and categorized by Maimonides in his *Book of Mitzvot* and his *Mishneh Torah*. Numbers in black represent the positive commandments; numbers in red represent the prohibitions.

	mitzvah numbers	source in Torah
FOUNDATIONAL MITZVOT (82 MITZVOT)		
Belief in and knowledge of G-d	**1**	Exodus 20:2
Unity of G-d	**2**	Deuteronomy 6:4
To love G-d	**3**	Deuteronomy 6:5
To fear G-d	**4**	Deuteronomy 6:13
To cleave to G-d and emulate G-d's ways	**6, 8**	Deuteronomy 11:22
To sanctify G-d's name	**9, 63, 65**	Leviticus 22:32; Deuteronomy 12:4
Laws regarding prophecy	**172, 27, 29, 64**	Deuteronomy 18:15, 18:20-22, 6:16
Prohibitions against idolatry and idolatrous practices	**1, 2, 3, 4, 5, 6, 7, 10, 11, 12, 13, 14, 15, 16, 17, 18, 19, 20, 21, 22, 25, 26, 28, 30**	Exodus 20:3-5, 20:20, 23:13; Leviticus 18:3, 18:21; 19:4, 20:23, 26:1; Deuteronomy 7:25-26, 13:4, 13:7-12, 16:21-22, 18:20
Not to pursue heretical ideas or immoral thoughts	**47**	Numbers 15:39
Not to blaspheme or swear falsely in G-d's name	**60, 61, 62**	Exodus 20:7, 22:27; Leviticus 19:12
Not to tolerate the existence of idolatry in the Holy Land	**185, 186, 187, 23, 24, 48, 49, 50, 51**	Exodus 23:32-33; Deuteronomy 7:2, 12:2, 13:13-18, 20:16-18
Prohibitions against sorcery, necromancy, and soothsaying	**8, 9, 31, 32, 33, 34, 35, 36, 37, 38, 310**	Exodus 22:17; Leviticus 19:31; Deuteronomy 18:10-11
To love one's fellow as oneself	**206, 207, 302**	Leviticus 19:17-18; Deuteronomy 10:19
To give charity to the poor	**195, 232**	Deuteronomy 15:7-11
To admonish a friend who is doing something wrong	**205**	Leviticus 19:17
Not to embarrass, insult, or curse a fellow	**251, 252, 303, 317**	Exodus 22:20; Leviticus 19:14, 19:17, 25:17

	mitzvah numbers	source in Torah
Not to gossip or speak negatively of others	**301**	Leviticus 19:16
Not to take revenge or hold a grudge	**304, 305**	Leviticus 19:18
Not to deal harshly with a widow or an orphan	**256**	Exodus 22:21
To study and teach Torah	**11**	Deuteronomy 6:7
To honor sages and elders	**209**	Leviticus 19:32
To follow the rulings of the sages of each generation in all matters of Torah law	**174, 312**	Deuteronomy 17:8-11
Not to add to or subtract from the mitzvot	**313, 314**	Deuteronomy 13:1
To confess and repent one's failings	**73**	Numbers 5:6-7

MITZVOT THAT FOSTER OUR RELATIONSHIP WITH G-D ON A DAILY BASIS (10 MITZVOT)

	mitzvah numbers	source in Torah
The daily readings of the Shema	**10**	Deuteronomy 6:7
Prayer	**5**	Exodus 23:25
Grace after meals	**19**	Deuteronomy 8:10
The priestly blessing	**26**	Numbers 6:22-27
To bind *tefillin* on the arm and head	**12, 13**	Deuteronomy 6:8
To affix a *mezuzah* on the doorposts of the home	**15**	Deuteronomy 6:9
To write a Torah scroll	**18**	Deuteronomy 31:19
To tie *tzitzit* on the corners of one's garment	**14**	Numbers 15:37-41
The covenant of circumcision	**215**	Genesis 17:9-14; Leviticus 12:3

	mitzvah numbers	source in Torah

SHABBAT, THE FESTIVALS, AND THE JEWISH CALENDAR (36 MITZVOT)

	mitzvah numbers	source in Torah
To observe the Shabbat	**154, 155, 320, 321, 322**	Exodus 20:8–11, 23:12, 16:29; 35:3
To set the Jewish calendar based on the lunar and seasonal cycles	**153**	Exodus 12:2
To cease work on Rosh Hashanah, Yom Kippur, and the festival days of Passover, Shavuot, Sukkot, and Shemini Atzeret	**159, 160, 162, 163, 165, 166, 167, 323, 324, 325, 326, 327, 328, 329**	Exodus 12:16; Leviticus 16:29, 23:21, 23:24–25, 23:28, 23:35–36
To rejoice on the festivals	**54**	Deuteronomy 16:14
To sound the shofar on Rosh Hashanah	**170**	Numbers 29:1
To fast on Yom Kippur	**164, 196**	Leviticus 16:29
To dwell in the *sukkah* and take the "four kinds" on Sukkot	**168, 169**	Leviticus 23:40–42
To eat matzah and refrain from leavened foods on Passover	**156, 158, 197, 198, 199, 200, 201**	Exodus 12:15–20, 13:3, 13:7; Deuteronomy 16:3
To tell the story of the Exodus on the first night of Passover	**157**	Exodus 13:8
The counting of the *omer*	**161**	Leviticus 23:15–16
To proclaim a day of prayer and fasting when a calamity threatens the community	**59**	Numbers 10:9

MARRIAGE AND FAMILY (16 MITZVOT)

	mitzvah numbers	source in Torah
To marry	**213, 355**	Deuteronomy 24:1, 23:18
A husband's obligations to provide sustenance, companionship, and intimacy	**214, 262, 311**	Exodus 21:10; Deuteronomy 24:5
To procreate	**212**	Genesis 1:28
To abstain from intimate relations while a woman is in a state of *nidah* (the period during and following menstruation)	**346**	Leviticus 18:19
Laws of divorce	**222, 356**	Deuteronomy 24:1–4

	mitzvah numbers	source in Torah
Laws of *yibum* (levirate marriage) and *chalitzah*	**216, 217, 357**	Deuteronomy 25:5–10
To honor and revere one's parents	**210, 211, 318, 319**	Exodus 20:12, 21:15, 21:17; Leviticus 19:3

FORBIDDEN RELATIONS (41 MITZVOT)

	mitzvah numbers	source in Torah
Not to commit adultery	**347**	Exodus 20:13
The laws of the *sotah* (wayward wife)	**223, 104, 105**	Numbers 5:11–31
The penalties for falsely accusing one's wife of adultery	**219, 359**	Deuteronomy 22:13–19
Prohibitions against intermarriage	**52, 53, 54, 55**	Deuteronomy 7:3, 23:4, 23:8–9
Prohibitions against incest and other forbidden relations	**330, 331, 332, 333, 334, 335, 336, 337, 338, 339, 340, 341, 342, 343, 344, 345, 348, 349, 350, 351, 352, 354**	Leviticus 18:6–18, 18:22–23; Deuteronomy 23:3
Marriages that are forbidden to a Kohen	**158, 159, 160**	Leviticus 21:7
The penalties for rape	**218, 358**	Deuteronomy 22:28–29
The penalties for seducing a virgin	**220**	Exodus 22:15–16
Prohibition against any amorous contact with a person with whom relations are forbidden	**353**	Leviticus 18:6
Prohibitions against castration (in both humans and animals)	**360, 361**	Leviticus 22:24; Deuteronomy 23:2

FOOD AND DIET (46 MITZVOT)

	mitzvah numbers	source in Torah
Laws defining kosher and non-kosher animal species	**149, 150, 151, 152, 172, 173, 174, 175, 176, 177, 178, 179**	Leviticus 11:1–23; 11:41–44; 20:25; Deuteronomy 14:3–20
Laws governing the slaughter of animals for food (*shechitah*)	**146, 147, 101, 180**	Leviticus 17:13, 22:28; Deuteronomy 12:21, 14:21
Not to eat flesh torn from a living animal	**182**	Genesis 9:4; Deuteronomy 12:23
Not to eat the flesh of an animal with a terminal illness or injury	**181**	Exodus 22:30
Not to eat the flesh of an animal that killed a person	**188**	Exodus 21:28

	mitzvah numbers	source in Torah
Not to eat blood	**184**	Leviticus 17:10–12
Not to eat the sciatic nerve and other proscribed veins and fats	**183, 185**	Genesis 32:33; Leviticus 7:23
Not to combine meat and milk	**186, 187**	Exodus 23:19, 34:26; Deuteronomy 14:21
To send away the mother bird before taking its chicks or eggs	**148, 306**	Deuteronomy 22:6–7
Not to eat the fruit of a tree's first three years	**192**	Leviticus 19:23
Not to eat the products of the hybrid sowing of grain in a vineyard	**193**	Deuteronomy 22:9
Not to eat from the grain of the new season before the 16th of Nisan	**189, 190, 191**	Leviticus 23:14
Not to drink wine used in idol worship	**194**	Deuteronomy 32:38
Not to eat and drink like a glutton and a drunkard	**195**	Leviticus 19:26; Deuteronomy 21:20
Laws governing personal vows	**94, 95, 157**	Numbers 30:2–17; Deuteronomy 23:24
Laws of the nazirite	**92, 93, 202, 203, 204, 205, 206, 207, 208, 209**	Numbers 6:1–21

DRESS AND GROOMING (7 MITZVOT)

	mitzvah numbers	source in Torah
Not to wear a garment containing a mixture of wool and linen	**42**	Deuteronomy 22:11
Prohibitions against cross-dressing	**39, 40**	Deuteronomy 22:5
Not to tattoo or mutilate one's body	**41, 45**	Leviticus 19:28; Deuteronomy 14:1
Not to completely remove the hair of the temples or the beard	**43, 44**	Leviticus 19:27

AGRICULTURAL LAWS (62 MITZVOT)

	mitzvah numbers	source in Torah
Prohibitions against mixing different species of plants or animals	**215, 216, 217, 218**	Leviticus 19:19; Deuteronomy 22:9–10
Not to muzzle an animal while it is working	**219**	Deuteronomy 25:4

	mitzvah numbers	source in Torah
Tithes and other gifts to the Kohen and the Levite	**80, 81, 82, 125, 126, 127, 129, 131, 132, 133, 143, 144, 133, 134, 135, 136, 137, 148, 153, 154**	Exodus 22:28, 23:19, 34:20; Leviticus 22:1–16; Numbers 15:17–21, 18:11–16, 18:21–32; Deuteronomy 12:17, 18:3–4, 26:1–13
Tithes and other agricultural gifts to the poor	**120, 121, 122, 123, 124, 130, 210, 211, 212, 213, 214**	Leviticus 19:10, 23:22; Deuteronomy 14:28, 24:19–21
The "second tithe" and the "fourth year of planting" eaten in Jerusalem	**119, 128, 141, 142, 143, 150, 151, 152**	Leviticus 19:23–25; Deuteronomy 12:17–18, 14:22–26, 26:14
To cease working the land during the sabbatical year	**134, 135, 220, 221, 222, 223**	Exodus 23:10–11; Leviticus 25:1–7
To suspend debts in the sabbatical year	**141, 230, 231**	Deuteronomy 15:1–3, 15:9
Observances of the jubilee year	**136, 137, 140, 224, 225, 226**	Leviticus 25:8–13
Laws governing the sale of land in the Holy Land	**138, 139, 227**	Leviticus 25:14–16; 25:23–31

THE HOLY TEMPLE AND THE TEMPLE SERVICE (148 MITZVOT)

	mitzvah numbers	source in Torah
To build the Holy Temple as a place dedicated to the service of G-d	**20, 84, 85, 79, 80, 86, 89, 90**	Exodus 25:8, 25:15, 20:22–23; Deuteronomy 12:11–14, 12:26
To guard the Holy Temple and honor its sanctity	**21, 22, 31, 67, 68,**	Leviticus 17:3–5, 19:30; Numbers 5:2, 18:2–5
The three annual pilgrimages to the Holy Temple	**52, 53, 83, 156**	Exodus 23:14–17; Deuteronomy 12:5–6, 16:16
To gather the entire nation at the Holy Temple once every seven years to hear the Torah read by the king	**16**	Deuteronomy 31:10–13
To light the menorah in the Holy Temple	**25**	Exodus 27:20–21
To offer *ketoret* (incense) in the Holy Temple	**28, 82, 85**	Exodus 30:7–9, 30:34–38
To bake and display the "showbread"	**27**	Exodus 25:30; Leviticus 24:5–9
Additional mitzvot pertaining to the Temple service performed by the Kohanim	**24, 29, 30, 32, 33, 34, 36, 88, 89, 69, 70, 71, 73, 74, 75, 76, 81, 87, 88, 138, 149, 163, 164, 165**	Exodus 28:2, 28:28, 28:32, 29:8–9, 29:33, 30:19–20; Leviticus 6:3–6, 6:9, 6:16, 10:6–7, 10:9–11; 16:2, 21:6, 21:8, 21:12, 21:17–23; 22:2; Numbers 7:9; Deuteronomy 18:6–8

	mitzvah numbers	source in Torah
Mitzvot pertaining to the appointment and service of the *Kohen Gadol* (high priest)	35, 38, 40, 83, 84, 161, 162	Exodus 30:22–33; Leviticus 6:13–15, 21:10–15
Mitzvot pertaining to the Levites and their service in the Holy Temple	23, 183, 72, 169, 170, 228, 229	Leviticus 25:32–34; Numbers 4:19, 18:23, 35:1–8; Deuteronomy 12:19, 18:1–2
Mitzvot pertaining to the *korbanot* (animal and meal offerings) brought in the Holy Temple	63, 66, 67, 124, 139, 145, 146, 147	Leviticus 1:1–17, 2:1–10, 3:1–17, 6:10, 6:23; Deuteronomy 12:17
The annual half-shekel contributed by each Jew for the communal offerings	171	Exodus 30:11–16
The daily communal offerings brought in the Holy Temple	39	Numbers 28:1–8
The additional offerings brought on Shabbat, Rosh Chodesh, and the festivals	41, 42, 43, 44, 45, 46, 47, 48, 50, 51	Leviticus 23:4–37; Numbers 28:9–29:39
The Yom Kippur service in the Holy Temple	49	Leviticus 16:3–34
The Passover offering	55, 56, 57, 58, 115, 116, 117, 118, 119, 121, 122, 123, 125, 126, 127, 128	Exodus 12:3–10, 12:43–48, 23:18, 34:25; Numbers 9:10–14; Deuteronomy 16:4
Offerings of the firstborn and the tithes of kosher animals	78, 79, 108, 109, 144	Leviticus 27:32–33; Numbers 18:17; Deuteronomy 12:17, 15:19
Sin and guilt offerings	64, 65, 68, 69, 70, 71, 72, 102, 103, 112	Leviticus 4:13–21, 4:27–35, 5:1–26, 6:17–7:7
Not to bring a blemished, ritually impure, or disqualified offering	61, 86, 90, 91, 91, 92, 93, 94, 95, 96, 97, 100, 120, 130, 131, 132, 140	Leviticus 7:17–19, 19:6–8, 22:20–25, 22:30; Numbers 28:31; Deuteronomy 12:15, 14:3, 17:1, 23:19
To only offer an animal that is older than eight days	60	Leviticus 22:27
Not to offer leaven or honey upon the altar	98	Leviticus 2:11
To salt all the offerings	62, 99	Leviticus 2:13
Laws governing animals consecrated as offerings, and donations to the Holy Temple	87, 114, 115, 116, 117, 118, 145, 106, 107, 110, 111, 113, 114, 155	Leviticus 5:14–16, 22:14, 27:1–29, 27:33; Deuteronomy 15:19, 23:22

	mitzvah numbers	source in Torah
LAWS OF RITUAL PURITY (30 MITZVOT)		
Ritual impurity caused by contact with a corpse or grave	107, 108, 113	Numbers 19:1–22
Ritual impurity caused by contact with carrion or vermin	96, 97	Leviticus 11:8, 11:24–40
Ritual impurity caused by bodily emissions	74, 75, 99 , 104, 105, 106	Leviticus 15:1–33
Laws of ritual purification following childbirth	76, 100	Leviticus 12:1–8
Laws of *tzaraat* ("leprosy" of the person, home, or garment)	77, 101, 102, 103, 110, 111, 112, 307, 308	Leviticus 13:1–59, 14:1–32, 14:33–57; Deuteronomy 24:8
Ritual impurity pertaining to food and drink	98	Leviticus 11:34
That a ritually impure person should not enter the Holy Temple or partake of sanctified food	77, 78, 129	Leviticus 7:20–21, 12:4; Numbers 5:2–3; Deuteronomy 23:11
That a Kohen should avoid becoming ritually impure through contact with a corpse or grave	166, 167, 168	Leviticus 21:1, 21:11
To purify oneself by immersing in a mikveh	109	Leviticus 11:36, 15:16
PROTECTION AND PRESERVATION OF LIFE (15 MITZVOT)		
Not to murder	289, 292, 295	Exodus 20:13; Numbers 35:12, 35:31
Not to stand by while another person's life is threatened	247, 293, 297	Leviticus 19:16; Deuteronomy 25:12
Laws pertaining to an accidental killing	182, 225, 296	Numbers 35:11, 35:22–25, 35:32; Deuteronomy 19:2–7
The law of *eglah arufah* (communal responsibility for an unsolved murder)	181, 309	Deuteronomy 21:1–9
Not to kidnap	243	Exodus 20:13, 21:16
Not to hit or assault a fellow	300	Deuteronomy 25:3
To remove any life-endangering elements from one's property	184, 298	Deuteronomy 22:8

	mitzvah numbers	source in Torah

FINANCIAL AND PROPERTY LAWS (60 MITZVOT)

	mitzvah numbers	source in Torah
Laws governing payment for damages caused by one's person or property	**236, 237, 238, 240, 241**	Exodus 21:18–19, 21:28–36, 22:4–5
Not to steal or rob	**239, 244, 245**	Exodus 21:37–22:3; Leviticus 19:11, 19:13
To return a stolen object	**194**	Leviticus 5:23
Not to defraud	**208, 246, 250, 253, 271, 272**	Exodus 22:20; Leviticus 19:35–36, 25:14; Deuteronomy 19:14, 25:13
Not to withhold money owed to others	**247, 248**	Leviticus 19:11, 19:13
Not to mislead with bad advice or to abet someone committing a wrong	**299**	Leviticus 19:14
Not to covet another's property, or contrive to acquire what belongs to another	**265, 266**	Exodus 20:14; Deuteronomy 5:18
To return a lost object to its owner	**204, 269**	Exodus 23:4; Deuteronomy 22:1-3
To assist in unloading an overburdened animal or lifting a fallen load	**202, 203, 270**	Exodus 23:5; Deuteronomy 22:4
Laws of buying and selling	**245**	Leviticus 25:14
Laws pertaining to the treatment of slaves and indentured servants	**196, 232, 233, 234, 235, 233, 254, 255, 257, 258, 259, 260, 261**	Exodus 21:2–11, 21:26–27; Leviticus 25:39–55; Deuteronomy 15:12–18, 23:16–17
Laws governing employees' rights and privileges	**200, 201, 238, 267, 268**	Leviticus 19:13; Deuteronomy 23:25–26, 24:15
Laws governing the responsibilities of guardians, renters, and borrowers	**242, 243, 244**	Exodus 22:6–14
To lend money to one who is in need of a loan, and laws governing loan collection, pawned objects, and interest	**197, 198, 199, 142, 234, 235, 236, 237, 239, 240, 241, 242**	Exodus 22:24–26; Leviticus 25:35–37; Deuteronomy 15:3, 23:20–21, 24:6, 24:10–13, 24:17
Laws governing monetary disputes	**246**	Exodus 22:8

THE EXECUTION OF JUSTICE (34 MITZVOT)

	mitzvah numbers	source in Torah
To establish courts of law and appoint qualified judges	**176, 284, 315**	Exodus 22:27; Deuteronomy 1:15–17; 16:18
Not to pervert justice or accept bribes	**273, 274**	Exodus 23:8; Leviticus 19:15
To treat all persons equally before the law	**177, 275, 276, 277, 278, 280**	Exodus 23:6, 23:3; Leviticus 19:15; Deuteronomy 1:17, 24:17
Laws governing witnesses' testimony	**178, 179, 180, 285, 286, 287, 288, 291**	Exodus 20:13, 23:1; Leviticus 5:1; Numbers 35:30; Deuteronomy 13:15, 17:6, 19:15–19, 24:16
Laws governing the taking of oaths	**7, 249**	Leviticus 19:11–12; Deuteronomy 10:20
Laws governing the weighing of evidence and the handing down of verdicts and sentences	**175, 224, 226, 227, 228, 229, 230, 279, 281, 282, 283, 290**	Exodus 21:20, 23:1–2, 23:7; Leviticus 19:15, 20:10, 20:14; Deuteronomy 19:21, 21:22, 22:24, 25:1–3
Not to punish a rape victim, or one who was forced to commit a transgression against their will	**294**	Deuteronomy 22:25–26

GOVERNMENT AND WARFARE (21 MITZVOT)

	mitzvah numbers	source in Torah
Laws governing the appointment of a king and other leaders	**17, 173, 316, 362, 363, 364, 365**	Deuteronomy 17:14–20; Exodus 22:27
Laws governing the conduct of war	**190, 191, 192, 193, 221, 56, 57, 58, 263, 264**	Deuteronomy 3:22, 7:21, 20:1–20, 21:10–14, 23:7, 23:13–15
To remember the evil of Amalek	**188, 189, 59**	Deuteronomy 25:17–19
Not to live in the land of Egypt	**46**	Deuteronomy 17:16

END OF LIFE (5 MITZVOT)

	mitzvah numbers	source in Torah
To bury the dead	**231, 66**	Deuteronomy 21:23
To mourn the death of a close relative	**37, 171**	Leviticus 21:2–3; Deuteronomy 14:1
Laws of inheritance	**248**	Numbers 27:8–11

THE PROPHETS OF ISRAEL

"A fundamental principle of our faith," writes Maimonides, "is that G-d communicates to mankind by prophecy." In the words of Deuteronomy (18:18): "I will raise up for them a prophet from amongst their brethren … and I will place My word in his mouth, and he will speak to them all that I will instruct him."

An equally fundamental principle in Judaism is that a prophet never comes to add, subtract, or change any of the divine commandments (mitzvot) of the Torah. Rather, the role of the prophet is to inspire the people to follow in the ways of G-d; to exhort an individual or community to repent a wrongdoing; to warn of a future calamity and how it can be avoided; and to provide hope with divine promises of future salvation. The prophets also expounded on classical Torah themes, providing depth and clarity to precepts such as prayer, charity, and justice.

 TALMUD, *MEGILAH 14a*

Forty-eight prophets and seven prophetesses prophesied for the people of Israel.

Were there not many more prophets? But these are the prophets whose prophecies were recorded as relevant for future generations.

The seven prophetesses were: Sarah, Miriam, Deborah, Hannah, Abigail, Huldah, and Esther.

[SEE CHARTS ON PAGES 58, 158, AND 188]

 NUMBERS 11:16–29

And G-d said to Moses: "Assemble for Me seventy men of the elders of Israel, whom you know to be the people's elders and officers … and I will emanate from the spirit that is upon you and bestow it upon them; and they will bear the burden of the people with you…"

There remained two men in the camp, the name of one was Eldad and the name of the second was Medad, and the spirit rested upon them…. The lad ran and told Moses, and said, "Eldad and Medad are prophesying in the camp." Joshua the son of Nun, Moses' servant from his youth, responded and said, "Moses, my master, arrest them!"

Moses said to him: "Are you jealous for me? If only all of G-d's people were prophets, that G-d would bestow His spirit upon them."

 TALMUD, *MAKOT 23b–24a*

Six hundred and thirteen mitzvot were said to Moses…. Then King David came and expressed them as eleven principles, as it is written (Psalms 15): "Who shall sojourn in Your tent? Who shall dwell on Your holy mount? The one who walks with integrity, works righteousness, and speaks truth in their heart; who has not slander on their tongue, has not done evil to their fellow, and has not brought disgrace upon their kinsmen; in whose eyes a vile person is despised, and who honors the G-d-fearing; who promises to their own detriment and does not retract; who puts not their money to usury, and does not take a bribe against the innocent. One who does these shall not falter forever."

Isaiah came and expressed them as six, as it is written (Isaiah 33:15): "Who walks in righteousness, and speaks honestly; who despises the profits of oppression, who shakes off their hands from the support of bribes, who stops their ears from the hearing of blood, and shuts their eyes from looking upon evil."

Micah came and expressed them as three, as it is written (Micah 6:8): "It has been told to you, O man, what is good, and what G-d seeks of you: only to do justice, to love charity, and to walk modestly with your G-d."

Isaiah came again, and expressed them as two, as it is written (Isaiah 56:1): "So said the Lord: Keep justice, and do righteousness."

Habakkuk came and expressed them as one principle, as it is written (Habakkuk 2:4): "The righteous person lives by their faith."

II SAMUEL 11:27–12:13

Nathan's parable

As related in the Book of Samuel, King David had coveted Bathsheba's beauty and arranged to have her husband Uriah killed in battle so that he could marry her. In the wake of this incident, Nathan was dispatched to David.

The thing that David had done was bad in the eyes of G-d. G-d sent Nathan to David, and he came to him and said to him:

"There were two men in one city, one rich, and one poor. The rich man had very many flocks and herds. The poor man had nothing, save one little ewe lamb which he had bought and reared, and it grew up together with him and his children; of his bread it would eat and from his cup it would drink, and in his bosom it would lie, and it was to him like a daughter.

"There came a wayfarer to the rich man, and he spared to take of his own flock and of his own herd to prepare for the guest that had come to him; and he took the poor man's lamb, and prepared it for the man that had come to him."

David's rage was exceedingly inflamed at the man, and he said to Nathan: "As G-d lives, the man who has done this deserves to die! And the ewe lamb he shall repay fourfold, because he did this thing, and because he had no pity."

And Nathan said to David: "You are the man...."

Said David to Nathan: "I have sinned against G-d."

ISAIAH 1:1–27

The vision of Isaiah the son of Amoz which he prophesied on Judah and Jerusalem, in the days of Uzziah, Jotham, Ahaz, and Hezekiah, kings of Judah:

Hear, O heavens, listen earth, for G-d has spoken; children I have raised and exalted, and they have rebelled against Me.

An ox knows its owner and a donkey its master's crib; Israel does not know, My people do not consider.

Woe, O sinful nation, a people heavy with iniquity, evildoing seed, corrupt children. They have forsaken G-d, they provoked the Holy One of Israel, they drew backward.

Why when beaten do you continue to rebel? Every head is with illness and every heart with malaise. From the sole of the foot until the head there is no unblemished spot, wounds and contusions and lacerated sores; they have not been sprinkled, nor bandaged, nor softened with oil.

Your land is desolate, your cities burnt with fire; foreigners devour your soil before you, and it is desolate as a conquered land.

The daughter of Zion is left as a hut in a vineyard, as a lodge in a cucumber field, as a besieged city. Had not the Lord of Hosts left us a remnant, we would be like Sodom, we would resemble Gomorrah.

Hear the word of G-d, officers of Sodom; give ear to the law of our G-d, people of Gomorrah! What use to Me are your many sacrifices? says G-d. I am sated with burnt-offerings, with rams and the fat of fattened cattle; I desire not the blood of bulls and sheep and he-goats. When you come to show yourselves before Me, who asked this of you, to trample My courts?

Bring no longer a vain meal-offering, it is smoke of abomination to Me; New Moons and Sabbaths, calling convocations ... they are a bother to Me; I am weary of bearing them. And when you spread out your hands, I will hide My eyes from you; also when you profuse in prayer, I am not listening, as your hands are filled with blood.

Cleanse yourselves, purify yourselves, remove the evil of your deeds from before My eyes; cease to do evil.

Teach yourselves goodness, seek justice, strengthen the robbed; do justice for the orphan, fight for the widow.

Come now, says G-d, let us prove ourselves; If your sins be as scarlet, they shall be whitened as snow; if they be as red as crimson, they shall become as wool....

Zion shall be redeemed through justice, and her returnees through charity.

Ezekiel's prophecy, wall painting from Duro Europos Synagogue (detail), Syria, 244 CE

EZEKIEL 37:1–14

Prophecy of the dry bones

The hand of G-d was upon me; and He carried me out in the spirit of G-d, and He set me down in the midst of the valley; and it was full of bones.

He made me pass by them round and round; and behold, there were very many in the open valley, and behold, they were exceedingly dry.

And He said to me: "Son of man, can these bones live?" And I said, "O Lord G-d, You know."

And He said to me: "Prophesy unto these bones. Say to them: 'Dry bones! Hear the word of G-d…. Behold, I will bring spirit into you and you will live. I will lay sinews upon you, and I will bring up flesh upon you, and I will cover you with skin, and I will put breath in you, and you will live; and you will know that I am G-d.'"

I prophesied as I was commanded. As I prophesied there was a sound, and behold a commotion, and the bones came together, bone to its bone.

I looked, and behold there were sinews on them, and flesh came up upon them, and the skin covered them above; but there was no spirit in them.

And He said to me: "Prophesy to the spirit; prophesy, O son of man, and say to the spirit, 'So says the Lord G-d: From the four winds come, O spirit, and breathe into these slain ones that they should live.'"

I prophesied as He commanded me. And spirit entered into them, and they lived, and stood up upon their feet, a very great army, exceedingly so.

He said to me: "Son of man! These bones, they are the whole house of Israel. Behold, they say: Our bones are dried, our hope is lost, we are cut off to ourselves.

"Therefore, prophesy and say unto them, 'So says the Lord G-d: My people, behold, I will open your graves, and I will raise you up from your graves; and I will bring you to the soil of Israel. And you will know, My people, that I am G-d…. I will put My spirit into you and you will live, and I will set you down on your own soil; and you will know that I, G-d, have spoken it and done it. So says G-d.'"

ELIE WIESEL, EXCERPTED FROM
FIVE BIBLICAL PORTRAITS, PP. 40–64

Elijah

Such is the biblical portrait of Elijah ... inflexible, monolithic, a destroyer of false idols and their worshippers.... Wherever he appears, one breathes the fury and flame of heaven....

Let us read from Scripture: There were kings in Israel and Judea, and most of them were mediocre and selfish; some were even worse. In a house divided against itself, spirituality was first to go. Leaders emerged and disappeared in endless wars, intrigues, plots and counterplots. Wars and alliances with Phoenicians and Assyrians, usually for the wrong motives, resulted in increased degradation, idolatry, and more idolatry. The G-d of Israel was a stranger in His own land.

The most wicked of the kings was Ahab.... To secure his alliance with the Phoenicians, Ahab married the Phoenician princess Jezebel, daughter of Priest and King Ethbaal of Sidon. Under her influence, he built pagan temples [and] opened his palace to false prophets....

[Elijah] challenged King Ahab to a public confrontation.... The entire population was invited to Mount Carmel, especially the false prophets: 400 Baal worshippers and 450 of Jezebel's house-prophets, so to speak. Facing this assembly was one man, Elijah, who believed in one G-d, the G-d of Israel.

And Elijah spoke, and what he said made sense: "You cannot serve both G-d and Baal; you cannot be both Jewish and anti-Jewish; you cannot believe in your own destiny and in someone else's. You must commit yourself, take a stand.... If G-d is G-d, follow Him; if Baal is G-d, follow him."

The people, says the text, did not reply: already then, people preferred to wait, and join the winner.

Elijah himself directed the staging.... Two oxen were brought, and Elijah asked his opponents to choose one and offer it in sacrifice, according to their tradition.

Then he would do the same, except that both rites included an offering by fire, which comes from G-d alone. "Well," said Elijah, "let us see your god and mine at work."

The other side accepted the challenge, and lived to regret it. Courteous, Elijah allowed the prophets of Baal to open the contest. They built their altar and prayed for fire. But there was no fire. The priests and prophets implored Baal with all their might ... Baal remained mute, absent. At this point, Elijah began to mock them: "Perhaps you are not shouting loudly enough! He is asleep—or away! Wake him up...." They howled and shouted, and lacerated their flesh in collective madness for hours and hours. Finally, at dusk, they admitted defeat.

Then came Elijah's turn. He "rebuilt" the altar with twelve stones to illustrate the unity of Israel's twelve tribes. And he implored G-d's help: "G-d of Abraham, Isaac, and Jacob, prove to us here that You are the G-d of Israel.... Answer me, G-d."

And the entire people saw G-d's answer; the entire people saw a fire that came down from heaven to accept and consume Elijah's offering. The story does not end here. After Elijah's victory, he ordered the people to massacre all the false prophets....

As for Elijah, things were not any easier for him afterwards.... For having defined himself as being alone—alone against his entire people—Elijah will be admonished by G-d.... There is irony: G-d was angry at Elijah for having obeyed Him too well. And so it was time for him to leave and ascend to heaven.

Only to return after having been cast into a totally different role. The post-biblical or post-ascension Elijah has undergone an astonishing metamorphosis. Talmudic legend now represents him as the friend and companion to all those who lack friendship, comfort, and hope. To the cynic, he brings certainty; to the wanderer, a spark of light and warmth. To the sage, a teacher; to the dreamer, a dream: that is Elijah. His visits—or his revelations—are rewards in themselves....

The chastising preacher has become the prophet of consolation. As angel and protector of Israel, he dominates time and space: he is everywhere at the same time. He cannot be described, since his disguises are numerous. Sometimes he appears as an Arab, or a Persian, a Roman, a horseman, a soldier, and even as a woman of questionable trade. On one occasion he had to save Rabbi Meir. Roman soldiers chased him and were about to close in on him when they saw him being picked up by a streetwalker! No, impossible. They turned around and gave up the chase....

Another story: A certain Rabbi Nahum of Gamzu went on a mission to Rome, bearing Jewish gold, to bribe the emperor into a friendlier attitude towards Judea. On his way he stopped at an inn, where thieves stole his gold and put sand in its place. Imagine the rage of the emperor when he opened the box and found sand. Reb Nahum was sentenced to death for lèse-majesté. *Gam zu letova*, said Reb Nahum, repeating his favorite expression: "Whatever is being done is for the best." This time he was right—for Elijah appeared disguised as a courtesan (some say an adviser) and told the emperor: "Wait, this man brought you a precious gift! More precious than gold! His sand has powers; it is a mighty weapon, try it!" He did—and the sand miraculously turned into a weapon capable of destroying the enemy's walls. The emperor rewarded Reb Nahum by offering him a box filled with gold and precious stones. On his way home he stopped in the same inn and was met by the same thieves—who were astonished to see him alive, and rich. They wanted to know what had happened in Rome. He told them. Then they filled ten boxes with the same sand and brought it to the emperor, who used it in battle and saw that it was worthless. And of course, the thieves were jailed, condemned, and hanged....

Much emphasis is placed on the secret knowledge [Elijah] communicates to the chosen few. There is even a book attributed to him—*Tana d'bei Eliyahu*—containing his presumed teachings at a school bearing his name....

But sages and saints are not the only ones to be visited by Elijah. They alone are privileged to see him, but he sees everybody. He loves poor people, pious people, simple people. "G-d looked about among all the qualities to bestow upon Israel and found none better than ... poverty," he once declared. He visits all Jewish homes at least once a year during the Passover Seder service, and attends all circumcision ceremonies: any Jew entering Jewish society must be welcomed by him....

Gilui Eliyahu ("revelation of Elijah") is more than a concept; it is an adventure close to the Messianic one. Lurianic scholars evoke him in ecstasy. The Baal Shem Tov's companions dedicate their dreams to him. Of all the prophets, it is Elijah who sets the imagination on fire. Why? Because Malachi links him irrevocably to the Messiah? Because of the expression *Veheshiv lev avot al banim*—"he will reconcile children and their parents"? Because he sent a letter to Yehoram ben Yehoshafat seven years after his death? Why has he, of all the prophets, become the symbol of consolation? Why Elijah and not Jeremiah, nor Isaiah? Why has his legend left such an imprint on our mystical quest throughout the generations from and into exile, from and to Jerusalem?

Elijah: the great hero, the romantic rescuer, the personification of chivalry, faith, and courage, especially in midrashic and Hasidic tales. In that literature we are struck by a strange factor: whenever a stranger appears, he takes on the identity of Elijah. At first Elijah is unknown, then the unknown becomes Elijah. A stranger utters a true word, performs a true deed: it must be Elijah. A man with no name or trade emerges from nowhere to accomplish a secret mission, it must be Elijah. The best proof is that he disappears as soon as his work is completed. And his disappearance is as mysterious as his appearance. He responds to our inner need: he is the tenth man for the *minyan*, the secret emissary who advises the prince to revoke his evil decree,

Elijah Carried off to Heaven, Marc Chagall, France, 1957

the compassionate Gentile who stops the hangman at the last minute, the mysterious traveler who arrives at the right moment, at the right place, to prove to a despairing person or a despairing community that hope is forever possible and it has an ever-changing face.

But one day he will come and stay. On that day he will accompany the Messiah, with whose destiny he is linked. One cannot fulfill his mission without the other. For the Messiah to come, he must be preceded—and announced—by Elijah.

In the meantime, he consoles and occasionally cures the sick. He encourages the helpless. He takes risks and defies enemies to safeguard Jewish survival. We have no better defender in heaven than Elijah. He is linked to Jewish suffering and speaks about it to G-d. In fact, he is the chronicler, the historian of Jewish suffering. He takes note of every tragic event, every massacre, every pogrom, every agony, and every tear; thanks to him, nothing is lost. His most magnificent role is that of witness; he is the memory of the Jewish people....

THE BOOK OF PSALMS

If the Five Books of Moses encapsulate the historical, ideological, and legal foundations of Judaism, the Tehilim, or Book of Psalms, embodies Judaism's emotive heart. Tehilim is timeless: composed nearly 3,000 years ago—primarily by King David in the Holy Land—its 150 psalms express the yearnings, tribulations, and exultations of the Jewish experience in every land and century. Psalms form an integral part of every Jewish prayer, and are read, wept, and sung at every occasion from a birth to a funeral. Whenever a Jew has need to plead for divine assistance, celebrate a triumph, or simply talk to G-d, it is the verses of Tehilim that give voice to the outpourings of his or her soul.

PSALMS 1

Fortunate is the man who did not walk in the counsel of the wicked, who stood not in the path of sinners, who did not sit in the company of scorners.

Only in the teaching of G-d is his desire, and in His Torah he meditates day and night.

He shall be as a tree planted upon rivulets of water, which brings forth its fruit in its season, and its leaves do not wilt, and all that it does prospers.

Not so the wicked; they are like chaff driven off by the wind.

Therefore, the wicked shall not stand up in judgment, and the sinners in the community of the righteous.

For G-d knows the way of the righteous; and the way of the wicked shall be lost.

PSALMS 23

A song of David: G-d is my shepherd; I shall not want.

He makes me lie down in green pastures; He leads me beside still waters.

He restores my soul; He leads me in paths of righteousness for sake of His name.

Though I walk in the valley of the shadow of death, I fear no evil, for You are with me; Your rod and Your staff, they comfort me.

You set a table before me in the presence of my adversaries; You anointed my head with oil; my cup runs over.

May only goodness and kindness pursue me all the days of my life; and I will dwell in the house of G-d for length of days.

PSALMS 44

For the conductor, interpreted for the sons of Korah:

O G-d, with our ears we heard, our forefathers told us, what deeds You performed in their days, in the days of old.

By Your hand, You displaced nations and planted them; You punished kingdoms and drove them out.

For not by their sword did they inherit the land, neither did their arm deliver them; rather by Your right hand and Your arm and the light of Your countenance, for You favored them.

The Shepherd (detail), Reuven Rubin, Land of Israel, 1940

You are my King, O G-d; command the salvations
of Jacob!

With You, we will gore our adversaries;
with Your name, we will trample those who
rise up against us.

For I do not trust in my bow, neither will my sword
save me.

For You saved us from our adversaries; You put our
enemies to shame.

We prided ourselves in G-d all day long; and we will
give thanks to Your name forever, always.

Although You have forsaken us and put us to shame,
and You do not go out in our hosts.

You make us retreat from before the adversary,
and our enemies plunder for themselves.

You deliver us as sheep for meat;
You have scattered us among the nations.

You sell Your people without gain, nor did You profit
from their price.

You make us a mockery to our neighbors,
a scorn and a derision to our surroundings.

You make us a byword among the nations,
a head-shake among the kingdoms.

All day long, my disgrace is before me, and the shame
of my face has covered me. From the voice of the

one who taunts and blasphemes, from before the
enemy and avenger.

All this has befallen us; yet we have not forgotten
You, neither have we been false to Your covenant.

Our heart has not turned back, nor have our steps
turned away from Your path.

Even when You crushed us in a place of serpents,
and You covered us with the shadow of death.
Have we forgotten the name of our G-d, have we
spread our palm to an alien deity?

Would G-d not have searched this out? For He knows
the secrets of the heart.

It is for You that we are killed all day long, that we
are regarded as sheep for the slaughter.

Awaken, O Lord, why do you sleep? Arouse Yourself,
forsake us not forever.

Why do You hide Your face, forget our affliction and
oppression?

For our soul is cast down to the dust, our belly
cleaves to the earth.

Arise to help us, redeem us for the sake of Your
kindness.

🔊 PSALMS 104

My soul, bless G-d!

My Lord G-d, You are verily great; with splendor and
beauty You have clothed Yourself.

Who dons light like a robe; who spreads the heavens
like a tapestry.

Who roofs His lofts with water, who makes clouds
His chariot; who traverses upon wings of wind.

He makes the winds His messengers; flaming
fire His ministers.

He set the earth upon its foundations;
lest it ever falter.

You covered the watery depths like a garment; above
the mountains are stood the waters.

From Your shout they flee; from the sound of
Your thunder they rush off.

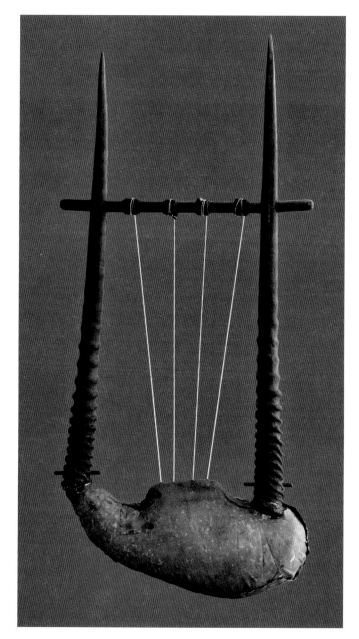

*Biblical harp reconstruction, Moshe Frumin, Israel, circa 2005,
based on the image depicted on the Bar Kochba
era coin, 132–136 CE*

They climb the mountains, they descend the valleys;
    to this place You established for them.
You set a boundary for them that they may not cross;
    lest they return to cover the earth.
Who sends forth wellsprings along the riverbeds;
    between the mountains they traverse.
They water every beast of the field; the wild ones
    quench their thirst.
Upon them the birds of heaven dwell; from between
    the branches they give voice.
He waters the mountains from His lofts; from the
    fruit of Your works is the earth satiated.
He grows fodder for cattle, and herbage to be
    worked by man; to bring forth bread from the
    earth.
And wine that will gladden the heart of the human,
    oil to brighten the face; and bread that sustains
    the human heart.
The trees of G-d are satiated; the cedars of Lebanon
    which He planted.
There birds do nest; the stork makes her home
    in the cypresses.
The high mountains are for the gazelles; the rocks
    shelter the badgers.
He made the moon to mark times; the sun knows
    its setting.
You set darkness and night becomes; in it do crawl
    all beasts of the forest.
The lions roar for prey; to request their food
    from G-d.
The sun shines and they gather in; and lie down
    unto their dens.
Man goes forth to his doings; to his labors until
    evening.
How manifold are Your works, O G-d! You made them
    all with wisdom; the world is filled with Your
    possessions.
This sea is great and wide; there are creeping things
    and innumerable beasts, both small and large.

There the ships go; You formed this leviathan with
    which to sport.
They all look to You with hope, to give their food
    in its time.
You give them and they gather it; You open Your hand
    and they are sated with goodness.
You hide Your countenance and they are frightened;
    You gather in their spirit and they perish and
    return to their dust.
You send forth Your spirit and they are created,
    and You renew the face of the earth.
The glory of G-d shall be forever; G-d shall rejoice
    in His works.
Who looks upon the earth and it quakes;
    He touches the mountains and they smoke.
I shall sing to the Lord while I am alive;
    I shall make songs to my G-d as long as I exist.
May my speech be pleasing to Him;
    I shall rejoice in G-d.
May sins cease from the earth and the wicked be no
    more; my soul shall bless G-d. Praise G-d!

PSALMS 121

A song of ascents. I raise my eyes to the mountains;
    from where will come my help?
My help is from G-d, maker of heaven and earth.
He will not allow your foot to falter; your guardian
    will not slumber.
Behold, the guardian of Israel neither slumbers
    nor sleeps.
G-d is your guardian; G-d is your shadow,
    at your right hand.
The sun shall not smite you by day, nor the moon
    at night.
G-d will guard you from all evil; He will guard
    your soul.
G-d will guard your goings and your comings,
    from now and to eternity.

THE WISDOM OF SOLOMON

 SELECTED SAYINGS FROM PROVERBS

Know Him in all your ways. (3:6)

[The Torah's] ways are ways of pleasantness, and all its paths are peace. It is a tree of life for those who grasp on to it, and those who support it are fortunate. (3:17–18)

Go to the ant, you sluggard; see her ways and become wise. (6:6)

Reprove not a scorner lest he hate you; reprove a wise man and he will love you. (9:8)

Love covers all sins. (10:12)

The blessing of G-d will bring riches, and toil will add nothing to it. (10:22)

The righteous person is the foundation of the world. (10:25)

The innocence of the honest guides them; the treacherous are robbed by their own contortions. (11:3)

Riches will not avail on the day of wrath; but charity will save from death. (11:4)

In every distress will be a gain. (14:23)

Jealousy rots the bones. (14:30)

A gentle reply turns away wrath. (15:1)

Everything G-d made for His sake, also the wicked for the day of evil. (16:4)

A person's heart plans their way, but G-d prepares their steps. (16:9)

Before ruin comes pride. (16:18)

Better a piece of dry bread and tranquility with it, than a house full of meat of strife. (17:1)

Even a fool, when he keeps silent, is considered wise. (17:28)

The soul of man is a lamp of G-d. (20:27)

Do not remove an ancient boundary that your forefathers set. (22:28)

When your enemy falls, do not rejoice, and when he stumbles, let your heart not exult. (24:17)

Have your quarrel with your friend, but do not divulge another's secret. (25:9)

If your enemy is hungry, feed him bread, and if he is thirsty, give him water to drink; for you will be scooping coals upon his head. (25:21–22)

Do not answer a fool according to his folly, lest you too become like him. (26:4)

Without wood the fire goes out; so without a grumbler the quarrel quiets down. (26:20)

One who digs a pit will fall into it; one who rolls a stone, it will come back to him. (26:27)

Do not boast for tomorrow, for you do not know what the day will bear. (27:1)

Let a stranger praise you, not your own mouth. (27:2)

As in water face answers to face, so is the heart of a man to a man. (27:19)

Where there is no vision, a people perish. (29:18)

SELECTED SAYINGS FROM ECCLESIASTES

Vanity of vanities, said Koheleth; vanity of vanities, all is vanity. What profit has man in all his toil that he toils under the sun?

A generation goes and a generation comes, but the earth stands forever…. All the rivers flow into the sea, and the sea is not filled…. What was is what will be, what was done is what will be done, and there is nothing new under the sun. (1:2–9)

הֲבֵל הֲבָלִים הַכֹּל הָבֶל:

Ecclesiastes, Ben Shahn,
United States, 1965

More knowledge, more pain. (1:18)

I have seen that there is an advantage in wisdom over folly, as the advantage of light over darkness. (2:13)

He has made everything beautiful in its time; also the world He put into their hearts, save that man should not find out the work that G-d did from beginning to end. (3:11)

All came from the dust, and all returns to the dust. (3:20)

Two are better than one, as they have good reward for their toil. For if they fall, one will lift up his friend; but woe to the one who falls and has no second one to lift him up. Also, when two lie together, they will have warmth; but how will one alone have warmth? (4:9–11)

Better a poor and wise child, than an old and foolish king. (4:13)

It is better that you should not vow, than that you vow and do not pay it. (5:4)

Even the king is subservient to the field. (5:8)

One who loves silver is not sated by silver.... With the increase of wealth its eaters increase, and what is the advantage to its master, except seeing it with his eyes? (5:9–10)

The sleep of the laborer is sweet, whether he eat little or much; but the satiety of the rich does not allow him to sleep. (5:11)

There is a grievous evil that I saw under the sun: riches kept by their owner for his own harm. (5:12)

As he came out of his mother's womb, naked shall he return to go as he came; nothing will he carry of his toil that can be taken with his hand. (5:14)

It is better to go to a house of mourning than to go to a house of feasting, for that is the end of every man, and the living should take it to their heart. (7:2)

One corresponding to the other, G-d made. (7:14)

There is no righteous man on earth who does only good and errs not. (7:20)

A live dog is better than a dead lion. (9:4)

Experience life with a wife that you love ... for that is your portion in life, and in your toil that you toil under the sun. (9:9)

The race does not belong to the swift, nor the battle to the mighty; neither do the wise have bread, nor do the understanding have riches, nor the knowledgeable, favor; for time and fate will overtake them all. (9:11)

Wisdom is better than weapons. (9:18)

Even in your thought, do not curse a king, nor in your bedrooms should you curse a wealthy man; for the bird of the heaven will carry the voice, and the winged creature will tell the matter. (10:20)

Send forth your bread upon the waters, for after many days you will find it. (11:1)

In the morning sow your seed, and in the evening do not withhold your hand; for you know not which will succeed, this or that, or whether both of them will be equally good. (11:6)

The end of the matter, everything having been heard: Fear G-d and keep His commandments, for this is the whole of man. (12:13)

🎧 SELECTIONS FROM SONG OF SONGS

The voice of my lover, here he is coming, leaping over the mountains, skipping over the hills. My lover is like a gazelle, or a fawn of hinds; here he is, standing behind our wall, watching from the windows, peering from the cracks.

My lover called out and said to me: Arise, my loved one, my fair one, and go forth! For behold, the winter is over, the rain is over and gone. The blossoms have appeared in the land, the time of singing has arrived, and the voice of the turtledove is heard in our land! (2:8–12)

On my bed at night I sought him whom my soul loves; I sought him but I did not find him.

I shall arise now and go about the city, in the market places and in the city squares. I will seek him whom my soul loves; I sought him, but I did not find him.

The watchmen who patrol the city found me. Have you seen him whom my soul loves...?

I adjure you, O daughters of Jerusalem, by the gazelles or by the hinds of the field: Lest you awaken and lest you arouse the love, until it is desirous. (3:1–5)

You are beautiful, my beloved, you are beautiful. Your eyes are like doves behind your kerchief. Your hair is like a flock of goats that streamed down from Mount Gilead.

Your teeth are like a flock of even-shorn sheep coming up from the washing, all of whom are perfect, and there is not a bereaved one among them.

Your lips are like a scarlet thread, and your speech is pretty; your temple is like a section of pomegranate behind your kerchief.

Your neck is like the Tower of David, built as a citadel; a thousand shields hanging on it, all the quivers of the mighty men.

Your two breasts are like two fawns, twins of a gazelle, who feed among the lilies.

Until the day spreads and the shadows flee, I betake myself to the mountain of myrrh and to the hill of frankincense....

A locked garden is my sister, my bride; a locked spring, a sealed fountain. (4:1–12)

I am asleep, but my heart is awake. The sound of my lover knocking: Open for me, my sister, my friend, my dove, my perfect one; for my head is full of dew, my locks with the drops of the night.

I have taken off my shirt; how can I put it on? I have washed my feet; how can I soil them?

My beloved withdrew his hand from the latch, and my insides stirred over him. I arose to open for my beloved, and my hands dripped with myrrh, and my fingers with flowing myrrh, upon the handles of the lock.

I opened for my beloved, but my beloved had eluded and was gone; my soul went out when he spoke; I sought him, but I did not find him; I called him, but he did not answer me. (5:2–6)

Set me as a seal on your heart, as a seal on your arm. For love is fierce as death, jealousy is harsh as the grave; its coals are coals of fire, a blazing flame!

Many waters cannot extinguish love, and rivers cannot drown it. Should a person offer all the wealth of his house for love, they would verily scorn him. (8:6–7)

 MIDRASH RABBAH ON SONG OF SONGS

Your eyes are like doves—From the moment that a dove recognizes its mate, it never exchanges it for another. So, too, from the moment that the people of Israel recognized G-d, they did not exchange Him for any other. Also: A dove, even if you take away its hatchlings from under it, will never forsake its nest. So, too, although the Holy Temple was destroyed, the people of Israel still keep the three annual pilgrimage festivals.

Your hair is like a flock of goats that streamed down from Mount Gilead—This mountain (Mount Sinai) from which you streamed forth, you made it a monument (*gal*) and testament (*eid*) for the nations of the world. *Your teeth are like a flock of even-shorn sheep*—These are the evenly paced words of the Torah's commandments, the 248 positive mitzvot and the 365 prohibitions.

Your temple is like a section of pomegranate—Even your empty ones [*reikaneich*, a play on *rakateich*, "your temple"] are full of good deeds as a pomegranate is full of seeds.

Your neck is like the Tower of David—As the neck channels vitality to the body, so is the Holy Temple the conduit of vitality to the people of Israel. *Built as a citadel* [*talpiot:* literally, "mound of mouths"]—It is the mound toward which all mouths are directed in prayer.

Your two breasts are like two fawns—These are Moses and Aaron, who nourished the people of Israel with the milk of Torah. *Twins of a gazelle*—as they were equal in greatness. *Who feed among the lilies*—Jochebed and Miriam, who sustained the children of Israel in Egypt.

I am asleep, but my heart is awake—The community of Israel says to G-d: Although I am asleep regarding the mitzvot, my heart is awake to acts of kindness. Although I am asleep regarding the Holy Temple, my heart is awake to our synagogues and study halls. Although I am asleep regarding the end of the exile, my heart is awake to the redemption.

Talmud and Midrash

*Shtender (study stand),
Odobesti, Romania,
late 19th–early 20th century*

The terms Talmud *("learning") and* Midrash *("exposition") describe a process that began at Sinai and continues to this day: the process of studying, interpreting, and extrapolating from the text of the Written Torah and applying it to the task of living our lives and developing our world in accordance with the divine will. This symbiosis of divine revelation and human intellectual toil is what we call the "Oral Torah."*

More specifically, "The Talmud" is a 60-volume work, the product of discussions and debates by hundreds of sages over the course of several centuries conducted in great yeshivahs of Babylonia and the Land of Israel more than 1,500 years ago (see pp. 108–109). "The Midrash" is a series of works, dating from the same period, containing expositions on the Bible that complement the legal, historical, and inspirational narratives of the Talmud.

In this section, we will cite a number of texts that illuminate the history and nature of the Oral Torah, present examples of the Talmudic methodology, and sample a few drops from the vast "sea of the Talmud" and its contemporary works.

NOTE: THROUGHOUT THIS BOOK, THE SYMBOL
INDICATES A CITATION FROM THE TALMUD OR MIDRASH

CECIL ROTH, *A SHORT HISTORY
OF THE JEWISH PEOPLE, CHAPTER 12*

The importance in Jewish life of the Talmud is not by any means purely academic. It comprises the accumulated wisdom of the Jewish people over many generations. No aspect of Hebrew thought, and no subject of human interest, is unrepresented in it. The period of its redaction coincided with the growth of independent centers of life in far-distant regions, cut off politically and linguistically from the former nuclei. The Jewish people was about to enter on an entirely different phase of its being, in countries of which their fathers had never heard, in callings with which they had previously been unfamiliar, in the face of difficulties hitherto unimaginable.

But they possessed, to bring with them into their new existence, a code, not merely of religion or of law, but of civilization. The way of life which the Talmud so minutely illustrated and prescribed made the whole people of Israel one, wheresoever they might be found and into however many political fractions they might be

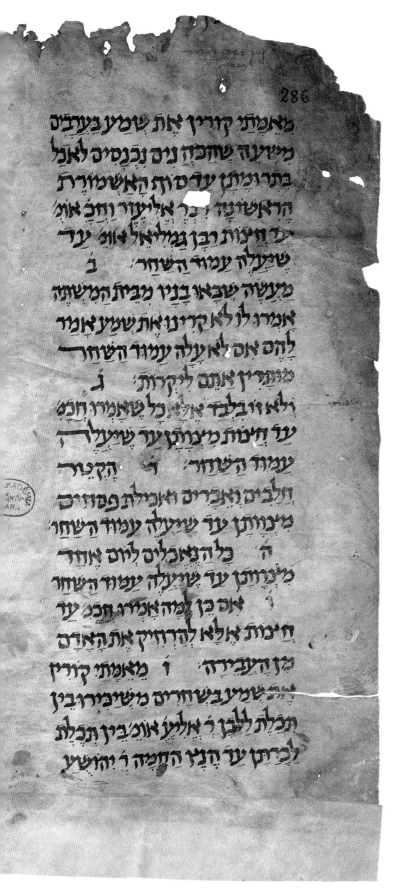

*Mishnah, the Kaufmann manuscript,
Land of Israel or Italy, 10th or 11th century*

divided. It gave them the characteristic imprint which distinguished them from others, as well as their remarkable power of resistance and cohesion. Its dialectic sharpened their wits, and conferred upon them a preternatural mental acuteness.

But, though it may seem an exaggeration, there was more in it even than this. For the Talmud gave the persecuted Jew of the Middle Ages another world into which he could escape, when the vicissitudes of that in which he lived had become too great to bear. It gave him a fatherland, which he could carry about with him when his own land was lost. And, if he was able to maintain his identity in the course of the long centuries to come, under conditions such as no other people has ever been able to surmount, it is with the Talmud … that the credit lies.

 ABRAHAM JOSHUA HESCHEL
THE EARTH IS THE LORD'S, PP. 46–47

"Once I noticed," writes a Christian scholar who visited the city of Warsaw during the First World War, "a great many coaches on a parking-place but with no drivers in sight. In my own country I would have known where to look for them. A young Jewish boy showed me the way: in a courtyard, on the second floor, was the *shtibl* of the Jewish drivers. It consisted of two rooms: one filled with Talmud-volumes, the other a room for prayer. All the drivers were engaged in fervent study and religious discussion…. I then found out and became convinced that all professions, the bakers, the butchers, the shoemakers, etc., have their own *shtibl* in the Jewish district; and every free moment which can be taken off from their work is given to the study of the Torah. And when they get together in intimate groups, one urges the other: '*Sog mir a shtickl Torah*—Tell me a little Torah.'"

An old book saved from the countless libraries recently burned in Europe, now at the YIVO Library in New York, bears the stamp, "The Society of Wood-Choppers for the Study of Mishnah in Berditshev."

THE ORAL TORAH

 FIVE COMPONENTS OF THE ORAL TORAH

■ The meaning of the text of the Written Torah, as handed down through the generations.

■ Laws and principles not contained within the text but communicated to Moses at Mount Sinai.

■ Interpretations and expositions of the text that are derived by the sages using the Oral Torah's rules of Torah exegesis, with differences of opinion among the sages in matters of law decided by majority view.

■ Ordinances enacted by the sages of each generation as "safeguards" for the laws of the Torah, in accordance with the authority vested in them by the Torah.

■ Ordinances enacted by the sages of each generation for the sake of the common good in light of the specific needs and circumstances of the time, in accordance with the authority vested in them by the Torah.

From Maimonides' introduction to the Mishnah

 DEUTERONOMY 17:8–11

When a matter eludes you in judgment, between blood and blood, between law and law, or between affliction and affliction, matters of dispute in your city gates; you shall arise and go up to the place that G-d will choose. You shall come to the Levite priests, and to the judge who will be in those days, and you shall inquire, and they will tell you the words of judgment….

According to the law that they instruct you, and according to the judgment which they say to you, you shall do; you shall not divert from the word they tell you, right or left.

 ETHICS OF THE FATHERS, *CH. 1, MISHNAH 1*

Moses received the Torah from Sinai and gave it over to Joshua, Joshua to the Elders, the Elders to the Prophets, and the Prophets gave it over to the men of the Great Assembly. They said three things: Be deliberate in judgment, establish many disciples, and make safeguards to the Torah.

 TALMUD, *GITTIN 60b*

It is written (Exodus 34:27), "Write down these words." It is also written (ibid.), "By the mouth of these words." This comes to teach us: the words that were given in writing, you are not allowed to teach them orally; and the words that were taught orally, you are not allowed to put them in writing.

 TALMUD, *SANHEDRIN 34a*

"My words are like fire, says G-d, and like a hammer that shatters a stone" (Jeremiah 23:29). As the hammer explodes many particles, so does one verse of Scripture diverge into many meanings.

 TALMUD, *ERUVIN 13b*

For three years the School of Shamai and the School of Hillel were disputing. These said, "The law is as we say," and these said, "The law is as we say." A voice issued forth from heaven and proclaimed: "These and these are both the words of the living G-d."

 MAIMONIDES, *INTRODUCTION TO MISHNEH TORAH*

All the commandments were given to Moses at Mount Sinai together with their explanation, as it says (Exodus 24:12), "I will give you the tablets of stone, the Torah, and the mitzvah." "The Torah" refers to the Written Torah; "the mitzvah," to its explanation.

Moses personally transcribed the entire Torah before his passing. But he did not transcribe its explanations; rather, he instructed them to the elders and to Joshua and to the rest of Israel. This is why it is called the "Oral Torah."

From the days of Moses until R. Judah ha-Nasi, no one composed a text for the purpose of disseminating the Oral Torah in public. Rather, in each generation, the head of the court or the prophet of that generation would make personal notes of the teachings they received from their teachers, and teach them orally. Similarly, each person would write down for themselves, according to their ability, the teachings they heard regarding the explanation of the Torah, its laws, and the new concepts that were deduced in each generation using one of the thirteen rules of Biblical exegesis and accepted by the high court.

So it continued until the time of R. Judah ha-Nasi. He collected all the teachings, all the laws, and all the explanations and commentaries that were handed down from Moses and which were taught by the courts in each generation concerning the entire Torah. From all these, he composed the text of the Mishnah. He taught it publicly to the sages and revealed it to the Jewish people, who all wrote it down, and disseminated it everywhere.

Why did R. Judah do this and not leave matters as they were? Because he saw that the students of Torah were becoming fewer, new troubles were constantly arising, the Roman Empire [which was suppressing the study and practice of Judaism] was spreading throughout the world and becoming more powerful, and the Jewish people were being dispersed to the far ends of the earth. He therefore composed a single text that would be available to everyone, so that it could be learned quickly and would not be forgotten.

 R. JOSEPH ALBO, EXCERPTED FROM *IKARIM 3:23*

Any written text can be understood in multiple ways, to the extent that it can mean one thing to one person and the complete opposite to another person. As Maimonides writes in his *Letter on the Resurrection of the Dead*, the verse (Deuteronomy 6:4), "Hear O Israel, G-d is our G-d, G-d is one" is understood by Jews as affirming the absolute unity of G-d, but is interpreted by Christians as a reference to the trinity.

Therefore, in order to preserve the integrity of the Torah and ensure that it is understood in the manner that G-d intended, the meaning of the Written Torah was explained to Moses, who explained it to Joshua, and so on, generation after generation. These explanations could not be written down, because if they were, the meaning of this text, too, would be open to interpretation, requiring an explanation of the explanation, and so on, *ad infinitum*. As indeed happened when the Mishnah—which is the explanation of the Written Torah—was written down: its own meaning became subject to debate, requiring its own explanation, which is the Talmud, compiled by Rav Ashi as the exposition of the Mishnah. The Talmud itself subsequently required explanation, and numerous commentaries with differing opinions, as well as commentaries on those commentaries, were composed. All this makes it clear that no written Torah can be complete without an accompanying oral explanation; this is what is called the "Oral Torah."

In addition, the Torah must address all times and all new arising circumstances, which are too numerous to be written in a book. Therefore, Moses was given at Sinai general principles and pathways, which are concisely alluded to in the Torah, by which the sages of each generation would extract the newly arising particulars. These are the "Thirteen Rules of Torah Exegesis" enumerated in the *beraita* of R. Ishmael.

Also, because it is possible that there will arise differences of opinion among the sages of Israel regarding things that were not handed down by tradition but were extracted by one of the Thirteen Rules, or by other means of logical deduction, the divine wisdom ordained to grant the authority of deciding the matter to the majority of sages in each generation. As the Torah states (Exodus 23:2), "Follow the majority ruling," and also instructs (Deuteronomy 17:11), "You shall not divert from the word they tell you, to the right or to the left."

the chain of tradition

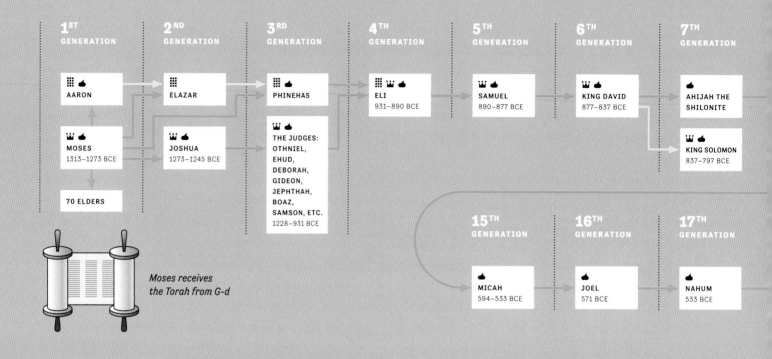

1ST GENERATION	2ND GENERATION	3RD GENERATION	4TH GENERATION	5TH GENERATION	6TH GENERATION	7TH GENERATION
AARON	ELAZAR	PHINEHAS	ELI 931–890 BCE	SAMUEL 890–877 BCE	KING DAVID 877–837 BCE	AHIJAH THE SHILONITE
MOSES 1313–1273 BCE	JOSHUA 1273–1245 BCE	THE JUDGES: OTHNIEL, EHUD, DEBORAH, GIDEON, JEPHTHAH, BOAZ, SAMSON, ETC. 1228–931 BCE				KING SOLOMON 837–797 BCE
70 ELDERS						

Moses receives the Torah from G-d

15TH GENERATION	16TH GENERATION	17TH GENERATION
MICAH 594–533 BCE	JOEL 571 BCE	NAHUM 533 BCE

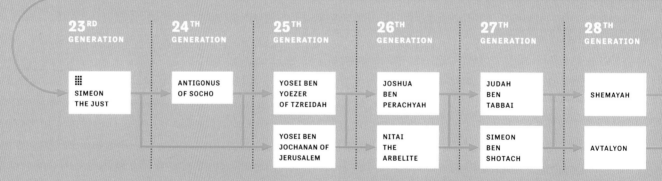

23RD GENERATION	24TH GENERATION	25TH GENERATION	26TH GENERATION	27TH GENERATION	28TH GENERATION
SIMEON THE JUST	ANTIGONUS OF SOCHO	YOSEI BEN YOEZER OF TZREIDAH	JOSHUA BEN PERACHYAH	JUDAH BEN TABBAI	SHEMAYAH
		YOSEI BEN JOCHANAN OF JERUSALEM	NITAI THE ARBELITE	SIMEON BEN SHOTACH	AVTALYON

▦ high priest
♚ king, ruler, or political leader
☙ prophet
→ son and disciple
→ disciple
dates: years active (when known)

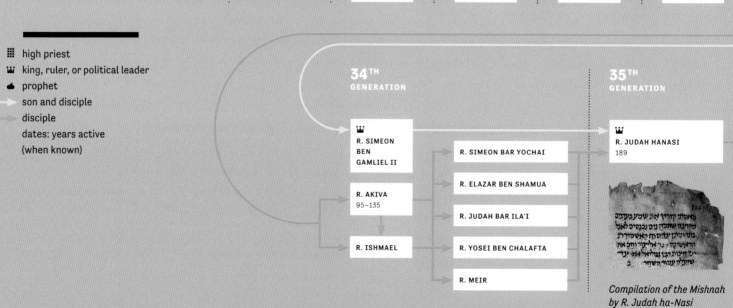

34TH GENERATION			35TH GENERATION
R. SIMEON BEN GAMLIEL II	R. SIMEON BAR YOCHAI		R. JUDAH HANASI 189
R. AKIVA 95–135	R. ELAZAR BEN SHAMUA		
	R. JUDAH BAR ILA'I		
R. ISHMAEL	R. YOSEI BEN CHALAFTA		
	R. MEIR		

Compilation of the Mishnah by R. Judah ha-Nasi

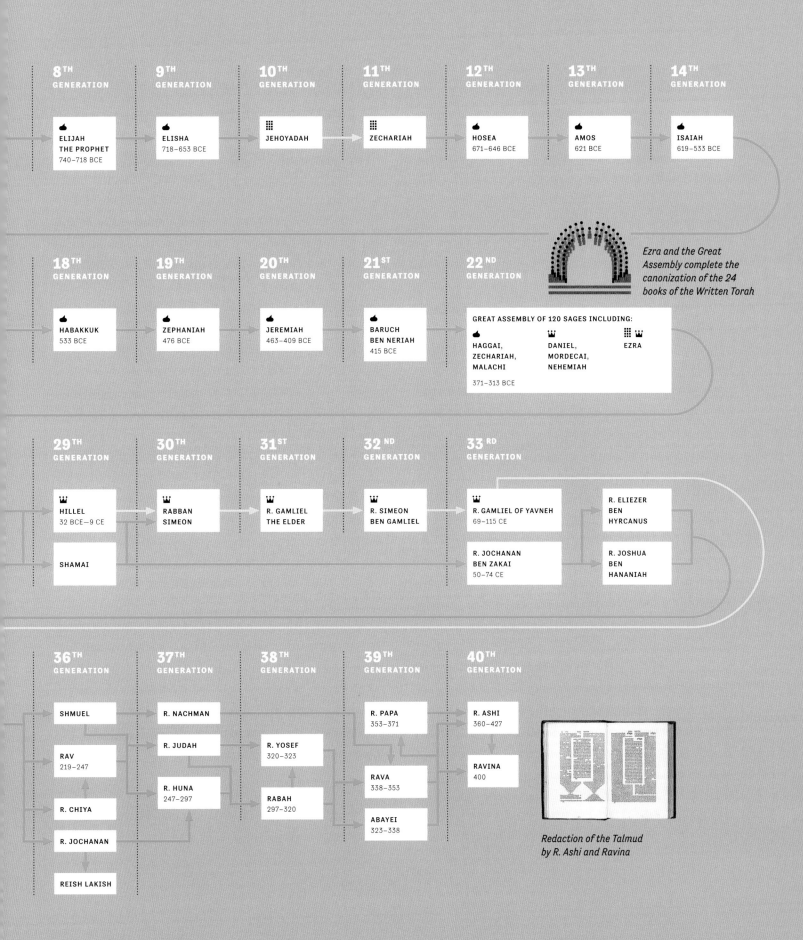

8TH GENERATION	9TH GENERATION	10TH GENERATION	11TH GENERATION	12TH GENERATION	13TH GENERATION	14TH GENERATION
ELIJAH THE PROPHET 740–718 BCE	ELISHA 718–653 BCE	JEHOYADAH	ZECHARIAH	HOSEA 671–646 BCE	AMOS 621 BCE	ISAIAH 619–533 BCE

18TH GENERATION	19TH GENERATION	20TH GENERATION	21ST GENERATION	22ND GENERATION
HABAKKUK 533 BCE	ZEPHANIAH 476 BCE	JEREMIAH 463–409 BCE	BARUCH BEN NERIAH 415 BCE	

Ezra and the Great Assembly complete the canonization of the 24 books of the Written Torah

GREAT ASSEMBLY OF 120 SAGES INCLUDING:

HAGGAI, ZECHARIAH, MALACHI   DANIEL, MORDECAI, NEHEMIAH   EZRA

371–313 BCE

29TH GENERATION	30TH GENERATION	31ST GENERATION	32ND GENERATION	33RD GENERATION	
HILLEL 32 BCE–9 CE	RABBAN SIMEON	R. GAMLIEL THE ELDER	R. SIMEON BEN GAMLIEL	R. GAMLIEL OF YAVNEH 69–115 CE	R. ELIEZER BEN HYRCANUS
SHAMAI				R. JOCHANAN BEN ZAKAI 50–74 CE	R. JOSHUA BEN HANANIAH

36TH GENERATION	37TH GENERATION	38TH GENERATION	39TH GENERATION	40TH GENERATION
SHMUEL	R. NACHMAN		R. PAPA 353–371	R. ASHI 360–427
RAV 219–247	R. JUDAH	R. YOSEF 320–323		RAVINA 400
R. CHIYA	R. HUNA 247–297	RABAH 297–320	RAVA 338–353	
R. JOCHANAN			ABAYEI 323–338	
REISH LAKISH				

Redaction of the Talmud by R. Ashi and Ravina

R. ISAIAH HOROWITZ
SHENEI LUCHOT HABERIT, 1:25a

The blessing recited before studying Torah concludes with the words, "Blessed are you, G-d, who gives the Torah." In truth, G-d has already given us the Torah (at Mount Sinai); yet we refer to Him as one who perpetually "gives the Torah," in the present tense. This matter requires some elaboration.

It is written (Deuteronomy 5:19): "These words G-d spoke to your entire assembly at the mountain … a great voice that did not cease." Rashi explains the meaning of the words *velo yasaf*, "did not cease," in accordance with the translation by Onkelos, in the sense that "it did not stop," as it is a powerful voice that endures forever. Rashi also offers a second interpretation of the words *velo yasaf*—"it did not any more," meaning that G-d did not again speak openly and publicly as He did at Sinai.

There is a profound significance in these two interpretations, as they are simultaneously true. The divine voice spoke the Torah at Sinai and "did not any more," as all the subsequent laws and edicts instituted by the sages throughout the generations were not explicitly commanded by the Almighty. At the same time, "it did not stop," for everything was included, in potential form, within that voice. It is only that "for everything there is a time and season" (Ecclesiastes 3:1), and the time had not yet come for that potential to emerge into actuality. For that depends on the initiative of those down here below, in accordance with their nature and their abilities, and in accordance with the qualities of the souls of each generation. Following the revelation at Sinai, the sages of each generation were roused to actualize from that potential in accordance with the time and season. Thus, the sages did not invent anything from their own minds, Heaven forbid, but rather actualized the divine intent.

TANA D'BEI ELIYAHU
ELIYAHU ZUTA, CHAPTER 2

I was once traveling on the road when a person encountered me on the way to doing a mitzvah. This person had Scripture, but he did not have Mishnah. He said to me, "Master, Scripture was given to us at Mount Sinai; Mishnah was not given to us at Mount Sinai." I said to him, "Both Scripture and Mishnah issued from the mouth of the Almighty. What is the difference between them? The following parable was said to explain this:

"There was a king who had two beloved servants. He gave a measure of wheat to one of them, and a measure of wheat to the other. He also gave each a bundle of flax. The wise one among them took the flax and wove a beautiful cloth out of it; he took the wheat and made fine flour from it, sifting it, milling it, kneading it, and baking it. He arranged it on a table and spread the beautiful cloth over it, setting it aside for when the king would come. The foolish servant did nothing. Then the king arrived and said to his two servants, 'My children, present to me what I have gifted you.' The first one brought out the bread made of fine flour on a table with a beautiful cloth spread over it; the other brought out the wheat in a box with the bundle of flax on top of it…. Now, which of the servants is more precious to the king…?

"When the Almighty gave the Torah to the people of Israel, He gave it as wheat from which to make fine flour, and as flax from which to weave a cloth, by means of the rules of Torah exposition: a general clause followed by a specific clause; a specific clause followed by a generality; a sequence of general, specific, and general clauses; [and so on.]"

THE TALMUDIC DIALECTIC

 R. JOSEPH B. SOLOVEITCHIK
FROM A TALK DELIVERED IN 1971

I enter the classroom, which is crowded with boys who could be, as far as age is concerned, my grandchildren. I enter the classroom as an old man, with a wrinkled face and eyes reflecting fatigue and the sadness of old age. It's a very strange sadness: the melancholy of remembering things which disappear, which no longer exist. I sit down, and opposite me are rows of young boys with beaming eyes, beaming faces, clear eyes, radiating the joy of being young.

I always enter the class in a very pessimistic mood; I always enter in despair. I ask myself: Can there be a dialogue between an old teacher and young students? Between a *rebbe* in his Indian summer and boys enjoying the spring of their lives?

I start the *shiur*; the door opens, and another old man walks in and sits down. He is older than I am. All the students call me the Rav, but he is older than the Rav. He is the grandfather of the Rav; his name is Reb Chaim Brisker, without whom no *shiur* can be delivered nowadays. Then, the door opens quietly again and another old man comes in, he is older than Reb Chaim, he lived in the 17th century. What's his name? Shabsai Kohen—the famous Shach—who must be present when *dinei mamonos* (property law) is being discussed; when we study [the Talmudic tractates] *Bava Metzia* and *Bava Kama*. And then, more visitors show up. Some of the visitors lived in the 11th century, some in the 12th century, some in the 13th century, some lived in antiquity. Rabbi Akiva, Rashi, Rabbeinu Tam, the Raavad, the Rashba; more and more come in.

I introduce them to my pupils and the dialogue commences. The Rambam (Maimonides) says something, the Raavad disagrees; and sometimes he's very nasty. Very sharp, harsh language he uses against the Rambam. A boy jumps up to defend the Rambam against the Raavad, and the boy is fresh—you know how young boys are fresh—so the language he uses is improper.

So, I correct him. And another jumps up with a new idea; the Rashba smiles gently. I try to analyze what the young boy meant, another boy intervenes, we call upon the Rabbeinu Tam to express his opinion, and suddenly a symposium of generations comes into existence.

Generations! Young boys, 22, 23, 24 years of age, there are boys who are just 18 years old in my class: one generation. Then my generation, then the generation of Reb Chaim Brisker, then the generation of the Shach, then the generation of the Rashba, the Ramban, the generation of the Rambam, the generation of Rabbeinu Tam, the generation of Rashi, and then, I mean there is no end! What about Rav Hai Gaon? What about Rabbi Akiva, Rabbi Elazar, Rabban Yochanan ben Zakai?

We all speak one language; "the entire earth was one language and singular words" (Genesis 11:1). We all chat, we all laugh, we all enjoy the company, and we all pursue one goal; we all are committed to a common vision, and we all operate in the same categories. There is *mesorah* collegiality, friendship, comradeship between old and young, between antiquity, middle-ages, and modern times.

This unity of generations, this march of centuries, this conversation of generations, this dialogue between antiquity and present will finally bring the redemption of the Jew.

Let me tell you that at the conclusion of three and sometimes four hours, I emerge young and elated, younger than my pupils. They are tired, exhausted, some of them yawn. I feel happy. I have defeated age. I have defeated oldness; I emerge young, less fatigued, less exhausted than my young pupils.

We belong to the same *mesorah* community, where generations meet. Where hands, no matter how wrinkled and parchment-dry one hand is and how soft and wan the other hand is, grasp each other and unite in a community where the great dialogue continues.

Talmud and commentaries

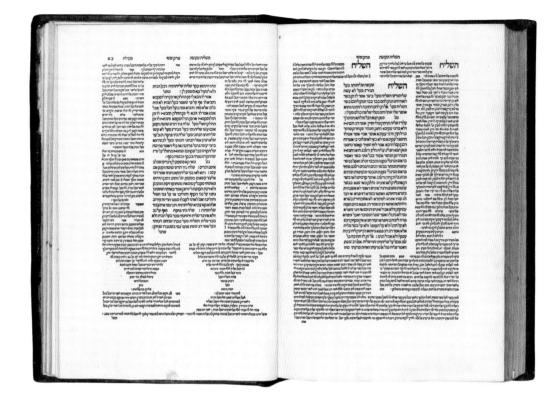

The Bomberg Talmud,
Venice, 1519–1549.
Daniel Bomberg produced
the first complete printed edition
of the Babylonian Talmud.

THE ORIGINAL HYPERTEXT The complexity of the Talmudic text, and the variety of approaches among the commentaries, make the study of Talmud an immersive and challenging intellectual journey. The distinctive format of the Talmudic *daf* (folio page) was created to enable a simultaneous consultation of numerous Talmudic commentaries. On an oversize page (typically 11 by 16 inches), the text of the Talmud is laid out in the center of the page, with surrounding blocks of text containing the major commentaries. Additional commentaries are presented, in similar format, as addendums following the text. A single volume of Talmud will thus contain close to 100 different works authored over the course of 1,800 years.

Ⓐ **MISHNAH** The first official transcription of the Oral Torah, compiled by R. Judah ha-Nasi toward the end on the 2nd century CE (see citation from Maimonides on p. 186).

Ⓑ **GEMARA** Analysis and interpretation of the Mishnah, as well as other Halachic and Agadic discussions by the Talmudic sages who studied and taught in the great yeshivahs of Babylonia and the Holy Land in the 3rd, 4th, and 5th centuries. Also includes citations from Mishnaic sages (called *beraitot*) not included in the Mishnah.

Ⓒ **RASHI** The most important commentary on the Talmud, explaining the basic meaning of its often obscure wording. Composed by R. Solomon Yitzchaki (1040–1105).

Ⓓ **TOSAFOT** Anthology of commentaries by dozens of sages who lived in Western Europe in the 12th and 13th centuries, including a number of Rashi's disciples and descendants. The Tosafists explain the Talmudic text, often challenging Rashi's explanations, and labor to reconcile seemingly inconsistent passages. The analytical and dialectical style of Tosafot strongly influenced the manner in which the Talmud has been studied over the centuries.

Ⓔ **R. HANANEL** First running commentary on the Talmud. Authored by R. Hananel of Kairouan (c. 965–1055; see biographical note on p. 114).

Ⓕ **BACH** Glosses on the Talmud, Rashi, and Tosafot by R. Joel Sirkis (c. 1560–1640).

Ⓖ **GRA** Glosses and brief notes by R. Elijah, the "Gaon of Vilna" (1720–1797).

Ⓗ **GILYON HASHAS** Notes by R. Akiva Eiger of Posen (1761–1837).

Ⓘ **MASORET HASHAS** Cross-references showing where specific passages and rulings are discussed elsewhere in the Talmud.

Ⓙ **EIN MISHPAT** References indicating where key Talmudic statements are cited in the various Halachic codes.

Ⓚ **TORAH OHR** References for Biblical citations.

יציאות השבת פרק ראשון שבת כ:

Contemporary Talmud folio page, published by Oz Vehadar, United States and Israel, 1988–2007
Page shown: Tractate Shabbat 20b

TORAH EXEGESIS METHODOLOGIES

Central to the Sinaic tradition are the methods of Torah exposition, by means of which the particulars of Torah law are derived. There are dozens of such rules, including *The Thirteen Methods of Torah Exegesis* cited by the Mishnaic sage R. Ishmael, and the *Thirty-Two Methods* attributed to his contemporary, R. Yosei the Galilean. This overview describes some of these rules, and presents examples of how they are used to expound the meaning of the Biblical text.

KAL VACHOMER (*"LENIENT AND STRICT"*)

RULE When we have two laws or situations, and the more lenient or less obvious one has a certain stringency, then certainly the more stringent law or the more obvious circumstance will also have this stringency.

A corollary to this rule is the rule that "It is sufficient for the derived law to be as the source law," meaning that if law B is derived from law A by means of a *kal vachomer*, law B can be no stricter than law A.

EXAMPLE Exodus 23:5 reads: "When you see the donkey of your enemy collapsing under its burden, and you are inclined to desist from assisting him, assist must you assist with him."

Does this mean that the obligation to assist in unloading a collapsed beast of burden applies only to the animal of an enemy? The principle of *kal vachomer* dictates that if you are required to assist an enemy in such a situation, you are certainly required to assist a friend.

How about the case where both your enemy and your friend require such assistance? Must you first help your friend, as this is the "stronger" or more obvious obligation? Here the rule, "It is sufficient for the derived law to be as the source law," applies. Because the *source* of the obligation is the case of the enemy's animal, and the obligation to unload a friend's animal is derived from it, the derived obligation cannot be greater than the source obligation.

RIBU AND MI'UT (*"ADDITION AND SUBTRACTION"*)

RULE The Torah is very precise with its wording. If a verse contains an extra word or even an extra letter, this is to teach us a new law or detail. Certain words or phrases—such as "also," "and" (which in Hebrew is indicated by adding the letter *vav* to a word), or the repetition of a word, indicate an *addition* to the law. Other words or phrases—such as "if," "but," or when a word is spelled "deficiently" (in Hebrew, certain words can be spelled with or without certain letters)—indicates the *exclusion* of a certain circumstance from this law.

EXAMPLE In the law cited above from Exodus 23:5, the phrase "assist must you assist with him" contains both an "addition" and a "subtraction." The repetition, "assist must you assist" teaches us that "if one unloads the animal and loads it [and it collapsed again], unloads it and loads it, even four or five times, one is still obligated [to assist]." On the other hand, the phrase "*with* him" teaches us that "if [the owner of the animal] went and sat off to a side and said, 'Since you are commanded to unload, go ahead and unload,' one is not obligated."

GEZEIRAH SHAVAH
(*"DERIVING FROM COMMON WORDING"*)

RULE When the same word or phrase appears in two different places, the meaning in one place can be extrapolated to the second place.

EXAMPLE Deuteronomy 6:8 instructs on the mitzvah of tefillin: "You shall bind them as a sign on your hand, and they shall be phylacteries between your eyes." Yet the head-tefillin are not worn literally between the eyes, but rather above the forehead, centered between the eyes. This is derived from the fact that the phrase "between your eyes" also appears in Deuteronomy 14:1, where it carries that meaning. There, the Torah instructs, "Do not make a baldness between your eyes for the dead," forbidding the idolatrous practice of tearing out the hair in the front-center of one's head as a sign of mourning.

KELAL U'PERAT (*"GENERALITY AND PARTICULARITY"*)

RULE The premise behind this rule is that the word order in the Torah is precise. When a verse contains both general and particular terms, the order in which they are placed will teach us how the law should be applied. This rule has three variations:

1) *General and particular*: When a generality is followed by particulars, the law is limited to those particulars only.

2) *Particular and general*: When particulars are followed by a generality, the law applies to everything included in the generality.

3) *General, particular, and general*: When the verse begins with a generality, followed by particulars, followed by a second generality, then the law includes anything that is *similar* to the particularities cited.

EXAMPLE *General and particular*: Deuteronomy 22:11 states, "Do not wear a blend of woven threads, wool and linen together." Here we have a generality ("a blend of woven threads"), followed by a particular ("wool and linen together"). This means that the particular clause defines the general clause: the Torah is only forbidding the wearing of a wool and linen combination. (Had the Torah reversed the order and said, "wool and linen together, a blend of threads," it would have been understood to mean that all mixed fibers are forbidden, with wool and linen being the example).

Particular and general: When the Torah commands that a person's animals should rest on Shabbat, it writes, "your ox and your donkey and all your animals" (Deuteronomy 5:14). Because this is formulated as particulars followed by a generality, the law applies to "all your animals," not just oxen and donkeys.

General, particular, and general: The law of the "unpaid guardian" (Exodus 22:6–8) details the responsibilities of a person who is taking care of another's property as a favor, and the procedures to be followed in case the property is damaged or lost. Essentially, the unpaid guardian is responsible for losses arising out of outright negligence and for losses following the guardian's unauthorized use of the property, but is absolved of responsibility for losses through theft or natural disaster. There are also various oaths that unpaid guardians are required to take when they claim that the object was lost or stolen.

The Torah introduces these laws as follows: "If a person gives to his fellow money or utensils to watch…" The structure of this sentence is: a generality ("if a person gives to his fellow"), followed by particulars ("money or utensils"), followed by a generality ("to watch").

Now, this same sentence could have also have been formulated as a "general and particular" (e.g., "If a person gives his fellow to watch money or utensils"), in which case the laws enumerated in these verses would have applied to "money and utensils" only. Alternatively, if the verse would have been written as "particular and general" (e.g., "If money and utensils are given by a person to his fellow to watch"), the law would have applied to anything that is placed under an unpaid guardian's responsibility. Instead, we have a "general, particular, and general" format, which dictates that "we only include what is similar to the particulars." Not just those two particulars, but also not everything. Rather, the particulars are to be viewed as examples that define what should be included in the general clauses.

In this case, the Talmud provides two criteria for something to be considered "similar to the particulars": 1) it is moveable 2) it has intrinsic monetary value. A basket of fruit, for example, is neither money nor a utensil, but meets these two criteria. A house or a field has intrinsic monetary value but is not moveable, so it is not included. A document is moveable, but is not considered to have intrinsic monetary value (other than the cost of the parchment), so it is not included in this specific set of laws.

THE SUGYA

The *sugya* (literally, "topic") is the basic unit of the Talmudic narrative. A *sugya* will typically begin with a Mishnah or a citation from a Mishnah, and then proceed to ask a series of questions regarding the wording of the law, its source in the Torah, the reasoning behind it, how this law compares and contrasts with other Mishnaic rulings, and what additional principles and laws can be derived from it. The *sugya* will also explore the differences of opinion between Mishnaic sages (*tana'im*), as well as differing interpretations and conclusions by post-Mishnaic sages (*amora'im*), citing proofs and counter-proofs from other Mishnaic sources.

The following treatment is a summary of some of the main points discussed in the first two pages of the Talmudic tractate *Bava Metzia* and in the major Talmudic commentaries, known as the *sugya* of *Shnayim ochazin be-talit* ("Two people are holding on to a garment").

THE CASES

CASE 1 Two people are holding on to a garment. One says, "I found it," and the other says, "I found it." (This case involves a garment whose owner cannot be identified, and therefore belongs to its finder.)

RULING Each of the two litigants swears an oath that "no less than half of it belongs to me." The garment is then divided between them. (*Mishnah, Bava Metzia 1:1*)

CASE 2 Two people conduct a business transaction in which a donkey is traded for a cow. It is later discovered that in the interim, the cow gave birth to a calf. The cow was in a public pasture at the time, and neither of the litigants claims to know if the birth occurred before the transaction (in which case the calf belongs to the seller of the cow), or after the transaction (in which case it belongs to the buyer).

RULING The value of the calf is divided between the litigants. No oaths are required. (*Mishnah, Bava Metzia 8:4, as per Mishneh Torah, Laws of Sales, 20:11*)

CASE 3 An ox gores a cow, and we subsequently find the cow's newborn calf lying dead beside it. However, we do not know if the calf was stillborn before the cow was gored, or if it was born dead as a result of the goring. What is the extent of the liability of the owner of the ox for the loss of the calf?

RULING The Talmud cites two opinions regarding this case. The first opinion is that of Sumchus, who says that the two litigants "split the difference," with the owner of the ox paying half of the amount that would have been due if there was no doubt (similar to case #2). The second opinion is that of other (unnamed) sages, who rule that the owner of the ox does not have to pay anything for the calf, unless the owner of the cow can prove that it died as a result of the goring. (*Mishnah, Bava Kama 5:1, as per Talmud, ad loc., 46b*)

CASE 4 Two people entrusted funds with a third person. One of them deposited 100 *zuz*, and the other one deposited 200 *zuz*. Now, each one is claiming that the larger sum belongs to them.

RULING The funds are placed under the guardianship of the court and are not released to either party until one of them can provide proof that the larger sum is theirs. If neither brings proof (or admits the truth), the money remains in the court's possession "until Elijah the Prophet comes." (*Mishnah, Bava Metzia 3:1*)

CASE 5 There is a boat out in the water over which two people are claiming ownership. Neither can provide any proof of ownership or prior possession to support their claim.

RULING The court does not involve itself in this case. "Whichever one is stronger prevails," unless the other can prove their claim. (*Talmud, Bava Batra 34b*)

SIMILAR SCENARIOS, DIFFERENT OUTCOMES

In all five cases, a property—either an object or a sum of money—is claimed by two parties, neither of whom can provide conclusive proof that it belongs to them. Yet in each case, the court reaches a different conclusion, resulting in five different rulings:

In case 1, the property is divided, but only after each party swears an oath.

In case 2, the property is divided without an oath.

In case 3, we have two rulings: either the property is divided without an oath (Sumchus' ruling), or it remains in the possession of the plaintiff (the sages' ruling).

In case 4, the property is not released to either party.

In case 5, the court refuses to get involved. Whichever party manages to seize the property first keeps it, unless and until the other can establish proof of ownership.

What is the logic behind these diverse rulings?

THREE CRITERIA

In considering how to act in cases of "property whose ownership is in doubt," the court asks itself the following questions:

a) In whose possession does the property currently reside? Is it in the possession of one of the two litigants, is it in both their possessions, or is it in neither's possession?

b) Is one of the two litigants certainly lying? Or is it possible that both have legitimate claims to the property, and that dividing it will actually give each their rightful due?

c) Is there an objective dilemma that is being presented to us, or is our doubt regarding the ownership of the object wholly the product of the litigants' arguments?

Based on these three criteria, we will be able to explain the five rulings cited above.

THE MUCHZAK

A cardinal governing principle in property cases (derived from Exodus 24:14) is that the burden of proof lies with the plaintiff. In the words of the Talmud, "The one who seeks to take out from the possession of his fellow, he is the one who must provide proof." So the first thing that the court needs to establish is: Who is the *muchzak*, or "possessor," in whose possession the property currently resides?

Among all the cases cited here, there is one case in which there is a clear *muchzak*—case 3. The money is in the possession of the owner of the goring ox. So, we tell the owner of the cow: If you wish to take out money from the *muchzak*'s pocket, you need to provide proof that their ox was the cause of your calf's death. Until you do, the property remains with its current possessor. This explains the ruling of "the sages" in case 3. (Sumchus' opinion is more complex, and will be understood after the other cases are discussed).

TWO POSSESSORS

Now let us consider case 1. Who is the *muchzak* here? Two people walk into the courtroom holding on to a garment, each claiming that they found it. There are no witnesses who saw what happened, and no proof of prior ownership or possession. But both are holding on to it. So both are *muchzakim.* Each is attempting to "take out from the possession of his fellow." Since both have equal rights to this garment, the court decides to divide it between them.

But the court has a problem. If any time that two people are in equal possession of an object, and neither can prove it is theirs, the object will be divided, then what is to prevent a person from grabbing hold of an object that another person has found and claiming an equal share in the windfall? Hence the required oath. Swearing falsely in a court of law is a very grave sin (a violation of one of the Ten Commandments), and it is

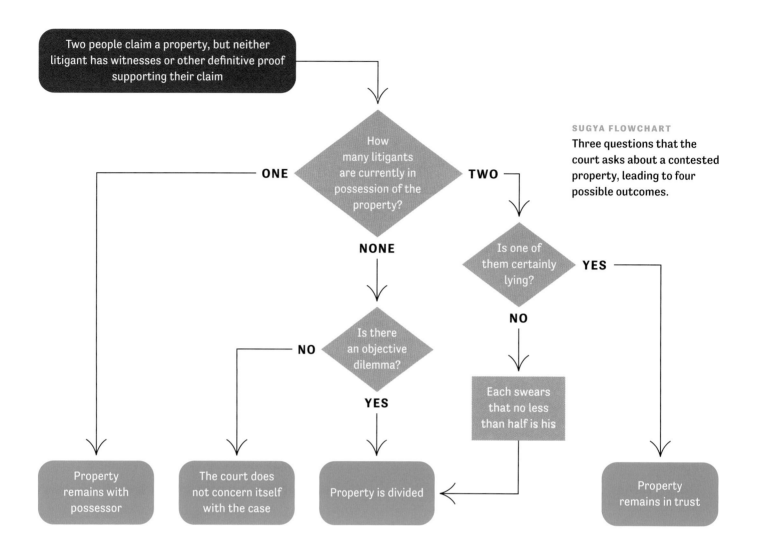

SUGYA FLOWCHART
Three questions that the court asks about a contested property, leading to four possible outcomes.

assumed that the prospect of violating such a severe prohibition would deter anyone who may be tempted to make a quick profit at the expense of their fellow.

There is another question that the court asks before it decides to divide the property between the litigants: Is one of the two litigants certainly lying? Or is it possible that both have legitimate claims to the property? If the court is certain that one of the two parties is lying, it will not rule to divide the disputed property between them, as this would be rewarding the thief. In the case of the found garment, it is possible that both of them saw it, rushed to grab it, and picked it up together, and that each honestly believes that they got it first. As long as there exists the *possibility* that the division is not depriving a *muchzak* of their rightfully held property, the court will proceed with it, as the only equitable solution for a case of two "possessors."

Notice, as well, that the oath is worded in such a way that the two oaths do not contradict each other. Each one swears that "no less than half of it belongs to me"—language that is consistent with each one's initial argument, but also with the court's ruling. Indeed, the court would never allow an oath which it knows to be false to be taken.

TWO POSSESSORS, ONE LIAR

With case 4, we have another scenario in which the contested property is in the possession of both litigants. While they are not physically holding on to it, the person to whom they entrusted their funds is holding the money for them, in effect, acting as their agent. Legally, this makes them both *muchzakim* of the property.

However, in this case, one of them is certainly lying. Therefore, the court cannot rule that the contested funds should be divided, as there is no possibility that this settlement would reflect the truth, and it would actually reward the thief. But neither can the court refrain from dealing with the matter, as it has two people standing before it, each of whom is a *muchzak* seeking to prevent the other from taking property that is in their possession. The only possible ruling, therefore, is for the property to be held in trust until such time as its rightful owner can be determined.

NO POSSESSORS, NO OBJECTIVE DILEMMA

We have examined one case in which there is one *muchzak*, and two cases in which both litigants are *muchzakim*. Now we turn to consider the third possibility: What about cases in which *neither* party is in possession of the property?

In such cases, there is another factor that the court considers: Is the dilemma that we have regarding the ownership of this property a product of objective circumstances, or is it wholly the product of the litigants' arguments?

Let us look at case 5. A boat sits in the water, and two people claim ownership over it. It is not in the possession of either of them, nor can any one of them produce any proof that connects them to it. Other than their arguments, there is nothing before the court that indicates any connection between the boat and any one of the litigants. If a third person were to walk in and claim ownership, we would have as much—or rather, as little—cause to think that it is theirs.

With neither a *muchzak*, nor any objective circumstances pointing to either of the two litigants as possible owners of the property, the court has no basis on which to concern itself with the case, and no basis on which to prevent one of them from taking possession of it.

NO POSSESSORS, BUT OBJECTIVE DILEMMA

Case 2 also has no *muchzak*. The newborn calf, born in a public pasture, is not in the possession of either one of the litigants. But unlike the free-floating boat,

there are objective circumstances that establish the litigants' respective claims to ownership. We know that it belongs to one of them. The dilemma before the court exists independently of their arguments.

In such a case, it is incumbent on the court to devise a solution, however imperfect. That solution is to divide the disputed property, so that the true owner will get at least half their due. Neither litigant claims to know when the calf was born; rather, each is saying, "Maybe it's mine." So there is no basis to the fear that we might be rewarding a thief's dishonesty (as in case 4). For the same reason, there is no reason to require an oath, whose purpose is to deter untruthful claims. It is the circumstances themselves, not the litigants' arguments, that are dictating our course of action.

SUMCHUS' OPINION

Now we can also understand Sumchus' ruling in case 3. Sumchus takes the principle of "objective dilemma" one step further, applying it even to the case where only one of the litigants is a *muchzak*. If the dilemma of ownership is a product of objective circumstances, and neither litigant claims to know what has actually transpired, why should the fact that the property happens to be in one person's possession place that person at an advantage? The other sages, however, maintain that the overriding principle remains that property cannot be extracted from a *muchzak* without definitive proof.

In fact, there is some discussion in the Talmud and the commentaries as to whether the sages who disagree with Sumchus in case 3 might do so also in case 2, ruling that the calf should not be divided, but rather awarded to the seller of the cow. According to this view, although the calf is not physically in the possession of the seller, the fact that it originally belonged to the seller (as a fetus in its mother's womb) makes the seller the *muchzak*, granting them possession of the calf unless the buyer can prove that it was born after the sale.

THE ART OF THE PARABLE

 MIDRASH RABBAH, *VAYIKRA 4:6*

A group of people were traveling in a boat. One of them took an awl and began to drill a hole beneath himself.

His companions said to him: "Why are you doing this?" Replied the man: "What concern is it of yours? Am I not drilling under my own place?"

Said they to him: "But the water that will come up will drown us all!"

 MIDRASH RABBAH, *BEREISHITH 5:10*

When iron was created, all the trees started trembling. Said iron to the trees: "Why are you afraid? If none of you provide a handle for my blade, you cannot be hurt."

 TALMUD, *TAANIT 5b*

A man was traveling through the desert. He was hungry, thirsty, and tired. He came upon a tree that was laden with luscious fruit and gave plentiful shade; under the tree ran a spring of water. He ate of the fruit, drank of the water, and rested in the shade. When he was about to leave, he turned to the tree and said:

"Tree, O tree, with what should I bless you?"

"Should I bless you that your fruit be sweet? Your fruit is already sweet.

"Should I bless you that your shade be plentiful? Your shade is plentiful. That a spring of water should run beneath you? A spring of water runs beneath you.

"There is one thing with which I can bless you: May the Almighty grant that all the saplings planted from your seeds should be like you."

 MIDRASH TEHILIM, *PSALM 39*

The king of Persia fell ill and was on the verge of death. The physicians said to him, "Your only cure is if they bring you the milk of a lioness, from which we will prepare a cure for you."

There was a man there who said to the king, "If you wish it, I will go. Just give me ten goats." The king in-

structed his servants and they gave him the goats.

The man went to a lion's lair where there was a lioness nursing her cubs. On the first day he stood at a distance, and threw her one goat, which she ate. On the second day he moved a bit closer and threw her another goat. So he did day after day, until he was playing with her. He took from her milk and went.

When he was halfway back he went to sleep. In his dream he saw all the limbs of his body fighting with each other.

The feet said: "None of the body's limbs compare to us! Had we not walked, he would not have been able to bring the milk."

Said the hands: "There are none who compare to us. If we had not milked the lioness, he could not have done anything."

Said the eyes: "We are above you all. If we had not shown him the way, nothing could have been done."

The heart called out and said: "I am above you all. If I had not given the counsel, nothing would have been accomplished."

Said the tongue: "If not for me, what could any of you have accomplished?"

Responded all the limbs: "How dare you compare yourself to us! You sit locked away in a dark place. You don't even have a bone, like the other limbs."

The tongue answered them: "Today you will all admit that I am king and ruler over you."

The man heard all these words and he was afraid. He woke from his sleep and went on his way. Arriving at his destination, he went into the king and said to him, "Here, I brought you the milk of a bitch."

The king was enraged, and ordered that the man be hanged. As they were taking him to the gallows, all his limbs were weeping. Said the tongue to them, "Did I not tell you that you are all worthless? If I save you, will you admit that I am your king?" Said they, "Yes."

Immediately, the tongue said, "Take me back to the

Converse,
David Asher Brook,
Sydney, Australia, 2015

king." They took him back. Said the man to the king, "Why did you instruct to hang me? This is my reward?" Said the king, "Because you brought a bitch's milk to hasten my death." Said the man, "What do you care, as long as it will heal you? Furthermore, a lioness is also called a bitch." They took the milk from him and tested it, and found it to be of a lioness.

Said the limbs to the tongue: "We concede to you that you spoke the truth."

Thus it is stated (Proverbs 18:21): "Death and life are in the hand of the tongue."

💬 **MIDRASH RABBAH,** *VAYIKRA 4:5*

There was a king who had an orchard in which there were beautiful fruits. The king placed two guardians in it; one was lame and the other was blind. The king said to them: "Take care of these beautiful fruits."

A while later, the king came to the orchard, and said to them, "Where are the beautiful fruits?"

Said the blind one, "Your majesty, am I then able to see?" Said the lame one, "Your majesty, am I then able to walk?"

Now this king was a wise man. What did he do with them? He placed the lame one on the shoulders of the blind one, and said to them: "This is what you did to eat the fruits."

So, too, in the World to Come, G-d says to the soul, "Why did you sin?"

Says the soul, "Master of the world! I did not sin. The body sinned. From the moment that I left the body, I am like a pure bird flying through the air. How would I sin before You?"

G-d says to the body, "Why did you sin?"

Says the body, "Master of the world! I did not sin. The soul sinned. From the moment that it left me, I am like a stone that has been cast to the ground. How would I sin before You?"

What does G-d do with them? He brings the soul and inserts it into the body, and judges them as one.

Halachah (Torah law)

Halachah is the "bottom line" of Torah, the juncture where it interfaces with the hard surface of reality. It is in the field of Halachah that all the principles, ideas, and arguments that the student of Torah has grappled with are brought to bear on the question: What should we do, in the here and now, in these specific circumstances?

Halachah addresses the entire existence of the Jew. In everything we do—from waking to bedtime, from birth to burial—there is a G-dly, holy way to do it; in every dilemma we face, there is a divinely ordained set of rules by which we navigate. It is by means of Halachah that the Torah not only informs but also transforms human life and the physical world, shaping them in accordance with the divine will.

NOTE: THROUGHOUT THIS BOOK, THE SYMBOL INDICATES A HALACHIC CITATION

 DEUTERONOMY 30:11–14

For this mitzvah, which I command you this day, is not mysterious to you, nor is it far away.

It is not in heaven, that you should say, "Who will go up to heaven for us and get it for us, and teach it to us so that we can do it?"

Nor is it across the sea, that you should say, "Who will cross to the other side of the sea for us and get it for us, and teach it to us so that we can fulfill it?"

Rather, the matter is very near to you, in your mouth and in your heart, to do it.

 SHULCHAN ARUCH, *ORACH CHAYIM, 1:1*

Be strong as a lion to get up in the morning to serve your Creator, so that it is you who wakes the dawn.

[*Gloss*] The verse "I set G-d before me always" (Psalms 16:8) is a primary principle of the Torah, and of the attainments of the righteous who walk before G-d. For one cannot compare how a person sits and moves about and conducts themself when they are alone in their home, to how a person sits and moves about and conducts themself when standing before a great king…. How much more so when a person takes to heart that the great king, the Holy One, blessed be He, whose presence fills the entire world, stands over them and observes their deeds….

[Such a person] will not be intimidated by those who mock their service of the Creator.

TALMUD, *BERACHOT 8a*

From the day that the Holy Temple was destroyed, the only thing that G-d has in His world are the four cubits of Halachah.

Synagogue of R. Joseph Caro (1488–1575, author of Shulchan Aruch), Safed, Israel

 R. SHALOM JOSEPH HERCSZTARK
CITED IN *MOFET HADOR, P. 24*

The Error

R. Yechezkel Landau, author of the Halachic work *Noda bi-Yehudah*, served as the rabbi of Prague from 1754 to 1793. Once, a group of scholars who wished to contest his rabbinic qualifications presented him with a complex question in Torah law, construed in such a way so as to mislead him and embarrass him with an incorrect ruling. The ruse was successful, and the rabbi decided the case incorrectly. Immediately his detractors pounced on him, showing that his verdict contradicted Torah law.

Said R. Yechezkel: "I am certain that this case is not actually relevant, and that you have invented it in order to embarrass me."

He then explained: "Whenever a human being of flesh and blood is called upon to decide a matter of Torah law, we are confronted with a basic dilemma: How is the finite and error-prone human mind given the authority to determine what is the divine will? But the Torah itself declares that 'it is not in heaven,' and has been given to us to study and comprehend. When a person puts aside all selfish considerations and completely surrenders their mind to serve the Torah, the Almighty guarantees that the result will be consistent with His will.

"However," concluded R. Yechezkel, "this guarantee applies only to an actual Halachic question, when a rabbi is called upon to determine what it is that G-d desires to be done under a given set of circumstances; but not if the rabbi's personal honor is the only issue at hand. Had you presented me with a real question, I am certain that I would not have erred, because I know that I approached the matter with no interest other than to serve the divine will. But because your case was only a hypothetical question, my mind was just like every other mind, great or small—limited and manipulable."

THE HALACHIC CODES

MISHNAH

COMPILED BY
R. Judah ha-Nasi, c. 189 CE
STRUCTURE Six orders,
63 tractates, 523 chapters,
4,184 *mishnayot*
PRIMARY FEATURES First
codification of Halachah, which
until then was transmitted by
oral tradition from *beit-din*
(court of Torah law) to *beit-din*.

1. SEEDS

Shema, daily prayers, and
blessings on food

Agricultural gifts to the Kohen,
Levite, and the poor

Charity

Forbidden hybrids

The sabbatical year

2. APPOINTED TIMES

Shabbat and the festivals

The Jewish calendar

3. WOMEN

Marriage and divorce

Forbidden sexual relations

Vows

4. DAMAGES

Torts

Loans and usury

Partnerships and transactions

Criminal law

Judicial procedures

Idolatrous practices

Ethics

5. SACRAMENTS

The Holy Temple and the
Temple service

Donations to the Holy Temple

Kosher dietary laws

6. PURITIES

Ritual purity

Mikveh

Nidah

MISHNEH TORAH

COMPILED BY
R. Moses ben Maimon
(Maimonides), c. 1177
STRUCTURE 14 books,
83 sections, 1000 chapters
PRIMARY FEATURES
First and only work to
systematically codify all the
Halachot of the Torah.

1. KNOWLEDGE

Belief, knowledge, love,
and awe of G-d

Character and ethics

Torah study

Idolatrous practices

Repentance

2. LOVE

Shema, daily prayers, and
blessings on food

Tefillin, Mezuzah, and Torah scrolls

Tzitzit

Circumcision

3. TIMES

Shabbat and the festivals

The Jewish calendar

4. WOMEN

Marriage and divorce

5. SANCTITY

Forbidden sexual relations

Kosher dietary laws

6. SEPARATION

Vows

Donations to the Holy Temple

7. SEEDS

Agricultural gifts to the Kohen,
Levite, and the poor

Charity

Forbidden hybrids

The sabbatical year

8. SERVICE

The Holy Temple
and the Temple service

9. OFFERINGS

The *korbanot* (animal and
meal offerings) brought in the
Holy Temple

10. PURITY

Ritual purity

Mikveh

11. DAMAGES

Torts

Criminal law

12. ACQUISITIONS

Partnerships and business
transactions

13. CIVIL LAWS

Loans and usury

Renters and bailees

Monetary disputes

Inheritance

14. JUDGES

Judges and judicial procedures

Burial and mourning

Kings and government

The Messianic redemption

TUR & SHULCHAN ARUCH

COMPILED BY

R. Jacob ben Asher, c. 1340
R. Joseph Caro, c. 1563
R. Moses Isserlis, c. 1571

STRUCTURE Four "columns,"
1,705 sections

PRIMARY FEATURES Provides
rulings based on the hundreds
of Halachic works produced up
until its time. Unlike *Mishneh
Torah*, however, it includes
only laws that currently apply,
omitting those connected with
the Temple service.

The original codification,
commonly referred to as *Tur*,
was authored by R. Jacob
ben Asher, who grouped the
laws into four primary topics
or *turim* ("rows" or "columns").
Sephardic Halachist R. Joseph
Caro wrote an extensive
commentary on the *Tur*,
and summarized his
conclusions in his *Shulchan
Aruch* ("Set Table"), to which
R. Moses Isserlis appended
glosses reflecting the rulings
and customs followed by
the Ashkenazic communities.
Shulchan Aruch and its
attendant commentaries
form the basis for almost
all subsequent Halachic
discussion.

1. ORACH CHAYIM

WAY OF LIFE
(697 SECTIONS)

1–7	Morning routine
8–24	Tzitzit
25–45	Tefillin
46–149	Morning prayer, Shema, and public Torah reading
150–156	The synagogue
157–216	Mealtime blessings and rituals
217–231	Other blessings
232–234	Afternoon prayer
235–239	Evening prayer
240–241	Modesty
242–416	Shabbat
417–428	Rosh Chodesh and the Jewish calendar
429–494	Passover, the *omer* count, and Shavuot
495–548	General festival observances
549–580	Fast days and the Three Weeks
581–603	Rosh Hashanah
604–624	Yom Kippur
625–669	Sukkot
670–685	Hanukkah
686–697	Purim

Ⓑ Ⓕ

2. YOREH DE'AH

INSTRUCTOR OF KNOWLEDGE
(403 SECTIONS)

1–138	Kosher dietary laws
139–158	Idolatrous practices
159–177	Loans and usury
178–182	Idolatrous practices
183–200	Marital separation during menstruation
201–202	Mikveh
203–239	Vows and oaths
240–244	Honoring parents and teachers
245–246	Torah study
247–259	Charity
260–266	Circumcision
267	Servants
268–269	Converts
270–284	Torah scrolls
285–291	Mezuzah
292–304 306–333	Hybrids and other agricultural laws
305	Redemption of the firstborn
334	Excommunication
335–339	Visiting the sick
340–403	Burial and mourning

Ⓑ Ⓓ Ⓖ Ⓗ

PRIMARY COMMENTARIES ON SHULCHAN ARUCH

Ⓐ Sma (R. Joshua Falk, 1555–1614)

Ⓑ Taz (R. David Segal, 1586–1667)

Ⓒ Chelkat Mechokek (R. Moses Lima, c. 1605–1658)

Ⓓ Shach (R. Shabetai ha-Kohen, 1621–1662)

Ⓔ Beit Shmuel (R. Samuel of Fiyorda, c. 1630–1700)

Ⓕ Magen Avraham (R. Abraham Gombiner, c. 1637–1683)

Ⓖ Kereti u-Peleti (R. Jonathan Eibeschutz, 1694–1764)

Ⓗ Pri Megadim (R. Joseph Teomim, 1727–1792)

Ⓘ Ketzot ha-Choshen (R. Aryeh Leib Heller, 1745–1812)

3. EVEN HA-EZER

STONE OF SALVATION
(178 SECTIONS)

1–14	Marriage
15–26	Forbidden sexual relations
27–65	Marriage
66–118	The *ketubah* (marriage contract) and the financial obligations between husband and wife
119–155	Divorce
156–176	Levirate marriage and *chalitzah*
177–178	Rape, seduction, and adultery

Ⓑ Ⓒ Ⓔ

4. CHOSHEN MISHPAT

BREASTPLATE OF JUDGMENT
(427 SECTIONS)

1–38	Judges and judicial procedures
39–152	Loans and financial disputes
153–188	Neighbors, partners, and agents
189–258	Sales and other transactions
259–275	Lost and ownerless property
276–289	Inheritance
290–306	Trustees and bailees
307–347	Renters and borrowers
348–377	Theft
378–427	Torts

Ⓐ Ⓑ Ⓓ Ⓖ Ⓘ

HALACHIC RESPONSA

queries in Torah law through the ages

> Jews are a scattered people, and from the earliest days of the Diaspora, queries in Torah law were dispatched to Halachic authorities who responded with written answers called *teshuvot*, or "responsa." This correspondence—which continues to this day—has produced a vast trove of Halachic literature, with some rabbinic responders authoring thousands of *teshuvot*. A typical responsum may run for many pages, citing and analyzing dozens of sources from the Talmud, the Talmudic commentaries, the Halachic codes and their commentaries, and previous responsa, and weighing the merits of several proposed solutions before rendering its decision. Presented here is a sampling of queries posed to different Halachists addressing issues of their time and place.

Atlanta
R. Tobias Gefen
1935 *Is Coca-Cola kosher?*

New York
R. Moshe Feinstein
1977 *Conjoined twins share a single six-chambered heart, and separating them would save the life of one of them but kill the other. Should the procedure be performed?*
1978 *When volunteers respond to a medical emergency on Shabbat, are they permitted to drive home after the emergency has been taken care of?*

Worms
R. Yair Bacharach
1699 *A woman committed adultery and fears that she is pregnant. Is she permitted to drink a potion that would terminate her pregnancy?*
1699 *When calculating one's earning for tithing (giving 10% to charity), may a person deduct their business expenses?*

Zurich
R. Mordecai Jacob Breisch
1963 *May a person undergo cosmetic surgery for the purpose of improving their appearance?*

Barcelona
R. Solomon ben Aderet (Rashba)
c. 1275 *Statements by the Talmudic sages describe the physical universe as finite in size, but Maimonides, in his* Guide for the Perplexed, *cites philosophical and scientific proofs that it is limitless. How should we address this contradiction?*
c. 1275 *Is it appropriate to inscribe the donor's name on a synagogue annex that he donated?*

Entre Rios
R. Joseph Aaron Taran
1894 *Is the Muscovy duck, a New World species, kosher?*

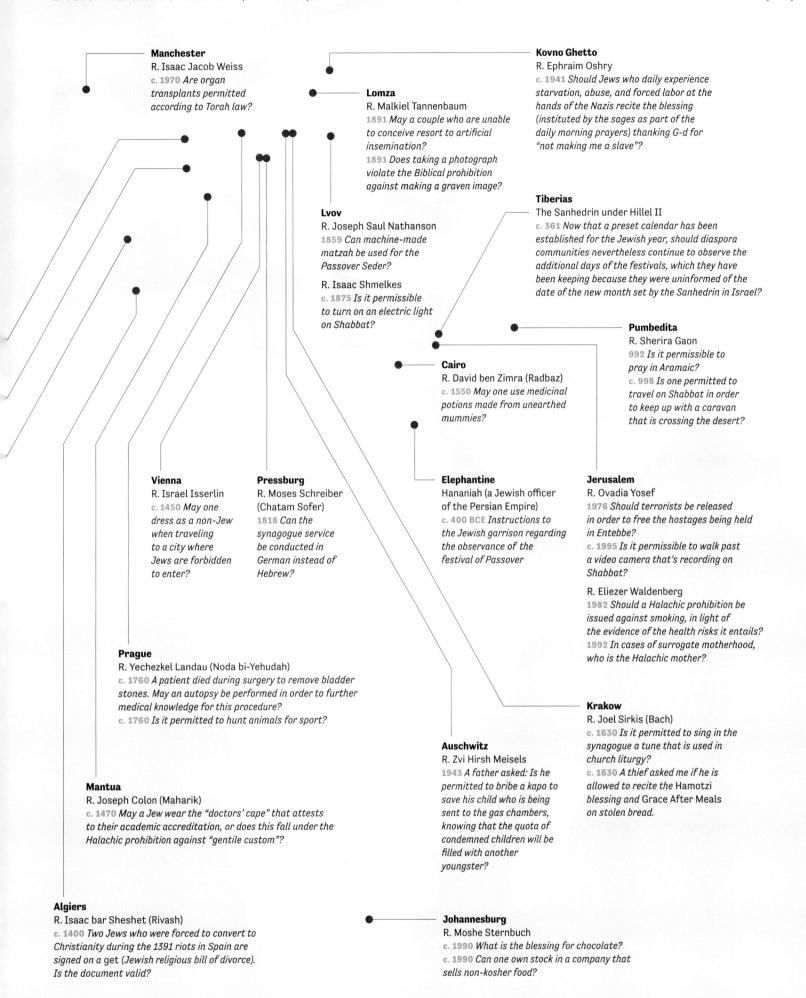

Manchester
R. Isaac Jacob Weiss
c. 1970 *Are organ transplants permitted according to Torah law?*

Kovno Ghetto
R. Ephraim Oshry
c. 1941 *Should Jews who daily experience starvation, abuse, and forced labor at the hands of the Nazis recite the blessing (instituted by the sages as part of the daily morning prayers) thanking G-d for "not making me a slave"?*

Lomza
R. Malkiel Tannenbaum
1891 *May a couple who are unable to conceive resort to artificial insemination?*
1891 *Does taking a photograph violate the Biblical prohibition against making a graven image?*

Lvov
R. Joseph Saul Nathanson
1859 *Can machine-made matzah be used for the Passover Seder?*

R. Isaac Shmelkes
c. 1875 *Is it permissible to turn on an electric light on Shabbat?*

Tiberias
The Sanhedrin under Hillel II
c. 361 *Now that a preset calendar has been established for the Jewish year, should diaspora communities nevertheless continue to observe the additional days of the festivals, which they have been keeping because they were uninformed of the date of the new month set by the Sanhedrin in Israel?*

Pumbedita
R. Sherira Gaon
992 *Is it permissible to pray in Aramaic?*
c. 998 *Is one permitted to travel on Shabbat in order to keep up with a caravan that is crossing the desert?*

Cairo
R. David ben Zimra (Radbaz)
c. 1550 *May one use medicinal potions made from unearthed mummies?*

Vienna
R. Israel Isserlin
c. 1450 *May one dress as a non-Jew when traveling to a city where Jews are forbidden to enter?*

Pressburg
R. Moses Schreiber (Chatam Sofer)
1818 *Can the synagogue service be conducted in German instead of Hebrew?*

Elephantine
Hananiah (a Jewish officer of the Persian Empire)
c. 400 BCE *Instructions to the Jewish garrison regarding the observance of the festival of Passover*

Jerusalem
R. Ovadia Yosef
1976 *Should terrorists be released in order to free the hostages being held in Entebbe?*
c. 1995 *Is it permissible to walk past a video camera that's recording on Shabbat?*

R. Eliezer Waldenberg
1982 *Should a Halachic prohibition be issued against smoking, in light of the evidence of the health risks it entails?*
1992 *In cases of surrogate motherhood, who is the Halachic mother?*

Prague
R. Yechezkel Landau (Noda bi-Yehudah)
c. 1760 *A patient died during surgery to remove bladder stones. May an autopsy be performed in order to further medical knowledge for this procedure?*
c. 1760 *Is it permitted to hunt animals for sport?*

Krakow
R. Joel Sirkis (Bach)
c. 1630 *Is it permitted to sing in the synagogue a tune that is used in church liturgy?*
c. 1630 *A thief asked me if he is allowed to recite the* Hamotzi *blessing and Grace After Meals on stolen bread.*

Auschwitz
R. Zvi Hirsh Meisels
1943 *A father asked: Is he permitted to bribe a kapo to save his child who is being sent to the gas chambers, knowing that the quota of condemned children will be filled with another youngster?*

Mantua
R. Joseph Colon (Maharik)
c. 1470 *May a Jew wear the "doctors' cape" that attests to their academic accreditation, or does this fall under the Halachic prohibition against "gentile custom"?*

Algiers
R. Isaac bar Sheshet (Rivash)
c. 1400 *Two Jews who were forced to convert to Christianity during the 1391 riots in Spain are signed on a get (Jewish religious bill of divorce). Is the document valid?*

Johannesburg
R. Moshe Sternbuch
c. 1990 *What is the blessing for chocolate?*
c. 1990 *Can one own stock in a company that sells non-kosher food?*

MEDICAL ETHICS

 DEUTERONOMY 4:15

Verily guard your lives.

 MAIMONIDES, *MISHNEH TORAH, LAWS OF CHARACTER, 4:1*

Maintaining a healthy and sound body is among the ways of serving G-d. For a person cannot understand or have any knowledge of the Creator if they are ill. A person should therefore avoid that which harms the body, and accustom themself to that which is healthful and strengthens the body.

 R. SCHNEUR ZALMAN OF LIADI *SHULCHAN ARUCH HARAV, LAWS OF INJURY, SEC. 4*

It is forbidden to strike another person, even if the person gave permission to hit them. For a person has no authority over their own body to injure it, or to humiliate it, or to cause it pain in any way.

 TALMUD, *BAVA KAMA 85a*

It is written (Exodus 21:19), "Heal he shall heal." This teaches us that a physician is granted license to heal.

 R. YOSEF YITZCHAK SCHNEERSOHN *SEFER HASICHOT 5705, P. 8*

The daughter-in-law of R. Menachem Mendel of Lubavitch (1789–1866) had fallen ill and the doctors were unanimous in their opinion that there was no hope of recovery. Said the Rebbe: "The Torah specifically grants permission to a doctor to heal. But nowhere is a doctor given the authority to decide that a human being is incurable. That is not in their jurisdiction."

 MAIMONIDES, *MISHNEH TORAH, LAWS OF THE FUNDAMENTALS OF TORAH, 5:1–6*

It is written regarding the mitzvot, "[You shall keep My statutes and My laws], which a person shall do and live by them" (Leviticus 18:5). [The Talmud (*Yoma* 85b) derives from this:] "Live by them"—not die by them.... For example, if a person falls ill and the physicians say that the cure involves transgressing a given Torah prohibition, we must do so, and use any of the Torah prohibitions as a remedy, with the exception of idol worship, forbidden sexual relations, and murder.

 MAIMONIDES, *MISHNEH TORAH, LAWS OF SHABBAT, 2:3 AND 2:18*

When we violate the Shabbat to care for a sick person whose life is in danger, the work should not be done by non-Jews or minors ... but by the leaders and sages.

If a building collapsed on Shabbat, we must clear the rubble, even if there is a doubt if anyone is there. If someone is found alive, but they have been crushed to the extent that it is impossible for them to recover, we continue to clear the rubble and rescue them, even if it is only to allow them to live for a short while.

 SHULCHAN ARUCH, *YOREH DE'AH, 339*

A dying person is like a live person in every respect... It is forbidden to take any action that would hasten their death. However, if there is something there that is hindering their death ... it is permissible to remove it, as long as no [life-shortening] action is being taken, only the removal of a hindrance.

 R. SHLOMO ZALMAN AUERBACH *MINCHAT SHLOMO, VOL. 1, RESPONSA 91:24*

Regarding the question of "quality of life," we have no yardstick by which to measure the value and importance of any life, not even the measure of the ability to study Torah and perform mitzvot. Indeed, the law is that we violate the Shabbat to save the life of a person who is aged, ill, deformed, uncommunicative, and senile, who cannot perform a single mitzvah and whose life is a burden and a source of suffering for their family ... nevertheless, even the greatest sage of the generation is commanded to make every effort to preserve this person's life, and to desecrate the Shabbat to do so....

Furthermore, even in the case that this sick person is suffering to such an extent that it is a mitzvah to pray for their death (as Ran writes in his commentary on Talmud, *Nedarim* 40a), at the same time, even as one prays for that person to be released from their suffering, one must actively preserve their life, desecrating the Shabbat numerous times....

There is, however, some confusion regarding the care of one who has the status of a *goses* [i.e., a terminally ill patient who is already in the process of dying]. Some believe that because we desecrate the Shabbat to treat such a patient, we are also obligated to coerce such a patient to accept medical treatment, since a person is not a master over their own life to relinquish even a single moment of it. However, in the case that the dying patient is experiencing great pain and suffering, or mental anguish, I would say that while nourishment and oxygen should be given even against the patient's will, it is permitted to refrain from medical treatments that cause suffering to the patient, if the patient demands this. Nevertheless, if the patient is a G-d-fearing person, it is desirable to explain to them that "a single moment of repentance and good deeds in this world is greater than all of the World to Come" (*Ethics of the Fathers*, 4:17).

 MICHAEL SCHULTZ AND GIL BAR-SELA
JOURNAL OF SUPPORTIVE ONCOLOGY,
VOL. 11, NO. 1, PP. 1–7

There are important differences between Western and Jewish ethics. Most significantly, we begin by noting this fundamental difference stated by the late Benjamin Freedman, Professor of Bioethics at McGill University: "... the distinction between an ethics whose foundational language is duty, as is true of the Jewish approach, and contrasting that with our common Western ethical approach, whose basis is rights."

In Judaism, one has a duty at all moments in life—whether to society, to family and friends, or to G-d. These duties devolve upon individuals and the collective, even against their will. In the Bible, they begin with Adam and Eve's duty upon creation "to work [the Garden] and protect it" (Genesis 2:15). The collective duties expand with the acceptance of the Ten Commandments and the Torah at Mount Sinai, following the Exodus from Egypt.

Making joint use of Western and Jewish approaches can be productive. "Secular bioethics ... has a great deal to say about procedural questions—who will decide—but relatively less about substantive questions—how to decide." Yet how and what to decide is the almost exclusive focus of Jewish bioethics. In this way, the two fields could be highly complementary.

If we narrow our focus from ethics to bioethics, we can consider what our duties are in relation to the Jewish system regarding questions of health. Judaism teaches that there is an obligation to seek healing. The obligation to seek healing finds its source in one of several possible texts in the Jewish tradition: "Just take care for yourself, and take great care of your life" (Deuteronomy 4:9); "Yet your blood of your own self I shall demand of you" (Genesis 9:5); and "Do not stand idly by the blood of your fellow," together with the presumption that "A person is their own relative" (Talmud, *Sanhedrin* 9b), meaning one must treat oneself at least as well as one treats one's fellow.

In Judaism, our bodies are not our own; rather, they are objects to be held in trust and used well on behalf of their true owner. G-d gave us the use of our body, but only on the condition that we care for it and seek medical treatment when necessary so that we can use it to fulfill our other duties.

BUSINESS ETHICS

The Talmud relates that "when a person is brought to their final judgment before the heavenly court, they are asked: Did you conduct your business dealings with honesty? Did you designate times for Torah study? Did you have children? Did you eagerly await the redemption?"

This Talmudic passage sheds light on what Judaism considers our most important tasks in life. Also noteworthy is the order in which the questions are posed: the very first question relates not to Torah learning, or raising a family, or striving for universal redemption, but to honesty in business! Indeed, business ethics occupies a major component of Halachah, and—as one of the citations in this section explains—is integral to the objective to "Love the Lord your G-d."

 LEVITICUS 25:14

When you sell something to your fellow, or make a purchase from the hand of your fellow, do not defraud one another.

 TALMUD, *BAVA METZIA 49b AND 50b*

A deviation of one-sixth [of the market value of a purchased item] constitutes fraud.... Less than a sixth, the sale stands; more than a sixth, the sale is nullified; a sixth, the sale stands but the deviation is refunded.

 MAIMONIDES, *MISHNEH TORAH, LAWS OF SALES, 15:3*

If a person sells real estate ... or movable property, and a defect is subsequently found in the property of which the purchaser was not aware, it may be returned, even if several years have passed, for the transaction was made under erroneous premises.... However, if the buyer uses the property after the blemish was discovered, this indicates that the buyer has accepted [the reduced value of their purchase], and no longer has the right to retract the sale.

 R. ACHAI GAON, *SHE'ILTOT, VAYECHI 36*

R. Safra was selling a donkey. A person came and wanted to purchase it. At that moment, R. Safra was reciting the Shema.

The person asked R. Safra, "Would you sell it to me for this amount?" R. Safra did not answer him.... So the buyer raised his offer and said, "Give it to me for this amount." R. Safra did not answer him.

When R. Safra finished reading the Shema, he said to him, "I decided in my mind to sell it to you when I heard your initial offer. I will not take more than that amount."

 TALMUD, *BAVA METZIA 83a*

Porters broke a barrel of wine belonging to Rabah son of R. Huna. Rabah confiscated their garments. The porters went to Rav.

Rav said to Rabah, "Give them their garments."

Said Rabah to Rav, "Is this the law?"

Official weight from Herod's reign, Jerusalem, Holy Land, 9 BCE

Said Rav to him, "Yes. As it is written, 'In order that you go on the path of the good' (Proverbs 2:20)."

He gave them their garments. The porters then said, "We are poor, and we worked all day; we are hungry and we have nothing."

Said Rav to Rabah, "Pay them their wages."

Said Rabah to Rav, "Is this the law?"

Rav said to him, "Yes. As it is written, 'and keep the ways of the righteous' (ibid.)."

 TALMUD, *ERUVIN 53b*

Said R. Joshua ben Hananiah: A little girl once got the better of me. I was traveling, and there was a path that cut across a field, and I took that path. This child said to me, "Rabbi, aren't you walking on someone's field?" I said to her, "I'm walking on a trodden path." Said she: "Thieves such as yourself have trampled it."

 EXODUS 22:24–26; DEUTERONOMY 24:10–11

When you lend money to My people, to the pauper with you, do not behave toward him as a creditor. Do not impose usury on him.

If you take your fellow's [night] garment as security, return it to him before the sun sets. For it is his only covering, it is his garment for his skin; in what shall he sleep? And it shall be that if he cries out to Me, I will hear, because I am compassionate….

When you make a loan of any sort to your fellow, do not enter his home to take his security. You shall stand outside; and your debtor shall bring the security to you outside.

 TALMUD, *BAVA METZIA 58b*

Just as there is fraud in sales, so there is fraud in words. A person should not say, "How much does this object cost?" when they have no intention of buying it.

 DENNIS PRAGER
THINK A SECOND TIME, PP. 15–16

Ever since I learned of this law as a college student, I have never regarded people who work in stores the same way as I did before…. Americans are frequently made aware of consumer rights, but this law makes it clear that there are also consumer obligations…. [It compels us] to see salespeople in a different light, transforming them from individuals whose sole function is to answer our questions into individuals with feelings and hopes for earning a living.

The ultimate genius of this law is that it forces us to establish something of an I-You relationship with the person behind the counter, rather than retaining the usual I-It relationship that we have with people whom we meet only in a service capacity.

Finally, this law can and ought to be applied to other areas of life. There are powerful ramifications to the principle that if you know that you are not going to buy, don't imply that you might, i.e., don't raise expectations you know you won't meet. One such ramification was made clear to me when a young woman, who had heard me speak about this law in a speech, told me how she wished the men whom she dated would live by the Storekeeper Law….

TALMUD, *YOMA 86a*

It is written (Deuteronomy 6:5), "You shall love the Lord your G-d." Meaning, the Name of Heaven should be made beloved because of you.

When a person who studies Scripture and Mishnah and attends upon Torah scholars is honest in business and speaks pleasantly to people, what do people then say? "Fortunate is the father who taught him Torah, fortunate is the teacher who taught him Torah! Woe unto people who have not studied the Torah! For this person, who has studied the Torah, look how fine his ways are, how righteous his deeds!" Of such a person the Torah says (Isaiah 49:3), "He said unto me: You are My servant, Israel, through whom I will be glorified."

But when a person who studies Scripture and Mishnah and attends on Torah scholars is dishonest in business and is discourteous in his relations with people, what do people say? "Woe unto so-and-so who studied the Torah, woe unto his father who taught him Torah, woe unto his teacher who taught him Torah! This person who studied the Torah, see how corrupt are his deeds, how ugly his ways!" Of him the Torah says (Ezekiel 36:20), "[They desecrated My holy name,] when it is said of them: These are G-d's people, who came out from His land."

 R. ELI SILBERSTEIN, *YOU BE THE JUDGE, PP. 7–12*

The most fundamental concept underlying any economic system is the principle of ownership. Purchases, loans, contracts, and torts are constructs that only have meaning when we accept the notion of ownership. Research demonstrates that children as young as three or four have a sophisticated understanding of rules of ownership and the bundle of rights they entail.

What is ownership? The 18th-century legal scholar William Blackstone presents a purely utilitarian view of ownership, as something devised in order to avoid social unrest and to stimulate progress (*Commentaries on the Laws of England*, vol. 2, ch. 1). The Torah's con-

cept of ownership is a more elemental one, seeing an intrinsic bond between owner and object. Consider the following statement:

"Forty days before a child is formed, a heavenly voice declares: This daughter of so-and-so will marry so-and-so. This house will belong to so-and-so. This field will belong to so-and-so" (Talmud, *Sotah* 2a).

Many are familiar with the first half of the statement; the term *bashert* (preordained soulmate) is part of the Jewish vernacular. Less common is the knowledge that our tradition maintains that the physical property that we own throughout our lives is also preordained.

Why is it important that every object that we will ever own has been assigned to us by Heaven? The Baal Shem Tov explains that every physical object contains a mystical reality, referred to in Jewish mysticism as a "divine spark"—a G-dly energy that constitutes the essential being of that object. Our task in life is to elevate these sparks from their state of obscurity and reveal the inherent divinity within the physical. This is accomplished by using the objects in which these sparks are contained to perform divine commandments.

Every individual is responsible for elevating the divine sparks associated with the spiritual roots of their soul. The objects containing those sparks become that person's physical possessions. Ownership represents the association between the soul and these divine sparks. When ownership of an object is transferred, it indicates that the sparks contained in the transferred object require the intervention of more than one soul in order to be elevated (*Keter Shem Tov*, 218; *Ohr Torah*, p. 101; *Likutei Sichot*, vol. 12, p. 118).

This Kabbalistic insight adds new meaning to the concept of ownership. It tells us that ownership is not merely a utilitarian convention; it signals an inherent relationship between property and proprietor. The law's function is not to create the concept of ownership (and then delimit the conditions in which it applies); rather, the law reveals this reality and responds to it.

ORDINANCES AND CUSTOMS

 **MAIMONIDES,** *INTRODUCTION TO COMMENTARY ON THE MISHNAH*

The fifth category [of the "Oral Torah"—see citation on p. 186] is laws governing societal norms, or practices that are useful to promote Torah values, which neither add to nor detract from a mitzvah, and on which the sages decided through investigation and consensus. These are called *takanot* (ordinances) and customs, and it is forbidden to transgress them.

There are many such ordinances mentioned in the Mishnah and the Talmud. For example, "Moses ordained for the people of Israel that they should inquire and expound the laws of Passover [prior to the festival]" (Talmud, *Megilah* 4a).... "Hillel instituted the *pruzbul*" (Mishnah, *Shevi'it* 10:3).... "The Sanhedrin in Usha ordained [that a person is obligated to provide financial support for his minor children]" (Talmud, *Ketuvot* 49b) ... and so on.

◗ TAKANOT OF R. GERSHOM

Among the historically significant rabbinic ordinances are those enacted by R. Gershom of Mainz, Germany, approximately 1000 CE, with the consensus of the heads of the major Ashkenazic communities of his day. These included:

- The prohibition of polygamy.

- A woman cannot be divorced against her will.

- A man traveling on business should not be absent from his home for more than eighteen months.

- A person who donates or sponsors a synagogue cannot prevent his enemy from praying there.

- It is forbidden to read another person's personal correspondence without their permission.

- It is forbidden to remind a penitent, or any of their descendants, of their past transgressions.

IMAGEIMAGE / ALAMY

THE MINHAG A significant part of Jewish practice is not mandated by Biblical or rabbinic law, but by *minhag* ("custom"). While based on Torah ideals and Halachic principles, *minhagim* arise spontaneously from Jewish life and are hallowed by generations of practice. These observances—such as eating dairy foods on Shavuot, dancing with the Torah on Simchat Torah, breaking a glass under the *chupah*, covering mirrors in a *shivah* house, or marking a Bar Mitzvah by being called up to the Torah—are no less integral to Jewish identity than the legal directives of Halachah. In the words of the great Halachist R. Solomon ben Aderet (1235–1310), "A Jewish custom is Torah."

The *kipah*, or head-covering, is an example of a *minhag* that became a hallmark of Jewish identity. In Jewish tradition, covering one's head is a sign of reverence, as well as a reminder of the One who stands above our "head" and understanding. Torah law requires that a person cover their head while praying or studying Torah; but over time it became customary for Jewish males to wear a head covering at all times.

Philosophy and beliefs

The first question a philosopher of Judaism might ask is: Does Judaism have a philosophy? The Torah is a way of life, a moral code, a charter of divine commandments and prohibitions. A defining feature of the founding event of Judaism, the giving of the Torah at Mount Sinai, was the people's response (Exodus 24:7), "We will do and we will hear"—first we will do what G-d instructs, and only after that we will learn and understand. So perhaps what a person thinks and believes is irrelevant, or at most unessential, to what it means to be a Jew?

But a closer examination of the mitzvot themselves reveals that while "we will do" precedes "we will hear," the latter is no less essential to embracing the Torah as the stuff and substance of our relationship with G-d. The mitzvot include the belief and knowledge of G-d—as well as the precepts to love and fear G-d, which can be optimally fulfilled only from a place of contemplation and understanding. Indeed, faith, knowledge, love, and awe are the cornerstones upon which the entire edifice of Judaism rests.

 R. ISAIAH HOROWITZ
SHENEI LUCHOT HABERIT, 1:40a

The Torah (Deuteronomy 4:39) states: "Know today, and bring unto your heart, that the Lord is the G-d." That is to say, know G-d with an in-depth knowledge and with logical proofs, in addition to the tradition received from your ancestors…. This is alluded to in the verse (I Chronicles 28:9), "Know the G-d of your fathers." Meaning: In addition to the faith established in your heart by your fathers—by the tradition handed down through the generations—you should also know on your own, by means of your own understanding.

This is also alluded to in the verse (Exodus 15:2), "This is my G-d, and I shall beautify Him; the G-d of my fathers, and I shall exalt Him." That is to say: When He is *my* G-d, due to my own knowledge and understanding, then *ve'anveihu* ["I shall beautify Him," which also can be read as a combination of the words] *ani vahu*, "I and Him"; meaning, I and Him are bonded together, so to speak, because my knowledge of Him is internalized in my heart. However, when I do not possess a knowledge of G-d that is the product of my own understanding, only the tradition that He is "the G-d of my fathers," then "I shall exalt Him"—G-d remains aloof and elevated from me, and I am distant from Him in the inner recesses of my heart.

Maimonides (R. Moses ben Maimon, 1135–1204) was
a seminal systemizer of Jewish philosophy and theology.
Below: An Israeli banknote honoring Maimonides
Left: 11th-century wood panel from the Torah ark
of the Ben Ezra Synagogue in Cairo, where Maimonides
is believed to have worshipped.

R. JOSEPH ALBO, *IKARIM 2:30*

A wise man was asked if he knows what G-d is. He replied, "If I knew Him, I would be Him." Only G-d can know His essence, though He reveals His reality to us through His deeds.... Our ultimate understanding of G-d is to appreciate the extent to which we cannot know Him.

R. JONATHAN SACKS
RADICAL THEN, RADICAL NOW, PP. 96–97

Judaism [is] structurally different from ... the other great attempt to understand the human condition: philosophy, the invention of ancient Greece. The Greek idea is of truth as system. The Jewish idea is of truth as story.

Time is the medium through which we learn, in which we make the long, slow journey from violence to justice, [from] oppression to freedom.... Judaism advances the daring idea that man and G-d are partners in the work of creation.

PRINCIPLES OF THE JEWISH FAITH

1 Belief in G-d. G-d is perfect in every way, and is not dependent on any other existence for anything; whereas all other existences, phenomena, and realities were created by G-d, and are utterly dependent upon Him for their existence.

2 The absolute oneness of G-d. There are no composite parts or aspects within G-d's being.

3 G-d is not physical, nor does He possess any physical properties.

4 G-d is timeless, primordial (i.e., preceded all other existences), and eternal.

5 It is imperative to worship G-d and obey His commandments, and not worship any other power or entity.

6 G-d communicates to humanity through prophecy.

7 The primacy of the prophecy of Moses.

8 The divinity of the Torah. The entire Torah now in our hands is the same Torah that was given to Moses by the Almighty.

9 The Torah—both the Written Torah and the Oral Torah—will never be changed, and nothing should be added to it or subtracted from it.

10 Divine providence. G-d knows and concerns Himself with everything that a person does.

11 G-d rewards those who fulfill the commandments of the Torah and punishes those who transgress them.

12 The coming of Mashiach (the Messiah) and the future Messianic era of divine goodness and perfection. To constantly await and anticipate its realization.

13 The resurrection of the dead. All who lived in the past will be brought back to life at a time of G-d's choosing.

Maimonides enumerates these 13 principles as "foundations" of Judaism

CREATION

The Torah's opening statement, "In the beginning G-d created the heavens and the earth," challenges our most basic conceptions of reality. The beginnings with which we are familiar—a child or nation is born, a tool is invented, a new era dawns—transpire out of the backdrop of some preexisting entity (a set of parents, a history, the laws of nature, time and space). But an absolute beginning means that everything, including the axioms, contexts, and abstractions that define reality for us, was created "something from nothing." Time and space are created entities, as are the very notions of cause and effect, beginning and purpose, even existence and nonexistence. Simply stated, creation *ex nihilo* means that everything that is, is solely because its Creator desires that it so be.

Everything that Judaism has to say to us is predicated on this fundamental truth: that G-d is the source and master of all, and nothing exists independently of Him; that G-d obviously can overrule the "laws of nature" by which He chose to order His work; that creation is a deliberate, purposeful act by G-d, meaning that our existence is likewise purposeful; that as the exclusive source of all, G-d is the sole arbiter of right and wrong and the ultimate author of, and authority for, the moral questions of life; and that everything that exists and occurs is, at its core, positive and good, as it is nothing other than the manifestation of G-d's desire that it be.

 GENESIS 1:1–3

In the beginning G-d created the heavens and the earth.

And the earth was desolate and void, and darkness on the face of the deep; and the spirit of G-d hovered upon the face of the waters.

And G-d said, "There shall be light"; and there was light.

 MIDRASH TEMURAH, *END OF CHAPTER 3*

A heretic asked R. Akiva: "Who created the world?"

Said R. Akiva: "G-d."

Said the man: "Prove it to me."

Said R. Akiva: "Come to me tomorrow."

On the next day R. Akiva said to him: "What are you wearing?"

Said the man: "A robe."

Said R. Akiva: "Who made it?"

Said he: "The weaver."

Said R. Akiva: "I do not believe you. Prove it to me."

Said he: "What is there to prove? Do you not see that it was made by a weaver?"

Said R. Akiva: "Do you not see that the world was made by G-d?"

 MAIMONIDES, *MISHNEH TORAH, LAWS OF THE FUNDAMENTALS OF TORAH, 1:1*

The foundation of all foundations and the pillar of all wisdom is to know that there is a Primary Existence, who brought every existence into being. All existences, in the heavens, in the earth, and what is between them, came into existence only from the truth of His existence.

 NACHMANIDES, *COMMENTARY TO GENESIS 1:1*

The Hebrew word *bara* ("created") refers to the creation of something from nothing. The meaning of this verse (Genesis 1:1) is: G-d created all creations out of absolute nothingness.

This is the root of our faith. One who does not believe this, and thinks that the world always existed, repudiates the core of Judaism, and has no Torah at all.

R. JONATHAN SACKS
RADICAL THEN, RADICAL NOW, PP. 70–71

The account of creation in the first chapter of Genesis is stunningly original, quite unlike any other in antiquity…. There are no contending forces, no battles of the gods, no capricious spirits. G-d speaks, and the universe comes into being. G-d is not in nature but above it, transcending it and ordering it according to His word. Nature has no will, or set of wills of its own.... This was an immense intellectual leap. It made possible for the first time the concept of science. If G-d created the world, then it is, in principle, intelligible. The mists of irrationality have been dispelled.

 R. NISSEN MANGEL, *FROM THE TRANSLATOR'S INTRODUCTION TO SHAAR HAYICHUD VEHAEMUNAH*

The central idea of this work, the pivot around which all the other concepts revolve, is the principle of the Divine Unity, expressed in the declaration, "Hear O Israel, G-d is our Lord, G-d is one."

The essential meaning of the doctrine of divine unity is the belief in absolute monotheism, i.e., there is but one G-d. It negates polytheism, the worship of many gods, and paganism, the deification of any finite thing or being or natural force; it excludes dualism, the assumption of two rival powers of good and evil, and pantheism, which equates G-d and nature.

The Hasidic understanding of the divine unity gives it a more profound meaning. R. Schneur Zalman of Liadi explains that divine unity does not only exclude the existence of other ruling powers besides the One G-d or of any plurality in Him, but it precludes any existence at all apart from Him. The universe appears to possess an existence independent from its Creator only because we do not perceive the creating force which is its *raison d'etre*.

All created things—the Kabbalists taught—exist only by virtue of the continuous flow of life and vitality from G-d. This creative process did not cease at the end of the six days of creation, but continues at every moment, constantly renewing all existence. Were this creating power to withdraw even a single moment, all existence would vanish into nothingness, exactly as before the six days of creation [R. Moses Cordovero, *Pardes Rimonim*, 6:8; R. Isaiah Horowitz, *Shenei Luchot ha-Berit*, 1:40b–41a; R. Israel Baal Shem Tov, *Keter*

Shem Tov, 194; R. Schneur Zalman of Liadi, *Shaar ha-Yichud veha-Emunah*, 1–3].

Thus, the true essence and reality of the universe and everything therein is but the divine power within it. It is only from the perspective of the created beings, who are incapable of perceiving their source, that they appear as independently existing entities. However, in relation to G-d, all creation is naught; there is no existence whatsoever apart from Him.

{ALSO SEE CITATION FROM TZEMACH TZEDEK ON P. 241}

 R. MENACHEM M. SCHNEERSON BASED ON *LIKUTEI SICHOT, VOL. 1, PP. 1–2*

The doctrine of perpetual creation is not just a cosmological truth, but one with practical significance to our lives.

At times, it may seem to us that the natural order of things is making it difficult, or impossible, to carry out our life's mission of making the material world a "vessel" for G-dliness. At such times, we should remember that in every moment of time, the world is being created out of absolute nothingness by the ten divine utterances spelled out in the Torah ("There shall be light," etc.). When we realize that the entirety of existence—including the very circumstances we now face—has no reality of its own, but derives solely from the ten utterances of the Torah, we also understand that the "reality" we now face cannot be inconsistent with the declaration "I am the Lord your G-d," or with any of the 613 mitzvot commanded by that selfsame Torah.

We also realize that we have no true cause for worry or stress over anything that is happening in our lives, whether these are spiritual or material "problems." For we remember that everything is coming directly from the Creator, who is the source of only good. When we recognize and live by this truth, we ultimately come to see the goodness in everything in a revealed way as well.

THE HUMAN BEING

 GENESIS 1:26, 2:7

And G-d said: "Let us make a human in our image, after our likeness...."

G-d Almighty formed the human of the soil of the earth, and He blew into his nostrils the breath of life; and the human became a living soul.

 MECHILTA, *EXODUS 20:14*

How were the Ten Commandments given? Five on one tablet, and five on the other tablet. On one tablet it says, "I am the Lord your G-d," and opposite it on the other tablet it says, "Do not murder." This teaches us that whoever spills blood, the Torah considers it as if they have diminished the stature of the Almighty.

 TALMUD, *SANHEDRIN 37a*

This is why G-d created mankind as a single individual:

To teach us that whoever destroys a single life, it is as if they destroyed an entire world; and whoever sustains a single life, it is as if they sustained an entire world.

For the sake of peace: So that no person could say to their fellow, "My ancestor is greater than yours."

So that the heretics could not say that there are numerous authorities in heaven.

To demonstrate the greatness of the Creator. When a human being stamps many coins with a single die, they are all identical. Yet G-d stamped every person with the template of the first human, and not one of them is identical to their fellow.

Therefore, every person is obligated to say: "The world was created for my sake."

 R. MORDECAI JOSEPH LEINER
MEI HASHILOACH, PARASHAT BEREISHITH

In declaring, "Let us make a human," the Creator invited all elements of creation to participate in the making of man. For it is through the human being that all other creations are elevated or debased.

 R. SCHNEUR ZALMAN OF LIADI
TANYA, CHAPTERS 1, 2, AND 9

Every Jew, whether righteous or wicked, possesses two souls.... One soul is from *kelipah* ["husks"—the forces of non-holiness that conceal G-dliness]. This is the soul that is clothed in the blood of the person to animate the body ... and from it stem all of a person's negative characteristics ... anger and haughtiness ... lust ... frivolity and cynicism ... and laziness and melancholy.... Also the Jew's naturally good traits derive from it....

The second soul in the Jew is literally a part of G-d above. As it is written (Genesis 2:7), "He blew into his nostrils a breath of life"....

Like two kings who battle over one city, each desiring to conquer it and reign over it—that is, to rule its inhabitants according to his will, that they should obey him in all that he decrees for them—so do the two souls, the divine soul and the animalistic soul from *kelipah*, battle each other over the body and all its limbs. The desire and will of the divine soul is that it alone should rule over the body and govern it, and that all the body's limbs should obey it, abnegate themselves completely to it, and serve as a vehicle for it.... Whereas the animal soul wants the very opposite. [It desires this, however,] for the person's own good, that the person should overpower it and defeat it.

 R. ABRAHAM ISAAC KOOK, *OROT, P. 119*

The human spirit finds stability only within a G-dly atmosphere. Its knowledge, feelings, vision, desires, and internal and external drives require humans to be divine beings. Only then will it achieve wholeness and its proper and fulfilling place in the world.

The person who seeks anything less than this greatness will consequently become confused and torn like a ship attempting to navigate a violent storm. The crashing breakers will toss them from one conflicting wave to another, depriving them of serenity and tranquility.

the lamp

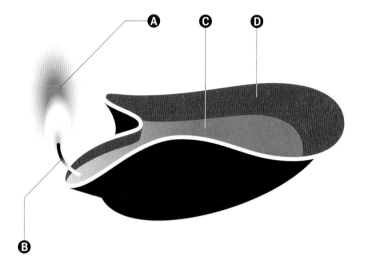

THE ANATOMY OF A METAPHOR "The soul of man is a lamp of G-d" (Proverbs 20:27). Hasidic teaching employs this Biblical metaphor to explain the dynamics of human life. Like the lamp, a human life has four primary components—FLAME, WICK, OIL, and CONTAINER—each indispensable to its function and purpose:

Ⓐ The FLAME is the SOUL—a divine spark dispatched on a mission to illuminate the world.

Ⓑ The soul, however, is pure divine energy, utterly aloof from the physical reality. It requires a WICK to hold it in existence and prevent it from dissipating to the transcendent nothingness which it craves. The "wick" is the physical BODY that holds the soul and tethers it to reality, transforming its transcendent energy into a source of tangible light.

Ⓒ But wick and flame alone will not produce a sustainable illumination. Without OIL to fuel their collaboration, the materialism of the body would smother the spiritual voice of the soul, and the spirituality of the soul would soon flee the materiality of physical life. The "fuel" of life is the MITZVOT—the divine actions that the body feeds to the soul in order to sustain it as an illuminating force in the world.

Ⓓ Finally, the CONTAINER that facilitates the interaction of our wick, flame, and oil is the PHYSICAL WORLD—the arena within which mitzvot can be performed and a human life can serve as a source of divine light. This is where body, soul, and mitzvot join as a brilliant lamp of G-d.

This person may submerge in the sludge of ego and insensitivity, and thus temporarily dim the light of life and delude themselves that they have found peace. It won't be long, however, before emotional pandemonium will resume in all its intensity.

R. ZADOK OF LUBLIN
TZIDKAT HATZADIK, 154

Just as we believe in G-d, we must consequently believe in ourselves: that G-d cares about us, that we do not labor in vain ... that we possess a divine soul, and that G-d takes pleasure and joy when we fulfill His desire.

TZVI FREEMAN

Monotheism can be a dangerous belief. Perhaps one of the most dangerous beliefs there is. Because it leaves no room for anything else. You could destroy the world with this belief.

There is another dangerous belief. That's belief in the human being. One who worships human intellect as the measure of all things has also proven himself capable of destroying the world with his beliefs. Because a human's mind cannot help but be bribed by his own ego.

For either of these beliefs—the belief in human beings and the belief in One G-d—to safely enter our world, the two concepts had to be married together.

For monotheism to work, a crucial fact about this One G-d must be accepted: That G-d is in love with this world He has made, and especially with the people He has placed upon it.

For human intellect to function safely, we must first accept that there is something beyond intellect, something eternally and immovably good and life-affirming Who determines what is true and what is not, what is right and what is wrong.

Look through the annals of history and you will see it: When this sort of belief has guided men and women, whatever religion they followed, those people brought peace, wisdom, and progress into the world. Today, we

Modulor (detail),
Le Corbusier, Paris, 1956

desperately need this marriage of beliefs. With it, we can heal our world.

Take a look at the opening of Genesis and you will see these two themes.

There are actually two narratives of creation there: The first is centered on the theme of G-d as creator, the second is focused on the theme of Adam, the first human being, created "in the divine image." Take one narrative without the other, and you've lost everything.

Even in the first narrative alone, take a closer look: G-d creates and then He declares each thing He makes to be good. When it's all done, it's declared "very good."

That's an essential part of the narrative: The Creator appreciates His creation. It has purpose and meaning to Him.

This world was not created for some apocalyptic finale, neither was its magnificence formed only to dissipate into ionized gas. It was created, as Isaiah says,

"not for desolation, but to be lived upon." And to find divine meaning in that life.

G-d loves life. Life is G-dly. The two, of necessity, go hand in hand.

 R. ADIN EVEN-ISRAEL (STEINSALTZ)
THE THIRTEEN PETALLED ROSE, PP. 52–53

Each individual soul is unique and special in terms of its essence, its capacity, and what is demanded of it. No two souls coincide in their actions, their functions, and their paths. No one soul can take the place of another, and even the greatest of the great cannot fill the special role, the particular place, of another who may be the smallest of the small.

From this notion derives Judaism's profound respect for human life. The life of a person is something that has no possible substitute or exchange; nothing and no one can take its place.

DIVINE PROVIDENCE

 JEREMIAH 32:19

[You, G-d,] who is great in counsel and mighty in work; as Your eyes are open to all the ways of mankind, to give to each according to his ways, and according to the fruit of his doings.

 ZOHAR, *VOL. 1, 15a*

There is not a single blade of grass on earth that does not have an angel in heaven that strikes it and commands it: Grow!

 R. MOSES ALSHICH, *BASED ON ALSHICH'S COMMENTARY TO PSALMS 113*

"G-d is exalted over all the nations; His glory is upon the heavens. Who is like the Lord our G-d, who dwells on high; who lowers to see in the heavens and in the earth" (Psalms 113:4–6).

The meaning of these verses is as follows:

To the nations of the world, "His glory is upon the heavens"—they exalt the Almighty so much that they place Him higher than both heaven and earth. While they acknowledge G-d as the source of all existence, they believe that He is too exalted to play any role in the lofty cosmos or in mundane earth. Rather, the forces of nature run the world, for better or for worse.

But the people of Israel deny this falsehood, proclaiming, "Who is like the Lord *our* G-d...." G-d indeed "dwells on high," transcending both heaven and earth; but at the same time, He "lowers to see in the heavens and in the earth"—neither the most lofty nor the most lowly are outside of G-d's providence.

 R. YOSEF YITZCHAK SCHNEERSOHN *SEFER HAMAAMARIM 5696, PP. 120–121*

The principle of "particular divine providence" (*hashgachah peratit*), as explained by our master the Baal Shem Tov, is not only that every detailed movement of

every creation is specifically ordained by the Creator, and that this divine attentiveness constitutes the very life and sustenance of this creation; but also that this specific event is related to the overall divine purpose in Creation.

For example, an individual blade of grass, deep in a forest or on a high mountain where no human being has ever traversed—each and every movement of that grass, to the right and to the left and back and forth, in every moment of its existence, is specifically ordained by divine providence, and plays a part in G-d's purpose in creating the world.

MACHINE LEARNING "Everything that a person sees or hears, they should derive from it a lesson in how to serve the Creator." This saying by the Baal Shem Tov is a corollary of the principle of Divine Providence. If every occurrence in G-d's world serves a purpose, then the fact that I have been made aware of a certain event or phenomenon is also providential.

The renowned ethicist R. Israel Meir Kagan (1838–1933, known as the "Chafetz Chayim") remarked on the lessons he derived from three of the innovations of the Industrial Age. The passenger train teaches us that a one-minute delay can disrupt many days of travel. The telegraph teaches us that every word is precious. And the telephone reminds us that what is said here, is heard there....

FREEDOM OF CHOICE

 DEUTERONOMY 30:15–19

See, I have given before you this day, life and good, and death and evil.

In that I command you this day, to love the Lord your G-d, to walk in His ways, and to keep His commandments, His statutes, and His laws....

I call the heaven and the earth as witnesses upon you upon this day: Life and death I have given before you, blessing and curse. You shall choose life, so that you shall live, you and your offspring.

 MAIMONIDES, *MISHNEH TORAH, LAWS OF REPENTANCE, 5:1–4*

Freedom of choice has been granted to every person. If a person wants to turn to the path of good and be righteous, the choice is theirs; and if a person wants to turn to the path of evil and be wicked, the choice is theirs....

This concept is a fundamental principle and a pillar of the Torah and its commandments. As it is written, "See, I have given before you this day, life [and good, and death and evil]".... Were the Almighty to decree that a person should be righteous or wicked, or if there were to be something in the essence of a person's nature that would compel them toward a particular path, a particular conviction, a particular character trait, or a particular deed... how could G-d command us through the prophets, "do this" and "do not do this"...? What place would the entire Torah have? And by what measure of justice would He punish the wicked and reward the righteous?

 R. JUDAH LOEW, *DERECH CHAYIM, 3:15*

If a person wants to sin, G-d does not stop them; rather, the person is allowed to do so. This is because the human being is created in the divine image, and in this man resembles the Creator.... Just as G-d does as He desires, so too is the human being given the autonomy to act as they desire; they have the power of choice.

 R. SAMUEL DE UCEDA
EXCERPTED FROM *MIDRASH SHMUEL, AVOT 3:21*

"All is foreseen, and autonomy is given" (*Ethics of the Fathers*, 3:21). Maimonides explains this *mishnah* as follows: "All is foreseen"—all of a person's deeds, everything they did and everything they are going to do, is known to G-d. This may lead us to say: Since the Almighty knows what a person will do, a person is compelled in their actions to be righteous or wicked. The *mishnah* therefore continues, "autonomy is given"—a person is free to do good or bad, and there is nothing at all that compels them.

Maimonides does not seem to resolve the contradiction. Rather, he states that a person must believe in both principles, despite the contradiction between them. We must believe that G-d knows the future, and also believe that this knowledge does not compel human action. It is only that we have no grasp on G-d's knowledge, which is beyond human understanding.

It seems to me, however, that there is no contradiction in the first place. The fact that on the day that a person is born G-d knows if they will be righteous or wicked does not in any way compel that person's behavior. G-d does not exist within time, so there is no "before" and "after" for G-d. G-d sees the future, and G-d sees what the person will choose.

The great sage R. Simeon ibn Duran answered the question [differently,] by explaining that everything has a positive and negative side. As the sages said, "One who is born under the influence of Mars will be a person who sheds blood—either a robber, or a butcher, or a surgeon, or a *mohel*" (Talmud, *Shabbat* 156a). The very thing that is foreseen by G-d, a person is able to direct its conclusion to a good deed or a bad deed.

 ZOHAR, *VOL. 2, 163a*

At the king's palace, outside, was a harlot, beautiful of visage and form. One day, the king said, "I wish to see my son's love for me." So he summoned that harlot and said to her, "Go and attempt to seduce my son, as I wish to see my son's love for me."

What does this harlot do? She pursues the prince, and proceeds to embrace him and kiss him and to entice him with all sorts of enticements. If the king's son is virtuous and obeys the directives of his father, he will reject her, and not listen to her, and drive her away. Then the father rejoices in his son, and invites him into his royal chambers, and bestows precious gifts and great honors on him.

Now, who is the cause of the great reward of the prince? I would say: the harlot.

 R. SHLOMO YOSEF ZEVIN
SIPUREI HASIDIM, GENESIS 4:7

R. Naphtali of Ropshitz once rebuked one of his children over some childish prank. When the child defended his behavior by blaming their *yetzer ha-ra* ("evil inclination"), the Hasidic master said, "On the contrary, you should learn from your evil inclination. He is doing exactly what the Almighty told him to do—to test your strength to resist him. So you, too, should do what G-d wants you to do."

"That is not a fair comparison," responded the child. "My evil inclination doesn't have an evil inclination enticing him not to do his job."

 R. SCHNEUR ZALMAN OF LIADI
TANYA, CHAPTER 12

It is written (Ecclesiastes 2:13), "I have found that there is an advantage to wisdom over folly, as the advantage of light over darkness." Meaning: Just as light has an innate advantage, power, and dominion over darkness—in that a small amount of physical light will banish a great deal of darkness, because darkness is spontaneously and automatically dispelled by light—so too, the great folly of the evil inclination in a person's heart is automatically dispelled by the wisdom of the divine soul.

 **DAVID AARON**
FROM A TALK GIVEN AT SINAI INDABA 2012

Why on earth are we here?

What is our mission? And why are we perfect for that mission?

Our mission is to choose good. But to choose good, you have to have a serious interest in bad.

In other words, what makes us perfect for our mission is that we're not perfect. What's so good about us is that we're not so good. But we can choose to be good.

For years I had a problem with G-d. It bothered me that G-d was always good, always kind, always loving, always honest, always happy, etc.

I wondered: Is G-d capable of acting kindly through choice, or does He *have* to be kind? Is G-d able to choose love over hate, peace over conflict? After all, G-d doesn't have an evil inclination.

If G-d is totally perfect and has no evil inclination, is He compulsively good? Is G-d not free to *choose* good?

Imagine two people—one who is naturally always good, and one for whom being good is often a struggle. I think we all intuit that the second person's goodness is of richer, more meaningful quality, because it's their choice (and not one that always comes easily).

Could G-d be missing this richer quality of the chosen good?

The answer is no. Because G-d has you and me. If we're willing to live our mission.

The Torah (Deuteronomy 4:35) teaches that there is *nothing at all* but G-d. And although we are not G-d, we are a part of Him. As it states in the Torah (ibid., 32:9), "A part of G-d is His people."

We are the part of G-d that is free and capable to battle evil and victoriously choose good.

G-d is good, always was good, and always will be good. But His almighty perfect goodness includes the possibility of freely choosing good. You and I are that part of G-d.

MASHIACH AND THE FUTURE REDEMPTION

Mashiach is much more than a Jewish belief; more, even, than a fundamental principle of Judaism. It is the ultimate realization of what Judaism aims to accomplish, and the animating spirit behind the whole of Jewish history, learning, and practice. Every mitzvah, every prayer, every effort to live a life of awareness and purpose, is another step in developing the world as a "home for G-d"—a place that embodies the goodness and perfection of its Creator.

 DEUTERONOMY 4:27–30, 30:3–8

G-d will scatter you among the nations; and you will remain few in number among the nations to where G-d will lead you....

And from there, you will seek the Lord your G-d, and you will find Him ... in the last of days, you will return to the Lord your G-d and listen to His voice.

G-d will return with your returnees ... and He will gather you from all the nations amongst whom G-d has scattered you. If your dispersed will be at the ends of the heavens, from there G-d will gather you, from there He will take you. G-d will bring you into the land that your ancestors have possessed, and you will possess it; and He will do you good and multiply you....

G-d will circumcise your heart, and the heart of your children, to love G-d with all your heart and with all your soul.... And you will return and listen to the voice of G-d, and fulfill all His commandments.

 ISAIAH 2:2–4

It shall come to pass, in the last days, that the mount of the house of G-d will be established atop the mountains and be exalted above the hills; and all nations will stream to it.

Many nations will go, and say: "Come, let us go up to the mountain of G-d, to the house of the G-d of Jacob; and He will teach us of His ways and we will walk in His paths." For from Zion shall go forth Torah, and the word of G-d from Jerusalem....

They will beat their swords into plowshares, and their spears into pruning hooks. Nation will not lift a sword upon nation, neither will they learn war anymore.

 ISAIAH 11:1–9

A shoot shall come forth from the stem of Jesse; and a twig shall sprout from his roots. The spirit of G-d will rest upon him; a spirit of wisdom and understanding, a spirit of counsel and might, a spirit of knowledge and fear of G-d.... He will judge the poor with equity, and decide with justice for the lowly of the land....

The wolf will dwell with the lamb, and the leopard will lie with the kid; a calf and a young lion and a fatling together, and a small child will lead them.... They shall neither harm nor destroy in all My holy mountain, for the world will be filled with the knowledge of G-d as waters cover the sea.

 MALACHI 3:23–24

Behold, I will send you Elijah the prophet, before the coming of the great and awesome day of G-d. And he will restore the heart of the parents to the children, and the heart of the children to their parents.

 **MAIMONIDES,** *MISHNEH TORAH,*
LAWS OF KINGS, 11:1–4 AND 12:5

The king Mashiach will arise and restore the sovereignty of the House of David to its former rule. He will build the Holy Temple and gather the dispersed of Israel. In his days, all the Torah's laws will be reinstated: the *korbanot* will be offered, and the sabbatical and jubilee years will be observed…. Anyone who does not believe in [Mashiach], or does not await his coming, denies not only the prophets, but also the Torah [of] Moses….

When there arises a king from the House of David, who studies Torah and fulfills the mitzvot like his father David, in accordance with the Written Torah and the Oral Torah; and he will compel all of Israel to walk in its ways and repair its breaches; and he will fight the battles of G-d; he is presumed to be Mashiach. If he does this and is successful, and he builds the Holy Temple in its place and gathers the dispersed of Israel, then he is definitely Mashiach. He will then improve the entire world to serve the Almighty together, as it is written (Zephaniah 3:9), "For then I will transform the nation to a pure language, that they all will call upon the name of G-d and serve Him with one purpose"….

In that time, there will be no hunger or war, no jealousy or rivalry. For the good will be plentiful, and all delicacies available as dust. The sole occupation of the world will be only to know G-d…. As it is written (Isaiah 11:9), "For the world will be filled with the knowledge of G-d, as waters cover the sea."

 NACHMANIDES, *BOOK OF REDEMPTION, 2:3 AND 3:1*

We await the redemption not in order to eat of the fruit of the Land of Israel and bathe in the hot springs of Tiberias…. Our hope is to attain the closeness of G-d, to be in His Sanctuary with His priests and prophets, and to achieve purity and holiness in the chosen land with the divine presence dwelling amongst us…. For then, in the days of Mashiach, the evil inclination will be annihilated, and we will comprehend the truth as it is.

This, and things much deeper and esoteric than what I have related, is the basis of our longing for Mashiach…. Indeed, the culmination and goal of all prophecies is the coming of Mashiach.

 BECHAYEI, *COMMENTARY TO GENESIS 1:2*

On the verse (Genesis 1:2), "The spirit of G-d hovered upon the waters," the sages expounded: "This is the soul of Mashiach" (*Bereishith Rabbah,* 2:4). Here the Torah addresses the end of time at the very beginning of time, telling us that the ultimate purpose of G-d's creation of the world is the era of Mashiach.

 R. JACOB SEKILI, *TORAT HAMINCHAH, 59*

Mashiach stands ready from the very beginning of Creation, "hovering upon the waters," awaiting only our return to G-d to be immediately revealed and actualized.

 R. ISAIAH HOROWITZ
SHENEI LUCHOT HABERIT, 2:364a

Every day, something of the redemption is realized.

 R. ISRAEL BAAL SHEM TOV
MEOR EINAYIM, END OF PARASHAT PINCHAS

Every soul contains a part of the soul of Mashiach, and it is the mission of each of us to cultivate and actualize their portion.

 R. JUDAH ARYEH LEIB ALTER
SEFAT EMET, VAYECHI 5635 AND 5631

The Torah relates that before his passing, Jacob said to his children, "Gather yourselves, and I will tell you that which will happen with you in the last of days" (Genesis 49:1). The Talmud (*Pesachim* 56a) explains that "Jacob wanted to reveal the Messianic 'end of days,' whereupon the divine presence departed from him." If this simply means that Jacob wished to reveal the date of Mashiach's arrival, what is so profound about this secret?

Untitled, Kazimir Malevich, Russia, circa 1916

ART TURNED TOWARD ETERNITY
Malevich's writings describe his Suprematist art as a striving for moral improvement and a quest toward an absolute where the spiritual and material do not clash with each other but exist in wholeness and indivisibility.

And what difference would this knowledge make?

But the deeper meaning is that Jacob wanted to reveal and fully explain to his children the purpose of *galut* (the exile)—its "end" in the sense of its objective. For the sufferings of *galut* are only due to our inability to fully see their purpose; hence we experience them as bad. If Jacob's children would have assimilated this truth, *galut* would have had no power over them. But then the things that need to be accomplished [through the challenges of *galut*] would not have been accomplished. This is why Jacob was not allowed to reveal it.

Nevertheless, the "end" of *galut* can be known, through faith. We believe that, in truth, nothing bad comes from G-d, and that *galut* is merely a concealment. Although we cannot perceive this with our senses, we can experience this truth through faith. Jacob desired that this truth should be revealed in a way that leaves no possibility of doubt. But it remained hidden, so that it requires effort on our part to discover it.

 R. SCHNEUR ZALMAN OF LIADI
TANYA, CHAPTERS 36–37

As is known, the sages have said that the purpose of the creation of this world is that "G-d desired to have a dwelling in the physical world".... For this purpose, the Almighty gave the Torah to Israel.... It is also known that the era of Mashiach, and especially the time of the resurrection of the dead, is the fulfillment and culmination of the creation of the world, for which purpose it was originally created.

Now, this ultimate perfection of the era of Mashiach and the resurrection depends on our actions and our work throughout the duration of the *galut*. For it is the mitzvah itself that generates its reward: when a person does a mitzvah, they draw down a flow of infinite divine light into the world, to be integrated into the material reality.

Jewish mysticism

How did our material and multifarious world emerge from the ineffable divine singularity? Are there "worlds" and realities other than our own, and what is their relationship to our existence? What is the deeper, spiritual significance of the stories and laws of the Torah?

The mystical teachings of Judaism are called sod *("secret teachings") and* kabbalah *("that which is received"). The tension between these two categorizations runs as a theme through the history of Jewish mysticism. The potency of these teachings carries their potential for misunderstanding and debasement, as well as their power to inspire and vitalize our service of our Creator. Hence the imperative to conceal but also to transmit; to cloak in layers of metaphor and explanation, but also disseminate the most intimate secrets of the divine wisdom.*

NOTE: THROUGHOUT THIS BOOK, THE SYMBOL INDICATES A CITATION FROM THE JEWISH MYSTICAL TEACHINGS

 ZOHAR, *VOL. 3, 152a*

R. Simeon [bar Yochai] said: Woe to the person who says that the Torah presents mere stories and ordinary words. If this were the case, we could compose a Torah right now with ordinary words, and better than any of them.... Rather, all the words of the Torah are sublime words and sublime secrets.

Come and see.... Of the angels it is written (Psalms 104:4), "He makes His angels spirits." But when angels descend here below, they clothe themselves in garments of this world. If they did not clothe themselves in garments of this world, they could not endure in this world, and the world could not endure them.

If this is so with angels, how much more so with the Torah, which created them and all the worlds, and for whose sake they all exist. In descending into this world, if the Torah did not clothe itself in garments of this world, the world could not endure....

Come and see: There is a garment that is visible to all. When the fools of the world see someone in a handsome garment, they look no further. Yet the significance of the garment is the body; and the significance of the body is the soul. So it is with the Torah. She has a body: the commandments of the Torah.... This body is clothed in garments—stories of this world. Fools look only at that garment, the story of the Torah; they know nothing more.... Those who know better look at the body within the garment. The truly wise, servants of the Supernal King, those who stood at Mount Sinai, look at the soul, the root of all, the real Torah. In the World to Come, they are destined to gaze at the soul of the soul of Torah....

As wine must be contained in a jar, so Torah must be contained in these garments. But look only to what is within the garments. All those words, all those stories, are garments.

Safed in the evening, Israel, 2014

 TALMUD, *HAGGIGAH 14b*

Four sages entered the orchard [of mystical knowledge]—Ben Azzai, Ben Zoma, Acher ["the other," a euphemism for Elisha ben Abuyah], and R. Akiva. Ben Azzai looked and died. Ben Zoma looked and went mad. Acher cut down the plantings [i.e., became a heretic]. R. Akiva entered in wholeness and peace and emerged in wholeness and peace.

 MAIMONIDES, *GUIDE FOR THE PERPLEXED, 1:71*

Even the Talmud, as you are well aware, was not originally committed to writing…. Now, if care was taken to avoid writing the Oral Torah in a book accessible to all because of the disadvantages in such a system, certainly, then, no portion of the esoteric teachings of Torah could be written, which would divulge these teachings to everyone.

These secrets, as I have explained earlier, were orally communicated by a few able people to others who were equally distinguished. As it says (Talmud, *Haggigah* 13a), "The secrets of the Torah can only be entrusted to skilled sages…." Nothing but a few remarks and allusions to these teachings are to be found in the Talmud and the Midrash. They are like small kernels enveloped in many husks, so that the reader is generally occupied with the husk and forgets that it encloses a kernel.

 R. ISRAEL BAAL SHEM TOV, *FROM A LETTER TO HIS BROTHER-IN-LAW, R. GERSHON KITOVER*

On Rosh Hashanah of the year 5507 [1746], my soul ascended to the higher worlds…. I rose level after level until I reached the chamber of the Messiah…. I asked the Messiah, "When will the master come?" He answered, "By this you will know: When your teachings will become known and revealed throughout the world, and your wellsprings will be spread to the outside."

THE KABBALISTS

The Jewish mystical tradition forms an integral part of the Torah's transmission from its very beginnings. The earliest Kabbalistic works are attributed to Abraham, the first Jew, or even earlier to Adam, the first man, and the Talmud and Midrashim incorporate many Kabbalistic passages. In Mishnaic times, the great sage R. Simeon bar Yochai taught the esoteric wisdom to a close circle of disciples. These discourses and discussions were recorded in the *Zohar*, which remains the most basic Jewish mystical text. Kabbalah, however, was the exclusive province of a relatively small number of sages who engaged in its study, and even fewer who dared to disseminate it.

That changed in the mid-16th century, when Safed, a city in the north of the Holy Land, became a center of Jewish mystical learning. At the hub of the Safed mystics were two great teachers of Kabbalah: R. Moses Cordovero ("Ramak"); and R. Isaac Luria, known by the acronym "Ari" ("The Lion"). Cordovero's encyclopedic *Orchard of Pomegranates* is a first-of-its-kind systematic explanation of the multitude of "worlds," *sefirot* (divine attributes), and concepts that populate Kabbalistic teaching. Ari, although his sojourn in Safed was cut short after only two years when he died in a plague at the age of 38, left behind numerous disciples and a vast body of teachings that revolutionized the study of Kabbalah. Ari also introduced many customs and prayers (including the Friday night *Kabbalat Shabbat* service) which left an indelible mark on Jewish life.

It was Ari who proclaimed that the restrictions on disseminating Kabbalistic teachings applied only in earlier generations, and that "in these times, it is permitted and obligatory to reveal this wisdom." A number of his disciples labored to record and publicize his teachings and to seed centers of Kabbalistic learning throughout the Jewish world.

EARLY KABBALISTIC TEXTS AND AUTHORS

VISION OF THE CHARIOT c. 429 BCE. The prophet Ezekiel's vision of the "divine chariot," recorded in the Biblical book of Ezekiel, is the origin for many Kabbalistic principles and ideas.

BAHIR c. 40 CE. A mystical exposition on the opening chapters of the Book of Genesis. Attributed to first-century sage R. Nechunia ben ha-Kanah.

SEFER YETZIRAH Attributed to the patriarch Abraham; transcribed by second-century sage R. Akiva. Describes how the Creator employed ten *sefirot* (divine attributes) and combinations of the letters of the Hebrew alphabet to create the world. Numerous commentaries were composed over the centuries to decipher its cryptic verses.

HEICHALOT A series of Kabbalistic Midrashim attributed to R. Ishmael ben Elisha, a colleague of R. Akiva.

ZOHAR The most fundamental work of Kabbalah. Records the teachings of second-century sage R. Simeon bar Yochai ("Rashbi") and his disciples. Its manuscripts were discovered and made public by R. Moses de Leon toward the end of the 13th century, but its texts were known and are cited in classical Jewish works going back to the Talmudic period.

RAAVAD R. Abraham ben David of Posquieres, c. 1125–1198, was a key link in the transmission of Kabbalah.

R. ISAAC THE BLIND c. 1160–1235; Provence, France. Son of Raavad; Nachmanides' teacher in Kabbalah.

HASIDIM OF ASHKENAZ School of Jewish mystics active in the German Rhineland in the 12th and 13th centuries; included R. Judah he-Chasid (1150–1217) and R. Elazar Rokeach of Worms (1176–1238).

NACHMANIDES 1195–1270; see biographical note on p. 114. Incorporated many Kabbalistic ideas into his commentary on the Torah.

ABULAFIA SCHOOL R. Abraham Abulafia and his disciples, active in 13th-century Italy, emphasized the practice of "Meditative Kabbalah" and the attainment of mystical union with G-d.

R. MENACHEM RECANATI 1223–1290, Italy. Authored an early Kabbalistic commentary on the Torah.

R. JOSEPH GIKATILLA c. 1248–1310; Spain. His *Shaarei Orah* ("Gates of Light") discusses the relationship between the names of G-d and the *sefirot*, and other mystical topics.

MAARECHET HA'ELOKUT "The Divine System." A foundational 14th-century Kabbalistic work of undetermined authorship, accompanied by a commentary—essentially a work in its own right—by R. Judah Chayat (c. 1500; Spain and Italy).

R. MEIR IBN GABBAI c. 1480–1540, Spain and Egypt. Author of *Avodat ha-Kodesh* ("Holy Service") and other foundational Kabbalistic works.

THE SAFED KABBALISTS

R. SOLOMON ALKABETZ c. 1500–1580. One of the early teachers of Kabbalah in Safed, his students included Caro and Cordovero, although Alkabetz later considered Cordovero his teacher. Known as the author of the mystical poem *Lecha Dodi* ("Come, my beloved, to meet the bride…"), sung to welcome the Shabbat.

R. JOSEPH CARO 1488–1575. Known primarily as a Halachist and Talmudic scholar (see p. 115 and p. 205), Caro was also an accomplished Kabbalist who recorded his mystical visions in his *Magid Meisharim*.

R. MOSES CORDOVERO 1522–1570; also known by the acronym "Ramak." Primary teacher of Kabbalah in Safed in the years 1550 to 1570. His most important work is the encyclopedic *Pardes Rimonim* ("Orchard of Pomegranates").

R. ABRAHAM GALANTE c. 1500–1560. Disciple of Alkabetz and Cordovero. Authored a number of important Kabbalistic works, including a commentary on *Zohar*.

ARI R. Isaac Luria, 1534–1572. Founder of the Lurianic School of Kabbalah, upon which almost all subsequent Jewish mystical teaching is predicated. His teachings were transcribed by R. Chaim Vital.

R. CHAIM VITAL 1543–1620. Originally a student of Cordovero; when Ari arrived in Safed in 1570, Vital became his leading disciple and the primary transcriber of his teachings.

R. ELIJAH DE VIDAS 1518–1587. Disciple of Cordovero and Ari. Author of the moral-mystical work *Reishit Chochmah* ("Genesis of Wisdom").

R. ELAZAR AZIKRI 1533–1600. Disciple of Alkabetz. Authored *Chareidim*, a Kabbalistic treatment of the 613 mitzvot. Composed the devotional poem *Yedid Nefesh* ("Soul Friend").

R. MOSES ALSHICH 1508–1593. Disciple of Caro, Cordovero, and Ari. Authored a popular commentary on Torah.

R. ISRAEL SARUG Active 1590–1610. Disciple of Ari who traveled extensively to introduce the Lurianic Kabbalah in Italy, the Balkans, Germany, Poland, Turkey, Egypt, and elsewhere.

R. SAMUEL DE UCEDA d. c. 1604. Disciple of Alkabetz, Ari, and Vital. Most famous for his *Midrash Shmuel*, a commentary on *Ethics of the Fathers*.

R. ISRAEL NAJARA c. 1555–1625. His father was a disciple of Ari. Najara's works include poetry, Kabbalistic discourses, Torah law, ethics, and responsa. Known as the composer of the Shabbat song *Kah Ribon Olam*. Served as the rabbi of Gaza.

R. MENACHEM AZARIAH DA FANO 1548–1620. Disciple of R. Israel Serug, who came to R. Menachem's native Italy to spread the Lurianic Kabbalah. Author of *Asarah Maamarot* ("Ten Utterances"), a voluminous and fundamental Kabbalistic work.

POST-SAFEDIAN KABBALISTS AND SCHOOLS

MAHARAL R. Judah Loew, 1520–1609. Mystic and philosopher who expressed Kabbalistic ideas in philosophical terms. There is a tradition that he used Kabbalistic formulae to create a *golem* (humanoid) to save the Jewish community of Prague from the frequent blood libels of the time. Maharal's Kabbalah appears to derive from earlier sources, as the Safedian Kabbalah had not yet reached Eastern Europe in his day.

SHALOH R. Isaiah Horowitz, 1560–1630. His magnum opus, *Shenei Luchot ha-Berit* ("Two Tablets of the Covenant"), blends Kabbalah, Talmudic discourse, Torah law and customs, Biblical commentary, and ethics. Shaloh served as a rabbi in numerous Jewish communities in both Europe and the Holy Land, including Dubna, Frankfurt, Prague, Jerusalem, Safed, and Tiberias. His works incorporate the teachings of Cordovero and Ari and their disciples.

R. NAFTALI HERTZ BACHARACH 17th century, Germany. Born in Poland, he traveled to the Holy Land to learn Kabbalah from the disciples of Ari. Authored *Emek ha-Melech* ("King's Dale"), a comprehensive exposition of Lurianic Kabbalah.

HASIDISM Founded by R. Israel Baal Shem Tov (1698–1760) and expounded by his disciple R. Dov Ber of Mezeritch (d. 1772). Predicated on the principles of Lurianic Kabbalah (see overview on pp. 232–236).

BETH-EL SCHOOL OF JERUSALEM Served as a center of Kabbalah for 250 years. Its leaders included R. Shalom Sharabi of Yemen (1720–1777), and R. Chaim Yosef David Azulai ("Chida," 1724–1806).

RAMCHAL R. Moses Chaim Luzzatto, 1707–1746, Italy and Holland. A prodigious author in areas of Kabbalah, philosophy, ethics, and poetry.

R. CHAIM IBN ATTAR 1696–1743; Morocco, Italy, and Jerusalem. Author of *Ohr ha-Chayim* ("The Light of Life") commentary on the Torah.

GRA SCHOOL OF KABBALAH R. Elijah of Vilna (the "Gaon of Vilna," 1720–1797) and his disciples. R. Elijah was a master of Talmud, Torah law, Hebrew grammar, and Kabbalah, as well as mathematics and the secular sciences. Kabbalists of the Gra School include R. Chaim of Volozhin (1749–1821), R. Menachem Mendel of Shklov (d. 1827), R. Eizik Haver (1789–1853), R. David Luria (1798–1855), and R. Shlomo Elyashiv (author of the *Leshem*, 1840–1926).

ABUHATZEIRA DYNASTY Founded by R. Jacob Abuhatzeira of Morocco, 1805–1880.

R. JUDAH ASHLAG 1885–1954; Poland, England, and Israel. Popularized the study of Kabbalah with a series of accessible works, including his *Sulam* ("Ladder"), a lucid explanation of the *Zohar*.

THE HASIDIC MOVEMENT

The Hasidic movement was founded by R. Israel Baal Shem Tov in 1734. It quickly spread throughout the Jewish world, energizing and revitalizing Jewish life.

Deriving its core ideas from the Zohar, the teachings of Ari, and those of later mystics such as Maharal and Shaloh, Hasidism stresses the mystical dimension of Torah, joyfulness in serving G-d, love of every Jew regardless of material or spiritual station, intellectual and emotional engagement in prayer, finding G-dliness in every aspect of one's existence, the elevation of the material universe, and the role of the tzadik *(righteous leader) in guiding a person's relationship with the Almighty. The Hasidic masters made these previously esoteric concepts accessible to all, empowering every individual to form a personal relationship with G-d and find spirituality, meaningfulness, and joy in their everyday endeavors.*

R. ISRAEL BAAL SHEM TOV, CITED IN
SEFER HATOLEDOT BAAL SHEM TOV, PP. 31–33

When I was five years old, I was orphaned from both my father and mother. The last words spoken to me by my holy father before his passing were, "Yisrolik, fear nothing but the Almighty alone."

In keeping with my father's words, I was drawn to walk the fields and the great, deep forest near our village, where I would review by heart what I had learned in *cheder*. Often, I would sleep over the night in the field or the forest. My guardians, who looked after me and several other orphan boys and girls, did not tolerate this behavior of mine, and dealt severely with me.

So passed two years. One morning, I heard in the forest the sound of a human voice, and came upon the figure of a Jew enveloped in tallit and tefillin, praying with a fervor such as I had never before witnessed.

I hid myself behind the trees and derived great pleasure from listening to the man praying. I decided that this holy man must be one of the thirty-six hidden *tzadikim* (righteous and saintly people) that are in the world. The *tzadik* concluded his prayers and began to read from the Book of Psalms in a melodious voice, following which he spent some time in ecstatic Torah study. He then gathered his books and his tallit and tefillin and placed them in a sack. At this point, I stepped out from my hiding place and walked toward him.

When the man saw me he asked, "What is a small child doing all alone in the forest? Are you not afraid to be in the forest all by yourself?"

I answered him, "I like the field and the forest, because there are no people, the great majority of whom are arrogant and dishonest. I am an orphan without father or mother. My father, peace be to him, said to

Portrait of a Rabbi,
Isidor Kaufmann, Vienna,
late 19th–early 20th century

me before his passing: 'Yisrolik, fear nothing but the Almighty alone.' So I'm not afraid of anything."

The man asked me if I was Reb Eliezer's son. When I replied that my father was indeed called by that name, the man took a volume of Talmud—the tractate *Pesachim*—from his sack, and studied with me for a while. I then joined him on his way, without knowing where we were going or the purpose of our journey.

In our wanderings, we would stop for different periods of time in various cities, towns, villages, and hamlets—sometimes for a few days, sometimes for a week or longer. I never learned the man's name. I would

study with him each day. He never accepted alms from anyone, yet he fed and clothed me and looked after my needs all the time. Three years passed in this manner.

One day we stopped in a small settlement, and the man said to me: "Not far from here, in the forest, lives a learned and pious Jew. I will leave you with him for a while." I lived in R. Meir's hut for four years. The people in the nearby village knew him only as a simple workman, a charcoal smelter.

In R. Meir's home I became familiar with the ways of the hidden *tzadikim* and their leader, the great sage and *tzadik* R. Adam Baal Shem. I was accepted into

founders of hasidic movements and dynasties

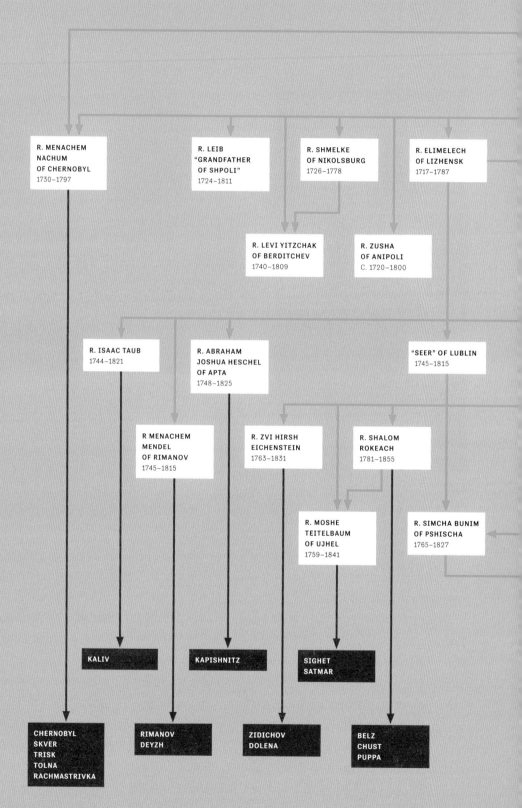

BRANCHES OF THE HASIDIC MOVEMENT
By the time of the passing of its second
leader, R. Dov Ber of Mezeritch,
in 1772, the Hasidic movement had spread
throughout Eastern Europe, with many
of R. Dov Ber's disciples establishing
followings in different towns and regions.
Thus were born the various branches or
schools within Hasidism, each with its
distinct customs and philosophy, and with
its own leader or "rebbe"—a position that
was passed down from father to son or
to a leading disciple. While some of these
Hasidic "dynasties" were tragically wiped
out in the Holocaust, many flourish to
this day. Depicted here are some of the
more well-known branches of the
Hasidic movement.

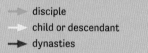

→ disciple
→ child or descendant
→ dynasties

R. MENACHEM NACHUM OF CHERNOBYL 1730–1797

R. LEIB "GRANDFATHER OF SHPOLI" 1724–1811

R. SHMELKE OF NIKOLSBURG 1726–1778

R. ELIMELECH OF LIZHENSK 1717–1787

R. LEVI YITZCHAK OF BERDITCHEV 1740–1809

R. ZUSHA OF ANIPOLI C. 1720–1800

R. ISAAC TAUB 1744–1821

R. ABRAHAM JOSHUA HESCHEL OF APTA 1748–1825

"SEER" OF LUBLIN 1745–1815

R MENACHEM MENDEL OF RIMANOV 1745–1815

R. ZVI HIRSH EICHENSTEIN 1763–1831

R. SHALOM ROKEACH 1781–1855

R. MOSHE TEITELBAUM OF UJHEL 1759–1841

R. SIMCHA BUNIM OF PSHISCHA 1765–1827

KALIV

KAPISHNITZ

SIGHET SATMAR

CHERNOBYL SKVER TRISK TOLNA RACHMASTRIVKA

RIMANOV DEYZH

ZIDICHOV DOLENA

BELZ CHUST PUPPA

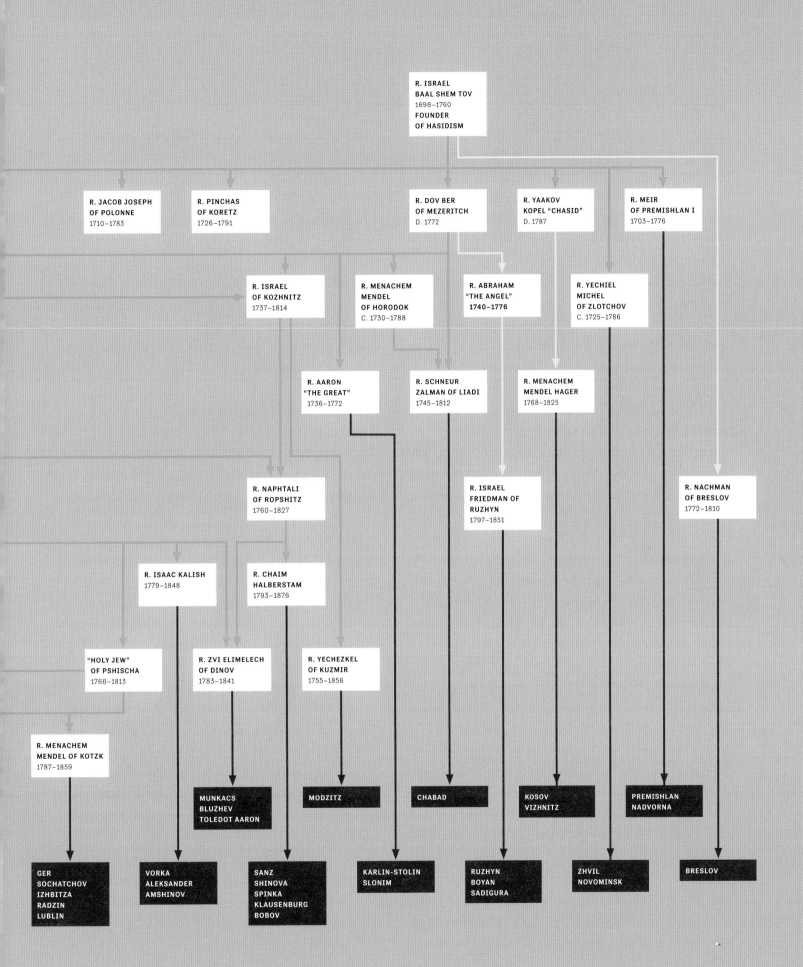

their society, and began journeying from town to town and from settlement to settlement on various missions that the society's leadership placed upon me. Before having attained sixteen years, I had gained a significant knowledge of the teachings of Kabbalah and would occasionally pray with the mystical meditations of the Lurianic tradition.

On my sixteenth birthday, Elul 18, 5474 [1714], I was in a small village. The local innkeeper was a simple Jew who could barely read the prayers and was completely ignorant of the meaning of their words. Yet he was an extremely devout Jew, whose custom was to say, regarding everything and on every occasion, "Blessed be He for ever and ever." His wife, the innkeeperess, would constantly avow, "Praised be His holy name."

That day, I went to meditate alone in the field in accordance with the practice, instituted by the early sages, to set aside time on one's birthday for private contemplation. Suddenly, I beheld Elijah the Prophet standing before me, a smile on his lips. In R. Meir's home, and in the company of other hidden *tzadikim*, I had occasionally merited a revelation of Elijah the Prophet, but never on my own; so I wondered at the reason for this unexpected vision. I also did not understand the significance of the prophet's smile.

Elijah said to me, "You are toiling mightily, investing great effort and concentration to meditate on the unifications of the Holy Names implicit in the verses compiled by King David. On the other hand, Aaron Shlomo the innkeeper and Zlateh Rivkah the innkeeperess are completely unaware of the unifications that emerge from their utterances, 'Blessed be He for ever and ever,' and 'Praised be His holy name.' Yet these words resonate through all the worlds, causing a greater stir than the unifications configured by the greatest *tzadikim*."

Elijah went on to explain to me the great pleasure that the Almighty derives from these words of gratitude and praise, especially by simple folk, reflecting a pure faith, wholesome heart, and a state of perpetual attachment to G-d.

From that point on I embarked upon a new method of serving G-d. Wherever I went, I would talk to people, inquiring after their health, their children, and their livelihood, and they would all reply with expressions of praise to the Almighty—"Thanks to G-d," "Blessed be His Name," and the like—each after his or her manner.

At a conference of the fellowship of hidden *tzadikim* it was resolved to adopt this method of divine service, which became the beginning of an approach that stressed the importance of brotherly love toward every Jew, regardless of their degree of Torah knowledge or spiritual attainment.

 R. ISRAEL BAAL SHEM TOV
HATAMIM, VOL. 8, P. 49–50

The Torah states (Exodus 23:5), "When you see the donkey of your enemy collapsing under its burden, and you are inclined to desist from assisting him, assist must you assist with him."

The Hebrew word for "donkey," *hamor*, also means "material." Thus, this verse also instructs us on our attitude toward the body and physicality:

When you see the hamor *of your enemy*—when you contemplate your physical self, you will initially see it as the enemy of your soul, hostile to your soul's strivings for G-dliness and spirituality.

Collapsing under its burden—you will also see that your body is resisting the tasks which the Creator placed upon it—the study of Torah and the fulfillment of the mitzvot—as it regards these tasks as a burden.

Your inclination may therefore be *to desist from assisting him*—to reject the body, suppress its instincts, and deny it its wants through fasting and other ascetic behavior.

Says the Torah, *assist must you assist with him*. Aid the material self with its "burden" by teaching it to recognize that the Torah is the vehicle for its own betterment and elevation.

THE SUPERNAL WORLDS

The opening chapter of the Book of Genesis describes G-d's creation of the world as a process. Ten divine utterances bring successively advanced forms of existence into being, as light is separated from darkness, matter is parted from spirit, and plant and animal life emerge from inanimate soil. Seven original days supply seven distinct characteristics to the created reality. The Kabbalists expound on this process, describing a multi-phased *seder hishtalshelut* ("order of devolution") by which the Creator generated—and continues to generate—the created reality. Our own physical and ostensibly independent world is but the last in a chain of interconnected worlds that link it to its supernal Source.

 NACHMANIDES, *COMMENTARY TO GENESIS 1:1*

The Torah speaks about the lower realms [i.e., the material world] and alludes to the higher [spiritual] realms.

 R. MENACHEM AZARIAH DA FANO
ASARAH MAAMAROT 1:3:22

Actually, the Torah speaks primarily of the higher worlds and alludes to the lower world.

 R. MOSES CORDOVERO, *PARDES RIMONIM, 14:1*

When discussing the different stages in the Creator's emanation of worlds and spheres of reality, we need to bear in mind an important distinction between our physical world and the higher spiritual realms. In a physical, time-bounded world, change and progression mean that the previous state no longer prevails. Wool becomes yarn, yarn becomes cloth, cloth becomes a coat; the person now has a coat, but the sheep is left bereft of its wool. Not so with a spiritual evolution, where all stages exist simultaneously, each on its own plane. There is no "before" and "after" in the temporal sense, but rather a hierarchy of realities that derive from and impact each other.

 ZOHAR, *VOL. 2, 184b*

The lower world always stands ready to receive ... and the upper world provides to it only in accordance with the state in which it stands. If the lower world is in a state of radiance, radiance shines down upon it from above. But if the lower world is in a state of gloominess, then the radiance it is given is constricted. Hence, "Serve G-d with joy" (Psalms 100:2), because human gladness draws a corresponding supernal gladness.

 R. CHAIM IBN ATTAR
OHR HACHAYIM, LEVITICUS 22:12

The four worlds

Know that our sages have said that G-d created four worlds, each higher than the other (*Zohar*, 2:155a). These are noted in the verse, "All that is called in My name and for My glory, I created it, I formed it, I also made it" (Isaiah 43:7). [*My name and*] *My glory* is the supernal world that is called the World of Emanation. *I created it* is the World of Creation. *I formed it* is the World of Formation. *I made it* is the World of Action.

You should also know that the radiance of G-d fills each and every world.... This is the secret of the four letters of the divine name *Havayah*—the letter *yud* is in Emanation, the first *hei* in Creation, and so on.

The sages also said (*Zohar*, 3:218b) that the vitality that operates within [us] is of the divine light, as it is written (Deuteronomy 32:9), "His people are G-d's portion...." They also said (*Zohar*, 1:80b) that the vital element within a person has four names attributed to it. There is an aspect of the soul that is called *nefesh* (vitality), an aspect called *ruach* (spirit), an aspect called *neshamah* (soul), and an aspect called *chayah* (life) ... which is also referred to as "the soul of the soul."

The practitioners of the true wisdom explain that *nefesh* is the part of the human soul that derives from the divine light in the World of Action, being of a greatly diminished spirituality, and the part of the soul that experiences the physical world; *ruach* is the part of the soul that derives from the divine light in the World of Formation; *neshamah* derives from the divine light of the World of Creation; and "the soul of the soul" derives from the light of the World of Emanation. We attain perfection by ascending from the lower level of spiritual life to the higher, this being the goal of man's creation.

{SEE "THE LADDER OF PRAYER" ON P. 272}

 R. SCHNEUR ZALMAN OF LIADI, *TANYA, CH. 36*

Our sages have said that the purpose of the creation of this world is that "G-d desired to have a dwelling in the lower worlds" (*Midrash Tanchuma, Naso* 16).

Obviously, regarding G-d, the distinction of "higher" and "lower" does not apply, as the Almighty pervades all realms of existence equally. The explanation of the matter, however, is as follows:

Before the world was created, G-d was exclusively and singularly one…. Insofar as G-d is concerned, it is still the same now. The change brought about by the act of creation relates only to those on the receiving end of the vitality that the Creator infuses into the created reality, which they receive via the many "garments" that conceal and obscure the divine light; [without these garments they would be unable to exist,] as it is written (Exodus 33:20), "For no man can see Me and live…."

This is the concept of the *hishtalshelut*, the downward descent of the worlds, level after level, by means of a multitude of "garments" that conceal the vitality that emanates from the Creator, until this physical and materialistic world—the lowest in degree, of which there is none lower in regard to the concealment of G-d's light—was created; a world of doubled and redoubled darkness, to the extent that it is full of evil—namely, elements that actually oppose the Almighty, declaring "I am, and there is nothing else besides me."

Clearly, however, the purpose of this devolution of

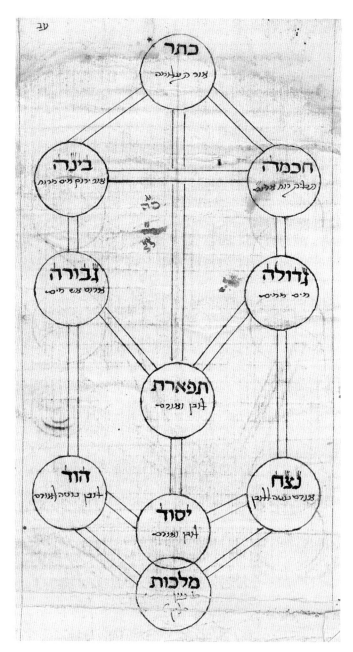

Diagram of the ten sefirot, Sefer Raziel ha-Mal'ach, Italy, 1650

the worlds and their descent from level to level is not for the sake of the higher spiritual worlds, since for them, this is a descent from the radiance of the divine countenance. Rather, the ultimate purpose is this lowest world, precisely because of its lowliness. For such was G-d's desire: that He should derive satisfaction when the forces opposing G-dliness are overcome and darkness is transformed into light; with the result that because of "the advantage of the light that comes from the darkness," the infinite light of G-d is revealed in the physical world with an even greater intensity than in the higher worlds.

THE SEFIROT

In the Jewish tradition, the statement (Deuteronomy 6:4) "G-d is one" means not just that there is only one G-d, but that there is no plurality within G-d's absolute singularity. Yet the Torah also speaks of G-d's kindness, compassion, power, justice, etc., implying the existence of divine traits, and even a divine "character."

The Kabbalists address this paradox by explaining that while G-d indeed transcends all characterization, G-d isolated from within His infinite and all-inclusive reality ten "attributes" ("ten substanceless *sefirot*," in the terminology of *Sefer Yetzirah*), via which He relates to His creations. The human being, created in the "image," mirrors these ten attributes in their own personality and character. Hence, "from my own flesh I perceive G-d" (Job 19:26)—by contemplating the inner workings of our own soul and personality, we gain insight into the Creator's relationship with our existence.

 MIDRASH RABBAH, *SHEMOT 3:6*

G-d said to Moses: You wish to know My name? I am called by My deeds. When I judge the creations, I am called *E-lohim*. When I battle the wicked, I am called *Tze-vaot*. When I abide with the sins of man, I am called *E-l Sha-dai*. When I have compassion upon my world, I am called *Y-H-V-H*.

 R. MEIR IBN GABBAI, *AVODAT HAKODESH, 1:8*

Just as G-d has the power of infinity, so does G-d have the power of finiteness. For should you say that He has the power of infinity but does not have the power of finiteness, you would be detracting from His perfection.

 R. JUDAH LOEW
GEVUROT HASHEM, INTRODUCTION 2

Our sages, of blessed memory, refer to G-d as "The Holy One".... The term "holy" denotes an entity that is apart and removed, and G-d is abstract in the ultimate sense of abstraction. But precisely because G-d is the ultimate abstraction, there is nothing that is excluded from Him.

A thing that has a definition, and is distinguished by certain characteristics, that same definition will exclude from it things that are outside of that definition. But because G-d has no definition at all, nothing is excluded from Him. Therefore, He knows everything and can do anything. All this is because G-d is not defined by any specific definitions; therefore, everything comes from Him.

 R. NAFTALI HERTZ BACHARACH
EMEK HAMELECH, SHAAR SHAASHU'EI HAMELECH

Before everything, it arose in His simple will the desire to create the worlds. For it is the nature of good to do good; and if there is no world, to whom would He do good?

 ZOHAR, *TIKUNIM, HAKDAMAH 2*

Elijah opened his discourse and said:

Master of the worlds, You are one, but not in the numerical sense. You are exalted above all the exalted, hidden from all the hidden; no thought can grasp You at all.

You are the one who has brought forth ten "garments," and we call them ten *sefirot*, through which to direct hidden worlds that are not revealed, and revealed worlds; and through them You conceal Yourself from man.

You are the one who binds them together and unites them; and inasmuch as You are within them, whoever separates one from another of these ten *sefirot*, it is as if they have effected a separation in You.

These ten *sefirot* proceed according to their order: one long, one short, and one intermediate.

It is You who directs them, but there is no one who directs You, neither above, nor below, nor from any side.

You have made garments for them, from which souls issue forth to man. You have made for them a number of bodies that are called "bodies" in comparison with the garments that cover them; and they are described in the following manner:

chesed (benevolence)—the right arm;

gevurah (severity, power)—the left arm;

tiferet (beauty, harmony)—the torso;

netzach (eternity, victory) and *hod* (splendor)—the two thighs;

yesod (foundation)—the end of the torso, the sign of the holy covenant;

malchut (sovereignty)—the mouth, which we call the Oral Torah;

chochmah (wisdom)—the brain, that is, the thought within;

binah (understanding)—the heart, by means of which the heart understands; concerning the latter two, it is written (Deuteronomy 29:28), "The hidden things belong to G-d";

supernal *keter* (crown) is the crown of kingship, concerning which it is said (Isaiah 46:10), "He declares the end from the beginning," and this is the skull [upon which are placed the] tefillin.

Within them is the Name whose numerical value is 45 (spelled יו״ד ה״א וא״ו ה״א), which is the path of *atzilut* [the world of Emanation]; and the watering of the tree [of the *sefirot*] with its arms and branches just as water irrigates a tree and it grows by that irrigation.

Master of the worlds, You are the cause of causes and effector of effects, who waters the tree through that fountain; and that fountain is as the soul to the body, which is the life of the body. In You, however, there is no similitude or likeness to anything within or without.

You created heaven and earth and brought forth from them the sun, the moon, the stars, and the planets; and on earth—the trees, the green herbage, the Garden of Eden, the grasses, the beasts, the cattle, the fowl, the fish, and mankind; in order to make known through them the supernal realms, how the higher and lower worlds are conducted, and how the higher worlds may be known from the lower; but there is no one who can know You at all.

Without You, there is no unity in the higher or lower realms, and You are known as the cause of all and the master of all.

Each *sefirah* has a specific name by which the angels are also called. You, however, have no known name, for You permeate all the names, and You are the perfection of them all. When You remove Yourself from them, all the names remain as a body without a soul.

You are wise, but not with a knowable wisdom; You are understanding, but not with a knowable understanding. You have no knowable place. [You vested Yourself in the *sefirot*] only to make known to mankind Your power and strength and to show them how the world is conducted through law and compassion, as there is righteousness and justice that are dispensed according to the deeds of man.

Law is *gevurah*; justice is the middle column; righteousness is the holy *malchut*; the "scales of righteousness" are the two supports of truth; the "measure of righteousness" is the sign of the holy covenant. All these are to show how the world is conducted, but not that You possess a knowable righteousness which is law, nor a knowable justice which is compassion, nor any of these attributes at all.

THE TZIMTZUM

The concept of the *tzimtzum*—G-d's "constriction" of His infinite self-expression so that the created reality could exist, if only in its own perception, as an entity distinct of its Creator—has its roots in a number of obscure Midrashic and Zoharic passages. But it was R. Isaac Luria who first expounded on this idea, making it a cornerstone of Kabbalistic teaching and the Jewish-mystical perspective on reality.

 ZOHAR, *VOL. 1, 15a*

At the beginning of the manifestation of the King's will, the lamp of darkness engraved engravings on the supernal clear sky. It emanated from the most concealed of all concealed things, from the secret of endlessness. A formless vapor was inserted into a circle that was neither white nor black nor red nor green, nor any color at all. When He began its measurements, He created bright colors that shone into the empty space and the engraving. From within the lamp a fountain spouted, from which the hues down below were colored.

 R. ISAAC LURIA, *EITZ CHAYIM 1:2*

Know that before the *sefirot* were emanated and the creations were created, a simple divine light filled the entirety of existence…. When it arose in His simple will the desire to create the worlds … G-d constricted His light, withdrawing it to the sides and leaving a void and an empty space in its center…. He then drew from the infinite light a single straight line from His circle of light, from the top downward, devolving as it descended into the empty space…. And within that "empty space" He emanated, created, formed, and made all the worlds.

 TZEMACH TZEDEK, *DERECH MITZVOTECHA, 94b*

It is written (I Samuel 2:3), "G-d is the G-d of minds." This implies the existence of two "minds."

The first mind is that G-d is the true reality, and all that is here below is regarded as naught, as it is nothing but a reflection [of the divine reality]…. This is how it is from G-d's perspective.

The second mind is the perspective of the creations. To them, it seems that they are real. They describe the creation of the world as "something from nothing"—meaning, that G-dliness is "nothing," as it is not graspable, and they are "something"….

Now, we say, "We concede to You" (I Chronicles 29:13). Meaning, we concede that the truth is how it is from G-d's perspective…. The fact that the world appears to be "something" is only due to the *tzimtzumim*, the "constrictions" [that] generate the "second mind"….

G-d is beyond these constrictions, and G-d is also the source of these constrictions. So, in the final analysis, G-d incorporates both "minds." Hence the verse states, "G-d is the G-d of minds."

 SHIMONA TZUKERNIK

The mystics tell us that G-d created the world through a process called *tzimtzum*, translated as "constriction." The Creator constricted His "infinite light" in order to create the world. But what does that mean?

A useful analogy is speech. All speech requires constriction—a withholding or hiding. When I exhale, there is no obstruction of the air between my lungs and the outside world. But in speech, there is an obstruction: a vibration with a vowel, an actual blockage with a consonant.

Beyond the physiological constriction that facilitates speech is a conceptual and emotional constriction. I can tell you only *this* idea and only in *this* way. I can share this emotion and not that emotion. In order to transmit this, I have to withhold all of that.

And that is an analogy of *tzimtzum*. To create the world, G-d did not make a new entity that is outside of Him. He created by withholding. G-d concealed all the other infinite potentials of His infinite being, so that a specific world could emerge.

INNER TORAH

According to *Zohar*, there are four general dimensions of Torah: *peshat,* or plain meaning; *remez,* allegory; *derush,* legal and homiletic exposition; and *sod,* the mystical (expressed by the acronym *pardes*, "orchard"). Hasidic teaching endeavors to uncover the "soul," or inner essence, of all four dimensions, revealing new depths in each and showing how all four aspects complement and fulfill each other.

In an essay titled *On the Essence of Chassidus,* the Lubavitcher Rebbe, R. Menachem M. Schneerson, presents one example of this dynamic. The *Modeh Ani* prayer, recited each morning upon awakening, has a plain meaning, alludes to a futuristic event, expresses a legal principle, and represents a mystical formula; and Hasidic teaching opens a window into the "soul" of each of these four dimensions.

I submit thanks before You, living and ever-enduring king,

that You have restored my soul within me with compassion;

great is Your faithfulness.

מוֹדֶה אֲנִי לְפָנֶיךָ מֶלֶךְ חַי וְקַיָּם
שֶׁהֶחֱזַרְתָּ בִּי נִשְׁמָתִי בְּחֶמְלָה, רַבָּה אֱמוּנָתֶךָ.

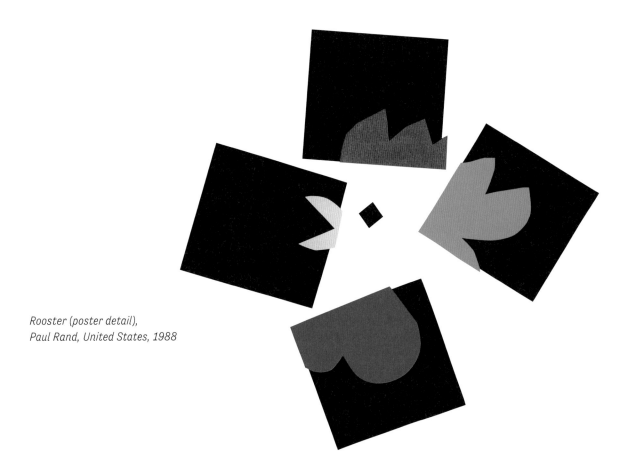

Rooster (poster detail),
Paul Rand, United States, 1988

dimensions of meaning in Modeh Ani

Four levels of interpretation	Hasidic teaching
PLAIN MEANING Every time we partake of one of the gifts of life (eat a food, smell a flower, etc.), we first recite a blessing expressing our gratitude to the Creator. Certainly, then, the gift of a new day of life calls for a blessing. A proper blessing, however, contains the sacred name of G-d, whereas in the *Modeh Ani* prayer we address G-d simply as "You." The reason for this is that *Modeh Ani* is said immediately upon awakening, even before we have washed our hands and performed our morning ablutions, and it is forbidden to mention the divine name when one is not in a state of cleanliness.	A "name" is a representation, a projected self that is extrinsic to the core self. When we address G-d by one of His names, we are relating to a specific projection of G-d's relationship with us. But when we relate to G-d as "You," we relate to G-d's essence. To evoke a divine name requires a standard of holiness commensurate to the expression of G-dliness that it represents. But in *Modeh Ani*, our very "I" addresses the very "You" of G-d. *Modeh Ani* can therefore be said in any state, as no impurity in the world can taint the *Modeh Ani* of the soul.
ALLEGORY One of the fundamental beliefs in Judaism is the resurrection of the dead, prophesied to occur in the Messianic World to Come. The Talmud (*Berachot* 57b) describes sleep as "one-sixtieth of death." So the *Modeh Ani* prayer, in which we thank the Almighty for "restoring my soul within me" after the minor death of sleep, is an allusion to the future resurrection.	Hasidic teaching elaborates on the principle of "perpetual creation": in every moment of time, the entirety of Creation is brought into being from a state of utter nothingness, as G-d continually imparts existence and life to everything that is. This gives us a deeper appreciation of the gratitude to G-d we express in *Modeh Ani*. Not only is our soul restored to our body each morning, but our body is also regenerated, as it will be in the future resurrection. Indeed, this occurs each and every moment of the day; our moment of awakening is simply a daily opportunity to tangibly experience and acknowledge this truth.
LEGAL EXPOSITION One of the 613 mitzvot of the Torah is the obligation to return an object that has been entrusted to us for safekeeping. This obligation is categorical: even in the case that the owner of the object has an outstanding financial obligation to us, this does not absolve us from the duty to return their property to them. This law is implicit in the *Modeh Ani* prayer. Every night, we entrust our soul to G-d. Often we are deficient in our obligations toward our Creator; yet, as we confirm in *Modeh Ani*, "great is Your faithfulness" —G-d returns the trust, regardless of our outstanding debts to Him.	To understand this law, we need to understand what a mitzvah is. There are logical mitzvot and suprarational mitzvot; social mitzvot and "religious" mitzvot. But these differentiations all pertain to a mitzvah's "garments," its outer packaging. At its core, every mitzvah is the infinite will of G-d. If the Torah commands to return the property of a fellow that has been placed in our trust, the logic of this mitzvah does not constitute its essence, which lies in the act itself.
MYSTICAL In the terminology of Kabbalah, "king" refers to G-d's involvement within the time and space of Creation, whereas "living and ever-enduring" describes G-d as He transcends time and space. In *Modeh Ani*, we attribute the restoration of our soul to the "living and ever-enduring king," implying that it is a product of the union of these two divine modalities.	There are no greater opposites than spirit and matter. Spirit expresses its subservience to a higher truth; matter proclaims its own being. The marriage of body and soul is thus an impossible union of opposites. Every breath of life is an expression of the infinite power of G-d, who both transcends and permeates existence.

Morals and character

Laws can obligate or forbid actions; it is quite another matter to mandate attitudes and feelings. The Torah, however, is not just a legal code; it is a wholistic guide to life, addressing character as well as behavior, social sensibilities as well as the inner life of the soul.

The internal-psychological component is an integral part of Torah in all its iterations: in Biblical verses such as "love your fellow as yourself" and "be wholesome with G-d"; in the Talmudic tractate of Avot ("Ethics of the Fathers"); in classic works such as R. Bachya ibn Pakudah's "Duties of the Hearts" and R. Elijah de Vidas' "Genesis of Wisdom"; and in the teachings of the Hasidic masters and of the founders of the 19th-century Musar movement.

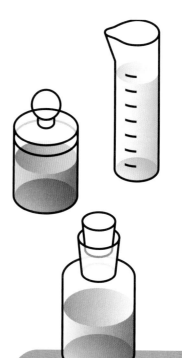

THE MODERN MUSAR MOVEMENT Founded in Vilnius, Lithuania, by R. Israel Lipkin Salanter (1810–1883), the Musar movement endeavored to bring a new emphasis to ethical behavior, character refinement, and spiritual self-improvement. Over the next two generations, various schools within this movement were established by R. Salanter's disciples, including the Kelm school, founded by R. Simcha Zisel Ziv (1824–1898), which emphasized orderliness, thoughtfulness, and dedication; the Slabodka school (R. Nathan Zvi Finkel, 1849–1927), which focused on the human being's striving for perfection; and the Novardok school (R. Yosef Yozel Horowitz, 1847–1919), which emphasized trust in G-d, and humility and self-effacement.

 ORCHOT TZADIKIM, *INTRODUCTION & PORTAL 14*

Building a character is like cooking a stew: You need greens and meat and water and salt and spices. Too little meat and the broth is thin; too much salt and it is inedible. But if you take from each in the right measure, then you will have a tasty dish.

So, too, with the traits of the human character. There are traits of which one should avail oneself in a large measure, such as humility and bashfulness and the like; and traits that should be employed only minutely, such as pride and brazenness and cruelty. One who carefully weighs and measures the amount to be taken of each trait will achieve goodness....

[For example:] Jealousy is an extremely negative trait, leading to virtually every vice and sin. Still, it has its positive uses. In the words of the sages (Talmud, *Bava Batra* 21a), "Jealousy among scholars increases wisdom." Similarly, when a person is jealous of the good deeds of their fellow and is driven to emulate them.

Jews in a Synagogue, Rembrandt van Rijn, Amsterdam, 1648

 MAIMONIDES, *MISHNEH TORAH,*
LAWS OF CHARACTER, 1:4

The correct path is the median temperament of each and every character trait that a person has. This is the trait that is equidistant from either of the extremes…. The early sages therefore instructed that a person should evaluate their traits and direct them along the middle path, so as to achieve wholeness.

For example … a person should not be overly stingy, nor squander their money; but should give charity according to their capacity and lend as is appropriate to one who is in need. A person should not be frivolous and jubilant, nor mournful and depressed; but should be tranquilly happy at all times and with a friendly demeanor.

The same applies to all of a person's traits. This path is the path of the wise, and the person whose traits are intermediate and balanced can be called wise.

 R. MOSES CHAIM LUZZATTO
PATH OF THE UPRIGHT, CH. 1

The basis of piety, and the root of wholesome service of the Creator, is for a person to clarify and verify what is their task in this world, and what should be their objective and striving in all that they toil all the days of their life.

 R. SIMCHA ZISEL ZIV OF KELM
CHOCHMAH UMUSAR, 1:122

People travel great distances to doctors in order to heal a physical ailment, but a spiritual ailment is seen not as an illness but merely as an imperfection. In truth, however, the body is only the garment of the soul. If it is justified to go to such trouble and expense for the sake of the garment, how much more so must be invested in the repair of the essence of the person, which is the soul.

ETHICS OF THE FATHERS

While all of the Talmud's sixty-three tractates include moral and ethical teachings, their primary focus is on a person's legal obligations under Torah law. The exception is the tractate *Avot* —"Fathers," commonly known as "Ethics of the Fathers"— which is wholly devoted to the cultivation of positive character traits and attitudes, imparting the Torah's guidance on how to approach our relationship with our Creator, with our fellows, and with the world in which we live.

SUMMER LEARNING It is customary to study *Ethics of the Fathers* on Shabbat afternoons during the summer months. One chapter is studied each Shabbat, beginning on the Shabbat after Passover and ending on the Shabbat before Rosh Hashanah, thereby completing the six-chapter course of study four times each year.

 SELECTED TEACHINGS FROM ETHICS OF THE FATHERS

The world stands on three things: Torah learning, service of G-d, and deeds of lovingkindness. (1:2)

Do not be like servants who serve their master in order to receive a reward; rather, be like servants who serve their master not for the sake of receiving a reward. (1:3)

Your home should be open wide, and the poor should be members of your household. (1:5)

Love work, loathe mastery over others, and avoid intimacy with the government. (1:10)

Be of the disciples of Aaron: a lover of peace, a pursuer of peace, one who loves the creatures and draws them close to the Torah. (1:12)

If I am not for myself, who will be for me? And when I am only for myself, what am I? And if not now, when? (1:14)

Say little and do much. (1:15)

Greet every person with a cheerful face. (1:15)

The world endures by virtue of three things: justice, truth, and peace. (1:18)

Which is the straight path that a person should choose for themselves? That which is harmonious for the one who does it and harmonious for mankind. (2:1)

Contemplate three things, and you will not fall into the hands of transgression. Know what is above you: an eye that sees, an ear that hears, and all your deeds are written in a book. (2:1)

Any learning that is not accompanied by work is destined to fail and to cause sin. (2:2)

Do not separate yourself from the community. (2:4)

Do not judge your fellow until you have stood in their place. (2:4)

A bashful person cannot learn; a short-tempered person cannot teach. (2:5)

In a place where there are no men, strive to be a man. (2:5)

Hillel saw a skull floating on the water. He said to it: Because you drowned others, you were drowned; and those who drowned you will in the end be drowned. (2:6)

More possessions, more worries. (2:7)

All your deeds should be for the sake of Heaven. (2:12)

Do not be wicked in your own eyes. (2:13)

It is not incumbent upon you to finish the job, but neither are you free to absolve yourself from it. (2:16)

Pray for the well-being of the government, for were it not for their fear of it, people would swallow each other alive. (3:2)

One who shames a fellow in public has no share in the World to Come. (3:11)

Silence is the safeguard of wisdom. (3:13)

If there is no Torah, there is no common decency;
if there is no common decency, there is no Torah.
If there is no wisdom, there is no fear of G-d;
if there is no fear of G-d, there is no wisdom.
If there is no knowledge, there is no understanding;
if there is no understanding, there is no knowledge.
If there is no flour, there is no Torah;
if there is no Torah, there is no flour. (3:17)

Who is wise? The one who learns from every person. Who is strong? The one who conquers their desires. Who is rich? The one who is satisfied with their lot. Who is honored? The one who honors others. (4:1)

One mitzvah brings another mitzvah; one transgression brings another transgression. (4:2)

Do not scorn any person, and do not discount any thing. For there is no person that does not have their hour, and no thing that does not have its place. (4:3)

Do not judge alone, for there is none qualified to judge alone, save for the One. (4:8)

Be humble before every person. (4:10)

Be a tail to lions rather than a head to foxes. (4:15)

Do not appease your friend at the height of their anger; do not comfort them while their dead still lies before them. (4:18)

Do not look at the vessel, but at what it contains. (4:20)

Envy, lust, and honor drive a person from the world. (4:21)

Against your will you are formed, against your will you are born, against your will you live, against your will you die. (4:22)

There are seven things that characterize a boor, and seven that characterize a wise person. A wise person does not speak before one who is greater than himself in wisdom or age. He does not interrupt his fellow's words. He does not hasten to answer. His questions are on the subject and his answers to the point. He responds to first things first and to latter things later. Concerning what he did not hear, he says, "I did not hear it." He concedes to the truth. With the boor, the reverse of all these is the case. (5:7)

There are four types of temperaments. One who is easily angered and easily appeased—their virtue cancels their flaw. One whom it is difficult to anger and difficult to appease—their flaw cancels their virtue. One whom it is difficult to anger and is easily appeased is a pious person. One who is easily angered and is difficult to appease is a wicked person. (5:11)

Any love that is dependent on something—when the thing ceases, the love also ceases. But a love that is not dependent on any thing never ceases. (5:16)

Be bold as a leopard, light as an eagle, fleet as a deer, and strong as a lion to do the will of your Father in heaven. (5:20)

Delve and delve into [the Torah], for all is in it; see with it; grow old and worn in it; do not budge from it, for there is nothing better. (5:21)

According to the pain is the reward. (5:21)

A person who learns something from their fellow, whether it is a single chapter, a single law, a single verse, a single word, or even a single letter, is obligated to act respectfully toward them. (6:3)

SELF AND FELLOW

 LEVITICUS 19:18

Love your fellow as yourself.

 TALMUD, *SHABBAT 31a*

A gentile came before Shamai and said, "I wish to convert to Judaism, on condition that you teach me the entire Torah while I stand on one foot." Shamai drove him away with the builder's yardstick he held in his hand.

He then came to Hillel. Hillel converted him, and said to him: "What is hateful to you, do not do to your fellow. This is the entire Torah; the rest is commentary—go and learn it."

 ETHICS OF THE FATHERS, *CHAPTER 5, MISHNAH 10*

There are four types of people. A person who says, "What is mine is yours, and what is yours is mine," is a boor. One who says, "What is mine is mine, and what is yours is yours," this is an intermediate character; others say that this is the character of [the evil city] Sodom. One who says, "What is mine is yours, and what is yours is yours," is a pious person. And one who says, "What is mine is mine, and what is yours is mine," is wicked.

 R. ISRAEL BAAL SHEM TOV, *HAYOM YOM, IYAR 5*

A soul may come down into the world and live seventy or eighty years for the sole purpose of doing a favor for another—even just a material favor, but especially a spiritual favor.

 R. SCHNEUR ZALMAN OF LIADI
TANYA, CHAPTER 32

When a person regards the body with disdain, and rejoices only in the joy of the soul, this provides a direct and easy path to the fulfillment of the mitzvah, "Love your fellow as yourself…." Because all [souls] are equal, having one father; which is why all Jews are called true brothers, due to their common source in the one G-d. It is only the bodies that are separate.

Indeed, those for whom the body is the primary thing and the soul is secondary cannot achieve true love and brotherhood among themselves, only a love that is dependent on some personal gain.

This is why Hillel the Elder said in regard to the fulfillment of this mitzvah, "This is the entire Torah; the rest is commentary." For the basis and root of the entire Torah is to raise up and exalt the soul above the body, reaching unto the source and root of all the worlds.

 R. SHALOM DOVBER OF LUBAVITCH
MAAMAR HEICHALTZU 5659, SEC. 4

Ultimately, all strife, conflict, and hatred are not for any particular reason, but because one person cannot tolerate the other person's existence…. A person may offer some sort of explanation why they hate the other person, but this explanation came later … the true reason for the hatred is the person's own egotism and self-importance. Their ego does not leave room for anyone else. The mere existence of another person detracts from their own existence, so they find it impossible to tolerate others.

 SIDDUR, *PRAYER RECITED BEFORE GOING TO SLEEP*

Master of the world, I hereby forgive anyone who has angered me or vexed me, or committed an offense against me, whether physically or financially, whether against my honor or anything else that is mine, whether unwillingly or willingly, whether mistakenly or deliberately, whether by speech or by deed, whether in this incarnation or in any other … may no person be punished on my account.

 R. ISRAEL BAAL SHEM TOV
MEOR EINAYIM, PARASHAH CHUKAT

Your fellow is your mirror. If your own face is clean, the image you encounter will also be flawless. If you look into a mirror and see a blemish, it is your own imperfection that you are seeing.

JOY AND HUMILITY

 PSALMS 100:2

Serve G-d with joy.

 R. HANOCH HENICH OF ALEKSANDER
CHASHAVAH LETOVAH, P. 90

Sadness is not a sin. But the spiritual numbness of the heart caused by sadness is worse than that of any sin.

 R. SCHNEUR ZALMAN OF LIADI
TANYA, CHAPTER 26

We now need to make known a major principle:

When two individuals are wrestling with each other, each striving to throw down the other, but one of them is lazy and lethargic, that person will be easily defeated and felled, even if they are stronger than their opponent. The same applies regarding the conquest of one's negative impulses: it is impossible to defeat them from a state of laziness and heaviness, which stem from melancholy and a dull heart, but only with the alacrity that derives from happiness and from a heart free from any trace of worry and sadness.

 R. NACHMAN OF BRESLOV
LIKUTEI MOHARAN II, 78 AND 112

There is no cause for despair, ever. A person must always believe that if it was in their ability to ruin it, it is in their ability to fix it.

 TALMUD, *BERACHOT 40a*

An empty vessel can receive; a full vessel cannot receive.

 R. SAMUEL DE UCEDA, *MIDRASH SHMUEL, AVOT 4:1*

How delectable is this expression that we find in the language of our sages, where a Torah scholar is referred to as a *talmid chacham* ("wise student" or "student of wisdom"). Indeed, one can never separate the word "student" from the word "wise." The moment a person stops thinking of themselves as a student, they can no longer be called wise.

 R. YOSEF YITZCHAK SCHNEERSOHN
SEFER HAMAAMARIM 5699, P. 101

It is written (Isaiah 29:19), "The humble increased their joy in G-d." The vessel for joy is *bitul*—humility and self-effacement. Where there is *bitul*, there is joy; conversely, egotism and self-regard are an impediment to joy.

This needs to be understood, as it would seem that humility and joy are two opposites. Humility entails putting oneself down and regarding oneself as inferior, whereas joy is the exultation of the soul. So how is humility a vessel and cause for joy?

But the truth is that humility is not synonymous with self-deprecation…. Rather, it means that a person contemplates how all the good they possess is a gift and an inheritance which they received…. This is the idea of humility: not to consider one's achievements as expressions of one's own greatness, but as a gift from the Creator.

Thus we are told that "Moses was exceedingly humble, more than any person on the face of the earth" (Numbers 12:3). Moses was cognizant of his own qualities, and was well-aware that his lofty spiritual level was unparalleled by any other person; but he was still humble. He recognized that all of these qualities were given to him from Above…. He felt that if another person would be endowed with the same abilities and qualities as he, the other would have equaled his achievements, or perhaps even surpassed them. It was this that led Moses to be the humblest man of all.

It is this kind of humility that brings true joy.

 VIKTOR FRANKL
MAN'S SEARCH FOR MEANING, PREFACE

Happiness cannot be pursued; it must ensue, and it only does so as the unintended side effect of one's personal dedication to a cause greater than oneself or as the by-product of one's surrender to a person other than oneself.

LOVE AND AWE

 DEUTERONOMY 30:20

Love the Lord your G-d … for He is your life.

 PSALMS 111:10

The beginning of wisdom is the fear of G-d.

 MAIMONIDES, *MISHNEH TORAH, LAWS OF THE FUNDAMENTALS OF TORAH, 2:2*

What is the path to the love and awe of G-d? When a person contemplates the Creator's great and wondrous deeds and creations, and through them appreciates His infinite and incomparable wisdom, he will come to love, praise, and glorify G-d, craving with tremendous desire to know the great Name…. Reflecting on these selfsame truths, a person will recoil in awe and fear, appreciating how the human being is a tiny, lowly, and dark creature, standing with their limited and flimsy intellect before One who is of perfect wisdom.

 MALBIM, *COMMENTARY TO GENESIS 20:11*

We may observe a person or a society that has great philosophers, has instituted a righteous way of life, has acclimated themselves with good character traits, and practices justice and charity—all in accordance with the reasoning of their intellect. Nevertheless, we cannot trust that at such time when their passions will be aroused, their intellect will conquer their passions. On the contrary, their intellect itself may lead them along the path of immorality and murder and every type of evil.

There is only one force within the human psyche that can ensure against sin, and that is the fear of the Almighty, who sees both what is revealed and what is hidden in the person and observes all their actions. Only this can ensure that at such time when a person's base inclinations overwhelm them, they will guard themselves from doing evil.

 R. BACHYA IBN PAKUDAH
DUTIES OF THE HEARTS, PORTAL 10: LOVE OF G-D

Understand and know that all that has been said in this work on the duties of the heart, on morals and spiritual nobility, are rungs and steps leading to this supreme objective…. Every duty and every good trait—whether it be rationally derived, stated in Scripture, or based on tradition—are all qualities and steps by which we ascend to this ultimate aim, and there is no level above or beyond it. Hence, the prophet [Moses], peace be unto him, attached it, in Deuteronomy (6:4–5), to the statement of the divine unity, declaring, "Hear O Israel, G-d is our Lord, G-d is One. And you shall love G-d…."

 MAIMONIDES, *MISHNEH TORAH, LAWS OF REPENTANCE, 10:1–2*

A person should not say: I will fulfill the mitzvot of the Torah and pursue its wisdom in order to receive all the blessings it contains, or in order to merit the life of the World to Come; and I will avoid the transgressions that the Torah warns against so that I may be saved from all the punishments contained in the Torah, or so that I will not be cut off from the life of the World to Come. It is not fitting to serve G-d in this manner….

One who serves the Almighty out of love fulfills the Torah and the mitzvot and follows in the paths of wisdom not for any reason in the world—not out of fear that something bad will happen to them, nor in order to acquire benefit. Rather, one does the truth because it is true, and ultimately, good will also come because of it.

 R. MENACHEM RECANATI
COMMENTARY ON TORAH, GENESIS 22:12

There are two types of fear of G-d: external fear and inner fear.

External fear is when a person is afraid to transgress the commandments lest they be punished for violating the divine decree. This fear is on a lower level than love.

Inner fear is when a person appreciates the great-

Mountain Fire, John Singer Sargent, The Alps, 1906–1907

ness of G-d, and the delight, richness, and glory of the divine abode, and is fearful and agitated by the thought: Perhaps I am unworthy of standing in the King's palace, as [the gulf between] G-d's greatness and my lowliness is shameful.... This fear is greater than love.

 ZVI YAIR, *MEIROSH TZURIM, P. 125*

Rush and recoil: a dialogue

Reb Abraham:
    The droplet yearns
for the source.
The spark craves
the great fire.
I can no longer bear
the darkness of this world.

Let us plunge
into the sea of nothingness.
Let the grains of our existence
melt within
His infinite being.

Reb Zalman:
    The One who first
carved my spark
from His blaze
desires not
the extinction of my candle
within His flame.
    Rather He seeks
the searing tremor of my soul
longing,
from afar, from the dark
toward His light.

TRUST

 DEUTERONOMY 8:11–18

Beware ... lest you eat and be sated, and build good houses and dwell therein; and your herds and your flocks multiply, your silver and gold increase, and all that you have increases.

And your heart will grow haughty; and you will forget the Lord your G-d.... And you will say in your heart: "My ability and the might of my hand have accumulated this wealth for me."

Remember the Lord your G-d; it is He who gives you the ability to make wealth.

 PSALMS 146:3–7

Do not trust in princes, in the human who has no salvation. His spirit departs, he returns to his soil; on that day, his plans are lost.

Fortunate is the one for whom the G-d of Jacob is their savior; whose hope is in the Lord their G-d, who made heaven and earth ... who keeps truth forever; who does justice for the oppressed; who gives bread to the hungry.

 R. BACHYA IBN PAKUDAH
DUTIES OF THE HEARTS, PORTAL 4: TRUST IN G-D

As we are speaking about a person's duty to serve the Almighty, it is fitting to discuss an imperative that is very necessary for the servant of G-d. This is *bitachon* (trust) in G-d in all one's affairs, which brings great advantages both religiously and materially.

Bitachon engenders ... absolute loyalty to one's Creator.... For one who does not rely on G-d is by necessity relying on something other than G-d.... The person who trusts in the Almighty is freed of their subservience to other people. That person will cease to pursue others, wait on them, flatter them, and bow to them, other than in the service of G-d. They will not fear animosity of others or be taken aback by their opposition, and will be unburdened of the debts incurred by their favors.

They will be free to rebuke the guilty without fear or shame, and need not participate in the conspiracies of their falsehoods....

Another advantage for the person who trusts in G-d.... If they are blessed with wealth, they will gladly and generously expedite their financial contributions toward Heaven and toward their fellows. And if they have no riches, they will see in their lack of wealth a kindness from the Almighty, in absolving them of the many obligations toward G-d and society it entails, and from the hassle of guarding and managing it.... Thus, the one who trusts in G-d enjoys the benefit of money—which is sustenance—but is free of the worries that the ownership of wealth brings.... Their money will not prevent them from trusting in G-d, as they do not rely on it, but rather see it as a deposit to be used for certain purposes for a certain limited time. If the money stays with them, it will not make them defiant, nor will they demand gratitude from those with whom they are obliged to share it, but will thank the Almighty for using them as a source of charity. And if the money is lost, they will not be pained by its loss, but will thank the Almighty for taking the deposit off their hands and relieving them of the responsibility.

These are all religious advantages. In a purely material sense, the person who trusts in G-d enjoys tranquility of both body and soul, and relief from difficult tasks and exhausting labor, from the service of kings and the exploitation of their subjects. They pursue a livelihood, but only in a manner that accords ultimate ease to their body, preserves their good name, provides leisure to their heart, and is most consistent with their religious needs and true beliefs. For this person knows that their choice of the material source of their livelihood will not add to their earnings nor subtract from it, save for their doing of G-d's will... They have no worries when they are left with unsold merchandise, are unable to collect a debt, or illness befalls them; for they know that the Creator manages their affairs and chooses what is best for them, better than they could choose for themselves.

2: JEWISH TEACHING / MORALS AND CHARACTER / TRUST

 SIFREI, *RE'EI 123*

"G-d will bless you in all that you do" (Deuteronomy 15:18). Because it says "G-d will bless you," I would have thought that a person can sit idle; so the verse says, "in all that you do."

 R. MOSES CHAIM LUZZATTO
PATH OF THE UPRIGHT, CHAPTER 21

Trust in G-d means that a person casts their burden entirely upon the Almighty, knowing that it is impossible for them to lack what was designated for them. As our sages taught (Talmud, *Beitzah* 16a), "All of a person's sustenance [for the year] is fixed from Rosh Hashanah...." Likewise, they said (Talmud, *Yoma* 38b), "No person can touch what is prepared for their fellow, even to the extent of a hair's breadth."

In truth, therefore, a person could have sat idle and their allotted share would have reached them, were it not for the duty that has been imposed on humanity, "By the sweat of your brow shall you eat bread" (Genesis 3:19). This is like a tax imposed on the human race that one cannot escape paying.... But it is not the effort expended in earning a living that produces one's livelihood. The effort is necessary, but once a person has put in the effort, they have discharged their obligation; there is now a vessel for the divine blessing, and a person need not consume their days in exertion and toil....

The true path is the path of the early pietists, who made their Torah learning their primary occupation and their work secondary, and succeeded in both (Talmud, *Berachot* 35b). For once a person does a minimal amount of work, they need only trust in their Master, and not be distressed by any worldly matters. Then will a person's mind be free and their heart ready for true piety and wholesome divine service.

 R. MENACHEM M. SCHNEERSON
FROM AN ADDRESS, JANUARY 15, 1981

Certain principles are so central to the foundation of this country that they were engraved on its coins and printed on its currency. One of these principles is the motto, "In G-d we trust."

The choice of the word "trust" is significant. The English language has a variety of words that express the concept of belief and faith; but the word "trust" implies more than an intellectual or emotional belief. When a person transfers funds into the hands of an individual or an organization to carry out their wishes, this is called a "trust." By the same token, "trust in G-d" implies that we *rely* on the Almighty and entrust all our concerns to Him.

The Talmud (*Berachot* 63a) states that, "A burglar at the mouth of his burrow calls out to G-d." This thief may believe in G-d, and not just as an abstract concept but as One who watches over him and who can help him; indeed, he prays to the Almighty to help him succeed in his thievery. But he does not trust and rely on G-d. Instead, he relies on his own logic, which tells him that G-d cannot provide his needs unless he defies G-d's own command and steals.

In a more subtle form, a person might insist that they believe in G-d and believe that Torah is the proper way of life, but when faced with a situation [that challenges their adherence to the Torah's instructions] they lack the confidence that they can rely on G-d's word. "In G-d we trust" means to entrust to G-d all matters of our life, the spiritual as well as the material.

 R. NACHMAN OF BRESLOV
OHR HA'EMET VEHA'EMUNAH, P. 21

The entire world is a very narrow bridge, and the main thing is not to be afraid at all.

DEALING WITH MISFORTUNE

 MAIMONIDES, *MISHNEH TORAH,*
LAWS OF FASTS, 1:1–3

It is a mitzvah to cry out to G-d and sound trumpets in the event of any calamity that befalls the community.… This practice is one of the paths of repentance, so that all will realize that the trouble occurred because of their bad deeds … [and] this will remove the trouble.… But if instead they say, "This thing that happened to us is merely a natural occurrence, a happenstance that happened"—this is a path of cruelty, as it causes them to remain attached to their bad deeds, and causes this trouble to spawn further troubles.

 MISHNAH, *BERACHOT 9:2*

Upon hearing good tidings, a person should say, "Blessed is the One who is good and does good." Upon hearing bad news, one should say, "Blessed is the True Judge."

 THE QUESTION, *ONCE UPON A CHASSID, P. 203*

A person once came to R. Dov Ber of Mezeritch with a question: The sages state (Mishnah, *Berachot* 9:5) that "a person is obligated to bless G-d for the bad just as they bless for the good." Is it possible to truly have that kind of faith? R. Dov Ber replied that his disciple, R. Zusha, could answer the question.

The man traveled to R. Zusha, who received him warmly and invited him into his home. The visitor decided to observe R. Zusha's conduct before posing his question, and was soon convinced that his host truly exemplified the Talmudic ideal that so puzzled him. R. Zusha's life was full of hardship, yet he was forever good-humored and cheerful and constantly expressing his gratitude to the Almighty for all His kindness.

The visitor finally posed his question to his host. "That is a very good question," said R. Zusha. "But why did the Rebbe send you to me? How would I know? He should have sent you to someone who has experienced suffering."

 R. SCHNEUR ZALMAN OF LIADI
TANYA, IGERET HAKODESH, 25

Our sages have said, "One who gets angry, it is as if they have worshipped idols" (*Zohar* 1:27b). The explanation of this statement is that a person gets angry only because, at the time of their anger, their faith [in G-d's absolute rule of the universe, to the exclusion of any other power or influence,] has departed from them. For if they were to truly believe that what happened to them came from the Almighty, they would not be angered at all. For although a human being possessed of free choice has cursed them or struck them or damaged their property—and this perpetrator is indeed culpable for punishment, both by human courts of law and by the heavenly court, for the evil of their choice—nevertheless, the hurt which the person has suffered had already been decreed from Above, and G-d has many emissaries to carry out His will.

 R. ELIEZER BERKOVITZ
FAITH AFTER THE HOLOCAUST, P. 68

The "reasoning" with G-d is a need of faith; it issues from the very heart of faith. When, in Elie Wiesel's *Night,* at the hanging of the little boy, someone asks, "Where is G-d now?" it is the right question to be asked. Not to ask it would have been blasphemy. Faith cannot pass by such horror in silence. Faith, because it is trust in G-d, demands justice of G-d. It cannot countenance G-d's involvement in injustice and cruelty. And yet, for faith, G-d is involved in everything under the sun. What faith is searching for is, if not to understand fully, at least to gain a hint of the nature of G-d's involvement.

This questioning of G-d with the very power of faith stands out as a guidepost at the earliest beginnings of the Jewish way in history. Abraham wrestled with G-d over the fate of Sodom and Gomorrah. We note how the man who in the humility of his piety sees himself as mere "dust and ashes," yet has the audacity to challenge G-d with the words: "The judge of all the

WHY DO THE RIGHTEOUS SUFFER? The Biblical book of Job tells the story of a generous and righteous man who suffers terrible loss and tragedy. Job's three friends come to comfort him, and in their ensuing conversations, the friends present various justifications for Job's suffering. Job rejects their arguments and demands an explanation from the Almighty. In the end, G-d appears in a whirlwind, chastises Job's friends, and responds to Job that no creature could possibly fathom the mind of its Creator.

Job, Jacob Steinhardt, Israel, 1957

earth shall not do justice?!" (Genesis 18:25). There is no contradiction here. The man of faith questions G-d because of his faith. It is the faith of Abraham in G-d that cannot tolerate injustice on the part of G-d.

This is also the essence of Job's dilemma. The sustained fire of his plaint is derived not from his personal plight, but from the passion of his faith. There is no weakening of faith with Job. On the contrary: it is the very power of faith that lends force to the accusation. What has happened to Job is wrong; it is terribly wrong because it is judged by the ideal of justice that Job formed for himself on the strength of his faith in G-d. That Job will not accept the arguments of his friends in defense of divine providence is not a matter of stubborn self-righteousness. What the friends attempt to do is to defend a wrong as justice. By doing so, without being aware of it, they degrade Job's faith.

 R. MENACHEM M. SCHNEERSON
FROM A LETTER TO ELIE WIESEL, APRIL 26, 1965

I obviously agree with you that the argument, "Would the judge of the entire world not do justice?" can be authentic and truly forceful only when it issues from the aching heart of a true believer. Indeed, we find that the first one to express this argument was our father Abraham, the great believer, and the father of the "believers who are the children of believers"....

I trust that you will agree with me that it is no coincidence that all the authentic questioners remained in their faith; indeed, it could not have been otherwise. For when the question is asked truly and sincerely, it is self-understood that such a deep feeling can only come from the conviction that true justice flows from a supra-human source—i.e., a source that is higher than both human understanding and human feeling. Indeed, for this reason the question agitates not only the emotions and the intellect, but also one's inner self and the very essence of one's being.

But after the initial storm abates, the [believing questioner] will inevitably realize that the entire premise—that one can seek to understand that which is higher than the intellect by using the intellect—has no place. Therefore, after a tumultuous and painful internal debate, he must in the end conclude that, "Despite all that, I believe!"—and, furthermore, more strongly than before.

SPEECH

 MAIMONIDES, *MISHNEH TORAH, LAWS OF CHARACTER, 7:1–2*

A person who gossips about another transgresses the Biblical prohibition, "Do not go about as a gossip-peddler amongst your people" (Leviticus 19:16).... What is a gossip-peddler? One who carries conversations from one person to another, saying, "So-and-so said such-and-such," or "This is what I heard about so-and-so"—even if it is true, such talk destroys the world.

There is an even greater sin, which is also included in this prohibition, and that is *lashon hara* ("evil talk").

THE STORYTELLER The classical philosophers refer to the human being as "the speaker," as they regard the human capacity for speech and communication as the distinguishing feature of humanity.

Hasidic teaching takes this a step further, seeing our faculty for speech as integral to our role as "a partner with G-d in the work of creation" (Talmud, *Shabbat* 10a). According to the Kabbalistic work *Sefer Yetzirah,* the words and letters of the divine utterances in the Book of Genesis ("There shall be light," etc.) form the building blocks of the created reality. We, too, create with speech, when we impart significance and meaning to G-d's creation by "telling stories"—weaving disparate objects and events into the narrative of a conscious, moral, and spiritual life.

This is when someone relates something negative about another person, even if they are speaking the truth. One who spreads lies about another transgresses [a different Biblical prohibition]—defamation (see Deuteronomy 22:13–21).

 TALMUD, *ARACHIN 15b*

Evil talk kills three people: the speaker, the listener, and the one who is spoken of.

 HAYOM YOM, *TISHREI 29*

One of the townspeople of Mezhibuzh had a quarrel with another, in the course of which he shouted at his opponent, "I will rip you apart like a fish!"

This event occurred in the Baal Shem Tov's synagogue. The Baal Shem Tov instructed his pupils to stand near him, hold each other's hands, and close their eyes. He then placed his holy hands on the shoulders of the two disciples next to him. Suddenly the disciples began to cry out in terror: they had seen that person actually dismembering the other person.

Every potential has an effect—either in a physical way, or on a more spiritual plane that can only be perceived with loftier and more sensitive senses.

 TALMUD, *BAVA METZIA 58b*

Oppressing someone with words is worse than defrauding them financially. The former is an affront to the person; the latter, only to their money. The former cannot be restituted; the latter can be restituted.

 TALMUD, *PESACHIM 3a*

A person should never allow a derogatory expression to pass their lips. For we find that the Torah deviated by adding eight extra letters in order not to use a derogatory word, when it said (Genesis 7:8), "From the animals that are pure and from the animals that are not pure."

3

Jewish Practice

"The primary thing is not learning, but action" (Ethics of the Fathers, 1:17). Notwithstanding the great emphasis that Jewish tradition places on the knowledge and understanding of the Torah's teachings, there is something it regards as greater yet: the actions and rituals that make those teachings a tangible reality of everyday life.

There are numerous Biblical mitzvot, rabbinic institutions, and community customs that comprise the Jewish way of life. In this section, we focus on a number of precepts that stand out as hallmarks of Jewish practice: prayer, charity, Shabbat, the kosher dietary laws, and the "signifiers" of Jewish identity—mezuzah, tefillin, and tzitzit.

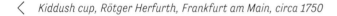

⟨ *Kiddush cup, Rötger Herfurth, Frankfurt am Main, circa 1750*

Israel Defense Forces soldier wearing tefillin, Israel, 2014

MENDY HECHTMAN

ETHICS OF THE FATHERS, *CH. 3, MISHNAH 17*

One whose wisdom is greater than his deeds, what is he comparable to? To a tree with many branches and few roots; comes a storm and uproots it, and turns it on its face…. But one whose deeds are more numerous than his wisdom, to what is he compared? To a tree with many roots and few branches, which all the storms in the world cannot move from its place.

 TALMUD, *KIDUSHIN 40b*

It already happened that R. Tarfon and the sages were assembled in the loft of the Nitzah House in Lod, and the query came before them: "Which is greater, learning or action?"

Said R. Tarfon: "Action is greater."

Said R. Akiva: "Learning is greater."

Concluded all: "Learning is greater, because learning brings to action."

 MIDRASH TANCHUMA, *SHELACH 15*

G-d did not leave off anything in the world in which He did not grant a mitzvah to the people of Israel.

A person goes out to plow? "Do not plow with an ox and a donkey together" (Deuteronomy 22:10). To sow? "Do not sow *kilayim* [hybrid plantings] in your vineyard" (ibid., verse 9). To reap? "When you reap your harvest in your field…" [leave the forgotten sheaf for the poor] (Deut. 24:19). Threshing? "Do not muzzle an ox when it is threshing" (ibid., 25:4). Kneading dough? "From the first of your kneading-bowl…" [lift up *challah* as a gift to the Kohen] (Numbers 15:20)…. Taking eggs from a nest? "Send away the mother bird" (Deut. 22:7). Slaughtering a wild animal or fowl? "Cover its blood with soil" (Leviticus 17:13). Planting a tree? "Observe its *orlah*" [by not partaking of its fruit for the first three years]

(ibid., 19:23). Burying one's dead? "Do not [mourn excessively by] cutting yourself" (Deut. 14:1). Getting a haircut? "Do not shave the corners of your head" (Leviticus 19:27). Building a house? "Make a fence" [for its roof], and "Inscribe [these words] on the doorposts of your home and on your city-gates" (Deut. 22:8 and 6:9). Covering yourself with a garment? "They shall make for themselves tzitzit" (Num. 15:38).

 R. MOSES AMIEL, *DRASHOT EL AMI, VOL. 3, P. 88*

To regard Judaism as a "religion" is to impose on it a terminology that is borrowed from other cultures, thereby reducing it to something that scarcely resembles authentic Judaism.

No religion encompasses the totality of the person. A religion suffices with a certain area of their personhood; the person's religion and the person's humanity remain two separate domains, neither of which encroaches on the other. If the religion is relegated to a specific place in the person's private life, it should be satisfied with that. Yet how far is this model from the original, authentic Judaism: the Judaism that is *torat chayim*, the "teaching of life"; the Judaism that is the soul of the Jewish nation. As the soul permeates the entire body, so does the Torah permeate us from head to toe…. There can be no differentiating between the "human being" and the "Jew" in us. All that is human in us is Jewish.

 MAIMONIDES
MISHNEH TORAH, LAWS OF REPENTANCE, 3:4

A person should always view themselves as equally balanced: half good and half evil. Likewise, one should see the entire world as half good and half evil. By committing a single transgression, one tips the scales for oneself, and for the entire world, to the side of guilt, and brings destruction upon it. And with a single good deed, one tips the scales for oneself, and for the entire world, to the side of merit, and brings it salvation.

Prayer

The verb "to pray" means to beseech and request. In a sense, this describes the activity of prayer: we appeal to G-d to grant us life and health, wisdom and forgiveness, protection and sustenance. We do so to acknowledge our dependence on G-d for the gifts of life, and because G-d desired that His relationship with us should not be one of unilateral bestowal from above, but the product of a dialogue between created and Creator.

But on a deeper level, the English word "prayer" is a mistranslation. The Hebrew term for prayer, tefilah*, actually means "connection" and "bond." At its heart, prayer is the striving of our soul to connect with its source on high, and the endeavor to bind our material life to its purpose and goal.*

 PSALMS 55:18

Evening, morning, and afternoon, I speak forth and yearn, and He hears my voice.

 MAIMONIDES, EXCERPTED FROM
MISHNEH TORAH, LAWS OF PRAYER, 1:1–8

It is a mitzvah to pray every day, as it is stated (Exodus 23:25), "You shall serve the Lord your G-d." Tradition teaches us that this service is prayer, as it is stated (Deuteronomy 11:13), "... to serve Him with all your heart," and our sages said (Talmud, *Taanit* 4:1), "What is the service of the heart? This is prayer."

The Torah does not prescribe the number of prayers or their formula, nor are there any fixed times for prayers according to Biblical law. Originally, a person who was eloquent would offer many prayers and requests; an inarticulate person would speak as well as they could. Some would pray once daily; others, several times. This is how it was from the time of our teacher Moses until Ezra.

When the people of Israel were exiled in the time of the wicked Nebuchadnezzar, they became interspersed in Persia and Greece and other nations. Consequently, when they would pray, they were limited in their ability to request their needs or to praise G-d in Hebrew, unless other languages were mixed in with it. When Ezra and his court saw this, they established a sequence of eighteen blessings: the first three praising G-d, the last three expressing gratitude, and the middle blessings containing requests that serve as general categories for the needs of each person and of the community as a whole. In this way, the prayers of those not fluent [in Hebrew] would be as complete as the prayers of the most eloquent.

They also ordained that the number of prayers should correspond with the [daily] offerings [that were brought in the Holy Temple]. Thus, there are three daily prayers: the *Arvit* (evening) prayer, the *Shacharit* (morning) prayer, and the [afternoon] *Minchah* prayer.

Meditation, Zalman Kleinman, Brooklyn, New York, 1985

Do our prayers induce G-d to "change His mind"?

■ G-d already knows everything we are experiencing, and our current reality is what He has already ordained for us. But the act of prayer elevates us and intensifies our bond with the Almighty to such an extent that we are no longer the same person to whom the previous state of affairs applied. G-d does not change through prayer; we change through prayer. *(R. Joseph Albo, d. 1444)*

■ The Almighty desired that His providence of our needs should come as His response to our actions and requests. When the reality changes as a result of prayer, this is not a change in the divine will, as the divine will is that we should effect this change. *(R. David Solomon Eibeschutz, 1755–1814)*

■ The divine attributes (*sefirot*)—benevolence, judgment, etc.—which the Creator ascribes to Himself to define His relationship with His creations, are extraneous to the divine essence, which transcends all modalities of divine conduct. The soul of man, on the other hand, is rooted in the very essence of G-d. The soul therefore possesses the power of prayer—the ability to connect with the supernal source of the *sefirot* and induce the generation of a "new will" from G-d. *(R. Schneur Zalman of Liadi, 1745–1812)*

KITZUR SHULCHAN ARUCH, *SECTION 12:2*

Before each prayer, a person should accept upon themselves the mitzvah to "love your fellow as yourself," and have in mind to love every Jew as their own self. For if there is divisiveness between the hearts of the Jewish people here below, Heaven forbid, then also above there is no unity. On the other hand, unity among our physical selves below causes a unity and bonding of our

souls above, by which our prayers are likewise united. And when our prayers are merged together, they are desirable to G-d.

 TALMUD, *BERACHOT 31a*

The sages taught: One should not stand to pray from a state of melancholy, or sloth, or mirth, or banter, or frivolity, or idle talk; but only out of the joy of a mitzvah.

 R. SHMUEL KAPLAN

Service of the heart

Guided by an inborn spiritual instinct, Jews from earliest times have given voice to the yearning that stirred their souls by turning to G-d in prayer. Indeed, the Talmud (*Berachot* 26b) credits our forefathers, Abraham, Isaac, and Jacob, with instituting our three daily prayers, over 3,500 years ago.

The individual striving to connect to G-d that they expressed was subsequently formalized in a Scriptural commandment to pray. Nevertheless, the manner in which the Torah communicates this commandment is significant. The Torah does not explicitly command us to pray; instead, it instructs "to serve G-d with all your heart." Our sages ask, "What is the service of the heart?" and answer, "This is prayer." By doing so, they also taught us what prayer is. It is not merely a recitation of words or an opportunity to make requests of the Almighty. It is "service of the heart," which Hasidic tradition explains to mean, "*in* one's heart, and *with* one's heart."

Such service is a revered part of our tradition. As the sages of the Mishnah relate (*Berachot* 5:1), "the devout ones of old used to pause for an hour before they began to pray," in order to reflect on the greatness of the Creator whom they were about to address.

The concept of meditative prayer, however, is not reserved for spiritual giants alone. On the contrary, the very structure of the prayer service was instituted to prompt such a process. With that intent in mind, our sages framed the twice-daily reading of the Shema with blessings whose recitation is intended to help the worshipper attain an appropriate state of mind and heart, and in due course they introduced further additions, such as the "Psalms of Praise" that precede the above blessings.

In this manner, Jews have prayed for thousands of years. With time, however, fresh and focused praying sometimes grew stale, and could even lapse into rapid reading by rote—a phenomenon our people's spiritual leaders labored to counter. Ari and Shaloh wrote, "Prayer without proper intent is like a body without a soul." When the founder of Hasidism, R. Israel Baal Shem Tov, strove to rejuvenate the Jewish world, he placed a renewed emphasis on *davening* (praying) with concentration and passion, establishing fervent prayer as a cornerstone of the movement he founded.

The sages of the Kabbalah employ the metaphor of a bird's flight to explain the process through which a mortal's divine service breaks free of worldliness and ascends aloft. To fly, a bird needs two wings. Similarly, our divine service rises upward through two catalysts: an ardent love of G-d and an earnest awe of G-d. It is told that the Baal Shem Tov once passed a house of prayer and learning, and exclaimed, "This *shul* is filled with prayers and Torah study!" The disciples who accompanied him were most impressed—until he explained that because these were mouthed mechanically, the *shul* had remained full of the words of prayer and Torah, lacking the wings of love and awe that would have borne them aloft.

The Alter Rebbe (R. Schneur Zalman of Liadi, founder of the Chabad branch of Hasidism) further developed the Baal Shem Tov's concept of prayer. He emphasized that for the passion and intensity of prayer to be authentic, it must result from a mature appreciation of the divine greatness and majesty. The understanding that follows is to be infused into one's prayers through disciplined meditation both before and in the course of *davening.* This activity in the mind will then hopefully trickle down into the heart and there give birth to a spiritual emotion, such as a love of G-d or an awe of G-d. Only in this manner, contends the Alter Rebbe, can the objective of praying "in one's heart and with one's heart" be genuine, impactful, and enduring.

Accordingly, a large part of the vast body of Chabad literature is devoted to explaining how the concept of G-d's majestic awesomeness is embedded within the deeper meanings of our prayers. It is a wakeful knowledge of these concepts that enables one to fully engage in a genuine "service of the heart."

This distinctive style of *davening,* in which the measured reading of the prayers is interspersed and enriched by deliberate meditation on related concepts, has long served as a hallmark of the Chabad Hasid. The previous Lubavitcher Rebbe's talks are replete with descriptions of vintage Hasidim who would spend hour after hour lost in their prayers. In fact, so vital is meditative prayer to the life-blood of a Hasid, that a Chabad *shul* was traditionally designed with a *chabadnitzeh*—an alcove or small room in which a *davener* could find a quiet corner to meditate and pray undisturbed.

For the Hasidic *davener*, the preparations begin long before the actual prayers, with an hour or more pondering the themes of the prayer book as illuminated by Hasidic teachings. This meditative focus continues during prayer, with lengthy pauses to further dwell on these teachings. A soft *nigun* (Hasidic melody) will emerge from under the Hasid's tallit, the melody and the words of the prayers merging into ecstatic harmony, as sentence after sentence, page after page, a soul voices its yearning for its Creator.

HANNAH'S PRAYER

Jewish bride in prayer (detail), England, 2014

The sages of the Talmud consider the prayer of Hannah, described in the first chapter of the Biblical book of Samuel, as a precedent-setting model for prayer. Hannah was a pioneer of prayer, establishing not only many of the methodologies of prayer, but also its essential nature and purpose.

🎧 I SAMUEL 1:1–17

There was a man from Ramathaim-Zophim, from Mount Ephraim, and his name was Elkanah…. He had two wives; the name of one was Hannah and the name of the second was Peninah. Peninah had children, but Hannah had no children.

And that man would go up from his city, every year, to prostrate himself and to slaughter [offerings] to the Lord of Hosts in Shiloh….

Hannah arose after she had eaten and drank; and Eli the Priest was sitting on the chair beside the doorpost of the temple of G-d.

She was grave in spirit; and she prayed to G-d, and she wept.

She vowed a vow, and said: "Lord of Hosts, if You will look upon the suffering of Your servant, and You will remember me, and You will not forget Your servant, and You will give Your servant a righteous son; I will give him to G-d all the days of his life…."

And it was as she prayed profusely before G-d, that Eli watched her mouth. Hannah was speaking in her heart, only her lips were moving and her voice was not heard; and Eli thought her to be a drunkard.

Eli said to her: "Until when will you be drunk? Cast off your wine from upon yourself!"

Hannah answered and said: "No, my lord, I am a woman of sorrowful spirit, and neither wine nor old wine have I drunk; I poured out my soul before G-d…."

Eli answered and said: "Go in peace, and the G-d of Israel will grant your request which you have asked of Him."…

principles derived from Hannah's prayer

"She was grave in spirit"	One should approach prayer only after placing oneself in a solemn state of mind.
"Hannah was speaking in her heart"	Prayer requires *kavanah*—focus and concentration of the heart.
"her lips were moving"	Prayer should be verbalized.
"her voice was not heard"	One should not pray loudly (unless this is the only way one can concentrate).
"neither wine nor old wine have I drunk"	It is forbidden to pray while drunk (as well as in other situations that inhibit mindfulness).
"I poured out my soul before G-d"	Prayer is the striving of the soul to connect with its source in G-d.
"If You will look upon the suffering of Your servant, and You will give Your servant a righteous son … I will give him to G-d"	The two cornerstones of prayer—asking G-d for our needs, and committing ourselves to G-d—are not a contradiction, but rather fulfill one another: we ask for the blessings of life in order to utilize them to serve the Almighty.

And it was after a period of time that Hannah conceived, and she bore a son. She called his name Samuel, [meaning,] "I asked him of G-d."

 ZOHAR, *VOL. 3, 143a*

The time of prayer is a time of battle.

 YANKI TAUBER

The paradox of prayer

A person praying is a standing paradox, a swaying contradiction, a self divided against itself.

Both body and soul are praying. The body prays for nourishment, health, protection, and comfort. The soul, a spark of the divine fire, prays because it yearns for its source and strives to be reabsorbed within it. The body is praying for life and existence. The soul is praying to escape life, to transcend existence.

Yet as prayer progresses, a harmony emerges. As the soul prays, climbing the heavens and shedding the husks of selfhood and need that hold it apart from its source in G-d, the body (who is praying on the same page as the soul) learns that spirituality, too, is a need; that transcendence is also a striving; that union with G-d is also an achievement. And the soul (who is praying on the same page as the body) learns that physical life, too, is divine; that existence is also a way of fusing with G-d; that achievement can be the ultimate self-abnegation, if one's achievements are harnessed to a higher, G-dly end.

Prayer reveals that the body needs the soul and the soul needs the body, and that both need to comprehend that the other's need is also their own.

This, ultimately, is the essence of prayer: to know our needs and comprehend their true objectives. To direct our minds and hearts to the One who implanted them within us, defined their purpose, and provides us with the means to fulfill it.

THE SHEMA

"The Shema" is the name given to a collection of three Biblical readings that articulate some of the primary principles and observances of Judaism. It is a distinct mitzvah to read the Shema every morning and evening. The sages incorporated the reading of the Shema into the daily morning and evening prayer services, along with special prayers called "blessings"—three for the morning Shema and four for its evening reading—that frame the Shema and amplify its message.

 DEUTERONOMY 6:4–9
FIRST PORTION OF THE SHEMA

Hear O Israel, G-d is our Lord, G-d is one.

[Blessed be the name of the glory of His kingship forever and ever.]

You shall love the Lord your G-d with all your heart, with all your soul, and with all your might. And these words that I command you today shall be upon your heart; teach them to your children, and speak of them when you sit in your home and when you travel on the way, when you lie down and when you rise up. Bind them as a sign on your arm, and they shall be *tefillin* between your eyes. Write them on the doorposts of your home, and on your gates.

 SELECTION FROM THE SHEMA BLESSINGS

G-d as Creator

Blessed are You, Lord our G-d, king of the universe. Who forms light and creates darkness, who makes peace and creates everything. Who illuminates the earth and those who dwell on it, with compassion. Who in His goodness, renews every day, constantly, the work of creation. How manifold are Your works, O G-d! You made them all with wisdom; the earth is filled with Your acquisitions.

The Praise of the Angels

His servants all stand in the celestial heights, and give voice together, with awe, the words of the living G-d and eternal king…. They all open their mouths in holiness and purity, with song and melody; they bless and praise, beautify and venerate, sanctify and coronate…. Together they call out … "Holy, Holy, Holy is the Lord of Hosts; the entire world is filled with His glory!"

Love of Torah

Our father, compassionate father, ever merciful, have mercy upon us. Instill in our hearts the understanding to comprehend and to conceive; to listen, to learn, and to teach; to keep and to do; and to fulfill all the words of the teachings of Your Torah, with love. Enlighten our eyes in Your Torah, attach our heart to Your commandments, and unite our hearts to love and fear Your name.

 VIKTOR FRANKL
MAN'S SEARCH FOR MEANING, PP. 137–138

Let me recall that which was perhaps the deepest experience I had in the concentration camp. The odds of surviving the camp were no more than one in twenty-eight, as can easily be verified by exact statistics. It did not even seem possible, let alone probable, that the manuscript of my first book, which I had hidden in my coat when I arrived at Auschwitz, would ever be rescued. Thus, I had to undergo and to overcome the loss of my mental child. And now it seemed as if nothing and no one would survive me; neither a physical nor a mental child of my own! So I found myself confronted with the question whether under such circumstances my life was ultimately void of any meaning.

Not yet did I notice that an answer to this question with which I was wrestling so passionately was already in store for me, and that soon thereafter this answer would be given to me. This was the case when I had to surrender my clothes and in turn inherited the worn-

the Shema and its blessings—primary themes

Preceding blessings		The Shema			Succeeding blessing(s)	
1st blessing	2nd blessing	**Deuteronomy 6:4–9**	**Deuteronomy 11:13–21**	**Numbers 15:37–41**	3rd blessing	evening only: 4th blessing*
The creation of light and darkness, and of the celestial luminaries and time cycles; the majesty of G-d's creation; the angels' praise of G-d.	G-d's love for us; our desire for the Torah and our ceaseless commitment to learning it.	**Unity of G-d; accepting the divine sovereignty; love of G-d; the mitzvot of Torah study, tefillin, and mezuzah.**	**The reward for fulfilling the mitzvot and the punishment for their transgression; the imperative to keep the mitzvot also when exiled from the Holy Land; G-d's promise of the Land to the Patriarchs.**	**The mitzvah of tzitzit; remembering the Exodus.**	Truth and faithfulness of G-d; the Exodus from Egypt and the splitting of the sea; praising G-d as the redeemer of Israel.	Prayer asking G-d to protect us while we sleep.

* Some communities recite an additional blessing after the 4th blessing of the evening Shema

out rags of an inmate who had already been sent to the gas chamber immediately after his arrival at the Auschwitz railway station. Instead of the many pages of my manuscript, I found in a pocket of the newly acquired coat one single page torn out of a Hebrew prayer book, containing the most important Jewish prayer, *Shema Yisrael*. How should I have interpreted such a "coincidence" other than as a challenge to live my thoughts instead of merely putting them on paper?

 LISA AIKEN, EXCERPTED FROM *THE HIDDEN BEAUTY OF THE SHEMA, PP. 17–19*

During World War II, many Jewish parents hid their children in Christian orphanages, in the hope that these would provide safe havens for them. Most of these parents perished in the ghettos and death camps, with the result that their orphans were not only bereft of their entire families, but also of their Jewish identity.

In May of 1945, Rabbi Eliezer Silver from the United States and Dayan Grunfeld from England were on a mission to the liberated camps when they were told that Jewish children had been placed in a monastery in Alsace-Lorraine. The rabbis went there to reclaim them, but the priest in charge refused to give up any child unless the rabbis could provide proof that the child was Jewish. The rabbis asked that they be allowed to come back in the evening, when the children were being put to bed.

That evening the rabbis came to the dormitory, where row upon row of little beds were arranged. The rabbis walked through the aisles, calling out: *Shema Yisrael, Ado-nai Elo-heinu, Ado-nai echad!* ("Hear O Israel, G-d is our Lord, G-d is one"). One by one, children burst into tears and cried out, "Mommy!" "Maman!" "Momma!" "Mamushka!" in each of their native tongues.

Many of the children had been mere toddlers when they were placed in the orphanage, and the intervening years had erased all memories of home. But they had not succeeded in erasing these children's memories of their Jewish mothers—now murdered—putting them to bed every night with the Shema on their lips.

THE THREE DAILY PRAYERS

	Prayer name	Time frame	Primary components of the prayer				
Morning prayer	*Shacharit*	First 1/3rd of the day, beginning at sunrise	Morning blessings	Readings describing the daily service in the Holy Temple	Hodu (introductory verses)	Psalms of Praise	Kaddish and Borchu ⦿
Afternoon prayer	*Minchah*	From half an hour after midday until sunset	—	Readings describing the daily service in the Holy Temple	—	Ashrei (Psalm 145)	—
Evening prayer	*Arvit* or *Maariv*	After nightfall, preferably before midnight	—	—	Introductory verses	—	Kaddish and Borchu ⦿

⦿ only when praying with a *minyan* (quorum of ten)

 TALMUD, *BERACHOT 26b*

R. Yosei the son of R. Chanina says: The [three daily] prayers were instituted by the Patriarchs.

R. Joshua the son of Levi says: The prayers were instituted to correspond to the daily communal offerings [in the Holy Temple].

There are teachings that support the view of R. Yosei the son of R. Chanina, and there are teachings that support the view of R. Joshua the son of Levi. In support of R. Yosei's view, we were taught:

Abraham instituted the morning prayer, as it is written (Genesis 19:27), "Abraham made-early in the morning, to the place where there he stood before G-d...." Isaac instituted the afternoon prayer, as it is written (ibid., 24:63),

"Isaac went out to converse in the field toward evening...." Jacob instituted the evening prayer, as it is written (ibid., 28:11), "He encountered the place and lodged the night there."

In support of R. Joshua's view, we were taught:

Why did the sages say that the morning prayer can be recited until ... four hours into the day? Because the daily morning offering was brought in the first four hours of the day. Why did they say that the [afternoon] Minchah prayer may be recited until evening? Because the daily afternoon offering can be brought until the evening.... And why did they say that the evening prayer has no fixed time [throughout the night]? Because the parts and the fats of the offerings which had not been consumed can be brought up [upon the altar] all night long.

Shema and its blessings	—	Amidah	Repetition of Amidah and Kedushah	Confession of sins	Kaddish	Public Torah reading (when applicable)	Aleinu
—	Kaddish	Amidah	Repetition of Amidah and Kedushah	Confession of sins	Kaddish	—	Aleinu
Shema and its blessings	Kaddish	Amidah	—	—	Kaddish	—	Aleinu

NOTES:

A fourth prayer, called *Musaf*, is added after the morning prayers on Shabbat, the festivals, the High Holidays, and Rosh Chodesh, in commemoration of the additional communal offering brought in the Holy Temple on these days. On Yom Kippur, a fifth prayer, called *Ne'ilah*, is added after the afternoon prayer.

The festive *Hallel* prayer (Psalms 113–118) is included in the morning services, following the repetition of the *Amidah,* on the festivals (excluding Rosh Hashanah and Yom Kippur), Hanukkah, and Rosh Chodesh.

The confession of sins and its associated prayers are not said on Shabbat, festival days, or on other special occasions.

Public Torah readings are held as part of the morning service on Shabbat, the festivals, Hanukkah and Purim, Rosh Chodesh, Tish'ah B'Av, and every Monday and Thursday. A short Torah reading is also conducted during the afternoon services (before the *Amidah*) on Shabbat, Yom Kippur, and fast days.

In the custom of some communities, Kaddish is not recited before *Borchu* in the evening service.

But in truth, [both opinions are correct.] The daily prayers were originally instituted by the Patriarchs, and the sages subsequently associated them with daily offerings.

 R. JACOB BEN ASHER, *TUR, ORACH CHAYIM, 232*

The Talmud (*Berachot* 6b) states: "A person should always be especially diligent with the *Minchah* prayer. Indeed, the prayer of Elijah the Prophet was answered only in the afternoon" (see I Kings 18:36–38).

In the morning, we pray before getting involved in our everyday tasks. Similarly, the time for the evening prayer is after the day's business is concluded. *Minchah,* however, comes in the middle of the day, when a person must interrupt everything in order to pray. This is why one who prays the afternoon prayer is especially rewarded.

 SELECTED PRAYERS

Adon Olam

Master of the world, who reigned before any
    creature was created

When by His will all things were made, then was
    His name called King

And after all shall cease to be, the Awesome One
    shall reign alone

He was, He is, and He shall be; in glory

He is one; there is no second to compare with Him
    or to be joined

Without beginning, without end; might and
    dominion are His

He is my G-d, my living redeemer
     my rock and lot in times of distress

He is my banner and my refuge; my portion, my cup
    on the day I call

In His hand I entrust my soul, when I sleep
    and when I awaken

With my soul and body, G-d is for me
    I shall not fear.

Recited or sung as a preface to the morning prayers, *Adon Olam*
is a poetic presentation of some of the foundational principles of
Judaism (see p. 216).

from the Ashrei prayer

Your kingship is a kingship of all worlds,
    and Your rule is in every generation.

G-d supports all who fall, and straightens
    all who are bent.

The eyes of all are expectant to You, and You give
    them their food in its time.

You open Your hand, and satisfy every living thing
    with favor.

G-d is righteous in all His ways, and kind
    in all His deeds.

G-d is near to all who call Him, to all who
    call Him in truth.

> **PATHWAYS OF PRAYER** Regarding the differences between various Jewish communities in the format of certain prayers, the Kabbalist R. Chaim Vital (1543–1620) writes: "My teacher [R. Isaac Luria] would say that there are twelve gates in heaven, corresponding to the twelve tribes of Israel, and each tribe's prayers ascend through its own gate; these are the gates [of Jerusalem] mentioned in the end of the book of Ezekiel.… Each gate is different, which is why there are differences in the prayers. Therefore, it is fitting that each person should maintain their custom in prayer, for perhaps they belong to a specific tribe whose prayer ascends through that specific gate. However, laws that are clearly stated in the Talmud apply equally for all tribes."

He does the will of those who fear Him,
    and He hears their cry and saves them.

G-d guards all who love Him, and He destroys
    all the wicked.

My mouth shall speak the praise of the Lord,
    and all flesh shall bless His holy name forever.

Ashrei, comprised primarily of Psalm 145 (with some additional verses from other psalms), is a central component of "Psalms of Praise," and is also recited prior to the *Amidah* of the afternoon prayers.

Psalm 148

Praise G-d! Praise G-d from the heavens;
    praise Him in the heights.

Praise Him, all His angels; praise Him, all His hosts.

Praise Him, sun and moon; praise Him,
    all stars of light.

Praise Him, heavens of heavens, and the waters
    that are above the heavens.

Let them praise the name of G-d, for He commanded
    and they were created.

He established them forever and for all time;
    He issued a decree that shall not be transgressed.

Praise G-d from the earth, sea-monsters
    and all deeps.

Fire and hail, snow and mist; the storm wind
     doing His bidding.
Mountains and all hills; fruit trees and all cedars.
Beasts and all cattle; creeping things and birds
     of wing.
Earthly kings and all nations; princes and all judges
     of the earth.
Youths and also maidens; old folks and young lads.
Let them praise the name of G-d, as His name
     alone is exalted; His splendor is upon
     earth and heaven.
He has raised the pride of His people, the praise
     of all His pious ones, the children of Israel,
     a people close to Him; praise G-d!

Psalm 148 is one of the "Psalms of Praise" of the morning service.

from the Aleinu prayer

We therefore hope to You, Lord our G-d, that we may speedily behold the glory of Your might, to remove abominations from the earth, and the idols will be utterly destroyed; to perfect the world under the sovereignty of the Almighty, and all of humanity will call in Your name; to turn to You all the evildoers of the earth. All the inhabitants of the world will recognize and know, that to You every knee shall bend, every tongue shall swear. Before You, Lord our G-d, they will kneel and prostrate themselves, and give honor to the glory of Your name; they will all accept upon themselves the yoke of Your kingdom, and You will soon reign over them forever. For kingship is Yours, and to all eternity You will reign in glory, as it is written in Your Torah (Exodus 15:18), "G-d will reign forever and ever." And it is said (Zechariah 14:9): "G-d shall be king over all the earth; on that day, G-d will be one, and His name, one."

Each of the three daily prayers concludes with *Aleinu*, comprised of two main sections. The first section extols the uniqueness of the Jewish people. The second section, cited here, gives voice to Judaism's universal message and its goal of a perfected world.

the blessings of the Amidah

PRAISE, REQUEST, GRATITUDE The *Amidah* is the crux of prayer; all other components of the service are there to frame it and lead into it. Recited while standing (*amidah*, in Hebrew), the *Amidah* is a series of blessings instituted by the sages as a standardized text with which to praise G-d, ask for our needs, and express our gratitude. On Shabbat and the festivals, when we do not concern ourselves with our personal needs, the thirteen middle blessings are replaced with a single blessing on the specialness and sanctity of the day.

Blessing type		Blessing theme
Praise	1	Lovingkindness
	2	Power
	3	Holiness
Request	4	Wisdom
	5	Repentance
	6	Forgiveness
	7	Redemption
	8	Healing
	9	Sustenance
	10	Ingathering of the exiles
	11	Justice
	12	Punishment of informers and apostates *
	13	Reward for the righteous
	14	Rebuilding of Jerusalem
	15	Speedy arrival of the Messiah
	16	Hear our prayers **
Gratitude	17	Acceptance of our service
	18	Thankfulness
	19	Peace

* The *Amidah* originally consisted of eighteen blessings. This blessing was added under the leadership of R. Gamliel of Yavneh (c. 74–115 CE), at a time when "informers and apostates" threatened the Jewish people.

** If a person has a specific request from G-d that they wish to articulate, it is inserted in the "Hear our prayers" blessing.

Evening Prayer, Yakov Payne,
Russia, 1918

the ladder of prayer

THE FOUR RUNGS OF JACOB'S LADDER Prayer is "a ladder stood on earth, whose top reaches the heavens" (Genesis 28:12; see citation from *Zohar* on p. 17). The Kabbalists and the Hasidic masters identified four distinct "rungs" in the ladder of prayer, by which we climb up from our earthly entanglements toward the objective of union with G-d. Depicted here are the four portions of the *Shacharit* morning prayer as they relate to the four cosmic "worlds," to the different levels of the soul, and to four stages in our relationship with G-d.

4th rung

PORTION OF PRAYER: Amidah

WORLD: Emanation

SOUL: *Yechidah* ("singularity")

RELATIONSHIP: Union

3rd rung

PORTION OF PRAYER: Shema and its blessings

WORLD: Creation

SOUL: *Neshamah* ("breath")

RELATIONSHIP: Understanding and appreciation

2nd rung

PORTION OF PRAYER: Psalms of Praise

WORLD: Formation

SOUL: *Ruach* ("spirit")

RELATIONSHIP: Love and awe

1st rung

PORTION OF PRAYER: Hodu (introductory verses)

WORLD: Action

SOUL: *Nefesh* ("animation")

RELATIONSHIP: Acknowledgement and submission

THE SYNAGOGUE

Prayer is a deeply personal communion with G-d, yet Jewish tradition also emphasizes the virtues of communal prayer. When we pray as a community, we compensate for each other's flaws and aggregate each other's merits; we rise above the narrow confines of individual identity, and reinforce our essential point of unity—which is also the point at which we are one with our source in our Creator. Our sages therefore teach that the Almighty is especially attentive to the prayers of the community.

Hence the synagogue—a place for the community to gather for the purpose of prayer. Synagogues existed throughout Jewish history, but it was following the destruction of the Holy Temple that their centrality to Jewish religious life developed. The synagogue became the *mikdash me'at* ("minor sanctuary")—the closest thing we have to a space sanctified by its dedication to divine service. The sages deemed the three daily prayer services to be representative of the daily offerings brought in the Temple, and many features of the synagogue reflect corresponding elements of the Holy Temple.

EZEKIEL 11:16

So said the Lord G-d: Although I have distanced them among the nations, and although I have scattered them among the countries, I have become for them a minor sanctuary in the lands where they have come.

Dome of the Great Synagogue of Florence, 1882

SAILKO

components of the synagogue

(A) THE EAST WALL

The front end of the synagogue is oriented in the direction of Jerusalem and the Holy Temple—the direction faced during prayer (see citation on p. 65). In the majority of the Jewish diaspora (i.e., Europe, North Africa, and the Americas), as well as in many of the large population centers in Israel, this direction is east.

(B) ARK & TORAH SCROLLS

In the center of the front wall is the holy ark (*aron ha-kodesh*) which holds the the Torah scrolls, reminiscent of the ark that housed the Torah in the Holy Temple (see p. 69). Before the ark hangs a curtain (*parochet*), often decorated with Biblical verses and/or Jewish themes, evoking the embroidered curtain that hung before the ark in the Temple.

The Torah scrolls (see p. 156) are kept covered at all times within a special mantle or case, and are uncovered only for the public readings. In keeping with the principle of "beautify the mitzvot," the Torah scroll is often decorated with a silver crown, an ornate pointer with which to follow the Torah reading, and other ornaments.

(C) THE READING TABLE

An important component of the synagogue service is the public reading from the Torah each Shabbat and on other special occasions (see p. 160). The table on which the Torah scroll is read is traditionally set in the center of the synagogue on a raised platform (*bimah*), so that all could better see and hear the reading—reminiscent of the giving of the Torah on Mount Sinai. Before or after the reading (depending on custom) the scroll is lifted up so that the congregation can see the text.

(D) THE LECTERN

According to Ashkenazic custom, the cantor (*chazan*) leads the prayers from the front of the synagogue, standing before a lectern (*amud*). In Sephardic communities, the prayers are led from the reading table in the center of the room. The one leading the prayers faces toward Jerusalem, like the rest of the congregation.

(E) THE MECHITZAH

Jewish law mandates the separation of men and women during communal prayer, to prevent the distractions that can arise in mixed company. Hence a partition (*mechitzah*) is set up to separate the men's and women's seating areas. In some synagogues, this is achieved by the construction of a "women's balcony" on a different level than the men's area.

(F) ETERNAL LIGHT

Many synagogues have a lamp hanging in front of the ark that is kept constantly burning—an allusion to the "western lamp" of the menorah in the Holy Temple, which burned round the clock. By the same token, custom dictates that the synagogue should be well lighted as a sign of honor, and in keeping with its role as a source of spiritual illumination. It is also customary to build a synagogue with high windows through which the heavens can be seen, in fulfillment of the verse (Isaiah 40:26), "Lift your eyes aloft, and see who created these!"

(G) SEATING

The seating arrangements in the synagogue vary from community to community. Depicted here is the classic Ashkenazic model, with rows of pews facing the front of the synagogue, and an "east wall" reserved for the elders of the community. In Sephardic synagogues, the congregants all face the reading table in the center. Yet another arrangement is the less formal *shtieble* model of seats around tables, which facilitates communal learning (see (I) below).

(H) ENTRANCE HALL

Tradition stipulates that one should not enter directly into the synagogue from the street, but should instead pass through an antechamber where one can properly compose themselves in preparation for prayer. The antechamber usually contains a washstand, as it is obligatory to wash one's hands before praying; both the antechamber and the washstand were features of the Holy Temple. Some Hasidic synagogues also have a "second room" (*cheder sheini*) reserved for meditative prayer. Modern synagogues usually include a social hall for Kiddush following services, and for community events.

(I) TORAH BOOKS

The Talmud distinguishes between a "synagogue" (*beit ha-keneset*) designated for prayer, and a "study hall" (*beit ha-midrash*) that serves as a place of Torah learning. In later generations the distinction was blurred, with synagogues also serving as places of Torah learning. Thus, in addition to shelves containing prayer books, and *Chumashim* (Bibles) from which to follow the Torah reading, most synagogues also have a collection of other Torah books. Many boast extensive libraries, and additional spaces reserved for classes and study.

Synagogue depicted is the classic Ashkenazic model

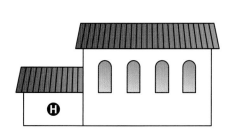

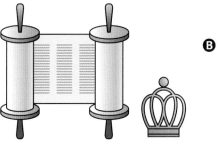

Torah scroll with Ashkenazic-style rollers and crown

Torah pointer

Torah scroll in Sephardic case

Altneuschul (Old-New Synagogue)
interior and exterior views, Prague, 1270

Portuguese Synagogue, Amsterdam, 1675

Touro Synagogue, Newport, Rhode Island, 1763

Ohel Jakob Synagogue, Munich, Germany, 2006

Charity

Charity is a fundamental mitzvah in Judaism. It is also an identifying characteristic of the Jewish people. No nation or people have done more to exemplify compassion, generosity, and the commitment to social justice.

Indeed, the very concept of "charity" has an entirely different meaning in Judaism. The Jewish term for charity, tzedakah, *actually means "righteousness" and "justice." Sharing one's blessings with those less fortunate than oneself is seen not as an act of magnanimity, but as a privilege and a duty—as the right and just thing to do.*

 **DEUTERONOMY 15:7–10**

If there be among you a needy person ... do not clench your heart, and do not close your hand, from your needy brother. Rather, open up your hand to him, and grant him sufficient for that which he is lacking.... For because of this thing, G-d will bless you in all your doings, and in all your endeavors.

 **MAIMONIDES,** *MISHNEH TORAH, LAWS OF CHARITY, 9:1–3*

In every city where Jews live, there must be appointed eminent, trustworthy individuals as trustees of a charity fund. These should circulate among the people every Friday, and collect from each and every one according to their assessment of what that person is able to give. They should then distribute the money ... to each pauper, sufficient for their nourishment for the next seven days....

We have never seen or heard of a Jewish community that does not have a charity fund.

 R. JACOB BEN ASHER, *TUR, YOREH DE'AH, 247*

Do not say to yourself, "Why should I reduce my wealth by giving to the poor?" Know that the money is not yours, but a deposit, to do with as the depositor wishes. And this is what G-d desires: that you dispense it to those who are poorer than you.

 SHULCHAN ARUCH, *YOREH DE'AH, 248:1*

Every person is obligated to give charity. Even a pauper who is himself supported by charity must give charity from what he receives.

 R. SCHNEUR ZALMAN OF LIADI
TANYA, CHAPTER 37

The sages greatly extolled the virtue of charity, declaring that it is "the equivalent of all the mitzvot" (Talmud, *Bava Batra* 9a). Throughout the Jerusalem Talmud, charity is called simply "the mitzvah." For it is the most primary of all actionable mitzvot, surpassing them all....

This is because every other mitzvah engages only one of the person's faculties [e.g., the mind, the emotions, the faculty of speech, the person's diet, mode of dress,

*Burial society charity box,
Bessarabia, early 20th century*

THE PUSHKEH A staple in every Jewish home, place of business, and house of worship is the *pushkeh* or charity box. The function of the charity box is to transform the act of giving from an occasional response to a request for help into a regular and frequent self-initiated activity. A coin or few are customarily placed in the *pushkeh* as a prequel to activities such as praying, lighting the Shabbat candles on Friday afternoon, preparing a meal, etc.

Maimonides writes: "When a person gives one thousand gold coins to a worthy recipient all at one time ... this does not cultivate in the benefactor the same spirit of generosity as does giving one coin on one thousand separate occasions. In the latter instance, the benefactor acts generously one thousand times, thereby implanting this trait in their personality. In the former instance, the individual is greatly inspired on but one occasion, after which the inspiration dissipates" (commentary on the Mishnah, *Ethics of the Fathers*, 3:15).

marital life, etc.], and only while the person is actually performing the mitzvah. But with charity, whereby a person gives away what they earned with their toil—the person's entire vitality is invested in the work they did, or in whatever occupation they engaged in, to earn this money. When the person now gives this money to charity, their entire vital self is elevated. Also ... with this money, the person could have acquired the nourishment that sustains their very life. Hence, the person has given their very life to G-d.

 GENESIS 18:17–19

And G-d said: "...Abraham will become a great and powerful nation, and all the nations of the earth will be blessed through him. For I know him, in that he will instruct his children and his household after him, and they will keep the way of G-d, to do charity and justice."

 TALMUD, *YEVAMOT 79a*

The Jewish people have three identifying traits: they are compassionate, bashful, and charitable.

 PSALMS 89:3

The world is built on benevolence.

 MIDRASH TANCHUMA, *MISHPATIM 9*

Said King David to the Almighty: "Master of the world! 'May the world be settled before G-d' (Psalms 61:8). Why don't You balance Your world, and make equal the rich and the poor?"

Replied G-d: "If such were the case, 'Who shall keep kindness and truth?' (ibid.). If all were rich or all were poor, how would there be an opportunity for human kindness?"

 MIDRASH RABBAH, *VAYIKRA 34:8*

More than the benefactor does for the pauper, the pauper does for the benefactor.

THE ACCIDENTAL MITZVAH The mitzvah of the "forgotten sheaf" (see infographic on facing page) provides an important insight into the divine commandments of the Torah, particularly the mitzvah of charity. What is most significant is the result of one's actions, not one's intentions in doing it, or even one's desire to do it. While there are many levels on which the mitzvah of charity can be performed, and much discussion of its effect on the character of the giver, in the final analysis, what matters most is the fulfillment of the recipient's need. The sages go so far as to say: "One who loses a coin which fell from his hand, and a pauper finds it and uses it to sustain himself, he has merited" the mitzvah of charity. (*Sifrei, Devarim 283*)

 SIFREI, *CITED IN TOSAFOT, TAANIT 9a*

It is written (Deuteronomy 14:22): "Tithe shall you tithe all the produce of your sowing that the field brings forth year by year." I might think that only "the produce of your sowing" must be tithed.... But then the verse could have simply said, "... the produce of your sowing." Why does it add the word "all"? This teaches us that also dividends, business gains, and all manners of profit should be tithed.

 MAIMONIDES, *MISHNEH TORAH, LAWS OF CHARITY, 10:7–14*

There are eight levels of charity, each greater than the next.

(1) The greatest level, above which there is none greater, is to support a fellow Jew by giving them a gift or loan, or entering into a partnership with them, or finding employment for them, in order to strengthen their hand until they no longer need to be dependent upon others.

(2) A lesser level of charity than this is to give to the poor without knowing to whom one gives, and without the recipient knowing from whom they received. For this is performing a mitzvah solely for the sake of Heaven. An example of this is the "anonymous fund" that was in the Holy Temple [in Jerusalem]. The righteous would contribute to it, and the worthy poor were sustained by it in secret. Giving to a charity fund is similar to this mode of charity, although one should not contribute to a charity fund unless one knows that the person appointed over the fund is trustworthy and wise and a proper administrator.

(3) A lesser level than this is when the giver knows to whom they gave, but the poor person does not know from whom they received. There were sages who used to walk about in secret and threw money in the doorways of the poor. It is worthy and truly good to do this if those who are responsible for distributing charity are not doing so properly.

(4) A lesser level than this is when the poor person knows from whom they received, but the giver does not know to whom they gave. There were sages who used to tie coins into their robes and cast them behind their backs, allowing the poor to come and take them, so that they should not be ashamed.

(5) A lesser level than this is when one gives to the poor person directly into their hand, but gives before being asked.

(6) A lesser level than this is when one gives after being asked.

(7) A lesser level than this is when one gives inadequately, but gives gladly and with a smile.

(8) A lesser level than this is when one gives with consternation.

agricultural tithes and gifts

SHARING THE BOUNTY OF THE LAND In Biblical Israel, most
people derived their livelihood from tilling the soil and
harvesting the produce of their fields, orchards, and vineyards.
The Torah mandates that certain portions of that yield be
earmarked for the poor, to support those who served in the Holy
Temple, and other religious goals. Depicted here are these
mandated gifts as they apply to a field of grain.

IN THE FIELD

CORNER OF FIELD
A corner of the field must be left unharvested,
for the poor to come and freely take
for themselves.

GLEANINGS
Stalks of grain that fall to the ground
during the harvest should be left there for
the poor to gather.

FORGOTTEN SHEAF
If a sheaf is forgotten in the field, one
should not return to retrieve it, but leave it
for the poor.

THE SABBATICAL YEAR

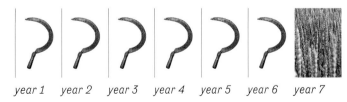

year 1   year 2   year 3   year 4   year 5   year 6   year 7

On the last year of the seven-year sabbatical cycle, the land is given
a rest, and there is no sowing or harvesting. Produce that grows
of its own accord (or from what was planted the previous year) must
be left free for the taking for all, human and animal alike.

FROM THE HARVEST

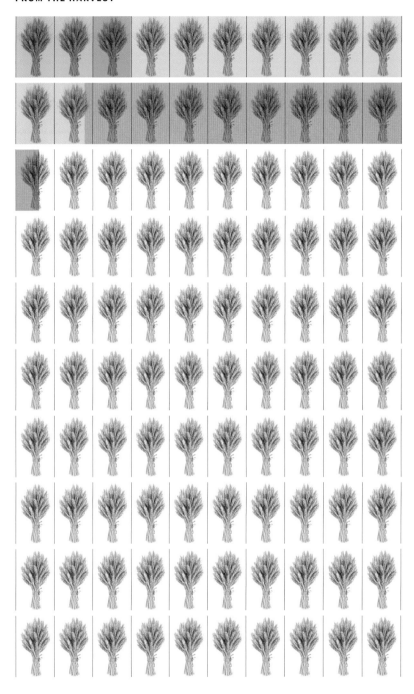

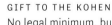

GIFT TO THE KOHEN
No legal minimum, but common practice according
to the Talmud is to give 2% of the harvest.

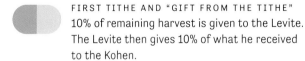

FIRST TITHE AND "GIFT FROM THE TITHE"
10% of remaining harvest is given to the Levite.
The Levite then gives 10% of what he received
to the Kohen.

SECOND TITHE
10% of what remains after the gift to the
Kohen and first tithe. In years 3 and 6 of the
sabbatical cycle, the second tithe is given to the
poor. In years 1, 2, 4, and 5, it is consumed by
the owner and their guests, but only in the holy
city of Jerusalem under conditions of ritual purity.

forms of charity

 TALMUD, *SOTAH 14a*

It is written: "After the Lord your G-d you shall walk" (Deuteronomy 13:5). But is it possible to walk behind the Divine Presence? Is it not already stated (ibid., 4:24) that "your G-d is a consuming fire"?

But the meaning of this is: Follow G-d's behavior. G-d clothes the naked, as it is written, "G-d made for Adam and for his wife coats of skin, and He clothed them" (Genesis 3:21); so should you clothe the naked.

G-d visits the sick, as it is written, "G-d appeared to [Abraham] in the Oaks of Mamre" (Genesis 18:1); so should you visit the sick.

G-d consoles mourners, as it is written, "It was after the death of Abraham that G-d blessed Isaac his son" (Genesis 25:11); so should you console mourners.

G-d buries the dead, as it is written, "He buried [Moses] in the valley" (Deuteronomy 34:6); so should you bury the dead.

 TALMUD, *SHABBAT 156b*

R. Akiva had a daughter. But astrologers said to him, "On the day that she enters the bridal chamber, a snake will bite her and she will die."

On the night of her wedding, she removed a brooch and stuck it into the wall. When she pulled it out the following morning, a poisonous snake came trailing after it; the pin had penetrated the eye of the serpent.

"Was there anything special that you did yesterday?" her father asked her.

"A poor man came to our door in the evening," she replied. "Everyone was busy at the banquet, and there was no one to attend to him. So I took the portion of food that was given to me and I gave it to him."

R. Akiva went out and quoted (Proverbs 10:2): "Charity delivers from death."

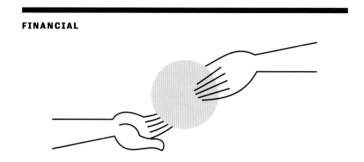

FINANCIAL

FINANCIAL ASSISTANCE This is the classic form of charity, extended individually or through a communal charity fund.

FEEDING THE HUNGRY The law is that when a person asks for financial assistance, it is prudent to investigate whether the need is genuine. But when a person says that they are hungry and asks for food, one must give immediately, without further investigation.

GIVING A LOAN A Talmudic maxim is that granting a loan is greater than charity, as charity is only for the poor, whereas a loan is for both the poor and the rich. Torah law mandates that loans to a fellow Jew must be interest-free.

REDEEMING CAPTIVES One of the highest forms of charity is to redeem someone from slavery or captivity. As a rule, funds raised for a specific purpose can be used for that purpose only; an exception to this rule is that all charitable funds can be used for redeeming captives.

PHYSICAL

HOSPITALITY TO GUESTS The Torah (Genesis 18) relates how Abraham interrupted a visit from G-d to offer food, drink, rest, and companionship to three desert wayfarers. The sages derive from this passage many of the laws of hospitality, as well as that "bringing guests into one's home is greater than greeting the Divine Presence" (Talmud, *Shabbat* 127a).

VISITING THE SICK This mitzvah includes caring for the sick person and praying for them. The Talmud (*Nedarim* 39b) states that visiting the sick "removes one-sixtieth of their illness."

BRINGING HAPPINESS TO BRIDE AND GROOM It is a special mitzvah to help a single person find a spouse, and to participate in a wedding in order to increase the joy of the bride and groom.

HONORING THE DECEASED Caring for the dead is called the "true kindness" (Genesis 47:29), because one does not expect any reciprocation from the recipient. For more on this mitzvah, see p. 423.

CONSOLING THE MOURNER For more on this mitzvah, see p. 427.

RETURNING A LOST OBJECT A person who finds an object that has distinctive features by which its owner could identify it is obligated to take the object, publicize the find, and care for it until its owner claims it (Deuteronomy 22:1–3).

ROADSIDE ASSISTANCE "When you see the donkey of your enemy collapsing under its burden … assist shall you assist with him" (Exodus 23:5). According to one opinion in the Talmud, this mitzvah is also a source of the obligation to alleviate the suffering of an animal.

SPIRITUAL

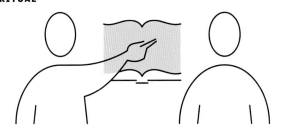

EDUCATING THE YOUNG For more on this mitzvah, see pp. 396–398.

TEACHING TORAH The Talmud (*Bava Metzia* 33a) notes that "a person's parents bring them into this world; but a person's teacher grants them life in this world, and life in the World to Come."

SPIRITUAL GUIDANCE The commandment (Leviticus 19:18) "love your fellow as yourself" implies that a person should not be satisfied with their own spiritual gains, but endeavor to achieve no less for their fellow. A person is therefore duty-bound to encourage and assist a fellow to repent a wrongdoing or to do a good deed.

THE THREE-WAY ENCOUNTER "When two people meet, something good should result for a third." The Lubavitcher Rebbe, R. Menachem Mendel Schneerson (1902–1994), would often quote this saying by his father-in-law and predecessor, R. Yosef Yitzchak Schneersohn (1880–1950). In his own encounters with people, the Rebbe always endeavored for the meeting to result in the doing of a mitzvah, particularly the mitzvah of charity. Each week, the Rebbe would stand for several hours and receive thousands of people for a few brief words of greeting and blessing, and give each of them a dollar bill for the purpose of serving as his agent to give it to the charity of the person's choice. In the photograph to the right, the Rebbe distributes coins to children as he enters his synagogue for the morning prayers, for the children to put in the charity box.

LEVI FREIDIN / JEM

The Lubavitcher Rebbe distributes coins to children, Brooklyn, New York, 1986

Shabbat

Shabbat is a weekly oasis in time, a bastion of tranquility and purpose amidst the turmoil and drudgery of the daily grind.

Shabbat serves as a guarantor of the freedom of the human spirit, as the touchstone of our partnership with G-d in creation, and as a bulwark of Jewish identity. Without Shabbat we are little more than cogs in the machine of existence, slaves to a paycheck or balance sheet, rootless itinerants in the trudge of history. Shabbat is our weekly encounter with the soul of existence—with the core of truth and meaning from which the entire week emanates and toward which it strives. Shabbat, say the sages of Israel, is "a taste of the world to come"—of the messianic goodness and perfection that is the goal of the whole of human endeavor.

"Six days you shall work," the people of Israel were commanded soon after their exodus from Egypt, "and on the seventh day you shall rest." "Remember the Shabbat day to sanctify it" begins the fourth of the Ten Commandments that form the core of Jewish faith and practice. "Call unto the Shabbat, delight; to the holy [day] of G-d, honored," exhorts the prophet Isaiah. Rest, sanctity, delight, and honor—these are the cornerstones of Shabbat observance, with which we incorporate the Shabbat reality into our lives.

Hanging Shabbat lamp,
the Netherlands, 18th century

Shabbat,
Natalya Goncharova,
Russia, circa 1909

Zemirot
(songs for the Shabbat meal)
in a Shabbat prayer book,
Germany, 1717

FREEDOM AND IDENTITY

Until a few short centuries ago, slavery was the daily reality for a large portion of humanity. But in many ways, modern man is no less a slave, subservient to a plethora of external and internal taskmasters: job, career, societal expectations, habits, addictions, and neuroses.

When Shabbat occupies one-seventh of a person's life, the result is more than a quantitative percentage of liberation. Shabbat provides an elevated vantage point from which the whole of one's existence assumes an entirely different nature and focus. No longer is the workday existence a closed, self-defining loop, its purpose obscured behind an ever-receding horizon. Rather, there is a weekly respite in which we experience a taste of the tranquility and perfection toward which our everyday endeavors are striving.

 DEUTERONOMY 5:13–15

Six days you shall labor; and do all your work.

The seventh day is Shabbat to the Lord your G-d. Do not do any work—you, and your son and your daughter, and your servant and your maidservant, and your ox and your donkey and all your animals, and the sojourner who is at your gates; in order that your servant and maidservant shall rest as you do.

You shall remember that you were a slave in the land of Egypt, and G-d took you out from there with a strong hand and with an outstretched arm. Therefore G-d commanded you to make the day of Shabbat.

 MECHILTA, *EXODUS 20:9*

It is written, "Six days … you shall do all your work." Is it then possible for a person to do all their work in six days? Rather, the meaning is: Rest on Shabbat as if all your work is done.

 MIDRASH RABBAH, *SHEMOT 1:28*

Moses saw that the children of Israel had no rest, so he went to Pharaoh and said: "If one has a slave and does not give him rest one day in the week, the slave will die. These are your slaves—if you do not give them one day a week, they will die." Said Pharaoh: "Go and do with them as you say." So Moses ordained for them the Shabbat day for rest.

 CHAIM NACHMAN BIALIK, *LETTERS, VOL. 5, P. 228*

The Jewish people will never relinquish the Shabbat, which is not only the foundation of their Jewishness, but also the foundation of their humanity. Without Shabbat, there would be no divine image in the world, nor, for that matter, any human image. For if work were an end unto itself, what would be the advantage of man over beast?

All civilized peoples received from the Jewish people, in one form or another, the concept of a day of rest, and it is this that imparted to them a modicum of humanity. Without it, the entire human race would never have emerged from primitivism. It is the Shabbat, not the cultivation of oranges or potatoes, that preserved our existence as a people throughout our wanderings. Shall we now, upon our return to the land of our ancestors, cast it aside as a useless object?

I speak not here about the observance of the mitzvot in general. Rather, I speak specifically about the observance of the Shabbat, which in my eyes is the equivalent not only of all 613 Jewish mitzvot, as our sages declared, but of the whole of the human spirit…. Without the Shabbat, there is no Jewish people, no Jewish homeland, and no Jewish culture. Shabbat is our culture.

 AHAD HA'AM

Even more than the Jewish people have preserved the Shabbat, the Shabbat has preserved the Jewish people.

*Light and Vessels, Avraham Loewenthal,
Safed, Israel, 2004*

HERMAN WOUK, *THIS IS MY G-D, PP. 44–46*

The pious Jew on the Sabbath does not travel, or cook, or use motors or electric appliances, or spend money, or smoke, or write. The industrial world stops dead for him. Nearly all the mechanical advantages of civilization drop away. The voice of the radio is still; the television screen is blank. The movies, the baseball and football games, the golf courses, the theatres, the nightclubs, the highways, the card tables, the barbecue pits—indeed most of the things that make up the busy pleasures of conventional leisure—are not for him. The Jewish Sabbath is a ceremony that makes steep demands to achieve a decisive effect. A Jew who undertakes to observe it is, from sundown on Friday to the end of twilight on Saturday, in a world cut off....

The Shabbat has cut most sharply athwart my own life when one of my plays has been in rehearsal or in tryout. The crisis atmosphere of an attempt at Broadway is a legend of our time, and a true one; I have felt under less pressure going into battle at sea. Friday afternoon, during these rehearsals, inevitably seems to come when the project is tottering on the edge of ruin. I have sometimes felt guilty of treason, holding to the Shabbat in such a desperate situation. But then, experience has taught me that a theater enterprise almost

always is in such a case. Sometimes it does totter to ruin, and sometimes it totters to great prosperity, but tottering is its normal gait, and cries of anguish are its normal tone of voice.

So I have reluctantly taken leave of my colleagues on Friday afternoon, and rejoined them on Saturday night. The play has never collapsed in the meantime. When I return I find it tottering as before, and the anguished cries as normally despairing as ever. My plays have encountered in the end both success and failure, but I cannot honestly ascribe either result to my observing the Shabbat.

Leaving the gloomy theater, the littered coffee cups, the jumbled scarred-up scripts, the haggard actors, the knuckle-gnawing producer, the clattering typewriter, and the dense tobacco smoke has been a startling change, very like a brief return from the wars.

My wife and my boys, whose existence I have almost forgotten in the anxious shoring up of the tottering ruin, are waiting for me, dressed in holiday clothes, and looking to me marvelously attractive. We have sat down to a splendid dinner, at a table graced with flowers and the old Shabbat symbols: the burning candles, the twisted challah loaves, the stuffed fish, and my grandfather's silver goblet brimming with wine. I have blessed my boys with the ancient blessings; we have sung the pleasantly syncopated Shabbat table hymns.

The talk has little to do with tottering ruins. My wife and I have caught up with our week's conversation. The boys, knowing that Shabbat is the occasion for asking questions, have asked them. We talk of Judaism. For me it is a retreat into restorative magic.

Shabbat has passed much in the same manner. The boys are at home in the synagogue, and they like it. They like even more the assured presence of their parents.... The telephone is silent. I can think, read, study, walk or do nothing. It is an oasis of quiet. My producer one Saturday night said to me, "I don't envy you your religion, but I envy you your Shabbat."

LIVING THE CYCLE OF CREATION

The opening chapters of the Book of Genesis describe how, with a series of ten divine utterances—"There shall be light," "The earth shall bring forth vegetation," etc.—G-d created the world in six days and rested on the seventh. By observing the Shabbat, we align our own creative efforts with the divine cycle of creation and rest, and bear testimony to the truth that the world has a Creator and a purpose. In doing so, says the Talmud, we become "a partner with G-d in creation."

 ZOHAR, *VOL. 2, 63b AND 88a*

Shabbat is both the end and the beginning of all. The toil and achievements of the preceding six days feed into Shabbat, where they are uplifted to their source. Then Shabbat generates, nourishes, and empowers the days of the following week.

 R. SCHNEUR ZALMAN OF LIADI
LIKUTEI TORAH, SHABBATH TESHUVAH 66c

Regarding Shabbat it is written (Exodus 31:17), "Six days G-d made the heaven and the earth ... and on the seventh day He ceased." This requires explanation, because G-d renews the work of creation every day, constantly bringing every thing from absolute nothingness into being. On Shabbat, too, the Creator renews the flow of divine vitality into the world. For were this flow to be withdrawn for one moment, Heaven forbid, the world would revert to nothingness.

The explanation is that on Shabbat the Almighty ceases to create via the "ten utterances," but continues to impart existence and vitality to all creations in the manner of divine thought.... By way of analogy, this is comparable to a person who pauses to rest from the work they have performed. While they were working, their talents and energies were invested in that action; then, when they rest, these revert to their source and are subsumed within it. Similarly, on Shabbat, the whole of Creation ascends from the realm of divine speech to become subsumed within the realm of divine thought.

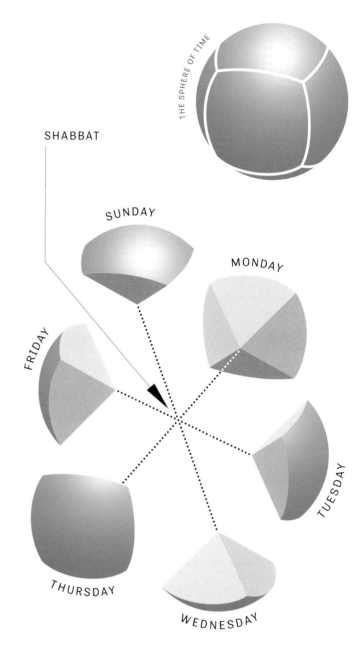

THE SPHERE OF TIME Kabbalistic master R. Joseph Gikatilla (13th century) describes the cycle of time as a sphere consisting of six segments, representing the six days of the week; Shabbat is the point that defines the center of the sphere, from which all six segments emanate and on which they turn.

Shaloh (R. Isaiah Horowitz, c. 1560–1630) expands on this model, pointing out that the center point possesses no volume or surface of its own, and yet precisely because of this, it serves as the point of origin and union for the six segments of the sphere. So too, Shabbat is in essence timeless, as time is defined by movement and flux, the very opposite of Shabbat's embodiment of tranquility and rest. Yet precisely because of its timelessness, Shabbat serves as the core and purpose on which the whole of time turns, and in which time's diverse segments unite and are sublimated.

👁 **JAY LITVIN**

When G-d blinks

Shabbat requires bravery and daring.

It challenges the very notion of consistency, of constancy. It is an affront to normalcy. It threatens reality, sanity, of waking in the morning to see the sun arise each day.

It flouts planning. Steps. Control of the world, ourselves. Of believing there is a self that is ours.

Shabbat is unknown. A turning left. The untrod path. The creative life in utero. It precludes tomorrow's monotony. Questions our next breath.

Shabbat reveals a world beyond. Of dreams. Where other forces rule. Where elephants climb through needles' eyes.

It is the pause between, the no-man's land, the dark of light, the in of out, the light of dark, the in-between.

Shabbat is vibration. The proof in rest of endless movement; the comma in perpetual

    motion,

    motion,

    motion.

Shabbat takes planning, preparation for submission, a yielding to the unknown, the irrepressible. A readiness, as best as we can, for that which is beyond, wild, in the hands of the Other.

It is an expedition, with the tools of civilization discarded, of gadgets and comfort left behind. It leads, with faith, forward, leaving behind reality's rhythm, groping without light in a world not of our making, illusion laid bare for a day, as we journey into nothingness, the world left on its own to breathe, to rest, to linger in the void.

What will be? What will be?

Shabbat is Kabbalah's proof. G-d's hidden habit revealed of recreating every moment the world anew. The affirmation of nothingness and some other force behind.

The place where artists live. From where inspiration sprouts. To where dreams head. From this void all things emerge. The blind fare best. And those who love to fly leap with closed eyes and held breath, anticipating their destination with uncertainty and thrill.

What will be?

Who will I be?

Will there be me?

This pulse is always there, everywhere. But on Shabbat it is ours. We enter cautiously its space, its time—welcoming the Other in our lives. Affirming what we know deep in ourselves but lack the courage to replace with it the normality of our lives, the illusion of our continuity.

And at its end, we emerge, blinking, startled, curious, bewildered by the world anew.

What's happened while we stayed away?

Strayed away?

Did something die?

Is there still me?

Without us, did it all go on?

Who mastered the world while we dreamt?

Or are we dreaming now?

Who mastered the world?

G-d.

With miracles, and masters it still.

Just for a moment, for these few hours in eternity, He let us in. We entered His reality. He allowed us to glimpse existence as it is when He blinks. He let us touch the place from which we too are born anew each moment, with infinite opportunity to become, to transform, to discover...

...with courage and daring.

The bravery of Shabbat.

The creative life sprung forth.

From nothing.

SHABBAT REST

Shabbat is more than a day off the job. Indeed, many typical "weekend" activities, such as home repairs and recreational travel, are inconsistent with Shabbat rest. On Shabbat, we cease to act on the world without, and redirect the flow of life and creativity to the soul within.

 R. JACOB ZVI MECKLENBURG
HAKETAV VEHAKABBALAH, EXODUS 35:1

Know that there is a difference between the Hebrew words *avodah* and *melachah*. *Avodah* refers to all of a person's actions, even if nothing is being changed or improved by the action; for example, when carrying a load of stones from place to place. The term *melachah*, however, only applies when we create something new from raw materials, changing it from its previous state and improving it. When a person's work makes the world more habitable, it is called *melachah*.

The work that the Creator did during the six days of creation is called *melachah*, not *avodah*. Therefore, the Torah specifically forbids the doing of *melachah* on Shabbat. Consequently, it is permitted to carry tables and chairs and food and drink [within the home] when they are needed for the enjoyment of Shabbat, despite the fact that it entails toil and exertion. On the other hand, writing just two characters on Shabbat is a desecration of Shabbat, because *melachah* was done.

 R. SHMUEL OF LUBAVITCH, BASED ON *SEFER HAMAAMARIM 5630, PP. 242–247*

The Talmud enumerates "forty minus one" (i.e., thirty-nine) types of work forbidden on Shabbat. These are the same thirty-nine creative actions that were involved in the construction of the Tabernacle that the people of Israel were commanded to build as a "dwelling place" for the divine presence in their midst. In other words, these are not mundane actions; they are noble actions, by which we develop the resources of our world into a home for G-d. Yet what is desirable and laudatory on the other six days of the week, we desist from on Shabbat. On Shabbat we cease from the task of developing our environment, and apply our creative endeavors to the development of our self and soul.

This is why the Talmud refers to this list of labors as "forty minus one," rather than simply stating that there are thirty-nine. The fortieth "creative work" is the spiritual work of nourishing and cultivating the soul, which continues, and is in fact given greater emphasis, on the holy day of Shabbat.

Construction of the Tabernacle, Jan Luyken, the Netherlands, 18th century

the thirty-nine works

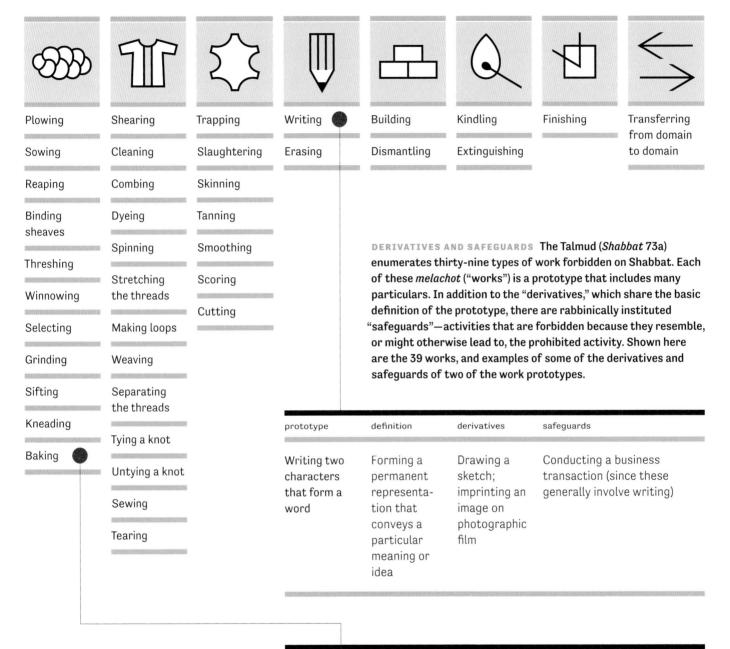

Plowing

Sowing

Reaping

Binding
sheaves

Threshing

Winnowing

Selecting

Grinding

Sifting

Kneading

Baking

Shearing

Cleaning

Combing

Dyeing

Spinning

Stretching
the threads

Making loops

Weaving

Separating
the threads

Tying a knot

Untying a knot

Sewing

Tearing

Trapping

Slaughtering

Skinning

Tanning

Smoothing

Scoring

Cutting

Writing

Erasing

Building

Dismantling

Kindling

Extinguishing

Finishing

Transferring
from domain
to domain

DERIVATIVES AND SAFEGUARDS The Talmud (*Shabbat* 73a) enumerates thirty-nine types of work forbidden on Shabbat. Each of these *melachot* ("works") is a prototype that includes many particulars. In addition to the "derivatives," which share the basic definition of the prototype, there are rabbinically instituted "safeguards"—activities that are forbidden because they resemble, or might otherwise lead to, the prohibited activity. Shown here are the 39 works, and examples of some of the derivatives and safeguards of two of the work prototypes.

prototype	definition	derivatives	safeguards
Writing two characters that form a word	Forming a permanent representation that conveys a particular meaning or idea	Drawing a sketch; imprinting an image on photographic film	Conducting a business transaction (since these generally involve writing)

prototype	definition	derivatives	safeguards
Baking or cooking raw food to make it edible	Effecting constructive change in a substance by means of heat	Boiling water; firing pottery; melting wax	When leaving food on the stove to stay warm during Shabbat, the heating element should be covered as a reminder that any action that advances the cooking process is forbidden.

HONOR AND DELIGHT

Rest, the central pillar of Shabbat observance, is buttressed by the auxiliary motifs of honor and delight. Throughout the week, honor is something that is accorded to the exceptional objects and activities of our lives; on Shabbat, the day itself is honored. Throughout the week, delight is something to be earned, rather than a value in its own right. For example, we eat in order to acquire the energy to do good deeds; to eat merely for the pleasure of eating borders on the hedonistic. On Shabbat, however, the pleasure derived from food is itself a mitzvah, a holy and spiritual act. For on Shabbat the very physicality of the world is holy. Instead of striving to improve and perfect the world, we relate to that which is already good and perfect in it.

Observances and customs whose purpose is to honor and to delight in the Shabbat:

■ Preparing for Shabbat during the preceding days of the week

■ Cleaning the house for Shabbat

■ Washing and grooming one's body before Shabbat

■ Dressing in freshly cleaned and pressed festive clothes

■ Lighting Shabbat candles before the onset of Shabbat to create a pleasant and peaceful atmosphere for the Shabbat meal

■ Eating three festive meals during the course of Shabbat that include foods that bring pleasure to the person

■ Setting the Shabbat table in a beautiful and luxurious manner

■ Singing of songs (*zemirot*) in honor of the Shabbat at the Shabbat table

■ Sleep

■ Marital relations

■ Setting aside of all workaday worries from one's mind

From *Shulchan Aruch, Orach Chayim, Laws of Shabbat*

 TALMUD, *SHABBAT 119a*

The Roman emperor asked R. Joshua ben Hananiah: "Why does your Shabbat cooking smell so delicious?"

Said he: "We have a special spice called 'Shabbat' which we put in it."

Said he: "Give me some of that spice."

Said he: "For those who observe the Shabbat, it is efficacious; for those who do not observe it, it is of no use."

*Shabbat at Tevye's,
Meyer Axelrod, Russia,
20th century*

 ELIE WIESEL
WISE MEN AND THEIR TALES, PP. 328–329

One can never speak enough of what Shabbat was like in the shtetl—and what it did for its inhabitants. Shabbat helped people endure the other six days of the week, often gray and dark, heavy with sorrow and anxiety. Hence the waiting for Shabbat, which actually began much earlier. Thursday evening or early Friday morning, the housewife would already be busy preparing the hallah, gefilte fish, and cholent, the traditional elements of a Shabbat meal in the shtetl. The white tablecloth, the white shirt: everything had to be ready, and everything was the housewife's responsibility. One easily forgets that we owe the gift of Shabbat to the queen of the home. *Shabbat malka,* the Shabbat queen. We couldn't wait for her arrival.

In the stores, business was conducted with haste. Sellers and customers were equally in a hurry to go home. Men would go to the ritual bath, the *mikveh,* then dress and prepare to be worthy of welcoming the Shabbat, already on the horizon. The first to spot her would be the beadle, the *shammash*: he would go around stores and homes shouting *"Yiden, greit zicht tzu Shabbes!"*—Jews, ready yourselves for the Sabbath! Or a variation on the same theme: *"Yiden, s'is bald Shabbes oif der velt!"*—Jews, it's almost Shabbat in the world!

At home, one did not need these reminders: the mother, mine too, lit the candles honoring Shabbat, one for each member of the family, and blessed them silently, with gestures of grace and tenderness. Suddenly, her face would be illuminated by a light coming from another world, from another time, a light at once frail and eternal. And her beauty was multiplied sevenfold. So that even now as I am writing these words, the tears well up in my throat.

In the shul also, everything was different. More luminous, the candelabras. More serene, the faces. More melodious, the prayers. The Talmud is right: on Shabbat, one gains an added soul, the *neshama yeteira….*

SHABBAT CANDLES

1

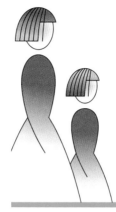

WHO LIGHTS The mitzvah of lighting Shabbat candles rests upon all members of the household. But it is the woman of the house, in her role as the mainstay of the home, who traditionally does the actual lighting. If there is no woman in the house, or if she is unable to light, a male member of the household lights the candles.

An age-old custom is that all women in the household should each light their own candle as well, including young girls from the age they can understand the significance of the mitzvah (about three years of age).

2

18 MIN

WHEN TO LIGHT The Shabbat candles are lit Friday evening, eighteen minutes before sunset. Certain communities have the custom to light them somewhat earlier. The latest that one may light the candles is sunset. On Shabbat, it is forbidden to kindle a flame, so to light a candle after sunset would be a desecration of Shabbat.

3

WHAT TO LIGHT Any candle or oil/wick combination that produces a clean and stable flame can be used for Shabbat candles. When it is not possible to light a flame (e.g., in a hospital), the blessing can be recited after turning on an electric light.

Married women light two candles, while unmarried women and girls light a single candle. Some women have a custom of lighting an additional candle for each of their children.

4

PREPARATION Set up the candles on or near the table where the Shabbat meal will be eaten.

Some families have the custom that the husband prepares the candles and singes the wicks, as his way of participating in the mitzvah.

Before lighting, put a few coins in a charity box.

5

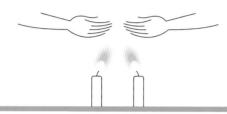

KINDLE THE FLAMES Light the candles. Young girls should light first, so that their mother can assist them if necessary.

Many have the custom to raise their hands above the candles in a gesture of welcome, signifying the welcoming of the Shabbat into the home.

6

RECITE THE BLESSING Cover your eyes and say the following blessing:

בָּרוּךְ אַתָּה ה׳ אֱלֹהֵינוּ מֶלֶךְ הָעוֹלָם אֲשֶׁר קִדְּשָׁנוּ בְּמִצְוֹתָיו וְצִוָּנוּ לְהַדְלִיק נֵר שֶׁל שַׁבָּת קֹדֶשׁ

TRANSLITERATION
Ba-ruch a-tah a-do-nai e-lo-hei-nu me-lech ha-o-lam a-sher ki-de-sha-nu be-mitz-vo-tav vi-tzi-va-nu le-had-lik ner shel sha-bat ko-desh

TRANSLATION
Blessed are You, Lord our G-d, king of the universe, who has sanctified us with His commandments, and commanded us to kindle the light of the holy Shabbat

7

PERSONAL PRAYER The time of candle lighting is an auspicious time for private prayer. From behind covered eyes, women throughout history have whispered prayers for health and happiness, and for children who will illuminate the world with their learning and observance of the Torah.

Uncover your eyes and gaze at the Shabbat lights. Turn to your loved ones and wish them "Shabbat Shalom" or "Good Shabbos." Embrace the light, peace, and joy you have generated, and welcome the Shabbat into your home.

KIDDUSH

The commandment to observe Shabbat begins by instructing us, "Remember the Shabbat day, to sanctify it" (Exodus 20:8). We fulfill this charge by proclaiming the sanctity of Shabbat over a cup of wine, the symbol of mystic joy. In the words of Maimonides, "Remember the Shabbat by proclaiming its sanctity…. Recite the Kiddush when the Shabbat enters, and the Havdalah when it departs."

THE FRIDAY NIGHT KIDDUSH

GENESIS 1:31–2:3 The sixth day. The heavens and the earth were finished, and all their hosts. G-d finished on the seventh day His work which He made; and G-d rested on the seventh day from all His work which He made. G-d blessed the seventh day, and He sanctified it; for in it He ceased from all His work, which G-d created to make.

BLESSING ON THE WINE Blessed are You, Lord our G-d, king of the universe, who creates the fruit of the vine.

KIDDUSH BLESSING Blessed are You, Lord our G-d, king of the universe, who has sanctified us with His commandments and has desired us; and has given us, in love and goodwill, His holy Shabbat as a heritage, in remembrance of the work of Creation; the first of the holy festivals, commemorating the Exodus from Egypt. For You have chosen us and sanctified us from among all the nations, and with love and goodwill, You have given us Your holy Shabbat as a heritage. Blessed are You, Lord, who sanctifies the Shabbat.

Kiddush cup, Rötger Herfurth, Frankfurt am Main, circa 1750

THE SHABBAT TABLE

(A) **SETTING THE TABLE**
The table is set with the best that the home has to offer, as we are welcoming royalty—the Shabbat queen—into our homes.

(B) **SHABBAT CANDLES**
Lit prior to the start of Shabbat, the Shabbat candles create an atmosphere of peace and holiness (see p. 296).

(C) **KIDDUSH** Recited on a goblet of wine, the Kiddush ("sanctification" of the day) consists of Biblical verses and a blessing that proclaim the role of Shabbat as a testament to G-d's creation of the world and our liberation from Egyptian slavery (see p. 297).

(D) **CHALLAH** Two whole challah loaves recall the double portion of manna that descended each Friday in honor of the Shabbat (see p. 44). The challah loaves are covered with a cloth during the recitation of the Kiddush—many households have a special embroidered "challah cover" for this purpose. Following Kiddush, the *Hamotzi* blessing is recited over the challah loaves, which are then cut into slices, dipped in salt, and distributed to all participants at the meal.

(E) **SHABBAT FISH**
The Shabbat meals traditionally include a fish course (see pp. 300–301).

(F) **MAIN COURSE**
The Shabbat meal traditionally includes a meat or poultry dish, to enhance one's enjoyment of the Shabbat. However, according to the *Code of Jewish Law,* "There is no particular obligation to eat meat and drink wine on Shabbat. It is only that most people enjoy eating meat more than other foods and enjoy drinking wine more than other beverages; so for them, it is proper to serve meat and wine to the extent that they are able to spend."

(G) **CHOLENT** (for the midday meal). The laws of Shabbat rest preclude lighting or extinguishing a fire, or cooking, from sunset Friday until nightfall the next evening. On the other hand, the mitzvah to delight in the Shabbat dictates that one should enjoy warm food at the Shabbat meals. The solution: To cook everything before Shabbat, and place the food on a stovetop (or other heating element) so that it stays warm until the meal. The fire or heating element is covered, as a reminder that it is forbidden to take any action that would aid in the cooking of the food (e.g., increasing or lowering the heat, stirring the pot, etc.).

Cholent or *hamin* is a traditional Shabbat stew that simmers overnight on a covered flame (or in a slow cooker) and is enjoyed at the midday Shabbat meal.

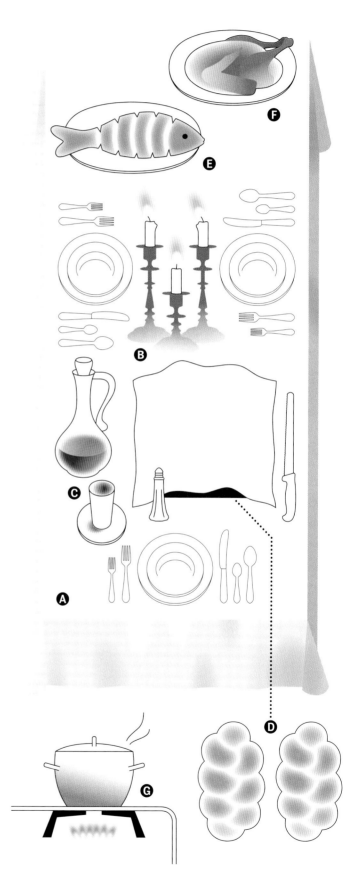

Friday Evening, Isidor Kaufmann, Austria, circa 1920

Challah cover,
Yair Emanuel, Israel, 2015

SHABBAT FISH

The custom to eat fish on Shabbat is an ancient one. The Talmud (*Shabbat* 119a) includes references to fish in its recommendations for how to honor and take pleasure in the Shabbat, and tells a story about a certain *Yosef Mokir Shabbat* ("Joseph who cherishes the Shabbat") who purchased a large fish in honor of the Shabbat and was richly rewarded as a result when he found a precious stone in its belly.

The virtues of Shabbat fish notwithstanding, the *Code of Jewish Law* rules that "it is proper to eat fish at each of the Shabbat meals, unless fish are harmful to one's constitution, or one dislikes them so that they accord discomfort rather than pleasure."

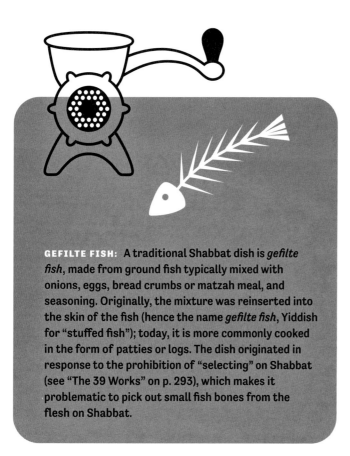

GEFILTE FISH: A traditional Shabbat dish is *gefilte fish*, made from ground fish typically mixed with onions, eggs, bread crumbs or matzah meal, and seasoning. Originally, the mixture was reinserted into the skin of the fish (hence the name *gefilte fish*, Yiddish for "stuffed fish"); today, it is more commonly cooked in the form of patties or logs. The dish originated in response to the prohibition of "selecting" on Shabbat (see "The 39 Works" on p. 293), which makes it problematic to pick out small fish bones from the flesh on Shabbat.

Various mystical explanations are given for the special status of fish as a Shabbat food:

■ The Hebrew word for "fish," דג (*dag*), has a numerical value (*gematria*) of seven (*R. Joseph Colon, c. 1420–1480*).

■ The Talmud relates that the great fish leviathan, created on the fifth day of creation, was preserved for the righteous in the World to Come. Shabbat is a foretaste of the Messianic era, described as "the day that is wholly Shabbat and tranquility for life everlasting" (*R. Moses Matt, 1540–1606*).

■ The souls of the righteous are said to be reincarnated in fish, and attain their elevation when the fish is eaten on Shabbat (*R. Yechiel Michel Epstein, d. 1706*).

■ In the Torah's account of creation, three things are the recipient of a special divine blessing: the fish are blessed on the fifth day of creation; the first man and woman on the sixth day; and the Shabbat on the seventh. The three blessings converge when we eat fish in honor of Shabbat (*R. Zvi Elimelech of Dinov, 1783–1841*).

■ Fish were the first living creatures to be created, and the only animals not to be corrupted in the generation of the Flood (*R. Menachem Mendel of Vorka, 1819–1868*).

■ Kosher meat and fowl must undergo various "refinements" before they can be eaten (the animal must be slaughtered in a ritually specific way; it must be inspected for certain flaws in its physiology; and the blood and certain veins of fat need to be removed). No such conditions, however, apply to the consumption of kosher fish. As such, the fish reflects the reality of Shabbat, in which everything is inherently holy and unified with its source (*R. Zadok of Lublin, 1823–1900*).

JEFFTAKESPICS2

DINA LEWIS

CLASSIC GEFILTE FISH

FISH INGREDIENTS

3 lbs. ground fish (mixture of pike, whitefish, and/or carp)

4 medium onions, peeled and ground

2 carrots, peeled and ground

2 stalks celery, peeled and ground

5 tsps. salt

1 tsp. pepper

3 to 5 tsps. sugar

1/2 cup matzah meal or bread crumbs

4 eggs, beaten

BROTH INGREDIENTS

2 carrots, peeled and sliced into chunks

3 onions, peeled and sliced

2 tsps. salt

1/2 tsp. pepper

6 to 8 cups water

Place broth ingredients in 8-quart pot. Bring to a boil, lower flame, and allow to cook for a few minutes.

Combine fish ingredients in a large mixing bowl and mix well. Bring broth to a rolling boil. Wet hands, fill palm with one scoop of fish mixture, and shape into a round or oval ball. Lower fish balls gently into boiling broth, leaving space between the balls. When all the balls are in the pot, lower flame and cook covered on medium heat for 1 to 1½ hours. After 1 hour, check water level and seasoning, and adjust if needed. Allow fish to cool before removing from pot.

Yields 10 to 12 portions

MOROCCAN SHABBAT FISH

6 to 8 servings of boneless fish fillets (approx. 2–3 lbs.)

3 red bell peppers, cut into strips

4 tomatoes, thickly sliced

6 to 8 large garlic cloves, coarsely chopped

1 or 2 chili peppers, cut into rings

1/2 cup olive oil

3 tbsp. sweet paprika

1/2 tsp. hot paprika

1/2 tsp. turmeric

1/2 tsp. cumin

salt to taste

1 bunch fresh cilantro

1 1/2 cups water

In large saucepan, heat 2–3 tsp. olive oil. Sauté tomato slices, bell pepper strips, chili pepper rings, and garlic.

Mix remaining oil with paprikas, turmeric, and cumin in a bowl. Coat each fish portion with oil and spice mixture, and place on top of sautéed vegetables. Salt fish and vegetables to taste. Pour remaining oil and spice mixture over fish. Add cilantro to pan.

Boil water and add to saucepan. Cover saucepan and simmer covered for 10 minutes. Uncover and simmer for an additional 5 to 10 minutes, or until fish reaches desired level of doneness. Serve hot or cold.

HAVDALAH

multisensory ritual

The close of the Shabbat is marked with Havdalah, a multisensory ritual employing the faculties of mind, speech and hearing, sight, smell, and taste.

Havdalah serves a dual, if paradoxical, function. It distinguishes Shabbat from the rest of the week, demarcating the boundaries "between the sacred and the mundane." It also serves to bridge these two domains, carrying over the tranquility and holiness of Shabbat to inform and empower the workday endeavors for the next six days of the week.

MIND *Havdalah* means "differentiation." The Havdalah ritual facilitates the mindful distinction between the holy and mundane areas of our lives, so that each can be fully itself and positively feed into and influence the other.

TASTE Havdalah is performed over a cup of wine, filled to overflowing to represent the overabundance of divine blessing, which is drunk at the conclusion of the ritual. Wine is the vehicle of revelation and delight, infusing our journey into the coming week with vitality and joy.

SMELL We recite a blessing thanking G-d for creating fragrant spices and herbs, and enjoy their aroma. On Shabbat we are each granted an "additional soul"; when that soul departs at the close of the holy day, we fortify ourselves with the most spiritual of our senses—the sense of smell.

SIGHT As we embark on a new week of creative engagement with the world, we express our gratitude to the Creator for a most elementary tool of human endeavor—fire and light—by reciting a blessing over a multi-wicked flame (representing manifold uses of fire) and enjoying its light.

SPEECH & HEARING We conclude the Havdalah ritual with the declaration: *Blessed are You, Lord our G-d, king of the universe, who differentiates between sacred and mundane, between light and darkness, between Israel and the nations, between the seventh day and the six work days. Blessed are You, Lord, who differentiates between sacred and mundane.* Verbalizing, or listening to the words being spoken, effects the transmission of an idea from the realm of thought into the realm of action.

Silver spice box, Russia, 1880

Havdalah candle, Safed, Israel, 2015

JERUSALEM TALMUD, *BERACHOT 8:5*

That first Shabbat, the night did not darken. Light reigned for 36 hours—twelve hours of the sixth day, twelve hours of Shabbat night, and twelve hours of Shabbat day.

When Shabbat ended and darkness began to encroach, Adam grew fearful. At that moment, the Almighty made two slates available to him, and he rubbed them against each other; fire emerged from them, and Adam proclaimed: "Blessed are You, G-d … who creates the lights of fire."

Said Shmuel: That is why we recite the blessing on fire on the night following the Shabbat, as that is when it was first created.

 R. JONATHAN SACKS,
COVENANT & CONVERSATION, TAZRIA 5776

There is a fundamental difference between the light of the first day of creation, and that of the eighth day. The light of the first day is the illumination G-d makes. The light of the eighth day is the illumination G-d teaches us to make. It symbolizes our "partnership with G-d in the work of creation" … how G-d empowers us to join Him in bringing light to the world.

On Shabbat we remember G-d's creation. On the eighth day we celebrate our creativity as the image and partner of G-d.

The Havdalah ritual in a book of Shabbat readings, Aaron Wolf Herlingen, Vienna, 1738

WHEN TO DO HAVDALAH: The Havdalah ritual is conducted after Shabbat ends at nightfall Saturday night. "Nightfall" is defined by Torah law as the time when three middle-sized stars are visible in the sky under natural conditions, and varies by location and by the time of the year. While there are various customs regarding how to calculate when we are certain that nightfall has occurred, one common approach is to wait until the sun has descended 8.5 degrees below the horizon, or approximately 40–50 minutes after sunset.

Food and diet

When we eat, we take a physical substance and absorb it into ourselves.
Its molecules bind with our molecules; the proteins and vitamins they
contain become the building blocks of our bodies, and the energy locked
within them drives the engine of our lives. We literally become what we
eat, and what we eat realizes its potential through us.

This, explain the sages, is why food and diet play such a dominant
role in the practice of Judaism. The kosher dietary laws, which govern
which foods are fit for Jewish consumption, are a universally recognized
feature of Jewish life. The Jewish calendar is a calendar of foods: the
wine and challah of the weekly Shabbat, the matzah and bitter herbs of
the Passover Seder, apple dipped in honey on Rosh Hashanah, blintzes on
Shavuot, latkes and sufganiot on Hanukkah, hamantaschen on Purim.
All major lifecycle events—marriage, brit, bar and bat mitzvah—are
celebrated with a festive meal. Even an ordinary meal on an ordinary day
is a sacred event, preceded and concluded with a berachah *(blessing),*
and approached with mindfulness and purpose.

NASA IMAGES

KOSHER IN SPACE Colonel Ilan Ramon was the first person to eat kosher meals in space. As Israel's first astronaut, Ramon felt that "I'm kind of a representative of all the Jewish community."

DAVE SANDER

Preparing fish at Benz's Gourmet, Brooklyn, New York, 2014

Manual on kosher slaughter, Isaac Lopez de Almeida, Amsterdam, 1671

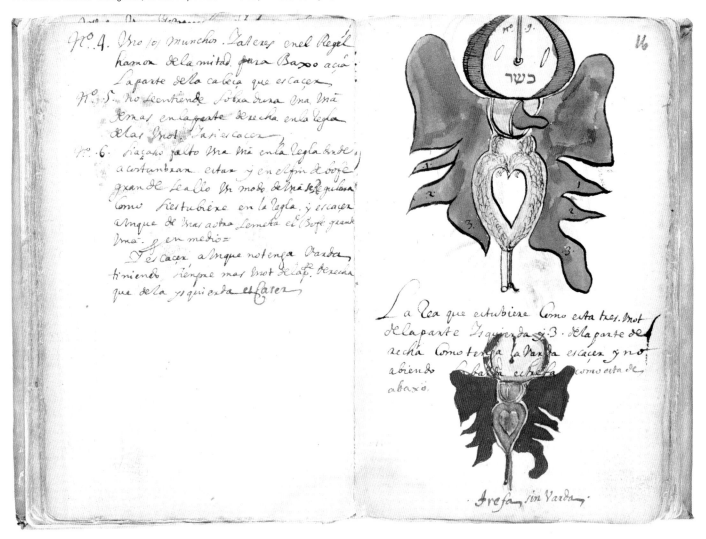

KOSHER

Stamp for marking foods as kosher, Rawicz, Poland, 19th century

Various reasons have been offered for the Torah's kosher dietary laws. Some point out the health benefits, or the adverse spiritual effects of consuming animals with a violent or predatory nature. Others dwell on the unifying effect these laws have on a dispersed people, and their role as a bulwark against assimilation. But perhaps the most basic reason is presented by the Torah itself, in the closing verses of its chapter on the dietary laws: "Sanctify yourselves and be holy ... to differentiate between the impure and the pure, between the animal that may be eaten and the animal that may not be eaten" (Leviticus 11:44–47).

"To differentiate" defines the human being's uniqueness as a moral creature. Morality — "holiness" in the Torah's terminology — is the capacity for setting boundaries: to live one's life with the understanding that there are things to be embraced and things to be rebuffed; elements of Creation to be developed and elevated, and elements that are beyond our ability to gainfully utilize. Sometimes the undesirability of a substance or activity is obvious; but if that's where it ends, we would be little more than cows avoiding the poison ivy. The true test of morality is when we accept that there is an objective "yes" and "no" in G-d's world, dictated not by human reason or utility, but by the creator and master of reality.

 MAIMONIDES
GUIDE FOR THE PERPLEXED, 3:35

The dietary laws train us in the mastery over our appetites. They accustom us to restrain both the growth of desire and the disposition to consider pleasure of eating and drinking as the end of man's existence.

 **NACHMANIDES**
COMMENTARY TO LEVITICUS 11:13

The birds that are forbidden by the Torah for consumption are all predators. The Torah tells us to avoid them because the trait of cruelty is in their blood ... and [consuming them] would impart the trait of cruelty to our hearts.

the basics of a kosher diet

ANIMAL PRODUCTS The meat, milk, and eggs of certain species of animal are permitted for consumption, while others are forbidden. In addition, a series of laws govern how the animal should be slaughtered and which parts of the animal may be eaten (see table on next page).

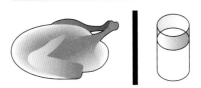

MEAT & MILK Meat and milk products are never combined. Separate utensils are used for each, and a waiting period is observed between eating them.

FRUIT, VEGETABLES & GRAINS All species of fruit, vegetables, and grains are kosher, but must be insect free. Certain restrictions apply to produce of the Land of Israel, which may require tithing before consumption (see p. 281).

COOKED OR PROCESSED FOODS Even a small trace of a non-kosher substance can render a food not kosher. In addition, certain foods must be cooked or produced by (or with the participation of) a Jew. As a result, all processed foods and eating establishments require certification by a reliable rabbi or kosher supervision agency.

IMPORTANT NOTE: The tables on this and the following pages present only a basic outline of the kosher dietary laws, whose details are quite complex.

 CHINUCH, *MITZVAH 451*

[One of the] reasons given for the commandment to slaughter an animal only by cutting its throat with a knife that was examined [and determined to be completely smooth] is that we should not cause undue suffering to the animal. The Torah permitted [the killing of] animals for human benefit and nourishment, but not to inflict pain on them unnecessarily. Indeed, the sages concluded that causing pain to animals is a Biblical prohibition.

 R. HAYIM HALEVY DONIN
TO BE A JEW, PP. 102–103

Critics [of the kosher dietary laws] have criticized its observance on the grounds that it tends to separate us from other peoples…. Yet in addition to whatever other merits or purposes *kashrut* may have, for all we know this too may be part of what the Almighty intended. For barriers to total social integration in a non-Jewish environment are also barriers to intermarriage and assimilation.

We find the connection between separation and *kashrut* even more explicitly delineated in the following passage (Leviticus 20:24–25): "I am the Lord your G-d, who has set you apart from the nations. And you shall differentiate the ritually pure beast and the impure, and between the ritually impure fowl and the pure."

kosher animals: signs and requirements

Food group	Identifying kosher signs	Examples of kosher species	Examples of non-kosher species
Land animals 	split hooves and chews its cud	bovines, sheep, goats, deer	pigs, rabbits, squirrels, bears, camels, horses
Fowl	the Torah lists 24 non-kosher species; in practice, we only eat fowl for which a tradition that it is kosher exists	domestic species of chickens, ducks, geese, turkeys, and pigeons	hawks, ravens, ostriches, storks, swan
Fish and seafood	fins and scales	salmon, tuna (most species), pike, flounder, carp, herring	catfish, lobster, shellfish, all water mammals
Reptiles, amphibians, worms, and insects	not kosher, with the exception of four types of locusts		

KOSHER LEXICON

KOSHER Hebrew for "fit." As applied to food, "kosher food" is food fit for consumption for a Jew in accordance with the Torah's dietary laws.

SHECHITAH Kosher slaughter. Land animals and fowl can be killed only by a specific method—cutting the throat with a smooth knife in an uninterrupted back-and-forth motion. Failure to follow this procedure in the smallest detail (for example, if the knife has a single nick in it that interrupts its smoothness) renders the animal unfit for consumption. A trained ritual slaughterer qualified to perform *shechitah* is called a *shochet.*

TREIF, TREIFAH Literally, "torn." An animal that has a life-threatening injury or disease, such as a punctured lung or a broken thighbone, rendering it unfit for consumption. In common usage, *treif* refers to any non-kosher food.

FLEISHIG or **BESARI** Literally, "meaty." Refers to meat and fowl and their byproducts, or utensils that are used for these foods. Such food or utensils must be kept separate from *milchig* (see below).

MILCHIG or **CHALAVI** Literally, "milky." Refers to foods containing milk or milk products, or utensils that are used for these foods. Such food or utensils must be kept separate from *fleishig* (see previous entry).

PAREVE Neutral food products containing no meat or milk or their derivatives, and utensils used exclusively for neutral foods. Pareve may be eaten or combined with either *fleishig* or *milchig.* Pareve foods include eggs, fish, grains, fruits, and vegetables.

SALTING Torah law forbids the consumption of blood. Therefore, before meat and fowl can be consumed, all blood must be extracted by a process involving rinsing the meat, soaking it in water, salting it, and a final triple rinsing.

KASHER, KASHERING Literally, "making fit." Utensils and equipment used with non-kosher food must be purged of the non-kosher taste they absorbed. The "kashering" method depends on the type of utensil and its mode of use, and may involve immersion in boiling water (*hagalah*) or heating it with a blowtorch (*libun*). Certain materials cannot be kashered.

YAYIN NESECH and **STAM YEINAM** The Torah forbids deriving benefit from anything associated with idolatry. Wine produced by idolaters is therefore forbidden, as it is suspect of being *yayin nesech*, wine offered as a libation to a pagan deity. As an additional precaution—and as a preventive measure against intermarriage—the sages also forbade any non-Jewish wine (*stam yeinam*). All wine therefore requires kosher certification that ensures it was produced under conditions that permit its consumption.

Shechitah (ritual slaughter)	Treifah (mortal injury or disease)	Blood	Additional restrictions
required	forbidden for consumption	forbidden, and must be extracted from meat by soaking and salting	Meat may not be combined with milk or milk products. The sciatic nerve and certain skeins of fat must be removed (applies only to certain species).
required	forbidden for consumption	forbidden, and must be extracted from meat by soaking and salting	Meat may not be combined with milk or milk products. Only eggs of kosher fowl are permissible for consumption.
not required	permitted	permitted	Should not be cooked or eaten together with meat.
—	—	—	In practice, most Jewish communities have not maintained the tradition that identifies the kosher locusts.

CHALAV YISRAEL Literally, "Jewish milk." The kosher laws mandate that a Torah-observant Jew must supervise the milking and consequent processing to ensure that only milk from kosher animals is used. Some Halachic authorities permit, under certain circumstances, to rely on government inspection as sufficient assurance.

BISHUL YISRAEL Literally, "Jewish cooking." The sages forbade eating food cooked by non-Jews, if the food cannot be eaten raw and it is a respectable food "that is served at a king's table." If a Jew participates in the cooking process, it is permitted.

PAS YISRAEL Literally, "Jewish bread." Bread baked with Jewish involvement. While many Halachic authorities permit commercially produced bread also when there is no Jewish involvement, it is meritorious to only eat pas yisrael.

YOSHON Literally, "old." The Torah instructs to refrain from consuming the current year's grain until after the 16th of Nisan, when the omer offering was brought in the Holy Temple. While there are different Halachic opinions as to whether this law applies to grain not grown by Jews in the Holy Land, many are careful to not use "new" grain harvested before this date.

TOIVELING Literally, "immersing." Utensils used for food preparation and eating must be immersed in a mikveh before their first use, if they were manufactured or previously owned by non-Jews.

KOSHER FOR PASSOVER Throughout the festival of Passover, it is forbidden to own, eat, or derive any benefit from leavened grain products (chametz). Foods with even the slightest trace of leaven are forbidden for consumption. Commercially produced foods used during the festival must therefore be certified "Kosher for Passover."

MEHADRIN This term, meaning "beautification" or "enhancement," is used to denote a higher standard in Jewish law. With regard to food, it implies that the kosher status is of a stricter standard.

GLATT Literally, "smooth." In its original context, this refers to meat from animals with smooth or defect-free lungs (in certain cases, adhesions on the lung can render an animal treif). In common usage, "glatt kosher" indicates a stricter standard of kosher in general (similar to mehadrin).

HASHGACHAH and HECHSHER Literally, "supervision" and "certified as fit." Due to the complex laws surrounding the kosher status of food products, various agencies or individual rabbis provide kosher supervision and certify products and eateries as kosher. Kosher certifiers use distinctive symbols to display their endorsement on the packaging of the product. Some well-known symbols include the OU and OK.

MINDFUL EATING

 TALMUD, *BERACHOT 55a*

As long as the Holy Temple stood, the altar atoned for the people of Israel. Now, a person's table atones for them.

 MAIMONIDES, *MISHNEH TORAH, LAWS OF CHARACTER, CHAPTER 4*

Maintaining a healthy and sound body is among the ways of G-d, as a person cannot understand or have any knowledge of the Creator if they are ill. Therefore, a person should avoid those things that harm the body, and accustom themselves to those things that impart wellness and vigor. To wit:

A person should never eat unless they are hungry, nor drink unless they are thirsty…. One should not eat until one's stomach is full, but should stop when one has eaten close to three-quarters of full satisfaction….

A person should exercise their body and exert themselves in a sweat-producing task each morning, and then rest for a while until they regain their composure, and only after that should they eat….

Overeating is like poison to any person's body. Most illnesses that afflict a person are caused by harmful foods, or by filling one's belly and overeating, even of healthful foods. Thus King Solomon proclaims in his wisdom (Proverbs 21:23), "One who guards their mouth and their tongue, guards their soul from distress."

 R. ISAAC LURIA, *SEFER HALIKUTIM, BEREISHITH*

This is the secret [of eating]…. When an animal eats grass and vegetation, the sparks [of divine energy] that they contain are refined and reincarnated in the [higher level] of animal life. And when a person eats meat, they [further] refine all those sparks that were refined by the animal…. This is what we should be mindful of when we eat: that we are refining all the sparks of holiness that are in the food.

Grace After Meals and other benedictions, Moravia, 1728

R. ISRAEL BAAL SHEM TOV
EXCERPTED FROM *KETER SHEM TOV, 194*

The writings of Ari cite a question posed by philosophers: How is it that the spiritual soul derives its vitality from physical food? Ari explains that this question derives from their ignorance of the roots of Creation. Our sages note that the world was created with ten divine utterances. When the Creator said, "The earth shall bring forth living animals" (Genesis 1:24), or, "The earth shall bring forth vegetation [and] fruit trees" (ibid., verse 11), and so on, these utterances brought all creations into being, and remain embedded within them, continually providing them with existence and vitality. When a person takes a fruit, or any other food—provided that this is a kosher food that G-d instructed to elevate from its material state to spirituality—and pronounces the blessing for the food, evoking the divine name with the proper mindfulness, this arouses and calls forth the divine vitality within the food.

Thus it is written, "It is not by bread alone that the human lives, but by all that comes forth out of the mouth of G-d that the human does live" (Deuteronomy 8:3). It is not by the physical bread itself that "the human" is vitalized—referring to the soul, as the body is merely the flesh of the human, while the soul is "the human"—but rather, "by all that comes forth out of the mouth of G-d." Meaning, when a person calls forth the divine vitality within the food, then their soul is nourished. For this was the divine intent in creation: that the sparks of holiness that were dispersed in the material realms when the Almighty was "creating worlds and destroying them" should be retrieved and elevated by human actions.

This is also the deeper meaning of the verse (Psalms 107:5), "Hungry and thirsty, their soul is enveloped in them." Here lies a great and awesome secret: When a person craves a food or drink, this is because a spark of their own soul is enveloped within that material substance. These sparks yearn to cleave to holiness, and therefore rouse the person to desire them. Every food or drink that a person consumes contains sparks of their own soul, which it is that person's mission to elevate.

 KITZUR SHULCHAN ARUCH, *SECTION 31*

Our sages, of blessed memory, have said: What is a pithy saying upon which major elements of the Torah depend? "Know Him in all your ways" (Proverbs 3:6). Meaning: Know the Creator also in your daily habits, in the things you do for the needs of your body, and do these things for His sake….

In eating and drinking: It goes without saying that one should not eat forbidden foods, Heaven forbid. But also regarding permitted foods, if a person is thirsty and hungry and eats and drinks solely for their pleasure, this is not ideal. Rather, one should have in mind that one is eating and drinking to have the energy to serve the Creator. Thus, a person should not eat anything that their palate craves, like a dog or a donkey does, but should rather eat things that are beneficial for the health of the body. There are conscientious individuals who, before they eat, say: "I now wish to eat in order to be healthy and strong for the sake of serving the Creator."

BLESSINGS ON FOOD

A primary feature of mindful eating is the practice of reciting *berachot* or "blessings" over food, acknowledging that G-d is the creator and provider of our sustenance. The Torah (Deuteronomy 8:10) instructs to bless and thank G-d after eating; hence the "Grace After Meals" recited after a meal. The sages instituted to recite a blessing before eating as well, in effect "asking permission" from the Almighty before we partake of His creation. There are six such blessings, each for a different group of foods.

1

NAME OF BLESSING: *Hamotzi*

TYPE OF FOOD: All forms of bread, including rolls, challah, matzah, bagels, pita, etc., if made of one of these five grains: wheat, barley, rye, oat, or spelt

BLESSING (IN HEBREW):

בָּרוּךְ אַתָּה ה׳ אֱלֹהֵינוּ מֶלֶךְ הָעוֹלָם הַמּוֹצִיא לֶחֶם מִן הָאָרֶץ

TRANSLITERATION: *Ba-ruch a-tah a-do-nai elo-hei-nu me-lech ha-o-lam ha-mo-tzi le-chem min ha-a-retz*

TRANSLATION: Blessed are You, Lord our G-d, king of the universe, who brings forth bread from the earth.

NOTE: *When the blessing Hamotzi is made on bread, it generally covers all other foods eaten in that meal, and no other blessings are made*

2

NAME OF BLESSING: *Mezonot*

TYPE OF FOOD: Foods other than bread that are made from one of the "five grains" listed above. Examples: cakes, cereals, pasta, cookies, etc.

BLESSING (IN HEBREW):

בָּרוּךְ אַתָּה ה׳ אֱלֹהֵינוּ מֶלֶךְ הָעוֹלָם בּוֹרֵא מִינֵי מְזוֹנוֹת

TRANSLITERATION: *Ba-ruch a-tah a-do-nai elo-hei-nu me-lech ha-o-lam bo-rei mi-nei me-zo-not*

TRANSLATION: Blessed are You, Lord our G-d, king of the universe, who creates various kinds of food

3

NAME OF BLESSING: *Hagafen*

TYPE OF FOOD: Wine and grape juice

BLESSING (IN HEBREW):

בָּרוּךְ אַתָּה ה׳ אֱלֹהֵינוּ מֶלֶךְ הָעוֹלָם בּוֹרֵא פְּרִי הַגֶּפֶן

TRANSLITERATION: *Ba-ruch a-tah a-do-nai elo-hei-nu me-lech ha-o-lam bo-rei pe-ri ha-ga-fen*

TRANSLATION: Blessed are You, Lord our G-d, king of the universe, who creates the fruit of the vine

4

NAME OF BLESSING: *Ha'eitz*

TYPE OF FOOD: Fruits from permanent trees
Examples: apples, oranges, peaches, grapes, raisins, and all nuts (except peanuts, which are a legume)

BLESSING (IN HEBREW):

בָּרוּךְ אַתָּה ה׳ אֱלֹהֵינוּ מֶלֶךְ הָעוֹלָם בּוֹרֵא פְּרִי הָעֵץ

TRANSLITERATION: *Ba-ruch a-tah a-do-nai elo-hei-nu me-lech ha-o-lam bo-rei pe-ri ha-eitz*

TRANSLATION: Blessed are You, Lord our G-d, king of the universe, who creates the fruit of the tree

5

NAME OF BLESSING: *Ha'adamah*

TYPE OF FOOD: All vegetables and greens, legumes, and some fruits such as bananas, melons, pineapples, and tomatoes

BLESSING (IN HEBREW):

בָּרוּךְ אַתָּה ה׳ אֱלֹהֵינוּ מֶלֶךְ הָעוֹלָם בּוֹרֵא פְּרִי הָאֲדָמָה

TRANSLITERATION: *Ba-ruch a-tah a-do-nai elo-hei-nu me-lech ha-o-lam bo-rei pe-ri ha-a-da-mah*

TRANSLATION: Blessed are You, Lord our G-d, king of the universe, who creates the fruit of the earth

6

NAME OF BLESSING: *Shehakol*

TYPE OF FOOD: All foods and drinks that do not belong to any of the previous five categories. Examples: meat, fish, milk and milk products, eggs, mushrooms, and water. Also, food from the previous categories that have been processed to the point that they no longer possess their original form, such as sugar and candy, fruit and vegetable juices, beer, etc.

BLESSING (IN HEBREW):

בָּרוּךְ אַתָּה ה׳ אֱלֹהֵינוּ מֶלֶךְ הָעוֹלָם שֶׁהַכֹּל נִהְיָה בִּדְבָרוֹ

TRANSLITERATION: *Ba-ruch a-tah a-do-nai elo-hei-nu me-lech ha-o-lam she-ha-kol ni-h'yah bi-d'va-ro*

TRANSLATION: Blessed are You, Lord our G-d, king of the universe, by whose word all things came to be

IMPORTANT NOTE: The above is only a most basic outline of the laws of *berachot*, whose details are quite complex, especially when dealing with food combinations consisting of ingredients from various groups.

Signs and identifiers

The human world is a fusion of abstract ideals and concrete matter, as the objects that populate our lives are infused with the function and significance we impart to them. A nation's flag, a historical document, a wedding ring—these are hallowed objects, suffused with the values and commitments they personify.

In this section we look at three mitzvot that exemplify the cheftza shel mitzvah, *the "object of a divine commandment": the* mezuzah, *a parchment scroll affixed to the doorpost of the Jewish home;* tefillin, *black leather boxes containing scriptural verses placed on the head and arm; and* tzitzit, *woolen threads tied to a four-cornered garment, worn as a reminder to observe the mitzvot. These signs and identifiers are holy objects, in which material, function, and mindful purpose join to create a physical embodiment of a divine ideal and desire.*

 MIDRASH TANCHUMA, *VA'EIRA 15*

Once there was a king who decreed: "The people of Rome are forbidden to go down to Syria, and the people of Syria are forbidden to go up to Rome." So too, when G-d created the world, He decreed: "The heavens are G-d's, and the earth is given to man" (Psalms 115:16).

But when the Creator desired to give the Torah, He rescinded the original decree, and said: "The lower realms may ascend to the higher realms, and the higher realms may descend to the lower realms. And I Myself shall begin." As it is written, "G-d came down on Mount Sinai" (Exodus 19:20); and then it says, "And to Moses He said: Go up to G-d" (ibid., 24:1).

 R. MENACHEM M. SCHNEERSON
BASED ON *LIKUTEI SICHOT, 1:40–41 AND 15:205*

The Talmud (*Yoma* 28b) relates that before the revelation at Sinai, our ancestors studied the Torah and fulfilled its precepts. What, then, was the significance of the "Giving of the Torah" at Mount Sinai?

The Midrash describes how, originally, there was a "decree" separating the higher, spiritual realms from the lower, material realms, until the Almighty revoked this decree at Sinai. The meaning of this is that before Sinai, a person could perform a holy and spiritual act, but while the action sanctified and elevated the person who performed it, it had no real effect on the physical world. In commanding us the mitzvot at Sinai, G-d empowered us to create "an object of a mitzvah"—a physical object through which a divine desire is actualized. Every time we do a mitzvah, the object with which it is performed is infused with holiness.

Jew in Black and White, Marc Chagall, Russia, 1914

MEZUZAH

Mezuzah in case, Central Europe, late 19th—early 20th century

Judaism embraces the totality of life. The mezuzah articulates this truth by defining the home—the kitchen, the bedroom, the children's playroom, the basement workshop—as a sacred space. A small parchment scroll, inscribed with verses affirming the unity and love of G-d and the commitment to study the divine wisdom and fulfill the divine commandments, is affixed to the doorway of every room, dedicating the myriad activities of home life to the purpose of making G-d a home in the world.

The doorway marks the boundary that separates the home from the street; at the same time, the doorway both restricts and facilitates the passage between the two domains. On this juncture of the personal and the public, of the familial and the foreign, we affix the mezuzah. The mezuzah thus serves a dual role: to guard and protect the Jewish home from all that may threaten it, materially or spiritually, from without; and to extend the positive influence of the sanctum we create within to the world at large.

MAIMONIDES, *MISHNEH TORAH, LAWS OF MEZUZAH, 6:13*

A person should be diligent in the observance of the mitzvah of mezuzah, as it is an obligation that is constantly incumbent upon everyone. Whenever a person enters or leaves the house, they will encounter the oneness of the divine name and be reminded of the love of G-d. This will rouse a person from their slumber and their obsession with the temporal vanities of the world, and bring them to recognize that there is nothing of enduring value save the knowledge of the Creator and following the paths of righteousness. The early sages said: "Whoever has tefillin on his head and arm, tzitzit on his garment, and a mezuzah on his doorway is as-

sured not to sin, as he has many reminders" (Talmud, *Menachot* 43b). These are the angels who will save a person from sinning, as it is stated (Psalms 34:8): "The angel of G-d camps around those who fear Him, and rescues them."

TALMUD, *AVODAH ZARAH 11a*

Onkelos the son of Kalonymus [and a nephew of the Roman emperor Titus] converted to Judaism. The emperor sent a contingent of soldiers to arrest him. He drew them in with teachings from the Scripture, and they converted. The emperor sent another contingent of Romans after him, saying to them, "Do not say any-

*Mezuzah case,
ceMMent Design, Jaffa,
Israel, 2018*

שְׁמַע יִשְׂרָאֵל יְדוָד אֱלֹהֵינוּ יְדוָד אֶחָד וְאָהַבְתָּ אֵת
יְדוָד אֱלֹהֶיךָ בְּכָל לְבָבְךָ וּבְכָל נַפְשְׁךָ וּבְכָל מְאֹדֶךָ וְהָיוּ
הַדְּבָרִים הָאֵלֶּה אֲשֶׁר אָנֹכִי מְצַוְּךָ הַיּוֹם עַל לְבָבֶךָ וְשִׁנַּנְתָּם
לְבָנֶיךָ וְדִבַּרְתָּ בָּם בְּשִׁבְתְּךָ בְּבֵיתֶךָ וּבְלֶכְתְּךָ בַדֶּרֶךְ
וּבְשָׁכְבְּךָ וּבְקוּמֶךָ וּקְשַׁרְתָּם לְאוֹת עַל יָדֶךָ וְהָיוּ לְטֹטָפֹת
בֵּין עֵינֶיךָ וּכְתַבְתָּם עַל מְזוּזֹות בֵּיתֶךָ וּבִשְׁעָרֶיךָ
וְהָיָה אִם שָׁמֹעַ תִּשְׁמְעוּ אֶל מִצְוֹתַי אֲשֶׁר אָנֹכִי
מְצַוֶּה אֶתְכֶם הַיּוֹם לְאַהֲבָה אֶת יְדוָד אֱלֹהֵיכֶם וּלְעָבְדוֹ
בְּכָל לְבַבְכֶם וּבְכָל נַפְשְׁכֶם וְנָתַתִּי מְטַר אַרְצְכֶם בְּעִתּוֹ
יוֹרֶה וּמַלְקוֹשׁ וְאָסַפְתָּ דְגָנֶךָ וְתִירֹשְׁךָ וְיִצְהָרֶךָ וְנָתַתִּי
עֵשֶׂב בְּשָׂדְךָ לִבְהֶמְתֶּךָ וְאָכַלְתָּ וְשָׂבָעְתָּ הִשָּׁמְרוּ לָכֶם
פֶּן יִפְתֶּה לְבַבְכֶם וְסַרְתֶּם וַעֲבַדְתֶּם אֱלֹהִים אֲחֵרִים
וְהִשְׁתַּחֲוִיתֶם לָהֶם וְחָרָה אַף יְדוָד בָּכֶם וְעָצַר אֶת
הַשָּׁמַיִם וְלֹא יִהְיֶה מָטָר וְהָאֲדָמָה לֹא תִתֵּן אֶת יְבוּלָהּ
וַאֲבַדְתֶּם מְהֵרָה מֵעַל הָאָרֶץ הַטֹּבָה אֲשֶׁר יְדוָד נֹתֵן לָכֶם
וְשַׂמְתֶּם אֶת דְּבָרַי אֵלֶּה עַל לְבַבְכֶם וְעַל נַפְשְׁכֶם וּקְשַׁרְתֶּם
אֹתָם לְאוֹת עַל יֶדְכֶם וְהָיוּ לְטוֹטָפֹת בֵּין עֵינֵיכֶם וְלִמַּדְתֶּם
אֹתָם אֶת בְּנֵיכֶם לְדַבֵּר בָּם בְּשִׁבְתְּךָ בְּבֵיתֶךָ וּבְלֶכְתְּךָ
בַדֶּרֶךְ וּבְשָׁכְבְּךָ וּבְקוּמֶךָ וּכְתַבְתָּם עַל מְזוּזוֹת בֵּיתֶךָ
וּבִשְׁעָרֶיךָ לְמַעַן יִרְבּוּ יְמֵיכֶם וִימֵי בְנֵיכֶם עַל הָאֲדָמָה
אֲשֶׁר נִשְׁבַּע יְדוָד לַאֲבֹתֵיכֶם לָתֵת לָהֶם כִּימֵי הַשָּׁמַיִם
עַל הָאָרֶץ

OUT OF RESPECT FOR ITS SANCTITY, THE DIVINE NAME IS NOT FULLY REPRODUCED IN THIS IMAGE

PARCHMENT AND COVER Mezuzah cases come in a great variety of materials and forms, including plain plastic cases, transparent cases that display the parchment scroll within, and cases of ceramic or precious metals exquisitely crafted in the spirit of "beautifying the mitzvah." Ultimately, however, the case is only for protection and decoration; the mitzvah of mezuzah is fulfilled with the mezuzah scroll inside it, which is inscribed with the first two sections of the Shema (Deuteronomy 6:4–9 and 11:13–21). If the scroll is not written according to the guidelines of Torah law, or if even a single letter is faded or cracked, the mezuzah is invalid.

thing to him." As they were taking him away, he said to them, "Let me tell you just an ordinary thing: The officer carries the torch before the captain, the captain carries the torch before the duke, the duke before the bishop, the bishop before the king. But does the king carry a torch for any person?" "No," they said. Said he, "Yet G-d carries the torch before Israel, as it is written (Exodus 13:21), *G-d went before them ... in a pillar of fire to illuminate for them*." They, too, converted.

The emperor sent another cohort after him, and said to them, "Do not converse with him at all." As they took him away, he saw the mezuzah that was fixed on the doorframe and he placed his hand on it, saying to them, "Now what is this?" Said they to him, "You tell us." Said he: "According to universal custom, the mortal king sits inside, and his servants keep guard on him on the outside. But the Almighty—His servants are inside their homes, and He guards them from without; as it is written (Psalms 121:8), *G-d shall guard your going and your coming, now and evermore*." They, too, converted to Judaism. The emperor sent for him no more.

❂ BASIC LAWS OF MEZUZAH

■ Two Torah sections, *Shema* (Deuteronomy 6:4–9) and *Ve'hayah im shamoa* (ibid., 11:13–21), are written on a single sheet of parchment by a trained Torah scribe.

■ It is customary to inscribe the divine name *Shadai* (which is also an acronym for the phrase "guardian of the doors of Israel") on the back of the parchment, opposite the space between the two sections. The inside of the scroll, however, should not contain anything other than the above Torah passages.

■ The mezuzah is folded by rolling it from the end of the written line to its beginning, so that a reader opening it encounters the beginning of the text.

■ The mezuzah is then placed in a protective case and affixed to the side post of the doorway with nails (or some other device that fixes it firmly in place).

■ Before affixing it to the doorpost, one should recite the blessing: *Blessed are You, Lord our G-d, king of the universe, who has sanctified us with His commandments and commanded us to affix a mezuzah.* When affixing a number of mezuzot one after the other, the blessing is made only once.

■ Every room in the house requires a mezuzah, if it meets the following criteria: it has a minimum area of four cubits by four cubits (approx. 36 square feet); the doorway has two doorposts and a lintel; the doorway is at least ten handbreadths (approx. 32 inches) high.

■ A doorless doorway does not require a mezuzah, according to some opinions. (In practice, we affix a mezuzah to such a doorway, but without reciting the blessing.)

■ A room whose designated use is of an undignified nature (e.g., a lavatory or bathroom) does not require a mezuzah.

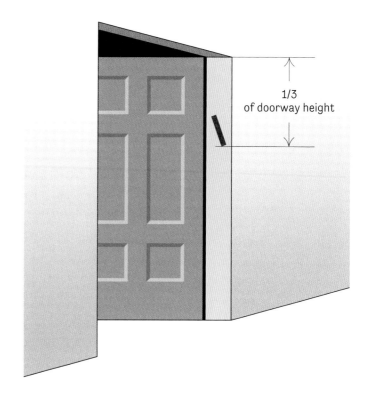

1/3 of doorway height

■ A room that has many doorways requires a mezuzah for each doorway, even though one generally enters and leaves through only one of them.

■ Only roofed dwellings require a mezuzah. However, all doorways leading to a room requiring a mezuzah likewise require a mezuzah. Mezuzahs are therefore affixed to gateways of courtyards, alleyways, and cities, when these lead to houses of human habitation.

■ The mezuzah is affixed within the doorway, at the lower part of the top third of the doorpost. It should be placed at the right-hand side as one enters the room.

■ According to some opinions, the mezuzah should be set upright; others, however, maintain that it should be set horizontally, to the width of the doorway. Our custom, therefore, is to place it diagonally, with the top of the mezuzah pointed to the inside of the room.

■ A mezuzah should be checked twice in seven years, to ensure that a letter has not become torn or faded. Some have the custom of checking their mezuzahs each year in the month of Elul, in preparation for the High Holidays.

From *Shulchan Aruch, Yoreh De'ah,* 285–291

TEFILLIN

"Place these words of Mine upon your hearts and upon your souls; bind them as a sign upon your hand, and they shall be as phylacteries between your eyes." Four times the commandment to wear tefillin is repeated in the Torah, indicating the four Torah passages that are inscribed on parchment scrolls and inserted in the tefillin: Exodus 13:1–10 and 13:11–16, and Deuteronomy 6:4–9 and 11:13–21.

The head-tefillin are placed above the forehead, and the hand-tefillin are placed opposite the heart and wound around the arm and hand—signifying the integration of our diverse faculties of mind, feeling, and deed, and their dedication to serving our Creator.

YIGAEL YADIN

*Tefillin, discovered at Qumran
in the Judean Desert, circa 1st century BCE*

 CHINUCH, *MITZVAH 422*

The four passages in the tefillin contain the following principles: the sovereignty of G-d, the oneness of G-d, and the Exodus from Egypt, from which follows the belief that G-d created the world and governs all that transpires here below. These are the foundations of the Jewish faith. We were therefore instructed to set these fundamental precepts ... upon our head between our eyes, and on our arm opposite our heart ... to reinforce our remembrance of them and increase our diligence in the ways of G-d.

 TALMUD, *BERACHOT 6a*

How do we know that G-d puts on tefillin? It is written (Isaiah 62:8): "G-d has sworn ... by His arm of might." ...

What is written in G-d's tefillin? The verse, "Who is like Your people Israel, one nation in the land" (I Chronicles 17:21).... G-d says to Israel: You have made Me singular in the world, with the proclamation [inscribed in the tefillin worn by the Jewish people,] "Hear O Israel, G-d is our Lord, G-d is one"; so I will make you a singular entity in the world.

what's in the tefillin

THE SCROLLS

Inside the tefillin are parchment scrolls on which four key Torah passages are handwritten by a specially trained scribe. In the hand-tefillin, the four passages are inscribed on a single scroll; in the head-tefillin, they are inscribed on four separate strips of parchment.

The four passages are:

Ⓐ "Sanctify to Me all the firstborn...." (Exodus 13:1–10)

Ⓑ "And it shall be when G-d will bring you into the land...." (Exodus 13:11–16)

Ⓒ "Hear O Israel...." (Deuteronomy 6:4–9)

Ⓓ "And it shall be, if you will hearken...." (Deuteronomy 11:13–21)

HAND-TEFILLIN

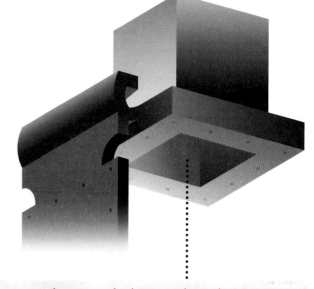

וידבר ידוד אל משה לאמר קדש לי כל בכור פטר כל רחם בבני ישראל באדם ובבהמה לי ה
את היום הזה אשר יצאתם ממצרים מבית עבדים כי בחזק יד הוציא ידוד אתכם מזה ולא
בחדש האביב והיה כי יביאך ידוד אל ארץ הכנעני והחתי והאמרי והחוי והיבוסי אשר נ
זבת חלב ודבש ועבדת את העבדה הזאת בחדש הזה שבעת ימים תאכל מצת וביום ה
את שבעת הימים ולא יראה לך חמץ ולא יראה לך שאר בכל גבלך והגדת לבנך ביום ז
ידוד לי בצאתי ממצרים והיה לאות על ידך ולזכרון בין עיניך למען תהיה תורת ידו
ידוד ממצרים ושמרת את החקה הזאת למועדה מימים ימימה

Ⓐ Ⓑ Ⓒ Ⓓ

THE BOXES

The boxes are made of the hide of a kosher animal and are colored black. The hand-tefillin has one large compartment; the head-tefillin has four compartments, for the four scrolls.

THE STRAPS

The straps used to bind the tefillin to the head and arm are made of the hide of a kosher animal and colored black. The hand-tefillin has an adjustable loop to tie on the upper arm; the head-tefillin has a larger, fixed loop to fit the head.

SHIN-DALET-YUD

The three Hebrew letters that spell the divine name *Shadai* ("almighty" and "all-sufficient") are represented in the tefillin: the letter *shin* appears on both sides of the head-tefillin box; the knot in the head-tefillin strap is in the shape of a *dalet*; and the knot of the hand-tefillin strap has the shape of a *yud*.

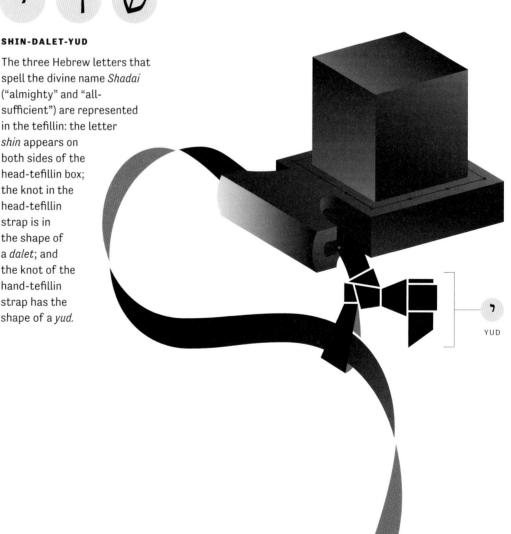

YUD

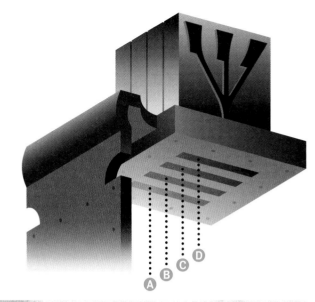

HEAD-TEFILLIN

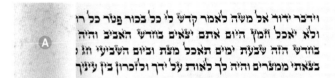

A
וַיְדַבֵּר יְדוָד אֶל מֹשֶׁה לֵּאמֹר קַדֶּשׁ לִי כָל בְּכוֹר פֶּטֶר כָּל רֶ
וְלֹא יֵאָכֵל חָמֵץ הַיּוֹם אַתֶּם יֹצְאִים בְּחֹדֶשׁ הָאָבִיב וְהָיָה
בַּחֹדֶשׁ הַזֶּה שִׁבְעַת יָמִים תֹּאכַל מַצֹּת וּבַיּוֹם הַשְּׁבִיעִי חַג ל
בְּצֵאתִי מִמִּצְרַיִם וְהָיָה לְךָ לְאוֹת עַל יָדְךָ וּלְזִכָּרוֹן בֵּין עֵינֶיךָ

B
וְהָיָה כִּי יְבִאֲךָ יְדוָד אֶל אֶרֶץ הַכְּנַעֲנִי כַּאֲשֶׁר נִשְׁבַּע לְךָ וְ
וְכָל פֶּטֶר חֲמֹר תִּפְדֶּה בְשֶׂה וְאִם לֹא תִפְדֶּה וַעֲרַפְתּוֹ וְכֹ
יְדוָד מִמִּצְרַיִם מִבֵּית עֲבָדִים וַיְהִי כִּי הִקְשָׁה פַרְעֹה לְשַׁלְּ
רֶחֶם הַזְּכָרִים וְכָל בְּכוֹר בָּנַי אֶפְדֶּה וְהָיָה לְאוֹת עַל יָדְכָה וּל

C
שְׁמַע יִשְׂרָאֵל יְדוָד אֱלֹהֵינוּ יְדוָד אֶחָד וְאָהַבְתָּ אֵת יְדוָ
נַפְשְׁךָ וּבְכָל מְאֹדֶךָ וְהָיוּ הַדְּבָרִים הָאֵלֶּה אֲשֶׁר אָנֹכִי מְצַ
לְבָנֶיךָ וְדִבַּרְתָּ בָּם בְּשִׁבְתְּךָ בְּבֵיתֶךָ וּבְלֶכְתְּךָ בַדֶּרֶךְ וּ
לְאוֹת עַל יָדֶךָ וְהָיוּ לְטֹטָפֹת בֵּין עֵינֶיךָ וּכְתַבְתָּם עַל מְזֻזֹת בּ

D
וְהָיָה אִם שָׁמֹעַ תִּשְׁמְעוּ אֶל מִצְוֹתַי אֲשֶׁר א
וְנָתַתִּי עֵשֶׂב בְּשָׂדְךָ לִבְהֶמְתֶּךָ וְאָכַלְתָּ וְשָׂבָעְתָּ הִשָּׁמְרוּ לָכֶ
יְכוּלָהּ וַאֲבַדְתֶּם מְהֵרָה מֵעַל הָאָרֶץ הַטֹּבָה אֲשֶׁר יְדוָד נ
בְּשִׁבְתְּךָ בְּבֵיתֶךָ וּבְלֶכְתְּךָ בַדֶּרֶךְ וּבְשָׁכְבְּךָ וּבְקוּמֶךָ וּכְתַבְתָּם

SHIN

THE TWO SHINS

Worked into the leather of the
head-tefillin box are two raised *shins*:
a standard three-headed *shin* on
the wearer's right side of the box,
and a unique four-headed *shin* on
the wearer's left side of the box.
These represent two forms of
"engraved letters": a protruding *shin*
on the right, and a recessed *shin*
formed by the three spaces
between the four raised stems
of *shin* on the left.

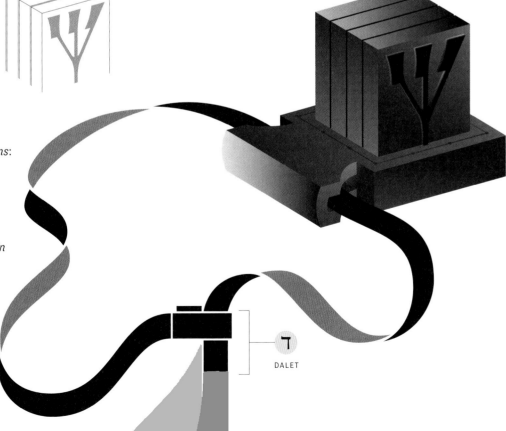

DALET

how to put on tefillin

1   **PLACEMENT OF THE HAND-TEFILLIN**
The hand-tefillin goes on the weaker arm—on the left arm
for a right-handed person, and on the right arm for a lefty.
   Roll up your sleeve so that the tefillin box is in direct
contact with your arm. Put your arm through the loop
formed by the knotted strap. Place the tefillin box up on
your biceps, just below the halfway point between the
shoulder and the elbow, directly across from your heart.

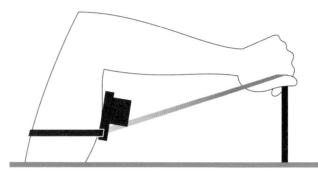

2   **BLESSING ON HAND-TEFILLIN**
Recite while tightening tefillin to your upper arm:

בָּרוּךְ אַתָּה ה׳ אֱלֹהֵינוּ מֶלֶךְ הָעוֹלָם אֲשֶׁר קִדְּשָׁנוּ
בְּמִצְוֹתָיו וְצִוָּנוּ לְהָנִיחַ תְּפִלִּין

TRANSLITERATION
*Ba-ruch a-tah a-do-nai elo-hei-nu me-lech ha-o-lam a-sher
ki-de-sha-nu be-mitz-vo-tav vi-tzi-va-nu le-ha-ni-ach tefillin*

TRANSLATION
Blessed are You, Lord our G-d, king of the universe,
who has sanctified us with His commandments,
and commanded us to put on tefillin

3   **TYING AND WRAPPING THE HAND-TEFILLIN**
After securing the tefillin to your upper arm, wrap the
tefillin strap seven times around your forearm, and once
around your palm.

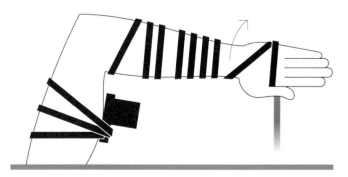

4   **PLACEMENT OF THE HEAD-TEFILLIN**
Place the head-tefillin box just above your forehead.
Center it directly above the point between your eyes.
The knot on the back of the loop should rest on the base of
your skull, and the two ends of the strap should hang
down the front of your torso, to the right and to the left.

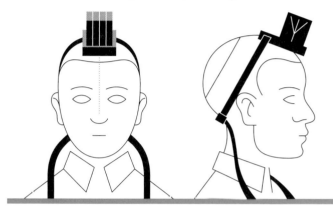

5   **BLESSING ON HEAD-TEFILLIN** (ASHKENAZIC CUSTOM)
Recite while adjusting head-tefillin in place:

בָּרוּךְ אַתָּה ה׳ אֱלֹהֵינוּ מֶלֶךְ הָעוֹלָם אֲשֶׁר קִדְּשָׁנוּ
בְּמִצְוֹתָיו וְצִוָּנוּ עַל מִצְוַת תְּפִלִּין

TRANSLITERATION
*Ba-ruch a-tah a-do-nai e-lo-hei-nu me-lech ha-o-lam a-sher
ki-de-sha-nu be-mitz-vo-tav vi-tzi-va-nu al mitz-vat tefillin*

TRANSLATION
Blessed are You, Lord our G-d, king of the universe,
who has sanctified us with His commandments,
and commanded us concerning the mitzvah of tefillin

6   **FINISH WRAPPING THE HAND-TEFILLIN**
Wrap the remainder of the arm-tefillin strap around
your middle finger and palm.

Note: There are variations in custom on how the hand-
tefillin are tied and wrapped. Presented here are general
directions. The illustrations reflect the Chabad custom.
   Tefillin are generally worn every day except Shabbat and
festivals for the morning prayer service. But the mitzvah
can be fulfilled by putting them on for even a brief moment
any time in the daytime. This is also an ideal time to recite
the Shema (see p. 266).

LIEL LEIBOVITZ
TABLET MAGAZINE, DECEMBER 30, 2015

The big guy made me do it.

It was late morning on a Wednesday in July, when Jerusalem oozes with a thick heat that traps you inside of it, like a fly in amber, and I was at the Kotel, waiting for the women in my family to conclude their visit to their side of the sacred stone wall. Call me a creep, but I've never really warmed up to the mossy old remnant: Every time I paid it a visit, my mind never failed to enumerate the many reasons for the wall's singular significance, but the heart was never roused from its slumber. Emotionally, standing at the foot of the wall was like gazing at the Mona Lisa—so set are we with an expectation of a transformative emotional experience that by the time we cram in with the masses and find ourselves in the presence of the real thing we can't help but feel disappointed.

As I'd done on each of my previous visits, I nodded respectfully at the wall. And just as it had done in the past, it stood there, craggy and quiet. That would've been it, I suppose, if the big guy hadn't intervened.

A sizable man, he stood there, five feet from the holiest, underneath a dark awning, and motioned for me to come near. His beard was red and his shirt white and dotted with sweat. "Put on tefillin," he said. It wasn't a question; it was a command.

Ordinarily, I would've nodded my head in that way those of us who live in big cities eventually develop to telegraph to panhandlers, perverts, and other violators of our physical space that we're too busy to give them the time of day but too benevolent to tell them straight up to get lost. But something about the big guy's invitation appealed. His tone was fatherly, as if he was gently persuading me to do something that was entirely to my benefit but that I, lacking the proper faculties, had failed to understand was necessary. I stepped forward and stood there in silence as the big guy wrapped the leather straps on my arm and placed the second black box on my head. He asked how long it had been; I said not since my bar mitzvah. The big guy chuckled. "That's what they all say," he bellowed. Then, he gave me a printout of a blessing and urged me to recite it while I looked at the wall.

I can't tell you what happened next, mostly because I don't understand it myself. Those of us who write about religion are doomed to live with the knowledge that we can describe everything about it—the customs, the rituals, the history, the feuds—except for that core feeling, the transcendent tremor that drives us to truly believe, that graceful feeling that, like sex and songs and other truly blessed things, cannot be captured by the hole-y nets of words. I'll say just that I felt something, something I never felt before, something joyful. The drive back to Tel Aviv was longer than usual that day, and dense with contemplation. By the time I was back in an earthlier realm, I had vowed to get myself a pair of tefillin immediately upon my return to New York and start putting them on every day.

Doing that—facilitated by my dear friend Menachem Butler—hardly helped me understand more. Every morning, for months now, I rise, wrap the straps around my arm and over my head, read the prayers, and fret: Am I doing this right? Is the ritual's force diminished by my disregard for so many other commandments? Can I truly clear my heart and my mind as I pray and maintain the purity of intention one desires when attempting to converse with the heavens? These are deep questions, and I've got no good answers. I put them on, even though I don't fully understand why.

Which, it turns out, is more or less the point.

You don't have to be much of a theologian to see how different tefillin are from most of the other signposts traditional Jews erect to identify themselves: A beautiful bit of hardware, it requires deed first and only then contemplation. The prayer, the meditation, come second; first come the leather straps.

This was the insight of Menachem Schneerson, the celebrated late Lubavitcher Rebbe and the great modern popularizer of tefillin. In 1967, shortly before the Six Day War, the Rebbe launched a global campaign, sending out emissaries—and, later, Mitzvah Tanks, Ryder trucks emblazoned with the Chabad logo—to entice Jewish men everywhere to roll up their sleeves and perform the act that, until then, was largely the domain of the meticulously observant. Jews being Jews, the Rebbe was immediately criticized: What, asked some of his detractors, was the point of a Jew putting on tefillin if he then hurried to the nearest diner and ordered a bacon cheeseburger for lunch?

The Rebbe was unfazed. Sometimes, he argued, commitment transcended understanding. That's why the Israelites, on the cusp of being presented with the Torah at Sinai, replied by saying *Na'aseh ve'nishmah*, we'll do first and only then listen. And that's why you put the arm tefillin on first; the head—the intellect—can only join in once the deed has begun.

Not that deed in and of itself is enough: Any system of faith predicated solely on blind obedience is likely to turn disastrous. But as I stood at my breakfast table, morning after morning, with the velvety tefillin pouch at hand, I found understanding slowly trickling in. Not, mind you, of any divine mysteries, nor of any hidden spiritual realms previously inaccessible; these will come later, if they come at all. What I felt was simpler than the intricate kabbalistic concepts associated with putting on tefillin; what I felt—what I continue to feel—is a sense of realignment, slight but ever so important. When I leave the house now, I do it after having surveyed the expanse of my universe and set the Lord at its center. I may then munch on that cheeseburger for lunch, but even eating the treyfest of treats, I still retain something of the *kavanah*, the intention, generated during those few moments of morningtime

consecration. Put simply, no matter how I choose to manifest my relationship with the Creator, I start each day by acknowledging that this relationship exists, that it matters, and that everything that follows in the day should be, in part, a reflection on how my thoughts and my actions conform to or challenge my faith.

In part, this should come as no surprise. Tefillin are, for lack of a better term, objects of spiritual technology, and like all great and groundbreaking technologies they work not so much by performing a particular function but by expanding our understanding of what is now possible. You needn't ever have boarded an airplane and flown across the ocean, for example, to be fully aware that the possibility of intercontinental travel exists; when you think of the world accessible to you, then, you think not only of your street or your block or the next town over but of China and England and Nigeria, too, which means that, however subtly, you see yourself as a citizen of the world. By putting on tefillin, you see yourself as a child of G-d, bound by his commandments and blessed by his love; what that actually means is entirely up to you to figure out, a lifelong task that's of singular importance and unparalleled pleasure.

And so I—a few cheeseburgers removed from the faith of my fathers, a pleasure-seeker who slinks back home after Friday night services only to binge on Netflix, an intermittent reader of the Talmud and *Mad* magazine, a frequent blasphemer, a flawed believer, brimming with doubt—continue to welcome each dawn with phylacterial devotion. It might not make me more religious, more insightful, more transcendent, a better Jew, but it sends me on my way each day with my eyes watching G-d. These days, that's nothing short of a miracle.

TZITZIT

The Hebrew word tzitzit *means "strings" or "fringes"; it also means "to look upon" and "peek through." Tzitzit is thus the Torah's name for the fringes it instructs us to tie on the four corners of our garments to serve as a visible reminder to resist sin and to fulfill the commandments of the Torah.*

Only a four-cornered garment requires tzitzit. Today, as most people don't wear four-cornered cloaks, we fulfill this mitzvah in two ways. The tallit gadol *("large garment") is a four-cornered prayer shawl in which we wrap ourselves during prayer. The* tallit katan *("small garment") is a smaller four-cornered garment worn under (or over) the shirt, which enables us to fulfill the mitzvah of tzitzit throughout the day.*

THE BLUE THREAD The Biblical description of tzitzit includes a "thread of blue" (*techelet*) to be incorporated in the fringes. According to the Talmud (*Sotah* 17a), blue is the color of the heavens, reminding the person of the divine sovereignty on high. The dye for this thread was extracted from a sea creature called *chilazon*, which surfaces only once in 70 years, making it a rare and precious commodity. The knowledge of the *techelet* was lost more than 1,000 years ago, and a Kabbalistic tradition holds that it will be rediscovered only in the Messianic era. A number of attempts have been made to revive the *techelet*, most famously by the Hasidic rebbe R. Gershon Hanoch Leiner of Radzin (1839–1891). Today, some communities use various forms of *techelet*, while most follow the established custom of using only white threads.

 NUMBERS 15:37–41

G-d spoke to Moses, saying:

Speak to the children of Israel and say to them: They shall make for themselves tzitzit on the corners of their garments, throughout their generations; and they shall put a thread of blue on the tzitzit of each corner.

This shall be tzitzit for you; you will see it, and you will remember all the commandments of G-d, and you will do them; and you shall not wander after your hearts and after your eyes, after which you go astray.

In order that you shall remember and do all My commandments, and you shall be holy to your G-d.

I am the Lord your G-d, who took you out of the land of Egypt to be your G-d; I am the Lord your G-d.

 RASHI, *NUMBERS 15:39*

"You will remember all the commandments of G-d." The *gematria* (numerical value) of the Hebrew word *tzitzit* is 600, and [each tzitzit has] eight threads and five knots, making 613 (the number of the mitzvot).

how tzitzit are tied

To tie tzitzit, four woolen strings are run through holes made near the corner of the garment, folded in half, and then tied, forming eight strings. One of the strings is longer than the others, and is wound around them. (When a blue string is used, two strings—one blue and one white—are used to form windings.) Depicted here are some of the various customs for tying tzitzit.

Ⓐ **STANDARD ASHKENAZIC** Five double knots separate 39 windings into groups of 7, 8, 11, and 13.

Ⓑ **SEPHARDIC** Five double-knots and 26 windings, in groups of 10, 5, 6, and 5. Each winding is inside a loop of its own.

Ⓒ **ARI AND CHABAD** The same as "Standard Ashkenazic," with the addition that the windings are inside loops containing three windings each. When a knot intersects a group of three, two separate loops are formed on both sides of the knot.

Ⓓ **R. AMRAM GAON** Two single knots frame 39 windings. The windings alternate between white and blue, changing every three windings.

Ⓔ **MAIMONIDES** Two double knots frame 39 windings. The first and last windings are white; the rest are blue. The windings are in loops of 3 except for the first and last three windings, which are grouped by color—one white and two blue.

Ⓕ **GRA** Five double-knots and 39 windings, in groups of 12, 12, 12, and 3. The windings alternate between white and blue every three windings.

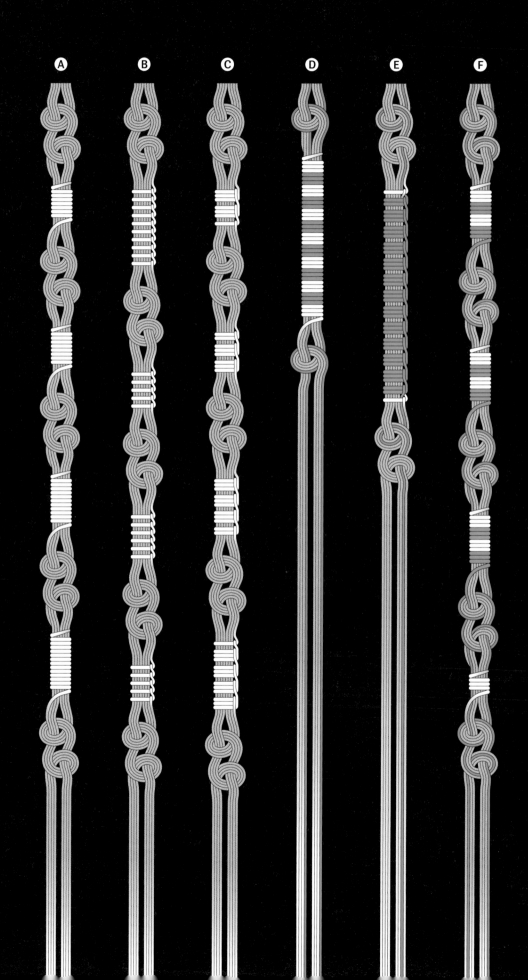

The Jewish Year

4

Time can be seen as linear, a unidirectional arrow that runs from point A to point B. But time is also experienced as a cycle, repeatedly returning to its starting point to traverse a pattern of familiar landmarks.

The Hebrew word for "year," shanah, means both "repetition" and "change," implying an ascending spiral that is both cyclical and progressive. There are the cycles of time: night and day; the weekly cycle of work and rest; the monthly lunar cycle of growth, fullness, regression, and rebirth; the solar seasons; and the annual landmarks of Passover freedom, High Holiday awe, and Purim joy. Yet there is also perpetual advancement and elevation, as "each year there descends from the divine supernal wisdom a new and renewed light that has never shined before … illuminating all the worlds" (Tanya, 4:14).

Our section on The Jewish Year *explores the dynamics of the Jewish calendar, and the observances and inner significance of the festivals and special days that mark its annual circuit through time.*

 LEVITICUS 23:4

These are the appointed times of G-d, callings of holiness, which you shall call forth in their appointed times.

R. MOSES ZACUTO
TIKUN SHOVAVIM, 17a

The holy days and festivals are days on which, in earlier times in Jewish history, there was a bestowal of loving-kindness and miraculous salvation from Above. When these time-junctures realign each year, that divine light shines forth once again, streaming in broad channels, increasing in radiance in all the worlds…. This is the deeper meaning of the verse (Esther 9:28), "These days are remembered and done, in each and every genera-

tion": when remembrance [of these historical events] is evoked here below, they are reenacted on high.

 R. YECHEZKEL PANET
COMMENTARY ON HAGGADAH, S.V. AVADIM HAYINU

By way of a parable: A king was traveling through the wilderness, and his child was thirsty. Instead of sending riders to fetch water, the king instructed that a well be dug at that very spot. For although there was no advantage to this method regarding the need for water in the present moment, in the future, a thirsty person passing by this spot would find water to drink.

See p. 42 for a map of Israel's journey from Egypt to the Holy Land and the annual calendar landmarks it produced.

‹ *Purim noisemaker, Poland, 19th century*

the annual cycle

● Fast days

* One day shorter
  in the Holy Land

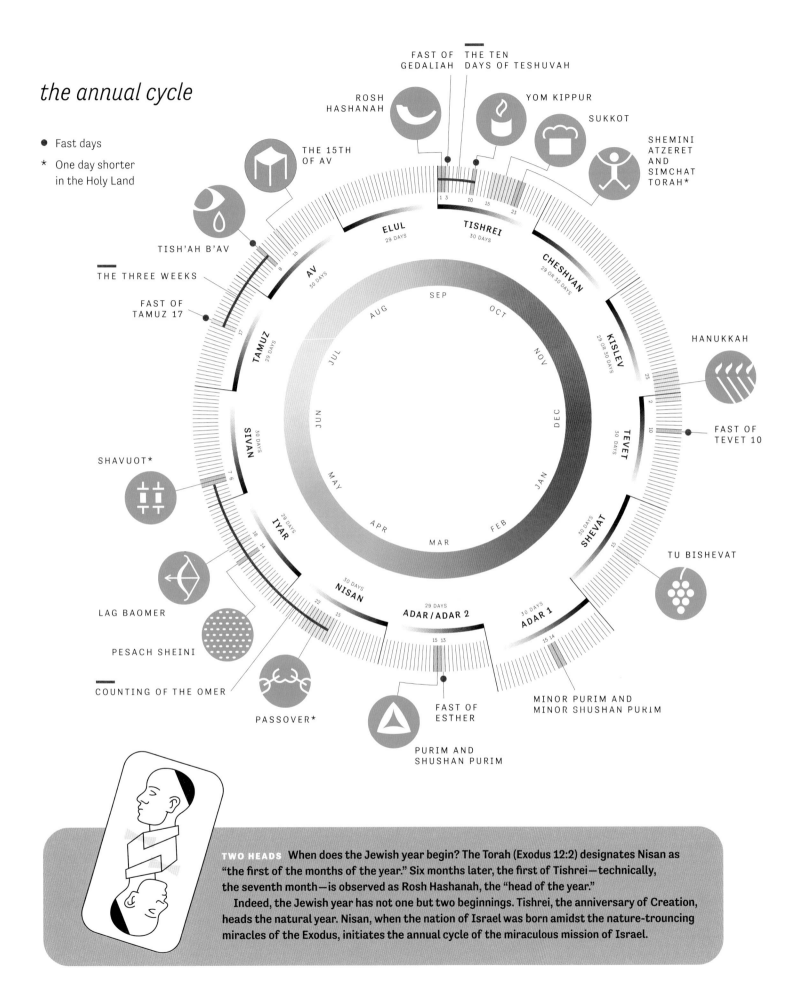

FAST OF GEDALIAH

THE TEN DAYS OF TESHUVAH

ROSH HASHANAH

YOM KIPPUR

SUKKOT

SHEMINI ATZERET AND SIMCHAT TORAH*

THE 15TH OF AV

TISH'AH B'AV

THE THREE WEEKS

FAST OF TAMUZ 17

HANUKKAH

FAST OF TEVET 10

SHAVUOT*

TU BISHEVAT

LAG BAOMER

PESACH SHEINI

COUNTING OF THE OMER

PASSOVER*

FAST OF ESTHER

MINOR PURIM AND MINOR SHUSHAN PURIM

PURIM AND SHUSHAN PURIM

ELUL
29 DAYS

TISHREI
30 DAYS

CHESHVAN
29 OR 30 DAYS

AV
30 DAYS

KISLEV
29 OR 30 DAYS

TAMUZ
29 DAYS

TEVET
30 DAYS

SIVAN
30 DAYS

SHEVAT
30 DAYS

IYAR
29 DAYS

NISAN
30 DAYS

ADAR / ADAR 2
29 DAYS

ADAR 1
30 DAYS

SEP
AUG
OCT
JUL
NOV
JUN
DEC
MAY
JAN
APR
FEB
MAR

TWO HEADS When does the Jewish year begin? The Torah (Exodus 12:2) designates Nisan as "the first of the months of the year." Six months later, the first of Tishrei—technically, the seventh month—is observed as Rosh Hashanah, the "head of the year."

Indeed, the Jewish year has not one but two beginnings. Tishrei, the anniversary of Creation, heads the natural year. Nisan, when the nation of Israel was born amidst the nature-trouncing miracles of the Exodus, initiates the annual cycle of the miraculous mission of Israel.

The Jewish calendar

Jewish time is a complex marriage of two seemingly incompatible systems—the lunar month and the solar year. On the mystical level, the solar cycle represents consistency and immutability, while the lunar cycle embodies flux and rebirth. The Torah insists that both systems should be incorporated into the Jewish experience of time, mirroring the truth that in our own lives, we have need for immutable truths as well as for innovation and self-reinvention.

SIGHTING THE MOON For seventeen centuries, the Jewish calendar was set month by month by the Sanhedrin, the 71-member tribunal that served as the highest authority of Torah law. Each month, witnesses who sighted the new moon would testify before the Sanhedrin, who would then proclaim and "consecrate" the new month. The Sanhedrin would also look for signs that the annual festival cycle was falling behind its mandated alignment with the seasons, and would decide if the addition of a 13th month to the year was warranted. But in the centuries following the destruction of the Second Temple, the deteriorating conditions in the Holy Land placed the continued functioning of the Sanhedrin in jeopardy, prompting Hillel II (who served as president of the Sanhedrin in the 4th century CE) to formulate the perpetual Jewish calendar depicted on pages 329 and 331.

 TALMUD AND RASHI, *SANHEDRIN 42a*

To the moon, G-d said: She shall be renewed each month. She is a crown of glory for [the people of Israel], a sign for them, who calculate [their calendar] by her, that they are destined to be renewed in their greatness, as she is renewed.

 TZEMACH TZEDEK, *OHR HATORAH, EMOR, P. 580*

The monthly "sanctification of the moon" prayer includes the phrase, "Just as I dance opposite you and cannot touch you...." What is the connection between dancing and the moon?

In a dance, the dancers begin by facing away from each other, then draw close, and then once again distance themselves. This is like the light of the moon. In the beginning of the [Jewish] month it receives [light] from the sun and becomes progressively more luminous, until the middle of the month. Then it begins to darken, so that by the [end of the month] it has become extremely small. Then, on the first of the new month, the moon is born anew. So it is with the union of the souls of Israel with G-dliness, whose relationship resembles that of the sun and the moon: distancing oneself, drawing near, distancing oneself, and so on.

{ALSO SEE CITATION FROM MIDRASH RABBAH ON P. 62}

the nineteen-year cycle of the Jewish calendar

19 SOLAR YEARS
228 MONTHS
6,939.75 DAYS

	YEAR 1	YEAR 2	YEAR 3	YEAR 4	YEAR 5	YEAR 6	YEAR 7	YEAR 8	YEAR 9	YEAR 10	YEAR 11	YEAR 12	YEAR 13	YEAR 14	YEAR 15	YEAR 16	YEAR 17	YEAR 18	YEAR 19
SOLAR YEAR	365.25 DAYS	365.25 DAYS	365.25 DAYS	365.25 DAYS	365.25 DAYS	365.25 DAYS	365.25 DAYS	365.25 DAYS	365.25 DAYS	365.25 DAYS	365.25 DAYS	365.25 DAYS	365.25 DAYS	365.25 DAYS	365.25 DAYS	365.25 DAYS	365.25 DAYS	365.25 DAYS	365.25 DAYS
JEWISH YEAR	353 DAYS	354 DAYS	385 DAYS	355 DAYS	353 DAYS	384 DAYS	355 DAYS	383 DAYS	355 DAYS	354 DAYS	385 DAYS	355 DAYS	354 DAYS	383 DAYS	355 DAYS	354 DAYS	383 DAYS	355 DAYS	385 DAYS
	YEAR 5777	YEAR 5778	YEAR 5779	YEAR 5780	YEAR 5781	YEAR 5782	YEAR 5783	YEAR 5784	YEAR 5785	YEAR 5786	YEAR 5787	YEAR 5788	YEAR 5789	YEAR 5790	YEAR 5791	YEAR 5792	YEAR 5793	YEAR 5794	YEAR 5795

OCT 3, 2016 · SEPT 21, 2017 · SEPT 10, 2018 · SEPT 30, 2019 · SEPT 19, 2020 · SEPT 7, 2021 · SEPT 26, 2022 · SEPT 16, 2023 · OCT 3, 2024 · SEPT 23, 2025 · SEPT 12, 2026 · OCT 2, 2027 · SEPT 21, 2028 · SEPT 10, 2029 · SEPT 28, 2030 · SEPT 18, 2031 · SEPT 6, 2032 · SEPT 24, 2033 · SEPT 14, 2034 · OCT 2, 2035

19 JEWISH YEARS
235 MONTHS
6,940 DAYS

LEAP YEAR

LUNAR MONTHS, SOLAR YEARS The Torah (Exodus 12:2) instructs that "the months of the year" should follow the waxing and waning of the moon, with each new moon marking the start of a new month. As the lunar cycle is approximately 29.5 days, the Jewish month alternates between 29 and 30 days. The Torah also instructs that the Jewish year should be kept aligned with the solar seasons, to ensure that the festival of Passover always occurs in "the month of spring" (Deuteronomy 16:1).

These two systems, however, are not easily synchronized. Twelve lunar months add up to a total of 354 days—about 11 days short of the 365.25-day solar cycle. To resolve this inconsistency, a 13th month is added every two or three years—seven times in a 19-year cycle.

Depicted above is the 19-year cycle that began on October 3, 2016.

SANCTIFICATION OF THE MOON Once a month, a special prayer called *kiddush levanah* ("sanctification of the moon") is recited in tribute to G-d's monthly renewal of the moon and His promised renewal of the Jewish people.

Kiddush Levana on Carroll Street, Zalman Kleinman, Brooklyn, New York, 1981

The High Holidays

The High Holidays, also called the "Days of Awe," are the most solemn days of the Jewish year. Two events inform the significance of this time-period—one universal, and the other a landmark of Jewish history.

The first day of Tishrei is the anniversary of the creation of the first man and woman, Adam and Eve. The day is accordingly marked as Rosh Hashanah, the "head of the year," when we recommit ourselves to the purpose for which we were created, and the Creator reaffirms His investment in His creation.

The second event relates to the aftermath of the Jewish people's betrayal of their covenant with G-d with the making of the Golden Calf (see p. 40). The forty days that Moses spent on Mount Sinai obtaining G-d's forgiveness—encompassing the whole of the month of Elul and the first ten days of Tishrei—are etched in time as days of repentance and divine compassion. Elul, the closing month of the Jewish year, is a time of soul-searching and reconciliation. This is followed by "ten days of repentance" that begin on Rosh Hashanah and culminate in Yom Kippur, our annual "day of atonement" on which we reconnect with the inviolable point of goodness at the core of our soul.

White cantor's cap, Galicia, early 20th century.
It is customary to wear white on the High Holidays, in evocation of the verse (Isaiah 1:18), "If your sins be as scarlet, they shall be whitened as snow." Also see note on "Kittel" on p. 408.

 **R. SCHNEUR ZALMAN OF LIADI**
LIKUTEI TORAH, RE'EI 32b

The king in the field

It is known that the month of Elul is a time when the "thirteen attributes of divine compassion" are revealed. Yet these are ordinary workdays, not holy days and festivals.

This can be explained with the following parable: Before a king enters the city, the people of the city go out to greet him and receive him out in the field. At that time, anyone who so desires is allowed to approach the king and greet him, and he receives them all with a pleasant countenance, showing a smiling face to all. Then the king enters the city, and the people follow him there. But afterwards, when the king is in the royal palace, one can enter into his presence only when given special permission, which is granted only to the elite of the nation and to special individuals. In the same way, the month of Elul is a time when we are received by the radiance of the divine presence "out in the field."

A prophet attempts to flee his mission to warn the city of Nineveh that it will be destroyed for its sins, is swallowed by a great fish, and lives to learn that what he considered the failure of his prophecy's fulfillment is in G-d's eyes its success. This Biblical account, which is read as part of the Yom Kippur afternoon service, conveys a number of lessons pertinent to the annual day of atonement: that to flee from G-d is, in effect, to flee to Him; the power of prayer to deliver a person, even from the belly of a fish in the depths of the sea; that *teshuvah* (repentance) redeems even the most corrupt of sinners; and G-d's boundless compassion for all of His creations.

Jonah thrown into the sea, Kennicott Hebrew Bible, La Coruña, Spain, 1476

ROSH HASHANAH

The Talmud defines the significance of Rosh Hashanah with three words: sovereignty, remembrance, and shofar. On Rosh Hashanah, we crown G-d king, committing ourselves to unite the whole of Creation under the divine sovereignty. Also on this day, the Almighty evokes the remembrance of each and every one of His creations and decides their fate for the coming year. And on Rosh Hashanah we fulfill the mitzvah of sounding the shofar (ram's horn), which heralds the divine coronation and recalls our merit before the divine throne.

The Hasidic masters note that the literal meaning of *Rosh Hashanah* is not "beginning of the year" but "head of the year." As the head controls the body, so do our actions and resolutions on Rosh Hashanah profoundly affect the entire year.

 PIRKEI D'RABBI ELIEZER, *CHAPTER 11*

When Adam stood on his feet, described in the divine likeness, all the creatures thought him their creator and came to bow to him. Said he to them: "You and I both, come, let us crown the one who created us and confer majesty on Him." For a king cannot crown himself; rather it is the populace who impart sovereignty to him. So Adam proclaimed G-d king, and all other creatures followed suit. And he declared (Psalms 93:1): "G-d has reigned, He is garbed in majesty."

 SIDDUR, *HIGH HOLIDAY LITURGY*

Let us proclaim the power of the holiness of this day
    as it is awesome and astounding.
In it Your kingship is exalted, Your throne with
    lovingkindness is established,
    and You are seated upon it in truth.
True, You are the judge, the indictor,
    the knower, and the witness
    who inscribes and seals, counts and calculates
    who remembers all forgotten things.
You open the book of remembrances, it reads itself,

and every man's signature is in it.
The great shofar is sounded, and a small still voice
    is heard; angels scurry, fear and trembling seize
    them, and they exclaim:
    The day of judgment is here
    for the hosts of the heavens to be reckoned
    in judgment
    as even they are not worthy in Your eyes
    in judgment
    and all inhabitants of the world will pass
    before You like a flock of sheep.
As a shepherd examines his flock
    passing his sheep under his staff
    so do You make pass, and count and calculate,
    and are mindful of every living soul.
    You allocate a portion for each of Your creations
    and inscribe the verdict of their judgment.
On Rosh Hashanah it is inscribed
    and on the Yom Kippur fast day it is sealed:
    How many will pass away
    and how many will be born.
Who will live, and who will die
    who in their allotted time
    and who before their time.
Who by water, and who by fire
    who by sword, and who by beast
    who by hunger, and who by thirst
    who by storm, and who by plague
    who by strangulation, and who by lapidation.
Who will rest, and who will wander
    who will find calm, and who will be preyed upon
    who will be tranquil, and who will suffer
    who will be impoverished, and who will be rich
    who will be brought low, and who will rise.
But repentance, prayer, and charity
    remove the harshness of the decree.

The *Unetaneh Tokef* prayer is based on the Talmudic descriptions of Rosh Hashanah as the annual heavenly day of judgment. Tradition connects it with the story of 11th-century sage R. Amnon of Mainz, who died a martyr's death after refusing the local bishop's demand that he convert to Christianity.

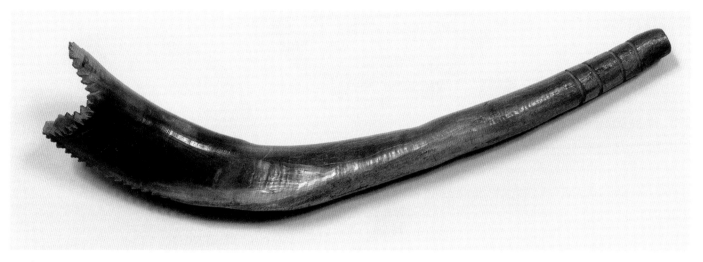

Shofar (engraved ram's horn), Europe, 18th—19th century

The significance of the shofar:

■ The shofar represents the call to repentance, proclaiming: "Awake, sleepers, from your sleep, and slumberers from your slumber; search your deeds, repent, and remember your Creator.... Look to your souls, and improve your ways." *(Maimonides, 1135–1204)*

■ It is the trumpet-blast of our coronation of G-d as our king. *(R. Yomtov Asevilli, c. 1260–1320)*

■ The ram's horn evokes the memory of the Binding of Isaac (see p. 11) and the merit of our self-sacrifice for G-d. *(R. Abahu, 3rd century)*

■ It reminds us of the shofar-blast at Mount Sinai, and of the sounding of the shofar that will herald the Messianic redemption. *(R. Saadia Gaon, 882–942)*

■ The sound of the shofar confuses the accusing angel Satan when he comes to present our sins before the heavenly court. *(R. Yitzchak, 4th century)*

■ The shofar is the cry of a child calling, "Father, father, save me!" *(R. Israel Baal Shem Tov, 1698–1760)*

■ The sound of the shofar, created when air is forced through its narrow end and emerges from its broadened end, represents the power that a soul achieves from within the strictures of physical life, as expressed by the verse (Psalms 118:5): "From the narrow straits I call to G-d; He answers me in the expanses of the Divine." *(Tzemach Tzedek, 1789–1866)*

R. ISRAEL BAAL SHEM TOV
KETER SHEM TOV, ADDENDA 194

A king had an only child, the apple of his eye. The king wanted his child to master different fields of knowledge and to experience various cultures, so he sent him to a faraway land and supplied him with a generous quantity of silver and gold. But the prince took up with bad company, fell to decadent ways, and squandered all his riches until he was left completely destitute. In his distress, he resolved to return to his father's house, and after much difficulty, he managed to arrive at the gates of his father's palace.

In the passage of time, the prince had forgotten the language of his native country, and he was unable to identify himself to the guards. In his despair, he emitted a loud, wordless cry. The king recognized the voice of his child and went out to him and embraced him and brought him into the palace.

G-d sends a soul down to this world to elevate itself through its fulfillment of Torah and mitzvot. But the soul becomes distracted by the material world, loses sight of its mission, and forgets its native language of spirituality and G-dliness. Having lost the ability to even articulate its desire to return home, it utters a simple cry to its Father in Heaven. This is the cry of the shofar, a simple, wordless cry from the very essence of the soul, that arouses G-d's compassion and restores us to His embrace.

 NEHEMIAH 8:2–10

Ezra the Priest brought the Torah before the congregation, both men and women, and all who could hear with understanding, on the first day of the seventh month....

Nehemiah said ... to all the people: "This day is holy to the Lord your G-d. Do not mourn or weep.... Go, eat succulent foods and drink sweet drinks, and send portions to whoever has nothing prepared, for this day is holy to our Lord. Do not be distressed, for the joy of G-d is your strength."

 JERUSALEM TALMUD, *ROSH HASHANAH 1:3*

Where is there a nation like this nation! Ordinarily, a person who has a judgment awaiting them dresses in black, shrouds themself in black ... as they do not know how their verdict will emerge. Not so the people of Israel: they dress in white, envelop themselves in white ... and eat and drink and rejoice, as they know that the Almighty will perform miracles for them.

TASHLICH Water symbolizes *chesed* (lovingkindness), and the perpetually open eye of the fish symbolizes G-d's unceasing providence. Hence the custom to recite the *Tashlich* prayer near a body of water, on or in the days following Rosh Hashanah. The *Tashlich* prayer also includes the verse requesting that G-d "return and have compassion for us, suppress our iniquities, and cast all [our] sins into the depths of the sea" (Micah 7:19).

TRADITIONAL ROSH HASHANAH FOODS On Rosh Hashanah it is the custom to eat foods that symbolize our prayers for a meritorious year. These include: Ⓐ apple dipped in honey ("renew for us a good and sweet year"); Ⓑ the head of a sheep or fish ("may we be a head and not a tail"); Ⓒ pomegranates ("may our merits be as numerous as a pomegranate's seeds"); and foods such as Ⓓ carrots, Ⓔ beets, Ⓕ dates, Ⓖ gourds, Ⓗ leeks, and Ⓘ black-eyed beans, whose names in Hebrew, Aramaic, Yiddish, Ladino, or other languages denote fruitfulness and victory. For example, the Yiddish term for carrots is *mehrn*, which also means "plentiful"; hence the custom in many communities to eat Ⓓ *tzimmes*, a sweet carrot stew, on Rosh Hashanah.

YOM KIPPUR

a day of fasting and prayer

1

ARVIT
Evening prayer

FAST BEGINS
BEFORE
SUNSET

SUNSET   NIGHTFALL

KOL NIDREI

The evening service is preceded by the solemn *Kol Nidrei* prayer. Technically, *Kol Nidrei* is a statement disavowing any extra-legal commitments we may make during the coming year and fail to fulfill—something the Talmud advises to do before Yom Kippur in order to avoid culpability for them. But the fact that *Kol Nidrei* is the opening prayer service of the holiest day of the year, and the moving ancient melody in which it is traditionally sung, lend it its aura of solemnity. The prayer assumed a particularly poignant character among the hidden Jews during the Spanish Inquisition, to whom it implied the renunciation of their coerced vows of fidelity to an alien faith.

"On this day He will atone for you, to purify you; from all your sins, you shall be cleansed before G-d. It is a sabbath of sabbaths for you ... one [day] a year" (Leviticus 16:30–34; see p. 40).

Yom Kippur, the annual "day of atonement," is when terrestrial man most resembles the supernal angel. For close to twenty-six hours, from several minutes before sunset on Tishrei 9 to after nightfall on Tishrei 10, we abstain from food and drink; nor do we bathe or anoint our bodies, wear leather shoes, or engage in marital relations. We spend the day in the synagogue, where five lengthy prayer services and the spiritual activity of *teshuvah* (repentance) engage our every waking moment.

Each of the five Yom Kippur prayers includes *viduy*, the confession of sins that is an integral part of the *teshuvah* process. Also included are *selichot,* "supplications for forgiveness," composed by the *payyetanim.*

 R. MOSHE CHAIM KLEINMAN
OHR YESHARIM, P. 181

R. Israel Baal Shem Tov heard about a cantor who would chant the *Al Cheit* (confession of sins) prayer on Yom Kippur in a joyous tune. The Baal Shem Tov asked

CELEBRATION
Many communities conclude the *Ne'ilah* service with joyous singing and dancing, expressing the confidence that our *teshuvah* has been accepted and that G-d has inscribed us in the book of life.

2
SHACHARIT
Morning prayer

3
MUSAF
Additional prayer added on Shabbat and holidays

4
MINCHAH
Afternoon prayer

5
NE'ILAH
"Closing of the Gates" prayer, unique to Yom Kippur

FAST ENDS AT NIGHTFALL

MORNING   SUNSET

YIZKOR
Following the Torah reading at the conclusion of the morning service, *Yizkor,* the memorial prayer for the dead, is said.

TEMPLE SERVICE
The *Musaf* service for Yom Kippur includes the *Avodah,* a detailed account of the special service performed by the High Priest in the Holy Temple on Yom Kippur, which included the offering of the *ketoret* in the Holy of Holies.

BOOK OF JONAH
The *Minchah* service includes the reading of the Biblical book of Jonah with its message on the power of prayer and repentance (see p. 333).

THE SHEMA
In the climactic finale of the *Ne'ilah* prayer, recited before an open ark as the sun sets on the holiest day of the year, the entire congregation calls out together: "Hear O Israel, G-d is our Lord, G-d is one."

SHOFAR
A single shofar blast at nightfall marks the end of the fast.

to meet the cantor, and asked him about his unusual practice.

Replied the cantor: "When the king's servants are cleaning the royal palace of the accumulated dirt and garbage in anticipation of the king's arrival, do they not do this work joyously?"

THE DYNAMICS OF TESHUVAH

 **MAIMONIDES**, *MISHNEH TORAH, LAWS OF TESHUVAH, 2:2–9 AND 7:3–4*

What is the process of *teshuvah*? That the person who committed a transgression should forsake the sin, resolve to never do it again, and regret their transgression…. The person should also verbally confess to G-d, and state what they have resolved….

Although *teshuvah* and calling out to G-d are desirable at all times, during the ten days between Rosh Hashanah and Yom Kippur it is even more desirable and will be immediately accepted, as it is stated (Isaiah 55:6): "Seek G-d when He is to be found; call to Him when He is near…."

Teshuvah and Yom Kippur only atone for sins between man and G-d; for example, if a person ate a forbidden food or engaged in forbidden sexual relations. However, sins between man and man—for example, a person who injures, curses, or steals from a fellow—are not forgiven until the person repays what is owed to their fellow…. The person must also appease those whom they have injured, repeatedly approaching them until they forgive them….

Teshuvah is not necessary only for sinful actions…. A person should also examine their negative character traits—anger, hatred, envy, frivolity, the pursuit of money and honor, gluttony, etc.—and do *teshuvah* for them….

Those who do *teshuvah* should not consider themselves as inferior to the righteous because of the sins and transgressions they committed. This is not so; rather, they are beloved and desirable before the Creator as if they had never sinned. Furthermore, their reward is great for having tasted sin and having separated from it, conquering their inclination. The sages said: "In the place where *baalei teshuvah* stand, even the completely righteous are not able to stand."

 TALMUD, *YOMA 86b*

Reish Lakish said: "Great is *teshuvah*, as it transforms a person's deliberate sins into errors."

But did not Reish Lakish say, "Great is *teshuvah*, as it transforms a person's deliberate sins into virtues"? This is no contradiction: The [latter] case is when one repents out of love; the [former] case is when one repents out of fear.

 TALMUD, *BERACHOT 10a*

In the neighborhood of R. Meir, there were thugs who caused him a great deal of distress. R. Meir prayed that they should die. His wife Beruria said to him: "What is your thinking? Is it because it is written (Psalms 104:35), 'Sins shall cease from the earth, and the wicked are no more'? But it doesn't say, 'sinners shall cease,' only that 'sins shall cease'…. Pray for them that they should repent, and then, as the verse concludes, 'the wicked are no more.'" R. Meir prayed for them, and they repented.

 R. SOLOMON IBN GABIROL *KETER MALCHUT, SECTION 38*

My G-d, if my sins are too great to forgive
What shall You do for Your great name?
And if I cannot hope for Your compassion
Who shall have mercy on me other than Yourself?
Therefore … should You seek out my sins
I shall flee from You to You
I shall hide from Your wrath in Your shadow.

 R. SCHNEUR ZALMAN OF LIADI *LIKUTEI TORAH, ROSH HASHANAH 60d AND 66c*

There is a common misconception that *teshuvah* is only for sinners…. In truth, *teshuvah* means "return," and refers to the return of all things to their root and source. The soul, which descends into this lowly world to become enmeshed in mundane and material things,

The Worms Machzor (High Holiday prayer book), Simcha ben Yehuda, Würzburg(?), Germany, 1272

yearns to return to its origin and source, to cleave to its Creator and to nullify its will before the divine will.

The Ten Days of Repentance and Yom Kippur were instituted not just for those who have sinned, but also for the perfectly righteous, as this is what human life is all about: the striving of the innermost essence of the heart to cleave to G-d.

 R. MENACHEM M. SCHNEERSON
LIKUTEI SICHOT, VOL. 2, P. 409

Teshuvah is commonly translated as "repentance." But in truth, the Hebrew word *teshuvah* has a different and even opposite meaning.

"Repentance" implies dismissing the past and starting anew. *Teshuvah* means "return." This expresses the idea that a person is intrinsically good, and intrinsically desires to do only good. The person is returning to their true, innermost self, and reestablishing its sovereignty over their life.

 R. ABRAHAM I. KOOK, *OROT HATESHUVAH, CH. 2*

The higher *teshuvah* is sparked by a flash of the all-encompassing good—the divine goodness that resides in all the worlds and is the vitalizing energy of Creation. The soul of the entire emanated reality appears before us in its splendor and holiness to the extent that the heart can absorb; for is not everything, in truth, good and correct? Does not everything that is good and correct in us derive from our correlation with the whole? How then can we be disconnected from the whole, detached and different, adrift as a meaningless speck of dust? It is from this recognition, which is a truly divine recognition, that *teshuvah* comes, on the individual as well as on the communal level.

Sukkot and Simchat Torah

While other festivals recall a specific event in Jewish history, the festival of Sukkot commemorates an entire epoch: the forty years that the people of Israel traversed the wilderness under the Almighty's special protection and care. Manna from heaven nourished them, the "well of Miriam" provided them with water, and miraculous "clouds of glory" sheltered them. On Sukkot, we replicate our ancestors' experience by dwelling in a sukkah—*a hut of temporary construction with a roof-covering of branches. For a full week, we exchange our regular home for a dwelling that leaves us at the mercy of the elements, demonstrating our trust in G-d's providence and protection.*

Another Sukkot observance is the taking of the "four kinds"—an etrog (citron), a palm frond, and myrtle and willow twigs. A central theme of Sukkot is unity, symbolized by the four kinds' bringing together of various types of plant life, various types within the community of Israel, and various components of our own psyche and physiology.

The seven days of Sukkot are immediately followed by the festival of Shemini Atzeret ("eighth day of assembly") and Simchat Torah ("rejoicing of the Torah"), observed as two separate days in the Diaspora and as a single day in the Land of Israel. This is the time of year when we conclude the annual Torah reading cycle (see p. 160) and begin it anew, amidst great joy and celebration.

Sukkah decorations,
Yair Emanuel, Israel, 2001–2011

Etrog container, Persia, early 20th century

Building the sukkah, Jerusalem, Israel, 2017

THE SUKKAH

 LEVITICUS 23:42–43

In *sukkot* (temporary shelters) you shall dwell for seven days.... In order that your generations should know that I made-dwell the children of Israel in *sukkot* when I took them out of the land of Egypt.

 TALMUD, *SUKKAH 11b*

R. Eliezer [ben Hyrcanus] says: These were the "clouds of glory" with which the Almighty protected the Israelites in the wilderness. R. Akiva says: They were actual shelters that they made for themselves.

◗ **TUR AND SHULCHAN ARUCH,** *ORACH CHAYIM, 639*

How does one fulfill the mitzvah of dwelling in the sukkah? One should eat, drink, sleep, relax, and live in the sukkah all seven days of the festival, both day and night, as one lives in one's own house on the other days of the year. For seven days, a person should make their home their temporary dwelling, and their sukkah, their permanent dwelling.

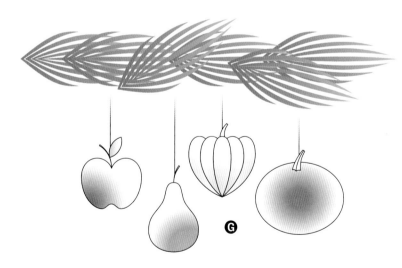

sukkah requirements

Ⓐ **ROOF COVERING**
The most important feature of the sukkah is the covering, called the *s'chach,* which consists of things that grow from the ground and are in their raw state. Common examples of *s'chach* are bamboo poles, evergreen branches, reeds, or palm leaves. Mats made of such materials can be used if they meet the Halachic requirements. There needs to be sufficient *s'chach* so that there is "more shade than sun" in the sukkah.

The sukkah should be directly under the open sky. If it is built under a tree or under any sort of roof or overhang, it is disqualified from use.

Ⓑ **THE WALLS**
The walls of the sukkah can be made of any material, as long as they are sturdy enough to withstand a common wind. Ideally a sukkah should have four full walls, but it is fit for use if it has a minimum of two walls plus at least part of a third wall (diagram shows one possible formulation for a minimally-walled sukkah).

Ⓒ **SUKKAH HEIGHT**
A sukkah should be at least ten handbreadths (approx. 33 inches) high, and should not exceed 20 arm-lengths (approx. 30 feet) in height.

Ⓓ **SUKKAH SIZE**
The area of the sukkah should be no less than seven handbreadths by seven handbreadths (approx. 23 x 23 inches). There is no limit to how long and wide a sukkah can be.

Ⓔ **CONSTRUCTION GAPS**
The walls of the sukkah do not need to reach all the way up to the *s'chach*: as long as they are the required ten handbreadths high, and the *s'chach* is placed no higher than twenty arm-lengths above the sukkah floor, there can be a vertical gap between the walls and the *s'chach*. If there is a horizontal gap between the *s'chach* and the walls of the sukkah, that gap must be less than three handbreadths (approx. 9.25 inches).

Ⓕ **THE "BENT WALL" RULE**
The part of the roof of the sukkah that adjoins its wall can be considered an extension of the wall. Thus, if one makes an opening in the center of a roofed structure and covers the opening with *s'chach,* the area directly under the *s'chach* can serve as a sukkah, provided that: (1) the area under the *s'chach* is the minimum sukkah size of 7 x 7 handbreadths; (2) the distance from the *s'chach* to the vertical wall is less than four arm-lengths (approx. 74 inches).

Ⓖ **SUKKAH DECORATIONS**
In keeping with the dictum of "beautifying the mitzvot," many have the custom of decorating the sukkah with fruit, posters, and other decorative hangings.

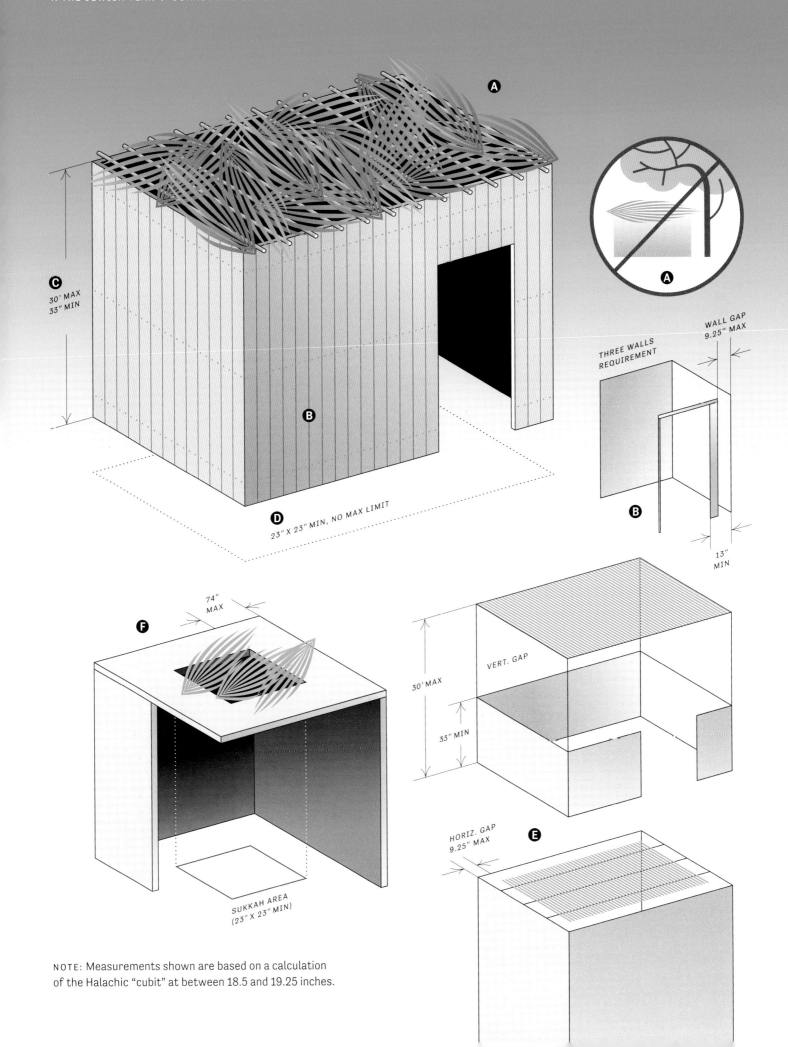

Ⓐ

Ⓒ
30' MAX
33" MIN

Ⓑ

Ⓓ
23" X 23" MIN, NO MAX LIMIT

THREE WALLS
REQUIREMENT

WALL GAP
9.25" MAX

Ⓑ

13"
MIN

74"
MAX

Ⓕ

30' MAX

VERT. GAP

33" MIN

SUKKAH AREA
(23" X 23" MIN)

HORIZ. GAP
9.25" MAX

Ⓔ

NOTE: Measurements shown are based on a calculation
of the Halachic "cubit" at between 18.5 and 19.25 inches.

THE FOUR KINDS

 LEVITICUS 23:40

You shall take for yourselves on the first day [of the festival of Sukkot], the fruit of a splendorous tree, the frond of a date palm, the branch of a braided tree, and willows of the brook; and you shall rejoice before the Lord your G-d for seven days.

MIDRASH RABBAH, *VAYIKRA 30:12 AND 14*

[The four kinds] represent the people of Israel. Just as the etrog has a taste and an aroma, so, too, does Israel include individuals who have both Torah [learning] and good deeds…. The date has a taste but does not have an aroma; so, too, does Israel include those who have Torah but do not have good deeds…. The myrtle has an aroma but not a taste; so, too, does Israel include those who have good deeds but do not have Torah…. The willow has no taste and no aroma; so, too, does Israel include those who do not have Torah and do not have good deeds…. Says the Almighty: Let them all bond together in one bundle and atone for each other.

"All my bones shall proclaim: G-d, who is like You!" (Psalms 35:10). This verse was said regarding the four kinds. The spine of the palm frond resembles a person's spine; the myrtle resembles the eye; the willow resembles the mouth; and the etrog resembles the heart.

TAKING THE FOUR KINDS

Tradition identifies the "four kinds" in Leviticus 23:40 as:

(A) Etrog—the citron fruit

(B) Lulav—an unopened palm frond

(C) Hadassim—a minimum of three myrtle twigs

(D) Aravot—two willow twigs

The lulav, hadassim, and aravot are bound together (customs in the manner in which they are arranged and tied vary from community to community). A blessing is recited over the four kinds, and then all four are held together and waved in all six directions: right, left, forward, up, down, and back.

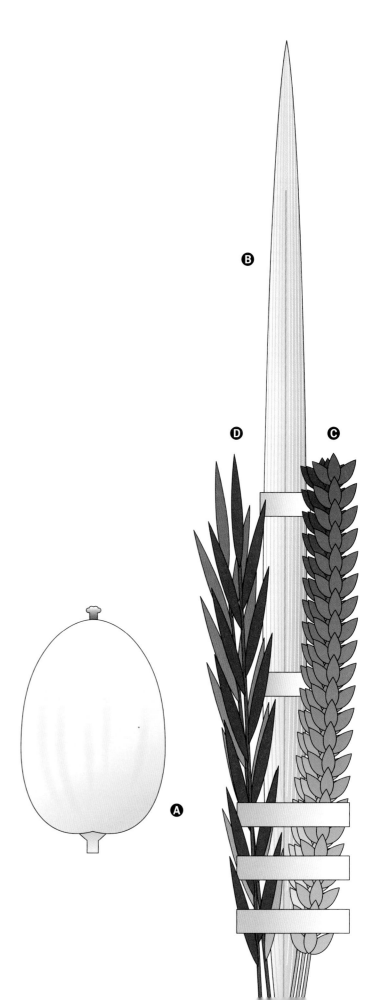

FESTIVAL JOY

 MAIMONIDES, *MISHNEH TORAH,*
LAWS OF FESTIVAL REST, 6:17–18

It is a mitzvah to rejoice on the eight days of Sukkot and on all the other festivals … as it is written (Deuteronomy 16:14), "You shall rejoice in your festival.…" Children are given roasted kernels, nuts, and sweets; women are given beautiful clothes and jewelry … men eat meat and drink wine.…

When one eats and drinks, one must also feed the stranger, the orphan, the widow, and other destitute people. But one who locks the doors of their courtyard and feasts and drinks with their children and wife but does not feed the poor and the unfortunate—this is not the joy of a mitzvah, but the joy of one's stomach.

 R. SHLOMO YOSEF ZEVIN
SIPUREI HASIDIM, FESTIVALS, STORY 124

The holy master, R. Pinchas of Koretz (1726–1791), was unhappy about the fact that people were always coming to him to seek his guidance and blessing, as he felt that this distracted him from his service of the Creator. So, he prayed that he should be detestable in the eyes of his fellows, in order that people should be disinclined to have anything to do with him.

And so it came to pass. R. Pinchas now lived a life of seclusion and poverty. The only time he came in contact with others was when he attended the synagogue for the communal prayers.

When the festival of Sukkot arrived, R. Pinchas had to hire a non-Jew to build his sukkah for him, as none of the town's Jews would help him. When R. Pinchas' wife tried borrowing the necessary tools to build the sukkah, none of their neighbors would lend them to her—so despised was he by all. It was with great difficulty that they succeeded in getting the sukkah built.

On the first night of the festival, at the conclusion of the prayer service in the synagogue, R. Pinchas tried to invite some guests to share the festival meal with him, but all refused him. Even those without a place to eat and desperate for an invitation turned him down, and he was forced to return home alone.

As he prepared to enter his sukkah, R. Pinchas began to recite the traditional invitation to the *ushpizin,* the supernal "guests" that visit the sukkah. R. Pinchas raised his eyes and saw the patriarch Abraham standing outside, keeping his distance. "Father Abraham!" he cried out, "Why do you not enter my sukkah? What is my sin?"

Replied Abraham: "I do not enter a place where there are no guests."

From that day onward, R. Pinchas changed his attitude. He prayed to G-d that he should once again find favor in the eyes of his fellows, and people resumed coming to him as before.

SUPERNAL GUESTS There is a tradition that the "seven shepherds" of the Jewish people—Abraham, Isaac, Jacob, Moses, Aaron, Joseph, and David—visit the sukkah on the seven days of the festival. A popular sukkah decoration is posters depicting the seven *ushpizin* ("guests"), as they are called, and the words of greeting to them that many have the custom to recite upon entering the sukkah.

SECOND HAKAFOT Outside of the Holy Land, where the festival of Shemini Atzeret is observed for two days, the second day is Simchat Torah, on which we conclude the annual Torah reading cycle and begin it anew and celebrate with *hakafot* (circling and dancing with the Torah scrolls—see texts on facing page). In Israel, where both Shemini Atzeret and Simchat Torah are observed on the same day, the custom developed to do a "second *hakafot*" on the evening following the festival, often with live music and dancing in the streets.

"Second Hakafot" in Maale Adumim, Israel, 2010

 MISHNAH, *SUKKAH 5:1–4 AND 4:9*

It is said: One who has not seen the joy of the water-drawing celebrations [in the Holy Temple on Sukkot], has not seen joy in their lifetime....

There was not a courtyard in Jerusalem that was not illuminated by the light of the water-drawing celebrations. The pious and men of achievement would dance before the people with lit torches in their hands, and say before them words of song and praise. The Levites would play with lutes, harps, cymbals, trumpets, and countless musical instruments, while standing upon the fifteen steps that descend into the women's courtyard [in the Holy Temple], corresponding with the fifteen "songs of ascents" in the Book of Psalms....

Two priests would stand at the upper gate ... with two trumpets in their hands. When the rooster crowed, they would blow a *tekiyah* [a steady blast], and a *teruah* [a broken blast], and a *tekiyah*....

How was the water libation done? A golden flask with a capacity of three *lugim* was filled from the Shiloah spring.... [The priest] ascended the ramp [of the altar] and turned to his left; two silver basins were there.... The [basins] had perforations like two narrow nostrils, one wider, and one narrower, so that both should run out together, [as] the western basin was for the water and the eastern one for wine.

 R. SHMUEL ELIEZER EIDELS
COMMENTARY ON TALMUD, SUKKAH 50b

The festival of Sukkot is when the world is allocated its water in the heavenly court. As is stated in [the Talmudic tractate] *Rosh Hashanah:* "Why does the Torah instruct to pour water on the altar on Sukkot...? So that the rains of the year should be blessed...." Hence the great joy that accompanied this mitzvah. For the world cannot survive without water, and every creature depends on the blessing of water.

 R. SAMSON RAPHAEL HIRSCH
COMMENTARY TO NUMBERS 29:19

Indeed, our ultimate joy comes not from remembering the gifts that G-d bestows on us on special occasions, but from the recognition that every life-sustaining drop of water is an agent of divine benevolence.

HAKAFOT

 SHULCHAN ARUCH, *ORACH CHAYIM, 669*

During the morning service of Simchat Torah, three Torah scrolls are taken out of the ark. From the first scroll is read from "And this is the blessing …" (Deuteronomy 33:1) until the end of the Torah; from the second scroll, from "In the beginning …" (Genesis 1:1) until "… which G-d created to make" (Gen. 2:3); and from the third, the reading, "On the eighth day …" (Numbers 29:35–30:1).

In both the evening and the morning services, all the Torah scrolls are taken out of the ark. Songs and prayers are said, in each place according to its custom,… and the reading platform of the synagogue is circled with all the Torah scrolls. It is also customary to increase the number of those called up to the Torah … the children, too, are called up to the Torah.

 R. YOSEF YITZCHAK SCHNEERSOHN
CITED IN *LIKUTEI SICHOT, VOL. 4, P. 1169*

The Torah wants to dance on Simchat Torah. But the Torah has no feet. On Simchat Torah, the Jew becomes the dancing feet of the Torah.

 R. ELIYAHU KI-TOV, EXCERPTED FROM *SEFER HATODAAH, VOL. 1, PP. 127–128*

Why do we conclude and celebrate the annual Torah reading cycle on Simchat Torah, rather than on Shavuot, the day that we received the Torah at Mount Sinai?

On Passover, we witnessed the miracles of the Exodus and the awesome punishments that the Almighty inflicted on the Egyptians. Fifty days later, we entered into the covenant of the Torah—an event punctuated by thunder and lightning so that the fear of G-d might always be upon us. This we celebrate with the festival of Shavuot.

In contrast, on Yom Kippur, G-d forgives our sins, and on Sukkot, we find shelter under the wings of G-d's providence and love. We immediately extend that love to the Torah on Simchat Torah. This covenant with the Torah is not accompanied by fear and trepidation, but by joy, song, and dance.

Another difference between Shavuot and Simchat Torah is that Shavuot comes fifty days after the Exodus on Passover, while Sukkot and Simchat Torah follow immediately after our repentance on Yom Kippur. For the strength of the penitent is greater than that of the righteous person. As a righteous nation, we required seven weeks to attain the gift of Torah; as penitents we can achieve it in seven days, creating a bond with G-d that does not weaken throughout the year for as long as the Torah's words are on our lips.

Simchat Torah hakafot flag,
Moshe Lipietz, Warsaw, circa 1905

Hanukkah

Hanukkah celebrates the triumph of light over darkness, of purity over adulteration, of spirituality over materialism.

In the second century BCE, *the Holy Land was ruled by the Seleucids (Syrian-Greeks), who sought to forcefully Hellenize the people of Israel. Against all odds, a small band of faithful Jews drove the Greeks from the land, reclaimed the Holy Temple in Jerusalem, and rededicated it to the service of G-d. A single cruse of ritually pure olive oil, enough to kindle the Temple's menorah for one day, burned for eight days, until new oil could be prepared.*

At the heart of the festival's observances is the nightly menorah lighting, commemorating the miracle of the oil. Hanukkah customs include the eating of foods fried in oil—latkes (*potato pancakes*) *and* sufganiot (*doughnuts*); *playing with the* dreidel; *and giving "Hanukkah gelt," gifts of money, to children.*

SPINNING LETTERS On Hanukkah it is customary to play with a *dreidel,* a spinning top on which are inscribed the Hebrew letters *nun, gimmel, hei,* and *shin*—an acronym for "a great miracle happened there." In the Land of Israel, the *shin* is replaced with a *pei,* to indicate the phrase, "a great miracle happened here." The *dreidel* recalls the time when the Hellenist rulers of the Holy Land forbade the study of Torah on the pain of death, and Jewish children would quickly replace their scrolls with a spinning toy when soldiers approached.

*Hanukkah Lamp,
the Netherlands(?), 19th century(?)*

THE STORY OF HANUKKAH

 MAIMONIDES
MISHNEH TORAH, LAWS OF HANUKKAH, 3:1–3

In the time of the Second Temple, the Hellenist rulers issued decrees against the Jewish people abolishing their faith and prohibiting them from studying the Torah and observing its commandments. They violated their property and their daughters, invaded the Holy Temple and wreaked destruction there, and contaminated the sacraments.

The Jews suffered greatly from the Greeks and their persecutions, until the G-d of our ancestors had mercy upon them and delivered them from their hand. The children of the Hasmoneans, the high priests, defeated the Greeks … and sovereignty returned to Israel for more than two hundred years, until the destruction of the Second Temple.

When the Jews defeated their enemies, it was the 25th of the month of Kislev. They entered the Holy Temple, and could not find any ritually pure oil in the sanctuary, with the exception of a single cruse that contained enough oil for just one day. They kindled the lamps [of the Temple's menorah] from it for eight days, until they could crush olives and produce pure oil.

The sages of that generation ordained that these eight days, beginning from the 25th of Kislev, should be days of rejoicing and praise of G-d, and that lamps should be lit in the evening in the doorways of the houses on each of these eight nights, to display and publicize the miracle. These days are called Hanukkah.

 MACCABEES, *BOOK I, CH. 2, VERSES 1–30*

The start of the Hasmonean revolt

In those days, there was a priest in Israel, and his name was Mattityahu the son of Jochanan…. He dwelt in Modi'in, and he had five sons: Jochanan, Simeon, Judah the Maccabee, Elazar, and Jonathan….

It came to pass that the king's officers came to Modi'in to forcefully remove the people from G-d's Torah and compel them to worship idols and offer sacrifices to them. Many of the people of Israel joined with them, but Mattityahu and his sons held strong.

The king's official said to Mattityahu: "See, you are a leader and an honored person amongst your people, and you have many sons and a large family. Now, you come first to carry out the king's command, as was done in all the provinces of his kingdom, and by all the people of Judah and Jerusalem, and you and your sons will find favor in the king's eyes, and gold and silver and precious gifts will be awarded to you."

Mattityahu raised his voice and said: "If indeed nation after nation of the king's subjects have turned away from their gods and obeyed his decree to betray the religion of their ancestors, not so shall it be with me and my family!... It is unthinkable for us to transgress the commandments of our G-d, and to violate His covenant with us…."

As he concluded speaking, a Jewish man approached the altar, in sight of all those standing there, to offer a sacrifice in accordance with the king's command.

Mattityahu saw this and his heart burned with zeal…. He ran toward the man and slew him near the altar. Also the king's official did he slay, and he destroyed the altar…. He then ran through the city, calling out with a great voice: "Whoever fears for G-d's Torah and holds fast to His covenant—follow me!" And all the people whom the Torah of G-d had touched their hearts followed Mattityahu, and they fled to the wilderness.

(SEE ALSO "THE GREEKS AND THE HASMONEANS," PP. 77–79)

 THE STORY OF JUDITH, EXCERPTED FROM *CHABAD.ORG, THE COMPLETE STORY OF CHANUKAH*

The town of Bethulia in the land of Judea came under siege by Holofernes, a mighty Syrian-Greek general, at the head of a large army. Holofernes was notorious for his cruelty in suppressing rebellions. When he captured a rebel stronghold, he showed no mercy to the men, women, and children sheltered there.

The Return of Judith to Bethulia,
Sandro Botticelli, Florence, circa 1472

The men of the beleaguered town fought bravely and desperately to repulse the repeated assaults by the superior enemy forces. Seeing that he couldn't take the fortified town by force, Holofernes decided to starve its inhabitants into submission. He cut off the food and water supply, and before long the town was indeed brought to the verge of surrender.

The desperate townspeople gathered in the marketplace and demanded of the town elders that, rather than die of hunger and thirst, they should surrender to the enemy. Uzziah, the commander of the defense forces, tried to calm the populace, without success. Finally, he pleaded, "Give us five more days. If no salvation comes by the end of five days, we will surrender. Just five more days...."

Reluctantly the people agreed, and slowly they dispersed. Only one person, a woman, remained in her place, as if riveted to it, and she addressed Uzziah and the elders. "Why do you test the Almighty, giving Him only five days in which to send us His help? Besides,

don't you know that surrender to Holofernes is worse than death?" So spoke Judith, the noble daughter of Jochanan the High Priest, father of the Hasmonean family. She was a young widow, blessed with extraordinary charm and beauty and known for her devoutness, modesty, and kindness. Her words made a deep impression on Uzziah and the elders.

"I have a plan," Judith said. "I ask your permission to leave town together with my maid. I shall go to Holofernes...."

Uzziah and the elders were shocked and dismayed. "Do you know what you are saying, Judith? Would you sacrifice your life and honor on the slim chance that you might soften Holofernes' heart? We cannot allow you to make such a sacrifice for us."

But Judith persisted. "It has happened before that the Almighty sent His salvation through a woman. As you well know, it was into the hands of Yael, the wife of Heber, that G-d delivered the Canaanite general Sisera...."

Judith passed through the gates of Bethulia, dressed in her best clothes, which she had not worn since her husband's death. A delicate veil all but hid her beautiful face. She was accompanied by her faithful maid, who carried a basket filled with rolls, cheese, and several bottles of old wine.

Presently they were stopped by sentries, who demanded to know who they were and who sent them. "We have an important message for your commander, the brave Holofernes," Judith said. "Take us to him at once."

"Who are you, and why are you here?" Holofernes asked when Judith was brought to his tent, his eyes feasting on the beauty of his unexpected visitor.

"I am but a plain widow from Bethulia. Judith is my name. I came to tell you how to capture the town, in the hope that you will deal mercifully with its inhabitants."

Judith told Holofernes that life in the besieged town had become unbearable for her, and that she had bribed the watchmen to let her and her maid out. She went on to say that she had heard of Holofernes' bravery and mighty deeds and wished to make his acquaintance. Finally she told Holofernes what he already knew, that the situation in the town was desperate. Yet, she said, their faith in G-d remained strong, and as long as they had faith, they would not surrender. On the other hand, she added, before long, every scrap of kosher food would be gone, and in desperation they would begin to eat the flesh of unclean animals, and then G-d's anger would be turned against them, and the town would fall. "I have arranged with the watchmen at the city's gates," concluded Judith, "that I would come to the gate every evening. I will tell them what is happening here, and they will tell me what is happening there."

Holofernes was captivated by the charming young widow who had so unexpectedly entered his life and was now offering him the key to the city. "If you are telling me the truth, and will help me capture the city, you will be my wife!" Holofernes promised. He gave orders that Judith and her maid were to have complete freedom to walk through the camp, and that anyone attempting to molest them would be put to death. A comfortable tent was prepared for the two women, next to his.

In the meantime, Holofernes, while awaiting the signal from Judith to storm the town, spent most of his time drinking, with and without his aides. When he was not completely drunk, he would send for Judith. She always came to his tent in the company of her maid.

On the third day, Judith said to Holofernes, "I have very good news, general. There is no kosher food left in the city now. Soon famine will drive them to eat their cats and dogs and mules…."

"Wonderful, wonderful! This surely calls for a celebration. Tonight we shall have a party, just you and I. I shall expect you as my honored guest."

That evening, when Judith entered Holofernes' tent, he bade her partake of the feast that had been laid out

for them. But Judith told him she had brought her own food and wine that she had prepared especially for that occasion. "My goat cheese is famous in all of Bethulia," Judith said. "I'm sure you will like it, General."

He did. He also liked the strong, undiluted wine she had brought. She fed him the cheese, chunk after chunk, and he washed it down with wine. Before long he was sprawled on the ground, dead drunk.

Judith rolled him over on his face. Then she uttered a silent prayer. "Strengthen me, O Lord, that I may bring Your deliverance to my people whom this cruel man vowed to destroy, and let the nations know that You have not forsaken us."

Judith unsheathed Holofernes' heavy sword, and brought it down on his neck with all her might.

For a moment she sat down to compose herself. Then she wrapped the general's head in rags, concealed it under her shawl, and calmly walked out and into her own tent. "Come quickly," she said to her maid, "but let us not arouse suspicion."

The two veiled women walked leisurely, until they reached the gates of the city. "Take me to Uzziah at once," she said to the sentry.

Uzziah could not believe his eyes when he stared at the gruesome prize Judith had brought him. "There is no time to lose," Judith said to the commander. "Prepare your men for a surprise attack at dawn. The enemy's camp is not prepared for it. When they run to their commander's tent, they will find his headless body, and they will flee for their lives."

This is precisely what happened. The enemy fled in confusion and terror, and thus the town of Bethulia was saved by the righteous and brave Judith.

HANUKKAH LIGHTS

 TALMUD, *SHABBAT 21b*

We have learned: The basic mitzvah is one light for each household. Those who enhance the mitzvah kindle a light for each person in the household.

For those who enhance beyond enhancement, [there are two approaches.] The sages of the School of Shamai say: On the first day, one kindles eight lights, and on each subsequent day, one light less. The sages of the School of Hillel say: On the first day, one kindles one light, and on each subsequent day, one additional light.

 R. YITZCHAK MEIR OF GER
CITED IN *LIKUTEI HARIM, VOL. 1, P. 117,*
AND *SEFAT EMET, HANUKKAH 5654*

HANUKKAH OUTREACH

This mass-produced menorah, stamped and folded from a single sheet of tin and costing only a few cents each to produce, was designed in 1973 by Tibor Kuferstein for the Chabad-Lubavitch movement, which distributes 350,000 Hanukkah lighting kits each year. The movement also erects thousands of large public menorahs in city squares and other public venues across the world.

Enhanced mode

The Talmud presents three possible ways to kindle the Hanukkah lights: the basic mitzvah, the enhanced way, and "enhanced beyond enhancement." In practice, everyone lights the Hanukkah menorah in the "enhanced beyond enhancement" manner—kindling one light on the first night of Hanukkah, two lights on the second night, and so on—a phenomenon which we do not find with any other mitzvah.

This is because the entire miracle of the oil was, in truth, unnecessary. According to Torah law, "The prohibition of impurity, if affecting the entire community, is waived" (Talmud, *Yoma* 6b). Technically, the menorah could have been lit with impure oil. The Almighty performed a miracle only to enable us to fulfill the mitzvah of lighting the Temple's menorah in the most optimal manner. Each Hanukkah, we reciprocate in kind, by making "enhanced beyond enhancement" the universally accepted norm for our mitzvah.

Two kinds of fire

Fire has two functions: it consumes, and it illuminates. Our service of the Creator also includes these two tasks: to vanquish evil, and to create good.

Therein lies the deeper significance of the debate between the sages of Shamai and the sages of Hillel. The Shamai school sees the primary function of the Hanukkah flames as the elimination of evil. After all, how can we do good when evil stands in our way? Thus, the number of flames decreases each night, signifying the progressive elimination of the negative. The Hillel school places the emphasis on doing good, reflected in the increase in the number of lights each night of the festival.

In practice, we follow the approach of Hillel. Our primary objective is to do good. When more good is created, the negative is automatically vanquished.

Kindling the Hanukkah lights during the Holocaust (detail), Westerbork Concentration Camp, the Netherlands, 1943

RUDOLF WERNER BRESLAUER

Trafalgar Square menorah, London, England, 2015

GARRY KNIGHT

menorah lighting tutorial

WHAT TO LIGHT Use a Hanukkah menorah that uses oil and wicks (preferably olive oil), or candles. If you don't have a menorah, you can just line up the correct number of candles in a straight row. (Electric menorahs are often used as holiday decorations or to raise awareness of the festival, but they do not fulfill the mitzvah of kindling the Hanukkah lights.)

WHERE TO LIGHT The Hanukkah lights are placed on the left side of a doorway (opposite the mezuzah), or in a window overlooking a public thoroughfare.

WHEN TO LIGHT The Hanukkah lights are kindled at night. Some communities light them at sunset; others after nightfall (approx. 20–30 minutes after sunset). In either case, the candles should be large enough (or there should be sufficient oil) to burn for 30 minutes after nightfall. One who was unable to kindle the lights in the beginning of the evening can do so later in the night, as long as members of the household are still awake.

On Friday evening, the lights must be lit before sunset (before lighting the Shabbat candles). On Saturday night, they can be lit only after the Shabbat ends at nightfall.

HOW TO LIGHT Kindle one light on the first night of Hanukkah, two lights on the second night, and so on until the eighth night, when eight lights are kindled. The lights are placed at the right end of the menorah. An additional light, the *shamash* ("servant candle") is used to kindle the lights, and is then placed in a designated place above or to the side of the lights.

Recite the blessings, and then kindle the lights. Begin with the newest light, and then proceed from left to right.

THE BLESSINGS On the first night, or if this is the first time you are kindling the Hanukkah lights this year, recite all three blessings. On all other nights, recite the first two blessings only.

1

בָּרוּךְ אַתָּה ה׳ אֱלֹהֵינוּ מֶלֶךְ הָעוֹלָם אֲשֶׁר קִדְּשָׁנוּ בְּמִצְוֹתָיו וְצִוָּנוּ לְהַדְלִיק נֵר חֲנֻכָּה

TRANSLITERATION

Ba-ruch a-tah a-do-nai e-lo-hei-nu me-lech ha-o-lam a-sher ki-de-sha-nu be-mitz-vo-tav vi-tzi-va-nu le-had-lik ner cha-nu-kah

TRANSLATION

Blessed are You, Lord our G-d, king of the universe, who has sanctified us with His commandments, and commanded us to kindle the Hanukkah light

2

בָּרוּךְ אַתָּה ה׳ אֱלֹהֵינוּ מֶלֶךְ הָעוֹלָם שֶׁעָשָׂה נִסִּים לַאֲבוֹתֵינוּ בַּיָּמִים הָהֵם בִּזְמַן הַזֶּה

TRANSLITERATION

Ba-ruch a-tah a-do-nai e-lo-hei-nu me-lech ha-o-lam she-a-sa ni-sim la-a-vo-tei-nu ba-ya-mim ha-heim bi-zman ha-zeh

TRANSLATION

Blessed are you, Lord our G-d, king of the universe, who performed miracles for our forefathers in those days, at this time

3

בָּרוּךְ אַתָּה ה׳ אֱלֹהֵינוּ מֶלֶךְ הָעוֹלָם שֶׁהֶחֱיָנוּ וְקִיְּמָנוּ וְהִגִּיעָנוּ לִזְמַן הַזֶּה

TRANSLITERATION

Ba-ruch a-tah a-do-nai e-lo-hei-nu me-lech ha-o-lam she-he-che-ya-nu ve-ki-yi-ma-nu ve-hi-gi-a-nu li-zman ha-zeh

TRANSLATION

Blessed are You, Lord our G-d, king of the universe, who has granted us life, sustained us, and enabled us to reach this occasion

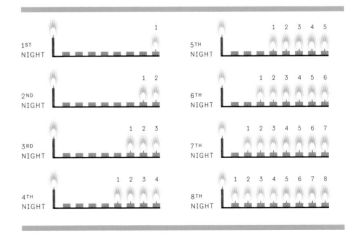

Tu BiShevat

The Talmud designates Tu BiShevat, *the 15th day of the month of Shevat, as the "New Year for Trees." Legally, this pertains to the different tithes that are given from the land's produce on different years of the sabbatical cycle (see p. 281). We mark the day by eating fruit, particularly the "seven fruits" with which the Land of Israel is blessed. We remember that "man is a tree of the field" (as per the Talmud's interpretation of Deuteronomy 20:19), and reflect on our responsibility as guardians of G-d's verdant world.*

Dried carob with seeds. Many communities have the custom of eating this hardy fruit on Tu BiShevat.

R. MENACHEM M. SCHNEERSON
IGROT KODESH, VOL. 1, PP. 247–248

What can we learn about our own existence from a tree?

A tree consists of three primary components: the roots, the body of the tree, and the fruit.

The roots are hidden underground, yet they are the foundation of the tree's existence, anchoring it to the ground and supplying it with water and nutrients from the soil. A tree with strong roots is secure against destruction by passing storms.

The body of the tree—its trunk, branches, and leaves—comprises the bulk of its presence and grandeur, visibly developing from year to year and displaying the tree's power and beauty.

But the ultimate goal of the tree is to produce fruit, as these contain the seeds that will sprout new trees, generation after generation.

"Man is a tree of the field," whose spiritual existence parallels these three components and their respective qualities:

The roots: This is the person's faith, by which he or she is bound to their Creator—their "place" and source of vitality. Even as a person grows in knowledge and achievements, these are grounded and nourished by their faith.

The trunk, branches, and leaves: This is the Torah that a person learns and the mitzvot they perform, to which a person should devote the bulk of their time and effort, and which constitute the most visible part of their spiritual existence.

The fruit: The ultimate goal, however, must be that a person does not suffice with their individual development, but also influences their fellows and their surroundings, seeding other "trees" that are strong in faith, in learning and good deeds, and who, in turn, influence others.

the seven fruits

According to Kabbalistic and Hasidic teaching, the seven fruits with which the Land of Israel is blessed in Deuteronomy 8:8—wheat, barley, grapes, figs, pomegranates, olives, and dates—are also seven fundamental traits in our psyche and personality.

1 WHEAT: Human spirit

In the Bible and in the words of the sages, wheat is described as the staple of the human diet. "Wheat" therefore represents our higher, spiritual strivings, which are the essence of our uniqueness as human beings.

2 BARLEY: Animal passion

In contrast to wheat, barley exemplifies animal fodder ("The barley and the straw for the horses and the mules"—I Kings 5:8). "Barley" thus represents our animal passions. In their raw state, our animalistic instincts oppose and may even corrupt our spiritual self, but when properly directed, they empower and intensify our positive strivings.

3 GRAPES: Joy

"When wine enters, the concealed emerges" (Talmud, *Eruvin* 65a). A joyless life may be complete in every way, but everything is in a subdued state; on the other hand, when a person is in a state of joy, their mind is keener, their loves are deeper, their fears more vivid, their desires more aggressive. "Grapes" is the joy that adds depth, color, and intensity to everything we do.

4 FIGS: Engagement

According to R. Nehemiah in the Talmud (*Berachot* 40a), the *Eitz ha-Daat*, the "Tree of Knowledge" in the Garden of Eden, was a fig tree. *Daat* is more than "knowledge" in the sense of information; it also implies involvement and attachment (as in the verse, "Adam knew his wife Eve"—Genesis 4:1). It means that we care, that we are invested in the task; that we are affected by what we are doing, for better or for worse.

5 POMEGRANATES: Action

Song of Songs (4:3) compares the people of Israel to a pomegranate; the Talmud (*Berachot* 57a) explains that "even the empty ones amongst you are full of good deeds, as a pomegranate is full of seeds." Indeed, the pomegranate exemplifies the paradox that a person can be "empty" yet also "full of good deeds." Each of the pomegranate's hundreds of seeds is encased in its own sac and is separated from the rest of the fruit; in the same way, it is possible for a person to do good deeds that remain isolated actions, with little or no effect on the person's character. Yet the sages see this as a praiseworthy trait. In other words, while "involvement" is integral to our humanity, at times we are called upon to employ an opposite trait—our ability to do what is good and right also when it runs contrary to our nature and our inclinations.

6 OLIVES: Struggle

The sages note that as the olive yields its oil only when pressed, so are our own purest talents and most illuminating potentials extracted from us by the pressures of life (*Midrash Rabbah, Shemot* 36:1). In the seven fruits of the soul, the "olive" is our ability to respond to the challenges of life in ways that surpass anything we might achieve under conditions of tranquility.

7 DATES: Perfection

"The *tzadik* (perfectly righteous person) blossoms like a date palm" (Psalms 92:13). The *Zohar* (3:16a) explains that there are date palms that bear fruit only after 70 years of undisturbed growth and development. Countering the olive in us is our "date"—our capacity for the perfection that only tranquility can produce. Even in the midst of our most ardent struggles, we can always find comfort and fortitude in the tranquil perfection that resides at the core of our souls.

Purim

*Hamantaschen,
poppy-seed-filled pastries
traditionally eaten on Purim*

Purim celebrates the salvation of the Jewish people, in the 4th century BCE, from Haman's plot "to destroy, kill, and annihilate all the Jews, young and old, infants and women, in a single day." Endorsed by the Persian emperor Ahasuerus, whose dominion extended from India to Ethiopia, Haman's decree boded the physical destruction of every Jew on the face of the earth.

As the Jewish sage Mordecai rallied the Jews to prayer and repentance, his cousin, Queen Esther, engineered Haman's downfall at a private wine party to which she invited the king and the minister. She prevailed upon Ahasuerus to hang Haman, and to issue a second decree empowering the Jews to defend themselves against their enemies. On Adar 13—the day selected by Haman's pur (lottery)—battles were fought throughout the empire between the Jews and those who tried to carry out Haman's decree, which was never actually revoked. The next day, Adar 14, became a day of celebration of the Jews' victory over their enemies. In the ancient walled capital, Shushan (Susa), where the battle went on for two days, victory was celebrated on Adar 15.

Mordecai and Esther instituted that these two days be observed as the festival of Purim—Adar 15 in walled cities, Adar 14 in all other communities—with public readings of the story of the miracle from the "Scroll of Esther"; sending food portions to friends; gifts of money to the poor; and a festive meal with inebriating drink (recalling the fateful wine party at which Esther turned Ahasuerus against Haman). The day before Purim is the "Fast of Esther," in commemoration of the fasts by Esther and the Jewish people as they prayed for G-d's salvation.

Ahasuerus and Haman at the Feast of Esther (detail), Rembrandt van Rijn, Amsterdam, 1660

 THE STORY OF PURIM,
EXCERPTS FROM THE SCROLL OF ESTHER

It was in the days of Ahasuerus; he is Ahasuerus who reigned from India to Ethiopia, one hundred twenty-seven provinces....

In the third year of his reign ... the king made for all the people located in Shushan the capital, both great and small, a banquet for seven days, in the court of the garden of the king's orchard....

On the seventh day, when the king's heart was merry with wine, he ordered ... to bring Queen Vashti before the king, in a royal crown, to show the peoples and the princes her beauty.... Queen Vashti refused to come at the king's behest.... The king became very angry, and his fury burned within him....

When King Ahasuerus' fury subsided, he remembered Vashti and what she had done, and what had been decreed upon her. The king's young men, his servants, said: "... Let the king appoint commissioners to all the provinces of his kingdom, and let them gather every young maiden of beautiful appearance to Shushan the capital.... The maiden who pleases the king, she shall reign instead of Vashti." The matter pleased the king, and he did so.

There was a Jewish man in Shushan the capital. His name was Mordecai the son of Jair the son of Shimi the son of Kish, a Benjamite.... He brought up Hadassah, that is Esther, his uncle's daughter, as she had neither father nor mother. The girl was of beautiful form and of beautiful appearance, and when her father and mother died, Mordecai took her to himself for a daughter.

When the king's order and his decree were heard, and when many maidens were gathered to Shushan the capital.... Esther was taken to the king's palace....

The king loved Esther more than all the women, and she won grace and favor before him more than all the maidens. He placed the royal crown on her head, and made her queen instead of Vashti....

But Esther did not disclose her lineage or her nationality, for so Mordecai had instructed her....

In those days, Mordecai was sitting in the king's gate. Bigthan and Teresh, two of the king's chamberlains ... sought to assassinate King Ahasuerus. The matter became known to Mordecai, and he told Queen Esther; and Esther told the king in Mordecai's name.

*Purim
noisemaker,
Poland,
19th century*

UNDERHANDED SPIN Two Jewish holidays—Hanukkah and Purim—are associated with a spinning toy. On Hanukkah we play with the *dreidel*, a spinning top inscribed with the message "A great miracle happened there." Purim has the *gragger*, a noisemaker that is spun when the wicked Haman's name is mentioned during the reading of the Scroll of Esther.

The *dreidel* is spun from above, whereas the *gragger* is rotated from underneath. This reflects the difference between the two holidays. On Hanukkah, the salvation of the Jewish people came "from above," via a series of supernatural miracles. On Purim, our salvation came "from below," by means of ordinary, even mundane events; in fact, the name of G-d does not appear in the entire Scroll of Esther. This was a hidden miracle, where the divine hand was concealed in what could easily be seen as a series of lucky coincidences.
(R. Zvi Elimelech of Dinov, 1783–1841)

The matter was investigated and found to be so, and they were both hanged on a gallows; and it was written in the king's book of chronicles.

After these events, King Ahasuerus promoted Haman the son of Hammedatha the Agagite and elevated him, and placed his seat above all the ministers who were with him. All the king's servants who were in the king's gate would kneel and prostrate themselves before Haman, for so had the king commanded concerning him. But Mordecai would not kneel and would not prostrate himself....

Haman saw that Mordecai would not kneel and prostrate himself before him, and Haman was filled with rage. It was contemptible in his eyes to lay hands on Mordecai alone, as they had told him Mordecai's nationality. Haman sought to destroy all the Jews who were throughout Ahasuerus' entire kingdom, Mordecai's people.... The *pur*—that is, the lot—was cast before Haman, from day to day and from month to month, to the twelfth month, which is the month of Adar.

Haman said to King Ahasuerus: "There is one nation, who are scattered and separated among the nations, throughout all the provinces of your kingdom. Their laws differ from those of every people, and they do not keep the king's laws. It is of no value for the king to allow them to exist. If it pleases the king, let it be written to destroy them, and I will weigh out ten thousand silver talents ... to bring into the king's treasuries."

The king took his ring off his hand and gave it to Haman the son of Hammedatha the Agagite, the enemy of the Jews. And the king said to Haman: "The silver is given to you, and the people, to do to them as you please." The king's scribes were summoned ... and letters were sent by the hand of the couriers to all the king's provinces: To destroy, kill, and annihilate all the Jews, young and old, infants and women, on one day, on the thirteenth day of the twelfth month, which is the month of Adar; and their spoils to be taken as plunder....

Mordecai knew all that had transpired. [He] rent his clothes, and put on sackcloth and ashes; and he went out into the midst of the city, and cried a loud and bitter cry....

Esther summoned Hathach, one of the king's chamberlains whom he had appointed before her, and she instructed him concerning Mordecai, to know what this was and why this was.... Mordecai told him all that had befallen him.... He gave him the copy of the writ of the decree that was given in Shushan, to show Esther and to tell her, and to instruct her to come before the king to beseech him and to plead with him for her people....

Esther said to Hathach, and she instructed him to tell Mordecai: "All the king's servants and all the people of the king's provinces know that any man or woman who comes to the king, into the inner court, who is not summoned, there is but one law for them, to be put to death; except the one to whom the king extends the golden scepter, that they may live. And I have not been summoned to come to the king these thirty days...."

Mordecai said to reply to Esther: "Do not imagine to yourself that you will escape in the king's palace from among all the Jews. For if you remain silent at this time, relief and rescue will arise for the Jews from elsewhere, and you and your father's household will perish; and who knows whether it was not for a time like this that you have attained royalty?"

Esther instructed to reply to Mordecai: "Go, assemble all the Jews who are to be found in Shushan, and fast on my behalf, and neither eat nor drink for three days, day and night; also I and my maidens will likewise fast. Then I will go to the king contrary to the law, and if I perish, I shall perish." Mordecai passed and did according to all that Esther had instructed him.

It was the third day. Esther clothed herself in royalty, and she stood in the inner court of the king's palace, opposite the king's chamber....

When the king saw Queen Esther standing in the court, she won favor in his eyes; and the king extended to Esther the golden scepter that was in his hand, and Esther approached and touched the end of the scepter.

The king said to her, "What concerns you, Queen Esther, and what is your request? Even to half the kingdom, it will be given to you."

Esther said, "If it pleases the king, let the king and Haman come today to the banquet that I have prepared for him." And the king said, "Rush Haman to do Esther's bidding"; and the king and Haman came to the banquet that Esther had prepared.

The king said to Esther during the wine banquet, "What is your request? It shall be granted to you...." Esther replied, "... Let the king and Haman come to the banquet that I will make for them, and tomorrow I will do the king's bidding."

Haman went out on that day happy and with a cheerful heart. But when Haman saw Mordecai in the king's gate, and he neither rose nor stirred for him, Haman was filled with wrath against Mordecai. Haman restrained himself; he came home, and sent for his friends and his wife Zeresh. Haman recounted to them the glory of his riches and the multitude of his sons, and all that the king had promoted him and that he had exalted him over the princes and the king's servants. And Haman said, "Queen Esther did not even bring anyone to the party that she made, except me, and tomorrow, too, I am invited to her with the king. But all this is worth nothing to me, every time I see Mordecai the Jew sitting in the king's gate."

Zeresh his wife and all his friends said, "Have a gallows made that is fifty cubits high; and in the morning, say to the king that they should hang Mordecai on it, and go with the king to the banquet joyfully." The matter pleased Haman, and he made the gallows.

That night, the king's sleep was disturbed. He ordered to bring the book of the records, the chronicles, and they were read before the king. It was found written that Mordecai had reported about Bigthana and Teresh ... who had sought to assassinate King Ahasuerus. The king said, "What honor and greatness was done to Mordecai on that account?" And the king's servants said, "Nothing was done for him."

And the king said, "Who is in the court?" Haman had come to the outside court of the king's house, to petition the king to hang Mordecai on the gallows that he had prepared for him....

Haman entered, and the king said to him, "What should be done for a man whom the king wishes to honor?" And Haman said to himself, "Whom would the king wish to honor more than me?" So Haman said to the King, "... Let them bring the royal raiment that the king wore, and the horse upon which the king rode, and the royal crown that was placed on his head. Let the raiment and the horse be delivered into the hand of one of the king's most noble princes, and let them dress the man whom the king wishes to honor. And let them parade him on the horse in the city square, and announce before him: So shall be done to the man whom the king wishes to honor!"

The king said to Haman, "Hurry, take the raiment and the horse as you have spoken, and do so to Mordecai the Jew, who sits in the king's gate. Let nothing fail of all that you have spoken...."

Haman took the raiment and the horse, and he dressed Mordecai. He paraded him in the city square and announced before him: "So shall be done to the man whom the king wishes to honor!"

Mordecai returned to the king's gate; Haman hurried home, mourning and with a covered head. Haman recounted to his wife Zeresh and to all his friends all that had befallen him, and his wise men and his wife Zeresh said to him: "If Mordecai is of the offspring of the Jews, now that you have begun to fall before him you will not prevail against him, but you will utterly fall before him."

While they were still talking to him, the king's chamberlains arrived, and they hastened to bring Haman to the banquet that Esther had prepared....

The king said to Esther also on the second day during the wine feast, "What is your petition, Queen Esther, and it shall be given to you. What is your request, even up to half the kingdom, and it shall be granted."

Queen Esther replied and said: "If I have found favor in your eyes, O king, and if it pleases the king, may my life be given me in my petition, and my people in my request. For we have been sold, I and my people, to be destroyed, killed, and annihilated...."

King Ahasuerus said, and he said to Queen Esther: "Who is this and where is he, who dared to do this?" Esther said, "A malevolent and hateful man, this evil Haman...!"

The king arose in his rage from the wine feast to the orchard garden; and Haman stood to beg for his life from Queen Esther, for he saw that evil was determined against him by the king.

The king returned from the orchard garden ... and Haman was falling on the couch upon which Esther was. The king said, "Will you even vanquish the queen with me in the house?" The word came out of the king's mouth, and Haman's face was covered.

Then said Harbonah, one of the chamberlains before the king, "Also, here are the gallows that Haman made for Mordecai, who spoke well for the king, standing in Haman's house, fifty cubits high!" And the king said, "Hang him on it!" They hanged Haman on the gallows that he had prepared for Mordecai, and the king's anger abated....

MASKED MIRACLE

A time-honored Purim custom is to dress up in disguises—an allusion to the fact that the miracle of Purim was disguised in natural "garments." This is also the significance behind a traditional Purim food, the *hamantasch*, a pastry whose filling is hidden within a three-cornered crust.

Jewish children in Purim costumes, Jerusalem, Israel, 2016

The king took off his ring, which he had removed from Haman, and gave it to Mordecai.... And King Ahasuerus said to Queen Esther and to Mordecai the Jew ... "You may write concerning the Jews, as you see fit, in the name of the king, and seal it with the king's ring. For the [original] writ that was written in the name of the king and sealed with the king's ring cannot be rescinded...."

And he wrote in the name of King Ahasuerus ... that the king had given to the Jews who are in every city the right to mobilize to protect their lives; to destroy, to kill, and to annihilate the entire host of every people and province that attacks them.... And for the Jews there was light and joy, and gladness and honor.... Many of the peoples of the land became Jews, for the fear of the Jews had fallen upon them.

In the twelfth month—which is the month of Adar—on the thirteenth day thereof, when the king's order and his edict drew near to be executed; on the day that the Jews' enemies looked forward to vanquishing them; it was overturned, that the Jews should vanquish their enemies. The Jews mobilized in their cities ... to wage battle against those who sought to harm them.... They slew their enemies, seventy-five thousand; but they did not lay their hands on the spoils. [This was] on the thirteenth of the month of Adar; they rested on the fourteenth thereof, and made it a day of feasting and joy. And the Jews who were in Shushan mobilized on the thirteenth thereof and on the fourteenth thereof, and rested on the fifteenth thereof, and made it a day of feasting and joy.

Mordecai inscribed these events; and he sent letters to all the Jews who were in all the provinces of King Ahasuerus, both near and far, to enjoin them to observe the fourteenth day of the month of Adar and the fifteenth day thereof, each and every year ... to make them days of feasting and joy, and sending food portions one to another, and gifts to the poor.

The Jews took upon themselves what they had commenced to do, and what Mordecai had written to them. Because Haman the son of Hammedatha the Agagite, the enemy of all the Jews, had devised to destroy the Jews, and he cast the *pur*—that is, the lot—to terrify them and to annihilate them.... Therefore, they called these days Purim, after the *pur*.... These days are remembered and done in every generation, in every family, every province, and every city. These Purim days shall never pass from amongst the Jews, and their remembrance shall not cease from their descendants.

The edict of Esther confirmed these matters of Purim, and it was inscribed in the Book.

Passover to Shavuot

The Exodus from Egypt and the Giving of the Torah at Mount Sinai—the two events occurring seven weeks apart in the spring of 1313 BCE—marked the birth of the Jewish people and the forging of their special relationship with G-d as a "kingdom of priests and a holy nation." We have chronicled these events and explored their significance in our section on Jewish History (see Exodus and Sinai, *pp. 22–39). In these pages, we will look at the observances of the two festivals by which these two events are "remembered and reenacted" each year: the festival of Passover, beginning on the 15th of Nisan, the anniversary of the Exodus; and the festival of Shavuot, observed fifty days later on the sixth day of Sivan, when we stood at Sinai and received the Torah. We will also look at the 49-day "counting of the omer" that connects the two festivals, and at two special dates—the "Second Passover" on Iyar 14, and Lag BaOmer on Iyar 18—occurring during this period.*

FREEDOM REDUX While the first day of Passover coincides with the anniversary of the Exodus, the seventh day of the festival is the day that the sea split for the people of Israel, marking their full liberation from Egyptian hegemony.

The last day of Passover—Day 7 in the Holy Land, Day 8 in the Diaspora—is also associated with the Messianic redemption (see pp. 225–227), which completes the process initiated by the Exodus from Egypt. A Hasidic custom, recently adopted by other communities as well, is to hold a festive "Mashiach's Meal," complete with matzah and four cups of wine, in the closing hours of Passover.

EXODUS 13:3–14

Moses said to the people: Remember this day, when you went out of Egypt....

Matzahs shall be eaten for the seven days. And no leaven of yours shall be seen ... throughout all of your borders.... You shall keep this statute at its appointed time, from year to year....

When your child will ask you tomorrow, saying, "What is this?" you shall say to them: "With a mighty hand G-d took us out of Egypt, out of the house of bondage."

The Birds' Head Haggadah, Southern Germany, circa 1300

*Omer calendar used in the
Tzedek ve-Shalom Synagogue
in Paramaribo, Suriname,
19th century*

*Had Gadya Suite, El Lissitzky, Russia, 1919.
"Had Gadya" (One Little Goat) is a popular hymn sung
at the conclusion of the Passover Seder.*

MATZAH AND LEAVEN

Matzah baking in Williamsburg,
Brooklyn, New York, 2006

FREEDOM FOOD Matzah, the unleavened bread, embodies the
story and the experience of the Exodus. It is the "bread of
poverty" that recalls our hardship under Egyptian slavery. It is
the "hasty bread" that did not have time to rise, reminiscent
of the sudden, drastic, overwhelming change that the Almighty
wrought in our lives. It is the "bread of faith," attesting to the
unquestioning devotion with which we followed G-d into the
wilderness and committed ourselves to be His people. It is the
"bread of healing" that liberates us from the crippling egotism
that enslaves our spirit and shackles our potential.

"*Shemurah* matzah" is made from grain that was closely
guarded from the time it was harvested and is prepared under
special conditions that ensure against even the slightest chance
of leavening. No more than 18 minutes may pass from when
the flour comes in contact with the water until the fully baked
product is removed from the oven. Many observe the custom
of using only handmade *shemurah* matzah for the Seder.

The burning of chametz, Jerusalem, Israel, 2014

THE WAR ON LEAVEN *Chametz*, or "leaven"—that is, any food in
which grain and water come in contact long enough to possibly
ferment—is the antithesis of the unleavened matzah. The Torah
forbids eating *chametz*, deriving benefit from it in any way, and
even having it in our possession for the duration of Passover.
In the weeks before the festival, the Jewish home is the scene
of an all-out effort to remove every last vestige of *chametz* from
the premises. On the night before Passover, we conduct
a solemn search for any remaining *chametz*; on the following
morning, we burn the proceeds of that search and renounce all
ownership of any leaven that may have escaped our notice.

Spiritually, leaven, whose primary feature is that it rises and
inflates itself, represents egotism, which is regarded by Jewish
teaching as the root of all negative character traits and as
the greatest impediment to the spiritual freedom to which we
aspire as our annual experience of the Exodus.

THE SEDER

The Passover Seder is many things in one: part family dinner, part ritualistic meal, part prayer service, part songfest, and part storytelling marathon. Constructed around the child's "four questions" and the story of the Exodus, it also incorporates the matzah and the bitter herbs, the "four cups" of wine, and a host of other mitzvot and customs. To accommodate all these observances and align them in the proper sequence, we conduct a *seder* (Hebrew for "order") consisting of the fifteen steps outlined in the following pages.

 PASSOVER HAGGADAH

The Four Questions

Why is this night different from all other nights?

On all nights, we do not dip even once; on this night, we dip two times (greens in salt-water, and bitter herbs in *haroset*).

On all nights, we eat leavened bread or matzah; on this night, only matzah.

On all nights, we eat any kind of vegetable; on this night, bitter herbs.

On all nights, we eat sitting or reclining; on this night, we all recline.

Passover, Matzah, and Maror

R. Gamliel would say: One who did not speak of these three things on Passover has not fulfilled their obligation (to tell the story of the Exodus). These are: the Passover offering, matzah, and the bitter herbs.

The Passover offering that our ancestors ate in the time that the Holy Temple stood, for what reason did they do so? Because the Omnipresent passed over our ancestors' homes in Egypt, as it is written (Exodus 12:27): "You shall say: It is a Passover-offering to G-d, because He passed over the houses of the children of Israel in Egypt when He struck the Egyptians with a plague, and He saved our houses...."

This matzah that we eat, for what reason? Because the dough of our ancestors did not have time to become

The Four Sons, Arthur Szyk, Lodz, Poland, 1934

FOUR CHILDREN In four different places—Exodus 12:26, 13:8, and 13:14; and Deuteronomy 6:20—the Torah instructs us to relate the story of the Exodus to our children. The Haggadah examines the differences in the wording of the four dialogues, and explains that the Torah is addressing four different types of children: the wise child, who notes the various rituals being practiced and desires to understand their purpose; the rebellious child, who feels alienated from the beliefs and practices of his elders; the simple child, who can only express mystification at the strangeness of it all; and "the child who doesn't know to ask," whose apathy is perhaps the most discouraging of all. The Torah enjoins us to respond to each child with a message that addresses their distinct natures and needs.

leavened before the king of all kings, the Holy One, blessed be He, revealed Himself to them and redeemed them, as it is written (Exodus 12:39): "They baked the dough that they took out of Egypt as matzah-cakes as it did not leaven, as they were driven out of Egypt; neither did they prepare provisions for themselves."

This bitter herb that we eat, for what reason? Because the Egyptians embittered our ancestors' lives in Egypt, as it is written (Exodus 1:14): "They made their lives bitter with hard labor, with mortar and with bricks, and with all manner of labor in the field; all the work they enslaved them with was crushing labor."

the fifteen steps of the seder

THE SEDER PLATTER

(A) The "shankbone"—a roasted bone with most of the meat removed, commemorating the Passover offering brought in the Holy Temple.

KADESH קַדֵּשׁ

1
SANCTIFY
Recite the kiddush over the **1st cup of wine**. We drink four cups of wine in the course of the Passover Seder, representing the "four expressions of redemption" in G-d's words to Moses (Exodus 6:6–7): "I will take out," "I will save," "I will redeem," and "I will take you as My people."

URCHATZ וּרְחַץ

2
CLEANSE
Ritually wash hands (as before eating bread), but without reciting a blessing.

KARPAS כַּרְפַּס

3
GREENS
Eat a small piece of vegetable (E) dipped in salt water (L), in order to arouse the curiosity of the children and prompt them to inquire about the unusual practices of the night. This ritual also has a dual symbolism: it is a sign of freedom, as eating dipped appetizers is a practice of royalty; on the other hand, *karpas*, the Hebrew word for "greens," is an acronym of the phrase "600,000 were subjected to crushing labor," and the salt water evokes the tears of the enslaved Israelites.

KICK BACK While drinking the four cups of wine and eating the three matzahs, we recline (lean to the left) as a sign of freedom and luxury.

YACHATZ יַחַץ

4
DIVIDE
Break the middle matzah (H) in half. The larger half (J) is put aside to be eaten at the end of the meal as the *afikoman* (step 12). The smaller half (K) is put back between the other two matzahs, and will serve as the symbolic "bread of poverty" over which we will tell the story of the Exodus.

Some communities have the custom of tying the *afikoman* to the shoulders of the children—reminiscent of the matzah that the Children of Israel carried out of Egypt "bundled in their robes upon their shoulders" (Exodus 12:34)—and appointing them as its guardians. Others hide the *afikoman* and reward the child who finds it with a prize. In both cases, the purpose is to keep the children engaged in the Seder.

MAGGID מַגִּיד

5
TELL
The children ask the "Four Questions." In response, tell the story of the Exodus, as provided in the Haggadah, which incorporates history, textual analysis, prayers, and songs. The Haggadah is read together, and all are encouraged to contribute insights and commentary. When the "ten plagues" (see p. 30) are mentioned, drops of wine are spilled into a broken dish.

Drink the **2nd cup of wine** at the conclusion of this step.

RACHTZAH רָחְצָה

6
WASH
Wash hands ritually, with a blessing.

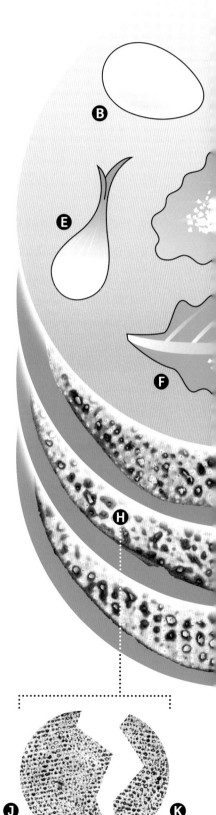

Ⓑ A hard-boiled egg, commemorating the "festival offering" brought in the Holy Temple on the three pilgrimage festivals of Passover, Shavuot, and Sukkot.

Ⓒ *Maror,* or "bitter herbs"; commonly romaine lettuce and/or horseradish.

Ⓓ *Haroset,* a paste made of apples, nuts, wine, and other ingredients.

Ⓔ "Greens"—a small piece of vegetable, commonly potato, onion, celery, or parsley.

Ⓕ More bitter herbs (same as *"Maror"* Ⓒ).

Ⓖ Ⓗ Ⓘ Three matzahs.

Ⓙ The larger half of the broken middle matzah.

Ⓚ The smaller half of the broken middle matzah.

Ⓛ Salt water.

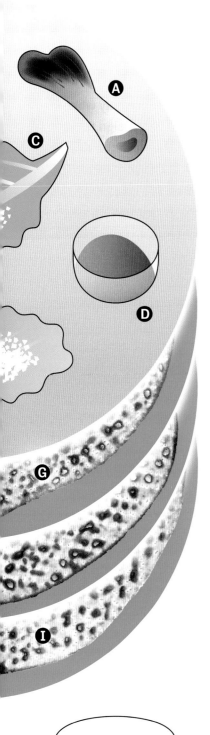

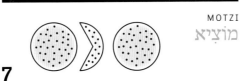

MOTZI
מוֹצִיא

7
NOURISHMENT
Recite the blessing *Hamotzi*—"Blessed are You G-d ... who brings forth bread from the earth"—while holding whole matzahs Ⓖ and Ⓘ, with the broken half Ⓚ between them.

MATZAH
מַצָּה

8
UNLEAVENED BREAD
Hold matzahs Ⓖ and Ⓚ, recite the special blessing over "the eating of matzah," and eat a piece from each of them.

According to *Zohar*, the half-matzah represents the redemption from Egypt, which was as "the light of the moon," whereas the whole matzah represents the future Messianic redemption, when "the light of the moon shall be as the light of the sun" (Isaiah 30:26).

MAROR
מָרוֹר

9
BITTERNESS
Recite the blessing for the *maror* ("bitter herb") Ⓒ, which recalls the bitterness of our slavery in Egypt. Before eating, dip the *maror* in *haroset* Ⓓ, evoking the "mortar and bricks" with which we labored.

KORECH
כּוֹרֵךְ

10
WRAP
Make a matzah-*maror* sandwich by dipping the second portion of bitter herbs Ⓕ in *haroset* Ⓓ and placing it between two pieces taken from the bottom matzah Ⓘ. This is in fulfillment of the opinion of the Mishnaic sage Hillel, who understood the commandment "upon matzah and bitter herbs you shall eat it" (Numbers 9:11) in this way.

(see step 4 above)

SHULCHAN ORECH
שֻׁלְחָן עוֹרֵךְ

11
SET TABLE
Eat the festive holiday meal.

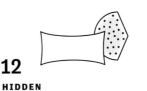

TZAFUN
צָפוּן

12
HIDDEN
Retrieve and eat the *afikoman* Ⓙ (see step 4 above). This additional portion of matzah represents the meat of the Passover offering, which was eaten as *afikoman* ("dessert") at the end of the meal.

BERACH
בָּרֵךְ

13
BLESS
Recite "Grace After Meals" over the 3rd cup of wine.

HALLEL
הַלֵּל

14
PRAISE
Recite the *Hallel* (psalms of praise), thanking G-d for the miracles of the Exodus, over the 4th cup of wine. A fifth cup, called the "Cup of Elijah the Prophet" (who, according to tradition, visits every Jewish home on the Seder night) is poured but not drunk, as it represents the future Messianic redemption. The door is opened, signifying our trust in G-d's protection on this "night of watching."

NIRTZAH
נִרְצָה

15
ACCEPTED
Having fulfilled the 14 active steps of the Seder as prescribed, we are confident that our deeds have been accepted by G-d. "Next Year in Jerusalem" and other traditional Passover songs are sung at the conclusion of the Seder.

THE COUNTING OF THE OMER

"This is your sign that I have sent you. When you take this people out of Egypt, you shall serve G-d on this mountain" (Exodus 3:12). These words, spoken to Moses at the burning bush, defined the purpose of the Exodus: to bring a nation of liberated slaves to Mount Sinai, where they would enter into a covenant with G-d and receive the Torah, committing themselves to the mitzvot that define their special relationship with the Almighty and their role as a "light unto the nations."

Tradition teaches that upon leaving Egypt, our ancestors counted the days in anticipation of this momentous encounter. The Torah subsequently institutionalized this seven-week count as the annual "counting of the *omer.*" Commencing on the second night of Passover—the day on which an offering of an *omer* of barley was brought in the Holy Temple—the 49-day count leads into the festival of Shavuot, which commemorates the giving of the Torah at Mount Sinai.

 **R. ELIYAHU KI-TOV,** *SEFER HATODAAH, VOL. 2, PP. 215–217*

According to the sages of the Kabbalah, the purpose of the seven-week *omer* count is to rectify any deficiencies in the seven *sefirot* or "traits" upon which the world is built.... The seven traits are: *chesed, gevurah, tiferet, netzach, hod, yesod,* and *malchut* (love, awe, compassion, ambition, humility, connectiveness, and receptiveness)....

The days of the *omer* count are especially suited for this rectification. For at the time that the Israelites came out of Egypt to become G-d's people, the gates of merit and purity were opened for them, and in the course of these 49 days, they were refined and elevated. From a nation of brick-makers and straw-gatherers in the service of Pharaoh, they were transformed into a chosen people devoted to the service of G-d.

This path of refinement was paved in the year of the Exodus, and each year at this time, the path is once again cleared for all who wish to traverse it....

Each of these seven character traits incorporates all seven within itself. For example, if love does not also include awe, it is not a productive love, only soft-heartedness; similarly, if love lacks the harmonizing effect of compassion, or any of the other traits. The same is true of all seven *sefirot*: each is complete only when it includes all seven. Thus, the Kabbalists assign to each of the 49 days of the counting of the *omer* the task of rectifying one aspect of one of the seven traits. The first week of the count is devoted to "love," with the first day of the week dedicated to "love in love," the second day to "awe in love," and so on with all seven weeks.

 HOW TO COUNT THE OMER

- The count begins on the second night of Passover and ends the day before Shavuot.

- Both the days and weeks are counted, as the Torah describes the count in terms of the days being counted as well as consisting of "seven complete weeks" and culminating in Shavuot, the "Festival of Weeks."

- Before counting, say: *Blessed are You, Lord our G-d, king of the universe, who has sanctified us with His commandments, and commanded us on the counting of the omer.*

- On the Jewish calendar, the day begins at nightfall and ends at nightfall of the following day. The count should therefore be conducted at the beginning of the night, or at least before daybreak. One who did not count at night may count throughout the day, but without reciting the blessing.

- One who misses an entire day of the count (both night and day) should continue counting on subsequent days, but without a blessing.

- Each day of the count represents another *sefirah*, or character trait (see facing page), and should be utilized for improving that aspect of one's character.

forty-nine steps to Sinai

TEXT OF OMER COUNT:

Today is ＿＿ days, which are ＿＿ weeks and ＿＿ days, to the *omer*

1 DAY	**2** DAYS	**3** DAYS	**4** DAYS	**5** DAYS	**6** DAYS	**7** DAYS 1 WEEK
LOVE IN LOVE	AWE IN LOVE	COMPASSION IN LOVE	AMBITION IN LOVE	HUMILITY IN LOVE	CONNECTIVENESS IN LOVE	RECEPTIVENESS IN LOVE
8 DAYS 1 1 WEEK & DAY	**9** DAYS 1 2 WEEK & DAYS	**10** DAYS 1 3 WEEK & DAYS	**11** DAYS 1 4 WEEK & DAYS	**12** DAYS 1 5 WEEK & DAYS	**13** DAYS 1 6 WEEK & DAYS	**14** DAYS 2 WEEKS
LOVE IN AWE	AWE IN AWE	COMPASSION IN AWE	AMBITION IN AWE	HUMILITY IN AWE	CONNECTIVENESS IN AWE	RECEPTIVENESS IN AWE
15 DAYS 2 1 WEEKS & DAY	**16** DAYS 2 2 WEEKS & DAYS	**17** DAYS 2 3 WEEKS & DAYS	**18** DAYS 2 4 WEEKS & DAYS	**19** DAYS 2 5 WEEKS & DAYS	**20** DAYS 2 6 WEEKS & DAYS	**21** DAYS 3 WEEKS
LOVE IN COMPASSION	AWE IN COMPASSION	COMPASSION IN COMPASSION	AMBITION IN COMPASSION	HUMILITY IN COMPASSION	CONNECTIVENESS IN COMPASSION	RECEPTIVENESS IN COMPASSION
22 DAYS 3 1 WEEKS & DAY	**23** DAYS 3 2 WEEKS & DAYS	**24** DAYS 3 3 WEEKS & DAYS	**25** DAYS 3 4 WEEKS & DAYS	**26** DAYS 3 5 WEEKS & DAYS	**27** DAYS 3 6 WEEKS & DAYS	**28** DAYS 4 WEEKS
LOVE IN AMBITION	AWE IN AMBITION	COMPASSION IN AMBITION	AMBITION IN AMBITION	HUMILITY IN AMBITION	CONNECTIVENESS IN AMBITION	RECEPTIVENESS IN AMBITION
29 DAYS 4 1 WEEKS & DAY	**30** DAYS 4 2 WEEKS & DAYS	**31** DAYS 4 3 WEEKS & DAYS	**32** DAYS 4 4 WEEKS & DAYS	**33** DAYS 4 5 WEEKS & DAYS	**34** DAYS 4 6 WEEKS & DAYS	**35** DAYS 5 WEEKS
LOVE IN HUMILITY	AWE IN HUMILITY	COMPASSION IN HUMILITY	AMBITION IN HUMILITY	HUMILITY IN HUMILITY	CONNECTIVENESS IN HUMILITY	RECEPTIVENESS IN HUMILITY
36 DAYS 5 1 WEEKS & DAY	**37** DAYS 5 2 WEEKS & DAYS	**38** DAYS 5 3 WEEKS & DAYS	**39** DAYS 5 4 WEEKS & DAYS	**40** DAYS 5 5 WEEKS & DAYS	**41** DAYS 5 6 WEEKS & DAYS	**42** DAYS 6 WEEKS
LOVE IN CONNECTIVENESS	AWE IN CONNECTIVENESS	COMPASSION IN CONNECTIVENESS	AMBITION IN CONNECTIVENESS	HUMILITY IN CONNECTIVENESS	CONNECTIVENESS IN CONNECTIVENESS	RECEPTIVENESS IN CONNECTIVENESS
43 DAYS 6 1 WEEKS & DAY	**44** DAYS 6 2 WEEKS & DAYS	**45** DAYS 6 3 WEEKS & DAYS	**46** DAYS 6 4 WEEKS & DAYS	**47** DAYS 6 5 WEEKS & DAYS	**48** DAYS 6 6 WEEKS & DAYS	**49** DAYS 7 WEEKS
LOVE IN RECEPTIVENESS	AWE IN RECEPTIVENESS	COMPASSION IN RECEPTIVENESS	AMBITION IN RECEPTIVENESS	HUMILITY IN RECEPTIVENESS	CONNECTIVENESS IN RECEPTIVENESS	RECEPTIVENESS IN RECEPTIVENESS

THE SECOND PASSOVER

The Second Passover comes one month after the first—on the 14th of Iyar. When the Holy Temple stood in Jerusalem, this day served as an opportunity for those who failed to bring the Passover offering on its appointed day. Today, we commemorate the day by eating matzah, and contemplate its significance as an opportunity to correct the failings and missed opportunities of the past.

The Second Passover also stands as a testament to the power of the human striving to connect with G-d. While all other Biblically-ordained "appointed times" are divine institutions ordained from Above, the Second Passover came in response to a petition by a group of people who were deeply pained by their inability to participate in the Passover offering, prompting the Almighty to institute a new mitzvah to address their need.

 NUMBERS 9:1–14

And G-d spoke to Moses in the Sinai desert, in the second year of their exodus from the land of Egypt, in the first month, saying: "The children of Israel should make the Passover offering in its appointed time. On the fourteenth of this month, in the afternoon, you shall make it in its appointed time; in accordance with all its decrees and laws you shall make it."

Moses spoke to the children of Israel to make the Passover offering.

They made the Passover offering in the first month, on the afternoon of the fourteenth day of the month, in the Sinai Desert; according to all that G-d had commanded Moses, so did the children of Israel do.

Now there were persons who had become ritually impure through contact with a dead body, and could not make the Passover offering on that day. They approached Moses and Aaron on that day. And these people said: "We are ritually impure through contact with a dead body. Why should we be deprived, and not be able to bring G-d's offering in its time, amongst the children of Israel?"

Moses said to them: "Wait here, and I will hear what G-d will command concerning you."

And G-d spoke to Moses, saying: "Speak to the children of Israel, saying: Any person who is contaminated by death, or is on a distant road, whether among you now or in future generations, shall make a Passover offering to G-d. They shall make it on the afternoon of the fourteenth day of the second month, and they shall eat it with matzahs and bitter herbs…. In accordance with all the statutes of the Passover offering, they shall make it."

 R. YOSEF YITZCHAK SCHNEERSOHN
HAYOM YOM, IYAR 14

The essence of the Second Passover is: There is no such thing as a lost case. There is always a second chance.

R. SHLOMO OF RADOMSK
TIFERET SHLOMO, PARASHAT MASSEI

When the desire for the Holy Land is roused in the depths of our heart, and our soul truly pines for the restoration of its glory, this will awaken the Almighty's compassion, and awaken the divine desire to swiftly bring the redemption…. As we find in the story of the Second Passover, when there were ritually impure individuals who had an immense desire to bring the Passover offering, and they cried from the inner walls of their hearts, "Why shall we be deprived from bringing G-d's offering!," the Almighty responded to their plea and gave the mitzvah of the Second Passover. Through their holy desire for connection with the Creator, they brought about the emergence of a new divine law. So, too, if such an intense desire for the Land and for the rebuilding of the Holy Temple will overwhelm our heart, G-d will certainly respond and fulfill it.

LAG BAOMER

The period between Passover and Shavuot is a time of anticipation and preparation, as we retrace our ancestors' journey to Mount Sinai. But it is also a time of mourning. The Talmud (*Yevamot* 62b) relates that 24,000 disciples of R. Akiva died in a plague during this time, because "they did not conduct themselves with respect for each other." Many communities have the custom not to perform marriages during certain parts of this period and follow other mourning observances.

But on Lag BaOmer, the 33rd day of the *omer* count, the mourning practices are suspended, children are taken out on outings, and the day is marked as a festive occasion.

There are two reasons for this joy. One is that the plague that raged among R. Akiva's disciples ceased on this day. A second reason is that it is the anniversary of the passing of 2nd-century sage R. Simeon bar Yochai, whose teachings heralded a new epoch in the dissemination of the mystical dimension of the Torah known as the "Kabbalah." As the day on which R. Simeon's life's work achieved its culmination (see citation from R. Yechiel of Glogau on p. 420), Lag BaOmer is celebrated as the holiday of the esoteric soul of Torah.

 TALMUD, *SHABBAT 33b*

R. Judah [bar Ila'i], R. Yosei, and R. Simeon [bar Yochai] were sitting, and Judah, a son of converts, was sitting near them. R. Judah said: "How fine are the works of [the Romans]! They have set up marketplaces, they have built bridges, they have erected bathhouses." R. Yosei was silent. R. Simeon said: "Everything that they did, they did only for themselves. They built marketplaces in order to place harlots in them. They built bathhouses to pamper themselves. They built bridges to collect tolls."

Judah the son of converts repeated their talk, which reached the government, which decreed: Judah, who exalted us, shall be promoted. Yosei, who was silent, shall be exiled. Simeon, who denounced us, shall be executed.

R. Simeon and his son [R. Elazar] hid in a cave. A carob tree and a wellspring were miraculously created for them. The whole day they studied Torah.... After twelve years, Elijah the Prophet stood at the entrance to the cave and exclaimed: "Who will inform the son of Yochai that the emperor is dead and his decree annulled?" So they emerged.

They saw people plowing and sowing. Said R. Simeon: "They forsake the eternal life [of Torah] and engage in temporal life?" Whatever met their gaze was immediately burnt. A heavenly voice proclaimed: "Have you come out to destroy My world? Return to your cave!" So they lived there another year.

[When they emerged,] wherever R. Elazar wounded, R. Simeon healed.... As the sun was setting on Shabbat eve, they saw an elderly man holding two bundles of myrtle branches and running at twilight. Said R. Simeon to his son: "See how precious the mitzvot are to Israel." And their minds were put at ease.

MYSTIC BOW On Lag BaOmer it is customary to take children to parks and fields to play with bows and arrows. One reason for this custom is that it was a sign of R. Simeon bar Yochai's greatness that a rainbow was not seen in his lifetime (the rainbow is the sign of the divine promise not to destroy the world for its sins; but R. Simeon's righteousness was sufficient, on its own merit, to protect the world).

Another reason is that the bow, which operates on the principle that the more it is drawn toward oneself the further it can reach, reflects the nature of the mystical teachings revealed by R. Simeon: The deeper one delves into the essence of things, the farther one can reach in understanding and impacting the most distant precincts of Creation.

SHAVUOT

Shavuot celebrates the day we stood at Mount Sinai and received the Torah from G-d (see "Giving of the Torah," pp. 36–39). It is a remarkably simple commemoration for so momentous an event. Passover has its matzah, Rosh Hashanah its shofar; in contrast, Shavuot has no special mitzvah to lend it grandeur and occasion. Indeed, what ritual could possibly capture Shavuot's essence—the revelation at Sinai, where we literally "saw the G-d of Israel" and apprehended the truth of all truths?

So, while there are a number of Shavuot customs that Jewish communities adopted through the generations, we essentially mark the day that forged our identity as G-d's people with the observances that are common to all the festivals: we refrain from work, recite the special prayers of the day, and enjoy a festive meal that brings joy to both body and soul.

When the Holy Temple stood in Jerusalem, however, there were two special services associated with Shavuot: the "two breads" offered on the altar in the Temple signifying the start of the wheat harvest; and the "first fruits" that the Jewish farmer brought as a

SINAIC REENACTMENT The public Torah reading for the morning of the first day of Shavuot includes the Ten Commandments and the account of the revelation at Sinai. Many synagogues make a special effort to encourage the entire community to come and listen to the reading, in replication of the original event at which the whole of the Jewish people—men, women, and children—were present.

gift to the priests, over which he proclaimed his gratitude to the Almighty for the land and its bounty. Today, we mention these offerings in the prayers of the day as we express our yearning to once again bring them to the rebuilt divine sanctuary.

◗ SHAVUOT CUSTOMS

■ On Shavuot night we stay awake and study Torah until daybreak. R. Isaac Luria compiled a learning program or *tikun* ("adornment" and "rectification") that includes readings from each *parashah* of the Torah, each book of the Bible, and each tractate of the Mishnah; a listing of the 613 mitzvot; and selections from *Zohar* and other Kabbalistic works.

■ In many communities, the Biblical book of Ruth is read on Shavuot. Ruth's journey of personal sacrifice in forsaking her former life and identity to join the people of Israel personifies the process we underwent as a people at Mount Sinai. Shavuot is also "the festival of harvest" (Exodus 23:16)—a dominant theme in the story of Ruth, which unfolds against the background of the barley harvest in ancient Judea. Finally, the birth of Ruth's great-grandson, King David—the culminating event of the Book of Ruth—as well as David's passing 70 years later, both occurred on Shavuot.

■ It is customary to eat dairy foods on Shavuot, in tribute to the nurturing quality of the Torah, which is compared to milk (Song of Songs 4:11). There is also a tradition that upon receiving the Torah, the Jews refrained from eating meat until they could prepare it in accordance with the newly-given dietary laws. Popular Shavuot foods are cheesecake and cheese blintzes.

■ Many have the custom to decorate the synagogue and the home with flowers and plants, in commemoration of the tradition that Mount Sinai was bedecked in greenery in honor of the giving of the Torah.

From Sefer ha-Todaah by R. Eliyahu Ki-Tov

MAREN CARUSO

CHEESE BLINTZES

BATTER

4	eggs
½	cup milk
½	cup water
1	cup flour
¼	cup sugar
1½	tsp. vanilla sugar
¼	tsp. salt
1	tbsp. oil

FILLING

8	oz. farmer cheese
4	oz. cream cheese
4	tbsp. honey or maple syrup
	juice of ½ lemon
1	egg yolk
	oil for frying

In a large mixing bowl, combine eggs, milk, and water. Blend well. Gradually add flour, then sugar, vanilla sugar, salt, and oil. Beat well until there are no lumps in the batter.

Using a paper towel or a basting brush, apply a thin coating of oil to a 7-inch skillet. Place skillet over medium heat, until skillet is hot but not smoking. Pour approximately ⅓ cup of batter into the skillet, tilting the skillet to swirl the batter so that it covers the bottom of the skillet. Fry on one side only until small bubbles form and the top is set. Bottom should be golden brown. When done, carefully loosen edges of blintz and slip out of skillet onto a plate. Repeat the above process, greasing the skillet as needed, until all the batter is used.

Combine the cheese filling ingredients in a mixer bowl or blender, and mix until smooth. Turn each blintz so that the golden side is up. Spoon 3–4 tablespoons of filling along one edge of the blintz to form a mound approximately 2 ½ inches long and 1 inch wide. Roll once to cover filling. Fold in the sides of the blintz and continue rolling until completely closed.

Heat 2 tablespoons of oil in the skillet. Place each blintz seam side down in the skillet, and fry 2 minutes on each side.

Yields 12 blintzes. Serve with sour cream and blueberries.

The Three Weeks

For more than eight centuries the Holy Temple stood in Jerusalem, serving as the point of contact between heaven and earth. So central is this edifice to our relationship with G-d that nearly two-thirds of the mitzvot (divine commandments in the Torah) are contingent upon its existence. The Temple's destruction is regarded as the greatest tragedy of Jewish history, and its rebuilding will mark the ultimate redemption—the restoration of harmony within G-d's creation, and between G-d and His creation.

A full three weeks of the Jewish year—the three weeks "between the strictures" of Tamuz 17 and Av 9—are designated as a time of mourning over the destruction of the Holy Temple and the resultant galut, *the physical exile and spiritual displacement in which we still find ourselves.*

But the 9th of Av, the day that the Holy Temple was set aflame, is also, by tradition, the birthday of Mashiach, the promised redeemer. The destruction itself holds the seeds of reconstruction and redemption.

The Arch of Titus (detail), Rome, 82 CE

JEBULON

Tish'ah B'Av, Maurycy Minkowski, Paris, 1927

 **R. CHAIM OF VOLOZHIN,**
CITED IN AVNEI CHEIN, 1:791

The Talmud (*Taanit* 30b) states: "Those who mourn Jerusalem merit to behold its joy." The question is asked: Would it not be more correct to say, "*will* merit to behold its joy," in the future tense?

This question can be answered based on Rashi's commentary on Genesis 37:35. Citing the words "[Jacob] refused to be consoled," Rashi explains: "Because a person is not consoled over the living." Over one who has truly died, a person is eventually consoled, because it has been decreed that the dead should be forgotten; as it is written (Psalms 31:13), "I was forgotten as the dead are forgotten by the heart." But when a person is only thought to be dead but is, in fact, still alive (as was the case with Joseph), those who mourn that person are not consoled.

The same is true regarding Jerusalem: Were it that she was truly and hopelessly dead, Heaven forbid, we would have long forgotten her, as every loss is eventually forgotten. But seeing that some two thousand years have elapsed, yet Jerusalem and the Land of Israel have not been forgotten from our hearts, this is a sure sign that they still live within us.

According to this, it is indeed fitting that our sages spoke in the present tense when they said, "Those who mourn Jerusalem merit to behold its joy." Even as we weep and mourn, we simultaneously experience its joy. For there is no greater joy than the knowledge that the hope of Jerusalem has not died in us.

{FOR MORE ON THE HOLY TEMPLE, SEE PP. 64–73}

THREE WEEKS OF MOURNING

TAMUZ 17	TAMUZ 18	TAMUZ 19	TAMUZ 20	TAMUZ 21
FAST DAY				
Begin mourning practices: e.g., no weddings or other joyful events, no music and dancing, no haircuts or shaving.				First of the "Three of Rebuke" readings from the Prophets. JEREMIAH 1:1–2:3

TAMUZ 22	TAMUZ 23	TAMUZ 24	TAMUZ 25	TAMUZ 26	TAMUZ 27	TAMUZ 28
						Second of the "Rebuke" readings. JEREMIAH 2:4–28

TAMUZ 29	AV 1	AV 2	AV 3	AV 4	AV 5	AV 6
	The "Nine Days" of increased mourning practices begin. No meat or wine, no bathing for pleasure, etc.					SHABBAT OF VISION Third "Rebuke" reading. ISAIAH 1:1–27 Most mourning practices suspended in honor of the Shabbat.

AV 7	AV 8	AV 9 (TISH'AH B'AV)
		FAST DAY The Book of Lamentations and *kinot* (elegies) are read in the synagogue. Additional mourning practices include sitting on a low stool, and studying only somber portions of Torah.

THREE WEEKS CALENDAR Shown here is the example of a year in which the Three Weeks begin on Tuesday. When Tamuz 17 and Av 9 fall on Shabbat, the fast is postponed to Sunday.

The mourning customs vary from community to community. Presented here is the custom followed by most Ashkenazic communities. Sephardic communities are generally more lenient, applying the mourning practices only in the week of Tish'ah B'Av (beginning Av 7 in the example above).

 MIDRASH RABBAH, *EICHAH 1:29*

"All her pursuers caught her between the strictures" (Lamentations 1:3). Meaning, in the calamitous days between the 17th of Tamuz and the 9th of Av.

 MISHNAH, *TAANIT 4:6*

Five things happened to our ancestors on the 17th of Tamuz, and five on the 9th of Av.

On the 17th of Tamuz:

The tablets [inscribed with the Ten Commandments] were broken [see p. 40];

the daily offerings in the Holy Temple were disrupted;

the city walls of Jerusalem were breached;

Apostomus burned the Torah;

and an idol was placed in the Temple sanctuary.

On the ninth of Av:

It was decreed that our ancestors should not enter the Holy Land [see "The Spies" on p. 45];

both the first and second Temples were destroyed;

the town of Betar was captured [see p. 84];

and the city [Jerusalem] was plowed under.

From when the month of Av begins, we decrease in joy.

TISH'AH B'AV

 R. LEVI YITZCHAK OF BERDITCHEV
CITED IN *OHR HATORAH, NACH, VOL. 2, P. 1097*

There was a father who had a child who was very dear to him. The father made a precious suit of clothes for his child, but the child did not take proper care of it and engaged in improper activities, and the suit was torn to pieces. The father made a second suit, but the child destroyed that one as well. So the father made a third suit of clothes, and put it away for safekeeping. From time to time, the father shows the suit to his child and says to him: "Look! If you conduct yourself properly, you will be given this suit to wear."

This is why the Shabbat before Tish'ah B'Av is called "The Shabbat of Vision." On this day, each of us is shown a vision of the future Third Temple.

SELECTIONS FROM THE BOOK OF LAMENTATIONS

How she sits alone! The city once so populous, she has become like a widow. Great among the nations, a princess among the provinces, has become tributary.

Weep does she weep in the night, and her tears are upon her cheek; she has no comforter among all her lovers. All her friends have betrayed her, they have become enemies to her.

Judah was exiled in affliction and great servitude; she settled among the nations and found no haven. All her pursuers caught her between the strictures.

The roads of Zion are mournful, empty of the festival pilgrims; all her gates are desolate, her priests moan; her maidens grieve, and she, it is bitter for her…. Gone from the daughter of Zion is all her splendor….

Behold and see … is there any pain like my pain which has been dealt to me, which G-d has anguished me on the day of His fierce anger?

From above He has hurled fire into my bones, and it broke them; He has spread a net for my feet, He has turned me back, He has made me desolate….

For these things I weep; my eye, my eye sheds wa-

ter, for the comforter who restores my soul is removed from me….

G-d is just, for I have defied His word….

What shall I compare to you, O daughter of Jerusalem? What can I liken to you, that I may comfort you, O maiden of Zion? For your ruin is as vast as the sea; who can heal you…?

Arise, keen in the night, at the beginning of the watch-hour; pour your heart like water before the face of the Lord; lift up your hands to Him for the lives of your infants, who are faint with hunger at the head of every street.

See, G-d, and look, to whom you have done this! Would women devour their own offspring, their dandled infants? Would priest and prophet be slain in the sanctuary of G-d?

In the streets, on the ground, lie young and old; my maidens and my youths have fallen by the sword. You have slain them in the day of Your anger; You have slaughtered without mercy….

Though I cry out and plead, He shuts out my prayer…. So I said: My eternity is lost, and my hope from G-d….

This I reply to my heart; therefore, I have hope: The kindness of G-d never ends; His mercies never cease….

Let us search and examine our ways, and let us return to G-d. Let us lift up our hearts to our [raised] hands, to G-d in heaven….

Remember, O G-d, what has befallen us; behold and see our disgrace. Our heritage has been turned over to strangers, our houses to foreigners….

For this our heart has become ill, for these things our eyes have gone dark. For Mount Zion, which has become desolate; foxes prowl over it.

But You, G-d, remain forever; Your throne endures through the generations. Why should you forget us for an eternity, forsake us so long? Restore us to You, O G-d, and we shall return. Renew our days as before.

DON ISAAC ABARBANEL
COMMENTARY TO JEREMIAH 2:24

It turned out that the day set for the expulsion of the Jews from Spain was the 9th of Av. The king did not know anything about the nature of this day; it was as if he had been led from Heaven to set this time.

R. JUDAH HALEVI, *TISH'AH B'AV ELEGY*

Zion, would you not inquire after the welfare of your imprisoned, those seeking your welfare, the remnant of your flock...? Those prisoners of longing, letting fall tears like the dew on Mount Hermon, longing to let them fall on your mountains....

If only I could wander in the places where G-d was revealed to your envoys and seers! Who shall make wings for me, that I may roam afar, that the broken pieces of my heart may flutter among your broken hills? I would fall to my face upon your soil, treasure your stones, cherish your dust....

O Zion, the perfection of beauty ... in you are bound the souls of your friends. They who rejoice in your tranquility, who are pained by your desolation, who weep over your ruins. From the pit of captivity they strive for you; they prostrate themselves, each from their place, toward your gates. The flocks of your multitudes, who were exiled and scattered from mountain to hill, and did not forget your walls. They cling to your skirts, they struggle to rise and grasp the branches of your palm tree.

Babylon and Egypt; can their greatness compare to yours, can their vain vapor compare to your innocence and light...? They shall fade and vanish, all the idolatrous kingdoms. But your power is forever, your crown for all generations.

Your G-d has desired you as an abode; fortunate is the man who chooses to draw near and dwell in your courtyards. Fortunate is the one who waits, and will arrive, to behold the rising of your light, and upon whom your dawn will break. To behold the goodness of your chosen ones, to exult in your joy, when you are restored to your youthfulness of yore.

TALMUD, *MAKOT 24b*

Again it happened that R. Gamliel, R. Elazar ben Azariah, R. Joshua, and R. Akiva went up to Jerusalem... When they reached the Temple Mount, they saw a fox emerging from the place of the Holy of Holies. The others started weeping; R. Akiva laughed.

Said they to him: "Why are you laughing?"

Said he to them: "Why are you weeping?"

Said they to him: "A place so holy that it is said of it, 'The stranger that approaches it shall die' (Numbers 1:51); now foxes traverse it, and we should not weep?"

Said he to them: "That is why I laugh.... Uriah prophesied, 'Zion shall be plowed as a field; Jerusalem shall become heaps, and the Temple Mount like the high places of a forest' (Micah 3:12). And Zechariah prophesied, 'Old men and women shall yet sit in the streets of Jerusalem' (Zechariah 8:4). As long as the prophecy of Uriah had not been fulfilled, I feared that the prophecy of Zechariah may not be fulfilled. But now that Uriah's prophecy has been fulfilled, it is certain that Zechariah's prophecy will be fulfilled."

With these words they responded to him: "Akiva, you have consoled us! Akiva, you have consoled us!"

JERUSALEM TALMUD, *BERACHOT 2:4*

On the day that the Holy Temple was destroyed, a Jew was plowing his field when his cow suddenly called out. An Arab was passing by and heard the call of the cow. Said the Arab to the Jew: "Son of Judah! Unyoke your cow, free the stake of your plow, for your Holy Temple has now been destroyed." The cow then called a second time. Said the Arab to the Jew: "Son of Judah! Yoke your cow, reset the stake of your plow, for Mashiach has now been born."

The Western Wall at Sunset

Prayer at the Western Wall

Lifecycle Milestones

5

"The human being is a miniature universe," declare the sages of Israel. The saga of an individual lifespan—birth, maturation, marriage, pro-creation, achievement, and legacy, and then the passing to a new state of being in the World to Come—mirrors the story of a people, of mankind, and of Creation as a whole. As Judaism commemorates the milestones of national and universal history, so does it establish the practices and rituals that infuse meaning into the stepping stones of our individual progress from womb to grave and beyond.

ECCLESIASTES 3:1–8

To every thing there is a season, a time to every purpose under the heavens:

A time to give birth and a time to die; a time to plant and a time to uproot what is planted.

A time to kill and a time to heal; a time to break and a time to build.

A time to weep and a time to laugh; a time to mourn and a time to dance.

A time to cast stones and a time to gather stones; a time to embrace and a time to refrain from embracing.

A time to search and a time to lose; a time to keep and a time to cast away.

A time to rend and a time to mend; a time to be silent and a time to speak.

A time to love and a time to hate; a time for war and a time for peace.

ETHICS OF THE FATHERS, *CH. 5, MISHNAH 22*

Five years is the age [to begin] the study of Scripture. Ten, for the study of Mishnah. Thirteen, for the obligation to observe the mitzvot. Fifteen, for the study of Talmud. Eighteen, for marriage. Twenty, to pursue [a livelihood]. Thirty, for strength. Forty, for understanding. Fifty, for counsel. Sixty, for sagacity. Seventy, for elderliness. Eighty, for power. Ninety, for meditation. At one hundred years, it is as if one has died and passed away and has been negated from the material world.

Chair of Elijah, Dermbach, Germany, circa 1768

AGATHA ROWLAND

Badeken (traditional veiling of the bride), Toronto, Canada, 2015

Ecclesiastes,
The Cervera Bible,
Spain, 1300

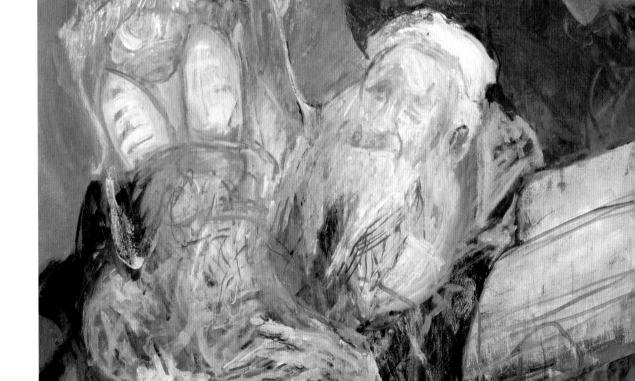

Old Man with Torah (detail), Hyman Bloom, Boston, 1999

Birth and childhood

One of the most important statements Judaism makes is that each and every person is singularly indispensable to the divine purpose in Creation. The very fact that a person was born means that no other person who ever lived, nor any other person who ever will live, can accomplish what he or she can accomplish. Only this person has been entrusted by his or her Creator with the unique set of circumstances and abilities required to fulfill their individual mission in life.

Hence the special joy that a birth evokes. On the day that a child emerges from the womb, we have no way of knowing if their life will be long or short, tranquil or challenge-ridden; if his or her achievements will garner universal acclaim, or fail to be appreciated by an oblivious world. But one thing we know: our world has been brought one step closer to the fulfillment of its destiny and purpose.

 MIDRASH TANCHUMA, *PEKUDEI 3*

At the moment that a child is conceived … the soul protests, "Master of the world! I am quite satisfied with the world I inhabited since You created me. I am holy and pure, hewn from Your throne of glory. Why do You wish to make me enter this putrid drop?"

The Creator says to the soul, "The world to which I am sending you is better for you than the one in which you have dwelt. When I formed you, I formed you only for this seminal drop…."

Why does the infant cry when it comes out from the womb? Over the loss of its place of tranquility and comfort, and the world it has departed.

 TZEMACH TZEDEK
DERECH MITZVOTECHA 140a–b

When the soul enters the body, this is a "descent for the sake of ascent." Before the soul came into this world, it stood before G-d, as it is written (I Kings 17:1), "By the life of G-d, before whom I stood." To "stand" implies to remain on the same level, never rising or falling, like the angels, who also "stand" before the Divine, with the same love and awe from the time of their creation….

But when the soul comes down into the body, into a place of spiritual darkness and constriction, and it overcomes the concealments of the material world, the soul becomes a "journeyer," ascending level after infinite level…. For the source of the physical creation is even higher than the spiritual, as it derives from the all-encompassing truth of G-d that transcends both the finite and the infinite.

An amulet containing Psalm 121 (see p. 179), traditionally hung above the doorway of the room of a newborn infant, Jerusalem, Land of Israel, 1863

 TALMUD, *NIDAH 30b*

The child in its mother's womb is taught the entire Torah. But as it emerges into the open air, an angel comes and slaps the child on the mouth, and makes it forget....

The child does not leave the womb until it is made to swear the following oath: "Be righteous and do not be wicked. And even if the entire world tells you that you are righteous, regard yourself as if you were wicked."

 TZEMACH TZEDEK
AS CITED IN *OPENING THE TANYA,* P. 44

What is the purpose of this oath? Does not the soul desire only good? It is the human being, saddled with a physical body and nature, that is susceptible to evil, not his or her spiritual essence. So why administer this oath to the soul?

The explanation is that this oath represents not only a promise, but also an empowerment. Every soul possesses the necessary powers to overcome the evil inclination and "not be wicked"; however, these powers reside in the transcendent essence of the soul, and are often beyond the reach of its conscious self. The oath that the soul takes has the effect of stimulating these potentials and making them accessible to its everyday life. Indeed, the Hebrew word for "made to swear" in this Talmudic passage, *mashbi'in*, can also read as *masbi'in*, "is fortified."

 R. JOSEPH B. SOLOVEITCHIK
REFLECTIONS OF THE RAV, VOL. 1, P. 61

Every Jew comes into the world with a natural responsiveness to Torah teaching. Every Jew begins with a share in Torah that was vested in them before their birth; and though the person is made to forget it, it is preserved in the deep recesses of their soul, waiting to be awakened by study and a favorable environment.

THE CHILD IN JUDAISM

 MECHILTA D'RASHBI, *EXODUS 19*

When the Torah was given to the people of Israel at Mount Sinai, the Almighty demanded a guarantee that they would not forsake it. Said the people of Israel: "The heaven and the earth will be our guarantors."

Said G-d: "They won't last forever."

Said they: "Our parents will guarantee it."

Said G-d: "They are busy."

Said they: "Our children will guarantee it."

Said G-d: "These are excellent guarantors."

 R. DR. J.H. HERTZ, *COMMENTARY TO GENESIS 15:2*

Abraham's agonizing cry, "My Lord G-d! What will You give me, if I go childless?" (Genesis 15:2), enables us to look into the soul of the Patriarch. Of what value are earthly possessions to him, if a worthy child who would continue his work after him is denied him?

This attitude of the father of the Jewish people toward the child—that it is the highest of human treasures—has remained that of his descendants to the present day. Among the most enlightened nations of antiquity, the child had no right, no protection, no dignity of any sort. In Greece, for example, weak children were generally exposed on a lonely mountain to perish. The Roman historian Tacitus deemed it a contemptible prejudice of the Jews that "it is a crime amongst them to kill any child!" The rabbis (Talmud, *Shabbat* 119b), on the other hand, spoke of little children as "the Messiahs of mankind," i.e., the child is the perennial regenerative force in humanity, because in the child, the Almighty continually gives mankind a chance to make good its mistakes.

 R. ELIEZER GOLDSCHMIDT, *EZER MISHPAT, P. 9*

The rulings of Torah law regarding child custody are not intended to benefit the parents, but the children. A son or daughter is not an object over which the father or mother has rights. The father and mother have no rights, only obligations; namely, the obligation to raise and educate their children.

 R. MENACHEM M. SCHNEERSON
FROM A TALK, JANUARY 1990

Children have a strong sense of themselves as the center of the universe, and are convinced that everything exists to serve them. There are, of course, negative aspects to such self-centeredness; but the feeling itself—that the individual human being plays the central role in the purpose of Creation—is a positive one. Indeed, the Talmud states, "Every person is obligated to say: For my sake was the world created." The purpose of education is to weed out the negative repercussions of this attitude, and direct it toward its proper expression: that a person should appreciate that their every thought and deed is of real, even global, significance.

Self-portrait by Julie Voigt (age 9), United States, circa 2010

BRIT MILAH

The Talmud (Shabbat 130a) states that "every mitzvah for whose sake the people of Israel sacrificed their lives in times of persecution—for example, the rejection of idol-worship, and the practice of circumcision —remains with them to this day." Indeed, brit milah, *Hebrew for "the covenant of circumcision," has remained a standard-bearer of Jewish identity through 3,800 years of Jewish history, also among Jews who exhibited little or no other identification with their heritage.*

 GENESIS 17:9–11, 17:24, 21:4

G-d said to Abraham: "… This is My covenant (*brit*) which you shall keep, between Me and you and your descendants after you: to be circumcised, every male among you… it will be a covenant-sign between Me and you…."

And Abraham was ninety-nine years old when he was circumcised….

Abraham circumcised his son Isaac at the age of eight days, as G-d had commanded him.

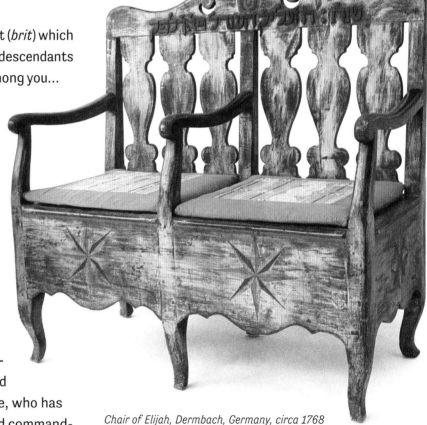

Chair of Elijah, Dermbach, Germany, circa 1768

SEAT OF HONOR The highest honor given at a *brit* is to serve as the *sandak*, the one who holds the baby on their lap while the *mohel* performs the circumcision. The chair on which the *sandak* sits is called "The Chair of Elijah the Prophet," in reference to the tradition that the prophet Elijah attends every *brit* (see citation from *Zohar* on p. 393). Many synagogues have an ornate, throne-like chair reserved for this purpose.

CHINUCH, *MITZVAH 2*

The mitzvah of circumcision is fulfilled by cutting off the foreskin that covers the tip of the male organ, and pushing back the membrane beneath it. Two blessings are recited. The *mohel* (circumciser) says, "Blessed are You, Lord our G-d, king of the universe, who has sanctified us with His commandments, and commanded us regarding circumcision." The child's father says, "Blessed are You … and commanded us to enter him into the covenant of our father Abraham."

Among the core reasons for this mitzvah is that G-d desired that His people should be distinguished bodily, just as they are distinguished spiritually. He set this distinction in the crowning glory of the human body—the organ that facilitates the continuity of the species.

The perfection of the human body is achieved by the removal of the foreskin, which is extraneous to it. But the Creator desired that this perfection be achieved by human action, rather than creating man perfect from the womb, in order to indicate to us that spiritually, too, it is in our hands to perfect our soul through our actions.

 MIDRASH TANCHUMA, *TAZRIA 5*

Tyrannus Rufus the wicked asked R. Akiva: "Which is better—the works of G-d, or the works of humans?"

Said R. Akiva: "The works of humans are better...."

Said Tyrannus Rufus to him: "Why do you circumcise yourselves?"

Said R. Akiva: "I knew that this was what you were going to ask me. That is why I anticipated you by saying that human works are better than works of G-d."

R. Akiva brought him sheaves of grain and loaves of white bread, and said to him: "Those are G-d's work, and these are the work of humans; are these loaves not better than the sheaves?"

UNINVITEDS WELCOME Have you ever gone to a party uninvited? If you've attended a traditional *brit*, chances are that the answer is yes. But don't worry: this is not a breach of etiquette. Traditionally, one does not invite people to attend a *brit*, but simply notifies them of the time and place. This is because it is considered improper to decline an invitation to such a holy occasion.

Said Tyrannus Rufus: "If circumcision is desirable to G-d, why isn't a child born circumcised?"

Said R. Akiva: "And why does his umbilical cord come out with him, leaving him hanging by his belly, and his mother needs to cut it? But the answer to your question—why isn't a child born circumcised—is that G-d gave the mitzvot to the people of Israel for us to be refined by them."

HERMAN WOUK
EXCERPTED FROM *THIS IS MY G-D, PP. 123–125*

Voltaire spoke with scorn of a G-d who could care whether or not people cut off their children's foreskins; thus summing up in one entertaining image the whole skeptical reaction to religious form. Spinoza, an equally severe skeptic, was not as funny as Voltaire; in fact there was little fun in him; but he was the profounder of the two. "So great importance do I attach to this sign," said he, "I am persuaded that it is sufficient by itself to maintain the separate existence of the nation for ever."

Circumcision has lately become respectable, after serving as a joke about Jews for centuries. It turns out to be sound hygiene. On the recommendation of medical science, informed people everywhere are now cutting off their children's foreskins. But for Jews, circumcision today, as in the past four thousand years, is not a detail of hygiene. It is the old seal of the pledge between Abraham and his Creator, a sign in the flesh, a mark at the source of life. The levellers like to say that when you strip off men's clothes, nobody can tell the beggar from the king; but naked or dead, the Jew is recognizable for what he is. The medical endorsement is not the glory of Judaism. It is a footnote.

We circumcise our sons on the eighth day after birth, as Abraham did Isaac, except when a doctor puts off the day for a delicate child. The ordinary infant of eight days passes through the operation easily, sleeping most of the time. Done with skill, the cut causes little pain, and it heals in a couple of days.

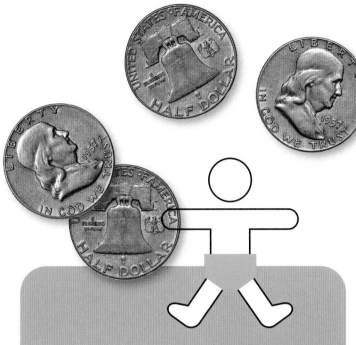

REDEMPTION OF THE FIRSTBORN While a *brit* is a fairly common event in a Jewish community, not many people have had the occasion to participate in a *pidyon ha-ben*, the "redemption of the firstborn" ritual performed on the 31st day following the birth of a firstborn boy. The ritual begins with the following dialogue:

"My Israelite wife has borne me this firstborn son."

"Which do you want, your firstborn son, or the five silver coins you are obligated to give me for the redemption of this firstborn son of yours?"

"I want my firstborn son. Here you have five silver coins for the redemption, as required of me."

A *pidyon ha-ben* is a relatively rare event because it is performed only for a firstborn male child, and only if neither of the child's parents is a Kohen or Levite. But despite its esoteric nature, this is an important mitzvah—one of the first mitzvot given to the Jewish people while they were still in Egypt, as related in the 13th chapter of the Book of Exodus.

The ritual serves as a reminder that when G-d smote the firstborn of Egypt, the Israelite firstborn were spared. As a result, the Jewish firstborn were consecrated to perform the service in the Holy Temple. Although the tribe of Levi subsequently replaced the firstborn in that role, the firstborn still "belong" in principle to the Temple service, and must be redeemed with the gift to the Kohen stipulated in the Torah: five shekels (approx. 100 grams) of silver. While the redemption can be performed with any object of equivalent value, the custom is to reenact the Biblical method by using five silver coins. A festive meal follows the ceremony, to celebrate this unique mitzvah.

The event is what we call a *bris*, the Hebrew word for covenant. Ideally the father should do the circumcision himself, as Abraham did. In universal practice he appoints a highly skilled *mohel*, or circumciser, to do it. Performing hundreds of such ceremonies every year, the mohel attains experience in this operation which many surgeons will candidly admit they cannot match. Mohels use, of course, all existing medical safeguards and antisepsis.

 ZOHAR, *VOL. 1, 93a*

Every time a child is brought to be entered into the covenant of circumcision, Elijah comes there.... We therefore learned that a chair should be prepared in his honor, and one should announce: "This is the chair of Elijah...."

See, originally it is written [that Elijah accused,] "The children of Israel have forsaken Your covenant" (I Kings 19:10). So G-d said to him: By your life! At every occasion that My children will stamp this holy mark in their flesh, you will be present there, and the same mouth that testified that "Israel has forsaken" shall testify that Israel upholds the covenant.

{SEE "ELIJAH," ON PP. 173–175}

 R. JOSEPH BECHOR SHOR
COMMENTARY TO GENESIS 17:24

The Torah relates the age of Abraham at the time of his circumcision in order to teach us that if a person wasn't circumcised at the age of eight days, he can still do so even at an advanced age, like Abraham.

R. JUDAH LOEW, *DERASHOT MAHARAL, DERUSH AL HATORAH*

Three things are designated as "covenants" between G-d and the people of Israel: the Torah, Shabbat, and circumcision. The Torah binds the mind of the Jew to G-d; Shabbat is the bond of the soul; and circumcision binds the body of the Jew to its Creator.

NAMING

MIDRASH RABBAH, *VAYIKRA 32:5*

In the merit of four things the Children of Israel were redeemed from Egypt: They did not change their names and their language; they did not speak badly of each other; and no promiscuity was found among them.

R. CHAIM VITAL
SHAAR HAGILGULIM, INTRODUCTION 23

When a person is born, and their father and mother call their child by a name that arises in their minds, this is not random or arbitrary. Rather, G-d places in their mouth the name that is needed for this soul.

R. SCHNEUR ZALMAN OF LIADI
LIKUTEI TORAH, BEHAR 41c

Before the soul enters the body, it has no name … nor does a lifeless body have any use for a name. Rather, the function of the name is to join the soul with the body. The vitalizing energy that emanates from the soul to give life to the body is rooted in the name.

NAMING CUSTOMS

■ Boys are named at the *brit*. Girls are named at the Torah reading in the synagogue soon after birth, and a *kiddush* or festive meal is held to mark the occasion.

■ It is the custom to honor one's parents, ancestors, or mentors by naming one's children after them. In Ashkenazic communities it is the custom not to name a child after a living family member. The Sephardic custom, however, is to honor the child's living grandfather or grandmother by giving their name to the child.

■ Naming the child is the sole prerogative of the parents. Other family members or friends should not pressure or even advise the parents regarding the name.

A SELECTION OF POPULAR JEWISH NAMES

Aaron (m); *variations* Aharon, Aron; biblical; name of the brother of Moses and the ancestor of the Kohanim ("priests" who served in the Holy Temple); means "exalted"; *Hebrew spelling* אַהֲרֹן

Abigail (f); *var* Avigayil; biblical prophetess and wife of King David; means "my father is joy"; *heb* אֲבִיגַיִל

Abraham (m); *var* Avraham, Avrohom, Avi; biblical; name of the first Jew; means "father of a multitude of nations"; *heb* אַבְרָהָם

Adam (m); biblical; name of first man; means "man"; *heb* אָדָם

Aidel (f); *var* Eidel, Adel, Adelle; Yiddish for "refined"; *heb* אײדל

Akiva (m); name of Talmudic sage; Aramaic form of the name Yaakov (Jacob); *heb* עֲקִיבָא

Amadio (m); Ladino for "love of G-d"; *heb* אמאדיו

Asher (m); *var* Osher; biblical; name of the father of one of the twelve tribes of Israel; means "fortunate"; *heb* אָשֵׁר

Aviva (f); Hebrew for "spring"; *heb* אֲבִיבָה

Baruch (m); *var* Boruch; biblical prophet; means "blessed"; *heb* בָּרוּךְ

Baila (f); *var* Bella; Yiddish for "white"; also a form of the biblical name Bilhah, one of Jacob's wives; *heb* בײלא

Batsheva (f); *var* Bathsheba; biblical; mother of King Solomon; means "daughter of oath"; *heb* בַּת שֶׁבַע

Benjamin (m); *var* Binyomin; biblical; father of one of the twelve tribes of Israel; means "son of the right"; often given together with the name Ze'ev ("wolf"), the symbol of the tribe of Benjamin; *heb* בִּנְיָמִין

Chaim (m); *var* Chayim, Haim, Hayyim; Hebrew for "life"; *heb* חַיִּים

Daniel (m); *var* Doniel; biblical; name of Judean prince during the Babylonian exile; means "G-d is my judge"; *heb* דָנִיֵּאל

David (m); *var* Dovid; biblical; name of the king of Israel and ancestor of the Messiah; means "beloved"; *heb* דָּוִד

Deborah (f); *var* Devorah, Doba; biblical prophetess and leader of Israel; means "bee"; *heb* דָּאבע, דְּבוֹרָה

Dinah (f); *var* Dina, Deena; biblical; name of the daughter of Jacob and Leah; means "judgment"; *heb* דִּינָה

Elijah (m); *var* Eliyahu, Eli; biblical prophet; means "the Almighty is my G-d"; *heb* אֵלִיָּהוּ

Ephraim (m); *var* Efraim, Efrayim; biblical; name of Joseph's second son and of one of the tribes of Israel; means "fruitful"; *heb* אֶפְרַיִם

Esther (f); *var* Ester; biblical prophetess and savior of the Jewish people during the events of Purim; means "hidden"; also Persian for "star"; *heb* אֶסְתֵּר

Fraida (f); *var* Frayda, Fraidel; Yiddish for "joy"; *heb* פריידא, פריידל

Gento (m); Ladino for "good name"; *heb* ג'ענטו

Golda (f); Yiddish for "golden"; *heb* גּוֹלְדָה, גולדא

Hadassah (f); biblical; another name of Esther; means "myrtle"; *heb* הֲדַסָּה

Hannah (f); *var* Chana, Chanah; biblical prophetess and mother of the prophet Samuel; means "grace"; *heb* חַנָּה

Havah (f); *var* Chavah, Eve, Eva; biblical; name of first woman; means "life-giver" and "home"; *heb* חַוָּה

Hayah (f); *var* Chaya, Chayah; Hebrew for "living"; *heb* חַיָּה

Isaac (m); *var* Yitzhak, Yitzchak, Yitzchok, Aizik; biblical; name of one of the three patriarchs of the Jewish people; means "will laugh" and "will rejoice"; *heb* יִצְחָק, אייזיק

Israel (m); *var* Yisrael, Yisroel; biblical; name given by G-d to the patriarch Jacob, and to the Jewish people as a whole; means "divine ruler" and "wrestles with G-d"; *heb* יִשְׂרָאֵל

Jacob (m); *var* Yaakov, Yakov; biblical; name of one of the three patriarchs of the Jewish people; means "to grasp at the heel" and "will follow"; *heb* יַעֲקֹב

Jamila (f); Judeo-Arabic for "beautiful"; *heb* ג'אמילה

Joseph (m); *var* Yosef, Yosei, Yossi; biblical; Jacob and Rachel's first son; means "will increase"; *heb* יוֹסֵף

Judah (m); *var* Yehudah, Yudy; biblical; name of father of one of the 12 tribes of Israel; also used to refer to the Jewish people as a whole; means "will acknowledge" and "will submit to G-d"; *heb* יְהוּדָה

Judith (f); *var* Judy, Yehudit, Yudit, Yehudis; biblical; feminine form of Judah; *heb* יְהוּדִית

Leah (f); *var* Laya; biblical; name of one of the four matriarchs of the Jewish people; means "weary"; *heb* לֵאָה

Leib (m); *var* Laib, Laibel, Loeb, Loew; Yiddish for "lion"; often given together with its Hebrew equivalent, Aryeh, and/or together with Judah; *heb* לייב, לייבל

Levy (m); *var* Levi; biblical; name of Jacob's third son and ancestor of the priestly tribe; means "joined" and "companion"; *heb* לֵוִי

Maimon (m); Judeo-Arabic for "fortune"; *heb* מַימוֹן

Mazal (f); Hebrew for "fortune"; *heb* מַזָּל

Meir (m); *var* Mayer, Meyer; name of Talmudic sage; Hebrew for "luminary"; *heb* מֵאִיר

Menachem (m); *var* Menahem; biblical; means "consoler"; often given together with its Yiddish form, "Mendel"; *heb* מְנַחֵם

Michael (m); *var* Michoel; biblical; name of angel; means "who is like G-d?"; *heb* מִיכָאֵל

Michal (f); biblical; name of the daughter of King Saul and wife of King David; means "who is like G-d?"; *heb* מִיכַל

Miriam (f); *var* Miryam, Mirel; biblical prophetess and sister of Moses and Aaron; means "bitter"; *heb* מִרְיָם, מירל

Moshe (m); *var* Moishe, Moses; biblical; name of the leader who took the Children of Israel out of Egypt and received the Torah from G-d; means "drawn"; *heb* מֹשֶׁה

Naomi (f); *var* Naami, Nomi; biblical; name of Ruth's mother-in-law; means "pleasant" and "sweet"; *heb* נָעֳמִי

Nissim (m); Hebrew for "miracles"; *heb* נִסִּים

Ovadiah (m); *var* Obadiah; biblical prophet; means "servant of G-d"; *heb* עֹבַדְיָה

Rahamim (m); *var* Rachamim; Hebrew for "compassion"; *heb* רַחֲמִים

Rachel (f); *var* Rochel, Rakhel, Raquel; biblical, name of one of the four matriarchs of the Jewish people; means "ewe"; *heb* רָחֵל

Rebecca (f); *var* Rivkah, Riva; biblical, name of one of the four matriarchs of the Jewish people; means "yoke" or "captivating"; *heb* רִיבָה, רִבְקָה

Ruth (f); *var* Rus; biblical; name of the Moabite convert to Judaism who was King David's ancestor; means "replete" or "friendship"; *heb* רוּת

Saadia (m); *var* Sa'adya, Se'adya; Hebrew/Aramaic for "G-d's help"; *heb* סַעֲדְיָה

Sarah (f); *var* Sara, Suri; biblical, name of the first matriarch of the Jewish people; means "ruler" and "princess"; *heb* שָׂרָה

Shaina (f); *var* Shayna, Shaindel; Yiddish for "beautiful"; *heb* שיינא, שיינדל

Shalom (m); *var* Sholom; Hebrew for "peace"; *heb* שָׁלוֹם

Samuel *var* Shmuel; biblical prophet and leader; means "granted from G-d"; *heb* שְׁמוּאֵל

Shoshana (f); Hebrew for "rose" or "lily"; *heb* שׁוֹשַׁנָּה

Shulamith (f); *var* Shulamis, Shulamit, Shlomit; biblical; name of the maiden lauded in Song of Songs; means "peace"; *heb* שׁוּלַמִּית, שְׁלוֹמִית

Simcha; (m/f); Hebrew for "happiness"; *heb* שִׂמְחָה

Solomon (m); *var* Shlomo, Shloime; biblical; king of Israel and builder of the first Holy Temple; means "peace"; often given together with its Yiddish form, Zalman; *heb* שְׁלֹמֹה

Tamar (f); biblical; name of the daughter-in-law of Judah and ancestor of King David; means "date palm"; *heb* תָּמָר

Yael (f); *var* Jael; biblical; name of the woman who slew the Canaanite general Sisera; means "ibex"; *heb* יָעֵל

Yenta (f); *var* Yentel; Yiddish for "noble"; *heb* יענטל, יענטא

Zalman (m); Yiddish form of Solomon; *heb* זַלְמָן

EDUCATION

Many have marveled at the Jewish commitment to education, and the resultant high level of literacy in Jewish communities of every age and locale. A pupil of the eleventh-century scholar Peter Abelard observed: "A Jew, however poor, if he had ten sons he would put them all to letters, not for gain, as the Christians do, but to the understanding of G-d's Law, and not only his sons, but his daughters."

For the Jew, education is much more than a tool for earning a living or for social advancement, or even for intellectual enrichment. Rather, it is deemed indispensable to the goal of raising one's child to be a proper Jew, and to the equally fundamental goal of developing and refining the child's character. Indeed, the sages of Israel taught, "Common decency is antecedent to Torah."

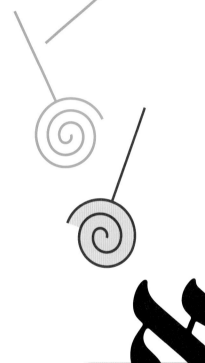

SWEET LEARNING The day that a child begins their Jewish schooling is celebrated in a way designed to foster a love of learning in the child's heart. The letters of the *aleph-bet* are coated with honey for the child to lick, imparting the message that "G-d's Torah is wholesome, restoring the soul … rejoicing the heart … enlightening the eyes … sweeter than honey and the drippings of honeycombs" (Psalms 19:8-11); a modern twist on this custom is to write the letters in icing on cupcakes baked for the occasion. As the teacher guides the child through their first encounter with the holy letters, candies are thrown down from above, which the child is told are being cast by the heavenly angel Michael.

 **DEUTERONOMY 6:6–7**

And these words, which I command you this day, shall be upon your heart; you shall teach them thoroughly to your children, and you shall speak of them when sitting in your home and when walking on the road, when you lie down and when you rise.

 **TALMUD,** *KIDUSHIN 29a*

A father is obligated to circumcise his son, to redeem him [if he is a firstborn], to teach him Torah, to find a wife for him, and to teach him a profession. Some say that a father is also obligated to teach his child to swim.

 **ETHICS OF THE FATHERS,** *CH. 4, MISHNAH 20*

One who learns Torah in his childhood, what is this comparable to? To ink inscribed on fresh paper. One who learns Torah in his old age, what is this comparable to? To ink inscribed on erased paper.

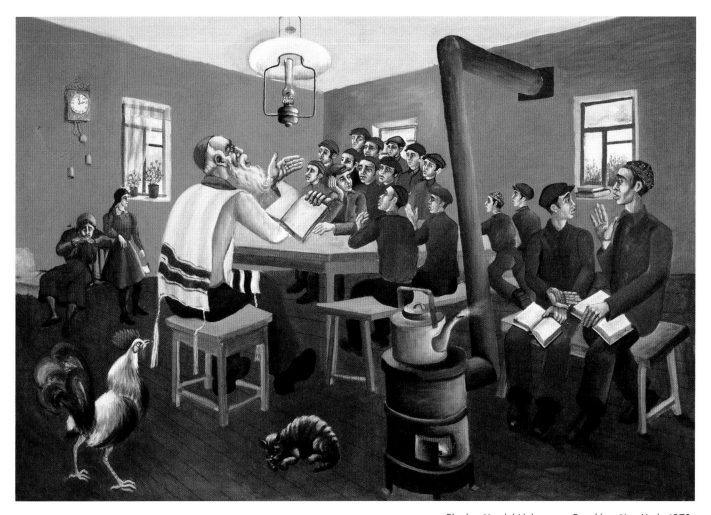

Cheder, Hendel Lieberman, Brooklyn, New York, 1970s

 TALMUD, *BAVA BATRA 21a*

Indeed, there is a certain individual who must be remembered for the good, and his name was Joshua ben Gamla; were it not for him, the Torah would have been forgotten from Israel.

For at first, if a child had a father, his father taught him Torah; if he had no father, he did not learn Torah.... Then they made an ordinance that teachers of children should be appointed in Jerusalem.... Still, if a child had a father, the father would take him up to Jerusalem and have him taught there, and if not, he would not go up to learn. They subsequently ordained that teachers should be appointed in every district, and pupils were accepted at the age of sixteen or seventeen. But a student whose teacher got angry with him would rebel and leave the school. Until Joshua ben Gamla came and ordained that teachers of young children should be appointed in every district and every town, and that children should enter school at the age of six or seven.

 R. ELIJAH OF VILNA
COMMENTARY TO PROVERBS 22:6

We cannot escape our innate personality ... but we can choose how to channel it and utilize it—either for positive, or negative, or neutral ends. The Talmud (*Shabbat* 156a) says that a person who is born with a "martian" nature—i.e., with the inclination to spill blood—can turn out to be a medic, or a gangster, or a butcher, or a *mohel*.

This is the meaning of the verse (Proverbs 22:6), "Educate the child in accordance with their way; even when they grow old, they will not turn away from it." If we direct a child in a path that is consistent with their nature, they will not abandon it later in their lives. If, however, we compel a child to follow a path that is inconsistent with their nature, the child may listen to us now, in deference to our authority, but afterward, when they grow older, they will turn away from the education we gave them.

ALTER KACYZNE

Girls' cheder, Bielsko-Biala, Poland, 1926

 CHATAM SOFER
COMMENTARIES ON TALMUD, BAVA BATRA 21a

Those who teach Torah to children must be exceedingly devout and G-d-fearing ... because words that emanate from a reverent heart penetrate the hearts of the young listeners and instill in them love and awe of G-d. The opposite is also true: The teacher may be an accomplished scholar and pedagogue, but if their heart is not true to G-d, their work is fraudulent and they destroy their charges.

With this principle in mind, we can understand the sequence of verses (Deuteronomy 6:6–7): "These words that I command you this day shall be upon your heart," and only then, "You shall teach them to your children."

 R. SAMSON RAPHAEL HIRSCH
PRINCIPLES OF EDUCATION, VOL. 2, PP. 56–57

Why is it so difficult for parents to instill in their children the foundational value of uncoerced acceptance of authority and discipline? Perhaps the true reason for this phenomenon is that self-discipline may be the

one trait that children do not see exemplified by their parents. If our children see us only in the guise of authority figures—as instructors and enforcers—from whom will they learn the trait of obedience?

Jewish parents, however, have the advantage of leading a Jewish way of life, which is suffused with joyous, freely chosen obedience and self-discipline, and where the mitzvot (divine commandments) serve as the foundations of all positive character traits. In the eyes of a child, the Torah constitutes the "parents" of his or her parents, and the joy with which their parents subordinate themselves to the discipline of Torah and adhere to its imperatives and prohibitions in their day-to-day lives is an amazing educational model for the child to emulate, among many other positive traits.

This approach also applies beyond the context [of the Torah's instructions]. The rules that we impose on our children should flow from our own self-discipline. When we are thoughtful in the manner in which we allow or forbid a child to do something, and when we happily give the child the autonomy to do as he or she wishes [when appropriate], we demonstrate that whatever we permit or prohibit is not a product of a transient mood, the result of our desire for control, or due to our stubbornness. Rather, the child sees that our instruction is a result of careful consideration and serious thought.

 R. SHALOM DOVBER OF LUBAVITCH
HAYOM YOM, TEVET 22

In the same way that putting on *tefillin* every day is a Biblical mitzvah that applies to every Jewish man, regardless of whether he is a great Torah scholar or a simple person, so too it is an absolute duty for every person to spend a half hour every day thinking about the education of children, and to do everything in their power, and more than what is in their power, to influence children to follow in the proper path.

THE JEWISH BIRTHDAY

The sages taught that on a person's birthday, their "mazal"—the channel of spiritual sustenance connecting their soul with its source on high—operates in a heightened and more potent manner. Because this is the day on which our individual mission in life was inaugurated, the resources we are granted to accomplish this mission are available to us in a more powerful way. Any good resolutions made on this day, and any new initiatives we undertake, are especially empowered to succeed.

UPSHERIN In Jewish tradition, a child's third birthday signals an important milestone in his or her education. The child begins to be trained to recite the Shema and the blessings over food, and to participate in the doing of various mitzvot and Jewish customs.

For a Jewish boy, an age-old custom is to mark this transition with a celebration—called an *upsherin* in Yiddish, and a *chalakah* by Sephardic Jews. The child, whose hair is left unshorn for the first three years of life, receives his first haircut, leaving his *peyot* (Biblically mandated side-locks), and is encouraged to begin wearing a kipah and tzitzit.

For girls, this is the age at which many communities have the custom for a girl to begin lighting her own Shabbat candle. Many also mark this event with a party for family and friends to celebrate the child's formal start of her Jewish education.

 HAYOM YOM, *NISAN 11*

On the day of their birthday, a person should spend some time in seclusion, bring to mind recollections from the past and contemplate them, and repent and rectify those things that require correction.

HOW TO CELEBRATE YOUR JEWISH BIRTHDAY

■ Arrange to be called up to the Torah in the synagogue on the Shabbat before your Jewish birthday.

■ Give extra charity on this day. (If your birthday is on Shabbat or a festival day, do so on the preceding day.)

■ Pray with increased concentration, and read from the Book of Psalms.

■ Read and study the chapter in Psalms that corresponds with the years of your life (e.g., on your 30th birthday study Psalm 31, as you are entering your 31st year).

■ Study Torah texts (in addition to your regular study schedule).

■ Learn a text from the mystical portion of the Torah, and repeat it to others.

■ Find a way to lovingly and respectfully have a positive influence on another person.

■ Set aside a time for private contemplation and stocktaking of the previous year, resolving to correct any wrongdoings and to find ways to improve yourself.

■ Undertake a new mitzvah or positive practice in honor of your birthday.

■ Get together with family and friends to joyously celebrate and express your gratitude to G-d.

A ten-point program suggested by the Lubavitcher Rebbe, R. Menachem M. Schneerson

Bar and Bat Mitzvah

A Jewish girl attains adulthood at age twelve; a Jewish boy one year later, at age thirteen. This is the age at which, according to Torah law, a person's faculty of daat *(intellectual maturity and self-awareness) has developed to the point that she or he is responsible for their actions.*

In Judaism, responsibility is not a burden, but a privilege; obligation is not bemoaned, but celebrated. Hence, the day on which a Jew becomes Bar or Bat Mitzvah—i.e., obligated to fulfill the divine commandments of the Torah—is a joyous day for the young man or woman, for their family and friends, and for the community as a whole.

 TZVI FREEMAN, *CHABAD.ORG*

Bar Mitzvah: Myths and Facts

MYTH: A Bar Mitzvah is an event.
FACT: A Bar Mitzvah is a person. The term *bar mitzvah* is Hebrew for "one who is obligated to fulfill the commandments."

MYTH: To become Bar Mitzvah, you must be called to the Torah and make a big party.
FACT: To become Bar Mitzvah, you must reach the age of thirteen for a boy, or twelve for a girl. (According to the sages of the Talmud, the mind of a girl matures earlier than that of a boy.) The custom of making a feast to celebrate the occasion goes back many centuries, but the nature of the celebration varies from community to community.

MYTH: It is a custom since the days of Moses that the Bar Mitzvah boy reads the entire Shabbat Torah reading in public.
FACT: The tradition to be called to the Torah on the occasion of one's Bar Mitzvah is mentioned in the ancient Midrash. Having the Bar Mitzvah boy perform the entire reading is a recent custom that seems to have arisen in 19th-century Germany.

MYTH: Bar Mitzvah training consists of at least one year learning how to read the Torah.
FACT: Bar Mitzvah training consists of twelve or thirteen years of learning how to do mitzvahs, and why. And it continues for the rest of one's life.

MYTH: The idea that a person becomes an adult at such an early age is a holdover from agrarian times.
FACT: Establishing adulthood at these ages is progressive to this day. Twelve/thirteen is when a girl or boy begins to develop her or his own mind. The reason boys are generally considered men at around eighteen is because that is the age they can carry arms and go to war. The Jewish nation is based not on the power of battle, but on the power of the mind.

 R. MENACHEM M. SCHNEERSON, *RESHIMOT #19*

The age of majority for Jews is thirteen…. This stands in contrast to the laws of other nations, whereby one reaches the age of majority at the age of twenty, twenty-one, or the like.

The reason for this: The other nations were formed when people abandoned their nomadic existence as herdsmen to settle on a land, banded together to choose a leader, and organized militarily to defend their territory; following which they established a legal system.

Regarding the people of Israel, the opposite is true. Immediately upon being liberated from bondage in Egypt, while still in an uninhabitable wilderness, they began a life defined by the Torah and mitzvot.... This was the foundation and beginning of their becoming a people.

Accordingly, a Jewish boy does not attain maturity at age twenty, when he has the physical prowess to contribute to his country's existence by defending it in war; but at the age of thirteen, when he is mature enough to understand the great privilege and responsibility of being a part of the Jewish people.

Bat Mitzvah celebration (detail), Miami Beach, Florida, 2015

CELEBRATING JEWISH WOMANHOOD A recent trend in many communities is the development of Bat Mitzvah celebrations that highlight the distinctly feminine mitzvot and teachings of Judaism.

Bar Mitzvah at the Western Wall, Jerusalem, Israel, 2013

BAR MITZVAH AND TEFILLIN The age of Bar Mitzvah is the point at which a Jew becomes obligated to fulfill the mitzvot, the divine commandments of the Torah. While other mitzvot are observed earlier as well, for educational purposes, tefillin are different in that one begins to wear them only upon attaining the maturity of mind required to properly appreciate their sacredness; hence the connection between Bar Mitzvah and tefillin. For more on tefillin, see pp. 319–324.

Marriage

*Jewish wedding ring,
Italy, 17th century*

In Judaism, the primary edifice is not the synagogue or the study hall, but the family home. Little wonder, then, that no event in Jewish life is celebrated with greater joy and enthusiasm than a marriage. When a child is born, the traditional blessing to the parents is, "May you merit to raise him/her to Torah, the marriage canopy, and good deeds"; indeed, the very first blessing and commandment issued to the first man and woman upon their creation by G-d was to marry and bear children (Genesis 1:28). In the teachings of Judaism, marriage is described as the ultimate abode for the divine presence, and as the "eternal edifice" that houses and perpetuates the myriad particulars of Jewish tradition and practice.

 ZOHAR, *VOL. 1, 91b*

When the Creator brings forth souls into the world, all souls include both a male and a female aspect, which are bound together as one entity.... Then, when they descend [into the physical world], they are separated ... and are vested in two separate bodies.

When the time comes for them to marry, G-d, who knows each soul and spirit, unites them as they were originally unified.... Thus it is written (Ecclesiastes 1:9), "There is nothing new under the sun."

 MIDRASH RABBAH, *BEREISHITH 68:4*

A Roman princess asked R. Yosei ben Chalafta: "In how many days did G-d create the world?"

Said he to her: "In six days."

Said she to him: "And from then until now, what does He do?"

Said he to her: "He sits and matches couples."

Said she to him: "This is G-d's vocation? I, too, can do that. How many servants and maids do I have! In a fleeting moment I can pair them."

Said he to her: "For you it may be easy. For the Almighty it is as difficult as the splitting of the sea." R. Yosei ben Chalafta left her and went.

What did she do? She took a thousand slaves and a thousand slave girls, lined them up in two rows, and announced: "You marry him, and you marry her."

The next morning they appeared before her—this one with a wound in his head, that one with a drooping eye, and that one with a broken leg.

Said she to them: "What happened to you?"

The one said, "I don't want him," and the other said, "I don't want her...."

Immediately she sent for R. Yosei ben Chalafta and said to him: "Rabbi, your Torah is true, beautiful, and praiseworthy. Everything that you said was well said."

Ketubah (marriage contract), Livorno, Italy, 1698

THE KABBALAH OF MAN AND WOMAN

In the mystical teachings of Judaism, gender is not just a fact of existence, but its central dichotomy: the union of male and female is the most prominent metaphor in Kabbalistic thought. Understanding what it means to be male and female lends insight into the nature of the relationship between G-d and His creation; and understanding the mystical perspective on the dynamics of G-d's creation informs the way we engage in our closest relationships.

 GENESIS 1:27, 2:18, 2:21–24

G-d created man in His image, in the image of G-d He created him; male and female He created them....

And G-d said: "It is not good that man should be alone; I will make him a helpmate opposite him...."

G-d made fall a slumber upon the man, and he slept; and He took one of his sides ... and built [it] into a woman; and He brought her to the man. And the man said: "This time she is bone of my bones and flesh of my flesh. She shall be called *ishah* (woman), as she was taken from *ish* (man)."

Therefore a man shall leave his father and his mother; and he shall cleave to his wife, and they shall become one flesh.

 R. ISAAC ARAMA
AKEIDAT YITZCHAK, BEREISHITH 8

The divine wisdom desired that the joining of husband and wife should not be solely for the sake of the perpetuation of the species, as is the case with other living creatures, but that they should have a uniquely personal relationship, which would reinforce their mutual love and fellowship, to aid one another in all aspects of their lives.... This is why the Creator formed the woman out of "one of [Adam's] sides," unlike all other species

[in which the male and female were originally formed as two distinct entities]: so that they should be of one essence, thereby intensifying the love and fellowship between them.

 R. JUDAH LOEW, *BE'ER HAGOLAH, 5:4*

There are those who regard the union of husband and wife as a shameful thing; some go so far as to declare it the disgrace of the human being. The Torah (Genesis 2:25) refutes this notion. Indeed, is it possible that the process of procreation, upon which the continued existence of the world is predicated, should be a disgraceful thing? Is it not an insult to the Creator to suggest that His world is built upon a depraved foundation? In truth, there is nothing depraved in the union of a man with his wife in and of itself, but only when a person intends it to satisfy their lust and their evil inclination.

 ZOHAR, *VOL. 3, 81a–b*

It is written, "He is in one" (Job 23:13). Why "*in* one"? Should it not say, "He *is* one"? [But] G-d does not dwell, nor is G-d found, only in one who is one.... When is a person one? When a person is in the union of intimacy.... This is why a person must make his wife happy at this time, so that her desire is one with his, and their minds are directed to the same place.... When male and

The Talmud (*Sotah* 17a) notes that *aish*, the Hebrew word for fire, with the addition of the letter *yud*, spells *ish*, "man," while the same word, but with the addition of the letter *hei*, spells *ishah*, "woman." The significance of this is that when a man and a woman are meritorious, the divine presence—represented by the letters *yud-hei*—dwells within their union; when they are not, they are consumed by the fire of their opposite natures.

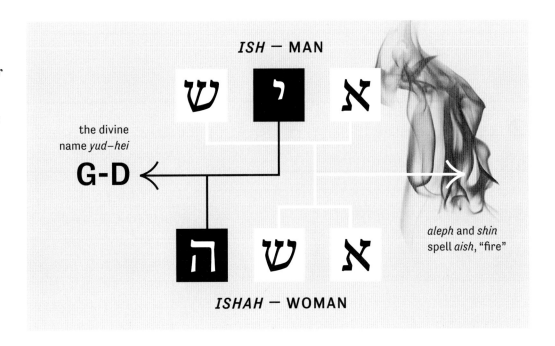

ISH — MAN

the divine
name *yud–hei*

G-D

aleph and *shin*
spell *aish*, "fire"

ISHAH — WOMAN

female unite [in this way], they become one in soul as well as in body; they are one person. And G-d dwells in the oneness.

 R. ISAIAH HOROWITZ,
SHENEI LUCHOT HABERIT, 1:102b

Know my children and heed these words carefully: From each sanctified intimacy there is positive result. Even when a woman does not conceive, there is an arousal in the heavens above and a soul issues forth.

 R. SCHNEUR ZALMAN OF LIADI
BASED ON *TORAH OHR, BEREISHITH 5b*

In the cosmic sense, too, "it is not good that man should be alone." If the sum of G-d's relationship with our existence were that of a Creator who bestows being, vitality, and goodness upon His creation, that would limit G-d to a "male" or giving role. G-d, too, desires a "helpmate opposite him"—a world that both challenges and facilitates the divine flow from above, thereby partnering with Him to create the home that He desires.

 R. DR. ABRAHAM J. TWERSKI

Love is a word that in our culture has almost lost its meaning. It is told that the Rebbe of Kotzk once came across a young man who was clearly enjoying the dish of fish he was eating, and asked him, "Young man, why are you eating that fish?"

The young man says, "Because I love fish."

"Oh, you love the fish! That's why you took it out of the water, killed it, and boiled it…. Don't tell me that you love the fish. You love yourself. And because the fish tastes good to you, you took it out of the water, killed it, and boiled it."

So much of love is fish love. A young man and a young woman fall in love. What does that mean? It means that he saw in this woman someone who he felt could provide him with all of his physical and emotional needs. And she saw in this man someone who she feels could do the same. And this is love. But each one is looking out for their own needs. It's not love for the other. The other person becomes a vehicle for my gratification.

Too much of what is called love is fish love. In truth, love is not what I'm going to get, but what I'm going to give. We had an ethicist, Rabbi Dessler, who said: People make a serious mistake in thinking that you give to those whom you love. The truth is, you love those to whom you give.

His point is that when I give something to you, I've invested myself in you. And since self-love is a given—everybody loves themselves—now there is part of me in you that I love. So true love is a love of giving, not a love of receiving.

◉ R. SIMON JACOBSON

Why do we fall in love?

What lies behind the attraction between the genders? Where does our sexuality come from?

In this article, I would like to look at two approaches to that question. One is the prevalent, contemporary, scientific approach. We will then contrast that with the Torah approach—specifically, the Kabbalistic-Hasidic perspective on Torah.

There are, of course, numerous secular-scientific theories of sexuality. Let us examine what is probably the most dominant one: the biological or evolutionary theory, which is based on the idea that "the survival of the fittest" is the primary force in nature. From this perspective, our attraction derives from the fact that the perpetuation of the species is achieved through a physical relationship between a male and a female. The male will therefore seek out the female who is most fertile and will bear the healthiest offspring; the female will seek a male who provides the healthiest seed, is the most virile, and will protect the young.

This theory explains why men and women seek out and mate with each other. It also explains that certain features are extremely enticing to the opposite gender because they indicate signs of fertility or health that are important for the perpetuation of the species.

What this theory essentially says is that behind the beauty and the sensuality of love, there is a primal force: the need to exist and to perpetuate that existence. Since the human being is an animal with a certain degree of sophistication, human sexuality has evolved to address that sophistication. People are not prepared to think of themselves merely as production machines to bear children, so evolution and biology have conspired to imbue the physical union not only with pleasure, but also with a mystique that compels us along the romantic journey.

Gazing into a loved one's eyes across a candlelit table for two, one may think that one has risen above a survival-of-the-fittest mode of existence, but, in truth, this "rising higher" is just nature's way of packaging that drive. Two human beings courting each other are essentially the same as two bees courting each other. One bee will buzz a certain way or give off a certain scent, but what it comes down to is that these are tactics to attract a mate and bear offspring. By the same token, the accouterments of human courtship—the romance, the flowers, the music, the moonlight—are really just nature's way of getting two people together.

Nature is ruthless. Nature must prevail. So nature finds the means to get a male and a female to mate. This, basically, is the scientific approach to physical attraction.

The Torah's conception of human sexuality is completely different: we are driven to search for our divine image, for our quintessential self.

In the opening chapters of Genesis, the Torah describes man as originally having been created as a "two-sided" being: "Male and female He created them, and He called their name 'man.'" The Creator then split this two-sided creature into two, and ever since, the divided halves of the divine image seek and yearn for each other.

They're not half individuals; man is a full-fledged personality and woman is a full-fledged personality. But there are elements in their transcendental persona that remain incomplete if they don't find each other. There's something missing in each of them; they were once part of a greater whole.

To put it in more mystical terms, they're really searching to become one with G-d. When man and woman come together and unite in a marital union, they recreate the divine image in which they were originally formed.

The teachings of Kabbalah take this a step further, seeing the male-female dynamic not just as two gen-

Jewish Wedding (detail), Jozef Israëls, the Netherlands, 1903

ders within a species, but rather two forms of energy: an internal energy and a projective energy. Feminine energy and masculine energy coexist in every person and in every part of nature. Even G-dliness is sometimes described in the feminine and sometimes in the masculine. Contrary to the common perception of the "patriarchal" G-d of the Bible, many of the divine attributes are feminine, such as the *Shechinah*.

So what we have here is a split of two energies and a striving to become one whole. Not that we've ever been completely disconnected, but consciously or unconsciously, we can go off on our own individual, narcissistic, even selfish path. And here, there's a voice inside us saying: I yearn for something greater. When a man is attracted to a woman, or a woman to a man, it may seem to be a very biological urge; but from a Jewish, Torah perspective, this is only a physical manifestation of a very deep, spiritual attraction.

This is not to say that the Torah's concept of sexuality is not intrinsically tied in to the objective of creating new life. It certainly is. But perpetuation of the species is not the sole end of our sexuality. Rather, it's the other way around: the divine nature of our sexuality—the fact that the union of male and female completes the divine image in which we were created—is what gives us the power to bring life into the world.

So there is something divine about the union itself. Halachah (Torah law) sanctifies marriage even without the possibility of offspring, such as in the case of a couple who are beyond childbearing age, or who are physically unable to bear children. If the physical union was simply the mechanism for childbearing, one might argue, "Hey, no perpetuation of the species, what's the point of marriage and intimacy? Just a selfish pleasure? Where's the holiness?"

The answer: In and of itself, the unity of male and female is a divine act, a divine experience.

THE JEWISH WEDDING

A Jewish wedding consists of two stages: *kidushin* (betrothal) and *nisu'in* (marriage). In Biblical and Talmudic times, these were two separate events. In recent centuries, it became the custom to conduct the *nisu'in* immediately following the *kidushin*, so that the wedding ceremony incorporates both stages. The following is a brief overview of the components of a traditional Jewish wedding, as well as some of the customs followed in different Jewish communities.

Ⓐ CHUPAH The wedding ceremony is held under a wedding canopy, called a *chupah,* symbolizing the home that the couple are committing themselves to jointly create. In many communities, the custom is to set up the *chupah* under the open sky, alluding to G-d's blessing to Abraham (Genesis 15:5) to make his descendants as numerous as the stars of the heavens.

Ⓑ VEIL Before being escorted to the *chupah*, the groom covers the bride's face with a veil. The bride remains veiled for the duration of the wedding ceremony, affording her privacy at this sacred time. This custom has its origins with the Jewish matriarch Rebecca, who covered her face upon meeting her groom Isaac (Genesis 24:65), and serves as a tribute to the modesty that is a hallmark of the Jewish woman. According to Sephardic custom, the

groom does not veil the bride; instead, a *tallit* is draped over the heads of the groom and bride during the recitation of the "seven blessings." In some communities, this also serves as the *chupah* itself.

Ⓒ KITTEL The groom wears a *kittel*, the white garment traditionally worn on Yom Kippur. The *kittel* alludes to the purity of the heavenly angels as well as to the shrouds of the dead, evoking feelings of awe and repentance. The sages teach that a person's wedding day is a personal "day of atonement," in which their sins are forgiven and they are granted a new start on life. Many have the custom that the groom and bride fast on their wedding day (until after the ceremony), as this is their personal Yom Kippur.

Ⓓ THE ESCORTS Two couples (usually, the respective parents of the bride and the groom) escort the groom and the bride to the *chupah*. The groom is led to the *chupah* first, where he awaits the arrival of his bride. According to Sephardic custom, the bride stops a few feet before the *chupah,* the groom comes out to greet her, and the two walk together to the *chupah.* In Ashkenazic weddings, the bride circles the groom seven times, symbolically creating the sacred space of their marital home. Another custom is for the escorts to carry torches or candles, symbolic of the

"lightning and flames" that accompanied the giving of the Torah at Mount Sinai (Exodus 19:16–18)—an event that marked the wedding of the Divine Groom and the Bride Israel. According to the Kabbalistic tradition, the souls of the deceased ancestors of the bride and groom are also present at the *chupah*.

Ⓔ KIDUSHIN The groom places a ring on the bride's finger, and says: "You are hereby consecrated to me with this ring, in accordance with the law of Moses and Israel." This action, with the bride's acceptance and acquiescence, creates the *kidushin*-bond between them. They are now husband and wife.

Ⓕ THE WITNESSES For the *kidushin* to be valid, it must be observed by two witnesses, who are designated for this task.

Ⓖ KETUBAH A marriage contract, called a *ketubah*, is drawn up prior to the wedding, and is read aloud under the *chupah* and given to the bride (see p. 403).

Ⓗ THE SEVEN BLESSINGS A series of seven blessings are recited over a cup of wine. The blessings recall the creation of the first man and woman and their union in the Garden of Eden, and ask the Almighty to bless the couple with "joy and happiness, gladness and song, jubilation and delight, love and fellowship, harmony and friendship." The groom and bride both drink from the cup.

Ⓘ BREAKING THE GLASS At the conclusion of the "seven blessings," a glass is broken to commemorate the destruction of the Holy Temple, in fulfillment of the vow, "If I do not arouse [the memory of] Jerusalem at the height of my joy" (Psalms 137:6). The breaking of the glass also represents Moses' breaking of the tablets following the giving of the Torah at Mount Sinai.

Ⓙ THE YICHUD ROOM The bride and groom adjourn to the *yichud* room, where they spend a few minutes alone. *Yichud* means "seclusion," and the act of being in a room alone together completes the *nisu'in* stage of the wedding. In Ashkenazic communities, the bride and groom enter the *yichud* room immediately following the recitation of the seven blessings under the *chupah*; the Sephardic custom is for the seclusion to take place after the wedding reception.

Ⓚ THE OFFICIATING RABBI In contrast to other religious or secular ceremonies, in a Jewish wedding the attending clergyman does not "marry" the couple, as the marriage bond is created by the actions of the groom and bride. Rather, the role of the officiating rabbi is to oversee the process and ensure that all the ritualistic requirements are adhered to.

MARITAL LIFE AND MIKVEH

 DEUTERONOMY 24:5

When a man weds a new wife, he shall not go out in the army, nor shall any such matter be imposed on him; he shall remain free for his home for one year, and make happy his wife whom he has wed.

 TALMUD, *NIDAH 31b*

Why did the Torah ordain the state of *nidah* for seven days [following menstruation]? Because being in constant contact with his wife, a man might develop an apathy toward her. The Torah therefore ordained: Let her be ritually impure for seven days, in order that she shall be as cherished by her husband as at the time that she first entered the bridal chamber.

 SACRED LETTER, *ADVICE TO A YOUNG MAN BEFORE HIS WEDDING, ATTRIBUTED TO NACHMANIDES*

Begin with words that draw her heart, settle her mind, and lift her spirits. This way, your mind and hers will be in one place and bond together in harmony. Speak to her of different things, some of them to awaken her desire and love, some to draw her to an awe of Heaven, toward goodness and modesty. For if both of you will focus your minds and hearts toward Heaven at this time, you will be granted children whose character permits entry to spirituality and purity.

 RIVKAH SLONIM
TOTAL IMMERSION, PP. XXIII–XXXV

The mikveh

To the uninitiated, a modern-day mikveh looks like a miniature swimming pool. Its ordinary appearance, however, belies its primary place in Jewish life. In Jewish law, constructing a mikveh takes precedence even over building a synagogue. In fact, a group of Jewish families living together do not attain the status of a community if they do not have a communal mikveh. This is so for a simple reason: private and even communal prayer can be held in virtually any location, but Jewish married life, and therefore the birth of future generations in accordance with Halachah (Torah law), is possible only where there is access to a mikveh. It is no exaggeration to state that the mikveh is the touchstone of Jewish life and the portal to a Jewish future.

The world's natural bodies of water—its oceans, rivers, wells, and spring-fed lakes—are mikvehs in their most primal form. They contain waters of divine source, and thus, tradition teaches, the power to purify. But these waters may be inaccessible or dangerous, not to mention the problems of inclement weather and lack of privacy. Jewish life therefore necessitates the construction of mikvehs ("pools"), and indeed this has been done by Jews in every age and circumstance.

Briefly: A mikveh must be built into the ground or as part of a ground-connected building, using materials and construction methods prescribed by Torah law. The mikveh must contain a minimum of 200 gallons of rainwater that was gathered and channeled into the mikveh pool in accordance with a highly specific set of regulations. The casual observer will often see only one pool—the one used for immersion. In reality, most mikvehs are comprised of two (or more) adjoining pools. The accumulated rainwater is kept in one pool, and there is a variety of Halachic methods by which the legal status of a mikveh is extended to the adjacent immersion pool, which is drained and refilled regularly with tap water (see infographic on p. 413). Modern-day mikveh pools are equipped with filtration and water-purification systems. The mikveh waters are commonly chest high and kept at a comfortable temperature. Access to the pool is achieved via stairs. (Mikvehs accessible to the handicapped or infirm are equipped with lifts.)

The mikveh as an institution is the victim of a popular misconception. Immersion in water is naturally associated with physical hygiene. But the mikveh never was a monthly substitute for a bath or shower. In fact,

The besieged Jews in Masada (see p. 83) used this mikveh in the first century CE

Halachah stipulates that one must be scrupulously clean before immersing. To facilitate this requirement, preparation areas—with baths and showers, shampoos, soaps, and other cleansing and beauty aids—are a staple of the modern mikveh.

Until a relatively short time ago, most mikvehs could best be described as utilitarian: function, not comfort, dictated their style. A new awareness among modern Jewish women, the rabbinate, and community leaders over the last few decades has sparked a new trend in mikveh construction. Beautiful, even lavish, mikvehs—complete with elegant foyers and waiting rooms, fully equipped preparation areas, and well-designed mikveh pools—are being built around the world. Some mikvehs rival luxurious European spas and offer patrons more amenities than they could enjoy at home.

Today, it is not just a Jewish metropolis that can boast a mikveh. In remote, even exotic, locations there are kosher and comfortable mikvehs, and rabbis and rebbetzins willing and able to assist any woman in their use.

The primary uses of mikveh today are delineated in Jewish law and date back to the dawn of Jewish history. Mikveh is an integral part of conversion to Judaism. It is used, though less widely known, for the immersion of new pots, dishes, and utensils before they are utilized by a Jew. The mikveh concept (in the form of the manual pouring of water over the body) is also the focal point of the *taharah*, the purification rite before the body of the deceased is laid to rest and the soul ascends on high. But the most important and general usage of mikveh is for purification by the menstruant woman.

For the menstruant woman, immersion in a mikveh is part of a larger framework known as "family purity" (*taharat ha-mishpachah*). Family purity is a system predicated on the woman's monthly cycle. From the onset of menstruation and for seven days after its end, until the woman immerses in the mikveh, husband and wife may not engage in sexual relations. To avoid violation of this law, the couple should curtail their indulgence in actions they find arousing, putting a check on direct physical contact and refraining from physical manifestations of affection. The technical term for a woman in this state is *nidah* (literal meaning: "to be separated").

Exactly a week from when the woman has established the cessation of her flow, she visits the mikveh. Immersion takes place after nightfall of the seventh day and is preceded by a requisite cleansing to ensure that the waters of the mikveh envelop each and every part of the body. After immersing once, while standing in the waters of the mikveh, the woman recites the

the making of a mikveh

blessing for ritual purification and then, in accordance with widespread custom, immerses twice more. Many women use this auspicious time for personal prayer and communication with G-d. After immersion, woman and husband may resume marital relations.

When all is said and done, an understanding of the ultimate reason for the framework of family purity and its culminating point—immersion in the mikveh—is impossible. We observe these laws simply because G-d so ordained. Still, there are insights that can help add dimension and meaning to our mikveh experience.

Water is the primary source and vivifying factor of all life as we know it. Judaism teaches that these same attributes are mirrored in its spiritual function. Water has the power to restore and replenish life to our essential, spiritual selves.

The mikveh personifies both the womb and the grave: the portals to life and afterlife. In both, the person is stripped of all power and prowess. In both, there is a mode of total reliance, complete abdication of control. Immersion in the mikveh can be understood as a symbolic act of self-abnegation, the conscious suspension of the self as an autonomous force. In so doing, we signal a desire to achieve oneness with the source of all life, to return to a primeval unity with G-d. In keeping with this theme, immersion in the mikveh is described not only in terms of purification, revitalization, and rejuvenation, but also, and perhaps primarily, as rebirth.

In years gone by, menstruating women were a source of consternation and fear. At best they were avoided, at worst they were shunned and cast aside. Often, menstruating women were blamed for tragedy and mishap, as if they had polluted the environment with their breath or gaze. This was a simplistic, if not misguided, response to a complex phenomenon whose rhyme and reason eluded the primitive mind. In those societies, peace could be made with menstruation only by ascribing it to evil and demonic spirits, and by the adaptation of a social structure that facilitated its avoidance.

Ritual purification is achieved by immersing in a "mikveh," Halachically defined as a naturally gathered pool of water. Water that was held in a container loses this ritually-cleansing quality. This rule essentially disqualifies ordinary tap water for use in filling a mikveh. The most common method of obtaining ritually purifying water is to channel rainwater into the mikveh-pool in a way that carefully avoids it being "contained" at any point of its progress from raincloud to pool.

Rainfall, however, is intermittent, and in some places, only seasonal; while considerations of hygiene and comfort call for the ability to regularly change the water in the immersion pool. Most modern mikvehs, therefore, incorporate one or more of a variety of Halachic solutions that enable the conversion of ordinary tap water into ritually-cleansing naturally-pooled water. Illustrated here are three common methods for creating a mikveh in a way that allows for the immersion pool to be emptied and refilled without a new supply of rainwater.

1

Two pools are constructed side by side, with a connecting hole in the wall between them. One pool holds the rainwater. The other pool, which will serve for immersion, is then filled with tap water to above the level of the connecting hole. Because the water in the immersion pool is now "connected" Ⓐ with the water in the rainwater pool, it becomes the extension of the rainwater pool and shares its ritualistic qualities.

2

As in method 1, two pools are constructed side by side. After the rainwater pool is filled, tap water is added to it in a way that the overflow fills the adjoining immersion pool. As the tap water enters the rainwater pool, it is "seeded" Ⓑ within it and attains the status of its ritually cleansing water.

3

The two pools are built as a single deep pool, with a dividing floor between them. In the floor are connecting holes and a removable stone slab. After the bottom pool is filled with rainwater, the slab is put in place, and the upper pool is filled with tap water. One advantage in this method is that because the two pools essentially form a single mikveh, the "seeding" Ⓑ is accomplished by adding tap water to a rainwater mikveh rather than by passing through it.

NOTE As an additional Halachic safeguard—employed in all three methods—the tap water is not run directly into the pool, but first flows over a stretch of porous ground Ⓒ, which has the effect of reinstating its natural status. The same is also done for the rainwater, just in case it was in some way compromised as it flowed from the roof through the drainpipe.

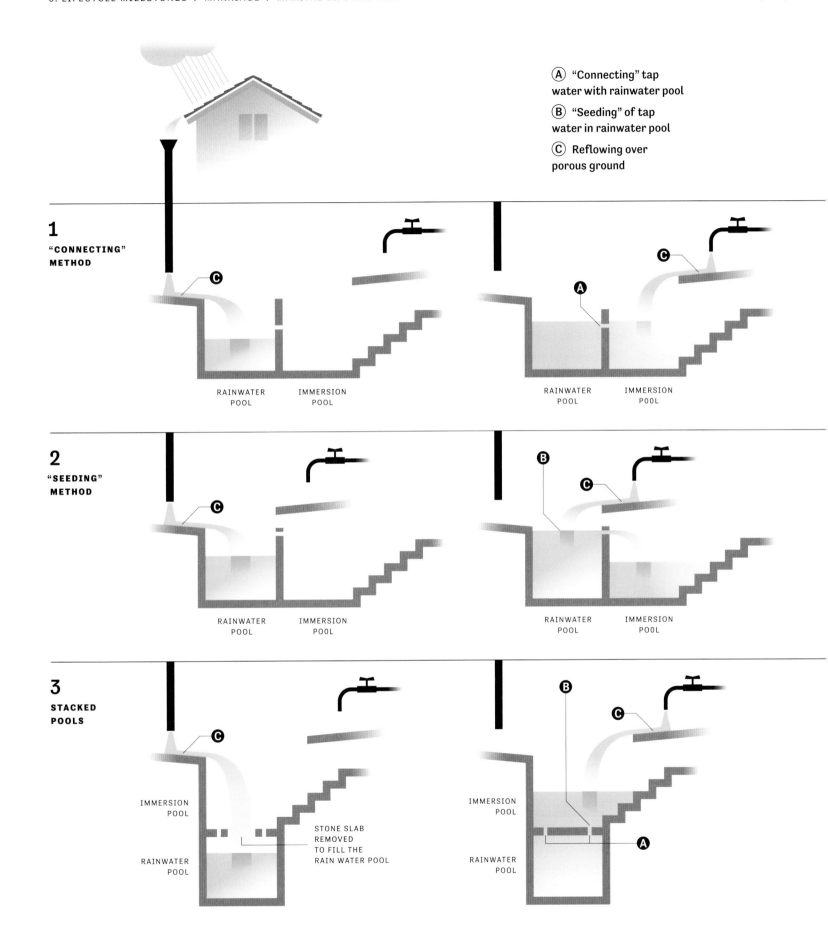

Ⓐ "Connecting" tap water with rainwater pool

Ⓑ "Seeding" of tap water in rainwater pool

Ⓒ Reflowing over porous ground

1
"CONNECTING" METHOD

RAINWATER POOL   IMMERSION POOL

RAINWATER POOL   IMMERSION POOL

2
"SEEDING" METHOD

RAINWATER POOL   IMMERSION POOL

RAINWATER POOL   IMMERSION POOL

3
STACKED POOLS

IMMERSION POOL

RAINWATER POOL

STONE SLAB REMOVED TO FILL THE RAIN WATER POOL

IMMERSION POOL

RAINWATER POOL

IMPORTANT NOTE: The laws pertaining to mikveh construction are extremely complex and include many requirements not covered in this diagram.

Viewed against this backdrop, the Jewish rhythm in marriage is perceived by many as a throwback to archaic taboos, a system rooted in antiquated attitudes and a ubiquitous form of misogyny. In truth, family purity is a celebration of life and our most precious human relationships. It can be understood most fully only within a deeper notion of purity and impurity.

Judaism teaches that the source of all *taharah*, "purity," is life itself. Conversely, death is the harbinger of *tumah*, "impurity." All types of ritual impurity, and the Torah describes many, are rooted in the absence of life or some measure—even a whisper—of death.

When stripped to its essence, a woman's menses signals the death of potential life. Each month a woman's body prepares for the possibility of conception. The uterine lining is built up—rich and replete, ready to serve as a cradle for life—in anticipation of a fertilized ovum. Menstruation is the shedding of the lining, the end of this possibility.

The presence of potential life within fills a woman's body with holiness and purity. With the departure of this potential, impurity sets in, conferring upon the woman a state of impurity or, more specifically, the state of *nidah*. Only immersion in the mikveh has the power to change this status.

In ancient times, *tumah* and *taharah* were central and determining factors in Jewish religious life. There were numerous types of impurities, and a commensurate number of purification processes, though mikveh immersion was the culmination of the purification rite in every case. The status of a Jew, whether he or she was ritually pure or impure, regulated a person's involvement in all areas of ritual. Most notably, *tumah* made entrance into the Holy Temple impossible and thus sacrificial offering inaccessible.

In our day, in this post-Temple period, the power and interplay of ritual status has all but vanished, relegating this dynamic to obscurity. There is, however, one arena in which purity and impurity continue to be pivotal. In this connection only is there a Biblical mandate for mikveh immersion—and that is regarding human sexuality. To understand why this is so, we must first understand how the Torah views sexuality.

The alleged incompatibility of sexuality and spirituality is a notion that, while foreign to Torah thought, is attributed by many to Judaic philosophy under the larger and completely mythical rubric of a "Judeo-Christian" creed. Few concepts have done more harm than this widespread misapprehension. In stark contrast to Christian dogma—where marriage is seen as a concession to the weakness of the flesh, and celibacy is extolled as a virtue—the Torah accords matrimony an exalted and holy position. Within that consecrated union, the expression of human sexuality is a mandate, a mitzvah. In fact, it is the first mitzvah in the Torah and one of the holiest of all human endeavors.

Moreover, human lovemaking signals the possibility and potential for new life—the formation of a new body and the descent from heaven of a new soul. In their fusing, man and woman become part of something larger; in their transcendence of the self, they draw on, and even touch, the Divine. They enter into a partnership with G-d; they come closest to taking on the divine attribute of creator. In fact, the sacredness of the intimate union remains unmitigated even when the possibility of conception does not exist. In the metaphysical sense, the act and its potential remain linked.

Human sexuality is a primary force in the lives of a married couple. It is the unique language and expression of the love they share, from which flow the blessings of trust, stability, and continuity. In reaffirming their commitment, in their intimacy, the couple adds to the vibrancy and health of their society, of humanity, and ultimately, to the fruition of the divine plan of a world perfected by man.

In this light, it becomes clear why marital relations are often referred to as the Holy Temple of human

Mikveh Rachel, designed by Pascal Arquitectos,
Mexico City, Mexico, 2011

continues to be, contingent on ritual purity. While we cannot presently serve G-d in a physical Temple in Jerusalem, we can erect a sacred shrine within our lives. Immersion in the mikveh is the gateway to the holy ground of conjugality.

The laws of family purity are a divine ordinance. It is a difficult commandment, a discipline that makes demands on our time, our psyche, and our emotions. It is a force at odds with the flesh, a way of life that the average person would not likely choose or devise. It calls for the subservience of our most intimate desires to the bidding of a higher authority.

And therein lies the mitzvah's potency. The knowledge that it is sourced in something larger than the self—that it is not based on the emotions or the subjective will of one or the other of the marriage part-

ners—allows *taharat hamishpachah* to work for the mutual benefit of woman and husband. Ironically, this "unfathomable" mitzvah reveals its blessings to us more than almost any other, in daily, palpable ways. Its rewards are commensurate with the challenge of observance.

Trite as it may sound, mikveh offers couples the possibility of repeated "honeymoons" during the course of their marriage. Boredom can beleaguer any relationship and chip away at its foundation. The mandatory monthly separation fosters feelings of longing and desire—at the very least, a sense of appreciation—which is followed by the excitement of reunion.

The man-woman relationship thrives on a model of withdrawal and return. The Torah teaches that Adam and Eve in their original form were created as an androgynous being. Subsequently, G-d separated them, thus granting them independence on the one hand and the possibility for a chosen union on the other. Men and women have been pulling apart and coming together ever since. The mikveh system grants the married couple this necessary dynamic. Within their commitment to live together and be loyal to each other forever, within their monogamy and security, there is still this spring-like mechanism at work.

For many women, their time as a *nidah* also offers them a measure of solitude and introspection. There is, additionally, an empowering feeling of autonomy over their bodies and, indeed, over the sexual relationship they share with their spouses. There is strength and comfort in the knowledge that human beings can neither have their every whim nor be had at whim.

The benefits brought to married life by the practice of family purity have been recognized by numerous experts, Jew and non-Jew alike. To be sure, this type of analysis, as any other, is subject to argument and critique. Ultimately, however, mikveh's powerful hold on the Jewish people—its promise of hope and redemption—is rooted in the Torah and flows from a belief in G-d and His perfect wisdom.

Work and retirement

Our working lives are sometimes seen as a necessary encumbrance, a daily eight-hour debt to be rendered in return for our subsistence and the opportunity to do or experience something of greater significance in our "free" time. The Jewish view of work insists otherwise. If, by divine providence, our lives are so ordered that the bulk of our waking hours are devoted to a particular task, then value must and can be found in that activity itself.

The Hasidic masters teach that work is the greatest blessing that has been bestowed upon us, for it is the vehicle by which we become "a partner with G-d in creation." The Creator regards His world as a work in progress, and the opportunities and challenges He plants along our life's pathways call forth from us the talent and the creativity, the commitment and the passion, that form our unique, indispensable partnership in G-d's grand endeavor.

 JOB 5:7

Man is born to toil.

 ETHICS OF THE FATHERS, *CH. 4, MISHNAH 1*

"If you eat of the toil of your hands, fortunate are you, and good it is for you" (Psalms 128:2). *Fortunate are you*—in this world; *and good it is for you*—in the world to come.

 TALMUD, *PESACHIM 113a*

Skin carcasses in the street to earn a living ... rather than depending on the charity of others.

 R. BACHYA IBN PAKUDAH
DUTIES OF THE HEARTS, 4:3

Some people are more suited for physical labor, others for craftsmanship, still others for commerce, and so on. If you find yourself drawn toward a particular vocation, know that this is because your Creator has imbued you with that nature and proclivity—in the same way that the wading bird was given its long legs and beak, and the lion its claws. Employ it to earn your livelihood, accept its satisfactions and its hardships, and do not spurn it when it momentarily fails you but trust that the Almighty will provide for you all the days of your life. And bear in mind that you are doing it to fulfill the command of your Creator, as it is written (Genesis 2:15): "G-d Almighty took the human, and He placed him in the Garden of Eden to work it and to keep it."

*Professor Herman Branover in his Liquid Metal Magnetohydrodynamics Research Center
at Ben-Gurion University in Be'er Sheba, Israel, 1981*

Yemenite Jews constitute one of the oldest Jewish communities outside of the Land of Israel, and their unique traditions and culture predate both the Sephardic and Ashkenazic diasporas. Originally populating hundreds of towns and villages across southern Arabia, the great majority of today's 530,000 Yemenite Jews live in Israel (see "The Yemenite Aliyah" on p. 95), with smaller communities in the U.S. and Great Britain and only a handful remaining in Yemen.

קליעה תימנית אמנותית
YEMENITE ARTISTIC PLAITING

1950s postcard showing Yemenite-born artisan Tzivia Qarawani of Rosh Ha-Ayin, Israel

PROVERBS 31:10–31

A woman of valor, who can find?
    For her price is beyond pearls....
She seeks wool, and flax,
    and works it with the will of her hands.
She makes like merchants' ships
    bringing her bread from afar.
She rises while it is yet night
    and gives prey to her household
    and a ration to her maidens.
She plots a field and buys it
    with the fruit of her hands
    she plants a vineyard.
She girds her loins with might
    and strengthens her arms....
    her lamp does not go out at night....
She spreads her palm to the pauper
    she extends her hands to the needy....
She opens her mouth with wisdom
    and the teaching of kindness is upon her tongue.
She oversees the ways of her household
    and eats not the bread of idleness....
Charm is false and beauty is vain
    a G-d-fearing woman, she is to be praised.
Give her of the fruit of her hands
    and her own works will praise her in the gates.

R. MENACHEM M. SCHNEERSON
BASED ON A SERIES OF TALKS DELIVERED IN THE SUMMER OF 1980

The Torah considers old age a virtue and a blessing. Throughout the Torah, the term "old" (*zakein*) is synonymous with "wise." The Torah instructs us to honor all elderly, regardless of their scholarship and piety, because the many trials and experiences that each additional year of life brings yield a wisdom which the most accomplished young prodigy cannot equal.

This is in marked contrast to the prevalent attitude in the "developed" countries of today's world, where old age is a liability. Youth is seen as the highest credential in every field from business to government, where a younger generation prefers to "learn from their own mistakes" rather than build upon the life experience of their elders. At age fifty, a person is considered "over the hill" and is already receiving hints that their position would be better filled by someone twenty-five years their junior. In many companies and institutions, retirement is mandatory at age sixty-five or earlier.

Thus society dictates that a person's later years be marked by inactivity and decline. The aged are made to feel that they are useless, if not a burden, and had best confine themselves to retirement villages and nursing homes. After decades of achievement, their knowledge and talents are suddenly worthless; after decades of contributing to society, they are suddenly undeserving recipients, grateful for each time the younger generation takes off from work and play to drop by for a half-hour chat and the requisite Father's Day necktie.

On the face of it, the modern-day attitude seems at least partly justified. Is it not a fact that a person weakens as they advance in years? But this, precisely, is the point: Is a person's worth to be measured by their physical prowess, by the number of man-hours and intercontinental flights that can be extracted from them per week? If a person's physical strength has waned while their sagacity and insight have grown, do we view this as an improvement or a decline?

Indeed, a twenty-year-old can dance the night away while his grandmother tires after a few minutes. But the human being was not created to dance for hours on end. The human being was created to make the world purer, brighter, and holier than it was before he or she arrived on the scene. Seen in this light, the spiritual maturity of the aged more than compensates for any decrease in physical strength.

At the basis of the institution of "retirement" is the notion that life is composed of productive and nonproductive periods. Torah, however, recognizes no such distinction between life's phases. It sees productivity as the very essence of life, making the very concept of a "nonproductive life-period" an oxymoron. There are marked differences between childhood, adulthood, etc., but these differ in the manner, not the fact, of a person's productivity. Retirement and the passive enjoyment of the fruits of one's labor have their time and place—in the World to Come. In the words of the Talmud (*Eruvin 22a*), "Today is the time to do; tomorrow, to receive the reward." The very fact that the Almighty has granted a person a single additional day of bodily life means that he or she has not yet concluded their mission in life, that there is still something for them to accomplish in this world.

Death and the afterlife

One of the fundamental beliefs of Judaism is that life does not begin with birth, nor does it end with death. The human soul is "a part of G-d above" (Job 31:2) that is placed within the body for a period of time and then returns to its source. Furthermore, body and soul will be reunited in a future World to Come in which "death will be vanquished forever" (Isaiah 25:8).

At the same time, Judaism does not make light of the value of physical life, nor of the tragedy of its termination by death. Indeed, our temporal, physical world is seen as the focal point of the whole of Creation, and as the state in which the purpose of life is fulfilled.

This duality informs the Jewish approach to death: on the one hand, an appreciation of the infinite value of every moment of physical life, and profound grief and mourning upon its termination; on the other hand, the consolation that comes from the knowledge that the soul of a loved one lives on, and continues to be a vital presence in our lives.

 ECCLESIASTES 12:7

The dust returns to the earth as it was, and the spirit returns to G-d who gave it.

 SIDDUR, *DAILY MORNING PRAYER*

My G-d: The soul You have given within me, it is pure. You created it, You formed it, You breathed it into me, You preserve it within me; and You will take it from me, and return it to me in the future [world] to come.

ETHICS OF THE FATHERS, *CH. 4, MISHNAYOT 16–17*

R. Yaakov would say: This world is like an antechamber before the World to Come. Prepare yourself in the antechamber, so that you may enter the palace.

He would also say: A single moment of repentance and good deeds in this world is greater than all of the World to Come. And a single moment of gratification in the World to Come is greater than all of this world.

 R. YECHIEL OF GLOGAU
NEZER HAKODESH, BEREISHITH 96:4

The anniversary of the passing (*yahrzeit*) of a righteous person is regarded in Jewish tradition as an auspicious time and as a day of celebration. For this is the day on which all the person's deeds and achievements converge together, fulfilling and completing each other, and exert the fullness of their combined impact in the heavens above and in our world below.

Funeral, Solomon Yudovin, Russia, 1927

 MIDRASH TANCHUMA, *VAYAK'HEL 1*

It is written (Ecclesiastes 7:1), "Better is the day of death than the day of one's birth."

This can be explained with a parable: Two ships laden with merchandise are sailing the ocean, one coming in to harbor and the other going out, and the people praised the one coming in. Some stood there and wondered: Why do you praise this one and not the other? They replied: "We are praising the ship that came in, because we know that it went out in peace and has returned in peace. As for the one now going out, we do not know what its fate will be."

 LAND OF DIAMONDS, *A FOLK PARABLE*

A man heard rumors that far across the sea, there was a land where diamonds were as plentiful as dust. So he took leave of his family and set out to make his fortune.

He discovered that everything that was said about this land was indeed true! Diamonds of all sizes were strewn around everywhere; even the sand consisted of billions of tiny glittering gems. He wasted no time in stuffing his pockets with stones and pebbles. He soon learned, however, that these pebbles were utterly worthless in this place. The currency with which people paid for goods and services was schmaltz (chicken fat). No one was bothered by the stench that emanated from their pocketbooks and money closets; a reeking establishment exuded the sweet aura of old money.

Once he overcame the disappointment of his lost dream, our traveler turned out to be an ambitious and resourceful fellow. He worked hard for many years, invested wisely, and became one of the wealthiest people in the land. He then wrote to his family that he was

Pouch of earth from the Mount of Olives,
Jerusalem, Land of Israel, 1920s

HOLY SOIL Jews throughout the ages yearned to be buried in
the Land of Israel (see citation from Maimonides on p. 93).
For those buried elsewhere, it is customary to place earth from
the Holy Land in the grave.

returning home with great riches. He loaded his fortune
on a fleet of ships and set sail for his hometown.

Family and friends eagerly awaited the wealthy man
at the seaport. Of course, there was nothing that could
be done with his shiploads of schmaltz other than to
dump them into the sea.

But later that day, a few grains of sand fell from
his trouser cuffs and sparkled on the floor. He and his
family never again wanted for anything in their lives.

The soul, in its abode on high, hears wondrous tales of a
faraway land. To get there, it must embark on a perilous
journey, but great treasures are free for the taking.
A coin given to charity, a prayer uttered, a candle lit
to usher in the Shabbat—the spiritual realms, lacking
physical bodies and a material reality, can only dream
of such riches.

The soul descends into the material world and discovers that everything that had been said about it is
true. Wherever one turns, there await countless opportunities to do divine deeds called mitzvot. Yet the

value of these diamonds is not appreciated in this alien
place. Riches of an entirely different sort beckon, so
that when the time comes to return, many a soul finds
itself lugging home shiploads of fetid schmaltz.

But no soul can traverse our world without picking
up at least a few mitzvot along the way—gems that
enrich the heavens and make the entire trip more than
worth its while.

 TALMUD, *SHABBAT 153a*

R. Eliezer said: "Repent one day before your death."

His disciples asked him: "Does a person know which
day they will die?"

Said R. Eliezer: "Certainly, then, a person should repent today, for perhaps tomorrow they will die. Hence,
all their days they are repenting."

 **LAWS PERTAINING TO THE FINAL
MOMENTS OF LIFE**

■ A person who is dying should recite *viduy* (confession
of sins): "I acknowledge before You, Lord my G-d and
the G-d of my fathers, that my healing and my death
are in Your hands. May it be Your will that You heal me a
complete healing. But if I shall die, may my death atone
for all failings, sins, and crimes I committed before You.
Grant me a portion in the Garden of Eden, and may I
merit the World to Come preserved for the righteous."

■ The person should ask forgiveness from anyone they
have wronged, and forgive those who have wronged
them.

■ The dying person then recites the Shema: "Hear O
Israel, G-d is our Lord, G-d is one."

■ If the dying person is unable to speak, they should
say the *viduy* and Shema in their thoughts. If the person
is unconscious, those present should say it for them.

■ One is not allowed to leave a dying person, so that
their soul should not depart while they are alone.

TAHARAH AND BURIAL

◗) R. YECHIEL TUKACHINSKY
GESHER HACHAYIM, 5:1

All who handle the dead must be aware that they are dealing with a sacred entity. The human body is not only the container that served the exalted soul, but has itself become sanctified with a holiness of its own, like a Torah scroll.

Water jug used for the taharah purification ritual with imprint of burial society, Transylvania, late 19th–early 20th century

SACRED PRIVILEGE Every Jewish community has a *Chevra Kadisha* ("Holy Society") that is entrusted with the care and burial of the body of the deceased. It is considered a great privilege to be admitted into this society, and traditionally, the greatest sages and most prestigious members of the community served in it.

◗) LAWS OF JEWISH BURIAL

■ Jewish law is unequivocal in its insistence that the body, in its entirety, be buried in the earth, returning it to the soil of which it was formed. It is forbidden to cremate the body, even in the case that the deceased expressed a desire that this be done. Similarly, Jewish practice forbids embalming the body. Autopsies are likewise forbidden, except in extreme circumstances.

■ From the moment of passing until the burial, the body should not be left unattended. A *shomer* ("guardian") remains with (or near) the body at all times. Every effort should be made to conduct the funeral and burial as soon as possible after the passing.

■ The *taharah* ("purification") is a cleansing ritual performed by the *Chevra Kadisha,* in which the body is cleaned and groomed, and water is ritually poured over it.

■ The body is then dressed in plain white shrouds, called *tachrichim*, emphasizing that death erases all distinctions between rich and poor and all differences in social status.

■ The body must be treated with dignity, never as a lifeless, unfeeling object. No casual conversation is allowed in its presence, and it remains covered at all times, even while it is being cleaned. Only men prepare a man's body for burial, and only women tend to a woman's body.

■ There is no displaying or "viewing" the body, as this is considered an affront to its dignity.

■ It is a mitzvah to carry the body to the burial, and for the community to accompany it on its journey.

■ Following the burial, the Kaddish prayer is recited, and the traditional words of consolation are spoken to the mourners.

From The Jewish Way in Death and Mourning by R. Maurice Lamm

MOURNING AND MEMORIAL

Mourning the death of a next of kin (parent, sibling, child, or spouse) is a mitzvah, one of the divine commandments of the Torah, and the community is enjoined to participate in the mourners' grief and to comfort them. At the same time, the traditional mourning observances emphasize our acceptance of the divine decree—our acknowledgment that the end of physical life marks the completion of the soul's mission in this world, and that G-d alone is the "true judge" of life and the course it takes. Jewish tradition specifies a series of customs and practices designed to aid the soul in its elevation to the World of Truth, and to guide those who have suffered the loss through the various stages of mourning, consolation, and memorial.

 MIDRASH MISHLEI, *SECTION 31*

It happened that one Shabbat afternoon, while R. Meir was lecturing at the study hall, his two sons died. What did their mother do? She laid them on the bed and covered them with a sheet.

After Shabbat, R. Meir arrived from the study hall and said to her, "Where are my two sons?"

Said she to him, "They went to the study hall."

Said he to her, "But I looked in the study hall and I did not see them."

She handed him a cup of wine for Havdalah. [After reciting Havdalah] he again asked, "Where are my two sons?"

Said she to him, "They went somewhere and will soon return."

She served him dinner. After he recited *Grace After Meals*, she said, "My teacher, I have a question to ask."

Said he to her, "Ask."

Said she to him, "A while ago someone left an item with me for safekeeping, and now he has come to collect it. Shall we return the item or not?"

Said he to her, "My daughter, is not a custodian required to return the deposit to its master?"

Said she to him, "My teacher, if not for your words, I could not have brought myself to return it."

What did she do next? She grasped his hand, led him up to that room, brought him near the bed, and removed the sheet from over them; and he saw the two of them lying dead upon the bed. He began to weep, saying, "My children, my children! My teachers, my teachers!" (Meaning, my children in the natural sense, and my teachers who enlightened my eyes with words of Torah.)

At that moment, she said to him, "Rabbi Meir, my teacher, did you not tell me that we are required to return the deposit to its master? 'G-d has given, and G-d has taken' (Job 1:21)." With these words, she consoled him, and his mind was eased and settled.

 R. JOSEPH ALBO, *IKARIM 4:40*

It is written (Deuteronomy 14:1), "You are children of G-d; you shall not gash yourselves, nor shall you make any baldness between your eyes for the dead."

Yahrzeit reminder, Transylvania, early 20th century.
The homemade wall-hanging contains parents' names and dates of passing, serving as a reminder
to perform the memorial observances on the anniversaries of their passing.

MEMORIAL FLAME In Jewish tradition, the flame
symbolizes the soul, embodying its spiritual upward
striving on the one hand, and on the other hand, the
material attachments that fuel a soul's ability to
illuminate its surroundings (see "The Lamp" on p. 220).
Hence the custom of memorializing the departed
soul with a kindled lamp or candle.

DIRECTED UPWARD Kaddish is the emblematic mourner's prayer, recited at the gravesite immediately after burial, in the house of mourning, during the year following the passing, and on its every anniversary thereafter. Significantly, however, the Kaddish includes no mention of death or mourning. Rather, it extols the "name" of G-d (i.e., G-d's conduct), "in the world that He created in accordance with His will," and asks the Almighty to accept our prayers for peace and redemption. The recitation of this ancient prayer is among the deeds performed by the mourner for the merit and elevation of the soul of the departed.

On the face of it, it would seem that the very opposite should be the case: that [the fact that "you are children of G-d"] is a reason to be pained and to mourn excessively over a death. Indeed, the death of a child of a king would be more cause for mourning than that of an ordinary person. Imagine that a person says to their friend, "Don't feel so bad about that ring you lost, because it had a precious gem set in it"!

But the meaning of the verse is as follows: Because you are children of G-d and a holy and treasured people, it is not fitting that you should mourn a death excessively. For that would indicate that you believe that the deceased is hopelessly gone, and you are therefore mourning them as you would an earthen pot that was shattered beyond repair.

But it is not so in the case of a death…. For the soul enters into the treasure house of G-d. Therefore, there is no cause to be excessively pained over this, only as a person would be pained over their friend's parting from them to travel to a distant place…. There should be no doubt that the soul, being holy, will be joined with the holy angels on high. In this way, the Torah indicates that the soul endures after death.

 R. MENACHEM M. SCHNEERSON
IGROT KODESH, VOL. 25, PP. 4–5

An element of solace … is expressed in the traditional text [of the words of consolation spoken to a mourner], hallowed by scores of generations of Torah and tradition among our people: *May the Omnipresent comfort you among the mourners of Zion and Jerusalem.*

At first glance, the connection between [an individual death and the mourners of Zion and Jerusalem] is puzzling. But the primary consolation embodied by this phrase is in its inner content. Namely, that just as the grief over Zion and Jerusalem is shared by all Jews, wherever they may be … so too is the grief of a single individual or family. The consolation lies in the fact that the entire nation shares in their grief, for as our sages have taught, all of the Jewish people comprise one integral organism.

Another point … is that just as the Almighty will most certainly rebuild the ruins of Zion and Jerusalem and gather the dispersed of Israel from the ends of the earth through our righteous Mashiach, so too regarding the grief of the individual, G-d will certainly fulfill the prophecy (Isaiah 26:19), "Awaken and rejoice, you who repose in the dust." Great will be the joy when all will be rejoined at the time of the resurrection of the dead.

There is also a third point: In regard to Zion and Jerusalem, the Romans were only able to vanquish the wood and stone and silver and gold of the Temple. But over its inner spiritual essence, contained within the heart of each and every Jew, the nations of the world have no dominion, and this endures eternally. So too, regarding the loss of the individual. Death overpowers only the physical body and its concerns. The soul, however, is eternal; it has only ascended to the world of truth. That is why every good deed [performed by the mourner] that accords with the will of the Giver of Life adds to the soul's delight and to its merit and good.

From a letter written to Israeli general Ariel Sharon in 1967, following the tragic death of Sharon's 11-year-old son, Gur.

stages in Jewish mourning

from the passing until the burial

BEREAVEMENT & KERIAH This is the most intense phase of mourning. At this point, one should not attempt to console the mourner; it is a time of silence, not of words. The sole focus is on caring for the body of the deceased and arranging the funeral and burial.

During this period (according to current practice, at the beginning of the funeral) the next of kin perform *keriah*, making a tear in their clothing as a sign of mourning.

7 days

SHIVAH The mourners stay in the house of mourning (preferably, the home of the deceased) and do not work; they sit on low stools, wear their torn garments, and do not wear leather footwear. It is a mitzvah to visit the mourners during *shivah* to comfort them and to talk about the life and good deeds of the deceased.

30 days

SHELOSHIM After "getting up" from *shivah* and resuming the everyday routines of life, certain mourning practices are continued until thirty days from the day of burial. These include refraining from wearing new clothes, getting a haircut or shaving, and participating in festive events. (In the case of one who is mourning the loss of a parent, some of these practices are observed for twelve months.)

1 year

KADDISH & "MERITING THE SOUL" Kaddish is recited by the mourner for eleven months from the day of the burial. Throughout the first year, one increases in charity, Torah study (particularly the study of Mishnah), and other good deeds, for the merit of the departed soul.

annually

YAHRZEIT & YIZKOR Every year, the *yahrzeit* is observed on the anniversary of the passing on the Jewish calendar. Kaddish is recited, and additional good deeds to merit the soul (charity, Torah learning, etc.) are performed. It is also customary to visit the grave of the departed on or in proximity to the *yahrzeit*.

Four times a year (on Yom Kippur, Shemini Atzeret, Passover, and Shavuot) a special memorial service, known as *Yizkor*, is held in the synagogue, and charity is pledged in memory of the departed.

THE GRAVESITE

Visiting the grave of an ancestor or a loved one is both a sign of respect for the departed and a way of sustaining the soul-to-soul bond that physical death does not sever. The sages also teach that "the souls of the righteous descend as guardians over their graves, and are aware of all that transpires in this world."

Indeed, the custom of visiting the grave of a righteous person goes back to Biblical times. The book of Genesis relates that Jacob erected a monument over the gravesite of his beloved wife Rachel, the purpose of which, according to the Midrash, was "that her place of burial would be known, so that those being exiled should come there to pray." The Talmud also describes how Caleb (one of the Spies) visited the Cave of the Patriarchs in Hebron to pray for success in his mission.

 ZOHAR, *VOL. 2, 141b*

When those in this world are in distress, and they come to the gravesite [of the *tzadik*], the *nefesh* [the aspect of the soul that remains near the grave] is aroused, and it rouses the [higher aspect of the soul called] *ruach*, which rouses the souls of the Patriarchs ... and the Almighty has mercy on the world.

 R. NISSIM GERONDI
DERASHOT HARAN, DERUSH 8

When the Holy Temple stood [in Jerusalem], that holy abode served as a receptacle for the divine wisdom and prophecy, and as the conduit by which these qualities flowed to the whole of Israel. In the same way, the prophets and the pious individuals serve as receptacles of divine wisdom and prophecy, and as the conduits by which these qualities are imparted to those of their generation who are worthy of it, even to those who have no connection with them, simply by the virtue of

their presence in the world ... how much more so to those who are close to them and have a relationship with them.

This is not only the case during their lifetimes, but after their passing as well.... For the remains of the righteous, having served as vessels for the divine effluence during their lifetime, retain this exalted quality. This is why our sages say that it is proper to visit the graves of the righteous and to pray there, as prayers said in such a place are graciously received on high.

 R. CHAIM ELAZAR SPIRA OF MUNKACS
RESPONSA, 1:68

There is much discussion among the Halachic authorities about the custom to pray at the graves of the righteous, since the Torah (Deuteronomy 18:10–11) forbids worshipping the dead as an idolatrous practice. Maharil writes that "when visiting the graves of the righteous to pray there, one should not address oneself to the dead, but rather request of the Almighty to have mercy on us in

Praying at the gravesite of the Lubavitcher Rebbe, R. Menachem M. Schneerson, Cambria Heights, Queens, New York, 2014

the merit of the righteous who are buried there."

Certainly the intent is not that one may not address the souls of the righteous at all, since that would contradict numerous accounts in the Talmud and the writings of our sages that explicitly speak of asking the souls of the departed to intercede on our behalf before G-d. The Talmud also speaks of sages who visited the gravesite of someone they had wronged to beg forgiveness from the soul, and who otherwise communicated with the souls of the departed for a variety of purposes.... Rather, the point is that we do not pray to the souls of the righteous requesting that they help us in our time of need, as that would smack of idolatry, Heaven forbid. The only power to whom we pray to fulfill our needs is G-d. We do, however, ask the souls of the righteous to also pray for us and to beseech the Almighty to help us, in the same way that we ask them to appeal to G-d on our behalf during their lifetimes, as sanctioned and indeed recommended by the Torah.

Hasidic teaching enumerates five reasons or "levels" for visiting the gravesite of one's rebbe:

■ Visiting a gravesite serves as a reminder of the mortality of physical life, rousing a person to repentance.

■ The grave of a righteous person is a place of holiness and purity, making it an opportune place for prayer.

■ When the grave is that of a loved one or someone very close to the visitor, the emotions that are aroused open one's heart to come close to G-d.

■ Because of the heightened presence of the soul at the place of burial, a person visiting the gravesite of their spiritual master will experience the sense of self-abnegation they felt in the *tzadik*'s presence when the *tzadik* was still alive.

■ The visitor's soul bonds with the soul of the *tzadik*.

From *Kuntres ha-Hishtatchut* by R. DovBer of Lubavitch

THE AFTERLIFE IN JEWISH TRADITION

 TALMUD, *ERUVIN 22a*

It is written (Deuteronomy 7:11), "[You shall keep the mitzvah, the decrees, and the laws,] which I command you today to do them." This is to say: *today to do them*—and not to do them tomorrow; *today to do them*—and tomorrow to receive their reward.

 CHINUCH, *MITZVAH 171*

Many people misunderstand the concept [of divine retribution]. They assume that it is similar to human behavior, whereby people recompense each other's deeds, good for good and bad for bad. It is not so with G-d, Heaven forfend. With G-d there is only goodness, lovingkindness, and compassion…. [Rather,] the reward or the punishment is the consequence of the person's actions, good or bad…. By way of example: A person is traveling on a smooth, clear road, but fails to follow it properly and gets hurt by the thorns growing on the roadside. Is this traveler being "punished" for straying from the road, or are they simply suffering the consequences of their misguided action?

 R. JOSEPH ALBO, *IKARIM 4:33*

We need to explain the nature of the reward and punishment experienced by the soul after death:

When the soul parts from the body, it now uninhibitedly craves to realize its innate nature and cognizance, which is to serve its Creator. At the same time, the soul also gravitates to that which it has become habituated to while in the body.

Therefore, a person whose deeds were for the sake of Heaven … [and] who truly related to spiritual things and divine matters, that soul will, upon parting from the body, experience great delight when it sees [its life's strivings] agree with the divine realities as they are…. For the divine apprehension of which the soul was capable while alive, in relation to the truth of the divine reality as it is, is only like a dream relative to a waking reality. Hence the soul's experience is like one who dreams of a great pleasure, and then wakes to experience this delight in reality…. In the same vein, if while alive the soul strove to serve the Creator, fulfill the mitzvot, and pursue justice and charity, it will experience an amazing delight in the world of souls, where the angels and supernal beings all exist in perfection in this mode….

If, however, a person pursued only their desires and physical pleasures, and their soul turned away from doing the will of G-d and accommodated its actions to the nature of the body, which is opposed to the soul's own true nature; when this soul is separated from the body, it still longs for those things to which it was accustomed and feels a desire for them, yet it has no instruments with which to obtain them. On the other hand, by reason of its own nature, the soul desires to unite with the spiritual, and will experience a longing for it; yet it has not learned the means to achieve this, nor is it accustomed to the service of G-d. For these spiritual delights can only be experienced by one who has prepared themselves for them…. As it is written (Daniel 2:21), "He gives wisdom to the wise."

Accordingly, this soul will be simultaneously drawn in two directions, upwards and downwards, the one by reason of its nature, the other by reason of habit and custom. But it will have no instruments for obtaining the lower desires and no conditioning to obtain the higher. This causes great pain and suffering to the soul, greater than any pain in the world or any kind of fracture—more pain than the burning of fire or cold and terrible frost, more than the wounds of knives and swords or the stings of snakes and scorpions….

 R. SCHNEUR ZALMAN OF LIADI
LIKUTEI TORAH, MATOT 86b

All the punishments of the Torah, while manifesting the divine attribute of judgment, are in essence divine kindnesses, as it is through them that the soul achieves its rectification.

No. 12,
Mark Rothko, New York, 1951

 R. CHAIM VITAL
SHAAR HAGILGULIM, INTRODUCTION 16

Know that a person needs to fulfill all 613 mitzvot in action, speech, and thought.... If a person does not fulfill all 613 in these three aspects, they have to be reincarnated until they complete them.

Also know that a person is obligated to study the Torah on all four levels—namely, its basic, allegorical, homiletic, and mystical meanings. A person likewise needs to be reincarnated until they achieve this.

 **R. SHLOMO OF RADOMSK**
TIFERET SHLOMO, PARASHAT VAYEISHEV

A soul comes down into this world in order to rectify the damage it did in a previous reincarnation.... [For example,] Reuben was the reincarnation of the soul of Cain who murdered his brother Abel. This is why when Joseph's brothers plotted to kill him, it was Reuben who intervened to save him.

 R. MOSES CORDOVERO, *SHIUR KOMAH 84*

Should you wonder: How, then, will we know the purpose for which we entered this world—which mitzvah we need to scrupulously perform or which transgression we must especially avoid? The answers to these questions are naturally ingrained in us. We will feel a natural affinity and longing to do a certain mitzvah. Or, our evil inclination will work especially hard to entice us to do that sin which we stumbled on in the past [incarnation].

TZEMACH TZEDEK
DERECH MITZVOTECHA, 14b–15b

Regarding the reward that a person attains through the doing of the mitzvot, there are two forms: one is the Garden of Eden, and the other is the resurrection of the dead, may it be speedily in our day.

Maimonides elaborates on the concept of the "World to Come," which according to him, is the Garden of Eden. These are his words (in brief):

"Just as colors are incomprehensible to a blind person, and sounds to a deaf person, so is it impossible for a physical being to comprehend the pleasures of the soul … which are utterly unrelated to physical pleasures. This is the World to Come, where our souls perceive the knowledge of the Creator…. This is the ultimate end and the greatest good—to inhabit this glorious and elevated state infinitely…. As for the resurrection of the dead, this is a fundamental principle of the Mosaic faith … but know that the human being will by necessity die, and [the body] will disintegrate and return to the elements of which it is composed."

This is the gist of Maimonides' words, and his intent is that the resurrection of the dead is a temporary state [in order to reward the body for its endeavors in this world], after which the soul will return to the Garden of Eden, which is the ultimate end and the true good that is called the "World to Come"….

Nachmanides, however, disagrees [with Maimonides' approach], and brings clear proofs [from the words of the sages]. His view is that the resurrection of the dead is the ultimate end, and that this is the great good that is called the "World to Come." As for the Garden of Eden, which is a delight for souls and disembodied minds, this is indeed a very lofty level, as Maimonides says—and even loftier, level beyond level; nevertheless, it is only

a temporary abode for the soul from the time of its departure from the body in this world until the time of the resurrection. [After the resurrection] is the World to Come, which is infinitely greater [than the Garden of Eden] in regards to the delight in the revelation of G-dliness. This view also holds true according to the teachings of Kabbalah.

On the face of it, however, this is not understood. How could the delight of a soul within a body be greater and more glorious than the delight of a soul that is removed from the material? For it is known that the spiritual is loftier and more perfect than the physical….

[The explanation lies in understanding the difference between "wisdom" and "desire." In the human psyche, desire is more primal than intellect; so too, by way of analogy, the divine desire is a more transcendent expression of G-dliness than the divine wisdom.] The delight that the soul enjoys in the Garden of Eden derives from its comprehension of the divine wisdom of the Torah…. But the World to Come, which is the post-resurrection world, is the reward of the mitzvot, which are the embodiment of G-d's desire. And the delight contained in the divine desire of the mitzvot is far loftier than the delight reflected in the divine wisdom of the Torah….

And because it is higher, it can descend much lower, so low that the body too can delight in it—unlike the delight of the Garden of Eden, which can only be experienced by souls without bodies. For the very beginning is embedded in the very end.

APPENDICES

authors and works cited in this book

Aaron, R. David b. 1957. Founder of the Isralight Institute in Jerusalem. International speaker and author of seven books, including *Endless Light, Seeing G-d,* and *Love Is My Religion*.

R. Aba bar Kahana 3rd-century Talmudic sage. Immigrating to the Land of Israel from Babylonia, he brought with him many Agadic teachings.

R. Abahu c. 279–320; Caesarea, Land of Israel. Talmudic sage who was a disciple of R. Jochanan.

Abarbanel, Don Isaac See biographical information on p. 115.

R. Achai Gaon c. 680–756 CE; Babylonia and Israel. One of the greatest Torah scholars of the Geonic era. His *She'iltot* ("Queries") is the first known Halachic work composed in post-Talmudic times.

Adams, John 1735–1826; Quincy, Massachusetts. Political theorist and leader in the American Revolution. He co-authored the U.S. Declaration of Independence with Thomas Jefferson, and served as second president of the United States (1797–1801).

Ahad Ha'am Pen name of Hebrew writer Asher Zvi Ginsberg, 1856–1927. A leading voice in the movement for cultural or spiritual Zionism, which strived for "a Jewish state and not merely a state of Jews."

Aiken, Lisa Author and speaker. Served as chief psychologist at Lenox Hill Hospital in New York City from 1982 to 1989.

Akeidat Yitzchak See **Arama, R. Isaac**.

R. Akiva d. c. 135; Bnei Brak, Israel. A key personality in the history of the Torah's transmission through the generations. R. Akiva was a descendant of converts to Judaism, and an illiterate shepherd until the age of 40, when he was "discovered" by his employer's daughter Rachel, who promised to marry him if he would devote his life to the study of Torah. After 24 years of study, he returned home as an accomplished sage with thousands of students. Much of the material in the Mishnah and the Midrashim is based on the teachings his disciples received from him. He was cruelly executed by the Romans for defying their ban on teaching Torah.

al-Dhahiri, Zechariah c. 1531–1608; Yemen. Jewish poet and scholar. Traveled extensively across the Holy Land and throughout Asia, and recorded his experiences in a Hebrew rhymed prose narrative which he included in his *Sefer ha-Musar* ("Book of Moral Instruction").

Albo, R. Joseph c. 1380–1444, Spain. Author of the Jewish-philosophical classic *Ikarim* ("Book of Fundamentals"). The work stresses three fundamental aspects of Jewish belief: the existence of G-d, the divine origin of the Torah, and reward and punishment.

Alfasi See biographical note on "R. Isaac Alfasi" on p. 114.

Alkabetz, R. Solomon See biographical note on p. 231.

Alon, Gedaliah 1902–1950; Noted Israeli historian.

Alshich, R. Moses See biographical note on p. 231.

Alter, R. Judah Aryeh Leib See **Sefat Emet**.

Amiel, R. Moses 1882–1945. A chief proponent of Religious Zionism. Served in rabbinical positions in Lithuania and Antwerp before being elected chief rabbi of Tel Aviv in 1936.

Amos Biblical book recording the prophecies of Amos; see p. 158.

R. Amram Gaon d. 875. Head of the yeshivah in Sura, Babylonia. In response to a request from the Jewish community in Spain, he wrote out the text of the daily prayers, adding Halachic decisions, comments on customs, and other materials, which became known as *Seder Rav Amram Gaon*.

Arama, R. Isaac 1420–1494; Spain. Author of *Akeidat Yitzchak* ("The Binding of Isaac"), a series of philosophic and mystical essays on the Bible.

Ari Master Kabbalist R. Isaac Luria, 1534–1572. See biographical note on p. 231.

Aruch A dictionary of the Talmud and Midrashim by R. Nathan ben Yechiel, c. 1035–1105, of Rome, Italy.

Asevilli, R. Yomtov c. 1250–1330; Spain. Known by the acronym "Ritva." Served as rabbi of Saragossa and Seville, and responded to many Halachic queries. Mostly known for his lucid commentary on the Talmud. Also authored a defense of Maimonides' *Guide for the Perplexed*.

Auerbach, R. Shlomo Zalman 1910–1995; Jerusalem. Recognized as one of the prominent Halachic authorities of the 20th century. Wrote extensively on the interface of Torah law with medical ethics and modern technology.

Avot d'Rabbi Nathan A commentary on and an elaboration of *Ethics of the Fathers* bearing the name of the 2nd-century Mishnaic sage R. Nathan.

Azulai, R. Chaim Yosef David See **Chida**.

Baal Shem Tov, R. Israel 1698–1760; founder of the Hasidic movement. See pp. 232–236.

Bach Acronym for *Bayit Chadash*, a commentary by R. Joel Sirkis (1561–1640, Poland) on the Halachic code *Tur* (see p. 205). He also authored textual notes on the Talmud, and many responsa.

Bacharach, R. Naftali Hertz See biographical note on p. 231.

Bacharach, R. Yair 1639–1702; Worms, Germany. Author of many Halachic works, as well as works of natural philosophy (early sciences) and poetry.

Bahir Early Kabbalistic work. See p. 230.

Bar Kapara 2nd–3rd century Talmudic sage. Student of R. Judah ha-Nasi.

Bar-Sela, Gil Israeli professor and physician. Currently serves as head of the cancer center at the Emek Medical Center in Afula, Israel.

Bar Yochai, R. Simeon See p. 375.

Bartenura R. Ovadiah Bartenura; c. 1445–1524; Italy and Jerusalem. His commentary on the Mishnah appears in almost every printed edition.

Bechayei R. Bechayei (or Bachya) ben Asher; 1255–1340; Spain. Also referred to as "Rabbeinu Bechayei." His commentary on Torah is a synthesis of elucidation, allegory, homilies, and mysticism.

Bechor Shor, R. Joseph 12th century; Orleans, France. Prominent Tosafist, also known for his commentary on the Bible.

Ben Ish Chai Work containing lectures on the weekly Torah reading with mystical discussion and practical Halachah. Authored by R. Joseph Chaim of Baghdad, 1834–1909.

Ben-Gurion, David 1886–1973. One of the founders of the modern State of Israel and its first prime minister.

Ben Zimra, R. David 1479–1573. Known by the acronym "Radbaz." Served as chief rabbi of Egypt and later on the rabbinical court of Safed. He was also a successful businessman and independently wealthy. Authored a classic commentary to Maimonides' *Mishneh Torah*, and many Halachic responsa.

Benjamin of Tudela 12th century; Spain. Traveled across Europe, the Holy Land, the Middle East, and North Africa, visiting virtually every medieval Jewish community. He recorded his travels in his *Masa'ot Binyamin*.

Beresovsky, R. Shalom Noach 1911–2000; Belarus and Israel. Rebbe of the Slonim branch of Hasidism. Is best known for his popular seven-volume collection of Hasidic teachings titled *Netivot Shalom* ("Pathways of Peace").

Berkovitz, R. Eliezer 1908–1992. Held rabbinical positions in Germany, England, Australia, and the United States, and served as chairman of the department of Jewish philosophy at Hebrew Theological College in Skokie. Authored more than 20 books in English, Hebrew, and German.

Bialik, Chaim Nachman 1873–1934; Odessa and Tel Aviv. A pioneer of modern Hebrew poetry, he is regarded as Israel's national poet.

Breisch, R. Mordecai Jacob 1895–1976. Served as rabbi in various communities in Poland and Germany. After the rise of Nazism, he fled to Switzerland where he served as chief rabbi.

Cahill, Thomas b. 1940; New York. American scholar and writer, best known for his *The Hinges of History* series, in which he recounts formative moments in Western civilization.

Caro, R. Joseph Author of the *Shulchan Aruch* (see p. 205). See biographical note on p. 115.

Chafetz Chayim See **Kagan, R. Israel Meir**.

R. Chaim Brisker R. Chaim Soloveitchik; 1853–1918; Volozhin and later Brisk (Brest-Litovsk), Belarus. A scion of the renowned Soloveitchik rabbinical dynasty, and founder of the distinctive method of Talmud study known as the "Brisker Methodology." His disciples included many of the last century's great Talmudists: his sons R. Moshe (1879–1941, later in New York) and R. Yitzchak Ze'ev ("R. Velveleh Brisker," 1886–1959, Jerusalem); R. Boruch Ber Leibowitz (1862–1939) of Slabodka; R. Isser Zalman Meltzer (1870–1953, Slabodka and Jerusalem); R. Elchanan Wasserman (1874–1941), head of the Novardok yeshivah; R. Chaim Ozer Grodzinski (1863–1940) of Vilna; and R. Shimon Shkop (1860–1939) of Telshe and Grodno. Many of R. Chaim's descendants serve as rabbis and heads of yeshivahs in Israel, Europe, and the U.S.

R. Chaim of Volozhin 1749–1821. A protégé of R. Elijah of Vilna. Author of the philosophical and Kabbalistic work *Nefesh ha-Chayim* ("Soul of Life"). In 1803, he founded the famed yeshivah of Volozhin, which would produce many of the leading Torah scholars of the next century and a half, including Netziv, R. Chaim Brisker, and R. Abraham Isaac Kook.

Chatam Sofer R. Moses Schreiber; 1762–1839; Pressburg, Slovakia. Preeminent leader of Hungarian Jewry. Known as "Chatam Sofer" after his works by that name, which include Halachic responsa, Talmudic exposition, and Biblical commentary.

Chida R. Chaim Yosef David Azulai; 1724–1806; Jerusalem. Noted bibliophile and a prolific writer in many areas of Torah. His *Shem ha-Gedolim* ("Name of the Greats") includes short biographies of some 1,500 Torah authors and their works.

Chidushei ha-Rim See **R. Yitzchak Meir of Ger**.

Chinuch ("Book of Education") An overview of the reasons behind each of the 613 Biblical commandments and the ethical lessons they convey. Composed in the 13th century by an anonymous author who identifies himself only as "a Levite from Barcelona."

R. Chiya See "Aliyahs of Talmudic Sages" on p. 94; also see entry for **Tosefta**.

Chronicles Biblical book; see p. 159. In the Greek and Latin translations of the Bible, it is divided into two books, I Chronicles and II Chronicles.

R. Chunya See **R. Huna**.

Colon, R. Joseph c. 1420–1480; Italy. Known by the acronym "Maharik." His authoritative Halachic responsa circulated throughout the Jewish diaspora.

Cordovero, R. Moses See biographical note on p. 231.

Crescas, R. Hasdai c. 1340–1411; Spain. Author of *Ohr Hashem* ("Light of G-d"), a defense of classical Jewish theology in the face of the popularity of Aristotelian philosophy among medieval Jewish scholars.

Da Fano, R. Menachem Azariah See biographical note on p. 231.

De Uceda, R. Samuel See biographical note on p. 231.

De Vidas, R. Elijah See biographical note on p. 231.

Deborah Prophetess and Israelite leader in the era of the Judges. See p. 54.

Derashot ha-Ran A collection of eight discourses exploring a series of fundamental ideas in Jewish philosophy including creation, free choice, prophecy, the chosenness of the people of Israel, nature and miracles, the mitzvot, and Torah learning. Authored by 14th-century sage R. Nissim Gerondi.

Dershowitz, Alan b. 1938; New York. Lawyer, jurist, political commentator, and author. Professor of law at Harvard University for half a century. Advocate for the State of Israel, and an activist civil liberties lawyer.

Dessler, R. Elijah 1892–1953; United Kingdom and Israel. Spiritual counselor of the Ponevezh Yeshivah, and a leading voice of the Musar movement. His writings were published under the title *Michtav me-Eliyahu*.

Deuteronomy Fifth of the Five Books of Moses; see p. 158 and p. 163.

Dimont, Max I. 1912–1992; Missouri. Historian and author. In 1962, he published the critically acclaimed *Jews, G-d and History*, which has sold over 1.5 million copies.

Donin, R. Hayim Halevi 1928–1983. Served as rabbi in Southfield, Michigan, and as Adjunct Professor of Judaic Studies at the University of Detroit. Author of the highly acclaimed *To Be A Jew: A Guide to Jewish Observance in Contemporary Life*.

R. DovBer of Lubavitch 1773–1827; Russia. Second rebbe of the Chabad-Lubavitch branch of Hasidism.

Duties of the Hearts See **Ibn Pakudah, R. Bachya.**

Ecclesiastes Biblical book; see p. 159 and pp. 180–182.

Edelstein, Yuli b. 1958. A "refusenik" in the Soviet Union, he later served as Speaker of the Knesset (Israeli parliament) in the years 2013–2020.

Eibeschutz, R. David Solomon 1755–1814. Served as a rabbi in a number of communities in the Polish-Lithuanian commonwealth before making aliyah and settling in Safed, Israel. Authored numerous Halachic, Talmudic, and Kabbalistic works, many of which are still in manuscript.

Eibeschutz, R. Jonathan 1690–1764. A child prodigy who developed into one of the great rabbinic leaders of his time. Served as *dayan* (rabbinical judge) in Prague and later as the rabbi of the prestigious "three communities" of Altona, Hamburg, and Wandsbek. Was falsely accused of being a secret follower of the false messiah Shabbetai Zvi, involving him in one of the greatest controversies to engulf the Jewish world in the 18th century. He wrote voluminously in many areas of Jewish thought, including commentaries on *Shulchan Aruch* and popular expositions on the Bible.

Eidels, R. Shmuel Eliezer 1555–1631; Poland. Known by the acronym "Maharsha." His commentaries on both the Halachic and Agadic portions of the Talmud are a staple of Talmudic study.

Eiger, R. Akiva 1761–1837; Posen, Poland. Known for his sharp intellect. Authored commentaries on the Mishnah, Talmud, and *Shulchan Aruch*.

Ein Yaakov An extraction of the Agadic material in the Talmud, together with commentaries. Compiled by R. Jacob ibn Habib, c. 1460–1516, of Zamora, Spain and Salonica, Greece.

R. Eliezer R. Eliezer ben Hyrcanus; 1st century CE; Lod, Israel. Also known as "R. Eliezer the Great." R. Eliezer was an illiterate farm worker in his father's fields when he ran away to study in the academy of R. Jochanan ben Zakai, where he developed into a leading Torah scholar. R. Akiva was his disciple. The Midrash *Pirkei d'Rabbi Eliezer* is attributed to him.

Elijah the Prophet Active 740–718 BCE; Land of Israel. See pp. 173–175.

R. Elijah of Vilna See note on "Gra School" on p. 231, and under "Vilna" on p. 120.

Emek ha-Melech See biographical note on "R. Naftali Hertz Bacharach" on p. 231.

Encyclopedia Talmudit Encyclopedia summarizing all Talmudic and Halachic topics and technical terms. The first volume was published in 1947 under the editorship of R. Shlomo Yosef Zevin. The project is still ongoing, with more than 40 volumes published to date.

Epstein, R. Yechiel Michel d. 1706; Frankfurt, Germany. Author of *Kitzur Shaloh*, a work summarizing the teachings of the monumental work *Shenei Luchot ha-Berit* (see note on "Shaloh" on p. 231), with additional material by the author (not to be confused with a later R. Yechiel Michel Epstein, 1829–1908, author of *Aruch ha-Shulchan*).

Esther Biblical book; see p. 159 and pp. 361–365.

Ethics of the Fathers One of the 60 tractates of the Talmud, citing ethical and moral teachings from 14 generations of Torah sages, from Simeon the Just (4th century BCE) to R. Judah ha-Nasi (2nd century CE). See sample teachings on pp. 246–247.

Exodus The second of the Five Books of Moses; see p. 158 and p. 161.

Ezekiel Biblical book containing the prophecies of Ezekiel; see p. 158 and p. 172.

Ezra Active c. 348–315 BCE; Jerusalem, Israel. Spiritual leader of the Jewish community at the beginning of the Second Temple era, and head of the Great Assembly. Author of the Biblical book Ezra-Nehemiah.

Ezra, Book of Biblical book; see p. 159.

Falk, R. Joshua 1555–1614. A disciple of R. Moses Isserlis. Authored important commentaries on *Tur* and *Shulchan Aruch* (see p. 205). Served on the "Council of Four Lands," a central body of Jewish authority in Poland.

Fastag, Azriel David d. 1942; Warsaw. A member of the Modzitz branch of Hasidism, and a composer of Hasidic melodies. Most famous for the *Ani Maamin* tune he composed in a cattle car as he was being taken to Treblinka.

Feinstein, R. Moshe 1895–1986. Served as rabbi of Lubań, Belarus for sixteen years. Moved to New York in 1937, where he gained eminence as a leading Halachic authority of the 20th century.

Five Books of Moses First part of the Bible, and the core text of Judaism. See pp. 161–163.

Frank, Anne See biographical note on p. 134.

Frankl, Viktor See biographical note on p. 134.

Freeman, Tzvi b. 1955; Atlanta, Georgia. Rabbi, computer scientist, and writer. His books include *Bringing Heaven Down to Earth* and *Men, Women and Kabbalah*. He is a senior editor at Chabad.org.

Gafni, Isaiah b. 1944. Professor of Jewish history at Hebrew University of Jerusalem and president of Shalem College.

R. Gamliel of Yavneh Served as president of the Sanhedrin in the generation following the destruction of the Second Temple, approximately 74–115 CE.

Gefen, R. Tobias 1870–1970. Served as rabbi of the Shearith Israel Congregation in Atlanta, Georgia for 60 years. In 1935, he certified Coca-Cola as kosher after convincing the company to replace a non-kosher ingredient in its formula with a kosher substitute.

Genesis The first of the Five Books of Moses; see p. 158 and p. 161.

Geonim See entry for "Gaon; Geonim; Geonic" in *Glossary* (p. 444).

Gerondi, R. Nissim 1320–1376; Girona, Spain. Known by the acronym "Ran." Authored important Talmudic, Halachic, and philosophical works. See entry for **Derashot ha-Ran**.

R. Gershom of Mainz A seminal figure of early Ashkenazic Jewry. See p. 120 and p. 213.

Gikatilla, R. Joseph See biographical note on p. 230.

Goldschmidt, R. Eliezer 1909–1992; Hebron. Served on the Israeli Chief Rabbinate's highest Halachic court during the years 1951–1979.

Gombiner, R. Abraham See entry for **Magen Avraham**.

Gra R. Elijah of Vilna, 1720–1797. See note on "Gra School" on p. 231, and under "Vilna" on p. 120.

Guide for the Perplexed Philosophical work completed in 1190 by Maimonides (see biographical note on p. 114), employing Aristotelian and classical Arabic philosophy to present the fundamental principles of Judaism, explain narratives in the Torah, and offer rationalistic explanations for many of the mitzvot.

Halachic Midrashim Teachings of Mishnaic sages, from the schools of R. Akiva and his contemporary R. Ishmael (1st and 2nd century CE), containing textual exegeses of the Torah with focus on clarifying the resulting laws. Three primary works of this genre are *Mechilta* on Exodus, *Sifra* on Leviticus, and *Sifrei* on Numbers and Deuteronomy.

Halachot Gedolot A Geonic work on Jewish law, compiling the practical rulings arising from the Talmud. Attributed to either R. Shimon Kayyara or R. Yehudai Gaon, both of the 8th century.

R. Hananel See biographical note on p. 114.

Hanau, R. Zalman 1687–1746; Germany. Expert in Hebrew grammar and textual critic of Jewish liturgy.

R. Hanoch Henich of Aleksander 1798–1870; Poland. Senior disciple of R. Yitzchak Meir of Ger, whom he succeeded as the second leader of the "Ger" branch of Hasidism.

Hayom Yom An anthology of Hasidic aphorisms and customs arranged according to the days of the year, compiled in 1942 by the Lubavitcher

Rebbe, R. Menachem Mendel Schneerson, culled from the writings and talks of his father-in-law and predecessor, R. Yosef Yitzchak Schneersohn.

Heller, R. Aryeh Leib See **Ketzot ha-Choshen**.

Hercsztark, R. Shalom Joseph d. 1924. Served as rabbi of Jozefow, Poland.

Hertz, J. H. 1872–1946, London. Chief rabbi of the British Empire from 1914 until his passing. Edited a comprehensive commentary on the Torah popularly known as "The Hertz Chumash."

Herzl, Theodor 1860–1904; Vienna. Journalist, activist, and founder of modern political Zionism. Deeply affected by the Dreyfus Affair (see *Glossary* entry on. p. 444), he campaigned for the establishment of a Jewish State as a solution to the problem of antisemitism.

Heschel, Abraham Joshua 1907–1972; New York. Professor of Jewish ethics and mysticism at the Jewish Theological Seminary of America in New York. Active in the struggle for civil rights in the U.S. in the 1950s and 1960s. His published works include *Man Is Not Alone*, *G-d in Search of Man*, *The Sabbath*, and *The Prophets*.

Hillel Hillel the Elder; c. 110 BCE–10 CE; Babylonia and Israel. A descendant of King David, Hillel served as president of the Sanhedrin (highest court of Torah law), a position filled thereafter almost exclusively by his descendants. His devotion to Torah study under conditions of extreme poverty in his early years as a student became legendary; he was also famed for his approachability and tolerance. Hillel tended toward the lenient position in his rulings on Torah law, in contrast with the more stringent approach of his colleague Shamai. Each of them gathered a following of like-minded disciples, which developed into two schools of Torah thought and law—the "School of Hillel" and the "School of Shamai."

Hillel II 4th century; Israel. Descendant of Hillel the Elder, and one of the last to preside over the Sanhedrin before its operation was discontinued by the Romans. Formulated the Jewish perpetual calendar (see "Sighting the Moon" on p. 330).

Hirsch, R. Samson Raphael 1808–1888; Germany. Founder of the *Torah Im Derech Eretz* approach to Judaism, advocating a symbiosis of Torah learning with secular sciences and engagement with the modern world. His commentaries on the Bible contain his philosophical and psychological insights into the Biblical narratives and his novel system of Hebrew philology. He also authored *Horeb*, a philosophical exploration of the mitzvot; and *Nineteen Letters on Judaism*.

Horowitz, R. Isaiah See biographical note on "Shaloh" on p. 231.

House of Hillel; House of Shamai See entry for **Hillel**.

R. Huna Two different Talmudic sages, both of whom were originally from Babylonia but later moved to the Land of Israel, bear this name. One lived in the late 3rd century and the other in the mid-4th century. Both are also referred to as "R. Chuna" and "R. Chunya."

Hutner, R. Yitzchak 1906–1980; Poland, U.S., and Israel. Dean of the Rabbi Chaim Berlin Yeshivah in New York, which he built up into one of the premier institutions of Torah learning in the United States. His primary work is the ten-volume *Pachad Yitzchak*, in which he draws on the writings of Maharal, Ramchal, Gra, and the teachings of Hasidism.

Ibn Attar, R. Chaim See biographical note on p. 231.

Ibn Daud, R. Abraham c. 1110–1180; Spain. Rabbi, astronomer, historian, and philosopher. Best known as the author of *Sefer ha-Kabbalah*, which chronicles the transmission of the Oral Torah through the generations, and Jewish history in Spain.

Ibn Duran, R. Simeon 1361–1444; Spain and Algiers. Halachist, philosopher, physician, astronomer, mathematician, communal leader, and prolific author. Also known by the acronym "Rashbatz," and by the name of his work of Halachic responsa, *Tashbetz*.

Ibn Ezra R. Abraham ibn Ezra; 1092–1167; Spain, Italy, and France. Author of a classic commentary on the Bible as well as works of poetry, philosophy, medicine, astronomy, and other topics.

Ibn Gabbai, R. Meir See biographical note on p. 230.

Ibn Gabirol, R. Solomon See biographical note on p. 114.

Ibn Janach, R. Jonah 11th century; Cordoba and Zaragoza, Spain. Composed a groundbreaking listing of Hebrew words arranged by root, and a handbook of Hebrew grammar.

Ibn Labrat, Dunash c. 920–990; Babylonia and Spain. Hebrew philologist and poet, who disputed some of the grammatical interpretations of his contemporaries Menachem ibn Saruk and R. Saadia Gaon. Rashi occasionally quotes his interpretations.

Ibn Pakudah, R. Bachya 11th century; Spain. Author of *Duties of the Hearts*, the first systematic work of Jewish ethical philosophy. The work consists of ten "gates" exploring ten principles of inner spiritual life: unity of G-d, divine providence, worship, trust, sincerity, humility, repentance, self-examination, asceticism, and love. Originally written in Judeo-Arabic, the work is also known by its Hebrew title, *Hovot Halevavot*.

Ikarim See **Albo, R. Joseph**.

R. Isaac bar Sheshet 1326–1408. Known by the acronym "Rivash." Served as rabbi in Barcelona and other communities in Spain. Settled in Algiers after fleeing the anti-Jewish riots of 1391. His Halachic responsa, which quote from sources no longer extant, served in part as a basis for the *Shulchan Aruch* (see p. 205).

R. Isaac the Blind See biographical note on p. 230.

Isaiah Biblical book containing the prophecies of Isaiah; see p. 158 and p. 171.

R. Ishmael R. Ishmael ben Elisha; d. c. 130 CE; Kfar Aziz, Israel. Colleague of R. Akiva. The Midrash *Mechilta* is based on his teachings. Executed by the Romans during the Bar Kochba revolt.

Isserlin, R. Israel 1390–1460; Austria. A foremost Ashkenazic Talmudist and Halachist who attracted students from throughout Europe. His *Terumat ha-Deshen* served as a source for many of R. Moses Isserlis' glosses on the *Shulchan Aruch* (see p. 205). He also wrote an important supercommentary on Rashi.

Isserlis, R. Moses 1530–1572; Krakow. Also known as "Rema." See note on "Krakow" on p. 120, and on "Shulchan Aruch" on p. 205.

R. Jacob Ben Asher c. 1269–1343; Germany and later Spain. Also known as "Tur," after his monumental codification of Halachah (see description on p. 205). He also wrote a commentary on the Torah that includes many fascinating acrostics and gematrias (numerical correlations) connecting the Torah's words with their Midrashic explanations and narratives.

Jacobson, Simon b. 1956; Brooklyn. Served as one of the "oral scribes" entrusted to memorize and transcribe the teachings of the Lubavitcher Rebbe, R. Menachem Mendel Schneerson, and to prepare initial drafts of the Rebbe's essays and discourses. Author of the best-selling book *Toward a Meaningful Life*, and founder of the Meaningful Life Center.

Jeremiah Biblical book containing the prophecies of Jeremiah; see p. 158.

Jerusalem Talmud Version of the Talmud composed in the Holy Land in the 3rd and 4th centuries CE. See p. 109 and pp. 184ff.

Job Biblical book; see p. 159.

R. Jochanan R. Jochanan bar Naphcha; c. 180–280 CE. As a young boy, he studied under R. Judah ha-Nasi. He later moved to Tiberias, where he established an academy and became renowned as the leading scholar in the Land of Israel. Over the course of his long life, he laid the foundations for the Jerusalem Talmud.

R. Jochanan ben Zakai c. 40 BCE–80 CE; Israel. A disciple of both Hillel and Shamai. Served as vice-president of the Sanhedrin in the period before and after the destruction of the second Holy Temple, guiding the adjustment of Jewish religious life in the wake of that catastrophic loss. His disciples included R. Eliezer ben Hyrcanus and R. Joshua ben Hananiah.

Josephus c. 37–100; Jerusalem and Rome. Jewish historian. His two principal works, *Wars of the Jews* and *Antiquities of the Jews*, are considered primary sources for the events of the Second Temple era, including many that he personally participated in or witnessed.

Joshua Biblical book; see p. 158.

R. Joshua R. Joshua ben Hananiah; mid-1st to early 2nd century; Peki'in, Israel. A prominent disciple of R. Jochanan ben Zakai and a teacher of R. Akiva.

R. Joshua ben Korchah Second-century Mishnaic sage who was a disciple, and some say son, of R. Akiva.

R. Judah c. 190–299 CE; Pumbedita, Babylonia. A Talmudic sage (not to be confused with the Mishnaic sage R. Judah bar Ila'i, who is often cited as "R. Judah" without qualification) who studied under Rav and Shmuel. When Shmuel's hometown of Nehardea, along with its academy, was destroyed by invading armies from Palmyra in 259 CE, R. Judah reopened the academy in Pumbedita, where it continued to exist for many centuries as one of the flagship Torah institutions of the Jewish world.

R. Judah bar Ila'i 2nd century; Land of Israel. A disciple of R. Akiva, he is the sage most quoted by name in the Mishnah. The Midrashic work *Sifra* (also known as *Torat Kohanim*) is largely based on his teachings.

R. Judah Halevi See biographical note on p. 114.

R. Judah ha-Nasi c. 120–190 CE; Tiberias, Beth Shearim, and Sepphoris, Israel. President (*nasi*) of the Sanhedrin, and a direct descendant of King David and Hillel. His friendship with the Roman emperor Antoninus (usually identified as Marcus Aurelius) provided the Jewish community of the Land of Israel a peaceful respite that made it possible for him to redact and finalize the text of the Mishnah (see description by Maimonides on pp. 186–187). He is also known simply as "Rabbi" ("master" and "teacher" par excellence) in recognition of this accomplishment and of the great number of prominent sages who were his disciples.

Judges Biblical book; see p. 54.

Kaf ha-Chayim A commentary on *Shulchan Aruch* by R. Jacob Chaim Sofer, c. 1867–1939, of Baghdad and Jerusalem, incorporating rulings and customs of the Kabbalists and of later Sephardic Halachists.

Kagan, R. Israel Meir 1839–1933; Radun, Belarus. Foremost Halachist, ethicist, and leader and mentor of Eastern European Jewry in the late 19th and early 20th century. Known as *Chafetz Chayim* ("Desires Life"), after his first published work, a digest of laws pertaining to proper ethical speech. He also authored *Mishnah Berurah*, a commentary on the first section of the *Shulchan Aruch* (see p. 205).

Kaplan, R. Shmuel Director of Chabad-Lubavitch of Maryland since 1974. Serves on the executive committee of Merkos L'Inyonei Chinuch, the education and outreach arm of the Chabad-Lubavitch Movement, and on the executive committee of the Rohr Jewish Learning Institute.

Kedushat Levi See **R. Levi Yitzchak of Berditchev**.

Keli Yakar A popular commentary on the Bible, containing many philosophical and psychological insights, authored by R. Solomon Ephraim Luntshits, 1550–1619, of Poland and later Prague.

Ketzot ha-Choshen In-depth commentary by R. Aryeh Leib Heller (1745–1813; Galicia) on the financial and business law section of *Shulchan Aruch* (see p. 205). He also authored other intricate works on Torah law and the Talmudic dialectic.

Ki-Tov, R. Eliyahu 1912–1976. Israeli educator and community activist. In 1954 he left the political scene, dedicating the later years of his life to writing primers on Jewish practice and belief. His most popular works are *Sefer ha-Todaah* (published in English as "The Book of our Heritage") and *Ish Ubeito* ("The Jew and His Home").

Kings Biblical book; see p. 158. In the Greek and Latin translations of the Bible, it is divided into two books, I Kings and II Kings.

Kitzur Shulchan Aruch A basic digest of the *Shulchan Aruch* (see p. 205) written as a layman's guide for everyday Halachic conduct. Published by Hungarian rabbi R. Solomon Gantzfried in 1864.

Klatzkin, Shmuel b. 1952. Associate rabbi at Chabad of Greater Dayton, Ohio. Adjunct Professor at Antioch University, and senior editor of curriculum at the Rohr Jewish Learning Institute.

Kleinman, R. Moshe Chaim Early 20th century; Brisk, Belarus. Authored a compilation of teachings by the rebbes of the Slonim branch of Hasidism.

Kook, R. Abraham Isaac 1864–1935. First Ashkenazic chief rabbi of Israel in the modern era. His many works on Jewish thought and law are composed in a distinctive philosophical, mystical, and poetic style, and form the ideological underpinning for Religious Zionism.

Kovner, Abba 1918–1987; Lithuania and Israel. Fighter, poet, activist, and author. During the Holocaust he was instrumental in the Vilna ghetto underground and commanded a Jewish partisan brigade in the forest.

Kuzari See biographical note on "R. Judah Halevi" on p. 114.

Lamentations Biblical book; see p. 159 and p. 381.

Lamm, R. Maurice 1930–2016. Held the chair of professional rabbinics at Yeshiva University's RIETS rabbinical seminary in New York. Author of *The Jewish Way in Death and Mourning* and *The Jewish Way in Love and Marriage*.

Landau, R. Yechezkel 1713–1793; Poland and Bohemia. Author of an authoritative collection of responsa on Torah law titled *Noda bi-Yehudah* ("Renowned in Judah"), and other Halachic and Talmudic works.

Leibovitz, Liel b. 1976. Israeli-American journalist and author. Senior writer and executive producer of video and interactive media for *Tablet* magazine.

Leibowitz, Nechama 1905–1997; Latvia, Germany, and Israel. Biblical scholar who lectured for four decades at Tel Aviv University and was awarded the coveted Israel Prize for her work in furthering and popularizing Biblical study. Seven volumes of her thought-provoking "sheets" on the *parashah* (weekly Torah reading) have been published in the original Hebrew and in English translation.

Leiner, R. Mordecai Joseph 1801–1854; Poland. Founder of the Izhbitza-Radzin branch of Hasidism. His seminal work *Mei ha-Shiloach* expresses the doctrine that all events, including human actions, are absolutely under G-d's control.

R. Levi Yitzchak of Berditchev 1740–1809. Hasidic master, known for his all-encompassing love, compassion, and advocacy on behalf of the Jewish people. His teachings were published under the title *Kedushat Levi* ("The Holiness of Levi").

Leviticus Third of the Five Books of Moses; see p. 158 and p. 162.

Likutei Sichot ("Collected Talks") A 39-volume compilation of scholarly essays based on the talks of R. Menachem Mendel Schneerson, 1902–1994, the seventh Lubavitcher Rebbe, which he edited for publication. The essays demonstrate the unity of Torah by revealing the connective essence behind its Talmudic, Halachic, mystical, philosophical, and ethical aspects.

Lima, R. Moses c. 1604–1658, Lithuania. Served as rabbi in Slonim, Vilna, and Brisk. Authored glosses on the *Shulchan Aruch*, but passed away before the project was complete. The work, titled *Chelkat Mechokek,* was subsequently published by his son (see p. 205).

Lindsay, Lord Alexander 1812–1880; Scotland. The 25th Earl of Crawford. Traveled widely and was an avid art collector.

Litvin, Jay 1944–2004; Chicago and Israel. Writer and activist. Served as medical liaison for Chabad's Children of Chernobyl program and took a leading role in airlifting children from the nuclear contaminated areas. Founded and directed Chabad's Terror Victims program in Israel. Authored dozens of articles on Chabad.org.

Loew, R. Judah See biographical note for "Maharal" on p. 231.

Luria, R. Isaac See biographical note on "Ari" on p. 231.

Luther, Martin 1483–1546; Germany. Theologian and reformer who challenged the authority of the Roman Catholic Church and established the theological foundations of "Lutheran" Christianity.

Luzzatto, R. Moses Chaim See biographical note on "Ramchal" on p. 231.

Maarechet ha-Elokut Early Kabbalistic work; see note on p. 230.

Maccabees A series of post-Biblical books chronicling the Hasmoneans' revolt and their battles with the Syrian-Greeks. While certain Christian groups regard these books as part of the Bible, in Jewish tradition they are considered apocryphal ("external") to it, though recognized as a historical source. Claiming to be authored by Jason of Cyrene, it was probably composed in the first century BCE by a Jewish author.

Machberet See biographical note for "Menachem ibn Saruk" on p. 114.

Machzor Vitry *Piyyutim*, liturgical comments, and Halachic rulings compiled by R. Simcha of Vitry, d. 1105, of France, a disciple of Rashi.

Magen Avraham Commentary on *Shulchan Aruch* by R. Abraham Gombiner, c. 1637–1683, of Poland (see p. 205).

Maharal See biographical note on p. 231.

Maharsha see **Eidels, R. Shmuel Eliezer**.

Maharshal R. Solomon Luria; 1510–1574; Lublin, Poland. Talmudic commentator and Halachic authority. Taught and influenced many of the great Ashkenazic Halachists of his generation.

Maimonides See biographical note on p. 114.

Malachi Biblical book; see p. 159.

Malbim R. Meir Leibush Wisser, 1809–1879. Served as rabbi in Bucharest, Leczyca, Kherson, Mogilev, and Konigsberg; was also offered the rabbinate of New York City but passed away before being able to take up that post. His commentaries on all 24 books of the Bible combine textual analysis, philosophical and psychological insights, and Kabbalistic teaching.

Mangel, R. Nissen b. c. 1934; Hungary and New York. Survived Auschwitz as a child. Translator of the *Tehillat Hashem* prayer book and of portions of the *Tanya*, the seminal work of the Chabad Hasidism.

Masoretes See note on "Philology" on p. 154.

Matt, R. Moses c. 1551–1606. Served as rabbi and head of the yeshivah of Przemysl, Poland. Best known for his *Mateh Moshe*, which includes his lectures on Torah and laws and customs collected from the customs of his mentor, Maharshal (see above), and other sources.

Me'am Loez A multivolume encyclopedic commentary on Torah dealing with all areas of Jewish life. Originally written in Ladino (Judeo-Spanish). Begun by R. Jacob Culi, 1689–1732, chief rabbinical magistrate of Constantinople, with other prominent Turkish rabbis completing the work after his passing.

Mechilta see **Halachic Midrashim**.

Mechilta d'Rashbi A Halachic Midrash attributed to 2nd-century Mishnaic sage R. Simeon bar Yochai.

Mecklenburg, R. Jacob Zvi 1785–1865; Konigsberg, Prussia. His Biblical commentary *ha-Ketav veha-Kabbalah* ("Scripture and Tradition") demonstrates the indivisibility of the Written Torah and its counterpart, the Oral Torah.

R. Meir of Rothenburg c. 1215–1293. Also known by the acronym "Maharam." A leading Ashkenazic Halachic authority.

Meiri R. Menachem Meiri; 1249–1315; Southern France. Authored *Beit ha-Bechirah*, a broad commentary on the Mishnah and Talmud.

Meisels, R. Zvi Hirsch 1904–1974; Hungary. In Auschwitz, he served as spiritual mentor to thousands. Best known for his *Mekadshei Hashem* ("Sanctifiers of the Divine Name"), a collection of Halachic responsa from various rabbis killed during the Holocaust.

R. Menachem Mendel of Kotzk R. Menachem Mendel Morgenstern; 1787–1859; Poland. Prominent Hasidic leader who studied under the "Holy Jew" of Peshischa and R. Simcha Bunim of Peshischa, and refined their approach into a lifestyle demanding rigid devotion to high-level Torah study and the quest for truth, contrasting with many of his contemporaries' more populist approaches. His sayings and teachings, noted for their sharpness and unflinching honesty, are collected in his grandson R. Shmuel of Sochatchov's *Shem mi-Shmuel*, in R. Judah Aryeh Leib Alter of Ger's *Sefat Emet*, and in numerous other Hasidic works.

R. Menachem Mendel of Vorka 1819–1868; Poland. Second rebbe of the Vorka Hasidic dynasty. Known as "the silent" because he spoke little and tersely.

Metzudot A pair of commentaries on the Prophets and most of the Scriptures sections of the Bible by R. David Altschuler (18th century, Prague). *Metzudat David* explains the Biblical narrative, and *Metzudat Zion* explains the meaning of difficult words. The commentary was assembled and completed by Altschuler's son, R. Yechiel Hillel.

Michtav me-Eliyahu See **Dessler, R. Elijah**.

Midrash ha-Gadol Midrashic anthology attributed to R. David bar Amram al-Adani, 14th century, of Aden, Yemen.

Midrash Mishlei A Midrashic commentary on the Biblical book of Proverbs, composed in the Land of Israel or in Babylon approximately 800 CE.

Midrash Rabbah The most famous of the Midrashic compilations, citing the teachings of Talmudic sages from the Land of Israel from the 3rd and 4th centuries CE. "Midrash Rabbah" is in fact a collection of ten separate works, compiled between the 3rd and 12th centuries, containing textual exegeses, historical narratives, and moral teachings structured as commentaries on the Five Books of Moses and the five scriptural "scrolls" (Song of Songs, Ruth, Lamentations, Ecclesiastes, and Esther).

Midrash Tanchuma A foundational Midrashic work bearing the name of the 4th-century Talmudic sage it quotes.

Midrash Tehilim A Midrashic commentary on the Biblical book of Psalms. While the date of its composition has not been conclusively determined, it is cited as early as the 11th century by Rashi and in *Aruch*.

Midrash Temurah A short midrash, attributed to the Mishnaic sages R. Ishmael and R. Akiva. First published by Chida, it is also cited by Meiri as *Midrash Temurot*.

Minchat Shai A compilation by R. Yedidya Shlomo Norzi, c. 1560—1630, of Mantua, Italy, clarifying the Biblical text in matters of spelling, vocalization, and cantillation notes (see p. 157).

Mishnah; Mishnaic The Mishnah is the basic summary text of the laws of the Torah, and the first officially written text of any part of the "Oral Torah." It cites the teachings of the dozens of sages who lived and taught during the five generations from Hillel the Elder (first century BCE) to R. Judah ha-Nasi, who redacted the Mishnah at the end of the 2nd century CE. The Mishnah forms the basis for the subsequent 300 years of discussions and deliberations recorded in the Talmud, redacted in the 5th century CE. See p. 204, and description by Maimonides on pp. 186–187.

Mishnah Berurah See **Kagan, R. Israel Meir**.

Mishneh Torah Monumental codification of Torah law composed by Maimonides in the years 1168–1177. See biographical note on p. 114, and description of work on p. 204.

Morris, Benny b. 1948; Israel. Professor of history in the Middle East Studies department of Ben-Gurion University of the Negev.

R. Moshe ha-Darshan 11th century; Narbonne. Leader of French Jewry, renowned for his contribution to Midrashic literature. Rashi frequently quotes from his *Yesod*, a Midrashic work that is no longer extant.

Moss, Aron Teacher of Kabbalah, Talmud, and practical Judaism. Currently serves as rabbi of the Nefesh Synagogue in Sydney, Australia, and authors a popular weekly article on modern Jewish thought.

R. Nachman of Breslov 1772–1810; Ukraine. Founder of the Breslov Hasidic movement, whose fundamental ideas are contained in his *Likutei Moharan* ("Collected teachings of our master R. Nachman"). R. Nachman also authored a series of esoteric tales and parables that are studied for the mystical ideas they contain.

Nachmanides See biographical note on p. 114.

Najara, R. Israel See biographical note on p. 231.

R. Naphtali of Ropshitz 1760–1827. A prominent Hasidic leader in Galicia who greatly influenced the development of the movement there.

R. Nathan ben Yechiel See **Aruch**.

Nathanson, R. Joseph Saul 1808–1875; Lvov, Galicia. Halachist, author, and philanthropist.

Nefesh ha-Chayim See **R. Chaim of Volozhin**.

Nehemiah Biblical book; see p. 159.

Netziv R. Naphtali Zvi Judah Berlin; 1817–1893; Russia. Served as head of the famed yeshivah of Volozhin. Authored a popular commentary on the Bible and other Torah works.

Noam Elimelech Hasidic commentary on the Torah by R. Elimelech of Lizhensk, 1717–1787, pioneer of Hasidism in Poland and Galicia.

Noda bi-Yehudah See **Landau, R. Yechezkel**.

Numbers Fourth of the Five Books of Moses; see p. 158 and p. 162.

Ohr ha-Chayim See biographical note for "R. Chaim ibn Attar" on p. 231.

Onkelos Aramaic translation of the Bible authored by Onkelos, c. 35–120 CE, a Roman nobleman who converted to Judaism. The Talmud attests that his translation incorporates the interpretation of the Torah as received in the Sinaic tradition.

Orchot Tzadikim ("Ways of the Righteous") 15th-century collection of ethical teachings by an unknown author.

Oren, Michael b. 1955. Academic and author. Served as Israel's ambassador to the U.S. from 2009 to 2013.

Oshry, R. Ephraim 1914–2003; Lithuania and New York. While in the Kovno Ghetto, he responded to difficult Holocaust-related questions and later published them in five volumes under the title *Shaalot u-Teshuvot mi-Maamakim* ("Queries and Responses from the Depths").

Panet, R. Yechezkel 1783–1845. Hasidic leader and chief rabbi of Transylvania.

Papo, R. Eliezer 1785–1826. Rabbi of Selestria, Bulgaria. Author of *Peleh Yo'etz*, an encyclopedic compendium on Jewish ethics, morals, and personality development.

Passover Haggadah Compiled during the Talmudic era, it establishes the structure of the Passover Seder and incorporates verses from the Torah and Talmudic exegesis to tell the story of the Exodus. It has been published in thousands of editions and has spawned thousands of commentaries, making it one of the most published books in the history of literature.

Payyetanim Composers of liturgical poems (*piyyutim*), containing prayers, Midrashic expositions, and moral homilies. The earliest *payyetanim* lived in the Land of Israel in the 3rd to 8th centuries, and included Yosi ben Yosi (5th century), Yannai (5th or 6th century), and R. Elazar Hakalir (commonly believed to have lived in the 6th or 7th centuries, although some sources place him in the Mishnaic era).

Pesikta d'Rav Kahana A Midrashic work redacted in the Land of Israel approximately 500 CE.

Pirkei d'Rabbi Eliezer A Midrash bearing the name of Mishnaic sage R. Eliezer ben Hyrcanus, which expounds upon Biblical events from the Creation until the Israelites' journeys in the wilderness.

Prager, Dennis b. 1948; New York and California. Talk show host, author, and public speaker. Founder of PragerU, which produces videos on various political, economic, and philosophical topics.

Proverbs Biblical book; see p. 159 and p. 180.

Psalms Biblical book; see pp. 176–179.

Radak R. David Kimchi; 1160–1235; Narbonne, Provence. His works on Hebrew grammar are considered the most authoritative in the field. He also wrote commentaries on many Biblical books.

Radbaz See **Ben Zimra, R. David**.

Ralbag R. Levi ben Gershon; 1288–1344; France. Also known as "Gersonides." Philosopher, mathematician, astronomer, scientist, and inventor. His works include the philosophical treatise *Milchamot Hashem* ("Battles of G-d"), and a commentary on the Bible that presents his philosophical, ethical, and Halachic conclusions from the narrative.

Ramchal See biographical note on p. 231.

Ran See **Gerondi, R. Nissim**

Rashba R. Solomon ben Aderet 1235–1310; Barcelona. More than 3,000 of his responsa are extant, dealing with varied questions on Halachah and religious philosophy addressed to him from all over Europe. He also authored various Halachic and Talmudic works.

Rashbam R. Shmuel ben Meir; c. 1085–1160; Ramerupt, France. A grandson and disciple of Rashi (see next entry). In his commentaries on the Bible, he takes a strict *peshat* (plain meaning) approach and often differs from the approach of his illustrious grandfather. He also wrote commentaries on the Talmud, and was one of the founders of the "Tosafot" school of Talmudic learning.

Rashi R. Solomon Yitzchaki; 1040–1105; Troyes, France and Worms, Germany. Author of the most fundamental commentaries on the Bible and the Talmud, focusing on the straightforward meaning of the text.

Recanati, R. Menachem See biographical note on p. 230.

Reish Lakish R. Simeon ben Lakish; c. 200–275; Sepphoris, Israel. A gladiator and bandit leader in his youth, an encounter with R. Jochanan led him to embrace Torah learning and become one of the great Torah scholars of his time. He married R. Jochanan's sister and became his study partner. His debates with R. Jochanan are widely quoted in the Talmud.

Reishit Chochmah See biographical note on "R. Elijah de Vidas" on p. 231.

Ritva See **Asevilli, R. Yomtov**.

Rosenzweig, Franz 1886–1929, Germany. After almost converting to Christianity as a young student, he dedicated himself to Torah observance and wrote *The Star of Redemption*, a highly influential work of Jewish philosophy. He also collaborated on a German translation of the Bible with Martin Buber. He died at 43 of amyotrophic lateral sclerosis (ALS).

Rosh R. Asher ben Yechiel; 1250–1328; Germany and Spain. Best known for his *Piskei ha-Rosh,* which summarizes the Halachic points of each Talmudic discussion. He also authored commentaries on the Bible and Talmud, and over 1,000 Halachic responsa. His son was R. Jacob ben Asher, author of the Halachic code *Tur* (see p. 205).

Roth, Cecil 1899–1970; Oxford and Jerusalem. Professor of Jewish Studies at Oxford University. Authored some 600 works on Jewish scholarship, history, and art, and was general editor of the *Encyclopedia Judaica*.

R. Saadia Gaon 882–942; Egypt, Israel, and Babylonia. His *Emunot ve-De'ot* ("Beliefs and Opinions") is the earliest extant systematic work of Jewish philosophy, providing rational proofs for traditional Jewish beliefs. He also translated the Torah into Arabic and wrote Halachic and liturgical works.

Saba, R. Abraham c. 1440–1508. Studied Kabbalah under R. Isaac de Leon and served as rabbi in Castile, Spain. He lost his library and manuscripts when forced to flee the Spanish Expulsion and the forced conversion in Portugal. After many tribulations, he eventually found refuge in Adrianople, Turkey, where he rewrote some of his works from memory, including *Tzror ha-Mor*, a homiletical and mystical commentary on the Torah.

Sacks, Jonathan 1948–2020; London. Chief rabbi of the United Kingdom from 1991 to 2013. A prolific and influential author, his books include *Radical Then Radical Now* and *The Dignity of Difference*. Received the Jerusalem Prize for enhancing Jewish life in the Diaspora. Was knighted and made a life peer as Baron Sacks of Aldridge.

Salanter, R. Israel R. Israel Lipkin; 1809–1883; Lithuania. Spent his formative years in the town of Salant under the tutelage of R. Yosef Zundel Salanter. Founder of the Musar movement, which propagated a regimen of ethical and spiritual self-perfection (see p. 244).

Samuel Biblical book; see p. 158. In the Greek and Latin translations of the Bible, it is divided into two books, I Samuel and II Samuel.

R. Samuel of Fiyorda c. 1630–1700. Served as rabbi in Shidlov, Poland, and subsequently in Fürth (Fiyorda), Germany. Author of *Beit Shmuel*, a commentary on *Shulchan Aruch* (see p. 205).

Sarna, Jonathan b. 1955. Professor of American Jewish History at Brandeis University. Recognized as a leading commentator on this subject, he has written, edited, or coedited more than 30 books, including *American Judaism: A History*.

Schama, Simon b. 1945; London and New York. Professor of history and art history at Columbia University. The BBC commissioned him to write and present a five-part series called *The Story of the Jews*, broadcast in 2013.

Schneersohn, R. Yosef Yitzchak 1880–1950; Russia, Poland, and New York. Sixth rebbe of the Chabad-Lubavitch branch of Hasidism. He established, with immense self-sacrifice, an underground network of Jewish schools and religious institutions throughout the communist Soviet Empire. Upon arriving in America, he laid the foundation for the global renaissance of Torah-true Jewish life (see p. 140).

Schneerson, R. Menachem M. 1902–1994; USSR, Berlin, Paris, and New York. The towering Jewish leader of the 20th century, known as "the Lubavitcher Rebbe," or simply as "the Rebbe." Born in southern Ukraine, the Rebbe escaped Nazi-occupied Europe to the U.S. where he inspired and guided the revival of traditional Judaism after the Holocaust, impacting virtually every Jewish community the world over. The Rebbe often emphasized that the performance of just one additional good deed could usher in the era of Mashiach. His scholarly talks and writings have been printed in more than 200 volumes. Also see entry for "Likutei Sichot."

R. Schneur Zalman of Liadi 1745–1812, Belarus. Founder of the Chabad branch of Hasidism. His works include *Tanya*, often called "the bible of Hasidism"; and *Shulchan Aruch ha-Rav*, an expansion on the *Shulchan Aruch*.

Schultz, Michael Ordained as a rabbi in 2008, he currently serves as director of spiritual care service at Rambam Medical Center in Haifa, Israel, and on the executive board of the Israel Spiritual Care Association.

Seder ha-Dorot ("Order of the Generations") A comprehensive historical-Agadic chronicle composed by R. Yechiel Heilprin, c. 1660–1746, of Lithuania.

Seder Olam Attributed to 2nd-century Mishnaic sage R. Yosei ben Chalafta of Sepphoris, Israel. Chronicles Biblical and post-Biblical history from Creation to the Bar Kochba revolt.

Sefat Emet ("Edge of Truth") A classic of Hasidic teaching that includes commentaries on the Torah, Talmud, and *Shulchan Aruch* by R. Judah Aryeh Leib Alter, 1847–1905, third leader of the Ger branch of Hasidism.

Sefer Hasidim ("Book of the Pious") An ethical work by R. Judah he-Hasid, 1140–1217, of Germany, one of the initiators of the "Hasidim of Ashkenaz" movement that stressed piety and asceticism. He also authored a well-known ethical will (*tzavaah*).

Sefer Yetzirah Early Kabbalistic work; see p. 230.

Seforno R. Ovadiah Seforno, 1475–1550; Italy. Authored a popular commentary on the Bible.

Segal, R. David See **Taz**.

Segal, Moshe Zvi 1904–1984; Ukraine and Israel. Active in the Jewish underground opposing the British occupation of the Holy Land, he was famously arrested for blowing the shofar at the Western Wall. After the Six Day War, he was the first Jew to settle in the newly liberated Jewish Quarter of Jerusalem's Old City.

Sekili, R. Jacob 14th century; Spain and Babylonia. Prominent Torah scholar and Kabbalist who studied under Rashba. His weekly Shabbat discourses were published under the title *Torat ha-Minchah*.

Semag A work (full title, *Sefer Mitzvot Gadol,* meaning "Great Book of Commandments") explaining all 613 commandments of the Torah. Authored by the Tosafist R. Moses of Coucy (13th century, France), based on sermons he gave in his travels. The work is one of the earliest codifications of Halachah, and one of the first Hebrew books to be printed (Rome, 1473).

Senesh, Hannah See biographical note on p. 136.

Shaarei Teshuvah ("Gates of Repentance") One of several moralistic works by R. Jonah Gerondi (d. 1263, Spain).

Shabazi, R. Shalom 1619–c. 1720. The greatest of Yemenite Jewish poets. Some 850 of his poems and hymns are extant, written in Hebrew, Aramaic, and Arabic, and incorporating ethical and Kabbalistic teachings.

R. Shabetai ha-Kohen See **Shach**.

Shach (*Siftei Kohen*) Definitive commentary on the *Shulchan Aruch* by R. Shabetai ha-Kohen, 1621–1662, of Lithuania and Moravia (see p. 205).

Shaloh See biographical note on p. 231.

R. Shalom DovBer of Lubavitch R. Shalom DovBer Schneersohn; 1860–1920; Russia. Fifth rebbe of Chabad-Lubavitch. Established the *Tomchei Temimim* network of yeshivahs, which incorporate the study of the "revealed" (Talmudic-Halachic) and esoteric areas of Torah. His discourses are renowned for their explorations of Kabbalistic and Hasidic concepts.

Shamai d. approx. 10 CE; Jerusalem, Israel. A Mishnaic sage who served as vice-president of the Sanhedrin. Also see entry for "Hillel."

Shapira, R. Kalonymus See biographical note on p. 136.

Sharabi, R. Shalom 1720–1777; Yemen and Jerusalem. Known by the acronym "Rashash." An important expounder of the teachings of Ari (see p. 230), and the author of a Kabbalistic Siddur (prayer book).

Sharansky, Natan b. 1948; USSR and Israel. Spent many years in Soviet prison for his human rights activism and his desire to emigrate to Israel. Subsequently founded a political party in Israel and served in various ministerial positions in the Israeli government.

Shem mi-Shmuel Popular collection of Hasidic discourses by R. Shmuel Bornstein, 1855–1926, Hasidic rebbe of Sochatchov, Poland.

R. Sherira Gaon c. 906–1006; Pumbedita, Babylonia. His "Letter of R. Sherira Gaon" chronicles the transmission of the Torah in the 500-year period after the closing of the Talmud.

Shitah Mekubetzet Anthology of classical commentaries to the Talmud by R. Betzalel Ashkenazi, c. 1520–1592, who lived in Egypt and Israel.

R. Shlomo of Radomsk R. Shlomo Rabinowitz; c. 1801–1866; Poland. Founder of the Radomsk branch of Hasidism. His *Tiferet Shlomo* is a classic in Hasidic literature.

Shmelkes, R. Isaac 1828–1906. Served as head of the rabbinical court in Lemberg (Lvov), Galicia. His responsa were published under the title *Beit Yitzchak*, in which he also dealt with the application of Jewish law to modern technology, including the use of electricity on Shabbat.

R. Shmuel of Lubavitch R. Shmuel Schneersohn; 1834–1882; Russia. Fourth rebbe of the Chabad-Lubavitch branch of Hasidism. Known by the acronym "Maharash."

Shulchan Aruch 16th-century codification of Torah law. See p. 205 for a detailed description of this work.

Shulchan Aruch ha-Rav See **R. Schneur Zalman of Liadi**.

Siddur The Jewish prayer book; see entry for "Liturgy & Verse" on p. 154.

Sifrei See **Halachic Midrashim**.

Silberstein, Eli b. 1959. Founding codirector of Chabad of Ithaca, New York, and Chabad at Cornell University. He is the author of several JLI courses, and lectures widely on the intersection between Jewish law and mysticism.

Sirkis, R. Joel See **Bach**.

Slonim, Rivkah b. 1964; New York. Noted scholar, author, and lecturer. Serves as the associate director at the Rohr Chabad Center for Jewish Student Life at Binghamton University.

R. Solomon ben Aderet See **Rashba.**

R. Solomon bar Simeon 11th–12th centuries; Germany. In 1140, he wrote *Gezeirot Shenat Tatnu* ("Decrees of of the Year 4856"), a memoir that transcribes the testimony of victims and survivors of the Rhineland massacres during the First Crusade.

Soloveitchik, R. Joseph B. 1903–1993; Boston. Talmudist, philosopher, and a seminal figure of Modern Orthodox Judaism. Served at the helm of the rabbinical seminary at Yeshivah University in New York, in which capacity he ordained some 2,000 rabbis. His philosophy of Judaism is expressed in two landmark essays, *The Lonely Man of Faith* and *Halakhic Man*, and in numerous articles and talks.

Song of Songs Biblical book; see p. 159 and pp. 182–183.

Spira, R. Chaim Elazar 1871–1937. Chief rabbi of Munkacs, Hungary, and rebbe of the Munkacs branch of Hasidism. Most famous for his Halachic responsa, published as *Minchat Elazar*.

Steinsaltz, R. Adin Even-Israel 1937–2020; Jerusalem. Praised by *Time* magazine as a "once-in-a-millennium scholar." Authored a modern translation/elucidation of the entire Talmud, and numerous books and essays of Jewish scholarship, philosophy, Kabbalah, and Hasidism.

Sternbuch, R. Moshe b. 1926. Served as a rabbi in Johannesburg, South Africa. Currently heads the rabbinical court of the *Eidah ha-Chareidit* ("Hareidi Community") in Jerusalem.

Stories of R. Nachman See **R. Nachman of Breslov.**

Talmud A 60-volume compilation of teachings and deliberations by hundreds of Torah sages over a period of close to 300 years, from the 3rd through 5th centuries CE. See p. 109 and pp. 184ff.

R. Tam R. Jacob ben Meir; c. 1100–1171; Troyes and Ramerupt, France. Known as "Rabbeinu Tam." A grandson of Rashi and one of the primary Tosafists. His positions on matters of Torah law, and the ordinances he instituted, had a lasting influence on Jewish life in Europe.

Tana d'bei Eliyahu A Midrashic work attributed to Elijah the prophet.

Tanchuma see **Midrash Tanchuma**.

Tannenbaum, R. Malkiel 1847–1910. Chief rabbi of Lomza, Poland. Author of five volumes of Halachic responsa titled *Divrei Malkiel*.

Tanya Foundational work of the Chabad philosophy, authored by R. Schneur Zalman of Liadi.

Taran, R. Joseph Aaron 19th-century. Served as rabbi and *shochet* (ritual slaughterer) in Entre Ríos, Argentina.

Tauber, Yanki b. 1965; New York. Author, editor, and translator. Served as content editor of Chabad.org in the years 1999–2014. Compiler and editor of *The Book*, a new translation and anthologized commentary for the Five Books of Moses. Currently on the editorial staff of the Rohr Jewish Learning Institute. Rabbi Tauber is the compiler and editor of this volume.

Taz Commentary on the *Shulchan Aruch* by R. David Segal (1586–1667, Poland), titled *Turei Zahav* ("Rows of Gold"; on the section of *Orach Chayim*, the commentary is labeled *Magen David,* "Shield of David"). See p. 205. He also authored a supercommentary on Rashi.

Teomim, R. Joseph 1727–1792. Served as rabbi of Lvov, Galicia, and later in Frankfurt (Oder), Germany. Most famous for his *Pri Megadim* commentary on *Shulchan Aruch* (see p. 205).

Toldot Yaakov Yosef First printed work of Hasidic philosophy, by R. Jacob Joseph of Polonne, c. 1710–1784, a senior disciple of the Baal Shem Tov.

Torah Sheleimah Encyclopedic anthology of Talmudic and Midrashic commentaries on the Bible, the life's work of R. Menachem Mendel Kasher (1895–1983, Warsaw and Jerusalem). Forty-seven volumes have been published to date.

Tosafot; Tosafists Series of commentaries on the Talmud authored by a group of 12th- and 13th-century sages known as "the Tosafists." See p. 192.

Tosafot Yom Tov Commentary on the Mishnah by R. Yom Tov Lipman Heller, 1579–1654, Poland and Germany.

Tosefta A compendium of teachings by Mishnaic sages not included in the Mishnah proper. Compiled in the beginning of the 3rd century in the Land of Israel by R. Chiya and R. Oshiyah.

Tukachinsky, R. Yechiel 1871–1955. Dean of the Eitz Chaim Yeshivah in Jerusalem. Published many books and articles on Halachic issues. His most famous work is *Gesher ha-Chayim* ("Bridge of Life"), a treatise on the laws of burial and mourning.

Tur 14th-century codification of Torah law by R. Jacob ben Asher. See p. 205 for a detailed description of this work.

Twain, Mark Pen name of popular American author Samuel Langhorne Clemens, 1835–1910, of Hartford, Connecticut. Best known for his novels *The Adventures of Tom Sawyer* and *Adventures of Huckleberry Finn*.

Twerski, R. Dr. Abraham J. 1930–2021; Pittsburgh. A scion of the Chernobyl Hasidic dynasty. Founder of Gateway Rehabilitation Center. Author of 60 books on self-help and Judaism, and a pioneer in heightening awareness of the dangers of addiction, spousal abuse, and low self-esteem.

Tzafnat Paane'ach ("Decipherer of Secrets") Talmudic and Halachic writings, famed for their depth and terse style, by R. Joseph Rosen, 1858–1936, of Dvinsk (Daugapils), Latvia, known as "the Rogatchover Gaon."

Tzemach Tzedek R. Menachem Mendel Schneersohn; 1789–1866; Lubavitch, Belarus. Third leader of the Chabad-Lubavitch branch of Hasidism. Prolific author of Talmudic, Halachic, philosophical, and Hasidic works. Known as *Tzemach Tzedek* ("Scion of Righteousness") after his Halachic responsa and other works by that name.

Tzukernik, Shimona A native of South Africa. Creator of The Method, a therapeutic application of Kabbalah, and founder of Omek, a center devoted to in-depth transformational learning for women.

Vilnay, Zev 1900–1988; Jerusalem. A military topographer in the Haganah (the Jewish defense force in pre-1948 Israel) and the IDF, he wrote and lectured widely on Israeli geography, ethnography, history, and folklore.

Vital, R. Chaim See biographical note on p. 231.

Waldenberg, R. Eliezer 1915–2006; Jerusalem. Eminent authority on Jewish medical ethics. Served on the Supreme Rabbinical Court in Jerusalem, and as rabbi for the Shaare Zedek Medical Center.

Washington, George 1732–1799. Commander-in-chief of the Continental Army during the American War of Independence. Served as first president of the United States, 1789–1797.

Weiss, R. Isaac Jacob 1902–1989. A senior rabbi in Manchester, England, he was later appointed head of the rabbinical court of the *Eidah ha-Chareidit* ("Hareidi Community") of Jerusalem. His responsa, published under the name *Minchat Yitzchak,* discuss many contemporary technological and medical issues.

Wiesel, Elie See biographical note on p. 137.

Wouk, Herman 1915–2019; New York and California. Author of the Pulitzer-Prize-winning novel *The Caine Mutiny* and other bestselling works of literary fiction, he also wrote extensively on Jewish thought and practice. His most famous work in the latter category is *This Is My G-d* (1959).

Yaabetz, R. Joseph c. 1440–1508; Portugal and Italy. Witnessed the infamous Spanish Expulsion. Authored a commentary on *Ethics of the Fathers* as well as a number of Kabbalistic works.

Yair, Zvi Pen name of Hebrew poet Zvi Meir Steinmetz, 1915–2005, of Budapest and New York.

Yalkut Shimoni A voluminous Midrashic anthology covering all 24 books of the Bible. Compiled by R. Simeon ha-Darshan, 13th century, Frankfurt, Germany.

R. Yechiel of Glogau c. 1680–1730. Headed the yeshivah in Halberstadt, Germany. Authored *Nezer ha-Kodesh* ("Crown of Holiness"), a fundamental commentary on the Midrash *Bereishith Rabbah*.

R. Yitzchak When "R. Yitzchak" is mentioned without qualification in the Talmud, in Halachic discussions it refers to R. Yitzchak bar Acha, and in Agadic discussions, to R. Yitzchak bar Pinchas. Both lived in 4th-century Israel, were disciples of R. Jochanan, and frequently traveled to Babylonia.

R. Yitzchak Meir of Ger 1799–1866, Poland. Founder of the Ger branch of Hasidism. Renowned both as a brilliant Talmudist and a Hasidic master. His expositions and responsa were published under the title *Chidushei ha-Rim*.

Yosef, R. Ovadia 20th-century Sephardic leader. See biographical note on p. 115.

Zacuto, R. Moses c. 1620–1697; Italy. Served as a rabbi in Venice and later in Mantua. Considered one of the great Italian Kabbalists in the 17th century, his yeshivah was instrumental in disseminating R. Chaim Vital's manuscripts of Lurianic Kabbalah.

R. Zadok of Lublin R. Zadok ha-Kohen Rabinowitz; 1823–1900. A disciple of the Hasidic leaders R. Mordecai Joseph Leiner of Izhbitza and R. Leibel Eiger of Lublin, he succeeded the latter as rebbe in Lublin. Authored many works on Jewish law, Hasidism, Kabbalah, and ethics, as well as scholarly essays on astronomy, geometry, and algebra.

Zevin, R. Shlomo Yosef 1885–1978; Russia and Israel. Editor in chief of the *Encyclopedia Talmudit,* and author of numerous works of Torah scholarship and Jewish thought and lore.

Ziv, R. Simcha Zisel 1824–1898; Kelm, Lithuania. A disciple of R. Israel Salanter and one of the early leaders of the Musar movement (see p. 244).

Zohar Fundamental work of Kabbalah. See p. 230.

R. Zvi Elimelech of Dinov c. 1783–1841; Galicia. Known for his seminal Hasidic work *Benei Yisaschar*, he was influential in bringing the Hasidic movement to Galician and Hungarian Jewry.

glossary

AARON Elder brother of Moses. Served as *kohen gadol* ("high priest") during the Israelites' travels through the wilderness.

ABIHU Nadab and Abihu were the two eldest sons of Aaron. The Torah (Leviticus 9) describes how they died when "they came close to G-d" in the Tabernacle.

ABRAM Original name of Abraham, prior to G-d's instruction that his name be changed. *Abram* means "father of Aram," whereas *Abraham* is an acronym for *av hamon goyim,* "father of a multitude of nations."

ACHARONIM; ACHARON (sing.) Term for the "latter" Torah sages who followed after the period of the *Rishonim* ("early" sages, approx. 1000–1500). The basic distinction is that while the Halachic rulings of the *Rishonim* revolve around their understanding of the Talmud and their agreement or disagreement with other *Rishonim,* the *Acharonim,* as a rule, do not regard themselves as qualified to disagree with a *Rishon* unless other *Rishonim* support their view, and arrive at their rulings by analyzing and weighing the commentaries and rulings of the *Rishonim.*

ADAR Twelfth month of the Jewish calendar, or the sixth month counting from Tishrei (see "Two Heads" on p. 329). Corresponds to approximately February–March on the secular calendar. In Jewish leap years (see p. 331), there are two months called Adar: Adar I and Adar II.

AGADAH; AGADIC Non-legal Torah teachings, including ethics, homilies, narratives, etc. See infographic and notes on pp. 152–154.

AGAG Amalekite king whose life was spared by King Saul, and who was the ancestor of Haman.

AMALEK; AMALEKITES The first nation to attack the people of Israel after the Exodus. Regarded as the archenemy of Israel, and as the nemesis of divinity and holiness.

AMEN Means "true, affirmative." The traditional response after hearing a blessing recited by another.

ARAM NAHARAIM "Aram between the rivers," i.e., Mesopotamia.

ARCH OF TITUS A triumphal arch in Rome dedicated to the Emperor Titus to celebrate his victory over Jerusalem. On it is depicted the procession carrying the spoils looted from the destroyed Holy Temple; prominent among them is the menorah, the Temple's seven-branched candelabra.

ASHKENAZIM; ASHKENAZIC Refers to the Jewish communities who lived in Europe north of the Pyrenees and the Alps, and their descendants. These communities developed a set of customs and traditions distinct from the Jews of southern Europe, North Africa, and the Middle East (the Sephardic Jews). See pp. 117ff.

AUSCHWITZ Auschwitz-Birkenau was the largest Nazi concentration and extermination camp that operated during the Holocaust (see pp. 132–137). 1.5 million people, mostly Jews, were starved, tortured, and murdered in this camp. The term "Auschwitz" is sometimes used as synonymous with "the Holocaust."

AV Fifth month of the Jewish calendar, or the 11th month counting from Tishrei (see p. 329). Corresponds approximately to July–August.

BAR KOCHBA Jewish leader of a failed revolt against the Roman rulers of the Holy Land in the 2nd century. See p. 84 and p. 86.

BERAITA "Outside material"; a body of teachings by sages of the Mishnaic era not included in the Mishnah itself.

BETAR An ancient terraced farming village in the Judean highlands. The Betar fortress was the last stand of the Bar Kochba revolt, destroyed by the Roman army of Emperor Hadrian in the year 135. See p. 84.

BLOOD LIBEL A false accusation that Jews used the blood of non-Jews in religious rituals, especially in the preparation of Passover matzah. The libel was perpetrated throughout the Middle Ages and (sporadically) until the early 20th century.

BRIT; BRIT MILAH "Covenant" and "Covenant of Circumcision." The hallmark of G-d's covenant with the Jewish people, and a mitzvah incumbent on every Jewish male. See pp. 391–393.

CAIN Eldest son of Adam and Eve. As related in the 4th chapter of Genesis, Cain was a farmer and his younger brother Abel was a shepherd. Cain murdered Abel out of jealousy when G-d preferred Abel's offering over his.

CAVE OF THE PATRIARCHS Also called the "Machpelah Cave." Located in the city of Hebron, the cave and adjoining field were purchased by Abraham as a burial plot for his wife Sarah. In total, four prestigious couples are buried there: Adam and Eve, Abraham and Sarah, Isaac and Rebecca, and Jacob and Leah.

CHABAD Branch of Hasidism, founded in 1772 by R. Schneur Zalman of Liadi, emphasizing the role of the mind in assimilating divine truths and developing and guiding a person's emotions and behavior. The name "Chabad" is an acronym for the three intellectual faculties *chochmah, binah,* and *daat.* The movement is also called "Chabad-Lubavitch," or simply "Lubavitch," after the Russian town that served as its headquarters from 1813 to 1915.

CHALITZAH Biblically mandated ritual that absolves the brothers and the widow of a person who died childless from the obligation of one of the brothers to marry the widow; see entry for LEVIRATE MARRIAGE.

CHALLAH Lit., "loaf." Commonly refers to the bread (often braided) baked in honor of Shabbat and Jewish holidays. In Torah law, *challah* is a portion of dough given as a gift to a Kohen, who will eat it under conditions of ritual purity. As today such conditions rarely exist, the piece is separated from the dough and then burned.

CHEDER Lit., "room." Commonly refers to a traditional Torah school for young children.

CHOLENT Traditional Shabbat stew. See p. 298.

CHUPAH Wedding canopy; see p. 408.

COUNTING OF THE OMER See OMER.

CUBIT A measure of length used in Biblical and Talmudic times, and for Halachic purposes. It is defined as the distance from the average person's elbow to the tip of the middle finger. Various Halachic authorities put the length of the cubit at between 48 and 60 centimeters.

DREYFUS AFFAIR Alfred Dreyfus (1859–1935) was a French Jewish military officer who was wrongfully tried and convicted of treason against France in 1894. The trial and ensuing events are referred to as the "Dreyfus Affair" and roused awareness of the endemic antisemitism in 19th-century Europe.

EBER Great-grandson of Noah's son Shem, and ancestor of Abraham. A prophet and righteous man, he headed a school of study together with Shem. One of the meanings of the appellation "Hebrew" is "a descendant of Eber."

EGLAH ARUFAH Lit., "decapitated calf." The procedure mandated by the Torah as penitence for an unsolved murder (Deuteronomy 21:1–9).

ELUL Sixth month of the Jewish calendar, approximately August–September. It is also the last month of the Jewish year, when counting from Tishrei (see p. 329). The month of Elul is traditionally a time devoted to repentance and soul-searching in preparation for the "high holidays" of Rosh Hashanah and Yom Kippur.

EPHAH A measure of volume for grain or flour used in Biblical and Talmudic times, equal to approximately 25 liters.

ESAU Twin brother and nemesis of the patriarch Jacob. See p. 16.

EXILE, THE See entry for GALUT.

FLOOD, THE The great deluge that covered the earth during Noah's days, as related in the Book of Genesis, chapters 6–8.

FOUR CUBITS A measure of distance (see entry for CUBIT). Defined in Torah law as the area of a person's "personal space."

FOUR KINDS See p. 346.

GAON; GEONIM (pl.); **GEONIC; GAONATE** Title of the rabbis who headed the prestigious academies in Babylonia in the 6th to 11th centuries, and were recognized as the Torah authorities and spiritual leaders for the global Jewish community. See "The Geonic Era" on p. 109.

GALUT Lit., "exile." The state of physical and spiritual displacement experienced by the Jewish people for much of their history. See the "Diaspora" section of this book, pp. 104–148.

GARDEN OF EDEN Where Adam and Eve were placed by G-d upon their creation, from which they were expelled after partaking of the "Tree of Knowledge of Good and Evil" (as related in Genesis 3). "Garden of Eden" also refers to the spiritual reward that souls enjoy in the afterlife.

GEFILTE FISH Lit., "stuffed fish." A traditional Shabbat dish; see p. 300.

GOG AND MAGOG Protagonists of the apocalyptic battle against Israel and G-d prophesied in the Biblical book of Ezekiel (chapters 38–39) to occur before the Messianic redemption.

GOMORRAH See entry for SODOM.

GRACE AFTER MEALS A prayer, consisting of four blessings, recited after eating a meal.

GREAT ASSEMBLY A body of 120 prophets and sages who led the people of Israel during the return from Babylon to the Holy Land at the beginning of the Second Temple era (4th century BCE). Members included Haggai, Zechariah, Malachi, Mordecai, Ezra, Nehemiah, and Simeon the Just. The Great Assembly fixed the Biblical canon, standardized the text of the prayers, and enacted numerous other ordinances that became integral features of Jewish life to this day.

HADRIAN Roman emperor in the years 117–138; the Bar Kochba revolt took place under his rule. He outlawed the practice of Judaism and built a pagan temple on the site of the destroyed Holy Temple.

HAFTARAH Selected portions from the "Prophets" section of the Bible that are read following the public Torah reading on Shabbat and the festivals. The *haftarah* is thematically connected with the Torah reading of the week, or to the time of year in which it is read.

HAGAR Sarah's Egyptian maidservant, who later became Abraham's wife due to Sarah's childlessness, and gave birth to Ishmael. When Sarah insisted that Hagar and Ishmael be banished from Abraham's household because of Ishmael's negative influence on Isaac, G-d instructed Abraham to do as Sarah said.

HALACHAH; HALACHIC Lit., "the way"; i.e., Torah law. See pp. 152–154 and pp. 202–213.

HALLAH See entry for CHALLAH.

HAMOTZI The blessing recited before eating bread. See p. 312.

HASID; HASIDIM (pl.) Adherent of Hasidism (see following entry).

HASIDISM; HASIDIC Jewish revivalist movement founded in 1734 by R. Israel Baal Shem Tov. See pp. 232–236.

HAVAYAH Stand-in for the most sacred name of G-d, which consists of the four Hebrew letters *yud-hei-vav-hei* but is not pronounced due to its holiness. It is therefore a common practice to transpose its four letters as *Havayah* when referring to it in writing and conversation.

HAVDALAH Lit., "differentiation." Ritual marking the end of the Shabbat or festival day and the start of the mundane workdays. See p. 302.

HIGH HOLIDAYS Rosh Hashanah and Yom Kippur, the most solemn days of the Jewish year. Also called the "Days of Awe." See pp. 332–339.

HOLY OF HOLIES Heb. *kodesh hakodashim.* The innermost and most sacred chamber of the Tabernacle and, later, the Holy Temple. See p. 72.

HOREB Another name for Mount Sinai.

HOUSE OF DAVID The lineage of King David (907–837 BCE), designated as the monarchs and leaders of the Jewish people. Mashiach is prophesied to be a descendant of David.

ISHMAEL Eldest son of Abraham. See entry for HAGAR.

ISRAELITE Member of the Jewish people. In a more specific sense, the term refers to a Jew who is not a KOHEN or LEVITE (see their respective entries).

IYAR Second month of the Jewish calendar, or 8th month counting from Tishrei (see p. 329). Corresponds approximately with April–May.

JETHRO High priest of Midian and father-in-law of Moses. Abandoned his pagan vocation to worship G-d and joined the Israelites in the wilderness after the Exodus. Also known by six other names, including "Reuel" (see p. 27).

JUBILEE YEAR Occurring every fifty years, the jubilee year was a time to "proclaim liberty throughout the land and to all inhabitants thereof" in the Land of Israel (Leviticus 25:10). All indentured servants, including those who had sold themselves for lifetime labor, were set free, and all ancestral lands that had been sold reverted to their original owners.

JUDGES, THE A series of national leaders who led the people of Israel in the 12th to 9th centuries BCE, prior to the establishment of the Israelite monarchy. See pp. 54–55.

KABBALAH; KABBALISTIC The mystical dimension of the Torah. See pp. 228–243.

KETORET The incense offered in the Holy Temple. See pp. 70–71.

KIPAH Lit., "dome." The head covering (usually a skullcap) worn by Jewish males. See p. 213.

KISLEV Ninth month of the Jewish calendar, or the third month counting from Tishrei (see p. 329). Corresponds approximately with November–December.

KOHEN; KOHANIM (pl.) "Priest." Descendants of Aaron, who were appointed to perform the service in the Holy Temple. In the present day, the Kohanim perform the "priestly blessing" in the synagogue, and are honored there with being called first for the Torah reading. Certain Torah laws (e.g., the prohibition to marry a divorcee, or to have any contact with a dead body) pertain exclusively to Kohanim.

KOTEL "Wall." The Western Wall of the Temple Mount in Jerusalem; see p. 73.

LABAN Jacob's uncle and father-in-law. A notorious swindler in whose employ Jacob worked for 20 years. See p. 18.

LEAVEN; LEAVENED See p. 368.

LEVIRATE MARRIAGE The Biblically mandated obligation to marry the widow of a brother who died childless. The obligation, however, can be absolved by the *chalitzah* ritual (see Deuteronomy 25:5–10).

LEVITE Descendants of Levi, the third of Jacob's 12 sons, who served as spiritual leaders, and as priestly assistants in the Holy Temple.

MANNA The miraculous "bread from heaven" that sustained the people of Israel in their travels through the wilderness. See p. 44.

MASHIACH Lit., "anointed one." The Messiah. A fundamental principle of Judaism is that G-d will send a leader to return the dispersed people of Israel to their homeland, rebuild the Holy Temple, and usher in an era of universal peace, wisdom, and perfection. See pp. 225–227.

MATRIARCHS The four mothers of the Jewish people—Sarah, Rebecca, Leah, and Rachel. See "The First Jews," pp. 6–21.

MATZAH The unleavened bread eaten during the holiday of Passover. See p. 368 and p. 369.

MENORAH The golden seven-branched candelabrum kindled in the Holy Temple (see p. 69). May also refer to a candelabrum holding eight lights used during the Hanukkah festival (see p. 350 and pp. 355–357).

MESORAH Lit., "transmission." Refers to the Torah's laws and methodologies that were given to Moses and transmitted in an unbroken chain throughout Jewish history (see infographic on p. 188).

MESSIAH; MESSIANIC See MASHIACH.

MEZUZAH; MEZUZOT (pl.) Lit., "doorpost." A parchment scroll inscribed with Biblical verses affixed to the doorposts in a Jewish home or business. See pp. 316–318.

MIDRASH; MIDRASHIC; MIDRASHIM (pl.) General name given to explanations and expositions of Biblical verses cited by the sages of the Mishnaic and Talmudic eras. See pp. 152–154, p. 184, and pp. 200–201.

MIKVEH Lit., "pool." A ritual bathing pool used for the immersion of people or utensils as part of their transition to ritual purity. See pp. 410–415.

MINOR PURIM In a Jewish leap year, which has two months called Adar—Adar I and Adar II—the festival of Purim is observed in the second Adar. The 14th and 15th of Adar I, which are also days of celebration, are called "Minor Purim" and "Minor Shushan Purim."

MIRIAM Elder sister of Moses. A prophetess and leader during and after the Egyptian exile.

MISHNAH The first officially transcribed text of the "Oral Torah"; see Maimonides' description on p. 186, and table on p. 204. The term "Mishnah" refers to the work as a whole, while each of the 4,184 subsections that comprise it is also called a *mishnah* (pl. *mishnayot*).

MISHNAIC ERA The period during which the sages cited in the Mishnah lived and taught, approximately 100 BCE to 200 CE.

MITZVAH; MITZVOT (pl.) Lit., "commandment." A good deed or religious precept; specifically, one of the Torah's 613 divine commandments (see pp. 164–169), or of seven ordinances enacted by the rabbis.

MITZVAH TANK A vehicle, commonly a converted RV, used by the Chabad-Lubavitch movement as a mobile outreach center (see p. 140).

MOHEL Trained expert who performs *brit milah* (ritual circumcision). See pp. 391–393.

NADAB See entry for ABIHU.

NASI See entry for SANHEDRIN.

NAZIRITE A person who takes a vow to abstain from wine and to assume other self-imposed restrictions, as detailed in the 6th chapter of Numbers.

NEBUCHADNEZZAR Babylonian emperor who destroyed the first Holy Temple and exiled the Jewish people in the 5th century BCE.

NIGHTFALL On the Jewish calendar, the day begins at nightfall and ends at nightfall of the following evening. "Nightfall" is defined by Torah law as the point when three medium stars are observable in the nighttime sky with the naked eye (about 30 minutes after sunset).

NISAN First month of the Jewish calendar; also the 7th month counting from Tishrei (see p. 329). Corresponds approximately with March–April.

OMER Lit., "sheaf." A measure of volume for grain used in Biblical and Talmudic times, equal to approximately 2.5 liters. Also refers to a meal offering, consisting of this amount of barley flour, which was brought in the Holy Temple on the second day of Passover and inaugurated the 49-day "counting of the *omer*" culminating in the festival of Shavuot (see p. 372).

OMNIPRESENT, THE G-d is sometimes referred to as *Hamakom* (lit., "the Place"). As the Midrash (*Bereishith Rabbah*, 68:9) explains, "The world is not G-d's place; rather, G-d is the place of the world."

ORAL TORAH Collective name for the entire body of interpretation, exposition, and commentary that is part of the Torah's "chain of transmission" from Moses onward, in contrast to the "Written Torah" canonized by Moses and the later prophets. For more of the nature, role, history, and composition of the Oral Torah, see overview on pages 186–190. See also infographic on pp. 152–154.

PARASANG Heb. "*parsah*." A Talmudic unit of distance, covered by foot in approximately 72 minutes. It is the equivalent of approximately four kilometers.

PARTISAN Member of an armed group formed to fight secretly against an occupying force. Used in particular to refer to fighters against the German occupation during World War II.

PASSOVER OFFERING A yearling lamb or goat brought as an offering on the eve of Passover in the Holy Temple and eaten on Passover night during the Seder feast.

PATRIARCHS The three fathers of the Jewish people—Abraham, Isaac, and Jacob. See "The First Jews," pp. 6–21.

PESACH SHEINI The "Second Passover." See p. 374.

PHILISTINES A nation, oft-times belligerent toward the Jewish people, that occupied territory on the coast of the Mediterranean Sea southwest of Jerusalem, previously to and contemporaneously with the kingdoms of Israel.

PIYYUT; PIYYUTIM; PAYYETAN See entry for "Payyetanim" on p. 440.

PRIESTLY BLESSING A threefold blessing, consisting of the verses in Numbers 6:24-27, which the Kohanim (priests) are commanded to recite as a blessing to the Jewish people.

PRUZBUL A rabbinical ordinance enacted by Hillel the Elder in the first century BCE. When Hillel saw that people were avoiding giving loans close to the sabbatical year (which suspends all private debts) he instituted the *pruzbul* process, by which a lender submits their debt to a court of Torah law, making it a public debt and therefore redeemable.

R. An abbreviation for *Rabbi* ("my teacher"), *Rav, Rabban, Rebbe,* or *Reb* (see entries below). These are traditional honorifics for Torah teachers and leaders, particularly those upon whom the authority to decide matters of Torah law has been conferred.

RABBAN "Our teacher." A variation of the title "Rabbi," used primarily for heads of the Sanhedrin in the late Second Temple era and the centuries following.

RAV Lit., "teacher," "master," or "great one." A variant of the title "Rabbi." With the sages of the Talmudic era, "Rabbi" is used to denote the sages of the Mishnah and later sages who lived and taught in the Land of Israel, whereas "Rav" denotes the sages of Babylon. When applied to post-Talmudic sages, the two forms are used interchangeably.

REB A traditional Jewish title or form of address, less formal than "Rabbi," used also when the addressee is not a Rabbi.

REBBE A variant of the title "Rabbi." Generally used to refer to Hasidic leaders, as well as for schoolteachers and educators.

REDEMPTION, THE See entry for MASHIACH.

REFUSENIK A term referring to Soviet Jews who requested permission to immigrate to Israel and were refused, and were subsequently harassed and/or imprisoned by the Communist regime.

RELIGIOUS ZIONISM The centrality of the Land of Israel to the fulfillment of the Torah and to the Jew's relationship with G-d is a pervasive theme in both the Bible and the teachings of the sages, and is acknowledged by every branch and stream of Torah thought. Nevertheless, with the rise of the modern Zionist movement in the early 20th century, many leading Torah authorities opposed the movement because of its secularist and even anti-religious elements; a number of them also argued that the restoration of Jewish sovereignty must await the coming of the Messiah. In contrast, other Torah leaders chose to join forces with secular Zionism, believing that it was their duty to infuse it with the values of Torah and traditional Judaism, and seeing the establishment of a Jewish state in the Land of Israel as a preliminary stage toward the Messianic redemption.

RESURRECTION OF THE DEAD Heb. *techiyat ha-meitim*. Revival of the dead in the era of the future redemption; one of the fundamental beliefs of the Jewish religion.

REVISIONISTS Revisionist Zionism was a party within the Zionist movement, headed by Ze'ev Jabotinski (1880–1940). It was the chief ideological competitor to the dominant socialist Zionism, and the precursor of the more right-wing parties in Israeli politics.

RISHONIM Term for the "early" Torah sages and authors of the post-Geonic era. The era of the *Rishonim* is usually defined as the 500-year period from the early 11th century to the end of the 15th century. See also entry for ACHARONIM.

ROSH CHODESH Lit., "head of the month." The day or days that mark the start of a new month on the Jewish calendar. The first day of each month is observed as Rosh Chodesh; when a month has 30 days (the Jewish month can have 29 or 30 days), the last day of the month also serves as the first of the two Rosh Chodesh days for the following month.

ROSH HASHANAH Lit., "head of the year." The solemn New Year holiday, observed on the first and second days of the Jewish month of Tishrei. See pp. 334–337.

SABBATICAL YEAR Heb. *shemitah*, meaning "suspension." A Biblically mandated sabbatical year, occurring once every seven years, during which all agricultural work on the land ceases, indentured servants are freed, and personal debts are suspended (see Leviticus 25 and Deuteronomy 15).

SAMARITANS A people living in the Samaria region of the Holy Land since the end of the First Temple era, who practice a form of Judaism yet were historically hostile to the Jewish people. According to the Talmud, the Samaritans were a foreign people, also called Cuthians, whom the Assyrian conquerors brought in to populate the northern part of the Holy Land when they exiled the Ten Tribes (see p. 63). The Cuthians subsequently converted to Judaism, but the sages were divided on the question of whether their conversion was valid.

SANCTUARY Heb. *heichal*. The enclosed building of the Holy Temple, which was surrounded by an unroofed courtyard; see diagram on p. 68.

SANHEDRIN High court of Torah law. When unqualified, this term refers to the "Great Sanhedrin," consisting of 71 members, the highest legislative and judiciary authority in Judaism. The Sanhedrin was headed by a *nasi* (president). Under Roman rule its powers gradually eroded until the 4th century, when it ceased to operate.

SAUL First Israelite king; reigned 879–877 BCE.

SCIATIC NERVE A major nerve system in humans and other vertebrate animals, running from the spine down the leg. The Torah (Genesis 32) forbids the consumption of an animal's sciatic nerve, in commemoration of Jacob's battle with the angel with whom he wrestled all night, in the course of which Jacob's sciatic nerve was dislocated.

SCRIPTURES The third component of the *Tanach* (Jewish Bible)—see p. 159. "Scripture" and "the Scriptures" may also refer to the Bible as a whole.

SEA OF REEDS *Yam Suf* in Hebrew. The sea that miraculously split for the people of Israel following their exodus from Egypt. Popularly, though not conclusively, identified with the Red Sea (see map on p. 43).

SECOND PASSOVER See p. 374.

SEPHARDIM; SEPHARDIC Refers to the descendants of Jews who left Spain or Portugal after the 1492 expulsion, as well as the Jewish communities that developed in the Muslim-ruled world (with some significant exceptions: the Yemenite and Babylonian-Persian diasporas, for example, are not "Sephardim"). See pp. 112–116.

SHAVUOT Lit., "weeks." A one-day festival (two days outside of the Land of Israel) commemorating the giving of the Torah on Mount Sinai. See pp. 36–39 and 376–377.

SHECHEM (a) A city in northern Israel (Arabic name, "Nablus"). (b) Name of the son of Hamor, the governor of the city of Shechem. As related in Genesis 35, Shechem abducted and violated Jacob's daughter Dinah, spurring her brothers Simeon and Levi to kill all the city's men.

SHEKEL A unit of weight equivalent to approximately 10–12 grams. Also the name of a coin, containing that amount of silver, that served as a standard monetary unit in Talmudic times.

SHEM Son of Noah and ancestor of Abraham. He headed a Torah-study house together with his great-grandson Eber.

SHEMA Lit., "hear." Biblical verses expressing Judaism's most fundamental precepts; see pp. 266–267.

SHILOH A town in northern Israel where the Tabernacle (forerunner of the Holy Temple) was erected, and which served as the spiritual center for the people of Israel, for 369 years, from the days of Joshua until its destruction by the Philistines in 890 BCE.

SHIUR A class or lecture on a Torah subject.

SHIVAH Lit., "seven." The seven-day mourning period following the burial of a deceased next of kin.

SHOFAR The horn of a ram (or other kosher animal), sounded on Rosh Hashanah, and by custom also at the close of Yom Kippur and throughout the month of Elul. See p. 335.

SHOWBREAD Twelve uniquely shaped loaves of unleavened bread that were baked each Friday in the Holy Temple. See p. 70.

SHTETL Yiddish for "little town." Commonly refers to small market towns in pre-World War II Eastern Europe.

SHUL Yiddish for synagogue.

SINAI The mountain on which G-d gave the Torah to the people of Israel (see pp. 36–39). The term "Sinai" is often used to refer to that event, as well as to the chain of the Torah's transmission through the generations.

SIVAN Third month of the Jewish calendar, or the 9th counting from Tishrei (see p. 329). Corresponds approximately with May–June.

SODOM As related in Genesis 18–19, the evil cities of Sodom and Gomorrah were destroyed by G-d for their moral depravity and cruelty.

SPIES, THE Twelve spies sent by Moses to scout the Holy Land, whose negative report delayed the Israelites' entrance into the Land by 40 years; see p. 45.

SUKKAH Lit., "shed." A hut of temporary construction with a roof-covering of branches, in which the Torah (Leviticus 23:39–43) commands to dwell for the duration of the Sukkot festival; see pp. 342–345.

TABERNACLE Heb. *Mishkan*. The portable house of worship built by the people of Israel to accompany them in their journey in the wilderness, which served as the "dwelling" for the divine presence in the Israelite camp. It was the forerunner of the Holy Temple in Jerusalem.

TABLETS, THE Heb. *luchot*. Two stone tablets on which G-d inscribed the Ten Commandments and which Moses brought down from Mount Sinai. The tablets were kept in a specially built "ark" in the innermost chamber of the Holy Temple (the "Holy of Holies"). There were actually two sets of tablets, as the first were broken by Moses when he witnessed the people of Israel worshipping the Golden Calf; when G-d forgave Israel's sin, He instructed Moses to carve a second set of tablets. See pp. 36–41.

TALLIT Prayer shawl fringed with TZITZIT at its four corners; see p. 325.

TALMUDIC ERA The period in Jewish history when the sages of the Talmud lived and taught, approximately 200 to 500 CE. See note on p. 154 and overview on p. 109.

TAMUZ Fourth month of the Jewish calendar, or tenth month counting from Tishrei (see p. 329). Corresponds approximately with June–July.

TEFILLIN Lit., "prayer accessories." Small leather cubes containing parchment scrolls inscribed with the Shema and other Biblical passages, worn on the arm and head; see pp. 319–324.

TESHUVAH Lit., "return." Repentance, seen in Jewish teaching as a return to G-d and to one's true essence. See pp. 340–341.

THERESIENSTADT Town in northern Bohemia used from 1941 to 1945 by the Nazis as a ghetto and concentration camp, and as a transit camp for Jews being sent to Auschwitz and other extermination camps.

TISH'AH B'AV The ninth day of the Jewish month of Av, observed as a day of fasting and mourning over the destruction of the Holy Temple. See pp. 378–382.

TISHREI First month of the Jewish calendar, corresponding approximately with September–October. It is also the 7th month, counting from Nisan (see p. 329).

TITHES Portions of the field's produce that are earmarked for the poor, to support those who served in the Holy Temple, and other religious goals. See p. 281.

TORAH Lit., "teaching" and "instruction." In the narrow sense, the term refers to the Five Books of Moses. In its broader sense, "Torah" refers to the entire body of Jewish teaching deriving from the divine communication received by Moses at Mount Sinai and handed down and expounded upon through the generations. See pp. 149ff.

TORAH POINTER An instrument (often made of silver) used by the reader to follow the text of the Torah scroll, in order to avoid touching the parchment of the scroll, due to its sacredness. Also called a *yad* (Hebrew for "hand").

TOSAFISTS See note for "Tosafot" on p. 192.

TOWER OF BABEL An edifice whose building is described in Genesis 11:1–9 as the cause of the diversity of languages in the world and the dispersion of mankind over all the earth.

TZADIK; TZADIKIM (pl.) A perfectly righteous person.

TZITZIT An arrangement of knotted strings, mandated by the Torah to be attached to garments of four or more corners as a reminder to fulfill the 613 commandments of the Torah; see pp. 325 326.

UNIFICATIONS A Kabbalistic term referring to the uniting of cosmic and supernal forces through one's mystical devotions in prayer and the performance of mitzvot.

VOLTAIRE Pseudonym of François-Marie Arouet (1694–1778), a French Enlightenment writer, historian, and philosopher.

WELL OF MIRIAM A spring that miraculously accompanied the Israelites and provided them with water for the 40 years they traveled in the wilderness.

WRITTEN TORAH The 24 books of the Jewish Bible (see pp. 158–159) transcribed by Moses and the later prophets—in contrast with the body of teaching called the "Oral Torah," which was originally not written down (see pp. 186–190).

YESHIVAH; YESHIVAHS (pl.) Literally, "sitting" or "settling." A school for advanced Torah learning.

YOM KIPPUR Lit., "day of atonement." The holiest day on the Jewish calendar, occurring on the 10th of Tishrei, devoted to repentance and return to G-d; see p. 40 and pp. 338–339.

ZION Lit., "signpost" or "monument." A Biblical term for the city of Jerusalem, or the Land of Israel as a whole, and metonymically, for the Jewish people.

ZIONISM; ZIONIST The political movement, launched in the 19th century, advocating the restoration of the Jewish people to their homeland; see overview on pp. 96ff. Also see glossary entry for RELIGIOUS ZIONISM above.

additional sources and notes

General notes: As a rule, the sources for the citations in this book appear in the citation heading or following the citation, while the ideas presented in the introductory texts for each section or subsection are derived from the citations that follow them. Additional notations and/or sourcing, where appropriate, appear in the list below.

The English translations of the *berachot* (ritual blessings) on pages 296, 297, 312-313, 318, 322, 357, and 372 follow *Siddur Tehillat Hashem with English Translation* (Kehot, 2008). All other translations and adaptations are by Yanki Tauber, unless otherwise credited.

The information in the timelines, maps, and biographical data on pages 4–5, 20–21, 50–51, 58–59, 61, 62, 66–67, 74–75, 86–87, 94–95, 96–97, 106–107, 108–109, 114–115, 122–127, 133, 142–143, 146–147, 152–153, 188–189, 192, 204–205, 230–231, and 234–235 are drawn from the following sources: Talmud, *Sanhedrin* 97a–b; *Seder Olam Rabbah; Seder Olam Zuta; Zemach David* (Ganz); *Seder ha-Dorot* (Heilprin); *Shem ha-Gedolim* (Chida)*; Atlas Daat Mikra* (Elitzur; Kiel)*; Codex Judaica* (Kantor); *Daat Dorot* (Rozman); *A Historical Atlas of the Jewish People* (Barnavi); *The Illustrated Atlas of Jewish Civilization* (Bacon); *Atlas of the Jewish World* (de Lange); *Encyclopedia of Jewish History* (Shamir; Shavit); *Atlas of Modern Jewish History* (Friesel); *Masters of the Word* (Kolatch); *Daat Encyclopedia of Jewish Knowledge* (daat.ac.il); *Virtual Jewish History Tours* (JewishVirtualLibrary. org); *Jewish Timeline* (odyeda.com), and *Judaism Online* (SimpleToRemember. com). Additional notes and sourcing for these items appear under their respective page numbers in this list.

p. 2: **It has been posited...** See *Our Oriental Heritage* (Durant), p. 340; *The Gifts of the Jews* (Cahill); *Radical Then, Radical Now* (Sacks); et al.

p. 3: **Franz Rosenzweig** "The Builders," *Short Writings*, p. 119.

p. 6: **The fathers...** *Tanya*, ch. 18; *Torah Ohr, Va'eira* 55a; *Likutei Sichot*, 3:860 and 4:1068. **R. Yitzchak Hutner** *Pachad Yitzchak, Passover,* 49:3.

p. 7: Genesis 11:26–29, 16:15, 22:20–23, 25:1–2, 25:19–26, 35:22–26, 36:10–12, 41:50–52, and 46:8–27; Exodus 6:16–20; Numbers 26:59; Talmud, *Berachot* 16b and *Horayot* 6b.

p. 8: **Midrash Rabbah** The phrase "a mansion alight" (בירה דולקת) is understood in two ways by the classical commentaries on *Bereishith Rabbah*: (a) "alight" in the sense of going up in flames—i.e., Abraham was disconcerted by the chaos and violence consuming the world, and wondered, "Can it be that this mansion has no Master?"; (b) "alight" in the sense of illuminated; beholding the order and luminance of the universe, Abraham deduced that it must have a Master. See *Nezer ha-Kodesh, Eitz Yosef, Rashi*, and *Imrei Yosher* to *Bereishith Rabbah*, 39:1. **R. Judah bar Ila'i** *Bereishith Rabbah,* 42:8.

p. 9: *Ethics of the Fathers,* 5:3 and *Pirkei d'Rabbi Eliezer*, 26–31; for alternative listings of the "ten trials" see *Avot d'Rabbi Nathan* 33:2, and commentaries by Rashi, Maimonides, and Bartenura to *Ethics of the Fathers,* ad loc.

p. 12: **Zohar** 1:119b; also see *Likutei Torah (Ari), Vayeira*; Alshich to Genesis 22:1. **Maimonides** *Guide for the Perplexed,* 3:24; also see Radak and Bechayei to Genesis 22. **Nachmanides** Commentary to Genesis 22:1; also see Seforno, ad loc. **R. Nissim Gerondi** Commentary to Genesis 22:1; *Derashot ha-Ran*, 6. **R. Hasdai Crescas** *Ohr Hashem*, 2:2:6. **R. Abraham Isaac Kook** Letters, 2:379; also see essay by Binyamin Ish-Shalom, *Limmud ve-Siach, Beit Morashah*, 5756. **R. Menachem M. Schneerson** *Likutei Sichot*, 20:73–78.

p. 14: Bechayei to Genesis 25:27; Recanati, *Noach* 21 and *Vayechi* 37; Maharal, *Tiferet Yisrael*, 20; *Sefat Emet, Toledot* 5649 and 5652; *Likutei Sichot,* 3:856–857.

p. 15: Genesis 25, 27–35, 37, 46–49; *Seder Olam* 1–2; Talmud, *Megilah* 16b–17a; *Bereishith Rabbah* 68:5; Rashi to Genesis 25:30, 28:9, and 37:34; Chizkuni to Genesis 25:27.

p. 16: *Shemot Rabbah*, 21:1; Rashi to Genesis 25:22–26; Jerusalem Talmud, *Avodah Zarah,* 2:1; Alshich to Genesis 25:26; *Tanya*, ch. 9; *Torah Ohr, Vayishlach*.

p. 17: **Pesikta d'Rav Kahana** 23:2; also see *Tanchuma* and *Yalkut Shimoni, Vayeitzei*. **Bar Kapara** *Bereishith Rabbah*, 68:12. **Bereishith Rabbah** ad loc. **Zohar** 3:306b. **Maimonides** *Guide for the Perplexed*, 1:15. **R. Jacob ben Asher** *Baal ha-Turim*, Genesis 28:12. **R. Chaim ibn Attar** *Ohr ha-Chayim*, Genesis 28:14. **R. Moses Chaim Luzzatto** *Adir ba-Marom*, p. 50b. **R. Shalom Noach Beresovsky** *Netivot Shalom, Vayeitzei*.

p. 18: *Shenei Luchot ha-Berit*, 2:298b–301b; *Torah Ohr, Vayigash* 43c–44b; *Sefer ha-Maamarim 5746*, pp. 74–80; *Likutei Sichot*, 35:152–154.

p. 22: Ezekiel 16; see citation from Maimonides on p. 41.

p. 26: **Tanchuma** *Shemot* 8. **Ibn Ezra** commentary to Exodus 2:3. **R. Judah Loew of Prague** *Gevurot Hashem,* 18.

p. 28: **What's in a name** Also see *Shemot Rabbah,* 1:26.

p. 29: **R. Joshua ben Korchah** *Shemot Rabbah,* 2:5. **Tanchuma** *Shemot* 14. **Shemot Rabbah** 2:5. **Baal Shem Tov** *Sefer ha-Sichot 5702*, pp. 46–47.

pp. 30–31: Exodus 7:14–12:33; *Shemot Rabbah,* 9:9; Rashi to Exodus 8:14–15, 9:10, and 9:24; *Gevurot Hashem,* 32 and 34; *Ohr ha-Chayim* to Exodus 9:5; *Malbim* to Exodus 7:14 and 11:5; *Likutei Sichot,* 21:38–44; *New Studies in Exodus, Va'eira* 6.

p. 36: **Reverse Perception** *Likutei Sichot,* 6:119–122.

p. 38: **Maimonides** Also see *Kuzari,* 4:11. **Zohar** Also see *Mechilta, Yitro; Bamidbar Rabbah*, 13:15; *Az'harot* of R. Saadia Gaon; Nachmanides and Abarbanel to Exodus 20. **R. Judah Halevi** *Kuzari,* 1:25. **Ibn Ezra** Exodus 20:2 **Nachmanides** Exodus 20:2. **R. Schneur Zalman of Liadi** *Maamarei Admur ha-Zaken ha-Ketzarim*, p. 426.

p. 41: **Forty Times Three** Exodus 24:12–18; Deuteronomy 9:9–18; *Seder Olam*, 6; Rashi to Exodus 32:1, Exodus 33:11, and Deuteronomy 9:18. **Maimonides writes** *Guide for the Perplexed*, 3:32.

pp. 42–43: **The 42 encampments** Numbers 33. The locations of many of the places named and of the route of the Israelites' journey, including those of the crossing of the sea and of Mount Sinai, are the topic of much discussion and debate amongst the commentaries. The map on these pages primarily follows R. Aryeh Kaplan's estimations in his *The Living Torah* (pp. 333 and 843); also see *Atlas Daat Mikra*, pp. 118–119, *Daat Dorot*, p. 108, and *Atlas of Jewish Civilization*, pp. 15 and 17. For alternative views, see the Artscroll's Hebrew *Mikraot Gedolot* (Zuker edition), 2:1301 and 4:973–974; and the *Kol Menachem Chumash*, pp. 1097, 1099, and 1118. Regarding the switchback after encampment 4 and the route through the sea, see Rashi to Exodus 14:2, and Tosafot, *Arachin* 15a. **Route of the Spies** Rashi to Numbers 13:21–22. **Calendar in left column** Based on the Biblical accounts of these events as expounded by the Midrashim and commentaries and summarized in *Seder ha-Dorot*, years 2448 to 2488; regarding Kislev 25, see *Pesikta Rabati*, 6; regarding Sukkot, see Leviticus 23:39–43, and *Tur*, 1:625.

p. 46: **Nachmanides** Commentary to Numbers 22:23 **Meanings of the statement...** Talmud, *Bava Batra* 60a and *Sanhedrin* 105b; Rashi to Numbers 24:5.

p. 48: **The fulfillment of many mitzvot...** See *Shenei Luchot ha-Berit*, 1:264b (2nd gloss); Talmud, *Ketuvot* 110b; *Sifrei, Eikev* and *Re'ei*; Rashi to Deuteronomy 11:18; Nachmanides to Leviticus 18:25; Bechayei to Deuteronomy 11:18.

p. 53: Joshua 13–19; see commentaries to Genesis 49 and Deuteronomy 33; also see *Atlas Daat Mikra*, pp. 140–143; *Atlas of Jewish Civilization*, p. 18.

p. 54: **Deborah & Yael** Judges 4–5. **Ten songs** *Tanchuma, Beshalach* 10.

p. 56: I Samuel 8–16.

p. 61: **Map** I Kings 5:1–5.

p. 63: I Kings 11–12 and 16–17; *Seder ha-Dorot*, 3187; *Otzar Masaot*, p. 6.

p. 64: *Tanchuma, Naso* 16; *Shenei Luchot ha-Berit*, 2:340a.

pp. 68–73: Exodus 25, 27:1–8, 30:1–10; I Kings 7; Talmud, Tractate *Midot*, and *Tiferet Yisrael* commentary on the Mishnah, ad loc.; *Melechet ha-Mishkan* (Levin); also see transcript of Rebbe's remarks to Baruch Nachshon on the *keruvim*, 12/6/1979; *Likutei Sichot*, 21:164–172, and sources cited there. **Ark** Nachmanides to Exodus 25. **Menorah** *Likutei Torah, Behaalotecha* 29c; *Reshimot, Reshimat ha–Menorah*. **Table** Leviticus 24:5; *Chinuch*, Mitzvah 97. **Anatomy of the Temple** Bechayei to Exodus

25:9; *Shenei Luchot ha-Berit*, 2:324b; *Torat ha-Olah*, part 1; *Derech Mitzvotecha, Mitzvat Binyan Mikdash*; *Reshimot*, #81–85. **Holy of Holies** Rashi, *Chomat Anach*, and Malbim to II Kings 11:2; *Sefer ha-Maamarim 5643*, pp. 100–101. **Chamber of the Sanhedrin** *Mishneh Torah, Laws of Sanhedrin*, 1:3 and 5:1, and *Laws of Mamrim*, 1:1 and 1:4. **Temple Mount** *Mishneh Torah, Laws of Entering the Holy Temple*, 3:3; see *On the Mikveh Trail* by Aviva and Shmuel Bar-Am, published in *Times of Israel*, 25 March 2017. **Western Wall** *Shir ha-Shirim Rabbah*, 2:22.

p. 76: **The Writing on the Wall** Daniel 5; *Seder ha-Dorot* 3389.

pp. 77–78: Josephus' account closely follows the account in the Talmud (*Yoma* 69a). Josephus, however, identifies the Jewish high priest who met Alexander as "Jaddua," whereas in the Talmud's account it is Jaddua's grandson, Simeon the Just. Also see accounts of this event in *Sefer ha-Kabbalah*, *Zemach David*, and *Seder ha-Dorot*.

p. 81: **Sadduccee Calendar?** See Talmud, *Menachot* 65a–66a; *Reclaiming the Dead Sea Scrolls*, pp. 301–305. **Reign of Queen Shlomzion** Rashi, *Kidushin* 66a; *Seder ha-Dorot,* 3688; *Zemach David*, 3688.

p. 83: **The Last Holdout** Josephus, *Wars of the Jews*, 7:8.

p. 85: **Benjamin of Tudela** *Otzar Masaot*, pp. 25–29.

p. 91: *Chagall: Love, War, and Exile*, p. 30; *The Israel Review of Arts and Letters*, no. 114.

p. 92: **Sound the great shofar...** *Siddur, Daily Amidah*. **Throughout the Bible...** See Genesis 12:10, 13:1, and 46:4, Deuteronomy 1:25–26, Jeremiah 23:8, et al. **Land of Israel is higher...** Talmud, *Zevachim* 54b; *Sifrei, Shoftim*; Rashi to Genesis 45:9; et al. **Maharal** *Be'er ha-Golah,* 6:13.

p. 93: **Maimonides** *Seder ha-Dorot*, 4927.

p. 98: **Lord Alexander Lindsay** *Letters on Egypt, Edom, and the Holy Land*, vol. 2, p. 71. **The Old Yishuv** *A History of Palestine: From the Ottoman Conquest to the Founding of the State of Israel*, p. 104.

p. 99: **A Jewish custom...** See p. 213.

p. 100: **No Vote** See Ben-Gurion's letter to Dr. Alex Bein, November 11, 1972; article by Yitzchak Tesler, Ynet.co.il, May 11, 2019.

pp. 108–109: *The Steinsaltz Talmud, Berachot*, p. 56 (1970 ed.); *Aiding Talmud Study*, by Aryeh Carmell.

p. 110: **Philo of Alexandria** *Seder ha-Dorot*, 3781; *Codex Judaica*, 3800.

p. 111: **Jewish States** *Seder ha-Dorot*, 3804, 4757, and 4900; *Kuzari*, 1:1; *Atlas of Jewish Civilization*, p. 57.

pp. 112 and 117–121 Overviews by Dr. Shmuel Klatzkin.

p. 124: **R. Solomon bar Simeon** *Gezeirot Ashkenaz ve-Tzarfat*, pp. 24ff.; also see *Kuntres Gezeirot Tatnu* by R. Eliezer ben Nathan of Meinz (Raavan).

p. 128: **Humiliating Headgear** *Medieval Jewish Civilization*, pp. 73–74. **Martin Luther** *A History of the Jews*, p. 242.

p. 131 **Captive Audience** *Divided Souls*, p. 60.

p. 132: **A false vision called conscience...** *The Rise and Fall of the Third Reich*, ch. 4.

p. 137: **Elie Wisel** *Telling the Tale*, p. 43.

p. 138: **The Modern Era...** See *Igrot Kodesh Admor ha-Zaken*, pp. 396–397; *Sefer ha-Sichot 5752*, pp. 174–186. **George Washington** *George Washington and the Jews*, p. 37.

p. 140: See *Likutei Diburim*, 3:930ff.; *Sichot Kodesh 5723*, p. 188 (Shevat 10, 1963).

p. 141: **Aron Moss** Article on Chabad.org.

pp. 142–143: This timeline is an amalgamation of dozens of variant sources and estimates over four millennia, and should be viewed as a generalized overview of the shifts and migrations of Jewish populations through the vicissitudes of history rather than as a definitive tabulation. Sources include: **Biblical sources** Genesis 46; Exodus 12:37; Numbers 1 and 26; II Samuel 24; Ezra 2. **Post-Biblical sources** *The Population of Israel* (Bachi); *Demographic Trends in Israel and Palestine* (DellaPergola); *The Story of Civilization* (Durant); *Encyclopedia Judaica*, s.v. "Population" (Baron); *The Jews* (Finkelstein); *Universal Jewish Encyclopedia*, s.v. "Statistics" (Landman); *The Jewish Encyclopedia*, s.v. "Statistics" (Singer); *To Count a People*

(Marcus); *From Time Immemorial* (Peters); *JewishGen.org*; *Atlas of Modern Jewish History* (Friesel); *American Jewish Yearbook* (AJC); *The Berman Jewish DataBank* (JFNA); and *Jewish Timeline* (odyeda.com).

p. 144: **But the Jewish contribution...** See *Sefer ha-Sichot 5704*, p. 165. **John Adams** *The Works of John Adams*, vol. 9, pp. 608–609.

p. 145: **The Noahide Laws** Talmud, *Sanhedrin* 56b–59b; *Mishneh Torah, Laws of Kings*, 8:10–11 and 9:1; *Encyclopedia Talmudit*, vol. 3, pp. 393–396; *Likutei Sichot*, 5:145–147; *Torat Menachem Hitvaaduyot 5744*, 3:1431–1436.

p. 148: **The melody...** R. Schneur Zalman of Liadi, cited in *Sefer ha-Sichot 5702*, p. 122. **A particularly poignant example...** *Chassidic Ecstasy in Music*, p. 130.

p. 156: **The Torah Scroll** See *Shulchan Aruch* and commentaries, 2:271, 2:274, 2:279, and 2:282.

p. 157: **Vowel and Cantillation Marks** Nehemiah 8:8, as per Talmud, *Megilah* 3a; *Kuzari*, 3:31; *Responsa of Radbaz*, 3:1068 (643); *Masters of the Word*, vol. 1, ch. 7, and sources cited there; *Encyclopedia Talmudit*, vol. 20, pp. 596–617 and 685–749, and sources cited there; also see introduction to *Tikunei Zohar*, 4a–b.

p. 158–159: Talmud, *Bava Batra* 14b–15a.

p. 160: **The Annual Torah Reading Cycle** *Tur*, tables following section 428.

p. 163: **Seventy faces...** *Bamidbar Rabbah*, 13:15; *Zohar* 1:47b; et al.

p. 164: **Torah means instruction...** Maharal, *Gur Aryeh* to Genesis 1:1. **For two commandments...** Of the Ten Commandments proclaimed at Mount Sinai, only the first two were heard by all the people directly from G-d, while the other eight were communicated through Moses; see Deuteronomy 5:19–25; also see *Torah Sheleimah*, vol. 16, pp. 223–225, and sources cited there.

p. 170: **A fundamental principle...** *Mishneh Torah, Laws of the Fundamentals of Torah*, 7:1 and 9:1–2.

p. 176: See *Tanach Daat Mikra,* introduction to the Book of Psalms, pp. 15–18, and sources cited there. Additional citations from Psalms that appear in this book are on pages 108, 249, 250, 252, 260, 270–271, 279, et al.

p. 180: **The Wisdom of Solomon** See I Kings 3:5–14 and 5:9–14. **The soul of man...** See "The Lamp" on p. 220. **Ecclesiastes** Also see citations on pages 386, 420, et al.

pp. 188–189: This chart follows Maimonides' calculation in his introduction to *Mishneh Torah* of the 40 generations from Moses to the redaction of the Talmud; alternative calculations are presented by Abarbanel, *Sefer ha-Kaneh*, and *Machzor Vitri* (see *Daat Dorot*, pp. 63–64). The "chain of tradition" continues from the redaction of the Talmud to the present day, as documented in *The Letter of Sherira Gaon*, *Sefer ha-Kabalah*, *Seder ha-Dorot*, *Daat Dorot*, *Codex Judaica,* and *Jewish Timeline*.

pp. 194–195: *Sifra (Torat Kohanim),* beginning of Leviticus; Babylonian Talmud *Oz Vehadar* ed., addendum to *Berachot*, pp. 13–19; R. Saadia Gaon's commentary on Talmud, *Bava Metzia* 32a, *Menachot* 37b, *Bava Kama* 54a, and *Shavuot* 43a; Bartenura's commentary on the Mishnah, *Kilayim* 9:1.

pp. 196–199: Talmud and commentaries, *Bava Metzia* 2a–8a.

pp. 206–207: **Atlanta** *Karnei ha-Hod,* p. 244. **New York** *Assia Journal*, vol. IV, no. 1; *Igrot Moshe, Orach Chayim* 4:80. **Worms** *Chavat Ya'ir,* 31 and 224. **Zurich** *Chelkat Yaakov, Choshen Mishpat* 31. **Barcelona** *Responsa of the Rashba*, 1:9 and 1:581. **Entre Rios** *Zichron Yosef.* **Manchester** *Minchat Yitzchak*, 5:7. **Lomza** *Divrei Malkiel*, 4:107 and 3:58. **Kovno** *She'eilot u-Teshuvot mi-Maamakim*, 3:6. **Lvov** *Kuntres Bitul Modaah; Beit Yitzchak, Yoreh De'ah*, 1:120. **Tiberias** Talmud, *Beitzah* 4b. **Cairo** *Responsa of Radbaz*, 3:979 (548). **Pumbedita** *Otzar ha-Geonim*, vol. 2, pp. 4 and 157. **Vienna** *Terumat ha-Deshen*, 196. **Pressburg** *Chatam Sofer: Responsa*, 6:84. **Elephantine** *Aramaic Papyri of the Fifth Century*, pp. 60–65. **Jerusalem** *Torah Shebaal Peh Journal*, vol. 19 (1977), p. 9ff.; *Yabia Omer, vol. 9, Orach Chayim*, 35; *Tzitz Eliezer*, 15:39 and 20:49. **Prague** *Noda bi-Yehudah*, 2:B210 and 1:B10. **Mantua** *Responsa of Maharik*, 88. **Auschwitz** *Mekadshei Hashem*, vol. 1, p. 8. **Krakow** *Responsa of the Bach*, 1:127, and 2:1. **Algiers** *Responsa of Rivash*, 11. **Johannesburg** *ha-Berachot ke-Hilchatan*, 24; *Moadim u-Zemanim*, 3:269.

p. 210: **The Talmud relates...** *Shabbat* 31a.

p. 212: **You Be the Judge** JLI course, 2006.

p. 213: **Takanot of R. Gershom** See *Encyclopedia Talmudit*, vol. 17, pp. 757–772. **R. Solomon ben Aderet** *Torat ha-Bayit ha-Aroch*, 3:7 (32a); also see Tosafot, *Menachot,* 20b; Nachmanides, *Pesachim,* 7b. **The kipah...** See *Bach* on *Tur,* 1:2; *Shulchan Aruch* and commentaries, ad loc.

p. 214: See citation from Talmud on p. 36; *Tanya,* ch. 4.

p. 216: Maimonides' commentary on the Mishnah, introduction to *Perek Chelek.*

p. 217: See commentaries on Genesis 1:1 by Nachmanides, Ran, *Akeidat Yitzchak,* and Abarbanel; *Guide for the Perplexed*, 1:57, 2:25, and 3:10.

p. 220: **The Lamp** *Torah Ohr, Mikeitz* 33b–c; *Shaarei Orah, Shaar ha-Chanukah*, pp. 68ff.; *Igrot Kodesh*, vol. 4, p. 228; also see *Tanya*, chs. 19 and 35. **Tzvi Freeman** article on Chabad.org.

p. 222: **Alshich** Also see *Maamarei Admur ha-Tzemach Tzedek, Hanachot, 5614–5615,* p. 142. **Machine Learning** *Shem Olam*, part I, ch. 24 (*chasimat ha-sefer*); *Kol Yehudah*, p. 228; also cited in the name of R. Abraham Jacob of Sadigora in *L'kutei Bosar L'kutei, Avot* 1:17.

p. 225: *Likutei Sichot,* 28:131–137.

p. 227: **Art Turned Toward Eternity** Michail Grobman, *The Avant-Garde in Russia 1910–1930: New Perspectives*, pp. 25–27.

p. 229: **R. Israel Baal Shem Tov** *Ben Porat Yosef*, 100a–b; *Keter Shem Tov*, Citation 1.

p. 230: **In these times...** Introduction to *Shaar ha-Hakdamot; Tanya*, 4:26.

pp. 234–235: *Daat Dorot* (Rozman); *Hasidism Through the Generations* (Alfasi).

p. 239: **In the Jewish tradition...** See *Derech Mitzvotecha, Haamanat ha-Elokut.* **Ten substanceless sefirot** *Sefer Yetzirah*, 1:2. **Avodat ha-Kodesh** as quoted in *Sefer ha-Maamarim 5657*, p. 48.

p. 241: **Shimona Tzukernik** *How Did the Beginning Begin?*, a video presentation on TorahCafe.com.

pp. 242–243: Based on *Inyanah shel Torah ha-Chasidus*.

p. 244: **The Modern Musar Movement** *Torat ha-Musar* (Zaritzki).

p.246: **While all...** Talmud, *Bava Kama* 30a; *Biurim le-Pirkei Avot*, vol. 1, p. xviii–xix. **Summer Learning** *Avudraham, Seder Yemei ha-Omer; Shulchan Aruch*, 1:292:2.

p. 253: **Berachot 63a** This saying is from the Talmudic text as quoted in *Ein Yaakov* and appears as a gloss in the standard editions of the Talmud.

p. 255: **R. Menachem M. Schneerson** *Igrot Kodesh,* vol. 23, pp. 369–371.

p. 256: **The Storyteller** *Maharsha, Sanhedrin* 99b; *Likutei Sichot*, 15:96.

p. 260: **A mistranslation...** *Likutei Sichot*, 2:410.

p. 262: **R. Joseph Albo** *Ikarim*, 4:18 **R. David Shlomo Eibeschutz** *Arvei Nachal, Balak* 1. **R. Schneur Zalman of Liadi** *Torah Ohr*, 42b; *Likutei Sichot*, 29:184. **R. Shmuel Kaplan** introduction to *The Siddur Illuminated by Chassidus.*

p. 265: **Principles derived...** Talmud, *Berachot* 31a; *Likutei Sichot*, 19:291–297. **Zohar** As cited in *Likutei Torah, Balak,* 72a. **Yanki Tauber** Article on Chabad.org.

p. 266: **Blessed be...** This sentence is not part of the Biblical text, but an insertion instituted by the sages; see Talmud, *Pesachim* 56a.

p. 267: **Shema and its blessings** *Siddur*; Mishnah, *Berachot*, 1:4–5; Bartenura's commentary, ad loc.

p. 268: **Three daily prayers** *Siddur; Shulchan Aruch* and commentaries, 1:46–149 and 1:233–237.

p. 270: **Selected prayers** *Siddur.* **Pathways of prayer** *Pri Eitz Chayim*, introduction to *Shaar ha-Tefilah.*

p. 271: **Blessings of the Amidah** *Siddur; Mishneh Torah, Laws of Prayer,* 1:4, 2:1, and 2:5; *Shulchan Aruch*, 1:119:1.

p. 272: *Shaar ha-Kavanot, Tefilat ha-Shachar* 1; *Peri Eitz Chayim, Shaar ha-Tefilah; Megaleh Amukot, Vayeitzei; Shenei Luchot ha-Berit*, 2:291b–292a; *Ohr ha-Torah, Bamidbar* 1:5; *Derech Mitzvotecha*, 84b; *Sefer ha-Maamarim 5707*, p. 233; *Likutei Diburim,* 27.

p. 273: Talmud, *Berachot* 8a; *Mishneh Torah, Laws of Prayer*, 8:1; *Derashot ha-Ran*, 1; *Tefilah be-Tzibur*, ch. 4, and sources cited there.

p. 274: *Mishneh Torah, Laws of Prayer*, 11:1–5; *Nitei Gavriel, Ketivat ve-Hachnasat Sefer Torah*, ch. 8, and sources cited there; *Beit ha-Keneset ka-Halachah*, 8:2–4, 20:11–19, 20:22–28, 27:1, 29:1, 30:1–10, 30:16–17, 31:1, 33:1–2, and 33:8.

p. 278: *Likutei Sichot*, 2:410.

p. 279: **The Pushkah** See *Torat Menachem Hitvaaduyot 5748*, 4:343ff.

p. 280: **The Accidental Mitzvah** See *Likutei Sichot*, 15:261.

p. 281: Leviticus 19:9–10 and 25:1–7; Numbers 15:17–21 and 18:21–32; Deuteronomy 14:22–29 and 24:19–21; *Mishneh Torah, Laws of Gifts to the Poor*, 1:1–8; *Laws of Terumot*, 3:1–2 and 3:12; *Laws of Tithes*, 1:1; *Laws of the Second Tithe*, 1:1; *Laws of the Sabbatical Year*, 1:1 and 4:24.

pp. 282–283: **Feeding the Hungry** *Mishneh Torah, Laws of Gifts to the Poor*, 7:6. **Giving a Loan** Talmud, *Sukah* 49b; *Shulchan Aruch* 4:97:1, and Gra, ad loc.; Exodus 22:24. **Redeeming Captives** *Shulchan Aruch*, 2:252:1. **Hospitality** See Gersonides' commentary to Genesis 18. **Visiting the Sick** *Shulchan Aruch*, 2:335. **Bringing Happiness to Bride and Groom** See *Encyclopedia Talmudit*, vol. 9, pp. 136–143, and sources cited there. **Honoring the Deceased** *Midrash Tanchuma, Vayechi* 3. **Returning a Lost Object** *Shulchan Aruch*, 4:259. **Roadside Assistance** Talmud, *Bava Metzia* 32b. **Spiritual** See *Tanya*, ch. 32; *Likutei Sichot*, 2:580–581 and 5:148.

p. 284: **When two people meet...** *Igrot Kodesh*, vol. 10, p. 193.

p. 286: **A taste...** See Talmud, *Berachot* 57b; *Zohar* 1:48a; *Yalkut Reuveni, Yitro*, s.v. *Zachor*; et al.

p. 288: **Ahad Ha'am** From an article titled "Shabbat and Zionism," published in *ha-Shiloah*, vol. 3, no. 6 (Sivan 1898).

p. 290: **The sphere of Time** *Reishit Chochmah, Shaar ha-Kedushah*, 2; *Shenei Luchot ha-Berit*, 1:118a-120b; Maharal, *Tiferet Yisrael*, 40; *Reshimot*, #3.

p. 291: **Jay Litvin** Article on Chabad.org.

p. 292: **R. Shmuel of Lubavitch** Also see *Sefer ha-Sichot 5750*, 2:644ff., and footnote 25 there.

pp. 300–301: **Code of Jewish Law** *Shulchan Aruch ha-Rav*, 1:242:7. **R. Joseph Colon** Cited in *Leket Yosher*, vol. 1, *Laws of the Works of Shabbat*, 56. **R. Moses Matt** *Mateh Moshe*, 2:4:404. **R. Yechiel Michel Epstein** *Kitzur Shaloh*, 68b; also see *Maamarei Admur ha-Zaken Inyanim*, p. 410. This idea is often cited in the name of R. Isaiah Horowitz (Shaloh), but the source seems to be from the later work *Kitzur Shaloh* (based on various earlier Kabbalistic works), which consists of excerpts of Shaloh's teachings but also contains supplementary material from other Kabbalistic sources. **R. Zvi Elimelech of Dinov** cited in *Taamei ha-Minhagim*, 305. **R. Menachem Mendel of Vorka** cited in *Fun Di Chasidishe Oitzrois*, *Noach*. **R. Zadok of Lublin** *Pri Tzadik, Emor* 6. **Gefilte Fish** *The Spice and Spirit of Kosher-Jewish Cooking*, pp. 147–148.

p. 302: R. Simeon ibn Duran (Rashbatz), *Yavin Shemuah, Maamar Chametz*, 34c–d.

p. 306: **Maimonides** as cited by Hertz, Leviticus 11.

pp. 307–309: Leviticus 11; Deuteronomy 14; *Shulchan Aruch* and commentaries, 2:1–138; *Kitzur Shulchan Aruch*, 36–38, 46–47, 172.

pp. 312–313: *Shulchan Aruch ha-Rav, Seder Birchot ha-Nehenin; Siddur Tehillat Hashem with English Translation*, p. 86.

p. 317: **Parchment and Cover** *Shulchan Aruch* and commentaries, 2:288.

pp. 320–322: *Shulchan Aruch,* 1:25–45; *Taamei ma-Minhagim*, pp. 613–626; *Siddur Tehillat Hashem with English Translation*, pp. 11 and 640; *Responsa of Ritva*, 71.

p. 325: **The Blue Thread** *Encyclopedia Talmudit*, vol. 15, s.v. *Chilazon*; R. Gershon Hanoch Leiner, *Sefunei Temunei Chol*.

p. 326: *Kitzur Shulchan Aruch*, 9:5; *Maamar Mordechai, Orach Chayim*, 11:17; *Birkei Yosef*, 1:11:9; *Shulchan Aruch ha-Rav*, 1:11:30–31; *Taamei ha-Minhagim*, pp. 604–610; *Geonica*, vol. 2, p. 330–331; *Mishneh Torah, Laws of Tzitzit*, 1:6–8; *Yahel Ohr, Pinchas* 227a; tekhelet.com/tying-options.

p. 329: **Two Heads** *Yom Tov Shel Rosh Hashanah 5666*, pp. 156ff.

p. 330–331: *Mishneh Torah, Laws of the Sanctification of the Month,* 1:1–8, 4:1, 5:1–5, and 6:10–11; *Tur,* 1:426–428 (pp. 169b–172a); *Seder ha-Dorot,* 4118.

p. 332: **It is customary to wear white...** *Shulchan Aruch,* 1:610:4.

p. 334: **The Talmud...** *Rosh Hashanah* 34b. **R. Amnon of Mainz** See *Seder ha-Dorot,* 5001.

p. 335: **Maimonides** *Mishneh Torah, Laws of Repentance,* 3:4. **R. Yomtov Asevilli** Commentary on Talmud, *Rosh Hashanah* 16a. **R. Abahu** Talmud, *Rosh Hashanah* 16a. **R. Saadia Gaon** cited in *Avudraham, Taamei ha-Tekiot* **R. Yitzchak** Talmud, ibid. **R. Israel Baal Shem Tov** see citation on this page. **Tzemach Tzedek** *Derech Mitzvotecha,* p. 157a.

pp. 336–337: *Shulchan Aruch,* 1:583; *Siddur Torah Ohr,* p. 293 (*Machzor for Rosh Hashanah,* p. 200).

pp. 338–339: *Machzor for Yom Kippur; Likutei Sichot,* 4:1149–1154; *Kol Nidrei,* pp. 825–826, and sources cited there.

pp. 344–345: *Shulchan Aruch and commentaries,* 1:625–636.

p. 346: *Shulchan Aruch,* 1:651.

p. 347: **Supernal Guests** *Zohar,* 3:103b; *Chag ha-Asif,* ch. 4, footnote 2, and sources cited there.

p. 348: **Second Hakafot** *le-David Emet,* 26:6; *Orach Mishpat,* 1:142.

p. 350: **Spinning Letters** *Otzar Kol Minhagei Yeshurun,* p. 57.

p. 352: **The Story of Judith** The apocryphal *Book of Judith* places this event during the reign of Nebuchadnezzar, some three centuries prior to the Hasmonean rebellion; but in traditional Jewish sources, the story is associated with the events of Hanukkah, and Judith is identified as the daughter of Jochanan the High Priest. See *Kol-Bo,* 44; *Shulchan Aruch,* 1:670:2; *Zemach David,* 3622; *Encyclopedia Talmudit,* vol. 16, p. 368, and additional sources there; *Otzar Midrashim,* vol. 1, p. 192–193.

p. 357: *Shulchan Aruch and commentaries,* 1:671–673, 1:676, and 1:679; *Siddur Tehillat Hashem,* pp. 389 and 612.

p. 358: **The Talmud...** Mishnah, *Rosh Hashanah* 1:1; *Taanit* 7a. **Carobs** *Nitei Gavriel, Purim,* 5:8.

p. 359: *Sefer ha-Sichot 5750,* 1:273–285, and sources cited there.

p. 360: **Recalling the fateful wine party...** *Taamei ha-Minhagim,* 891. **Hamantaschen** *Nitei Gavriel, Purim,* 71:7, and sources cited there.

p. 362: **R. Zvi Elimelech of Dinov** cited in *Korban he-Ani, Mikeitz.*

p. 365: **Masked Miracle** *Shulchan Aruch,* 1:696:8; *Yalkut Yosef,* vol. 25, p. 199.

p. 366: **Kingdom of priests** Exodus 19:6. **Remembered and reenacted** see p. 328. **Freedom Redux** *Likutei Sichot,* 7:272–273.

p. 368: **Freedom Food** Deuteronomy 16:3; Rashi and Seforno, ad loc.; *Zohar,* 2:183b; Talmud, *Pesachim* 38b; *Shulchan Aruch and commentaries,* 1:453:4. **War on Leaven** Exodus 12:15–20; *Shulchan Aruch and commentaries,* 1:431–452.

pp. 369–371: *Passover Haggadah; Zohar, Tikunim,* 13; *Sefer ha-Minhagim,* 508–554. The order of the "Four Questions" is shown according to the Chabad custom; the order followed by other communities is: matzah, bitter herbs, dipping, reclining.

pp. 372–373: *Guide for the Perplexed,* 3:43; *Chinuch,* Mitzvah 307; Ran on Talmud, end of *Pesachim; Siddur Tehillat Hashem,* pp. 136–140.

p. 374: *Nitei Gavriel, Passover* 3:57.

p. 375: *Shulchan Aruch and commentaries,* 1:493; *Sefer ha-Todaah,* ch. 25; *Taamei ha-Minhagim,* 604–607; *Likutei Sichot,* 1:286 and 22:138; *Torat Menachem Hitvaaduyot 5711,* 2:50–58 and 77–81.

p. 376: **Shavuot celebrates...** *Likutei Sichot,* 28:80–83. **When the Holy Temple...** Leviticus 23:15–21; Numbers 28:26–27; Deuteronomy 26; Mishnah, *Bikurim* 1:3; *Musaf* prayer for Shavuot. **Sinaic Enactment** *Likutei Sichot,* 23:256.

p. 377: *The Spice and Spirit of Kosher-Jewish Cooking,* pp. 147–148.

p. 378: **Nearly two-thirds...** *Shenei Luchot ha-Berit,* 1:264b (2nd gloss).

p. 380: *Shulchan Aruch and commentaries,* 1:428:8 and 1:549–559. In the custom of some communities, verses 3:4 or 4:1–2 from the Book of Jeremiah are also included in the second of the "Three of Rebuke" readings.

p. 384: *Torat Menachem Hitvaaduyot 5749,* 4:150–151.

p. 386: **The human being...** *Midrash Tanchuma, Pekudei* 3. **From the material world...** see *Biurim le-Pirkei Avot,* vol. 1, pp. 318–319.

p. 388: See citations from Talmud on p. 219 and Steinsaltz on p. 221; also see *Likutei Sichot,* 24:178ff.

p. 389: **Psalm 121** *Raziel ha-Malach,* p. 43a; also see *Torat Menachem Hitvaaduyot 5747,* 2:37.

p. 390: **R. Menachem M. Schneerson** *Torat Menachem Hitvaaduyot 5750,* 2:139.

p. 391: **Seat of Honor** *ha-Manhig,* 129.

p. 392: **Uninviteds Welcome** *Sod Hashem,* 11a.

p. 393: **Redemption of the Firstborn** *Siddur Tehillat Hashem,* p. 460; Seforno to Exodus 13:15; *Bamidbar Rabbah,* 4:8.

p. 394: **R. Schneur Zalman of Liadi** also see *Devash le-Fi,* s.v. *Shem.* **Naming Customs** *Ziv ha-Sheimot,* and sources cited there.

p. 396: **A Jew however poor...** *Jews, G-d and History,* p. 261. **Common decency...** *Vayikra Rabbah,* 9:3. **Sweet Learning** *Kol-Bo,* 74; *Brent Spiegel,* ch. 16; also see *Torat Menachem Hitvaaduyot 5720,* 1:82–85.

p. 399: **Upsherin** *Nitei Gavriel, Tiglachat,* pp. 29–32, and sources cited there. **How to Celebrate your Jewish Birthday** *Sefer ha-Sichot 5748,* 2:406–407.

p. 400–401: **A Jewish girl...** Talmud, *Nidah* 45b; *Ethics of the Fathers,* 5:22. **In Judaism...** see *Likutei Sichot,* 3:921. **Bar Mitzvah and Tefillin** see *Encyclopedia Talmudit,* vol. 9, p. 510, and sources cited there.

p. 403: Mishnah, *Ketubot* 1:2; Talmud, ibid., 10a; *Shulchan Aruch,* 3:66:1–6; also see sources cited in *Encyclopedia Talmudit,* vol. 33, p. 3, footnotes 17 and 18.

p. 404: *Men, Women and Kabbalah,* by Tzvi Freeman.

p. 405: **R. Dr. Abraham J. Twerski** video on jinsider.com.

pp. 406–407: Essay by Rabbi Jacobson on meaningfullife.com.

p. 408: *Shulchan Aruch and commentaries,* 3:25–26, 34, 42, and 56; *Taamei ha-Minhagim,* 931–977; *Nitei Gavriel, Nisu'in,* chapters 5, 9, 13–17, 19–22, 32–33, and 36–38.

pp. 412–413: *Mikveh Mayim,* by R. Yirmiah Katz; *Igrot Kodesh,* vol. 3, p. 394.

p. 416: **The Hasidic masters teach** *Likutei Sichot,* 15:93ff.

p. 419: *Sichot Kodesh 5740,* vol. 3.

p. 420: **One of the fundamental...** see *Responsa of Radbaz,* 3:555 (985).

p. 421: **Land of Diamonds** See *Shem Olam,* part II, ch. 9.

p. 422: **Holy Soil** *Shulchan Aruch,* 2:363:1. **Final moments of life** *Shulchan Aruch,* 2:338–339; *Nitei Gavriel, Aveilut,* 1:15 and 3:14, and sources cited there.

p. 423: **Sacred Privilege** *Kolbo al Aveilut,* vol. 1, p. 175; *Nitei Gavriel, Aveilut* 1:42:1–2, and sources cited there.

p. 426: **Directed Upward** *Shulchan Aruch,* 2:376:4; *Shaar ha-Kavanot, Derushei ha-Kadish.*

p. 427: *Shulchan Aruch and commentaries,* 2:340–341, 2:375–376, and 2:380–395; *The Jewish Way in Death and Mourning,* chs. 1–5; *Nitei Gavriel, Aveilut,* 1:11, 1:53–63, 1:85–113, 2:1–11, 2:40, 2:51, 2:62–64, 2:70–79, and sources cited there.

p. 428: *Yefeh To'ar* on *Bereishith Rabbah,* 82:10; Genesis 35:19–20, *Bereishith Rabbah,* 82:10, and *Nezer ha-Kodesh,* ad loc.; Talmud, *Sotah* 34b, based on Numbers 13:22.

p. 430: **R. Schneur Zalman of Liadi** also see *Chinuch,* Mitzvah 595; *Shenei Luchot ha-Berit,* 1:14b.

p. 431: **All four levels...** see pp. 242–243.

bibliography

BIBLICAL, TALMUDIC, AND MIDRASHIC SOURCE TEXTS

Tanach [Jewish Bible]. Jerusalem: Koren, 2008.

Chumash Torat Chaim [Pentateuch with Onkelos and 11 commentaries: Saadia Gaon, R. Hananel, Rashi, Rashbam, Ibn Ezra, Radak, Nachmanides, Maharam, Chizkuni, Seforno, and *Chinuch*]. 7 vols. Jerusalem: Mosad Harav Kook, 1986.

Mikraot Gedolot ha-Maor [Pentateuch with 25 commentaries, incl. *Baal ha-Turim*, *Keli Yakar*, *Ohr ha-Chayim*, et al.]. 5 vols. Jerusalem: Hamaor, 1990.

Torah Sheleimah [Compendium of Talmudic and Midrashic Literature on the Pentateuch; incl. the Halachic Midrashim: *Mechilta*, *Sifrei*, and *Sifra*]. 45 vols. Compiled by Menahem Mendel Kasher. Jerusalem: 1926–1992.

Chumash Mikraot Gedolot: Zucker Edition. 5 vols. Brooklyn: Mesorah-Artscroll, 2014.

Mishnah with Commentaries [Bartenura, *Tosafot Yom Tov*, *Tiferet Yisrael*, et al.]. 14 vols. Vilnius: 1926.

Talmud Bavli [Babylonian Talmud; incl. Minor Tractates, *Tosefta*, and 143 commentaries: Rashi, *Tosafot*, Alfasi, Maimonides' commentary on the Mishnah, Ran, Rosh, Maharam, Maharshal, Maharsha, et al.]. 41 vols. Jerusalem: Oz Vehadar, 2017.

Jerusalem Talmud. 6 vols. New York: MP Press, 1959.

Seder Olam Rabbah v'Zuta. Hamburg: 1757.

Pirkei d'Rabbi Eliezer with Commentaries. Jerusalem: Zichron Aharon, 2006.

Midrash Rabbah with Commentaries. 6 vols. Jerusalem: Vagshal, 2001.

Midrash Tanchuma. 2 vols. Jerusalem: Eshkol, 1972.

Midrash Tanchuma—Buber edition. 2 vols. Vilnius: 1885.

Avot d'Rabbi Nathan [both versions]. New York: Feldheim, 1945.

Seder Eliyahu Rabbah v'Zuta. 2 vols. Vienna: 1900; Jerusalem: Vahrman, 1969.

Midrash Tehilim Shochar Tov. Buber edition. Vilnius: 1891.

Yalkut Shimoni. 2 vols. Jerusalem: Vagshal, 1960.

Sefer Yetzirah. Mantua: 1562.

Zohar and Zohar Chadash Matok mi-Devash. Translated and Elucidated by David Frish. 20 vols. Jerusalem: Machon Daat Yosef, 2005.

Passover Haggadah with 238 commentaries. Jerusalem: Eitz Chaim, 1957.

OTHER WORKS

Abarbanel, Isaac. *Commentary on the Earlier Prophets.* Pesaro: 1512.

———. *Commentary on the Pentateuch.* Venice: 1579.

Achai Gaon. *She'iltot.* Venice: 1546.

Adams, John. *The Works of John Adams.* 10 vols. Boston: Little Brown, 1850.

Adler, Shmuel Avraham. *Aspaklaria: An Encyclopedic Anthology of Jewish Thought.* 29 vols. Jerusalem: 1992.

Aiken, Lisa. *The Hidden Beauty of the Shema.* Brooklyn: Targum, 1997.

Albo, Joseph. *Ikarim* [Book of Principles]. Soncino: 1486.

al-Dahiri, Zechariah. *Sefer ha-Musar* [Book of Morals]. Bnei Brak: Yitzhari, 2008.

Alfasi, Isaac. *Hasidism Through the Generations.* 2 vols. Jerusalem: Machon Daat Yosef, 1995.

Alon, Gedaliah. *The Jews in Their Land in the Talmudic Age.* Cambridge: Harvard University Press, 1989.

Alshich, Moses. *Psalms with Commentary.* Lublin: 1886.

Alter, Judah Aryeh Leib. *Sefat Emet* [Edge of Truth]. 5 vols. Piotrkow: 1905–1908.

Alter, Samuel. *L'kutei Bosar L'kutei* [Gleanings After Gleanings]. 14 vols. New York: 1945–1960.

Alter, Yitzchak Meir. *Likutei ha-Rim* [Selected Teachings]. 2 vols. Beit Shemesh: 2010.

Altschuler, Moses. *Brent Spiegel* [Fiery Mirror]. Basel: 1602.

American-Israeli Cooperative Enterprise (AICE). *Jewish History Tours.* JewishVirtualLibrary.org: 1993–2000.

American Jewish Committee (AJC). *American Jewish Yearbook.* JPS, 1899–1993; AJC, 1994–2008; Springer, 2012–2020.

Amiel, Moses Avigdor. *Derashot El Ami* [Sermons to My People]. 3 vols. Warsaw: 1923–1929.

Arama, Isaac. *Akeidat Yitzchak* [Binding of Isaac]. 6 vols. Jerusalem: Amnon Gross, 2013–2015.

Asevilli, Yomtov. *Chidushei ha-Ritva* [Commentaries on the Talmud]. 26 vols. Jerusalem: Mosad Harav Kook, 2009.

———. *Responsa of Ritva.* Jerusalem: Mosad Harav Kook, 2008.

Auerbach, Shlomo Zalman. *Minchat Shlomo* [Solomon's Offering; responsa]. 3 vols. Jerusalem: Shaarei Ziv, 1986; Otzrot Shlomo, 1999.

Avudraham, David. *The Complete Avudraham.* Lisbon: 1490.

Azulai, Chaim Yosef David. *Birkei Yosef* [Lap of Joseph]. 2 vols. Vienna: 1860.

———. *Devash le-Fi* [Honey for My Mouth]. Livorno: 1801.

———. *le-David Emet* [Truth unto David]. Livorno: 1820.

———. *Shem ha-Gedolim* [Names of the Great]. Livorno: 1787.

Baal Shem Tov, Israel. *Keter Shem Tov* [Crown of the Good Name]. Brooklyn: Kehot, 1972.

Bacharach, Naftali Hertz. *Emek ha-Melech* [Vale of the King]. Amsterdam: 1648.

Bacharach, Yair. *Chavat Ya'ir* [Yair's Homestead]. Frankfurt-Am-Main: 1699.

Bachi, Roberto. *The Population of Israel.* Jerusalem: CICRED, 1974.

Bacon, Josephine. *The Illustrated Atlas of Jewish Civilization: 4000 Years of History.* London: Quantum Books, 2009.

Baer, S. *Elegies for Tish'ah be-Av.* Basel: 1896.

Barnavi, Eli (ed.). *A Historical Atlas of the Jewish People: From the Time of the Patriarchs to the Present.* New York: Hatchette Literature, 1992.

Barron, Stephanie; Tuchman, Maurice. *The Avant-Garde in Russia 1910–1930: New Perspectives.* Cambridge: MIT Press, 1980.

bar-Sheshet, Isaac. *Responsa of Rivash.* Istanbul: 1546.

Barzilai, Shmuel. *Chassidic Ecstasy in Music.* Frankfurt am Main: 2009.

Bechor Shor, Joseph. *Commentary on Torah.* 3 vols. Jerusalem: Hatechiyah, 1956.

ben-Aderet, Solomon. *Responsa of Rashba.* 8 vols. Jerusalem: Machon Yerushalayim, 1997.

———. *Torat ha-Bayit ha-Aroch* [Law of the House: long version]. Venice: 1608.

ben-Zimra, David. *Responsa of Radbaz.* 8 vols. Venice: 1749; Warsaw: 1882; Bnei Brak: 1978.

Beresovsky, Shalom Noach. *Netivot Shalom* [Pathways of Peace]. 7 vols. Jerusalem, 1985–2013.

Berkovitz, Eliezer. *Faith after the Holocaust.* New York: Ktav, 1973.

Besdin, Abraham. *Reflections of the Rav: Lessons in Jewish Thought adapted from the Lectures of Rabbi Joseph B. Soloveitchik.* Jerusalem: World Zionist Organization, 1979.

Bialik, Chaim Nachman. *Letters.* 5 vols. Tel Aviv: Devir, 1937–1938.

———. *Poems.* Tel Aviv: Devir, 1954.

Blau, Esther. *The Spice and Spirit of Kosher-Jewish Cooking.* Brooklyn: Lubavitch Women's Org., 1977.

Cahill, Thomas. *The Gifts of the Jews.* New York: Doubleday, 1998.

Carlebach, Elisheva. *Divided Souls: Converts from Judaism in Germany, 1500–1750*. New Haven: Yale University Press, 2001.

Carmell, Aryeh. *Siyata le-Gemarah* [Aiding Talmud Study]. Jerusalem: Feldheim, 1998.

Carmi, Mordecai. *Maamar Mordechai* [Word of Mordecai]. Livorno: 1784–1786.

Caro, Joseph; Isserlis, Moses. *Shulchan Aruch* [Code of Jewish Law] with 25 commentaries. 10 vols. New York: MP Press, 1976.

Chabad-Lubavitch Media Center. *Chabad.org* [Online Library of Torah and Judaism]. 1994–2020.

Colon, R. Joseph. *Responsa of Maharik*. Venice: 1509.

Cordovero, Moses. *Pardes Rimonim* [Orchard of Pomegranates]. Krakow: 1591–1592.

———. *Shi'ur Komah* [Measure of Stature]. Warsaw: Goldman, 1884.

Cowley, Arthur Ernest. *Aramaic Papyri of the Fifth Century*. Oxford: 1923.

Crescas, Hasdai. *Ohr Hashem* [Light of G-d]. Vienna: 1860.

Culi, Jacob; et al. *Me'am Loez* [Torah in the Vernacular]. 18 vols. Jerusalem: Ohr Chadash, 1967.

David of Lida. *Sod Hashem* [Divine Secret; laws and customs of *brit milah*]. Mantua: 1743.

Da Fano, Menachem Azariah. *Asarah Maamarot* [Ten Utterances]. Venice: 1597.

De Lange, Nicholas. *Atlas of the Jewish World*. Oxford: Equinox, 1984.

De Uceda, Samuel. *Midrash Shmuel* [Exposition of Samuel]. Venice, 1585.

De Vidas, Elijah. *Reishit Chochmah* [Genesis of Wisdom]. Warsaw: 1884.

Dershowitz, Alan. *The Vanishing American Jew*. New York: Touchstone, 1998.

Dessler, Elijah. *Michtav me-Eliyahu* [Letter from Elijah]. 5 vols. Jerusalem: Sifriati, 1994.

Dimont, Max I. *Jews, G-d and History*. New York: Signet Classics, 2004.

Donin, Hayim. *To Be a Jew: A Guide to Jewish Observance in Contemporary Life*. New York: Basic Books, 1972.

Dov Ber of Mezeritch. *Magid Devarav le-Yaakov* [He Tells His Word to Jacob]. Koretz: 1781.

Durant, Will and Ariel. *The Story of Civilization*. 11 vols. New York: Simon and Schuster, 1935–1975.

Eibeschutz, David Solomon. *Arvei Nachal* [Willows of the Brook]. 2 vols. Warsaw: 1905.

Eisenstein, J.D. *Otzar Masaot: A Compendium of Jewish Travels*. New York: 1926.

———. *Otzar Midrashim: A Library of Two Hundred Minor Midrashim*. 2 vols. New York: 1915.

Eliezer ben Nathan of Mainz (Raavan). *Kuntres Gezeirot Tatnu* [Booklet Describing the Decrees of the year 4856 (1096)]. Leipzig: 1854.

Elijah of Vilna. *Aderet Eliyahu* [Elijah's Cloak; commentaries on the Bible]. 4 vols. Jerusalem: 1988.

———. *Yahel Ohr* [Halo of Light; commentaries on Zohar]. Vilnius: 1882.

Elitzur, Yehudah; Kiel, Yehudah. *Atlas Daat Mikra* [Biblical atlas]. Jerusalem: Mosad Harav Kook, 1998.

Emden, Jacob. *Mor u-Ketziah* [Myrrh and Cassia]. 2 vols. Altona: 1761-1768.

Finkelstein, Louis. *The Jews: Their History, Culture, and Religion*. 2 vols. New York: Harper Brothers, 1949.

Frank, Anne. *The Diary of a Young Girl*. Amsterdam: Contact Publishing, 1947.

Frankl, Viktor. *Man's Search for Meaning*. Boston: Beacon Press, 1959.

Freeman, Tzvi. *Men, Women and Kabbalah*. Class One Press, 2004.

Friesel, Evyatar. *The Atlas of Modern Jewish History*. Jerusalem: Carta, 1990.

Ganz, David. *Zemach David* [Sprout of David; historical chronology]. Prague: 1592.

Ganzfried, Shlomo. *Kitzur Shulchan Aruch* [Abridged Code of Jewish Law]. Jerusalem: Mosad Harav Kook, 1974.

Gefen, Tobias. *Karnei ha-Hod* [Rays of Splendor]. St. Louis: Zaltz-Gelman, 1935.

Gerondi, Nissim. *Commentary on Torah*. Jerusalem: Machon Shalem, 1968.

———. *Derashot ha-Ran* [Discourses of R. Nissim]. Jerusalem: Mossad Harav Kook, 2016.

Gersonides, Levi. *Commentaries on Torah*. Mantua: 1576.

Gikatilla, Joseph. *Shaarei Orah* [Gates of Light]. Trento: 1661.

Ginzberg, Louis. *Geonica*. 2 vols. New York: JTS, 1909.

Glitzenshtein, Avraham Chanoch. *Sefer ha-Toledot Rabbi Israel Baal Shem Tov* [Biography of the Baal Shem Tov]. 2 vols. Brooklyn: Kehot, 1986.

Goldschmidt, Eliezer. *Ezer Mishpat* [Aid to Judgment]. Jerusalem: 2004.

Goldwurm, Hersh. *History of the Jewish People: The Second Temple Era*. Brooklyn: Mesorah Publications, 1982.

Goodman, Susan Tumarkin. *Chagall: Love, War, and Exile*. New Haven: Yale University Press, 2013.

Greenwald, Leopold. *Kolbo al Aveilut* [Compendium of the Laws of Mourning]. New York: Moriah, 1947.

Grossman, Mendel. *My Secret Camera: Life in the Lodz Ghetto*. San Diego: Gulliver Books, 2000.

Haberman, A.M. *Gezeirot Ashkenaz ve-Tzarfat* [The Decrees against the Jews of Germany and France]. Jerusalem: Tarshish, 1946.

Halevi, Judah. *The Kuzari*. Translated by Yehuda Even Shmuel. Tel Aviv: Dvir Publishing, 1972.

———. *Poems*. 5 vols. Tel Aviv: Yediot Acharonot, 1964.

Hayarchi, Abraham. *ha-Manhig* [Book of Jewish Customs]. Istanbul: 1619.

Heilman, Chaim Meir. *Beit Rebbi* [Our Rebbe's House]. 3 vols. Berditchev: Sheftil, 1902.

Heilprin, Yechiel Shlomo. *Seder ha-Dorot* [Order of the Generations]. 2 vols. Bnei Brak: Sifrei Ohr Hachaim, 2003.

Hertz, J. H. *The Pentateuch and Haftorahs: Hebrew Text with English Translation and Commentary*. London: Oxford University Press, 1937.

Herzl, Theodor. *The Jewish State*. Vienna: 1896.

Herzog College. *Daat: Online Encyclopedia of Jewish Knowledge*. Daat.ac.il: 1997–2020.

Heschel, Abraham Joshua. *The Earth Is the Lord's: The Inner World of the Jew in Eastern Europe*. New York: Farrar Straus Giroux, 1949.

Hirsch, Samson Raphael. *The Pentateuch: Translated and Explained with Commentary*. 5 vols. London: L. Honig & Sons, 1963.

———. *Yesodot ha-Chinuch* [Principles of Education]. 2 vols. Bnei Brak: Netzach, 1958–1968.

Hirschfeld, Fritz. *George Washington and the Jews*. Newark: University of Delaware Press, 2005.

Hirshovitz, A. L. *Otzar Kol Minhagei Yeshurun* [Treasury of Jewish Customs]. St. Louis: Moinister, 1918.

Horowitz, Isaiah. *Shenei Luchot ha-Berit* [Two Tablets of the Covenant]. 2 vols. Amsterdam: 1698; 4 vol. ed., Haifa: Yad Ramah, 1992.

Hutner, Isaac. *Pachad Yitzchak* [Awe of Isaac]. 8 vols. Brooklyn-Jerusalem: Gur Aryeh Institute, 1964–2008.

Ibn Attar, Chaim. *Ohr ha-Chayim* [Light of Life]. 2 vols. Venice: 1742.

Ibn Daud, Abraham. *Sefer ha-Kabbalah* [Book of Transmission]. Mantua: 1514.

Ibn Duran, Simeon. *Yavin Shemuah* [Comprehending the Teaching]. Livorno: 1744.

Ibn Gabbai, Meir. *Avodat ha-Kodesh* [Holy Service]. Krakow: 1577.

Ibn Gabirol, Solomon. *Keter Malchut* [Crown of Royalty]. Jerusalem: Mossad Harav Kook, 1950.

Ibn Halawa, Bechayei (or: Bachya) *Commentary on the Pentateuch*. 3 vols. Jerusalem: Mossad Harav Kook, 2006.

Ibn Pakudah, Bachya. *Hovot ha-Levavot* [Duties of the Hearts; bilingual edition]. Translated from Judeo-Arabic to Hebrew by Judah ibn Tibbon, and into English by Moses Hyamson. 2 vols. Jerusalem: Feldheim, 1970.

Isserlin, Israel. *Leket Yosher* [collection of rulings and customs recorded by a disciple]. 2 vols. Jerusalem: Machon Yerushalayim, 2010.

———. *Terumat ha-Deshen* [Uplifting of Ashes; responsa]. Venice: 1519.

Isserlis, Moses. *Torat ha-Olah* [Law of the Ascent-Offering]. Prague: 1670.

Jacob ben Asher. *Arbaah Turim* [Four Rows; code of Jewish law]. New York: MP Press, 1981.

Jacob Joseph of Polonne. *Ben Porat Yosef* [Joseph the Fertile Son]. Koretz: 1781.

Jewish Federations of North America. *Berman Jewish Databank*. JewishDataBank.org, 1986–2020.

Johnson, Paul. *A History of the Jews*. New York: Harper Perennial, 1988.

Josephus, Flavius. *Korot Yisrael bi-Tekufat Bayit Sheini u-Milchemet ha-Yehudim im ha-Roma'im.* [History of the Jews in the Second Temple Era and the Wars of the Jews with the Romans]. Jerusalem: Huminer, 1956.

———. *The Works of Josephus: Complete and Unabridged.* Translated by William Whiston. Peabody, MA: Hendrickson Publishers, 1987.

Kagan, Israel Meir. *Chafetz Chayim* [He Who Desires Life]. Vilna, 1877.

———. *Shem Olam* [Everlasting Name]. 2 vols. Warsaw: 1893–1898.

Kahana, Abraham. *ha-Sefarim ha-Chitzonim* [Biblical Apocrypha]. Tel Aviv: Mekorot, 1937.

Kamelhar, Yekutiel. *Mofet ha-Dor* [Wonder of the Generation; a biography of R. Yechezkel Landau]. Piotrkow: 1934.

Kantor, Mattis. *Codex Judaica: Chronological Index of Jewish History, Covering 5764 Years of Biblical, Talmudic, and Post-Talmudic History*. New York: Zichron Press, 2005.

Kaplan, Aryeh. *The Living Torah.* Jerusalem-New York: Moznaim, 1981.

Kaplan, Shmuel. *The Siddur Illuminated by Chassidus (Introduction).* Brooklyn: Sichos in English, 2013.

Katz, Y. *Mikveh Mayim* [Pool of Water]. 3 vols. Jerusalem: 2002.

Ketina, Jacob. *Korban he-Ani* [Pauper's Offering]. Lvov: 1882.

Kiel, Yehudah; et al. *Daat Mikra* [Knowledge of Scripture]. 30 vols. Jerusalem: Mosad Harav Kook, 1970–2003.

Ki-Tov, Eliyahu. *Sefer ha-Todaah* [Book of Knowledge; pubished in English as *Book of Our Heritage*]. 2 vols. Jerusalem: Yad Eliyahu Kitov, 1963–1972.

Kleinman, Moshe Chaim. *Ohr Yesharim* [Light of the Upright]. Ashdod: Birkat Yosef, 2002.

Kolatch, Yonatan. *Masters of the Word*. 2 vols. Jersey City: Ktav, 2006.

Kol-Bo [Compendium of Laws and Custom; author unknown]. Naples: 1490.

Kook, Abraham Isaac. *Igrot* [Letters]. 4 vols. Jerusalem: Mosad Harav Kook, 1985.

———. *Orach Mishpat* [Pathway of Judgment; Halachic responsa]. 4 vols. Jerusalem: Mosad Harav Kook, 1985.

———. *Orot* [Lights]. Tel Aviv: 1950.

———. *Orot ha-Teshuvah* [Lights of Repentance]. Jerusalem: 1925.

Kovner, Abba. *Scrolls of Fire*. Jerusalem: Keter, 1981.

Kramer, Gordon. *A History of Palestine: From the Ottoman Conquest to the Founding of the State of Israel*. Princeton University Press, 2011.

Lamm, Maurice. *The Jewish Way in Death and Mourning*. New York: J. David, 2000.

Landau, Yechezkel. *Noda bi-Yehudah* [Renowned in Judah; responsa]. 6 vols. Jerusalem: Machon Yerushalayim, 1994–2009.

Landman, Isaac. *The Universal Jewish Encyclopedia*. 10 vols. 1939–1943.

Leibowitz, Nechama. *Iyunim Chadashim ba-Mikra* [New Studies in the Pentateuch]. 5 vols. Tel Aviv: 1966–1996.

Leiner, Gershon Hanoch. *Sefunei Temunei Chol* [Treasures Hidden in the Sand]. Lublin: 1903.

Leiner, Mordecai Joseph. *Mei ha-Shiloach* [Waters of the Shiloah]. 2 vols. Vienna: 1860; Lublin, 1922.

Levin, Hanoch Henich. *Chashavah le-Tovah* [Thought It for the Good]. Piotrkow: 1929.

Levin, Moshe. *Melechet ha-Mishkan* [Making of the Tabernacle]. Tel Aviv: 1968.

Levner, Israel Benjamin. *Kol Agadot Yisrael* [Legends of Israel]. 2 vols. Warsaw: Tushia, 1912.

Lewin, Benjamin. *Otzar ha-Geonim* [Thesaurus of the Geonic Responsa and Commentaries]. 13 vols. Haifa: 1928–1944.

Lieberman, Y.M. *Chag ha-Asif* [Harvest Festival]. Bnei Brak: 1993.

Lindsay, Alexander. *Letters on Egypt, Edom, and the Holy Land*. 2 vols. London: 1838.

Lipkin, Chaim Isaac. *Taryag Mitzvot* [The 613 Mitzvot]. 6 vols. Bnei Brak: Netzach, 1962.

Litvin, Jay. Articles on Chabad.org, 1999–2004.

Loew, Judah. *Complete Works of Maharal*. 18 vols. Krakow; Prague; Jerusalem; Bnei Brak: 1582–1980.

Luria, Isaac; transcribed by Chaim Vital. *Eitz Chayim* [Tree of Life]. Koretz: 1782.

———. *Pri Eitz Chayim* [Fruit of the Tree of Life]. Koretz: 1785.

———. *Sefer ha-Likutim.* [Collected Teachings]. Jerusalem: 1913.

———. *Shaar ha-Gilgulim* [Portal of Reincarnations]. Frankfurt: 1684.

———. *Shaar ha-Kavanot* [Portal of Meditations]. Saloniki: 1852.

Luzzatto, Moses Chaim. *Adir ba-Marom* [Mighty in the Heights; commentaries on *Zohar*]. Warsaw: 1886.

———. *Mesilat Yesharim* [Path of the Upright]. Amsterdam: 1740.

Maimonides, Moses. *Commentary on the Mishnah.* Naples: 1492.

———. *Mishneh Torah and Sefer ha-Mitzvot*. 6 vols. Jerusalem: Pardes, 1955.

———. *Moreh Nevuchim* [Guide for the Perplexed]. Jerusalem: Mosad Harav Kook, 1977.

———. *Rambam la-Am* [Works of Maimonides, annotated]. 20 vols. Jerusalem: Mosad Harav Kook, 1961.

Mangel, Nissen. *Siddur Tehillat Hashem with English Translation.* Brooklyn: Kehot, 2006.

———. *Machzor for Rosh Hashanah with English Translation.* Brooklyn: Kehot, 1983.

———. *Machzor for Yom Kippur with English Translation.* Brooklyn: Kehot, 1983.

Marcus. J. R. *To Count a People*. Lanham: University Press of America, 1990.

Matt, Moses. *Mateh Moshe* [Staff of Moses]. Krakow: 1691.

Mecklenburg, Jacob Zvi. *ha-Ketav veha-Kabbalah* [Scripture and Tradition]. Nuremberg: J. Bulka, 1924.

Meisels, Zvi Hirsch. *Mekadshei Hashem* [Sanctifiers of the Name]. 2 vols. Chicago: International Printing Co., 1955.

Miller, Chaim. *Chumash with Commentary*. Brooklyn: Kol Menachem, 2003–2006.

Morris, Benny. *Righteous Victims: A History of the Zionist-Arab Conflict, 1881–1998*. New York: Knopf, 1999.

Museum of Jewish Heritage. *JewishGen.org*. 2003–2020.

Nachman of Breslov. *Likutei Moharan* [Collected Teachings of our Master R. Nachman]. Ostrog: 1808–1811.

———. *Ohr ha-Emet veha-Emunah* [Light of Truth and Faith]. Jerusalem: 1981.

Nachmanides. *Commentary on Torah*. 2 vols. Jerusalem: Mosad Harav Kook, 1959.

———. *Sefer ha-Geulah* [Book of Redemption]. London: Lifshitz, 1909.

Orchot Tzadikim [Paths of the Righteous; author unknown] Salonika: 1791.

Oren, Michael. *Six Days of War*. Oxford: Oxford University Press, 2002.

Oshri, Ephraim. *She'eilot u-Teshuvot mi-Maamakim* [Queries and Responses from the Depths]. 5 vols. New York: 1959–1979.

Panet, Yechezkel. *Commentaries on the Passover Haggadah*. Przemysl: 1894.

Papo, Eliezer. *Peleh Yo'etz* [Wondrous Counsel]. Bucharest: 1860.

Peters, Joan. *From Time Immemorial: The Origins of the Arab-Jewish Conflict over Palestine*. New York: Harper & Row, 1984.

Prager, Dennis. *Think a Second Time*. New York: ReganBooks, 1995.

Rabinovici, Ronen. *Jewish Timeline*. Odyeda.com, 2012.

Rabinowitz, Solomon. *Tiferet Shlomo* [Beauty of Solomon]. 2 vols. Piotrkow: 1890; Bedzin: 1909.

Rabinowitz, Zadok. *Pri Tzadik* [Fruit of the Righteous]. 7 vols. Lublin: 1901–1934.

———. *Tzidkat ha-Tzadik* [Righteousness of the Righteous]. Lublin: 1913.

Raziel ha-Malach [The Angel Raziel]. Amsterdam: 1701.

Recanati, Menachem. *Commentary on Torah*. Venice: 1523.

Rosenzweig, Franz. *Kleinere Schriften* [Short Writings]. Berlin: Schocken, 1937.

Roth, Cecil. *A Short History of the Jewish People*. London: East and West Library, 1948.

Roth, Cecil; et al. *Encyclopedia Judaica*. 22 vols. Jerusalem: Keter and Detroit: Gale, 1971–2006.

Roth, Norman. *Medieval Jewish Civilization: An Encyclopedia*. New York: Routledge, 2016.

Rozman, D. A. *Daat Dorot: The Order of the Generations and the Transmission of the Mesorah*. Jerusalem: Feldheim, 2005.

Saadia Gaon; et al. *Beraita of R. Ishmael's Thirteen Methods of Torah Exegesis with Commentaries*. Vilnius: Rohm, 1825.

Saba, Abraham. *Tzror ha-Mor* [Bundle of Myrrh]. Venice: Di Kbali, 1567.

Sacks, Jonathan. *Covenant and Conversation* [Online collection of articles and lectures at rabbisacks.org]. 2011–2020.

———. *Radical Then, Radical Now*. London: Continuum, 2000.

Sarna, Jonathan D. *American Judaism: A History*. New Haven: Yale University Press, 2004.

Schiffman, Lawrence. *Reclaiming the Dead Sea Scrolls*. New Haven: Yale University Press, 1995.

Schneersohn, Joseph Isaac. *Likutei Diburim* [Collected Talks]. 4 vols. Kfar Chabad: Kehot, 1973.

———. *Sefer ha-Maamarim 5680–5711* [Discourses, 1920–1950]. 18 vols. Brooklyn: Kehot, 1986.

———. *Sefer ha-Sichot 5700–5710* [Talks, 1940–1950]. 7 vols. Brooklyn: Kehot, 1992–2001.

Schneersohn, Shalom DovBer. *Sefer ha-Maamarim 5659* [Discourses 1899]. Brooklyn: Kehot, 1976.

———. *Yom Tov Shel Rosh Hashanah 5666*. [Series of discourses, 1906–1908]. Brooklyn: Kehot, 1970.

Schneersohn, Shmuel. *Torat Shmuel* [Teachings of Samuel]. 26 vol. Brooklyn: Kehot, 1993.

Schneerson, Menachem Mendel. *Biurim le-Pirkei Avot* [Elucidations on *Ethics of the Fathers*]. 2 vols. Brooklyn: Kehot, 1982–2000.

———. *Hagada Shel Pesach im Likutei Taamim, Minhagim, u-Biurim* [Passover Haggadah with Anthology of Explanations, Customs, and Elucidations]. 2 vols. Brooklyn: Kehot, 1991.

———. *Hayom Yom* [Today Is the Day; calendar of Hasidic aphorisms]. Brooklyn: Kehot, 1943.

———. *Igrot Kodesh* [Correspondence]. 32 vols. Brooklyn: Kehot, 1987–2015.

———. *Inyanah Shel Torat ha-Chasidut* [On the Essence of Hasidism]. Brooklyn: Kehot, 1972.

———. *Likutei Sichot* [Edited Talks]. 39 vols. Brooklyn: Kehot, 1964–2001.

———. *Reshimot* [Journal Notes]. 5 vols. Brooklyn: Kehot, 1994–2000.

———. *Sichot Kodesh 5710–5741* [Transcribed Talks, 1950–1981]. 52 vols. Brooklyn: 1985.

———. *Torat Menachem Hitvaaduyot 5742–5752* [Transcribed Talks, 1982–1992]. 43 vols. Brooklyn: Hanochos be-Lahak, 1993.

Schneur Zalman of Liadi. *Igrot Kodesh Admor ha-Zakein* [Correspondence]. Brooklyn: Kehot, 2012.

———. *Likutei Torah* [Collected Teachings; discourses]. Brooklyn: Kehot, 1972.

———. *Maamarei Admor ha-Zakein* [Discourses]. 28 vols. Brooklyn: Kehot, 1958–2008.

———. *Shulchan Aruch ha-Rav* [The Rav's Code of Jewish Law]. 6 vols. Brooklyn: Kehot, 1989.

———. *Siddur Torah Ohr*. Brooklyn: Kehot, 1987.

———. *Tanya* (parts I and II). Slavita: 1796.

———. *Tanya* (parts I–V, with English translation, notes, and introductions). London: Kehot, 1973.

———. *Torah Ohr* [Torah of Light; discourses]. Brooklyn: Kehot, 1975.

Schneuri, DovBer. *Kuntres ha-Hishtatchut*. 1944; (as part of *Sefer ha-Hishtatchut*) Brooklyn: Kehot, 1996.

———. *Shaarei Orah* [Gates of Light]. Brooklyn: Kehot, 1997.

Schreiber, Moses. *Chatam Sofer al ha-Shas* [Scribe's Seal; commentaries on the Talmud]. 18 vols. Jerusalem: 1988–2013.

Segal, Moshe Zvi. *Dor le-Dor* [Generation to Generation; an autobiography]. Tel Aviv: IDF Publications, 1985.

Sekili, Jacob. *Torat ha-Minchah* [Law of the Offering]. 2 vols. Safed: Baruch Chafetz, 1991.

Senesh, Hannah. *Yomanim, Shirim, Eduyot* [Diaries, Poems, Testaments]. Tel Aviv: Hakibutz Hameuchad, 1994.

Shahn, Ben. *Ecclesiastes: With Drawings by Ben Shahn, Engraved in Wood by Stephan Martin*. New York: Spiral Press, 1965.

Shamir, Ilana; Shavit, Shlomo. *Encyclopedia of Jewish History*. New York: Facts on File, 1986.

Shapira, Klonymous. *Aish Kodesh* [Sacred Fire]. Jerusalem: 1960.

Shapira, Nathan Noteh. *Megaleh Amukot* [Revealer of Depths]. Krakow: 1637.

Sharansky, Natan. *Defending Identity*. New York: Public Affairs, 2008.

Shirer, William. *The Rise and Fall of the Third Reich*. New York: Simon & Schuster, 1960.

Shmueli, Meir. *Beit ha-Keneset ka-Halachah* [The Synagogue in Torah Law]. Jerusalem: 2011.

Shtesman, Isaac. *Kol Nidrei*. Jerusalem: 2008.

Singer, Isidor; et al. *The Jewish Encyclopedia*. 12 vols. New York: Funk & Wagnalls, 1901–1906.

Sirkis, Joel. *Responsa of Bach*. 2 vols. Frankfurt am Main: 1697; Korets, 1775.

Slonim, Rivkah. *Total Immersion: A Mikvah Anthology*. Jerusalem: Urim, 2006.

Snyder, James. *The Jewish World: 365 Days.* New York: Harry N. Abrams, 2004.

Sperling, Avraham Yitzchak. *Taamei ha-Minhagim u-Mekorei ha-Dinim* [Reasons for Customs and Sources for Laws; with addendums by Shmuel Weinfeld]. Jerusalem: Eshkol, 1982.

Stein, Shacno. *Avnei Chein* [Gemstones]. New York: Posy-Shoulson, 1936.

Steinberg, Reuben. *Tefilah be-Tzibur* [Communal Prayer]. Brooklyn: 2011.

Steinsaltz, Adin Even-Israel. *Arba She'arim* [Four Gates]. Jerusalem: Koren, 2017.

———. *Biblical Images: Men and Women of the Book*. New York: Basic Books, 1984.

———. *Opening the Tanya*. San Francisco: Jossey-Bass, 2003.

———. *The Steinsaltz Talmud*. 44 vols. Jerusalem: Israel Institute for Talmudic Publications, 1970–2010.

———. *The Thirteen Petalled Rose*. New York: Basic Books, 1980.

Sternbuch, Moshe. *ha-Berachot ke-Hilchatan* [Blessings Properly Done]. Jerusalem: 1996.

———. *Moadim u-Zemanim* [Seasons and Times]. 9 vols. Jerusalem: 1961–1992.

Tauber, Yanki. *Beyond the Letter of the Law*. Brooklyn: VHH, 1995.

———. *The Inside Story*. 3 vols. Brooklyn: MLC, 2016–2019.

———. *Inside Time*. 3 vols. Brooklyn: MLC, 2015.

———. *Once Upon a Chassid*. Brooklyn: Kehot, 1994.

Tukachinsky, Yechiel Michel. *Gesher ha-Chayim* [Bridge of Life]. 3 vols. Jerusalem: 1960.

Twersky, Menachem Nachum. *Meor Einayim* [Light of the Eyes]. Slavita: 1798.

Tzemach Tzedek (Menachem Mendel of Lubavitch). *Derech Mitzvotecha* [The Path of Your Commandments]. Brooklyn: Kehot, 1970.

———. *Maamarei Admur ha-Tzemach Tzedek, Hanachot, 5614–5615* [Transcribed Discourses, 1854–1855]. Brooklyn: Kehot, 1997.

———. *Ohr ha-Torah* [Light of the Torah]. 41 vols. Brooklyn: Kehot, 1967.

Unterman, Isser Yehuda. *Shevet mi-Yehudah* [Ruler from Judah]. Jerusalem: Mosad Harav Kook, 1983.

Vilnay, Zev. *Legends of Palestine*. Philadelphia: JPS, 1932.

Volavkova, Hana. *I Never Saw Another Butterfly: Children's Drawings & Poems from Terezin Concentration Camp, 1942–44*. New York: Schocken, 1994.

Weinstock, Moses Yair. *Seder Olam ha-Shalem*. Jerusalem: 1956.

Wiesel, Elie. *Five Biblical Portraits*. Notre Dame: 1981.

———. *Telling the Tale: Essays, Reflections, and Poems*. St. Louis: Time Being Press, 1993.

———. *Wise Men and Their Tales: Portraits of Biblical, Talmudic, and Hasidic Masters*. New York: Schocken, 2003.

Wilhelm, Zushe. *Ziv ha-Sheimot* [Glory of Names]. Brooklyn: Moriah, 1988.

Wise, Doniel. *Shulchan Aruch ha-Kotzer* [The Concise Code of Jewish Law]. 2 vol. Kfar Chabad: Oholei Shem, 1990.

Wisser, Meir Leibush (Malbim). *Commentaries on the Bible*. 4 vols. Jerusalem: Pardes, 1957.

Wouk, Herman. *This Is My G-d*. Garden City: Doubleday, 1959.

Yaabetz, Joseph. *Ohr ha-Chayim* [Light of Life]. Przemysl: Zolkiew bei Saul Meyerhoffer, 1848.

Yair, Zvi (Zvi Meir Steinmetz). *Meirosh Tzurim* [From the Mountain Peaks; poems]. Tel Aviv: Eked, 1973.

Yosef, Ovadiah. *Yabia Omer* [Expressed Word; responsa]. 12 vols. Jerusalem: 1954–2008.

Yosef, Yitzchak. *Yalkut Yosef* [Joseph's Gleanings]. 40 vols. Jerusalem: 1997–2019.

Zacuto, Moses. *Tikun Shovavim* [Rectification of the Wayward]. Mantua: 1732.

Zalmanov, Shmuel (general editor). *Hatamim Journal*. 8 Issues. Warsaw: Tomchei Temimim, 1935–1938.

Zaritzki, David. *Torat ha-Musar* [The Teachings of Musar]. Tel Aviv: Moriah, 1959.

Zedaka, Judah. *Kol Yehudah* [Voice of Judah]. Jerusalem: 1995.

Zevin, Shlomo Yosef. *Sipurei Hasidim* [Hasidic Stories]. 2 vols. Jerusalem: Beit Hillel, 1955.

Zevin, Shlomo Yosef; et al. *Encyclopedia Talmudit*. 43 vols. Jerusalem: Yad Harav Hertzog, 1942–2020.

Zinner, Gavriel. *Nit'ei Gavriel* [Plantings of Gabriel]. 28 vols. Brooklyn: 1981–2009.

Ziv, Simcha Zisel. *Chochmah u-Musar* [Wisdom and Morals]. 2 vols. New York: Aber Press, 1957.

index

additional credits

This page contains additional accreditations and copyright information which, due to formatting constraints, do not appear alongside the images and texts or in the bibliography.

IMAGES

cover see entries for pages 1, 149, & 361 **title page** The Jewish Museum NY, Michael and Luz Zak Fund and Judaica Acquisitions Fund **1** Israel Museum, Jerusalem **3** Israel Museum / Nahum Slapak **4** *1313BCE:* Gilya / iStock.com *1273:* see p.52 *423BCE:* Engraving of Nebuchadnezzar; Wikimedia *355BCE:* see p.361 *139BCE:* Israel Museum / Elie Posner **5** *69:* see p.67 *133:* see p.1 *189:* see p.185 *219:* see p.192 *912:* Toledo Synagogue; Ivan Soto / 123RF.com *1492:* The Jewish Expulsion from Spain, Spain, Fototeca Storica Nazionale, c.1792; Hulton Archive via Getty Images *1933:* see p.132 *1967:* see p.67 **10** Artists Rights Society (ARS), New York / ADAGP, Paris; photo: RMN–Grand Palais / Art Resource, NY **12** Erich Lessing / Art Resource, NY **13** Israel Museum / Meidad Suchowolski **14, 15** stock.adobe.com **17** Lucien Krief Gallery, Jerusalem **19** Library of Congress **22** Paul Cliff / Manchester Museum **23** The Jewish Museum NY (thejewishmuseum.org) / Art Resource, NY **24** Penn Museum, image #150022 **29** acrylic on canvas, 34" x 44", robertshorepainter.com, by permission of Marietta Saravia-Shore **33** Granger Museum **35** The Milton Avery Trust / Artists Rights Society (ARS), NY; photo: Yares Art **37** adobe.com **40** Maurycy Gottlieb, Jews Praying in the Synagogue on Yom Kippur, 1878, oil on canvas, 245x192 cm.; Tel Aviv Museum of Art; gift of Sidney Lamon, NY, 1955; photo: Margarita Perlin **47** adobe.com **49** Bequest of Anna Ticho to The Israel Museum, Jerusalem; Photo: Israel Museum / Elie Posner **52** FALKENSTEINFOTO / Alamy **56** Smithsonian's National Museum of African Art **57** *Seal:* Dr. Eilat Mazar; photo: Ouria Tadmor *Epitaph:* Israel Museum **64** Israel Antiquities Authority; photo: Israel Museum / David Harris **65** Ariely / CC (Creative Commons) BY-SA 3.0 **66** *423BCE:* see p.4 *139BCE:* Seal of the High Priest, Jerusalem, 1st century CE; photo: Clara Amit, courtesy of the Israel Antiquities Authority **67** *69:* Beit HaShalom / CC BY-SA 3.0 *637:* Auguste Salzmann, 1854; The Metropolitan Museum of Art, NY *1948:* Divided Jerusalem, Ammunition Hill Museum Exhibit; photo: Avi Deror / Wikimedia *1967:* David Rubinger / GPO photos **69** *Western Wall:* Olesya / stock.adobe.com **70, 72** Bodleian Libraries, University of Oxford, MS. Poc. 295, fol. 184v & 198v **73** CC BY-SA 4.0 **76** National Gallery, London / Art Resource, NY **77** Classical Numismatic Group (cngcoins.com) / CC BY-SA 3.0 **83** CC BY-SA 4.0 **84** CC BY 2.0 **86–87** The National Library of Israel, Ms. Heb. 2380=28 **88** Los Angeles County Museum of Art (lacma.org); Marjorie and Leonard Vernon Collection, gift of Annenberg Foundation, acquired from Carol Vernon and Robert Turbin **91** Artists Rights Society (ARS), NY / ADAGP, Paris; photo: Israel Museum / Avshalom Avital **92** see p.69 **93** *Mizrach sign:* Gross Family Collection *Charity box:* Sydney Jewish Museum **94** *18th century BCE:* Machpelah Cave in Hebron; Hanan Isachar / Alamy *13th century BCE:* Seven Trumpets of Jericho, James Jacques Joseph Tissot; The Jewish Museum NY *4th century BCE:* Relief from Nimrud, Northern Iraq, 8th century BCE; Trustees of the British Museum *2nd century:* Tiberias from the South, c. 1862; Francis Frith / Library of Congress, LC-USZC4-8609 *13th century:* Interior of Ramban synagogue, Jerusalem; Ido Winter / Wikimedia *1740:* Jerusalem Jew, c. 1900–1910; Library of Congress, LC-DIG-ppmsca-13192 **95** *1881–1939:* Pioneer with Shovel, 1937; Rudi Weissenstein / The PhotoHouse *1881–1950:* Yemenite family walking through the desert to a reception camp near Aden, 1949; Zoltan Kluger / GPO photos *1934:* SS Exodus 1947; Hans Pinn / GPO photos *1948:* Aliyah of Iraqi Jews from Kurdistan; El Al Archives *1973:* Soviet Jewish dissident Anatoly B. Sharansky escorted by U.S. Ambassador Richard Burt during an East-West spy and prisoner exchange, Feb. 11, 1986; AP Photo *1984:* Jewish immigrants arriving in Israel from Ethiopia; Ilia Yefimovich / Getty **96** *Farmers:* Khan Museum, Hadera *Kindergarten:* Gisin Brothers / Museum of Rishon LeZion **97** *Engel House:* Yitzchak Kalter / Wikimedia *Fighters:* Kluger Zoltan / Government Press Office of Israel **98** Library of Congress, LC-USZ62-84235 **104** Alfredo Garcia Saz / Alamy **110** AF Fotografie / Alamy **114** *HaNagid:* Alhambra Palace, Granada; Jon Arnold Images Ltd. / Alamy *Maimonides:* see p.215 **115** *Mendes-Nasi:* Pastorino de Pastorini, Belgium, c.1558, bronze cast uniface medal, 62 mm.; courtesy of Busso Peus Nacht and The Jewish Museum in Cyberspace (amuseum.org) *Montefiore:* Corbis Historical / Getty **117** Artists Rights Society (ARS), New York / ADAGP, Paris; photo: Solomon R. Guggenheim Foundation / Art Resource, NY **119** International Center of Photography, Gift of Mara Vishniac Kohn, 2013 (MVK.2.2008) / Magnes Collection of Jewish Art and Life, University of California, 2018.15 **120** *Mainz:* mojolo / adobe.com *Prague:* see p.276 *Krakow:* Interior of the Old Synagogue in Kazimierz; Bart Van den Bosch / CC BY-SA 3.0 *Vilna:* Tower of Gediminas; Grigory Bruev / adobe.com **121** *Mezhibuzh:* BESHT Synagogue, c. 1915; Wikimedia *Warsaw:* Monument commemorating the Warsaw Ghetto uprising of 1943, by Leon Suzin and Nathan Rapoport, 1948; thauwald-pictures / adobe.com *Odessa:* Opera House; Artyom Knyaz / adobe.com *New York:* lucamedei / adobe.com **128** Heidelberg University, Cod. Pal. germ. 848, fol.355r **131** The Jewish Museum NY; Gift of Dr. Harry G. Friedman **132** United States Holocaust Memorial Museum; *Lodz Ghetto,* courtesy of Moshe Zilbar; *Yellow Star:* Gift of Ann West **134** *Frank:* Anne Frank House, Amsterdam *Frankl:* Imagno / Getty **135** The Jewish Museum in Prague **136** *Senesh:* Pritzker Family National Photography Collection, National Library of Israel, Abraham Schwadron Collection *Shapira:* Wikimedia **137** *Wiesel:* Sergey Bermeniev *Guard with stick:* The Jewish Museum in Prague **139** The Butcher Shop, George Segal, 1965, plaster, wood, metal, vinyl, acrylic sheet, 240.6 x 252.8 x 127.1 cm.; collection of the Art Gallery of Ontario 65/36; gift of the Women's Committee Fund, 1966 **141** Baruch Gorkin **146** *Lazarus:* William Kurtz / Library of Congress, LC-USZ62-53145 *Einstein:* Colorization by Michael W. Gorth **147** *Kissinger:* Gerald R. Ford Presidential Library *Streisand:* Herbert Dorfman / Corbis via Getty Images **149** Library of the Hungarian Academy of Sciences, Oriental Collection, Kaufmann A 50, fol. 1v **150** The Jewish Museum NY / Art Resource, NY **151** Library of Congress, LC-DIG-prokc-21861 **156** see title page **157** *Aleppo Codex:* Ben-Zvi Institute, Jerusalem / Ardon Bar Hama *Silver staves:* Sotheby's Inc. *Composite image of Torah Scroll:* Baruch Gorkin **160** Leon Levy Dead Sea Scrolls Digital Library, Israel Antiquities Authority; photo: Shai Halevi **163** Sotheby's, Inc. **172** Zev Radovan **175** Artists Rights Society (ARS), New York / ADAGP, Paris; photo: Haggerty Museum of Art, Marquette University, gift of Patrick and Beatrice Haggerty **177** Rubin Museum, Tel Aviv; photo: Sotheby's Inc. **178** *Coin:* see p.1 **181** Estate of Ben Shahn / VAGA at Artists Rights Society (ARS), NY **184** Museum of Jewish History in Russia, Moscow **185** see p.149 **192** Sotheby's, Inc. **203** Image Professionals GmbH / Alamy **205** Winner's Auction House, Jerusalem **211** Israel Antiquities Authority; photo: Israel Museum / Elie Posner **215** *Banknote:* Bank of Israel *Ark panel:* Jointly owned by the Walters Art Museum (funds provided by W. Alton Jones Foundation Acquisition Fund, 2000) and Yeshiva University Museum (funds provided by Jesselson Foundation) **221** F.L.C. / ADAGP, Paris / Artists Rights Society (ARS), New York **227** Solomon R. Guggenheim Foundation, Peggy Guggenheim Collection, Venice; acquisition confirmed in 2009 by agreement with the heirs of Kazimir Malevich **229** Shutterstock.com **233** Sotheby's Inc. **238** Moussaieff Manuscript Collection / Bar Ilan University Library **242** Paul Rand Charitable Trust **245** National Gallery of Art, Washington, D.C. **251** John Singer Sargent, Mountain Fire, ca. 1906-1907; opaque and translucent watercolor, 14 1/16 x 20in. (35.7 x 50.8cm); Brooklyn Museum, purchased by special subscription 09.831 **255** Bar-On Steinhardt Family / Israel Museum **257** Jewish Museum of Frankfurt **261** Chassidic Art Institute **272** Ekaterinburg Museum of Fine Arts **273** CC BY-SA 3.0 **276** *Portuguese Synagogue:* CC BY-SA 2.0 **277** *Ohel Jakob Synagogue:* Beit Hatfutsot, Oster Visual Documentation Center, Courtesy of Louis Davidson, Synagogues360 **279** Museum of Jewish History in Russia **286** Israel Museum / Elie Posner **287** *Shabbat:* Artists Rights Society (ARS), New York / ADAGP, Paris; State Museum of Fine Arts of the Republic of Tatarstan *Zemirot:* Israel Museum Jerusalem / Ardon Bar-Hama **289** Tzfat Gallery of Mystical Art (kabbalahart.com) **292** Artokoloro Quint Lox Limited / Alamy **297** see p.257 **299** *Friday Evening:* The Jewish Museum NY *Challah cover:* Emanuel Studio, Jerusalem **301** *Gefilte fish:* adobe.com **302** *Spice box:* Israel Museum / Elie Posner *Havdalah candle:* Safed Candle Store **303** Israel Museum Jerusalem / Ardon Bar-Hama **305** *Benz's Gourmet:* New York Times / Redux *Kashrut Manual:* Ets Haim–Livraria Montezinos, Amsterdam **306** The Jewish Museum NY **310** Royal Danish Library, Copenhagen, Cod. Heb. 32 **312-3** Mara Zemgaliete, Olivier Tabary, Maksim Shebeko, Ronny, Kreus, and denisk999 / adobe.com **315** Artists Rights Society (ARS), New York / ADAGP, Paris **316** The Jewish Museum NY / Art resource NY **317** *Mezuzah:* scribe Gad Sebag **319** The Israel Exploration Society / Israel Museum **327** The Jewish Museum NY **331** Chassidic Art Institute **332** Museum of Jewish History in Russia **333** Bodleian Libraries, University of Oxford, MS. Kennicott 1, fol. 305r **335** The Jewish Museum NY **336–7** boygostockphoto, Pepsona, Leonid Nyshko, zakiroff, Yanam, sriba3, cook_inspire, photocrew, and sarahdoow / adobe.com **338** Yom Kippur with the Rebbe, Zalman Kleinman / Chassidic Art Institute **339** *Book of Jonah:* see p.333 *The Shema:* BibleLandPictures.com / Alamy *Shofar:* mignic / iStock.com **341** The National Library of Israel **343** *Etrog Container:* The Jewish Museum NY / Art resource NY **349** Israel Museum **351** The Jewish Museum NY **353** Scala / Art Resource, NY **355** Baruch Gorkin **356** *Westerbrok:* Yad Vashem Photo Archive, Jerusalem **358** artmim / adobe.com **359** illustrart, egal, LordRunar, lucielang, dionisvero, nevena321, and Aviator70 / iStock.com **360** Baruch & Dena Gorkin **361** Pushkin State Museum of Fine Arts, Moscow **362** see p.327 **367** *Birds' Head Haggadah:* Israel Museum *Had Gadya:* The Jewish Museum NY *Omer Calendar:* Israel Museum / Elie Posner **369** Arthur Szyk Society, Burlingame, CA / CC BY-SA 4.0 **377** Breakfast Comforts / Weldon Owen International **379** Sotheby's Inc. **383** adobe.com **385** Feuchtwanger Collection, purchased and donated to the Israel Museum by Baruch and Ruth Rappaport of Geneva; photo: Israel Museum / David Harris **386** National Library of Portugal **387** *Old Man with Torah:* Hyman Bloom Estate **389** Kedem Auction House **390** ArtforSmallHands.com **391** see p.385 **393** *Coins:* Mark Kostich / adobe.com **397** Chassidic Art Institute **398** YIVO Institute for Jewish Research Archives, NY **401** *Bar Mitzvah:* Shutterstock.com **402** Collection of Eliezer Burstein, Lugano; photo: Israel Museum / Elie Posner **403** Sotheby's Inc. **407** Rijksmuseum, Amsterdam **411** Shutterstock.com **418** Israel Revealed to the Eye Archive, Badra Qarawani Album; Museum of Yemenite Jewish Heritage, Rosh ha-Ayin, Israel **421** Sepherot Foundation, Liechtenstein **422, 423** Museum of Jewish History in Russia **425** *Yahrzeit reminder:* Museum of Jewish History in Russia *Memorial flame:* Baruch Gorkin **431** Kate Rothko Prizel & Christopher Rothko / Artists Rights Society (ARS), New York; photo: Art Resource, NY **4-427** inforgaphics, diagrams, charts, maps, and uncredited illustrations: Baruch Gorkin.

TEXTS

78, 110, 130 *Jews, G-d and History* ©1962, 1990 Max I. Dimont; ©1994 Ethel Dimont; by permission of New American Library, an imprint of Penguin Publishing Group, a division of Penguin Random House LLC **103** *Six Days of War* © Michael Oren; by permission of the Oxford Publishing Limited through PLSclear **134, 249, 266** *Man's Search for Meaning* ©1959, 1962, 1984, 1992, 2006 Viktor E. Frankl; by permission of Beacon Press, Boston **144** *The Gifts of the Jews* ©1998 Thomas Cahill; by permission of Doubleday, an imprint of Knopf Doubleday Publishing Group, a division of Penguin Random House LLC **178** *Five Biblical Portraits* ©1981 Elie Wiesel; by permission of Georges Borchardt, Inc., on behalf of the author's estate **185** *The Earth is the Lord's* ©1949 Abraham Joshua Heschel; ©1977 Sylvia Heschel; by permission of Farrar, Straus & Giroux **220, 400** Articles by Tzvi Freeman © by chabad.org **245** *Faith after the Holocaust* © Eliezer Berkovitz; by permission of Maggid books, an imprint of Koren Publishers Jerusalem Ltd. **295** *Wise Men and Their Tales: Portraits of Biblical, Talmudic, and Hasidic Masters* by Elie Wiesel, © 2003 Elirion Associates, Inc.; by permission of Schocken Books, an imprint of Knopf DoubledayPublishing Group, a division of Penguin Random House LLC **307** *To Be a Jew* © Hayim Donin 1991, 2001, 2019; by permission of Basic Books, an imprint of Hachette Book Group, Inc.

THE ROHR JEWISH LEARNING INSTITUTE

Rabbi Moshe Kotlarsky
CHAIRMAN

Rabbi Efraim Mintz
EXECUTIVE DIRECTOR

ADVISORY BOARD OF GOVERNORS

Yaakov and Karen Cohen
POTOMAC, MD

Yitzchok and Julie Gniwisch
MONTREAL, QC

Barbara Hines
ASPEN, CO

Ellen Marks
S. DIEGO, CA

David Mintz, OBM
TENAFLY, NJ

George Rohr
NEW YORK, NY

Dr. Stephen F. Serbin
COLUMBIA, SC

Leonard A. Wien, Jr.
MIAMI BEACH, FL

PARTNERING FOUNDATIONS

Avi Chai Foundation

David Samuel Rock Foundation

Diamond Foundation

Estate of Elliot James Belkin

Francine Gani Charitable Fund

Goldstein Family Foundation

Kohelet Foundation

Kosins Family Foundation

Mayberg Foundation

Meromim Foundation

Myra Reinhard Family Foundation

Robbins Family Foundation

Ruderman Family Foundation

Schulich Foundation

William Davidson Foundation

World Zionist Organization

Yehuda and Anne Neuberger

Philanthropic Fund

Zalik Foundation

PRINCIPAL BENEFACTOR

George Rohr
NEW YORK, NY

PILLARS OF JEWISH LITERACY

Shaya and Sarah Boymelgreen
MIAMI BEACH, FL

Pablo and Sara Briman
MEXICO CITY, MEXICO

Zalman and Mimi Fellig
MIAMI BEACH, FL

Yosef and Chana Malka Gorowitz
REDONDO BEACH, CA

Shloimy and Mirele Greenwald
BROOKLYN, NY

Dr. Vera Koch Groszmann
S. PAULO, BRAZIL

Carolyn Hessel
NEW YORK, NY

Howard Jonas
NEWARK, NJ

David and Debra Magerman
GLADWYNE, PA

Yitzchak Mirilashvili
HERZLIYA, ISRAEL

David and Harriet Moldau
LONGWOOD, FL

Ben Nash
NEW JERSEY

Eyal and Aviva Postelnik
MARIETTA, GA

Clive and Zoe Rock
IRVINE, CA

Michael and Fiona Scharf
PALM BEACH, FL

Lee and Patti Schear
DAYTON, OH

Isadore and Roberta Schoen
FAIRFAX, VA

Yair Shamir
SAVYON, ISRAEL

SPONSORS

Jake Aronov
MONTGOMERY, AL

Moshe and Rebecca Bolinsky
LONG BEACH, NY

Daniel and Eta Cotlar
HOUSTON, TX

Meyer and Leah Eichler
BROOKLYN, NY

Steve and Esther Feder
LOS ANGELES, CA

Yoel Gabay
BROOKLYN, NY

Brian and Dana Gavin
HOUSTON, TX

Shmuel and Sharone Goodman
CHICAGO, IL

Adam and Elisheva Hendry
MIAMI, FL

Michael and Andrea Leven
ATLANTA, GA

Joe and Shira Lipsey
ASPEN, CO

Josef Michelashvili
GLENDALE, NY

Harvey Miller
CHICAGO, IL

Rachelle Nedow
EL PASO, TX

Peter and Hazel Pflaum
NEWPORT BEACH, CA

Abraham Podolak
PRINCETON JUNCTION, NJ

Dr. Ze'ev and Varda Rav-Noy
LOS ANGELES, CA

Zvi Ryzman
LOS ANGELES, CA

Larry Sifen
VIRGINIA BEACH, VA

Myrna Zisman
CEDARHURST, NY

Janice and Ivan Zuckerman
CORAL GABLES, FL